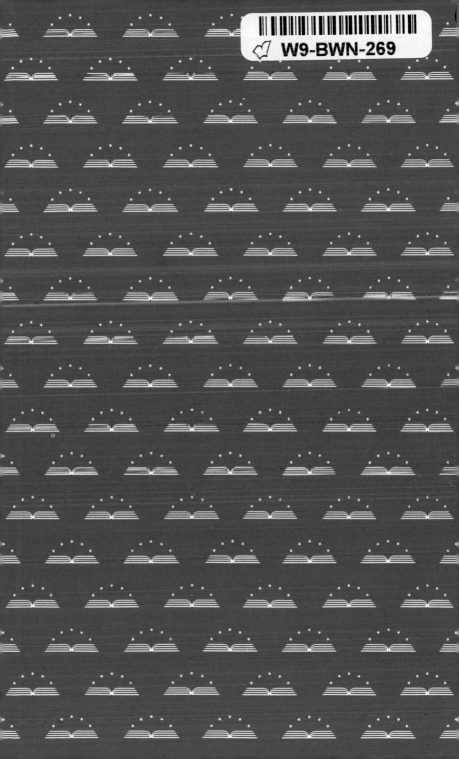

HENRY JAMES

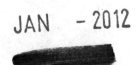

HENRY JAMES

COLLECTED TRAVEL WRITINGS: GREAT BRITAIN AND AMERICA

English Hours
The American Scene
Other Travels

THE LIBRARY OF AMERICA

The paper used in this publication meets the
minimum requirements for the American National Standard for
Information Sciences—Permanence of Paper for Printed
Library Materials, ANSI Z39.48—1984.

Distributed to the trade in the United States
by Penguin Putnam Inc.
and Canada by Penguin Books Canada Ltd.

Library of Congress Catalog Number: 93-9192
For cataloging information, see end of Index
ISBN 0—940450—76—3

Second Printing
The Library of America—64

Manufactured in the United States of America

RICHARD HOWARD
WROTE THE NOTES FOR THIS VOLUME

Grateful acknowledgment is made to the National Endowment for the Humanities, the Ford Foundation, and the Andrew W. Mellon Foundation for their generous support of this series.

Contents

Each section has its own table of contents.

St. Paul's from the Thames

ENGLISH HOURS

WITH NINETY-TWO ILLUSTRATIONS BY
JOSEPH PENNELL

Note

The papers gathered into this series, originally published in various periodicals, have already been reprinted —the earliest in date more than thirty years ago; the others, with the exception of two, more recently, in a volume entitled "Portraits of Places." They have been here once more placed together, for the great advantage they will be felt to derive from the company and support of Mr. Pennell's illustrations. Each article is marked in the list of Contents with its date and it is visible that the impressions and observations they for the most part embody had sprung from an early stage of acquaintance with their general subject-matter. They represent a good many wonderments and judgments and emotions, whether felicities or mistakes, the fine freshness of which the author has —to his misfortune, no doubt —sufficiently outlived. But they may perhaps on that account present something of a curious interest. I may add that I have again attentively looked them over, with a view to any possible amendment of their form or enhancement of their meaning, and that I have nowhere scrupled to rewrite a sentence or a passage on judging it susceptible of a better turn.

1905.   H. J.

3

Contents

List of Illustrations

Kensington Gardens

London

I

THERE is a certain evening that I count as virtually a first
impression—the end of a wet, black Sunday, twenty
years ago, about the first of March. There had been an earlier
vision, but it had turned to gray, like faded ink, and the occasion I speak of was a fresh beginning. No doubt I had mystic
prescience of how fond of the murky modern Babylon I was
one day to become; certain it is that as I look back I find
every small circumstance of those hours of approach and arrival still as vivid as if the solemnity of an opening era had
breathed upon it. The sense of approach was already almost
intolerably strong at Liverpool, where, as I remember, the
perception of the English character of everything was as

acute as a surprise, though it could only be a surprise without a shock. It was expectation exquisitely gratified, superabundantly confirmed. There was a kind of wonder, indeed, that England should be as English as, for my entertainment, she took the trouble to be; but the wonder would have been greater, and all the pleasure absent, if the sensation had not been violent. It seems to sit there again like a visiting presence, as it sat opposite to me at breakfast at a small table in a window of the old coffee-room of the Adelphi Hotel—the unextended (as it then was), the unimproved, the unblushingly local Adelphi. Liverpool is not a romantic city, but that smoky Saturday returns to me as a supreme success, measured by its association with the kind of emotion in the hope of which, for the most part, we betake ourselves to far countries.

It assumed this character at an early hour—or rather, indeed, twenty-four hours before—with the sight, as one looked across the wintry ocean, of the strange, dark, lonely freshness of the coast of Ireland. Better still, before we could come up to the city, were the black steamers knocking about in the yellow Mersey, under a sky so low that they seemed to touch it with their funnels, and in the thickest, windiest light. Spring was already in the air, in the town; there was no rain, but there was still less sun—one wondered what had become, on this side of the world, of the big white splotch in the heavens; and the gray mildness, shading away into black at every pretext, appeared in itself a promise. This was how it hung about me, between the window and the fire, in the coffee-room of the hotel—late in the morning for breakfast, as we had been long disembarking. The other passengers had dispersed, knowingly catching trains for London (we had only been a handful); I had the place to myself, and I felt as if I had an exclusive property in the impression. I prolonged it, I sacrificed to it, and it is perfectly recoverable now, with the very taste of the national muffin, the creak of the waiter's shoes as he came and went (could anything be so English as his intensely professional back? it revealed a country of tradition), and the rustle of the newspaper I was too excited to read.

I continued to sacrifice for the rest of the day; it didn't seem to me a sentient thing, as yet, to inquire into the

means of getting away. My curiosity must indeed have languished, for I found myself on the morrow in the slowest of
Sunday trains, pottering up to London with an interrupted-
ness which might have been tedious without the conversation of an old gentleman who shared the carriage with me,
and to whom my alien as well as comparatively youthful
character had betrayed itself. He instructed me as to the
sights of London, and impressed upon me that nothing was
more worthy of my attention than the great cathedral of St.
Paul. "Have you seen St. Peter's in Rome? St. Peter's is
more highly embellished, you know; but you may depend
upon it that St. Paul's is the better building of the two." The
impression I began with speaking of was, strictly, that of the
drive from Euston, after dark, to Morley's Hotel in Trafalgar
Square. It was not lovely—it was in fact rather horrible; but
as I move again through dusky, tortuous miles, in the greasy
four-wheeler to which my luggage had compelled me to
commit myself, I recognise the first step in an initiation of
which the subsequent stages were to abound in pleasant
things. It is a kind of humiliation in a great city not to know
where you are going, and Morley's Hotel was then, to my
imagination, only a vague ruddy spot in the general immensity. The immensity was the great fact, and that was a
charm; the miles of housetops and viaducts, the complication of junctions and signals through which the train made
its way to the station had already given me the scale. The
weather had turned to wet, and we went deeper and deeper
into the Sunday night. The sheep in the fields, on the way
from Liverpool, had shown in their demeanour a certain
consciousness of the day; but this momentous cab-drive was
an introduction to the rigidities of custom. The low black
houses were as inanimate as so many rows of coal-scuttles,
save where at frequent corners, from a gin-shop, there was a
flare of light more brutal still than the darkness. The custom
of gin—that was equally rigid, and in this first impression
the public-houses counted for much.

Morley's Hotel proved indeed to be a ruddy spot; brilliant,
in my recollection, is the coffee-room fire, the hospitable mahogany, the sense that in the stupendous city this, at any rate
for the hour, was a shelter and a point of view. My remem-

brance of the rest of the evening—I was probably very tired—is mainly a remembrance of a vast four-poster. My little bedroom-candle, set in its deep basin, caused this monument to project a huge shadow and to make me think, I scarce knew why, of "The Ingoldsby Legends." If at a tolerably early hour the next day I found myself approaching St. Paul's, it was not wholly in obedience to the old gentleman in the railway-carriage: I had an errand in the City, and the City was doubtless prodigious. But what I mainly recall is the romantic consciousness of passing under the Temple Bar, and the way two lines of "Henry Esmond" repeated themselves in my mind as I drew near the masterpiece of Sir Christopher Wren. "The stout, red-faced woman" whom Esmond had seen tearing after the staghounds over the slopes at Windsor was not a bit like the effigy "which turns its stony back upon St. Paul's and faces the coaches struggling up Ludgate Hill." As I looked at Queen Anne over the apron of my hansom— she struck me as very small and dirty, and the vehicle ascended the mild incline without an effort—it was a thrilling thought that the statue had been familiar to the hero of the incomparable novel. All history appeared to live again, and the continuity of things to vibrate through my mind.

To this hour, as I pass along the Strand, I take again the walk I took there that afternoon. I love the place to-day, and that was the commencement of my passion. It appeared to me to present phenomena, and to contain objects of every kind, of an inexhaustible interest; in particular it struck me as desirable and even indispensable that I should purchase most of the articles in most of the shops. My eyes rest with a certain tenderness on the places where I resisted and on those where I succumbed. The fragrance of Mr. Rimmel's establishment is again in my nostrils; I see the slim young lady (I hear her pronunciation) who waited upon me there. Sacred to me to-day is the particular aroma of the hair-wash that I bought of her. I pause before the granite portico of Exeter Hall (it was unexpectedly narrow and wedge-like), and it evokes a cloud of associations which are none the less impressive because they are vague; coming from I don't know where—from *Punch*, from Thackeray, from volumes of the *Illustrated London News* turned over in childhood; seeming connected with

St. Paul's

Mrs. Beecher Stowe and "Uncle Tom's Cabin." Memorable is a rush I made into a glover's at Charing Cross—the one you pass, going eastward, just before you turn into the station; that, however, now that I think of it, must have been in the morning, as soon as I issued from the hotel. Keen within me was a sense of the importance of deflowering, of despoiling the shop.

A day or two later, in the afternoon, I found myself staring at my fire, in a lodging of which I had taken possession on foreseeing that I should spend some weeks in London. I had just come in, and, having attended to the distribution of my luggage, sat down to consider my habitation. It was on the ground floor, and the fading daylight reached it in a sadly damaged condition. It struck me as stuffy and unsocial, with its mouldy smell and its decoration of lithographs and wax-flowers—an impersonal black hole in the huge general blackness. The uproar of Piccadilly hummed away at the end of the street, and the rattle of a heartless hansom passed close to my ears. A sudden horror of the whole place came over me, like a tiger-pounce of homesickness which had been watching its moment. London was hideous, vicious, cruel, and above all overwhelming; whether or no she was "careful of the type," she was as indifferent as Nature herself to the single life. In the course of an hour I should have to go out to my dinner, which was not supplied on the premises, and that effort assumed the form of a desperate and dangerous quest. It appeared to me that I would rather remain dinnerless, would rather even starve, than sally forth into the infernal town, where the natural fate of an obscure stranger would be to be trampled to death in Piccadilly and have his carcass thrown into the Thames. I did not starve, however, and I eventually attached myself by a hundred human links to the dreadful, delightful city. That momentary vision of its smeared face and stony heart has remained memorable to me, but I am happy to say that I can easily summon up others.

II

It is, no doubt, not the taste of every one, but for the real London-lover the mere immensity of the place is a large part of its savour. A small London would be an abomination, as it fortunately is an impossibility, for the idea and the name are beyond everything an expression of extent and number. Practically, of course, one lives in a quarter, in a plot; but in imagination and by a constant mental act of reference the accommodated haunter enjoys the whole—and it is only of him that I deem it worth while to speak. He fancies himself, as they say, for being a particle in so unequalled an aggregation; and its immeasurable circumference, even though unvisited and lost in smoke, gives him the sense of a social, an intellectual margin. There is a luxury in the knowledge that he may come and go without being noticed, even when his comings and goings have no nefarious end. I don't mean by this that the tongue of London is not a very active member; the tongue of London would indeed be worthy of a chapter by itself. But the eyes which at least in some measure feed its activity are fortunately for the common advantage solicited at any moment by a thousand different objects. If the place is big, everything it contains is certainly not so; but this may at least be said, that if small questions play a part there, they play it without illusions about its importance. There are too many questions, small or great; and each day, as it arrives, leads its children, like a kind of mendicant mother, by the hand. Therefore perhaps the most general characteristic is the absence of insistence. Habits and inclinations flourish and fall, but intensity is never one of them. The spirit of the great city is not analytic, and, as they come up, subjects rarely receive at its hands a treatment drearily earnest or tastelessly thorough. There are not many—of those of which London disposes with the assurance begotten of its large experience—that wouldn't lend themselves to a tenderer manipulation elsewhere. It takes a very great affair, a turn of the Irish screw or a divorce case lasting many days, to be fully threshed out. The mind of Mayfair, when it aspires to show what it really can do, lives in the hope of a new divorce case, and an indulgent providence—London is positively in certain ways the spoiled child of the world—abundantly recognises this particular aptitude and humours the whim.

The compensation is that material does arise; that there is a great variety, if not morbid subtlety; and that the whole of the procession of events and topics passes across your stage. For the moment I am speaking of the inspiration there may be in the sense of far frontiers; the London-lover loses himself in this swelling consciousness, delights in the idea that the town which encloses him is after all only a paved country, a state by itself. This is his condition of mind quite as much if he be an adoptive as if he be a matter-of-course son. I am by no means sure even that he need be of Anglo-Saxon race and have inherited the birthright of English speech; though, on the other hand, I make no doubt that these advantages minister greatly to closeness of allegiance. The great city spreads her dusky mantle over innumerable races and creeds, and I believe there is scarcely a known form of worship that has not some temple there (have I not attended at the Church of Humanity, in Lamb's Conduit, in company with an American lady, a vague old gentleman, and several seamstresses?) or any communion of men that has not some club or guild. London is indeed an epitome of the round world, and just as it is a commonplace to say that there is nothing one can't "get" there, so it is equally true that there is nothing one may not study at first hand.

One doesn't test these truths every day, but they form part of the air one breathes (and welcome, says the London-hater—for there be such perverse reasoners—to the pestilent compound). They colour the thick, dim distances which in my opinion are the most romantic town-vistas in the world; they mingle with the troubled light to which the straight, ungarnished aperture in one's dull, undistinctive housefront affords a passage and which makes an interior of friendly corners, mysterious tones and unbetrayed ingenuities, as well as with the low, magnificent medium of the sky, where the smoke and fog and the weather in general, the strangely undefined hour of the day and season of the year, the emanations of industries and the reflection of furnaces, the red gleams and blurs that may or may not be of sunset—as you never see any *source* of radiance you can't in the least tell—all hang together in a confusion, a complication, a shifting but irremovable canopy. They form the undertone of the deep, perpetual voice of the place. One remembers them when one's loyalty is on the defensive; when it is a question of introducing as many striking features as possible into the list of fine reasons one has sometimes to draw up, that eloquent catalogue with which one confronts the hostile indictment—the array of *other* reasons which may easily be as long as one's arm. According to these other reasons it plausibly and conclusively stands that, as a place to be happy in, London will never do. I don't say it is necessary to meet so absurd an allegation except for one's personal complacency. If indifference, in so gorged an organism, is still livelier than curiosity, you may avail yourself of your own share in it simply to feel that since such and such a person doesn't care for real richness, so much the worse for such and such a person. But once in a while the best believer recognises the impulse to set his religion in order, to sweep the temple of his thoughts and trim the sacred lamp. It is at such hours as this that he reflects with elation that the British capital is the particular spot in the world which communicates the greatest sense of life.

III

The reader will perceive that I do not shrink even from the extreme concession of speaking of our capital as British, and this in a shameless connection with the question of loyalty on the part of an adoptive son. For I hasten to explain that if half the source of one's interest in it comes from feeling that it is the property and even the home of the human race—Hawthorne, that best of Americans, says so somewhere, and places it in this sense side by side with Rome—one's appreciation of it is really a large sympathy, a comprehensive love of humanity. For the sake of such a charity as this one may stretch one's allegiance; and the most alien of the cockneyfied, though he may bristle with every protest at the intimation that England has set its stamp upon him, is free to admit with conscious pride that he has submitted to Londonisation. It is a real stroke of luck for a particular country that the capital of the human race happens to be British. Surely every other people would have it theirs if they could. Whether the English deserve to hold it any longer might be an interesting field of inquiry; but as they have not yet let it slip, the writer of these lines professes without scruple that the arrangement is to his personal taste. For, after all, if the sense of life is greatest there, it is a sense of the life of people of our consecrated English speech. It is the headquarters of that strangely elastic tongue; and I make this remark with a full sense of the terrible way in which the idiom is misused by the populace in general, than whom it has been given to few races to impart to conversation less of the charm of tone. For a man of letters who endeavours to cultivate, however modestly, the medium of Shakespeare and Milton, of Hawthorne and Emerson, who cherishes the notion of what it has achieved and what it may even yet achieve, London must ever have a great illustrative and suggestive value, and indeed a kind of sanctity. It is the single place in which most readers, most possible lovers, are gathered together; it is the most inclusive public and the largest social incarnation of the language, of the tradition. Such a personage may well let it go for this and leave the German and the Greek to speak for themselves, to express the grounds of *their* predilection, presumably very different.

When a social product is so vast and various it may be approached on a thousand different sides, and liked and disliked for a thousand different reasons. The reasons of Piccadilly are not those of Camden Town, nor are the curiosities and discouragements of Kilburn the same as those of Westminster and Lambeth. The reasons of Piccadilly—I mean the friendly ones—are those of which, as a general thing, the rooted visitor remains most conscious; but it must be confessed that even these, for the most part, do not lie upon the surface. The absence of style, or rather of the intention of style, is certainly the most general characteristic of the face of London. To cross to Paris under this impression is to find one's self surrounded with far other standards. There everything reminds you that the idea of beautiful and stately arrangement has never been out of fashion, that the art of composition has always been at work or at play. Avenues and squares, gardens and quays, have been distributed for effect, and to-day the splendid city reaps the accumulation of all this ingenuity. The result is not in every quarter interesting, and there is a tiresome monotony of the "fine" and the symmetrical above all, of the deathly passion for making things "to match." On the other hand the whole air of the place is architectural. On the banks of the

The end of a wet, black Sunday

Thames it is a tremendous chapter of accidents—the London-lover has to confess to the existence of miles upon miles of the dreariest, stodgiest commonness. Thousands of acres are covered by low black houses of the cheapest construction, without ornament, without grace, without character or even identity. In fact there are many, even in the best quarters, in all the region of Mayfair and Belgravia, of so paltry and inconvenient, especially of so diminutive a type (those that are let in lodgings—such poor lodgings as they make—may serve as an example), that you wonder what peculiarly limited domestic need they were constructed to meet. The great misfortune of London to the eye (it is true that this remark applies much less to the City) is the want of elevation. There is no architectural impression without a certain degree of height, and the London street-vista has none of that sort of pride.

All the same, if there be not the intention, there is at least the accident, of style, which, if one looks at it in a friendly way, appears to proceed from three sources. One of these is simply the general greatness, and the manner in which that makes a difference for the better in any particular spot; so that, though you may often perceive yourself to be in a shabby corner, it never occurs to you that this is the end of it. Another is the atmosphere, with its magnificent mystifications, which flatters and superfuses, makes everything brown, rich, dim, vague, magnifies distances and minimises details, confirms the inference of vastness by suggesting that, as the great city makes everything, it makes its own system of weather and its own optical laws. The last is the congregation of the parks, which constitute an ornament not elsewhere to be matched and give the place a superiority that none of its uglinesses overcome. They spread themselves with such a luxury of space in the centre of the town that they form a part of the impression of any walk, of almost any view, and, with an audacity altogether their own, make a pastoral landscape under the smoky sky. There is no mood of the rich London climate that is not becoming to them—I have seen them look delightfully romantic, like parks in novels, in the wettest winter—and there is scarcely a mood of the appreciative resident to which they have not something to say. The high things of

London, which here and there peep over them, only make the spaces vaster by reminding you that you are, after all, not in Kent or Yorkshire; and these things, whatever they be—rows of "eligible" dwellings, towers of churches, domes of institutions—take such an effective gray-blue tint that a clever water-colourist would seem to have put them in for pictorial reasons.

The view from the bridge over the Serpentine has an extraordinary nobleness, and it has often seemed to me that the Londoner twitted with his low standard may point to it with every confidence. In all the town-scenery of Europe there can be few things so fine; the only reproach it is open to is that it begs the question by seeming—in spite of its being the pride of five millions of people—not to belong to a town at all. The towers of Notre Dame, as they rise in Paris from the island that divides the Seine, present themselves no more impressively than those of Westminster as you see them looking doubly far beyond the shining stretch of Hyde Park water. Equally delectable is the large river-like manner in which the Serpentine opens away between its wooded shores. Just after you have crossed the bridge (whose very banisters, old and ornamental, of yellowish-brown stone, I am particularly fond of), you enjoy on your left, through the gate of Kensington Gardens as you go towards Bayswater, an altogether enchanting vista—a footpath over the grass, which loses itself beneath the scattered oaks and elms exactly as if the place were a "chase." There could be nothing less like London in general than this particular morsel, and yet it takes London, of all cities, to give you such an impression of the country.

IV

It takes London to put you in the way of a purely rustic walk from Notting Hill to Whitehall. You may traverse this immense distance—a most comprehensive diagonal—altogether on soft, fine turf, amid the song of birds, the bleat of lambs, the ripple of ponds, the rustle of admirable trees. Frequently have I wished that, for the sake of such a daily luxury and of exercise made romantic, I were a government-clerk living, in snug domestic conditions, in a Pembridge villa—let

me suppose—and having my matutinal desk in Westminster. I should turn into Kensington Gardens at their north-west limit, and I should have my choice of a hundred pleasant paths to the gates of Hyde Park. In Hyde Park I should follow the water-side, or the Row, or any other fancy of the occasion; liking best perhaps, after all, the Row in its morning mood, with the mist hanging over the dark red course, and the scattered early riders taking an identity as the soundless gallop brings them nearer. I am free to admit that in the Season, at the conventional hours, the Row becomes a weariness (save perhaps just for a glimpse once a year, to remind one's self how much it is like Du Maurier); the preoccupied citizen eschews it and leaves it for the most part to the gaping barbarian. I speak of it now from the point of view of the pedestrian; but for the rider as well it is at its best when he passes either too early or too late. Then, if he be not bent on comparing it to its disadvantage with the bluer and boskier alleys of the Bois de Boulogne, it will not be spoiled by the fact that, with its surface that looks like tan, its barriers like those of the ring on which the clown stands to hold up the hoop to the young lady, its empty benches and chairs, its occasional orange-peel, its mounted policemen patrolling at intervals like expectant supernumeraries, it offers points of real contact with a circus whose lamps are out. The sky that bends over it is frequently not a bad imitation of the dingy tent of such an establishment. The ghosts of past cavalcades seem to haunt the foggy arena, and somehow they are better company than the mashers and elongated beauties of current seasons. It is not without interest to remember that most of the salient figures of English society during the present century—and English society means, or rather has hitherto meant, in a large degree English history—have bobbed in the saddle between Apsley House and Queen's Gate. You may call the roll if you care to, and the air will be thick with dumb voices and dead names, like that of some Roman amphitheatre.

It is doubtless a signal proof of being a London-lover *quand même* that one should undertake an apology for so bungled an attempt at a great public place as Hyde Park Corner. It is certain that the improvements and embellishments recently enacted there have only served to call further

In the Park

attention to the poverty of the elements, and to the fact that this poverty is terribly illustrative of general conditions. The place is the beating heart of the great West End, yet its main features are a shabby, stuccoed hospital, the low park-gates in their neat but unimposing frame, the drawing-room windows of Apsley House, and of the commonplace frontages on the little terrace beside it; to which must be added, of course, the only item in the whole prospect that is in the least monumental—the arch spanning the private road beside the gardens of Buckingham Palace. This structure is now bereaved of the rueful effigy which used to surmount it—the Iron Duke in the guise of a tin soldier—and has not been enriched by the transaction as much as might have been expected.* There is a fine view of Piccadilly and Knightsbridge, and of the noble mansions, as the house-agents call them, of Grosvenor Place, together with a sense of generous space beyond the vulgar little railing of the Green Park; but, except for the impression that there would be room for something better, there is nothing in all this that speaks to the imagination: almost as much as the grimy desert of Trafalgar Square the prospect conveys the idea of an opportunity wasted.

None the less has it on a fine day in spring an expressiveness of which I shall not pretend to explain the source further than by saying that the flood of life and luxury is immeasurably great there. The edifices are mean, but the social stream itself is monumental, and to an observer not purely stolid there is more excitement and suggestion than I can give a reason for in the long, distributed waves of traffic, with the steady policemen marking their rhythm, which roll together and apart for so many hours. Then the great dim city becomes bright and kind, the pall of smoke turns into a veil of haze carelessly worn, the air is coloured and almost scented by the presence of the biggest society in the world, and most of the things that meet the eye—or perhaps I should say more of them, for the most in London is, no doubt, ever the realm of the dingy—present themselves as "well-appointed." Everything shines more or less, from the window-panes to the dog-

*The monument in the middle of the square, with Sir Edgar Boehm's four fine soldiers, had not been set up when these words were written.

collars. So it all looks, with its myriad variations and qualifications, to one who surveys it over the apron of a hansom, while that vehicle of vantage, better than any box at the opera, spurts and slackens with the current.

It is not in a hansom, however, that we have figured our punctual young man, whom we must not desert as he fares to the south-east, and who has only to cross Hyde Park Corner to find his way all grassy again. I have a weakness for the convenient, familiar, treeless, or almost treeless, expanse of the Green Park, and the friendly part it plays as a kind of encouragement to Piccadilly. I am so fond of Piccadilly that I am grateful to any one or anything that does it a service, and nothing is more worthy of appreciation than the southward look it is permitted to enjoy just after it passes Devonshire House—a sweep of horizon which it would be difficult to match among other haunts of men, and thanks to which, of a summer's day, you may spy, beyond the browsed pastures of the foreground and middle distance, beyond the cold chimneys of Buckingham Palace and the towers of Westminster and the swarming river-side and all the southern parishes, the hard modern twinkle of the roof of the Crystal Palace.

If the Green Park is familiar, there is still less of the exclusive in its pendant, as one may call it—for it literally hangs from the other, down the hill—the remnant of the former garden of the queer, shabby old palace whose black, inelegant face stares up St. James's Street. This popular resort has a great deal of character, but I am free to confess that much of its character comes from its nearness to the Westminster slums. It is a park of intimacy, and perhaps the most democratic corner of London, in spite of its being in the royal and military quarter and close to all kinds of stateliness. There are few hours of the day when a thousand smutty children are not sprawling over it, and the unemployed lie thick on the grass and cover the benches with a brotherhood of greasy corduroys. If the London parks are the drawing-rooms and clubs of the poor—that is, of those poor (I admit it cuts down the number) who live near enough to them to reach them—these particular grass-plots and alleys may be said to constitute the very *salon* of the slums.

I know not why, being such a region of greatness—great

towers, great names, great memories; at the foot of the Abbey, the Parliament, the fine fragment of Whitehall, with the quarters of the sovereign right and left—but the edge of Westminster evokes as many associations of misery as of empire. The neighbourhood has been much purified of late, but it still contains a collection of specimens—though it is far from unique in this—of the low, black element. The air always seems to me heavy and thick, and here more than elsewhere one hears old England—the panting, smoke-stained Titan of Matthew Arnold's fine poem—draw her deep breath with effort. In fact one is nearer to her heroic lungs, if those organs are figured by the great pinnacled and fretted talking-house on the edge of the river. But this same dense and conscious air plays such everlasting tricks to the eye that the Foreign Office, as you see it from the bridge, often looks romantic, and the sheet of water it overhangs poetic—suggests an Indian palace bathing its feet in the Ganges. If our pedestrian achieves such a comparison as this he has nothing left but to go on to his work—which he will find close at hand. He will have come the whole way from the far north-west on the green—which is what was to be demonstrated.

V

I feel as if I were taking a tone almost of boastfulness, and no doubt the best way to consider the matter is simply to say—without going into the treachery of reasons—that, for one's self, one likes this part or the other. Yet this course would not be unattended with danger, inasmuch as at the end of a few such professions we might find ourselves committed to a tolerance of much that is deplorable. London is so clumsy and so brutal, and has gathered together so many of the darkest sides of life, that it is almost ridiculous to talk of her as a lover talks of his mistress, and almost frivolous to appear to ignore her disfigurements and cruelties. She is like a mighty ogress who devours human flesh; but to me it is a mitigating circumstance—though it may not seem so to every one—that the ogress herself is human. It is not in wantonness that she fills her maw, but to keep herself alive and do her tremendous work. She has no time for fine discriminations.

Westminster

but after all she is as good-natured as she is huge, and the more you stand up to her, as the phrase is, the better she takes the joke of it. It is mainly when you fall on your face before her that she gobbles you up. She heeds little what she takes, so long as she has her stint, and the smallest push to the right or the left will divert her wavering bulk from one form of prey to another. It is not to be denied that the heart tends to grow hard in her company; but she is a capital antidote to the morbid, and to live with her successfully is an education of the temper, a consecration of one's private philosophy. She gives one a surface for which in a rough world one can never be too thankful. She may take away reputations, but she forms character. She teaches her victims not to "mind," and the great danger for them is perhaps that they shall learn the lesson too well.

It is sometimes a wonder to ascertain what they do mind, the best-seasoned of her children. Many of them assist, without winking, at the most unfathomable dramas, and the common speech of others denotes a familiarity with the horrible. It is her theory that she both produces and appreciates the exquisite; but if you catch her in flagrant repudiation of both responsibilities and confront her with the shortcoming, she gives you a look, with a shrug of her colossal shoulders, which establishes a private relation with you for evermore. She seems to say: "Do you really take me so seriously as that, you dear, devoted, voluntary dupe, and don't you know what an immeasurable humbug I am?" You reply that you shall know it henceforth; but your tone is good-natured, with a touch of the cynicism that she herself has taught you; for you are aware that if she makes herself out better than she is, she also makes herself out much worse. She is immensely democratic, and that, no doubt, is part of the manner in which she is salutary to the individual; she teaches him his "place" by an incomparable discipline, but deprives him of complaint by letting him see that she has exactly the same lash for every other back. When he has swallowed the lesson he may enjoy the rude but unfailing justice by which, under her eye, reputations and positions elsewhere esteemed great are reduced to the relative. There are so many reputations, so many positions, that supereminence breaks down, and it is difficult to be so rare that London can't match you. It is a part of her good-nature and one of her clumsy coquetries to pretend sometimes that she hasn't your equivalent, as when she takes it into her head to hunt the lion or form a ring round a celebrity. But this artifice is so very transparent that the lion must be very candid or the celebrity very obscure to be taken by it. The business is altogether subjective, as the philosophers say, and the great city is primarily looking after herself. Celebrities are convenient—they are one of the things that people are asked to "meet"—and lion-cutlets, put upon ice, will nourish a family through periods of dearth.

This is what I mean by calling London democratic. You may be in it, of course, without being of it; but from the moment you *are* of it—and on this point your own sense will soon enough enlighten you—you belong to a body in which a general equality prevails. However exalted, however able, however rich, however renowned you may be, there are too many people at least as much so for your own idiosyncrasies to count. I think it is only by being beautiful that you may really prevail very much; for the loveliness of woman it has long been noticeable that London will go most out of her way. It is when she hunts that particular lion that she becomes most dangerous; then there are really moments when you would believe, for all the world, that she is thinking of what she can give, not of what she can get. Lovely ladies, before this, have paid for believing it, and will continue to pay in days to come. On the whole the people who are least deceived are perhaps those who have permitted themselves to believe, in their own interest, that poverty is not a disgrace. It is certainly not considered so in London, and indeed you can scarcely say where—in virtue of diffusion—it would more naturally be exempt. The possession of money is, of course, immensely an advantage, but that is a very different thing from a disqualification in the lack of it.

Good-natured in so many things in spite of her cynical tongue, and easy-going in spite of her tremendous pace, there is nothing in which the large indulgence of the town is more shown than in the liberal way she looks at obligations of hospitality and the margin she allows in these and cognate matters. She wants above all to be amused; she keeps her books loosely, doesn't stand on small questions of a chop for a chop, and if there be any chance of people's proving a diversion, doesn't know or remember or care whether they have "called." She forgets even if she herself have called. In matters of ceremony she takes and gives a long rope, wasting no time in phrases and circumvallations. It is no doubt incontestable that one result of her inability to stand upon trifles and consider details is that she has been obliged in some ways to lower rather portentously the standard of her manners. She cultivates the abrupt—for even when she asks you to dine a month ahead the invitation goes off like the crack of a pistol—and approaches her ends not exactly *par quatre chemins*. She doesn't pretend to attach importance to the lesson conveyed in Matthew Arnold's poem of "The Sick King in Bokhara," that,

> Though we snatch what we desire,
> We may not snatch it eagerly.

London snatches it more than eagerly if that be the only way she can get it. Good manners are a succession of details, and I don't mean to say that she doesn't attend to them when she has time. She has it, however, but seldom—*que voulez-vous?* Perhaps the matter of note-writing is as good an example as another of what certain of the elder traditions inevitably have become in her hands. She lives by notes—they are her very heart-beats; but those that bear her signatures are as disjointed as the ravings of delirium, and have nothing but a postage-stamp in common with the epistolary art.

VI

If she doesn't go into particulars it may seem a very presumptuous act to have attempted to do so on her behalf, and the reader will doubtless think I have been punished by having egregiously failed in my enumeration. Indeed nothing could well be more difficult than to add up the items—the column would be altogether too long. One may have dreamed of turning the glow—if glow it be—of one's lantern on each successive facet of the jewel; but, after all, it may be success enough if a confusion of brightness be the result.

One has not the alternative of speaking of London as a whole, for the simple reason that there is no such thing as the whole of it. It is immeasurable—embracing arms never meet. Rather it is a collection of many wholes, and of which of them is it most important to speak? Inevitably there must be a choice, and I know of none more scientific than simply to leave out what we may have to apologise for. The uglinesses, the "rookeries," the brutalities, the night-aspect of many of the streets, the gin-shops and the hour when they are cleared out before closing there are many elements of this kind which have to be counted out before a genial summary can be made.

And yet I should not go so far as to say that it is a condition of such geniality to close one's eyes upon the immense misery; on the contrary, I think it is partly because we are irremediably conscious of that dark gulf that the most general appeal of the great city remains exactly what it is, the largest chapter of human accidents. I have no idea of what the future evolution of the strangely mingled monster may be; whether the poor will improve away the rich, or the rich will expropriate the poor, or they will all continue to dwell together on their present imperfect terms of intercourse. Certain it is, at any rate, that the impression of suffering is a part of the general vibration; it is one of the things that mingle with all the others to make the sound that is supremely dear to the consistent London-lover—the rumble of the tremendous human mill. This is the note which, in all its modulations, haunts and fascinates and inspires him. And whether or no he may succeed in keeping the misery out of the picture, he will freely confess that the latter is not spoiled for him by some of its duskiest shades. We are far from liking London well enough till we like its defects: the dense darkness of much of its winter, the soot on the chimney-pots and everywhere else, the early lamplight, the brown blur of the houses, the splashing of hansoms in Oxford Street or the Strand on December afternoons.

There is still something that recalls to me the enchantment of children—the anticipation of Christmas, the delight of a holiday walk—in the way the shop-fronts shine into the fog. It makes each of them seem a little world of light and warmth, and I can still waste time in looking at them with dirty Bloomsbury on one side and dirtier Soho on the other. There are winter effects, not intrinsically sweet, it would appear, which somehow, in absence, touch the chords of memory and even the fount of tears; as for instance the front of the British Museum on a black afternoon, or the portico, when the weather is vile, of one of the big square clubs in Pall Mall. I can give no adequate account of the subtle poetry of such reminiscences; it depends upon associations of which we have often lost the thread. The wide colonnade of the Museum, its symmetrical wings, the high iron fence in its granite setting, the sense of the misty halls within, where all the treasures lie—these things loom patiently through atmospheric layers which instead of making them dreary impart to them something of a cheer of red lights in a storm. I think the romance of a winter afternoon in London arises partly from the fact that, when it is not altogether smothered, the general lamplight takes this hue of hospitality. Such is the colour of the interior glow of the clubs in Pall Mall, which I positively like best when the fog loiters upon their monumental staircases.

In saying just now that these retreats may easily be, for the exile, part of the phantasmagoria of homesickness, I by no means alluded simply to their solemn outsides. If they are still more solemn within, that does not make them any less dear, in retrospect at least, to a visitor much bent upon liking his London to the end. What is the solemnity but a tribute to your nerves, and the stillness but a refined proof of the intensity of life? To produce such results as these the balance of many tastes must be struck, and that is only possible in a very high civilisation. If I seem to intimate that this last abstract term must be the cheer of him who has lonely possession of a foggy library, without even the excitement of watching for some one to put down the magazine he wants, I am willing to let the supposition pass, for the appreciation of a London club at one of the empty seasons is nothing but the strong expression of a preference for the great city—by no means so unsociable as it may superficially appear—at periods of relative abandonment. The London year is studded with holidays, blessed little islands of comparative leisure—intervals of absence for good society. Then the wonderful English faculty for "going out of town for a little change" comes into illimitable play, and families transport their nurseries and their bathtubs to those rural scenes which form the real substratum of the national life. Such moments as these are the paradise of the genuine London-lover, for he then finds himself face to face with the object of his passion: he can give himself up to an intercourse which at other times is obstructed by his rivals. Then every one he knows is out of town, and the exhilarating sense of the presence of every one he doesn't know becomes by so much the deeper.

This is why I pronounce his satisfaction not an unsociable, but a positively affectionate emotion. It is the mood in which he most measures the immense humanity of the place, and in which its limits recede furthest into a dimness peopled with possible illustrations. For his acquaintance, however numerous it may be, is finite; whereas the other, the unvisited London, is infinite. It is one of his pleasures to think of the experiments and excursions he may make in it, even when these adventures don't particularly come off. The friendly fog seems to protect and enrich them—to add both to the mystery and security, so that it is most in the winter months that the imagination weaves such delights. They reach their climax perhaps during the strictly social desolation of Christmas week, when the country-houses are crowded at the expense of the capital. Then it is that I am most haunted with the London of Dickens, feel most as if it were still recoverable, still exhaling its queerness in patches perceptible to the appreciative. Then the big fires blaze in the lone twilight of the clubs, and the new books on the tables say "Now at last you have time to read me," and the afternoon tea and toast, and the torpid old gentleman who wakes up from a doze to order potash-water, appear to make the assurance good. It is not a small matter either, to a man of letters, that this is the best time for writing, and that during the lamplit days the white page he tries to blacken becomes, on his table, in the circle of the lamp, with the screen of the climate folding him in, more vivid and absorbent. Those to whom it is forbidden to sit up to work in the small hours may, between November and March, enjoy a semblance of this luxury in the morning. The weather makes a kind of sedentary midnight and muffles the possible interruptions. It is bad for the eyesight, but excellent for the image.

VII

Of course it is too much to say that all the satisfaction of life in London comes from literally living there, for it is not a paradox that a great deal of it consists in getting away. It is almost easier to leave it than not to, and much of its richness and interest proceeds from its ramifications, the fact that all England is in a suburban relation to it. Such an affair it is in comparison to get away from Paris or to get into it. London melts by wide, ugly zones into the green country, and becomes pretty insidiously, inadvertently—without stopping to change. It is the spoiling, perhaps, of the country, but it is the making of the insatiable town, and if one is a helpless and shameless cockney that is all one is obliged to look at. Anything is excusable which enlarges one's civic consciousness. It ministers immensely to that of the London-lover that, thanks to the tremendous system of coming and going, to the active, hospitable habits of the people, to the elaboration of the railway-service, the frequency and rapidity of trains, and last, though not least, to the fact that much of the loveliest scenery in England lies within a radius of fifty miles—thanks to all this he has the rural picturesque at his door and may cultivate unlimited vagueness as to the line of division between centre and circumference. It is perfectly open to him to consider the remainder of the United Kingdom, or the British empire in general, or even, if he be an American, the total of the English-speaking territories of the globe, as the mere margin, the fitted girdle.

Is it for this reason—because I like to think how great we all are together in the light of heaven and the face of the rest of the world, with the bond of our glorious tongue, in which we labour to write articles and books for each other's candid perusal, how great we all are and how great is the great city which we may unite fraternally to regard as the capital of our race—is it for this that I have a singular kindness for the London railway-stations, that I like them æsthetically, that they interest and fascinate me, and that I view them with complacency even when I wish neither to depart nor to arrive? They remind me of all our reciprocities and activities, our energies and curiosities, and our being all distinguished together from other people by our great common stamp of perpetual motion, our passion for seas and deserts and the other side of the globe, the secret of the impression of strength—I don't say of social roundness and finish—that we produce in any collection of Anglo-Saxon types. If in the beloved foggy season I delight in the spectacle of Paddington, Euston or Waterloo—I confess I prefer the grave northern stations—I am prepared to defend myself against the charge of puerility; for what I seek and what I find in these vulgar scenes is at bottom simply so much evidence of our larger way of looking at life. The exhibition of variety of type is in general one of the bribes by which London induces you to condone her abominations, and the railway-platform is a kind of compendium of that variety. I think that nowhere so much as in London do people wear—to the eye of observation—definite signs of the sort of people they may be. If you like above all things to know the sort, you hail this fact with joy; you recognise that if the English are immensely distinct from other people they are also socially—and that brings with it, in England, a train of moral and intellectual consequences—extremely distinct from each other. You may see them all together, with the rich colouring of their differences, in the fine flare of one of Mr. W. H. Smith's bookstalls—a feature not to be omitted in any enumeration of the charms of Paddington and Euston. It is a focus of warmth and light in the vast smoky cavern; it gives the idea that literature is a thing of splendour, of a dazzling essence, of infinite gas-lit red and gold. A glamour hangs over the glittering booth, and a tantalising air of clever new things. How brilliant must the books all be, how veracious and courteous the fresh, pure journals! Of a Saturday afternoon, as you wait in your corner of the compartment for the starting of the train, the window makes a frame for the glowing picture. I say of a Saturday afternoon because that is the most characteristic time—it speaks most of the constant circulation and in particular of the quick jump, by express, just before dinner, for the Sunday, into the hall of the country-house and the forms of closer friendliness, the prolonged talks, the familiarising walks which London excludes.

There is the emptiness of summer as well, when you may have the town to yourself, and I would discourse of it—counting the summer from the first of August—were it not that I fear to seem ungracious in insisting so much on the negative phases. In truth they become positive in another manner, and I have an endearing recollection of certain happy accidents attached to the only period when London life may be said to admit of accident. It is the most luxurious existence in the world, but of that especial luxury—the unexpected, the extemporised—it has in general too little. In a very tight crowd you can't scratch your leg, and in London the social pressure is so great that it is difficult to deflect from the perpendicular or to move otherwise than with the mass. There is too little of the loose change of time; every half-hour has its preappointed use, written down month by month in a little book. As I intimated, however, the pages of this volume exhibit from August to November an attractive blankness; they represent the season during which you may taste of that highest kind of inspiration, the inspiration of the moment.

This is doubtless what a gentleman had in mind who once said to me, in regard to the vast resources of London and its having something for every taste: "Oh, yes; when you are bored, or want a little change, you can take the boat down to Blackwall." I have never had occasion yet to resort to this particular remedy. Perhaps it's a proof that I have never been bored. Why Blackwall? I indeed asked myself at the time; nor have I yet ascertained what distractions the mysterious name represents. My interlocutor probably used it generically, as a free, comprehensive allusion to the charms of the river at large. Here the London-lover goes with him all the way, and indeed the Thames is altogether such a wonderful affair that he feels he has distributed his picture very clumsily not to have put it in the very forefront. Take it up or take it down, it is equally an adjunct of London life, an expression of London manners.

From Westminster to the sea its uses are commercial, but none the less pictorial for that; while in the other direction—

taking it properly a little further up—they are personal, social, athletic, idyllic. In its recreative character it is absolutely
unique. I know of no other classic stream that is so splashed
about for the mere fun of it. There is something almost droll
and at the same time almost touching in the way that on the
smallest pretext of holiday or fine weather the mighty population takes to the boats. They bump each other in the narrow,
charming channel; between Oxford and Richmond they make
an uninterrupted procession. Nothing is more suggestive of
the personal energy of the people and their eagerness to take,
in the way of exercise and adventure, whatever they can get. I
hasten to add that what they get on the Thames is exquisite,
in spite of the smallness of the scale and the contrast between
the numbers and the space. In a word, if the river is the busi-
est suburb of London it is also by far the prettiest. That term
applies to it less, of course, from the bridges down, but it is
only because in this part of its career it deserves a larger
praise. To be consistent, I like it best when it is all dyed and
disfigured with the town, and you look from bridge to
bridge—they seem wonderfully big and dim—over the
brown, greasy current, the barges and the penny-steamers, the
black, sordid, heterogeneous shores. This prospect, of which
so many of the elements are ignoble, etches itself to the eye of
the lover of "bits" with a power that is worthy perhaps of a
better cause.

The way that with her magnificent opportunity London
has neglected to achieve a river-front is, of course, the best
possible proof that she has rarely, in the past, been in the
architectural mood which at present shows somewhat inexpensive signs of settling upon her. Here and there a fine fragment apologises for the failure which it doesn't remedy.
Somerset House stands up higher, perhaps, than anything
else on its granite pedestal, and the palace of Westminster
reclines—it can hardly be said to stand—on the big parliamentary bench of its terrace. The Embankment, which is admirable if not particularly interesting, does what it can, and
the mannered houses of Chelsea stare across at Battersea Park
like eighteenth-century ladies surveying a horrid wilderness.
On the other hand, the Charing Cross railway-station, placed
where it is, is a national crime; Millbank prison is a worse act

of violence than any it was erected to punish, and the waterside generally a shameless renunciation of effect. We acknowledge, however, that its very cynicism is expressive; so that if
one were to choose again—short of there being a London
Louvre—between the usual English irresponsibility in such
matters and some particular flight of conscience, one would
perhaps do as well to let the case stand. We know what it is,
the stretch from Chelsea to Wapping, but we know not what
it might be. It doesn't prevent my being always more or less
thrilled, of a summer afternoon, by the journey on a penny-
steamer to Greenwich.

VIII

But why do I talk of Greenwich and remind myself of one
of the unexecuted vignettes with which it had been my plan
that these desultory and, I fear, somewhat incoherent remarks
should be studded? They will present to the reader no vignettes but those which the artist who has kindly consented
to associate himself with my vagaries may be so good as to
bestow upon them. Why should I speak of Hampstead, as the
question of summer afternoons just threatened to lead me to
do after I should have exhausted the subject of Greenwich,
which I may not even touch? Why should I be so arbitrary
when I have cheated myself out of the space privately intended for a series of vivid and ingenious sketches of the particular physiognomy of the respective quarters of the town? I
had dreamed of doing them all, with their idiosyncrasies and
the signs by which you shall know them. It is my pleasure to
have learned these signs—a deeply interesting branch of observation—but I must renounce the display of my lore.

I have not the conscience to talk about Hampstead, and
what a pleasant thing it is to ascend the long hill which overhangs, as it were, St. John's Wood and begins at the Swiss
Cottage—you must mount from there, it must be confessed,
as you can—and pick up a friend at a house of friendship on
the top, and stroll with him on the rusty Heath, and skirt the
garden-walls of the old square Georgian houses which survive
from the time when, near as it is to-day to London, the place
was a kind of provincial centre, with Joanna Baillie for its

muse, and take the way by the Three Spaniards—I would never miss that—and look down at the smoky city or across at the Scotch firs and the red sunset. It would never do to make a tangent in that direction when I have left Kensington unsung and Bloomsbury unattempted and have said never a word about the mighty eastward region—the queer corners, the dark secrets, the rich survivals and mementoes of the City. I particularly regret having sacrificed Kensington, the once-delightful, the Thackerayan, with its literary vestiges, its quiet, pompous red palace, its square of Queen Anne, its house of Lady Castlewood, its Greyhound tavern, where Henry Esmond lodged.

But I can reconcile myself to this when I reflect that I have also sacrificed the Season, which doubtless, from an elegant point of view, ought to have been the central *morceau* in the panorama. I have noted that the London-lover loves everything in the place, but I have not cut myself off from saying that his sympathy has degrees, or from remarking that the sentiment of the author of these pages has never gone all the way with the dense movement of the British carnival. That is really the word for the period from Easter to midsummer; it is a fine, decorous, expensive, Protestant carnival, in which the masks are not of velvet or silk, but of wonderful deceptive flesh and blood, the material of the most beautiful complexions in the world. Holding that the great interest of London is the sense the place gives us of multitudinous life, it is doubtless an inconsequence not to care most for the phase of greatest intensity. But there is life and life, and the rush and crush of these weeks of fashion is after all but a tolerably mechanical expression of human forces. Nobody would deny that it is a more universal, brilliant, spectacular one than can be seen anywhere else; and it is not a defect that these forces often take the form of women extremely beautiful. I risk the declaration that the London season brings together year by year an unequalled collection of handsome persons. I say nothing of the ugly ones; beauty has at the best been allotted to a small minority, and it is never, at the most, anywhere, but a question of the number by which that minority is least insignificant.

There are moments when one can almost forgive the follies

of June for the sake of the smile which the sceptical old city puts on for the time and which, as I noted in an earlier passage of this disquisition, fairly breaks into laughter where she is tickled by the vortex of Hyde Park Corner. Most perhaps does she seem to smile at the end of the summer days, when the light lingers and lingers, though the shadows lengthen and the mists redden and the belated riders, with dinners to dress for, hurry away from the trampled arena of the Park. The population at that hour surges mainly westward and sees the dust of the day's long racket turned into a dull golden haze. There is something that has doubtless often, at this particular moment, touched the fancy even of the bored and the *blasés* in such an emanation of hospitality, of waiting dinners, of the festal idea, of the whole spectacle of the West End preparing herself for an evening six parties deep. The scale on which she entertains is stupendous, and her invitations and "reminders" are as thick as the leaves of the forest.

For half an hour, from eight to nine, every pair of wheels presents the portrait of a diner-out. To consider only the rattling hansoms, the white neckties and "dressed" heads which greet you from over the apron in a quick, interminable succession, conveys the overwhelming impression of a complicated world. Who are they all, and where are they all going, and whence have they come, and what smoking kitchens and gaping portals and marshalled flunkeys are prepared to receive them, from the southernmost limits of a loosely interpreted, an almost transpontine Belgravia, to the hyperborean confines of St. John's Wood? There are broughams standing at every door, and carpets laid down for the footfall of the issuing if not the entering reveller. The pavements are empty now, in the fading light, in the big sallow squares and the stuccoed streets of gentility, save for the groups of small children holding others that are smaller—Ameliar-Ann intrusted with Sarah Jane—who collect, wherever the strip of carpet lies, to see the fine ladies pass from the carriage or the house. The West End is dotted with these pathetic little gazing groups; it is the party of the poor—*their* Season and way of dining out, and a happy illustration of "the sympathy that prevails between classes." The watchers, I should add, are by no means all children, but the lean mature also, and I am sure these wayside joys are one of the reasons of an inconvenience much deplored—the tendency of the country poor to flock to London. They who dine only occasionally or never at all have plenty of time to contemplate those with whom the custom has more amplitude. However, it was not my intention to conclude these remarks in a melancholy strain, and goodness knows that the diners are a prodigious company. It is as moralistic as I shall venture to be if I drop a very soft sigh on the paper as I confirm that truth. Are they all illuminated spirits and is their conversation the ripest in the world? This is not to be expected, nor should I ever suppose it to be desired that an agreeable society should fail to offer frequent opportunity for intellectual rest. Such a shortcoming is not one of the sins of the London world in general, nor would it be just to complain of that world, on any side, on grounds of deficiency. It is not what London fails to do that strikes the observer, but the general fact that she does everything in excess. Excess is her highest reproach, and it is her incurable misfortune that there is really too much of her. She overwhelms you by quantity and number—she ends by making human life, by making civilisation, appear cheap to you. Wherever you go, to parties, exhibitions, concerts, "private views," meetings, solitudes, there are already more people than enough on the field. How it makes you understand the high walls with which so much of English life is surrounded, and the priceless blessing of a park in the country, where there is nothing animated but rabbits and pheasants and, for the worst, the importunate nightingales! And as the monster grows and grows for ever, she departs more and more—it must be acknowledged—from the ideal of a convenient society, a society in which intimacy is possible, in which the associated meet often and sound and select and measure and inspire each other, and relations and combinations have time to form themselves. The substitute for this, in London, is the momentary concussion of a million of atoms. It is the difference between seeing a great deal of a few and seeing a little of every one. "When did you come—are you 'going on'?" and it is over; there is no time even for the answer. This may seem a perfidious arraignment, and I should not make it were I not prepared, or rather were I not eager, to add two qualifications. One of these is that, cumbrously vast as the place may be, I would not have had it smaller by a hair's-breadth, or have missed one of the fine and fruitful impatiences with which it inspires you and which are at bottom a heartier tribute, I think, than any great city receives. The other is that out of its richness and its inexhaustible good humour it belies the next hour any generalisation you may have been so simple as to make about it.

Browning in Westminster Abbey

THE LOVERS of a great poet are the people in the world who are most to be forgiven a little wanton fancy about him, for they have before them, in his genius and work, an irresistible example of the application of the imaginative method to a thousand subjects. Certainly, therefore, there are many confirmed admirers of Robert Browning to whom it will not have failed to occur that the consignment of his ashes to the great temple of fame of the English race was exactly one of those occasions in which his own analytic spirit would have rejoiced, and his irrepressible faculty for looking at human events in all sorts of slanting coloured lights have found a signal opportunity. If he had been taken with it as a subject, if it had moved him to the confused yet comprehensive utterance of which he was the great professor, we can immediately guess at some of the sparks he would have scraped from it, guess how splendidly, in the case, the pictorial sense would have intertwined itself with the metaphysical. For such an occasion would have lacked, for the author of "The Ring and the Book," none of the complexity and convertibility that were dear to him. Passion and ingenuity, irony and solemnity, the impressive and the unexpected, would each have forced their way through; in a word, the author would have been sure to take the special, circumstantial view (the inveterate mark of all his speculation) even of so foregone a conclusion as that England should pay her greatest honour to one of her greatest poets. As they stood in the Abbey, at any rate, on Tuesday last, those of his admirers and mourners who were disposed to profit by his warrant for inquiring curiously may well have let their fancy range, with its muffled step, in the direction which *his* fancy would probably not have shrunk from following, even perhaps to the dim corners where humour and the whimsical lurk. Only, we hasten to add, it would have taken Robert Browning himself to render the multifold impression.

One part of it on such occasion is, of course, irresistible—the sense that these honours are the greatest that a generous nation has to confer and that the emotion that accompanies them is one of the high moments of a nation's life. The attitude of the public, of the multitude, at such hours, is a great expansion, a great openness to ideas of aspiration and achievement; the pride of possession and of bestowal, especially in the case of a career so complete as Mr. Browning's, is so present as to make regret a minor matter. We possess a great man most when we begin to look at him through the glass plate of death; and it is a simple truth, though containing an apparent contradiction, that the Abbey never takes us so benignantly as when we have a valued voice to commit to silence there. For the silence is articulate after all, and in worthy instances the preservation great. It is the other side of the question that would pull most the strings of irresponsible reflection—all those conceivable postulates and hypotheses of the poetic and satiric mind to which we owe the picture of how the bishop ordered his tomb in St. Praxed's. Macaulay's "temple of silence and reconciliation"—and none the less perhaps because he himself is now a presence there—strikes us, as we stand in it, not only as local but as social—a sort of corporate company; so thick, under its high arches, its dim transepts and chapels, is the population of its historic names and figures. They are a company in possession, with a high standard of distinction, of immortality, as it were; for there is something serenely inexpugnable even in the position of the interlopers. As they look out, in the rich dusk, from the cold eyes of statues and the careful identity of tablets, they seem, with their converging faces, to scrutinise decorously the claims of each new recumbent glory, to ask each other how he is to be judged as an accession. How difficult to banish the idea that Robert Browning would have enjoyed prefiguring and playing with the mystifications, the reservations, even perhaps the slight buzz of scandal, in the Poets' Corner, to which his own obsequies might give rise! Would not his great relish, in so characteristic an interview with his crucible, have been his perception of the bewildering modernness, to much of the society, of the new candidate for a niche? That is the interest and the fascination, from what may be termed the inside point of view, of Mr. Browning's having received, in this direction of becoming a classic, the only official assistance that is ever conferred upon English writers.

It is as classics on one ground and another—some members of it perhaps on that of not being anything else—that the numerous assembly in the Abbey holds together, and it is as a tremendous and incomparable modern that the author of "Men and Women" takes his place in it. He introduces to his predecessors a kind of contemporary individualism which surely for many a year they had not been reminded of with any such force. The tradition of the poetic character as something high, detached and simple, which may be assumed to have prevailed among them for a good while, is one that Browning has broken at every turn; so that we can imagine his new associates to stand about him, till they have got used to him, with rather a sense of failing measures. A good many oddities and a good many great writers have been entombed in the Abbey; but none of the odd ones have been so great and none of the great ones so odd. There are plenty of poets whose right to the title may be contested, but there is no poetic head of equal power—crowned and recrowned by almost importunate hands—from which so many people would withhold the distinctive wreath. All this will give the marble phantoms at the base of the great pillars and the definite personalities of the honorary slabs something to puzzle out until, by the quick operation of time, the mere fact of his lying there among the classified and protected makes even Robert Browning lose a portion of the bristling surface of his actuality.

For the rest, judging from the outside and with his contemporaries, we of the public can only feel that his very modernness—by which we mean the all-touching, all-trying spirit of his work, permeated with accumulations and playing with knowledge—achieves a kind of conquest, or at least of extension, of the rigid pale. We cannot enter here upon any account either of that or of any other element of his genius, though surely no literary figure of our day seems to sit more unconsciously for the painter. The very imperfections of this original are fascinating, for they never present themselves as weaknesses; they are boldnesses and overgrowths, rich roughnesses and humours, and the patient critic need not despair of digging to the primary soil from which so many disparities and contradictions spring. He may finally even put his finger on some explanation of the great mystery, the imperfect conquest of the poetic form by a genius in which the poetic passion had such volume and range. He may successfully say how it was that a poet without a lyre—for that is practically Browning's deficiency: he had the scroll, but not often the sounding strings—was nevertheless, in his best hours, wonderfully rich in the magic of his art, a magnificent master of poetic emotion. He will justify on behalf of a multitude of devotees the great position assigned to a writer of verse of which the nature or the fortune has been (in proportion to its value and quantity) to be treated rarely as quotable. He will do all this and a great deal more besides; but we need not wait for it to feel that something of our latest sympathies, our latest and most restless selves, passed the other day into the high part—the show-part, to speak vulgarly—of our literature. To speak of Mr. Browning only as he was in the last twenty years of his life, how quick such an imagination as his would have been to recognise all the latent or mystical suitabilities that, in the last resort, might link to the great Valhalla by the Thames a figure that had become so conspicuously a figure of London! He had grown to be intimately and inveterately of the London world; he was so familiar and recurrent, so responsive to all its solicitations, that, given the endless incarnations he stands for to-day, he would have been missed from the congregation of worthies whose memorials are the special pride of the Londoner. Just as his great sign to those who knew him was that he was a force of health, of temperament, of tone, so what he takes into the Abbey is an immense expression of life—of life rendered with large liberty and free experiment, with an unprejudiced intellectual eagerness to put himself in other people's place, to participate in complications and consequences; a restlessness of psychological research that might well alarm any pale company for their formal orthodoxies.

But the illustrious whom he rejoins may be reassured, as they will not fail to discover: in so far as they are representative it will clear itself up that, in spite of a surface unsuggestive of marble and a reckless individualism of form, he is quite

as representative as any of them. For the great value of
Browning is that at bottom, in all the deep spiritual and human essentials, he is unmistakably in the great tradition—is,
with all his Italianisms and cosmopolitanisms, all his victim-
isation by societies organised to talk about him, a magnificent
example of the best and least dilettantish English spirit. That
constitutes indeed the main chance for his eventual critic, who
will have to solve the refreshing problem of how, if subtleties
be not what the English spirit most delights in, the author of,
for instance, "Any Wife to any Husband" made them his perpetual pasture, and yet remained typically of his race. He was
indeed a wonderful mixture of the universal and the alem-
bicated. But he played with the curious and the special, they
never submerged him, and it was a sign of his robustness that
he could play to the end. His voice sounds loudest, and also
clearest, for the things that, as a race, we like best—the fascination of faith, the acceptance of life, the respect for its mysteries, the endurance of its charges, the vitality of the will, the
validity of character, the beauty of action, the seriousness,
above all, of the great human passion. If Browning had spoken for us in no other way, he ought to have been made sure
of, tamed and chained as a classic, on account of the extraordinary beauty of his treatment of the special relation between
man and woman. It is a complete and splendid picture of the
matter, which somehow places it at the same time in the
region of conduct and responsibility. But when we talk of
Robert Browning's speaking "for us" we go to the end of our
privilege, we say all. With a sense of security, perhaps even a
certain complacency, we leave our sophisticated modern conscience, and perhaps even our heterogeneous modern vocabulary, in his charge among the illustrious. There will possibly
be moments in which these things will seem to us to have
widened the allowance, made the high abode more comfortable, for some of those who are yet to enter it.

God's Providence House

Chester

IF THE Atlantic voyage be counted, as it certainly may, even with the ocean in a fairly good humour, an emphatic zero in the sum of one's better experience, the American traveller arriving at this venerable town finds himself transported, without a sensible gradation, from the edge of the New World to the very heart of the Old. It is almost a misfortune, perhaps, that Chester lies so close to the threshold of England; for it is so rare and complete a specimen of an antique town that the later-coming wonders of its sisters in renown—of Shrewsbury, Coventry, and York—suffer a trifle by comparison, and the tourist's appetite for the picturesque just loses its finer edge. Yet the first impressions of an observant American in England—of our old friend the sentimental tourist—stir up within him such a cloud of sensibility that

52

Chester Rows

while the charm is still unbroken he may perhaps as well dispose mentally of the greater as of the less. I have been playing at first impressions for the second time, and have won the game against a cynical adversary. I have been strolling and restrolling along the ancient wall—so perfect in its antiquity—which locks this dense little city in its stony circle, with a certain friend who has been treating me to a bitter lament on the decay of his relish for the picturesque. "I have turned the corner of youth," is his ceaseless plaint; "I suspected it, but now I know it—now that my heart beats but once where it beat a dozen times before, and that where I found sermons in stones and pictures in meadows, delicious revelations and intimations ineffable, I find nothing but the hard, heavy prose of British civilisation." But little by little I have grown used to my friend's sad monody, and indeed feel half indebted to it as a warning against cheap infatuations.

I defied him, at any rate, to argue successfully against the effect of the brave little walls of Chester. There could be no better example of that phenomenon so delightfully frequent in England—an ancient property or institution lovingly readopted and consecrated to some modern amenity. The good Cestrians may boast of their walls without a shadow of that mental reservation on grounds of modern ease which is so often the tax paid by the romantic; and I can easily imagine that, though most modern towns contrive to get on comfortably without this stony girdle, these people should have come to regard theirs as a prime necessity. For through it, surely, they may know their city more intimately than their unbuckled neighbours—survey it, feel it, rejoice in it as many times a day as they please. The civic consciousness, sunning itself thus on the city's rim and glancing at the little swarming towered and gabled town within, and then at the blue undulations of the near Welsh border, may easily deepen to delicious complacency. The wall enfolds the place in a continuous ring, which, passing through innumerable picturesque vicissitudes, often threatens to snap, but never fairly breaks the link; so that, starting at any point, an hour's easy stroll will bring you back to your station. I have quite lost my heart to this charming creation, and there are so many things to be said about it that

Shrewsbury

I hardly know where to begin. The great fact, I suppose, is that it contains a Roman substructure, rests for much of its course on foundations laid by that race of master-builders. But in spite of this sturdy origin, much of which is buried in the well-trodden soil of the ages, it is the gentlest and least offensive of ramparts; it completes its long irregular curve without a frown or menace in all its disembattled stretch. The earthy deposit of time has, indeed, in some places climbed so high about its base that it amounts to no more than a causeway of modest dimensions. It has everywhere, however, a rugged outer parapet and a broad hollow flagging, wide enough for two strollers abreast. Thus equipped, it wanders through its adventurous circuit; now sloping, now bending, now broadening into a terrace, now narrowing into an alley, now swelling into an arch, now dipping into steps, now passing some thorn-screened garden, and now reminding you that it was once a more serious matter than all this by the extrusion of a rugged, ivy-smothered tower. Its final hoary humility is enhanced, to your mind, by the freedom with which you may approach it from any point in the town. Every few steps, as you go, you see some little court or alley boring toward it through the close-pressed houses. It is full of that delightful element of the crooked, the accidental, the unforeseen, which, to American eyes, accustomed to our eternal straight lines and right angles, is the striking feature of European street scenery. An American strolling in the Chester streets finds a perfect feast of crookedness—of those random corners, projections and recesses, odd domestic interspaces charmingly saved or lost, those innumerable architectural surprises and caprices and fantasies which lead to such refreshing exercise a vision benumbed by brown-stone fronts. An American is born to the idea that on his walks abroad it is perpetual level wall ahead of him, and such a revelation as he finds here of infinite accident and infinite effect gives a wholly novel zest to the use of his eyes. It produces, too, the reflection—a superficial and fallacious one perhaps—that amid all this cunning chiaroscuro of its *mise en scène*, life must have more of a certain homely entertainment. It is at least no fallacy to say that childhood—or the later memory of childhood—must borrow from such a background a kind of anecdotical wealth. We all know how in the retrospect of later moods the incidents of early youth "compose," visibly, each as an individual picture, with a magic for which the greatest painters have no corresponding art. There is a vivid reflection of this magic in some of the early pages of Dickens' "Copperfield" and of George Eliot's "Mill on the Floss," the writers having had the happiness of growing up among old, old things. Two or three of the phases of this rambling wall belong especially to the class of things fondly remembered. In one place it skirts the edge of the cathedral graveyard, and sweeps beneath the great square tower and behind the sacred east window of the choir. Of the cathedral there is more to say; but just the spot I speak of is the best standpoint for feeling how fine an influence in the architectural line—where theoretically, at least, influences are great—is the massive tower of an English abbey, dominating the homes of men; and for watching the eddying flight of swallows make vaster still to the eye the large calm fields of stonework. At another point, two battered and crumbling towers, decaying in their winding-sheets of ivy, make a prodigiously designed diversion. One inserted in the body of the wall and the other connected with it by a short crumbling ridge of masonry, they contribute to a positive jumble of local colour. A shaded mall wanders at the foot of the rampart; beside this passes a narrow canal, with locks and barges and burly watermen in smocks and breeches; while the venerable pair of towers, with their old red sandstone sides peeping through the gaps in their green mantles, rest on the soft grass of one of those odd fragments of public garden, a crooked strip of ground turned to social account, which one meets at every turn, apparently, in England—a tribute to the needs of the "masses." *Stat magni nominis umbra.* The quotation is doubly pertinent here, for this little garden-strip is adorned with mossy fragments of Roman stonework, bits of pavement, altars, baths, disinterred in the local soil. England is the land of small economies, and the present rarely fails to find good use for the odds and ends of the past. These two hoary shells of masonry are therefore converted into "museums," receptacles for the dustiest and shabbiest of tawdry back-parlour curiosities. Here preside a couple of those grotesque creatures, *à la* Dickens, whom one finds squeezed into every cranny of English civilisation, scraping a thin subsistence, like mites in a mouldy cheese.

Next after its wall—possibly even before it—Chester values its Rows, an architectural idiosyncrasy which must be seen to be appreciated. They are a sort of Gothic edition of the blessed arcades and porticoes of Italy, and consist, roughly speaking, of a running public passage tunnelled through the second storey of the houses. The low basement is thus directly on the drive-way, to which a flight of steps descends, at frequent intervals, from this superincumbent verandah. The upper portion of the houses projects to the outer line of the gallery, where they are propped with pillars and posts and parapets. The shop-fronts face along the arcade and admit you to little caverns of traffic, more or less dusky according to their opportunities for illumination in the rear. If the picturesque be measured by its hostility to our modern notions of convenience, Chester is probably the most romantic city in the world. This arrangement is endlessly rich in opportunities for amusing effect, but the full charm of the architecture of which it is so essential a part must be observed from the street below. Chester is still an antique town, and mediæval England sits bravely under her gables. Every third house is a "specimen"—gabled and latticed, timbered and carved, and wearing its years more or less lightly. These ancient dwellings present every shade and degree of historical colour and expression. Some are dark with neglect and deformity, and the horizontal slit admitting light into the lurking Row seems to collapse on its dislocated props like a pair of toothless old jaws. Others stand there square-shouldered and sturdy, with their beams painted and straightened, their plaster whitewashed, their carvings polished, and the low casement covering the breadth of the frontage adorned with curtains and flower-pots. It is noticeable that the actual townsfolk have bravely accepted the situation bequeathed by the past, and the large number of rich and intelligent restorations of the old façades makes an effective jumble of their piety and their policy. These elaborate and ingenious repairs attest a highly informed consciousness of the pictorial value of the city. I indeed suspect much of this revived innocence of having recovered a freshness that never can have been, of

Chester High Street

having been restored with usurious interest. About the genuine antiques there would be properly a great deal to say, for they are really a theme for the philosopher; but the theme is too heavy for my pen, and I can give them but the passing tribute of a sigh. They are cruelly quaint, dreadfully expressive. Fix one of them with your gaze, and it seems fairly to reek with mortality. Every stain and crevice seems to syllable some human record—a record of lives airless and unlighted. I have been trying hard to fancy them animated by the children of "Merry England," but I am quite unable to think of them save as peopled by the victims of dismal old-world pains and fears. Human life, surely, packed away behind those impenetrable lattices of lead and bottle-glass, just above which the black outer beam marks the suffocating nearness of the ceiling, can have expanded into scant freedom and bloomed into small sweetness.

Nothing has struck me more in my strolls along the Rows than the fact that the most zealous observation can keep but uneven pace with the fine differences in national manners. Some of the most sensible of these differences are yet so subtle and indefinable that one must give up the attempt to express them, though the omission leave but a rough sketch. As you pass with the bustling current from shop to shop, you feel local custom and tradition—another tone of things—pressing on you from every side. The tone of things is somehow heavier than with us; manners and modes are more absolute and positive; they seem to swarm and to thicken the atmosphere about you. Morally and physically it is a denser air than ours. We seem loosely hung together at home as compared with the English, every man of whom is a tight fit in his place. It is not an inferential but a palpable fact that England is a crowded country. There is stillness and space—grassy, oak-studded space—at Eaton Hall, where the Marquis of Westminster dwells (or I believe can afford to humour his notion of not dwelling), but there is a crowd and a hubbub in Chester. Wherever you go the population has overflowed. You stroll on the walls at eventide and you hardly find elbow-room. You haunt the cathedral shades, and a dozen sauntering mortals temper your solitude. You glance up an alley or side-street, and discover populous windows and doorsteps. You

Interior of Chester Cathedral

roll along country roads and find countless humble pedestrians dotting the green waysides. The English landscape is always a "landscape with figures." And everywhere you go you are accompanied by a vague consciousness of the British child hovering about your knees and coat-skirts, naked, grimy, and portentous. You reflect with a sort of physical relief on Australia, Canada, India. Where there are many men, of course, there are many needs; which helps to justify to the philosophic stranger the vast number and the irresistible coquetry of the little shops which adorn these low-browed Rows. The shop-fronts have always seemed to me the most elegant things in England; and I waste more time than I should care to confess to in covetous contemplation of the vast, clear panes behind which the nether integuments of gentlemen are daintily suspended from glittering brass rods. The manners of the dealers in these comfortable wares seldom fail to confirm your agreeable impression. You are thanked with effusion for expending twopence—a fact of deep significance to the truly analytic mind, and which always seems to me a vague reverberation from certain of Miss Edgeworth's novels, perused in childhood. When you think of the small profits, the small jealousies, the long waiting, and the narrow margin for evil days implied by this redundancy of shops and shopmen, you hear afresh the steady rumble of that deep keynote of English manners, overscored so often, and with such sweet beguilement, by finer harmonies, but never extinguished— the economic struggle for existence.

The Rows are as "scenic" as one could wish, and it is a pity that before the birth of their modern consciousness there was no English Balzac to introduce them into a realistic romance with a psychological commentary. But the cathedral is better still, modestly as it stands on the roll of English abbeys. It is of moderate dimensions, and rather meagre in form and ornament; but to an American it expresses and answers for the type, producing thereby the proper vibrations. Among these is a certain irresistible regret that so much of its hoary substance should give place to the fine, fresh-coloured masonry with which Mr. Gilbert Scott, ruthless renovator, is so intelligently investing it. The red sandstone of the primitive structure, darkened and devoured by time, survives at many

On the Walls

points in frowning mockery of the imputed need of tinkering.
The great tower, however—completely restored—rises high
enough to seem to belong, as cathedral towers should, to the
far-off air that vibrates with the chimes and the swallows, and
to square serenely, east and west and south and north, its
embossed and fluted sides. English cathedrals, within, are apt
at first to look pale and naked; but after a while, if the proportions be fair and the spaces largely distributed, when you
perceive the light beating softly down from the cold clerestory
and your eye measures caressingly the tallness of columns and
the hollowness of arches, and lingers on the old genteel inscriptions of mural marbles and brasses; and, above all, when
you become conscious of that sweet, cool mustiness in the air
which seems to haunt these places as the very climate of Epis-
copacy, you may grow to feel that they are less the empty

shells of a departed faith than the abodes of a faith which may still affirm a presence and awaken echoes. Catholicism has gone, but Anglicanism has the next best music. So at least it seemed to me, a Sunday or two since, as I sat in the choir at Chester awaiting a discourse from Canon Kingsley. The Anglican service had never seemed to my profane sense so much an affair of magnificent intonations and cadences—of pompous effects of resonance and melody. The vast oaken architecture of the stalls among which we nestled—somewhat stiffly and with a due apprehension of wounded ribs and knees—climbing vainly against the dizzier reach of the columns; the beautiful English voices of certain officiating canons; the little rosy "king's scholars" sitting ranged beneath the pulpit, in white-winged surplices, which made their heads, above the pew-edges, look like rows of sleepy cherubs: every element in the scene gave it a great spectacular beauty. They suggested too what is suggested in England at every turn, that conservatism here has all the charm and leaves dissent and democracy and other vulgar variations nothing but their bald logic. Conservatism has the cathedrals, the colleges, the castles, the gardens, the traditions, the associations, the fine names, the better manners, the poetry; Dissent has the dusky brick chapels in provincial by-streets, the names out of Dickens, the uncertain tenure of the *h*, and the poor *mens sibi conscia recti*. Differences which in other countries are slight and varying, almost metaphysical, as one may say, are marked in England by a gulf. Nowhere else does the degree of one's respectability involve such solid consequences, and I am sure I don't wonder that the sacramental word which with us (and, in such correlatives as they possess, more or less among the continental races) is pronounced lightly and facetiously and as a quotation from the Philistines, is uttered here with a perfectly grave face. To have the courage of one's mere convictions is in short to have a prodigious deal of courage, and I think one must need as much to be a Dissenter as one needs patience not to be a duke. Perhaps the Dissenters (to limit the question to them) manage to stay out of the church by letting it all hang on the sermon. Canon Kingsley's discourse was one more example of the familiar truth—not without its significance to minds zealous for the good old fashion of "making

West Door, Chester Cathedral

an effort"—that there is an odd link between large forms and small emanations. The sermon, beneath that triply conse-crated vault, should have had a builded majesty. It had not; and I confess that a tender memory of ancient obligations to the author of "Westward Ho!" and "Hypatia" forbids my saying more of it. An American, I think, is not incapable of taking a secret satisfaction in an incongruity of this kind. He finds with relief that even mortals reared as in the ring of a perpetual circus are only mortals. His constant sense of the beautiful scenic properties of English life is apt to beget a habit of melancholy reference to the dead-blank wall which forms the background of our own life-drama; and from doubting in this fantastic humour whether we have even that modest value in the scale of beauty that he has sometimes fondly hoped, he lapses into a moody scepticism as to our place in the scale of "importance," and finds himself wondering vaguely whether this be not a richer race as well as a lovelier land. That of course will never do; so that when after being escorted down the beautiful choir in what, from the American point of view, is an almost gorgeous ecclesiastical march, by the Dean in a white robe trimmed with scarlet and black-robed sacristans carrying silver wands, the officiating canon mounts into a splendid canopied and pinnacled pulpit of Gothic stonework and proves—not an "acting" Jeremy Taylor, our poor sentimental tourist begins to hold up his head again and to reflect that so far as we *have* opportunities we mostly rise to them. I am not sure indeed that in the excess of his reaction he is not tempted to accuse his English neighbours of being impenetrable and uninspired, to affirm that they do not half discern their good fortune, and that it takes passionate pilgrims, vague aliens and other disinherited persons to appreciate the "points" of this admirable country.

Johnson's Statue, Lichfield

Lichfield and Warwick

To WRITE at Oxford of anything but Oxford requires, on
the part of the sentimental tourist, no small power of
mental abstraction. Yet I have it at heart to pay to three or
four other scenes recently visited the debt of an enjoyment
hardly less profound than my relish for this scholastic paradise. First among these is the cathedral city of Lichfield—the
city, I say, because Lichfield has a character of its own apart
from its great ecclesiastical feature. In the centre of its little
market-place—dullest and sleepiest of provincial market-
places—rises a huge effigy of Dr. Johnson, the *genius loci*,
who was constructed, humanly, with very nearly as large an
architecture as the great abbey. The Doctor's statue, which is
of some inexpensive composite painted a shiny brown, and of

no great merit of design, fills out the vacant dulness of the little square in much the same way as his massive personality occupies—with just a margin for Garrick—the record of his native town. In one of the volumes of Croker's "Boswell" is a steel plate of the old Johnsonian birth-house, by the aid of a vague recollection of which I detected the dwelling beneath its modernised frontage. It bears no mural inscription and, save for a hint of antiquity in the receding basement, with pillars supporting the floor above, seems in no especial harmony with Johnson's time or fame. Lichfield in general appeared to me indeed to have little to say about her great son beyond the fact that the smallness and the sameness and the dulness, amid which it is so easy to fancy a great intellectual appetite turning sick with inanition, may help to explain the Doctor's subsequent almost ferocious fondness for London. I walked about the silent streets, trying to repeople them with wigs and short-clothes, and, while I lingered near the cathedral, endeavoured to guess the message of its Gothic graces to Johnson's ponderous classicism. But I achieved but a colourless picture at the best, and the most vivid image in my mind's eye was that of the London coach facing towards Temple Bar with the young author of "Rasselas" scowling near-sightedly from the cheapest seat. With him goes the interest of Lichfield town. The place is stale without being really antique. It is as if that prodigious temperament had absorbed and appropriated its original vitality.

If every dull provincial town, however, formed but a girdle of quietude to a cathedral as rich as that of Lichfield, one would thank it for letting one alone. Lichfield Cathedral is great among churches, and bravely performs the prime duty of objects of its order—that of seeming for the time (to minds unsophisticated by architectural culture) the finest, on the whole, of all such objects. This one is rather oddly placed, on the slope of a hill, the particular spot having been chosen, I believe, because sanctified by the sufferings of certain primitive martyrs; but it is fine to see how its upper portions surmount any crookedness of posture and its great towers overtake in mid-air the conditions of perfect symmetry. The close is extraordinarily attractive; a long sheet of water expands behind it and, besides leading the eye off into a sweet

The Pool at Lichfield

green landscape, renders the inestimable service of reflecting the three spires as they rise above the great trees which mask the Palace and the Deanery. These august abodes edge the northern side of the slope, and behind their huge gate-posts and close-wrought gates the atmosphere of the Georgian era seems to abide. Before them stretches a row of huge elms, which must have been old when Johnson was young; and between these and the long-buttressed wall of the cathedral, you may stroll to and fro among as pleasant a mixture of influences (I imagine) as any in England. You can stand back here, too, from the west front further than in many cases, and examine at your ease its lavish decoration. You are perhaps a trifle too much at your ease; for you soon discover what a more cursory glance might not betray, that the immense façade has been covered with stucco and paint, that an effigy of Charles II., in wig and plumes and trunk-hose, of almost Gothic grotesqueness, surmounts the middle window; that the various other statues of saints and kings have but recently climbed into their niches; and that the whole expanse is in short an imposture. All this was done some fifty years ago, in the taste of that day as to restoration, and yet it but partially mitigates the impressiveness of the high façade, with its brace of spires, and the great embossed and image-fretted surface, to which the lowness of the portals (the too frequent reproach of English abbeys) seems to give a loftier reach. Passing beneath one of these low portals, however, I found myself gazing down as noble a church vista as any you need desire. The cathedral is of magnificent length, and the screen between nave and choir has been removed, so that from stem to stern, as one may say, of the great vessel of the church, it is all a mighty avenue of multitudinous slender columns, terminating in what seems a great screen of ruby and sapphire and topaz—one of the finest east windows in England. The cathedral is narrow in proportion to its length; it is the long-drawn aisle of the poet in perfection, and there is something grandly elegant in the unity of effect produced by this unobstructed perspective. The charm is increased by a singular architectural fantasy. Standing in the centre of the doorway, you perceive that the eastern wall does not directly face you, and that from the beginning of the choir the receding aisle deflects slightly

Lichfield from the East

to the left, in reported suggestion of the droop of the Saviour's head on the cross. Here again Mr. Gilbert Scott has lately laboured to no small purpose of *un*doing, it would appear—undoing the misdeeds of the last century. This extraordinary period expended an incalculable amount of imagination in proving that it had none. Universal whitewash was the least of its offences. But this has been scraped away and the solid stonework left to speak for itself, the delicate capitals and cornices disencrusted and discreetly rechiselled and the whole temple æsthetically rededicated. Its most beautiful feature, happily, has needed no repair, for its perfect beauty has been its safeguard. The great choir window of Lichfield is the noblest glass-work before the spell of which one's soul has become simple. I remember nowhere colours so chaste and grave, and yet so rich and true, or a cluster of designs so piously decorative and yet so vivified. Such a window as this seems to me the most sacred ornament of a great church; to be, not like vault and screen and altar, the dim contingent promise to the spirit, but the very redemption of the whole vow. This Lichfield glass is not the less interesting for being visibly of foreign origin. Exceeding so obviously as it does the range of English genius in this line, it indicates at least the heavenly treasure stored up in continental churches. It dates from the early sixteenth century, and was transferred hither sixty years ago from a decayed Belgian abbey. This, however, is not all of Lichfield. You have not seen it till you have strolled and restrolled along the close on every side, and watched the three spires constantly change their relation as you move and pause. Nothing can well be finer than the combination of the two lesser ones soaring equally in front with the third riding tremendously the magnificently sustained line of the roof. At a certain distance against the sky this long ridge seems something infinite and the great spire to sit astride of it like a giant mounted on a mastodon. Your sense of the huge mass of the building is deepened by the fact that though the central steeple is of double the elevation of the others, you see it, from some points, borne back in a perspective which drops it to half their stature and lifts them into immensity. But it would take long to tell all that one sees and

The Path to Haddon Hall

fancies and thinks in a lingering walk about so great a church
as this.

To walk in quest of any object that one has more or less
tenderly dreamed of, to find your way, to steal upon it softly,
to see at last, if it be church or castle, the tower-tops peeping
above elms or beeches—to push forward with a rush, and
emerge and pause and draw that first long breath which is the
compromise between so many sensations: this is a pleasure
left to the tourist even after the broad glare of photography
has dissipated so many of the sweet mysteries of travel; even
in a season when he is fatally apt to meet a dozen fellow pilgrims returning from the shrine, each as big a fool, so to
speak, as he ever was, or to overtake a dozen more telegraph-
ing their impressions down the line as they arrive. Such a
pleasure I lately enjoyed quite in its perfection, in a walk to
Haddon Hall, along a meadow-path by the Wye, in this interminable English twilight which I am never weary of admiring
watch in hand. Haddon Hall lies among Derbyshire hills, in a

region infested, I was about to write, by Americans. But I
achieved my own sly pilgrimage in perfect solitude; and as I
descried the gray walls among the rook-haunted elms I felt
not like a dusty tourist, but like a successful adventurer. I have
certainly had, as a dusty tourist, few more charming moments
than some—such as any one, I suppose, is free to have—that
I passed on a little ruined gray bridge which spans, with its
single narrow arch, a trickling stream at the base of the eminence from which those walls and trees look down. The twilight deepened, the ragged battlements and the low, broad
oriels glanced duskily from the foliage, the rooks wheeled and
clamoured in the glowing sky; and if there had been a ghost
on the premises I certainly ought to have seen it. In fact I did
see it, as we see ghosts nowadays. I felt the incommunicable
spirit of the scene with the last, the right intensity. The old
life, the old manners, the old figures seemed present again.
The great *coup de théâtre* of the young woman who shows you
the Hall—it is rather languidly done on her part—is to point
out a little dusky door opening from a turret to a back terrace
as the aperture through which Dorothy Vernon eloped with
Lord John Manners. I was ignorant of this episode, for I was
not to enter the place till the morrow, and I am still unversed
in the history of the actors. But as I stood in the luminous
dusk weaving the romance of the spot, I recognised the inevitability of a Dorothy Vernon and quite understood a Lord
John. It was of course on just such an evening that the romantic event came off, and by listening with the proper credulity,
I might surely hear on the flags of the castle court ghostly
footfalls and feel in their movements the old heart-beats. The
only footfall I can conscientiously swear to, however, is the
far from spectral tread of the damsel who led me through the
mansion in the prosier light of the next morning. Haddon
Hall, I believe, is one of the sights in which it is the fashion to
be "disappointed"; a fact explained in a great measure by the
absence of a formal approach to the house, which shows its
low, gray front to every trudger on the high-road. But the
charm of the spot is so much less that of grandeur than that
of melancholy, that it is rather deepened than diminished
by this attitude of obvious survival and decay. And for that
matter, when you have entered the steep little outer court

Haddon Hall

through the huge thickness of the low gateway, the present seems effectually walled out and the past walled in, even as a dead man in a sepulchre. It is very dead, of a fine June morning, the genius of Haddon Hall; and the silent courts and chambers, with their hues of ashen gray and faded brown, seem as time-bleached as the dry bones of any mouldering mortality. The comparison is odd, but Haddon Hall reminded me perversely of some of the larger houses at Pompeii. The private life of the past is revealed in each case with very much the same distinctness and on a scale small enough not to stagger the imagination. This old dwelling, indeed, has so little of the mass and expanse of the classic feudal castle that it almost suggests one of those miniature models of great buildings which lurk in dusty corners of museums. But it is large enough to be delectably complete and to contain an infinite store of the poetry of grass-grown courts looked into by wide, jutting windows and climbed out of by crooked stone stairways mounting against the walls to little high-placed doors. The "tone" of Haddon Hall, of all its walls and towers and stonework, is the gray of unpolished silver, and the reader who has been in England need hardly be reminded of the sweet accord—to eye and mind alike—existing between all stony surfaces covered with the pale corrosions of time and the deep living green of the strong ivy which seems to feed on their slow decay. Of this effect and of a hundred others— from those that belong to low-browed, stone-paved empty rooms where life was warm and atmospheres thick, to those one may note where the dark tower stairway emerges at last, on a level with the highest beech-tops, against the cracked and sun-baked parapet which flaunted the castle standard over the castle woods—of every form of sad desuetude and pictur- esque decay Haddon Hall contains some delightful example. Its finest point is undoubtedly a certain court from which a stately flight of steps ascends to the terrace where that daugh- ter of the Vernons whom I have mentioned took such happy thought for our requiring, as the phrase is, a reference. These steps, with the terrace, its balustrade topped with great ivy- muffled knobs of stone and its high background of massed woods, form the ideal *mise en scène* for portions of Shake- speare's comedies. "It's exactly Elizabethan," said my com- panion. Here the Countess Olivia may have listened to the fantastic Malvolio, or Beatrix, superbest of flirts, have come to summon Benedick to dinner.

The glories of Chatsworth, which lies but a few miles from Haddon, serve as a marked offset to its more delicate merits, just as they are supposed to gain, I believe, in the tourist's eyes, by contrast with its charming, its almost Italian shabbi- ness. But the glories of Chatsworth, incontestable as they are, were so effectually eclipsed to my mind, a couple of days later, that in future, when I think of an English mansion, I shall think only of Warwick, and when I think of an English park, only of Blenheim. Your run by train through the gentle Warwickshire land does much to prepare you for the great spectacle of the castle, which seems hardly more than a sort of massive symbol and synthesis of the broad prosperity and peace and leisure diffused over this great pastoral expanse.

Warwick Castle

The Warwickshire meadows are to common English scenery what this is to that of the rest of the world. For mile upon mile you can see nothing but broad sloping pastures of velvet turf, overbrowsed by sheep of the most fantastic shagginess, and garnished with hedges out of the trailing luxury of whose verdure great ivy-tangled oaks and elms arise with a kind of architectural regularity. The landscape indeed sins by excess of nutritive suggestion; it savours of larder and manger; it is too ovine, too bovine, it is almost asinine; and if you were to believe what you see before you this rugged globe would be a sort of boneless ball covered with some such plush-like integument as might be figured by the down on the cheek of a peach. But a great thought keeps you company as you go and gives character to the scenery. Warwickshire—you say it over and over—was Shakespeare's country. Those who think that a great genius is something supremely ripe and healthy and human may find comfort in the fact. It helps greatly to enliven my own vague conception of Shakespeare's temperament, with which I find it no great shock to be obliged to associate ideas of mutton and beef. There is something as final, as disillusioned of the romantic horrors of rock and forest, as deeply attuned to human needs in the Warwickshire pastures as there is in the underlying morality of the poet.

With human needs in general Warwick Castle may be in no great accord, but few places are more gratifying to the sentimental tourist. It is the only great residence he may have coveted as a home. The fire that we heard so much of last winter in America appears to have consumed but an inconsiderable and easily spared portion of the house, and the great towers rise over the great trees and the town with the same grand air as before. Picturesquely, Warwick gains from not being sequestered, after the common fashion, in acres of park. The village street winds about the garden walls, though its hum expires before it has had time to scale them. There can be no better example of the way in which stone walls, if they do not of necessity make a prison, may on occasions make a palace, than the prodigious privacy maintained thus about a mansion whose windows and towers form the main feature of a bustling town. At Warwick the past joins hands so stoutly with the present that you can hardly say where one begins and the

Chatsworth

other ends, and you rather miss the various crannies and gaps of what I just now called the Italian shabbiness of Haddon. There is a Cæsar's tower and a Guy's tower and half a dozen more, but they are so well-conditioned in their ponderous antiquity that you are at a loss whether to consider them parts of an old house revived or of a new house picturesquely superannuated. Such as they are, however, plunging into the grassed and gravelled courts from which their battlements look really feudal, and into gardens large enough for all delight and too small, as they should be, to be amazing; and with ranges between them of great apartments at whose hugely recessed windows you may turn from Vandyck and Rembrandt to glance down the cliff-like pile into the Avon, washing the base like a lordly moat, with its bridge, and its trees and its memories, they mark the very model of a great hereditary dwelling—one which amply satisfies the imagination without irritating the democratic conscience. The pictures at Warwick reminded me afresh of an old conclusion on this matter: that the best fortune for good pictures is not to be crowded into public collections—not even into the rela-

Guy's Cliff, Warwick

tive privacy of Salons Carrés and Tribunes—but to hang in
largely spaced half-dozens on the walls of fine houses. Here
the historical atmosphere, as one may call it, is almost a compensation for the often imperfect light. If this be true of most
pictures it is especially so of the works of Vandyck, whom you
think of, wherever you may find him, as having, with that
thorough good-breeding which is the stamp of his manner,
taken account in his painting of the local conditions and predestined his picture to just the spot where it hangs. This is in
fact an illusion as regards the Vandycks at Warwick, for none
of them represent members of the house. The very finest perhaps after the great melancholy, picturesque Charles I.—
death, or at least the presentiment of death on the pale
horse—is a portrait from the Brignole palace at Genoa; a
beautiful noble matron in black, with her little son and heir.
The last Vandycks I had seen were the noble company this
lady had left behind her in the Genoese palace, and as I
looked at her I thought of her mighty change of circum-

stance. Here she sits in the mild light of midmost England; there you could almost fancy her blinking in the great glare sent up from the Mediterranean. Intensity for intensity—intensity of situation constituted—I hardly know which to choose.

North Devon

FOR THOSE fanciful observers to whom broad England means chiefly the perfection of the rural picturesque, Devonshire means the perfection of England. I, at least, had so complacently taken for granted here all the characteristic graces of English scenery, had built so boldly on their rank orthodoxy, that before we fairly crossed the border I had begun to look impatiently from the carriage window for the veritable landscape in water-colours. Devonshire meets you promptly in all its purity, for the course of ten minutes you have been able to glance down the green vista of a dozen Devonshire lanes. On huge embankments of moss and turf, smothered in wild flowers and embroidered with the finest lace-work of trailing ground-ivy, rise solid walls of flowering thorn and glistening holly and golden broom, and more strong, homely shrubs than I can name, and toss their blooming tangle to a sky which seems to look down between them, in places, from but a dozen inches of blue. They are oversown with lovely little flowers with names as delicate as their petals of gold and silver and azure—bird's-eye and king's-finger and wandering-sailor—and their soil, a superb dark red, turns in spots so nearly to crimson that you almost fancy it some fantastic compound purchased at the chemist's and scattered there for ornament. The mingled reflection of this rich-hued earth and the dim green light which filters through the hedge is a masterpiece of produced beauty. A Devonshire cottage is no less striking an outcome of the ages and the seasons and the manners. Crushed beneath its burden of thatch, coated with a rough white stucco of a tone to delight a painter, nestling in deep foliage and garnished at doorstep and wayside with various forms of chubby infancy, it seems to have been stationed there for no more obvious purpose than to keep a promise to your fancy, though it covers, I suppose, not a little of the sordid side of life which the fancy likes to slur over.

I rolled past lanes and cottages to Exeter, where I had counted upon the cathedral. When one has fairly tasted of the pleasure of cathedral-hunting the approach to each new

A Devonshire Lane

possible prize of the chase gives a peculiarly agreeable zest to the curiosity. You are making a collection of great impressions, and I think the process is in no case so delightful as applied to cathedrals. Going from one fine picture to another is certainly good; but the fine pictures of the world are terribly numerous, and they have a troublesome way of crowding and jostling each other in the memory. The number of cathedrals is small, and the mass and presence of each specimen great, so that as they rise in the mind in individual majesty they dwarf all the commoner impressions of calculated effect. They form indeed but a gallery of vaster pictures; for when time has dulled the recollection of details you retain a single broad image of the vast gray edifice, with its head and shoulders, its vessel and its towers, its tone of colour, and its still green precinct. All this is especially true perhaps of one's sense of English sacred piles, which are almost alone in possessing, as pictures, a spacious and harmonious setting. The cathedral stands supreme, but the close makes, always, the *scene*. Exeter is not one of the grandest, but, in common with great and small, it has certain points in favour of which local learning discriminates. Exeter indeed does itself injustice by a low, dark front, which not only diminishes the apparent altitude of the nave, but conceals, as you look eastward, two noble Norman towers. The front, however, which has a gloomy impressiveness, is redeemed by two fine features: a magnificent rose-window, whose vast stone ribs (inclosing some very pallid last-century glass) are disposed with the most charming intricacy; and a long sculptured screen—a sort of stony band of images—which traverses the façade from side to side. The little broken-visaged effigies of saints and kings and bishops, niched in tiers along this hoary wall, are prodigiously black and quaint and primitive in expression; and as you look at them with whatever contemplative tenderness your trade of hard-working tourist may have left at your disposal, you fancy that they are broodingly conscious of their names, histories and misfortunes; that, sensitive victims of time, they feel the loss of their noses, their toes, and their crowns; and that, when the long June twilight turns at last to a deeper gray and the quiet of the close to a deeper stillness, they begin to peer sidewise out of their narrow recesses and to converse in some

Towers of Exeter Cathedral

strange form of early English, as rigid, yet as candid, as their features and postures, moaning, like a company of ancient paupers round a hospital fire, over their aches and infirmities and losses, and the sadness of being so terribly old. The vast square transeptal towers of the church seem to me to have the same sort of personal melancholy. Nothing in all architecture expresses better, to my imagination, the sadness of survival, the resignation of dogged material continuance, than a broad expanse of Norman stonework, roughly adorned with its low relief of short columns and round arches and almost barbarous hatchet-work, and lifted high into that mild English light which accords so well with its dull gray surface. The especial secret of the impressiveness of such a Norman tower I cannot pretend to have discovered. It lies largely in the look of having been proudly and sturdily built—as if the masons had been urged by a trumpet-blast, and the stones squared by a battle-axe—contrasted with this mere idleness of antiquity and passive lapse into quaintness. A Greek temple preserves a kind of fresh immortality in its concentrated refinement, and a Gothic cathedral in its adventurous exuberance; but a Norman tower stands up like some simple strong man in his might, bending a melancholy brow upon an age which demands that strength shall be cunning.

The North Devon coast, whither it was my design on coming to Exeter to proceed, has the primary merit of being, as yet, virgin soil as to railways. I went accordingly from Barnstaple to Ilfracombe on the top of a coach, in the fashion of elder days; and, thanks to my position, I managed to enjoy the landscape in spite of the two worthy aboriginals before me who were reading aloud together, with a natural glee which might have passed for fiendish malice, the *Daily Telegraph's* painfully vivid account of the defeat of the Atalanta crew. It seemed to me, I remember, a sort of pledge and token of the invincibility of English muscle that a newspaper record of its prowess should have power to divert my companions' eyes from the bosky flanks of Devonshire combes. The little watering-place of Ilfracombe is seated at the lower verge of one of these seaward-plunging valleys, between a couple of magnificent headlands which hold it in a hollow slope and offer it securely to the caress of the Bristol Channel.

Cliffs at Ilfracombe

It is a very finished little specimen of its genus, and I think that during my short stay there I expended as much attention on its manners and customs and its social physiognomy as on its cliffs and beach and great coast-view. My chief conclusion perhaps, from all these things, was that the terrible "summer question" which works annual anguish in so many American households would rage less hopelessly if we had a few Ilfracombes scattered along our Atlantic coast; and furthermore that the English are masters of the art of not losing sight of ease and convenience in the pursuit of the pastoral life—unlike our own people, who, when seeking rural beguilement, are apt but to find a new rudeness added to nature. It is just possible that at Ilfracombe ease and convenience weigh down the scale; so very substantial are they, so very officious and business-like. On the left of the town (to give an example) one of the great cliffs I have mentioned rises in a couple of massive peaks and presents to the sea an almost vertical face, all muffled in tufts of golden broom and mighty fern. You have not walked fifty yards away from the hotel before you encounter half a dozen little sign-boards, directing your steps to a path up the cliff. You follow their indications and you arrive at a little gatehouse, with photographs and various local gimcracks exposed for sale. A most respectable person appears, demands a penny and, on receiving it, admits you with great civility to commune with nature. You detect, however, various little influences hostile to perfect communion. You are greeted by another sign-board threatening legal pursuit if you attempt to evade the payment of the sacramental penny. The path, winding in a hundred ramifications over the cliff, is fastidiously solid and neat, and furnished at intervals of a dozen yards with excellent benches, inscribed by knife and pencil with the names of such visitors as do not happen to have been the elderly maiden ladies who now chiefly occupy them. All this is prosaic, and you have to subtract it in a lump from the total impression before the sense of the beguilement of nature becomes distinct. Your subtraction made, a great deal assuredly remains; quite enough, I found, to give me an ample day's refreshment; for English scenery, like most other English commodities, resists and rewards familiar use. The cliffs are superb, the play of light and shade upon them is a perpetual study, and the air a particular mixture of the breath of the hills and moors and the breath of the sea. I was very glad, at the end of my climb, to have a good bench to sit upon — as one must think twice in England before measuring one's length on the grassy earth; and to be able, thanks to the smooth foot-path, to get back to the hotel in a quarter of an hour. But it occurred to me that if I were an Englishman of the period, and, after ten months of a busy London life, my fancy were turning to a holiday, to rest and change and oblivion of the ponderous social burden, it might find rather less inspiration than needful in a vision of the little paths of Ilfracombe, of the sign-boards and the penny fee and the solitude tempered by old ladies and sheep. I wondered whether change perfect enough to be salutary does not imply something more pathless, more idle, more unreclaimed from that

Lynmouth

deep-bosomed nature to which the overwrought mind reverts with passionate longing; something after all attainable at a moderate distance from New York and Boston. I must add that I cannot find in my heart to object, even on grounds the most æsthetic, to the very beautiful and excellent inn at Ilfracombe, where such of my readers as are perchance actually wrestling with the question of "where to go" may be interested to learn that they may live *en pension*, very well indeed, at a cost of ten shillings a day. I have paid the American hotel-clerk a much heavier tax on a much lighter entertainment. I made the acquaintance at this establishment of that strange fruit of time the insular *table d'hôte*, but I confess that, faithful to the habit of a tourist open to the *arrière-pensée*, I have retained a more vivid impression of the talk and the faces than of our joints and side-dishes. I noticed here what I have often noticed before (the truth perhaps has never been duly recognised), that no people profit so eagerly as the English by the suspension of a common social law. A *table d'hôte*, being something abnormal and experimental, as it were, resulted apparently in a complete reversal of the supposed national characteristics. Conversation was universal—uproarious almost; old legends and ironies about the insular *morgue* seemed to see their ground crumble away. What social, what psychologic earthquake, in our own time, had occurred?

These are meagre memories, however, compared with those which cluster about that place of pleasantness which is locally known as Lynton. I am afraid I may seem a mere professional gusher when I declare how common almost any term appears to me applied to Lynton with descriptive intent. The little village is perched on the side of one of the great mountain cliffs with which this whole coast is adorned, and on the edge of a lovely gorge through which a broad hill-torrent foams and tumbles from the great moors whose heather-crested waves rise purple along the inland sky. Below it, close beside the beach where the little torrent meets the sea, is the sister village of Lynmouth. Here—as I stood on the bridge that spans the stream and looked at the stony backs and foundations and overclambering garden verdure of certain little gray old houses which plunge their feet into it, and then up at the tender green of scrub-oak and fern, at the colour of gorse and broom and bracken climbing the sides of the hills and leaving them bare-crowned to the sun like miniature mountains—I read an unnatural blueness into the northern sea, and the village below put on the grace of one of the hundred hamlets of the Riviera. The little Castle Hotel at Lynton is a spot so consecrated to supreme repose—to sitting with a book in the terrace-garden, among blooming plants of aristocratic magnitude and rarity, and watching the finest piece of colour in all nature, the glowing red and green of the great cliffs beyond the little harbour-mouth, as they shift and change and melt, the livelong day, from shade to shade and ineffable tone to tone—that I feel as if in helping it to publicity I were doing it rather a disfavour than a service. It is in fact a very deep and sure retreat, and I have never known one where purchased hospitality wore a more disinterested smile. Lynton is of course a capital centre for excursions, but two or three of which I had time to make. None is more beautiful than a simple walk along the running face of the cliffs to a singular rocky eminence whose curious abutments and pinnacles of stone have caused it to be named the

Lynmouth Lighthouse

Castle. It has a fantastic resemblance to some hoary feudal ruin, with crumbling towers and gaping chambers tenanted by wild sea-birds. The late afternoon light had a way, at this season, of lingering on until within a couple of hours of midnight; and I remember among the charmed moments of English travel none of a more vividly poetical tinge than a couple of evenings spent on the summit of this all but legendary pile in company with the slow-coming darkness and the short, sharp cry of the sea-mews. There are places whose very aspect is a story or a song. This jagged and pinnacled coast-wall, with the rock-strewn valley behind it, the sullen calmness of the unbroken tide at the dreadful base of the cliffs (where they divide into low sea-caves, making pillars and pedestals for the fantastic imagery of their summits), prompted one to wanton reminiscence and outbreak, to a recall of some drawing of Gustave Doré's (of his good time), which was a divination of the place and made one look for his signature under a stone, or, better still, to respouting, for sympathy and relief, some idyllic Tennysonian line that haunted one's destitute

The Castle, Lynton

past and that seemed to speak of the conditions in spite of being false to them geographically.

The last stage in my visit to North Devon was the long drive along the beautiful remnant of coast and through the rich pastoral scenery of Somerset. The whole broad spectacle that one dreams of viewing in a foreign land to the homely music of a postboy's whip I beheld on this admirable drive — breezy highlands clad in the warm blue-brown of heather-tufts as if in mantles of rusty velvet, little bays and coves curving gently to the doors of clustered fishing-huts, deep pastures and broad forests, villages thatched and trellised as if to take a prize for improbability, manor-tops peeping over rook-haunted avenues. I ought to make especial note of an hour I spent at midday at the village of Porlock in Somerset. Here the thatch seemed steeper and heavier, the yellow roses

on the cottage walls more cunningly mated with the crumbling stucco, the dark interiors within the open doors more
quaintly pictorial, than elsewhere; and as I loitered, while the
horses rested, in the little cool old timber-steepled, yew-
shaded church, betwixt the high-backed manorial pew and the
battered tomb of a crusading knight and his lady, and listened
to the simple prattle of a blue-eyed old sexton, who showed
me where, as a boy, in scantier corduroys, he had scratched
his name on the recumbent lady's breast, it seemed to me that
this at last was old England indeed, and that in a moment
more I should see Sir Roger de Coverley marching up the
aisle. Certainly, to give a proper account of it all, I should
need nothing less than the pen of Mr. Addison.

Wells and Salisbury

THE pleasantest thing in life is doubtless ever the pleasantness that has found one off one's guard—though if I was
off my guard in arriving at Wells it could only have been by
the effect of a frivolous want of information. I knew in a general way that this ancient little town had a great cathedral to
produce, but I was far from suspecting the intensity of the
impression that awaited me. The immense predominance of
the Minster towers, as you see them from the approaching
train over the clustered houses at their feet, gives you indeed
an intimation of its character, suggests that the city is nothing
if not sanctified; but I can wish the traveller no better fortune
than to stroll forth in the early evening with as large a reserve
of ignorance as my own, and treat himself to an hour of discoveries. I was lodged on the edge of the Cathedral lawn and
had only to pass beneath one of the three crumbling Priory
gates which enclose it, and cross the vast grassy oval, to stand
before a minster-front which ranks among the first three or
four in England. Wells Cathedral is extremely fortunate in being approached by this wide green level, on which the spectator may loiter and stroll to and fro and shift his standpoint to
his heart's content. The spectator who does not hesitate to
avail himself of his privilege of unlimited fastidiousness might
indeed pronounce it too isolated for perfect picturesqueness—too uncontrasted with the profane architecture of the
human homes for which it pleads to the skies. But Wells is in
fact not a city with a cathedral for central feature; it is a cathedral with a little city gathered at the base and forming hardly
more than an extension of the spacious close. You feel everywhere the presence of the beautiful church; the place seems
always to savour of a Sunday afternoon; and you imagine
every house tenanted by a canon, a prebendary or a precentor,
with "backs" providing for choristers and vergers.

The great façade is remarkable not so much for its expanse
as for its elaborate elegance. It consists of two great truncated
towers, divided by a broad centre bearing, beside its rich fret-
work of statues, three narrow lancet windows. The statues on

The Cathedral Lawn, Wells

this vast front are the great boast of the cathedral. They number, with the lateral figures of the towers, no less than three hundred; it seems densely embroidered by the chisel. They are disposed, in successive niches, along six main vertical shafts; the central windows are framed and divided by narrower shafts, and the wall above them rises into a pinnacled screen traversed by two superb horizontal rows. Add to these a close-running cornice of images along the line corresponding with the summit of the aisles and the tiers which complete the decoration of the towers on either side, and you have an immense system of images governed by a quaint theological order and most impressive in its completeness. Many of the little high-lodged effigies are mutilated, and not a few of the niches are empty, but the injury of time is not sufficient to diminish the noble serenity of the building. The injury of time is indeed being actively repaired, for the front is partly masked by a slender scaffolding. The props and platforms are of the most delicate structure, and look in fact as if they were meant to facilitate no more ponderous labour than a fitting-on of noses to disfeatured bishops and a rearrangement of the mantle-folds of straitlaced queens discomposed by the centuries. The main beauty of Wells Cathedral, to my mind, is not its more or less visible wealth of detail, but its singularly charming tone of colour. An even, sober, mouse-coloured gray invests it from summit to base, deepening nowhere to the melancholy black of your truly romantic Gothic, but showing as yet none of the spotty brightness of renovation. It is a wonderful fact that the great towers, from their lofty out-look, see never a factory chimney—those cloud-compelling spires which so often break the charm of the softest English horizons; and the general atmosphere of Wells seemed to me, for some reason, peculiarly luminous and sweet. The cathedral has never been discoloured by the moral malaria of a city with an independent secular life. As you turn back from its portal and glance at the open lawn before it, edged by the mild gray seventeenth-century deanery and the other dwellings, hardly less stately, which seem to reflect in their comfortable fronts the rich respectability of the church, and then up again at the beautiful clear-hued pile, you may fancy it less a temple for man's needs than a monument of his pride—less a fold for the flock than for the shepherds; a visible token that, besides the actual assortment of heavenly thrones, there is constantly on hand a "full line" of cushioned cathedral stalls. Within the cathedral this impression is not diminished. The interior is vast and massive, but it lacks incident—the incident of mon-uments, sepulchres and chapels—and it is too brilliantly lighted for picturesque, as distinguished from strictly architec-tural, interest. Under this latter head it has, I believe, great importance. For myself, I can think of it only as I saw it from my place in the choir during afternoon service of a hot Sun-day. The Bishop sat facing me, enthroned in a stately Gothic alcove and clad in his crimson band, his lawn sleeves and his lavender gloves; the canons, in their degree, with still other priestly forms, reclined comfortably in the carven stalls, and the scanty congregation fringed the broad aisle. But though scanty, the congregation was select; it was unexceptionably black-coated, bonneted and gloved. It savoured intensely in short of that inexorable gentility which the English put on with their Sunday bonnets and beavers and which fills

The Market Place, Wells

me—as a mere taster of produced tastes—with a sort of fond reactionary remembrance of those animated bundles of rags which one sees kneeling in the churches of Italy. But even here, as taster of tastes, I found my account. You always do if you throw yourself confidently enough, in England, on the chapter of accidents. Before me and beside me sat a row of the comeliest young men, clad in black gowns and wearing on their shoulders long hoods trimmed with white fur. Who and what they were I know not, for I preferred not to learn, lest by chance they should not be so mediæval as they looked.

My fancy found its account even better in the singular quaintness of the little precinct known as the Vicars' Close. It directly adjoins the Cathedral Green, and you enter it beneath one of the solid old gatehouses which form so striking an element in the ecclesiastical furniture of Wells. It consists of a narrow, oblong court, bordered on each side with thirteen small dwellings, and terminating in a ruinous little chapel. Here formerly dwelt a congregation of minor priests, established in the thirteenth century to do curates' work for the canons. The little houses are very much modernised; but they retain their tall chimneys, with carven tablets in the face, their antique compactness and neatness, and a certain little sanctified air as of cells in a cloister. The place is adorably of another world and time, and, approaching it as I did in the first dimness of twilight, it looked to me, in its exaggerated perspective, like one of those conventional streets represented on the stage, down whose impossible vista the heroes and confidants of romantic comedies come swaggering arm-in-arm and hold amorous converse with heroines perched at second-story windows. But though the Vicars' Close is a curious affair enough, the great boast of Wells is its episcopal Palace. The Palace loses nothing from being seen for the first time in the kindly twilight, and from being approached with an uncautioned mind. To reach it (unless you go from within the cathedral by the cloisters), you pass out of the Green by another ancient gateway into the market-place, and thence back again through its own peculiar portal. My own first glimpse of it had all the felicity of a *coup de théâtre*. I saw within the dark archway an enclosure bedimmed at once with the shadows of trees and heightened with the glitter of water. The picture

Glastonbury Abbey

was worthy of this agreeable promise. Its main feature is the
little gray-walled island on which the Palace stands, rising in
feudal fashion out of a broad, clear moat, flanked with round
towers and approached by a proper drawbridge. Along the
outer side of the moat is a short walk beneath a row of picturesquely stunted elms; swans and ducks disport themselves
in the current and ripple the bright shadows of the overclambering plants from the episcopal gardens and masses of wall-
flower lodged on the hoary battlements. On the evening of
my visit the haymakers were at work on a great sloping field
in the rear of the Palace, and the sweet perfume of the tumbled grass in the dusky air seemed all that was wanting to fix
the scene for ever in the memory. Beyond the moat and
within the gray walls dwells my lord Bishop, in the finest seat
of all his order. The mansion dates from the thirteenth century; but, stately dwelling though it is, it occupies but a subordinate place in its own grounds. Their great ornament,
picturesquely speaking, is the massive ruin of a banqueting-
hall erected by a free-living mediæval bishop and more or less

demolished at the Reformation. With its still perfect towers and beautiful shapely windows, hung with those green tapestries so stoutly woven by the English climate, it is a relic worthy of being locked away behind an embattled wall. I have among my impressions of Wells, besides this picture of the moated Palace, half a dozen memories of the romantic sort, which I lack space to transcribe. The clearest impression perhaps is that of the beautiful church of St. Cuthbert, of the same date as the cathedral, and in very much the same style of elegant, temperate Early English. It wears one of the high-soaring towers for which Somersetshire is justly celebrated, as you may see from the window of the train in rolling past its almost top-heavy hamlets. The beautiful old church, surrounded with its green graveyard, and large enough to be impressive, without being too large (a great merit, to my sense) to be easily compassed by a deplorably unarchitectural eye, wore a native English expression to which certain humble figures in the foreground gave additional point. On the edge of the churchyard was a low-gabled house, before which four old men were gossiping in the eventide. Into the front of the house was inserted an antique alcove in stone, divided into three shallow little seats, two of which were occupied by extraordinary specimens of decrepitude. One of these ancient paupers had a huge protuberant forehead, and sat with a pensive air, his head gathered painfully upon his twisted shoulders and his legs resting across his crutch. The other was rubicund, blear-eyed and frightfully besmeared with snuff. Their voices were so feeble and senile that I could scarcely understand them, and only just managed to make out the answer to my inquiry of who and what they were—"We're Still's Almshouse, sir."

One of the lions, almost, of Wells (whence it is but five miles distant) is the ruin of the famous Abbey of Glastonbury, on which Henry VIII., in the language of our day, came down so heavily. The ancient splendour of the architecture survives but in scattered and scanty fragments, among influences of a rather inharmonious sort. It was cattle-market in the little town as I passed up the main street, and a savour of hoofs and hide seemed to accompany me through the easy labyrinth of the old arches and piers. These occupy a large

Salisbury Cathedral

back yard, close behind the street, to which you are most prosaically admitted by a young woman who keeps a wicket and
sells tickets. The continuity of tradition is not altogether broken, however, for the little street of Glastonbury has rather an
old-time aspect, and one of the houses at least must have seen
the last of the abbots ride abroad on his mule. The little inn is
a capital bit of character, and as I waited for the 'bus under its
low dark archway (in something of the mood, possibly, in
which a train was once waited for at Coventry), and watched
the barmaid flirting her way to and fro out of the heavy-
browed kitchen and among the lounging young appraisers of
colts and steers and barmaids, I might have imagined that the
Merry England of the Tudors had not utterly passed away. A
beautiful England this must have been as well, if it contained
many such abbeys as Glastonbury. Such of the ruined columns and portals and windows as still remain are of admirable design and finish. The doorways are rich in marginal
ornament—ornament within ornament, as it often is; for the
dainty weeds and wild flowers overlace the antique tracery
with their bright arabesques and deepen the gray of the stonework as it brightens their bloom. The thousand flowers which
grow among English ruins deserve a chapter to themselves. I
owe them, as an observer, a heavy debt of satisfaction, but I
am too little of a botanist to pay them in their own coin. It
has often seemed to me in England that the purest enjoyment
of architecture was to be had among the ruins of great buildings. In the perfect building one is rarely sure that the impression is simply architectural: it is more or less pictorial and
romantic; it depends partly upon association and partly upon
various accessories and details which, however they may be
wrought into harmony with the architectural idea, are not
part of its essence and spirit. But in so far as beauty of structure is beauty of line and curve, balance and harmony of
masses and dimensions, I have seldom relished it as deeply as
on the grassy nave of some crumbling church, before lonely
columns and empty windows where the wild flowers were a
cornice and the sailing clouds a roof. The arts certainly hang
together in what they do for us. These hoary relics of Glastonbury reminded me in their broken eloquence of one of the
other great ruins of the world—the *Last Supper* of Leonardo.

Salisbury Spire

A beautiful shadow, in each case, is all that remains; but that shadow is the soul of the artist.

Salisbury Cathedral, to which I made a pilgrimage on leaving Wells, is the very reverse of a ruin, and you take your pleasure there on very different grounds from those I have just attempted to define. It is perhaps the best-known typical church in the world, thanks to its shapely spire; but the spire is so simply and obviously fair that when you have respectfully made a note of it you have anticipated æsthetic analysis. I had seen it before and admired it heartily, and perhaps I should have done as well to let my admiration rest. I confess that on repeated inspection it grew to seem to me the least bit *banal*, or even *bête*, since I am talking French, and I began to consider whether it does not belong to the same range of art as the Apollo Belvedere or the Venus de' Medici. I am inclined to think that if I had to live within sight of a cathedral and encounter it in my daily comings and goings I should grow less weary of the rugged black front of Exeter than of the sweet perfection of Salisbury. There are people by temper-

ament easily sated with beauties specifically fair, and the effect
of Salisbury Cathedral architecturally is equivalent to that of
flaxen hair and blue eyes physiognomically. The other lions of
Salisbury, Stonehenge and Wilton House, I revisited with undiminished interest. Stonehenge is rather a hackneyed shrine
of pilgrimage. At the time of my former visit a picnic-party
was making libations of beer on the dreadful altar-sites. But
the mighty mystery of the place has not yet been stared out of
countenance; and as on this occasion there were no picnickers
we were left to drink deep of all its ambiguities and intensities. It stands as lonely in history as it does on the great plain
whose many-tinted green waves, as they roll away from it,
seem to symbolise the ebb of the long centuries which have
left it so portentously unexplained. You may put a hundred
questions to these rough-hewn giants as they bend in grim
contemplation of their fallen companions; but your curiosity
falls dead in the vast sunny stillness that enshrouds them, and
the strange monument, with all its unspoken memories, becomes simply a heart-stirring picture in a land of pictures. It is
indeed immensely vague and immensely deep. At a distance
you see it standing in a shallow dell of the plain, looking
hardly larger than a group of ten-pins on a bowling-green. I
can fancy sitting all a summer's day watching its shadows
shorten and lengthen again, and drawing a delicious contrast
between the world's duration and the feeble span of individual experience. There is something in Stonehenge almost reas-
suring to the nerves; if you are disposed to feel that the life of
man has rather a thin surface, and that we soon get to the
bottom of things, the immemorial gray pillars may serve to
represent for you the pathless vaults beneath the house of history. Salisbury is indeed rich in antiquities. Wilton House, a
delightful old residence of the Earls of Pembroke, contains a
noble collection of Greek and Roman marbles. These are
ranged round a charming cloister occupying the centre of the
house, which is exhibited in the most liberal fashion. Out of
the cloister opens a series of drawing-rooms hung with family
portraits, chiefly by Vandyck, all of superlative merit. Among
them hangs supreme, as the Vandyck *par excellence*, the famous and magnificent group of the whole Pembroke family of
James I.'s time. This splendid work has every pictorial merit—

Stonehenge

design, colour, elegance, force and finish, and I have been vainly wondering to this hour what it needs to be the finest piece of portraiture, as it surely is one of the most ambitious, in the world. What it lacks, characteristically, in a certain uncompromising veracity, it recovers in the beautiful dignity of its position—unmoved from the stately house in which its author sojourned and wrought, familiar to the descendants of its noble originals.

An English Easter

I

It may be said of the English, as is said of the council of war in Sheridan's farce of *The Critic* by one of the spectators of the rehearsal, that when they *do* agree, their unanimity is wonderful. They differ among themselves greatly just now as regards the machinations of Russia, the derelictions of Turkey, the merits of the Reverend Arthur Tooth, the genius of Mr. Henry Irving, and a good many other matters; but neither just now nor at any other time do they fail to conform to those social observances on which respectability has set her seal. England is a country of curious anomalies, and this has much to do with her being so interesting to foreign observers. The national, the individual character is very positive, very independent, very much made up according to its own sentiment of things, very prone to startling eccentricities; and yet at the same time it has beyond any other this peculiar gift of squaring itself with fashion and custom. In no other country, I imagine, are so many people to be found doing the same thing in the same way at the same time—using the same slang, wearing the same hats and neckties, collecting the same china-plates, playing the same game of lawn-tennis or of polo, admiring the same professional beauty. The monotony of such a spectacle would soon become oppressive if the foreign observer were not conscious of this latent capacity in the performers for great freedom of action; he finds a good deal of entertainment in wondering how they reconcile the traditional insularity of the private person with this perpetual tribute to usage. Of course in all civilised societies the tribute to usage is constantly paid; if it is less apparent in America than elsewhere the reason is not, I think, because individual independence is greater, but because usage is more sparsely established. Where custom can be ascertained people certainly follow it; but for one definite precedent in American life there are fifty in English. I am very far from having discovered the secret; I have not in the least learned what becomes of that explosive personal force in the English character which is compressed and corked down by social conformity. I look with a certain awe at some of the manifestations of the conforming spirit, but the fermenting idiosyncrasies beneath it are hidden from my vision. The most striking example, to foreign eyes, of the power of custom in England is certainly the universal church-going. In the sight of the English people getting up from its tea and toast of a Sunday morning and brushing its hat, and drawing on its gloves, and taking its wife on its arm, and making its offspring march before, and so, for decency's, respectability's, propriety's sake, wending its way to a place of worship appointed by the State, in which it repeats the formulas of a creed to which it attaches no positive sense and listens to a sermon over the length of which it explicitly haggles and grumbles—in this exhibition there is something very impressive to a stranger, something which he hardly knows whether to estimate as a great force or as a great futility. He inclines on the whole to pronounce the spectacle sublime, because it gives him the feeling that whenever it may become necessary for a people trained in these manœuvres to move all together under a common direction, they will have it in them to do so with tremendous weight and cohesiveness. We hear a good deal about the effect of the Prussian military system in consolidating the German people and making them available for a particular purpose; but I really think it not fanciful to say that the military punctuality which characterises the English observance of Sunday ought to be appreciated in the same fashion. A nation which has passed through such a mill will certainly have been stamped by it. And here, as in the German military service, it is really the whole nation. When I spoke just now of paterfamilias and his *entourage* I did not mean to limit the statement to him. The young unmarried men go to church, the gay bachelors, the irresponsible members of society. (That last epithet must be taken with a grain of allowance. No one in England is literally irresponsible; that perhaps is the shortest way of expressing a stranger's, certainly an American's, sense of their cohesion. Every one is free and every one is responsible. To say what it is people are responsible *to* is of course a great extension of the question: briefly, to social expectation, to propriety, to

morality, to "position," to the conventional English conscience, which is, after all, such a powerful factor. With us
there is infinitely less responsibility; but there is also, I think,
less freedom.)

The way in which the example of the more luxurious classes
imposes itself upon the less luxurious may of course be noticed in smaller matters than church-going; in a great many
matters which it may seem trivial to mention. If one is bent
upon observation nothing, however, is trivial. So I may cite
the practice of banishing the servants from the room at breakfast. It is the fashion, and accordingly, through the length and
breadth of England, every one who has the slightest pretension to standing high enough to feel the way the social breeze
is blowing conforms to it. It is awkward, unnatural, troublesome for those at table, it involves a vast amount of leaning
and stretching, of waiting and perambulating, and it has just
that vice against which, in English history, all great movements have been made—it is arbitrary. But it flourishes for all
that, and all genteel people, looking into each other's eyes
with the desperation of gentility, agree to endure it for gentility's sake. My instance may seem feeble, and I speak honestly
when I say I might give others, forming part of an immense
body of prescriptive usage, to which a society possessing in
the largest manner, both by temperament and education, the
sense of the "inalienable" rights and comforts of the individual, contrives to accommodate itself. I do not mean to say
that usage in England is always uncomfortable and arbitrary.
On the contrary, few strangers can be unfamiliar with that
sensation (a most agreeable one) which consists in perceiving
in the rigidity of a tradition which has struck one at first as
mechanical a reason existing in the historic "good sense" of
the English race. The sensation is frequent, though in saying
so I do not mean to imply that even superficially the presumption is against the usages of English society. It is not, for
instance, necessarily against the custom of which I had it
more especially in mind to speak in writing these lines. The
stranger in London is forewarned that at Easter all the world
goes out of town, and that if he have no mind to be left to
some fate the universal terror of which half allures half appals
his curiosity, he too had better make arrangements for a

temporary absence. It must be admitted that there is a sort of unexpectedness in this prompt re-emigration of a body of people who but a week before were apparently devoting much energy to settling down for the season. Half of them have but lately come back from the country, where they have been spending the winter, and they have just had time, it may be supposed, to collect the scattered threads of town-life. Presently, however, the threads are dropped and society is dispersed as if it had taken a false start. It departs as Holy Week draws to a close, and remains absent for the following ten days. Where it goes is its own affair; a good deal of it goes to Paris. Spending last winter in that city, I remember how, when I woke up on Easter Monday and looked out of my window, I found the street covered overnight with a sort of snow-fall of disembarked Britons. They made for the other people an uncomfortable week of it. One's customary table at the restaurant, one's habitual stall at the Théâtre Français, one's usual fiacre on the cab-stand, were very apt to have suffered estrangement. I believe the pilgrimage to Paris was this year of the usual proportions; and you may be sure that people who did not cross the Channel were not without invitations to quiet old places in the country, where the pale fresh primroses were beginning to light up the dark turf and the purple bloom of the bare tree-masses to be freckled here and there with verdure. In England country-life is the obverse of the medal, town-life the reverse, and when an occasion comes for quitting London there are few members of what the French call the "easy class" who have not a collection of dull, moist, verdant resorts to choose from. Dull I call them, and I fancy not without reason, though at the moment I speak of their dulness must have been mitigated by the unintermittent presence of the keenest and liveliest of east winds. Even in mellow English country homes Easter-tide is a period of rawness and atmospheric acridity—the moment at which the frank hostility of winter, which has at last to give up the game, turns to peevishness and spite. This is what makes it arbitrary, as I said just now, for "easy" people to go forth to the wind-swept lawns and the shivering parks. But nothing is more striking to an American than the frequency of English holidays and the large way in which occasions for a "little change" are made use of. All this speaks to Americans of three things which they are accustomed to see allotted in scantier measure. The English have more time than we, they have more money, and they have a much higher relish for active leisure. Leisure, fortune, and the love of sport are felicities encountered in English society at every turn. It was a very small number of weeks before Easter that Parliament met, and yet a ten days' recess was already, from the luxurious Parliamentary point of view, a necessity. A short time hence we shall be having the Whitsuntide holidays, which I am told are even more of a season of revelry than Easter, and from this point to midsummer, when everything stops, is an easy journey. The men of business and the professional men partake in equal measure of these agreeable diversions, and I was interested in hearing a lady whose husband was an active member of the bar say that, though he was leaving town with her for ten days, and though Easter was a very nice "little break," they really amused themselves more during the later festival, which would come on toward the end of May. I thought this highly probable, and admired in their career such an effect of breeze-blown light and shade. If my phrase has a slightly ironical sound, this is purely accidental. A large appetite for holidays, the ability not only to take them but to know what to do with them when taken, is the sign of a robust people, and judged by this measure we Americans are sadly inexpert. Such holidays as we take are taken very often in Europe, where it is sometimes noticeable that our privilege is rather heavy on our hands. Acknowledgment made of English industry, however (our own stands in no need of compliments), it must be added that for those same easy classes I just spoke of things are very easy indeed. The number of persons obtainable for purely social purposes at all times and seasons is infinitely greater than among ourselves; and the ingenuity of the arrangements permanently going forward to disembarrass them of their superfluous leisure is as yet in America an undeveloped branch of civilisation. The young men who are preparing for the stern realities of life among the gray-green cloisters of Oxford are obliged to keep their terms but half the year; and the rosy little cricketers of Eton and Harrow are let loose upon the parental home for an embarrassing number of months. Happily the parental home is apt to be an affair of gardens, lawns and parks.

II

Passion Week, in London, is distinctly an ascetic period; there is really an approach to sackcloth and ashes. Private dissipation is suspended; most of the theatres and music-halls are closed; the huge dusky city seems to take on a still sadder colouring and a half-hearted hush steals over its mighty uproar. At such a moment, for a stranger, London is not cheerful. Arriving there, during the past winter, about Christmastime, I encountered three British Sundays in a row—a spectacle to strike terror into the stoutest heart. A Sunday and a "bank-holiday," if I remember aright, had joined hands with a Christmas Day and produced the portentous phenomenon to which I allude. I betrayed, I suppose, some apprehension of its oppressive character, for I remember being told in a consolatory way that I needn't fear; it would not come round again for another year. This information was given me on the occasion of that surprising interruption of one's relations with the laundress which is apparently characteristic of the period. I was told that all the washerwomen were intoxicated and that, as it would take them some time to revive, I must not count upon a relay of "fresh things." I shall not forget the impression made upon me by this statement; I had just come from Paris and it almost sent me spinning back. One of the incidental *agréments* of life in the latter city had been the knock at my door on Saturday evenings of a charming young woman with a large basket protected by a snowy napkin on her arm, and on her head a frilled and fluted muslin cap which was an irresistible advertisement of her art. To say that my admirable *blanchisseuse* was not in liquor is altogether too gross a compliment; but I was always grateful to her for her russet cheek, her frank expressive eye, her talkative smile, for the way her charming cap was poised upon her crisp, dense hair and her well-made dress adjusted and worn. I talked with her; I *could* talk with her; and as she talked she moved about and laid out her linen with a delightful modest ease. Then her light step carried her off again, talking, to the door, and with

a brighter smile and an "Adieu, monsieur!" she closed it behind her, leaving one to think how stupid is prejudice and
how poetic a creature a washerwoman may be. London, in
December, was livid with sleet and fog, and against this dismal background was offered me the vision of a horrible old
woman in a smoky bonnet, lying prone in a puddle of
whisky! She seemed to assume a kind of symbolic significance
and almost frightened me away.

I mention this trifle, which is doubtless not creditable to
my fortitude, because I found that the information given me
was not strictly accurate and that at the end of three months I
had another array of London Sundays to face. On this occasion, however, nothing occurred to suggest again the dreadful
image I have just sketched, though I devoted a good deal of
time to observing the manners of the lower orders. From
Good Friday to Easter Monday, inclusive, they were very
much *en evidence*, and it was an excellent occasion for getting
an impression of the British populace. Gentility had retired to
the background, and in the West End all the blinds were lowered; the streets were void of carriages, and well-dressed pedestrians were rare; but the "masses" were all abroad and
making the most of their holiday, so that I strolled about and
watched them at their gambols. The heavens were most unfa-
vourable, but in an English "outing" there is always a margin
left for a drenching, and throughout the vast smoky city, beneath the shifting gloom of the sky, the grimy crowds wandered with a kind of weather-proof stolidity. The parks were
full of them, the railway stations overflowed, the Thames embankment was covered. The "masses," I think, are usually an
entertaining spectacle, even when observed through the dis-
torting medium of London bad weather. There are indeed
few things in their way more impressive than a dusky London
holiday; it suggests so many and such interestingly related reflections. Even looked at superficially the capital of the Empire is one of the most appealing of cities, and it is perhaps on
such occasions as this that I have most felt its appeal. London
is ugly, dusky, dreary, more destitute than any European city
of graceful and decorative incident; and though on festal
days, like those I speak of, the populace is massed in large
numbers at certain points, many of the streets are empty

Baker Street

enough of human life to enable you to perceive their intrinsic want of charm. A Christmas Day or a Good Friday uncovers the ugliness of London. As you walk along the streets, having no fellow pedestrians to look at, you look up at the brown brick house-walls, corroded with soot and fog, pierced with their straight stiff window-slits, and finished, by way of a cornice, with a little black line resembling a slice of curbstone. There is not an accessory, not a touch of architectural fancy, not the narrowest concession to beauty. If I were a foreigner it would make me rabid; being an Anglo-Saxon I find in it what Thackeray found in Baker Street—a delightful proof of English domestic virtue, of the sanctity of the British home. There are miles and miles of these edifying monuments, and it would seem that a city made up of them should have no claim to that larger effectiveness of which I just now spoke. London, however, is not made up of them; there are architectural combinations of a statelier kind, and the impression moreover does not rest on details. London is pictorial in spite of details—from its dark green, misty parks, the way the light comes down leaking and filtering from its cloud-ceiling, and the softness and richness of tone which objects put on in such an atmosphere as soon as they begin to recede. Nowhere is there such a play of light and shade, such a struggle of sun and smoke, such aerial gradations and confusions. To eyes addicted to such contemplations this is a constant diversion, and yet this is only part of it. What completes the effect of the place is its appeal to the feelings, made in so many ways, but made above all by agglomerated immensity. At any given point London looks huge; even in narrow corners you have a sense of its hugeness, and petty places acquire a certain interest from their being parts of so mighty a whole. Nowhere else is so much human life gathered together, and nowhere does it press upon you with so many suggestions. These are not all of an exhilarating kind; far from it. But they are of every possible kind, and that is the interest of London. Those that were most forcible during the showery Easter season were certain of the more perplexing and depressing ones; but even with these was mingled a brighter strain.

I walked down to Westminster Abbey on Good Friday afternoon—walked from Piccadilly across the Green Park and

St. James's Park

through that of St. James. The parks were densely filled with
the populace—the elder people shuffling about the walks and
the poor little smutty-faced children sprawling over the dark
damp turf. When I reached the Abbey I found a dense group
of people about the entrance, but I squeezed my way through
them and succeeded in reaching the threshold. Beyond this it
was impossible to advance, and I may add that it was not
desirable. I put my nose into the church and promptly with-
drew it. The crowd was terribly compact, and beneath the
Gothic arches the odour was not that of incense. I gradually
gave it up, with that very modified sense of disappointment
that one feels in London at being crowded out of a place.
This is a frequent form of philosophy, for you soon learn that
there are, selfishly speaking, too many people. Human life is
cheap; your fellow mortals are too numerous. Wherever you
go you make the observation. At the theatre, at a concert, an
exhibition, a reception, you always find that, before you arrive, there are people enough in the field. You are a tight fit in
your place, wherever you find it; you have too many companions and competitors. You feel yourself at times in danger of
thinking meanly of the human personality; numerosity, as it
were, swallows up quality, and the perpetual sense of other
elbows and knees begets a yearning for the desert. This is the
reason why the perfection of luxury in England is to own a
"park"—an artificial solitude. To get one's self into the middle of a few hundred acres of oak-studded turf and to keep off
the crowd by the breadth, at least, of the grassy shade, is to
enjoy a comfort which circumstances make peculiarly precious. But I walked back through the profane pleasure-
grounds of London, in the midst of "superfluous herds," and
I found the profit of vision that I never fail to derive from a
great English assemblage. The English are, on the whole, to
my eyes so appreciably the handsomest people in Europe—
remembering always, of course, that when we talk of the frequency of beauty anywhere we talk of a minor quantity, more
small or less small—that it takes some effort of the imagination to believe that the appearance requires demonstration. I
never see a large number of them without feeling this impression confirmed; though I hasten to add that I have sometimes
felt it to be much shaken in the presence of a limited group. I

The Duke of York's Steps

suspect that a great English crowd would yield a larger percentage of *regular* faces and tall figures than any other. With regard to the upper class I suppose this is generally granted; but, with all abatements, I should extend it to the people at large. Certainly, if the English populace strike the observer as regular, nature, in them, must have clung hard to the higher ideal. They are as ill-dressed as their betters are well-dressed, and their garments have that sooty surface which has nothing in common with the continental costume of labour and privation. It is the hard prose of misery—an ugly and hopeless imitation of respectable attire. This is especially noticeable in the battered and bedraggled bonnets of the women, which look as if their husbands had stamped on them, in hob-nailed boots, as a hint of what may be in store for their wearers. Then it is not too much to say that two-thirds of the London faces, as the streets present them, bear in some degree or other the traces of alcoholic action. The proportion of flushed, empurpled, eruptive masks is considerable; a source of depression, for the spectator, not diminished by the fact that many of the faces thus disfigured have evidently been planned on lines of high superficial decency. A very large allowance is to be made, too, for the people who bear the distinctive stamp of that physical and mental degradation which comes from the slums and purlieus of this duskiest of modern Babylons—the pallid, stunted, misbegotten and in every way miserable figures. These people swarm in every London crowd, and I know of none in any other place that suggest an equal depth of degradation. But when such exceptions are taken the observer still notes the quantity and degree of facial finish, the firmness of type, if not always its fineness, the clearnesses and symmetries, the modelled brows and cheeks and chins, the immense contribution made to his impression, above all, by the elements of complexion and stature. The question of expression is another matter, and one must admit at the outset, to have done with it, that expression here in general lacks, even to strangeness, any perceptible intensity, though it often has among the women, and adorably among the children, an indescribable shy delicacy. I have it at heart, however, to add that if the English are handsomer than ourselves they are also very much uglier. Indeed I think all the

European peoples more richly ugly than the American: we are far from producing those magnificent types of facial eccentricity which flourish on soils socially more rank. American ugliness is on the side of physical poverty and meanness; English on that of redundancy and monstrosity. In America there are few grotesques; in England there are many—and some of them have a high plastic, historic, romantic value.

III

The element of the grotesque was very noticeable to me in the most marked collection of the shabbier English types that I had seen since I came to London. The occasion of my seeing them was the funeral of Mr. George Odger, which befell some four or five weeks before the Easter period. Mr. George Odger, it will perhaps be remembered, was an English Radical agitator of humble origin, who had distinguished himself by a perverse desire to get into Parliament. He exercised, I believe, the useful profession of shoemaker, and he knocked in vain at the door that opens but to the refined. But he was a useful and honourable man, and his own people gave him an honourable burial. I emerged accidentally into Piccadilly at the moment they were so engaged, and the spectacle was one I should have been sorry to miss. The crowd was enormous, but I managed to squeeze through it and to get into a hansom cab that was drawn up beside the pavement, and here I looked on as from a box at the play. Though it was a funeral that was going on I will not call it a tragedy; but it was a very serious comedy. The day happened to be magnificent—the finest of the year. The ceremony had been taken in hand by the classes who are socially unrepresented in Parliament, and it had the character of a great popular manifestation. The hearse was followed by very few carriages, but the *cortège* of pedestrians stretched away in the sunshine, up and down the classic decorum of Piccadilly, on a scale highly impressive. Here and there the line was broken by a small brass band— apparently one of those bands of itinerant Germans that play for coppers beneath lodging-house windows; but for the rest it was compactly made up of what the newspapers call the dregs of the population. It was the London rabble, the met-

ropolitan mob, men and women, boys and girls, the decent
poor and the indecent, who had scrambled into the ranks as
they gathered them up on their passage, and were making a
sort of solemn "lark" of it. Very solemn it all was—perfectly
proper and undemonstrative. They shuffled along in an interminable line, and as I looked at them out of the front of my
hansom I seemed to be having a sort of panoramic view of
the under side, the wrong side, of the London world. The
procession was filled with figures which seemed never to have
"shown out," as the English say, before; of strange, pale,
mouldy paupers who blinked and stumbled in the Piccadilly
sunshine. I have no space to describe them more minutely,
but I found the whole affair vaguely yet portentously suggestive. My impression rose not simply from the radical, or, as I
may say for the sake of colour, the revolutionary, emanation
of this dingy concourse, lighted up by the ironic sky; but
from the same causes I had observed a short time before, on
the day the Queen went to open Parliament, when in Trafalgar Square, looking straight down into Westminster and over
the royal procession, were gathered a group of banners and
festoons inscribed in big staring letters with mottoes and sentiments which might easily have given on the nerves of a
sensitive police department. They were mostly in allusion to
the Tichborne claimant, whose release from his dungeon they
peremptorily demanded and whose cruel fate was taken as a
pretext for several sweeping reflections on the social arrangements of the time and country. These signals of unreason
were allowed to sun themselves as freely as if they had been
the manifestoes of the Irish Giant or the Oriental Dwarf at a
fair. I had lately come from Paris, where the authorities have a
shorter patience and where revolutionary placards at the base
of the obelisk in the Place de la Concorde fall in with no
recognised scheme—such is the effect of the whirligig of
time—of the grand style or of monumental decorum. I was
therefore the more struck on both of the occasions I speak of
with the admirable English practice of letting people alone—
with the frank good sense and the frank good humour and
even the frank good taste of it. It was this that I found impressive as I watched the manifestation of Mr. Odger's under-

fed partisans—the fact that the mighty mob could march along and do its errand while the excellent quiet policemen— eternal, imperturbable, positively lovable reminders of the national temperament—stood by simply to see that the channel was kept clear and comfortable.

When Easter Monday came it was obvious that every one (save Mr. Odger's friends—three or four million or so) had gone out of town. There was hardly a pair of shutters in the West End that was not closed; there was not a bell that it was any use to pull. The weather was detestable, the rain incessant, and the fact that all your friends were away gave you plenty of leisure to reflect that the country must be the reverse of enlivening. But all your friends had gone thither (this is the unanimity I began by talking about), and to restrict as much as possible the proportions of that game of hide-and-seek of which, at the best, so much of London social life consists, it seemed wise to bring within the limits of the dull season any such excursion as might have been projected in commemoration of the first days of spring. After due cogitation I paid a little visit to Canterbury and Dover, taking Rochester by the way, and it was of this momentous journey that I proposed, in beginning these remarks, to give an account. But I have dallied so much by the way that I have come almost to my rope's end without reaching my first stage. I should have begun, artistically, by relating that I put myself in the humour for remote adventure by going down the Thames on a penny steamboat to the towers of Julius. This was on the Saturday before Easter, and the City was as silent as the grave. "London's lasting shame" was a memory of my childhood, and, having a theory that from such memories the dust of the ages had better not be shaken, I had not retraced my steps to its venerable walls. But the Tower—*the* Tower—is very good, and much less cockneyfied than I supposed it would seem to my maturer vision; very gray and historical, with the look that vivifies (rather lividly indeed) the past. I could not get into it, as it had been closed for Passion Week, but I was consequently relieved from the obligation to march about with a dozen fellow starers in the train of a didactic beefeater, and I strolled at will through the courts and the garden, sharing them only with the lounging soldiers of the garrison, who seemed to connect the place, for the backward-reaching fancy, with important events.

IV

At Rochester I stopped for the sake of its castle, which I espied from the railway-train as it perched on a grassy bank beside the widening Medway. There were other beguilements as well; the place has a small cathedral, and, leaving the creators of Falstaff and of the tale-telling Pilgrims out of the question, one had read about it in Dickens, whose house of Gadshill was a couple of miles from the town. All this Kentish country, between London and Dover, figures indeed repeatedly in Dickens; he expresses to a certain extent, for our later age, the spirit of the land. I found this to be quite the case at Rochester. I had occasion to go into a little shop kept by a talkative old woman who had a photograph of Gadshill lying on her counter. This led to my asking her whether the illustrious master of the house had often, to her old-time vision, made his appearance in the town. "Oh, bless you, sir," she said, "we every one of us knew him to speak to. He was in this very shop on the Tuesday with a party of foreigners—as he was dead in his bed on the Friday." (I should remark that I probably do not repeat the days of the week as she gave them.) "He 'ad on his black velvet suit, and it always made him look so 'andsome. I said to my 'usband, 'I *do* think Charles Dickens looks so nice in that black velvet suit.' But he said he couldn't see as he looked any way particular. He was in this very shop on the Tuesday, with a party of foreigners." Rochester consists of little more than one long street, stretching away from the castle and the river toward neighbouring Chatham, and edged with low brick houses, of intensely provincial aspect, most of which have some small, dull smugness or quaintness of gable or window. Nearly opposite to the shop of the old lady with the snubby husband is a little dwelling with an inscribed slab set into its face, which must often have provoked a smile in the great master of the comic. The slab relates that in the year 1579 Richard Watts here established a charity which should furnish "six poor travellers, not

Rochester Cathedral from the Medway

rogues or proctors," one night's lodging and entertainment gratis, and fourpence in the morning to go on their way withal, and that in memory of his "munificence" the stone has lately been renewed. The inn at Rochester had small hospitality, and I felt strongly tempted to knock at the door of Mr. Watts's asylum, under plea of being neither a rogue nor a proctor. The poor traveller who avails himself of the testamentary fourpence may easily resume his journey as far as Chatham without breaking his treasure. Is not this the place where little Davy Copperfield slept under a cannon on his journey from London to Dover to join his aunt Miss Trotwood? The two towns are really but one, which forms an interminable crooked thoroughfare, lighted up in the dusk, as I measured it up and down, with the red coats of the vespertinal soldier quartered at the various barracks of Chatham.

The cathedral of Rochester is small and plain, hidden away in rather an awkward corner, without a verdant close to set it off. It is dwarfed and effaced by the great square Norman keep of the adjacent castle. But within it is very charming, especially beyond the detestable wall, the vice of almost all the English cathedrals, which shuts in the choir and breaks the sacred perspective of the aisle. Here, as at Canterbury, you ascend a high range of steps, to pass through the small door in the wall. When I speak slightingly, by the way, of the outside of Rochester cathedral, I intend my faint praise in a relative sense. If we were so happy as to have this secondary pile within reach in America we should go barefoot to see it; but here it stands in the great shadow of Canterbury, and that makes it humble. I remember, however, an old priory gateway which leads you to the church, out of the main street; I remember a kind of haunted-looking deanery, if that be the technical name, at the base of the eastern walls; I remember a fluted tower that took the afternoon light and let the rooks and the swallows come circling and clamouring around it. Better still than these things I remember the ivy-muffled squareness of the castle, a very noble and imposing ruin. The old walled precinct has been converted into a little public garden, with flowers and benches and a pavilion for a band, and the place was not empty, as such places in England never are. The result is agreeable, but I believe the process was barbarous,

Rochester Castle

involving the destruction and dispersion of many interesting portions of the ruin. I lingered there for a long time, looking in the fading light at what was left. This rugged pile of Norman masonry will be left when a great many solid things have departed; it mocks, ever so monotonously, at destruction, at decay. Its walls are fantastically thick; their great time-bleached expanses and all their rounded roughnesses, their strange mixture of softness and grimness, have an undefinable fascination for the eye. English ruins always come out peculiarly when the day begins to fail. Weather-bleached, as I say they are, they turn even paler in the twilight and grow consciously solemn and spectral. I have seen many a mouldering castle, but I remember in no single mass of ruin more of the helpless, bereaved, amputated look.

It is not the absence of a close that damages Canterbury; the cathedral stands amid grass and trees, with a cultivated margin all round it, and is placed in such a way that, as you pass out from under the gatehouse, you appreciate immediately its grand feature—its extraordinary and magnificent length. None of the English cathedrals seems to sit more gravely apart, to desire more to be shut up to itself. It is a long walk, beneath the walls, from the gateway of the close to the farther end of the last chapel. Of all that there is to observe in this upward-gazing stroll I can give no detailed account; I can, in my fear to pretend to dabble in the esoteric constructional question—often so combined with an absence of other felt relations—speak only of the picture, the mere builded *scene*. This is altogether delightful. None of the rivals of Canterbury has a more complicated and elaborate architecture, a more perplexing intermixture of periods, a more charming jumble of Norman arches and English points and perpendiculars. What makes the side-view superb, moreover, is the double transepts, which produce the finest agglomeration of gables and buttresses. It is as if two great churches had joined forces toward the middle—one giving its nave and the other its choir, and each keeping its own great cross-aisles. Astride of the roof, between them, sits a huge Gothic tower, which is one of the latest portions of the building, though it looks like one of the earliest, so tempered and tinted, so thumb-marked and rubbed smooth is it, by the handling of

Canterbury Cathedral

the ages and the breath of the elements. Like the rest of the
structure it has a magnificent colour—a sort of rich dull yellow, a sort of personal accent of tone that is neither brown
nor gray. This is particularly appreciable from the cloisters on
the further side of the church—the side, I mean, away from
the town and the open garden-sweep I spoke of; the side that
looks toward a damp old clerical house, lurking behind a
brown archway through which you see young ladies in Gainsborough hats playing something on a patch of velvet turf; the
side, in short, that is somehow intermingled with a green
quadrangle—a quadrangle serving as a playground to a
King's School and adorned externally with a very precious
and picturesque old fragment of Norman staircase. This cloister is not "kept up"; it is very dusky and mouldy and dilapidated, and of course very sketchable. The old black arches and
capitals are various and handsome, and in the centre are tumbled together a group of crooked gravestones, themselves almost buried in the deep soft grass. Out of the cloister opens
the chapter-house, which is not kept up either, but which is
none the less a magnificent structure; a noble, lofty hall, with
a beautiful wooden roof, simply arched like that of a tunnel,
without columns or brackets. The place is now given up to
dust and echoes; but it looks more like a banqueting-hall than
a council-room of priests, and as you sit on the old wooden
bench, which, raised on two or three steps, runs round the
base of the four walls, you may gaze up and make out the
faint ghostly traces of decorative paint and gold upon the
brown ceiling. A little patch of this has been restored "to give
an idea." From one of the angles of the cloister you are recommended by the verger to take a view of the great tower,
which indeed detaches itself with tremendous effect. You see
it base itself upon the roof as broadly as if it were striking
roots in earth, and then pile itself away to a height which
seems to make the very swallows dizzy as they drop from the
topmost shelf. Within the cathedral you hear a great deal, of
course, about poor great Thomas A'Becket, and the special
sensation of the place is to stand on the spot where he was
murdered and look down at a small fragmentary slab which
the verger points out to you as a bit of the pavement that
caught the blood-drops of the struggle. It was late in the

Canterbury from the Meadows

afternoon when I first entered the church; there had been a service in the choir, but that was well over, and I had the place to myself. The verger, who had some pushing-about of benches to attend to, turned me into the locked gates and left me to wander through the side-aisles of the choir and into the great chapel beyond it. I say I had the place to myself; but it would be more decent to affirm that I shared it, in particular, with another gentleman. This personage was stretched upon a couch of stone, beneath a quaint old canopy of wood; his hands were crossed upon his breast, and his pointed toes rested upon a little griffin or leopard. He was a very handsome fellow and the image of a gallant knight. His name was Edward Plantagenet, and his sobriquet was the Black Prince. *"De la mort ne pensai-je mye,"* he says in the beautiful inscription embossed upon the bronze base of his image; and I too, as I stood there, lost the sense of death in a momentary impression of personal nearness to him. One had been further off, after all, from other famous knights. In this same chapel, for many a year, stood the shrine of St. Thomas of Canterbury, one of the richest and most potent in Christendom. The pavement which lay before it has kept its place, but Henry VIII. swept away everything else in his famous short cut to reform. Becket was originally buried in the crypt of the church; his ashes lay there for fifty years, and it was only little by little that his martyrdom was made a "draw." Then he was transplanted into the Lady Chapel; every grain of his dust became a priceless relic, and the pavement was hallowed by the knees of pilgrims. It was on this errand of course that Chaucer's story-telling cavalcade came to Canterbury. I made my way down into the crypt, which is a magnificent maze of low, dark arches and pillars, and groped about till I found the place where the frightened monks had first shuffled the inanimate victim of Moreville and Fitzurse out of the reach of further desecration. While I stood there a violent thunderstorm broke over the cathedral; great rumbling gusts and rain-drifts came sweeping through the open sides of the crypt and, mingling with the darkness which seemed to deepen and flash in corners and with the potent mouldy smell, made me feel as if I had descended into the very bowels of history. I emerged again, but the rain had settled down and spoiled the evening,

Interior Canterbury Cathedral

The Martyrdom, Canterbury

and I splashed back to my inn and sat, in an uncomfortable chair by the coffee-room fire, reading Dean Stanley's agreeable "Memorials of Canterbury" and wondering over the musty appointments and meagre resources of so many English hostels. This establishment had entitled itself (in compliment to the Black Prince, I suppose) the "Fleur-de-Lis." The name was very pretty (I had been foolish enough to let it attract me to the inn), but the lily was sadly deflowered.

Greenwich

London at Midsummer

I BELIEVE it is supposed to require a good deal of courage
to confess that one has spent the month of so-called social
August in London; and I will therefore, taking the bull by the
horns, plead guilty at the very outset to this poorness of
spirit. I might attempt some ingenious extenuation of it; I
might say that my remaining in town had been the most unexpected necessity or the merest inadvertence; I might pretend I liked it—that I had done it in fact for the perverse love
of the thing; I might claim that you don't really know the
charms of London until on one of the dog-days you have
imprinted your boot-sole in the slumbering dust of Belgravia,
or, gazing along the empty vista of the Drive, in Hyde Park,
have beheld, for almost the first time in England, a landscape
without figures. But little would remain of these specious
apologies save the bald circumstance that I had distinctly
failed to pack and be off—either on the first of August with
the ladies and children, or on the thirteenth with the members

133

of Parliament, or on the twelfth when the grouse-shooting began. (I am not sure that I have got my dates right to a day, but these were about the proper opportunities.) I have, in fact, survived the departure of everything genteel, and the three millions of persons who remained behind with me have been witnesses of my shame.

I cannot pretend, on the other hand, that, having lingered in town, I have found it a very odious or painful experience. Being a stranger, I have not felt it necessary to incarcerate myself during the day and steal abroad only under cover of the darkness—a line of conduct imposed by public opinion, if I am to trust the social criticism of the weekly papers (which I am far from doing), upon the native residents who allow themselves to be overtaken by the unfashionable season. I have indeed always held that few things are pleasanter, during very hot weather, than to have a great city, and a large house within it, quite to one's self. Yet these majestic conditions have not embellished my own metropolitan sojourn, and I have received an impression that in London it would be rather difficult for a visitor not having the command of a good deal of powerful machinery to find them united. English summer weather is rarely hot enough to make it necessary to darken one's house and denude one's person. The present year has indeed in this respect been "exceptional," as any year is, for that matter, that one spends anywhere. But the manners of the people are, to alien eyes, a sufficient indication that at the best (or the worst) even the highest flights of the thermometer in the United Kingdom betray a broken wing. People live with closed windows in August very much as they do in January, and there is to the eye no appreciable difference in the character—that is in the thickness and stiffness—of their coats and boots. A "bath" in England, for the most part, all the year round, means a little portable tin tub and a sponge. Peaches and pears, grapes and melons, are not a more obvious ornament of the market at midsummer than at Christmas. This matter of peaches and melons, by the way, offers one of the best examples of that fact to which a commentator on English manners from afar finds himself constantly recurring, and to which he grows at last almost ashamed of alluding—the fact that the beauty and luxury of

the country, that elaborate system known and revered all over
the world as "English comfort," is a limited and restricted, an
essentially private, affair. I am not one of those irreverent
strangers who talk of English fruit as a rather audacious *plaisanterie*, though I could see very well what was meant a short
time since by an anecdote related to me in a tone of contemp-
tuous generalisation by a couple of my fellow countrywomen.
They had arrived in London in the dog-days, and, lunching at
their hotel, had asked to be served with some fruit. The hotel
was of the stateliest pattern, and they were waited upon by a
functionary whose grandeur was proportionate. This personage bowed and retired, and, after a long delay, reappearing,
placed before them with an inimitable gesture a dish of
gooseberries and currants. It appeared upon investigation that
these acrid vegetables were the only things of succulence that
the establishment could undertake to supply; and it seemed to
increase the irony of the situation that the establishment was
as near as possible to Buckingham Palace. I say that the heroines of my anecdote seemed disposed to generalise: this was
sufficiently the case, I mean, to give me a pretext for assuring
them that on a thousand fine properties the most beautiful
peaches and melons were at that moment ripening either under glass or in warm old walled gardens. My auditors tossed
their heads of course at the fine properties, the glass and the
walled gardens; and indeed at their place of privation close to
Buckingham Palace such a piece of knowledge was but scantily consoling.

It is to a more public fund of entertainment that the desultory stranger in any country chiefly appeals, especially in
summer weather; and as I have implied that there is little encouragement in England to such an appeal it may appear remarkable that I should not have felt London, at this season,
void of all beguilement. But one's liking for London—a
stranger's liking at least—has at the best a kind of perversity
and infirmity often rather difficult to reduce to a statement. I
am far from meaning by this that there are not in this mighty
metropolis a thousand sources of interest, entertainment and
delight: what I mean is that, for one reason and another, with
all its social resources, the place lies heavy on the imported
consciousness. It seems grim and lurid, fierce and unmerciful.

And yet the imported consciousness accepts it at last with an active satisfaction and finds something warm and comfortable, something that if removed would be greatly missed, in its portentous pressure. It must be admitted, however, that, granting that every one is out of town, your choice of pastimes is not embarrassing. If you have happened to spend a certain amount of time in places where public manners have more frankness London will seem to you but scantily provided with innocent diversions. This indeed brings us back simply to that question of the absence of a "public fund" of amusement to which reference was just now made. You must give up the idea of going to sit somewhere in the open air, to eat an ice and listen to a band of music. You will find neither the seat, the ice, nor the band; but on the other hand, faithful at once to your interest and your detachment, you may supply the place of these delights by a little private meditation on the deep-lying causes of the English indifference to them. In such reflections nothing is idle—every grain of testimony counts; and one need therefore not be accused of jumping too suddenly from small things to great if one traces a connection between the absence of ices and music and the essentially hierarchical plan of English society. This hierarchical plan of English society is the great and ever-present fact to the mind of a stranger: there is hardly a detail of life that does not in some degree betray it. It is really only in a country in which a good deal of democratic feeling prevails that people of "refinement," as we say in America, will be willing to sit at little round tables, on a pavement or a gravel-walk, at the door of a café. The better sort are too "genteel" and the inferior sort too base. One must hasten to add too, in justice, that the better sort are, as a general thing, quite too well furnished with entertainments of their own; they have those special resources to which I alluded a moment since. They are persons for whom the private machinery of ease has been made to work with extraordinary smoothness. If you can sit on a terrace overlooking gardens and have your *café noir* handed you in old Worcester cups by servants who are models of consideration, you have hardly a decent pretext for going to a public-house. In France and Italy, in Germany and Spain, the count and countess will sally forth and encamp for the evening, under a row of coloured lamps, upon the paving-stones, but it is ten to one that the count and countess live on a single floor and up several pair of stairs. They are, however, I think, not appreciably affected by considerations which operate potently in England. An Englishman who should propose to sit down, in his own country, at a café door would find himself remembering that he is pretending to participations, contacts, fellowships the absolute impracticability of which is expressed in all the rest of his doings.

The study of these reasons, however, would lead us very far from the potential little tables for ices in—where shall I say?—in Oxford Street. But, after all, there is no reason why our imagination should hover about any such articles of furniture. I am afraid they would not strike us as at the best happily situated. In such matters everything hangs together, and I am certain that the customs of the Boulevard des Italiens and the Piazza Colonna would not harmonise with the scenery of the great London thoroughfare. A gin-palace right and left and a detachment of the London rabble in an admiring semicircle—these strike one as some of the more obvious features of the affair. Yet at the season of which I write one's social studies must at the least be studies of low life, for wherever one may go for a stroll or to spend the summer afternoon the comparatively sordid side of things is uppermost. There is no one in the parks save the rough characters who are lying on their faces in the sheep-polluted grass. These people are always tolerably numerous in the Green Park, through which I frequently pass, and are always an occasion for deep wonder. But your wonder will go far if it begins to bestir itself on behalf of the recumbent British tramp. You perceive among them some rich possibilities. Their velveteen legs and their colossal high-lows, their purple necks and ear-tips, their knotted sticks and little greasy hats, make them look like stage-villains of realistic melodrama. I may do them injustice, but consistent character in them mostly requires that they shall have had a taste of penal servitude—that they shall have paid the penalty of stamping on some weaker human head with those huge square heels that are turned up to the summer sky. Actually, however, they are innocent enough, for they are sleeping as peacefully as the most accomplished philanthropist, and it is their look of having walked over half England, and of being pennilessly hungry and thirsty, that constitutes their romantic attractiveness. These six square feet of brown grass are their present sufficiency; but how long will they sleep, whither will they go next, and whence did they come last? You permit yourself to wish that they might sleep for ever and go nowhere else at all.

The month of August is so uncountenanced in London that, going a few days since to Greenwich, that famous resort, I found it possible to get but half a dinner. The celebrated hotel had put out its stoves and locked up its pantry. But for this discovery I should have mentioned the little expedition to Greenwich as a charming relief to the monotony of a London August. Greenwich and Richmond are, classically, the two suburban dining-places. I know not how it may be at this time with Richmond, but the Greenwich incident brings me back (I hope not once too often) to the element of what has lately been called "particularism" in English pleasures. It was in obedience to a perfectly logical argument that the Greenwich hotel had, as I say, locked up its pantry. All well-bred people leave London after the first week in August, *ergo* those who remain behind are not well-bred, and cannot therefore rise to the conception of a "fish dinner." Why then should we have anything ready? I had other impressions, fortunately, of this interesting suburb, and I hasten to declare that during the period of good-breeding the dinner at Greenwich is the most amusing of all dinners. It begins with fish and it continues with fish: what it ends with—except songs and speeches and affectionate partings—I hesitate to affirm. It is a kind of mermaid reversed; for I do know, in a vague way, that the tail of the creature is elaborately and interminably fleshy. If it were not grossly indiscreet I should risk an allusion to the particular banquet which was the occasion of my becoming acquainted with the Greenwich *cuisine*. I would try to express how pleasant it may be to sit in a company of clever and distinguished men before the large windows that look out upon the broad brown Thames. The ships swim by confidently, as if they were part of the entertainment and put down in the bill; the light of the afternoon fades ever so slowly. We eat all the fish of the sea, and wash them down

Richmond

with liquids that bear no resemblance to salt water. We partake of any number of those sauces with which, according to the French adage, one could swallow one's grandmother with a good conscience. To touch on the identity of my companions would indeed be indiscreet, but there is nothing indelicate in marking a high appreciation of the frankness and robustness of English conviviality. The stranger—the American at least—who finds himself in the company of a number of Englishmen assembled for a convivial purpose becomes conscious of an indefinable and delectable something which, for want of a better name, he is moved to call their superior richness of temperament. He takes note of the liberal share of the individual in the magnificent temperament of the people. This seems to him one of the finest things in the world, and his satisfaction will take a keener edge from such an incident as the single one I may permit myself to mention. It was one of those little incidents which can occur only in an old society—a society in which every one that a newly arrived observer meets strikes him as having in some degree or other a sort of historic identity, being connected with some one or something that he has heard of, that he has wondered about. If they are not the rose they have lived more or less near it. There is an old English song-writer whom we all know and admire—whose songs are sung wherever the language is spoken. Of course, according to the law I just hinted at, one of the gentlemen sitting opposite must needs be his great-grandson. After dinner there are songs, and the gentleman trolls out one of his ancestral ditties with the most charming voice and the most finished art.

I have still other memories of Greenwich, where there is a charming old park, on a summit of one of whose grassy undulations the famous observatory is perched. To do the thing completely you must take passage upon one of the little grimy sixpenny steamers that ply upon the Thames, perform the journey by water, and then, disembarking, take a stroll in the park to get up an appetite for dinner. I find an irresistible charm in any sort of river-navigation, but I scarce know how to speak of the little voyage from Westminster Bridge to Greenwich. It is in truth the most prosaic possible form of being afloat, and to be recommended rather to the inquiring than to the fastidious mind. It initiates you into the duskiness, the blackness, the crowdedness, the intensely commercial character of London. Few European cities have a finer river than the Thames, but none certainly has expended more ingenuity in producing a sordid river-front. For miles and miles you see nothing but the sooty backs of warehouses, or perhaps they are the sooty faces: in buildings so utterly expressionless it is impossible to distinguish. They stand massed together on the banks of the wide turbid stream, which is fortunately of too opaque a quality to reflect the dismal image. A damp-looking, dirty blackness is the universal tone. The river is almost black, and is covered with black barges; above the black housetops, from among the far-stretching docks and basins, rises a dusky wilderness of masts. The little puffing steamer is dingy and gritty—it belches a sable cloud that keeps you company as you go. In this carboniferous shower your companions, who belong chiefly, indeed, to the classes bereft of lustre, assume an harmonious grayness; and the whole picture, glazed over with the glutinous London

Greenwich

mist, becomes a masterly composition. But it is very impressive in spite of its want of lightness and brightness, and though it is ugly it is anything but trivial. Like so many of the aspects of English civilisation that are untouched by elegance or grace, it has the merit of expressing something very serious. Viewed in this intellectual light the polluted river, the sprawling barges, the dead-faced warehouses, the frowsy people, the atmospheric impurities become richly suggestive. It sounds rather absurd, but all this smudgy detail may remind you of nothing less than the wealth and power of the British Empire at large; so that a kind of metaphysical magnificence hovers over the scene, and supplies what may be literally wanting. I don't exactly understand the association, but I know that when I look off to the left at the East India Docks, or pass under the dark hugely piled bridges, where the railway trains and the human processions are for ever moving, I feel a kind of imaginative thrill. The tremendous piers of the bridges, in especial, seem the very pillars of the Empire aforesaid.

It is doubtless owing to this habit of obtrusive and unprofitable reverie that the sentimental tourist thinks it very fine to see the Greenwich observatory lifting its two modest little brick towers. The sight of this useful edifice gave me a pleasure which may at first seem extravagant. The reason was simply that I used to see it as a child, in woodcuts, in school geographies, and in the corners of large maps which had a glazed, sallow surface and which were suspended in unexpected places, in dark halls and behind doors. The maps were hung so high that my eyes could reach only to the lower corners, and these corners usually contained a print of a strange-looking house perched among trees upon a grassy bank that swept down before it with the most engaging steepness. I used always to think of the joy it must be to roll at one's length down this curved incline. Close at hand was usually something printed about something being at such and such a number of degrees "east of Greenwich." Why east of Greenwich? The vague wonder that the childish mind felt on this point gave the place a mysterious importance and seemed to put it into relation with the difficult and fascinating parts of geography — the countries of unintentional outline and the lonely looking pages of the atlas. Yet there it stood the other day, the precise point from which the great globe is measured; there was the plain little façade with the old-fashioned cupolas; there was the bank on which it would be so delightful not to be able to stop running. It made me feel terribly old to find that I was not even tempted to begin. There are indeed a great many steep banks in Greenwich Park, which tumbles up and down in the most adventurous fashion. It is a charming place, rather shabby and footworn, as befits a strictly popular resort, but with a character all its own. It is filled with magnificent foreign-looking trees, of which I know nothing but that they have a vain appearance of being chestnuts, planted in long, convergent avenues, with trunks of extraordinary girth and limbs that fling a dusky shadow far over the grass; there are plenty of benches, and there are deer as tame as sleepy children; and from the tops of the bosky hillocks there are views of the widening Thames and the moving ships and the two classic inns by the waterside and the great pompous buildings, designed by Inigo Jones, of the old

Observatory, Greenwich

Hospital, which have been despoiled of their ancient pensioners and converted into a naval academy.

Taking note of all this, I arrived at a far-away angle in the
wall of the park, where a little postern door stood ajar. I
pushed the door open and found myself, by a thrilling transition, upon Blackheath Common. One had often heard, in
vague, irrecoverable, anecdotic connections, of Blackheath:
well, here it was—a great green, breezy place where lads in
corduroys were playing cricket. I am, as a rule, moved to disproportionate ecstasy by an English common; it may be cur-
tailed and cockneyfied, as this one was—which had lamp-
posts stuck about on its turf and a fresh-painted banister all
around—but it generally abounds in the note of English
breeziness, and you always seem to have seen it water-
coloured or engraved. Even if the turf be too much trodden
there is to foreign eyes an intimate insular reference in it and
in the way the high-piled, weather-bearing clouds hang over
it and drizzle down their gray light. Still further to identify
this spot, here was the British soldier emerging from two or

three of the roads, with his cap upon his ear, his white gloves in one hand and his foppish little cane in the other. He wore the uniform of the artillery, and I asked him where he had come from. I learned that he had walked over from Woolwich and that this feat might be accomplished in half an hour. Inspired again by vague associations I proceeded to accomplish its equivalent. I bent my steps to Woolwich, a place which I knew, in a general way, to be a nursery of British valour. At the end of my half-hour I emerged upon another common, where the water-colour bravery had even a higher pitch. The scene was like a chapter of some forgotten record. The open grassy expanse was immense, and, the evening being beautiful, it was dotted with strolling soldiers and townsfolk. There were half a dozen cricket matches, both civil and military. At one end of this peaceful *campus martius*, which stretches over a hilltop, rises an interminable façade—one of the fronts of the Royal Artillery barracks. It has a very honourable air, and more windows and doors, I imagine, than any building in Britain. There is a great clean parade before it, and there are many sentinels pacing in front of neatly kept places of ingress to officers' quarters. Everything it looks out upon is in the smartest military trim—the distinguished college (where the poor young man whom it would perhaps be premature to call the last of the Bonapartes lately studied the art of war) on one side; a sort of model camp, a collection of the tidiest plank huts, on the other; a hospital, on a well-ventilated site, at the remoter end. And then in the town below there are a great many more military matters: barracks on an immense scale; a dockyard that presents an interminable dead wall to the street; an arsenal which the gatekeeper (who refused to admit me) declared to be "five miles" in circumference; and, lastly, grogshops enough to inflame the most craven spirit. These latter institutions I glanced at on my way to the railway station at the bottom of the hill; but before departing I had spent half an hour in strolling about the common in vague consciousness of certain emotions that are called into play (I speak but for myself) by almost any glimpse of the imperial machinery of this great country. The glimpse may be of the slightest; it stirs a peculiar sentiment. I know not what to call this sentiment unless it be simply an admiration for the

The Thames at Greenwich

greatness of England. The greatness of England; that is a very off-hand phrase, and of course I don't pretend to use it analytically. I use it romantically, as it sounds in the ears of any American who remounts the stream of time to the head-waters of his own loyalties. I think of the great part that England has played in human affairs, the great space she has occupied, her tremendous might, her far-stretching rule. That these clumsily general ideas should be suggested by the sight of some infinitesimal fraction of the English administrative system may seem to indicate a cast of fancy too hysterical; but if so I must plead guilty to the weakness. Why should a sentry-box more or less set one thinking of the glory of this little island, which has found in her mere genius the means of such a sway? This is more than I can tell; and all I shall attempt to say is that in the difficult days that are now elapsing a sympathetic stranger finds his meditations singularly quickened. It is the imperial element in English history that he has chiefly cared for, and he finds himself wondering whether the imperial epoch is completely closed. It is a

moment when all the nations of Europe seem to be doing
something, and he waits to see what England, who has done
so much, will do. He has been meeting of late a good many
of his country-people—Americans who live on the Continent
and pretend to speak with assurance of continental ways of
feeling. These people have been passing through London, and
many of them are in that irritated condition of mind which
appears to be the portion of the American sojourner in the
British metropolis when he is not given up to the delights of
the historic sentiment. They have declared with assurance that
the continental nations have ceased to care a straw for what
England thinks, that her traditional prestige is completely extinct and that the affairs of Europe will be settled quite independently of her action and still more of her inaction.
England will do nothing, will risk nothing; there is no cause
bad enough for her not to find a selfish interest in it—there is
no cause good enough for her to fight about it. Poor old England is defunct; it is about time she should seek the most
decent burial possible. To all this the sympathetic stranger re-
plies that in the first place he doesn't believe a word of it, and
in the second doesn't care a fig for it—care, that is, what the
continental nations think. If the greatness of England were
really waning it would be to him as a personal grief; and as he
strolls about the breezy common of Woolwich, with all those
mementoes of British dominion around him, he vibrates quite
too richly to be distracted by such vapours.

He wishes nevertheless, as I said before, that England
would *do* something—something striking and powerful,
which should be at once characteristic and unexpected. He
asks himself what she can do, and he remembers that this
greatness of England which he so much admires was formerly
much exemplified in her "taking" something. Can't she "take"
something now? There is the *Spectator*, who wants her to occupy Egypt: can't she occupy Egypt? The *Spectator* considers
this her moral duty—inquires even whether she has a right
not to bestow the blessings of her beneficent rule upon the
down-trodden Fellaheen. I found myself in company with an
acute young Frenchman a day or two after this eloquent plea
for a partial annexation of the Nile had appeared in the super-
subtle sheet. Some allusion was made to it, and my com-

panion of course pronounced it the most finished example conceivable of insular hypocrisy. I don't know how powerful a defence I made of it, but while I read it I had found the hypocrisy contagious. I recalled it while I pursued my contemplations, but I recalled at the same time that sadly prosaic speech of Mr. Gladstone's to which it had been a reply. Mr. Gladstone had said that England had much more urgent duties than the occupation of Egypt: she had to attend to the great questions of—— What were the great questions? Those of local taxation and the liquor-laws! Local taxation and the liquor-laws! The phrase, to my ears, just then, sounded almost squalid. These were not the things I had been thinking of; it was not as she should bend anxiously over these doubtless interesting subjects that the sympathising stranger would seem to see England in his favourite posture—that, as Macaulay says, of hurling defiance at her foes. Mr. Gladstone may perhaps have been right, but Mr. Gladstone was far from being a sympathising stranger.

The Downs, Epsom

Two Excursions

I

THEY DIFFERED greatly from each other, but there was something to be said for each. There seemed in respect to the first a high consensus as to its being a pity that any stranger should ever miss the Derby day. Every one assured me that this was the great festival of the English people and that one didn't really know them unless one had seen them at it. So much, since it had to do with horse-flesh, I could readily believe. Had not the newspapers been filled for weeks with recurrent dissertations upon the animals concerned in the ceremony? and was not the event, to the nation at large, only imperceptibly less momentous than the other great question of the day—the fate of empires and the reapportionment of the East? The space allotted to sporting intelligence in a compact, eclectic, "intellectual" journal like the *Pall Mall Gazette*, had seemed for some time past a measure of the hold of such questions upon the native mind. These things, however, are very natural in a country in which in "society" you are liable to make the acquaintance of some such syllogism as the following. You are seated at dinner next a foreign lady who has on her other hand a communicative gentleman through whom she is under instruction in the art of the right point-of-view for English life. I profit by their conversation and I learn that this point-of-view is apparently the saddle. "You see, English life," says the gentleman, "is really English country life. It's the country that is the basis of English society. And you see, country life is—well, it's the *hunting*. It's the hunting that is at the bottom of it all." In other words "the hunting" is the basis of English society. Duly impressed with this explanation, the American observer is prepared for the huge proportions of the annual pilgrimage to Epsom. This pilgrimage, however, I was assured, though still well worth taking part in, is by no means so characteristic as in former days. It is now performed in a large measure by rail, and the spectacle on the road has lost many of its earlier and most of its finer features. The road has been given up more and more to the populace and the strangers and has ceased to be graced by the presence of ladies. Nevertheless, as a man and a stranger, I was strongly recommended to take it, for the return from the Derby is still, with all its abatements, a classic show.

I mounted upon a four-horse coach, a charming coach with a yellow body and handsome, clean-flanked leaders; placing myself beside the coachman, as I had been told this was the point of vantage. The coach was one of the vehicles of the new fashion—the fashion of public conveyances driven, for the entertainment of themselves and of the public, by gentlemen of leisure. On the Derby day all the coaches that start from the classic headquarters—"The White Horse" in Piccadilly—and stretch away from London toward a dozen different and well-selected goals, had been dedicated to the Epsom road. The body of the vehicle is empty, as no one thinks of occupying any but one of the thirteen places on the top. On the Derby day, however, a properly laden coach carries a company of hampers and champagne-baskets in its inside places. I must add that on this occasion my companion was by exception a professional whip, who proved a friendly and amusing cicerone. Other companions there were, perched in the twelve places behind me, whose social quality I made less of a point of testing—though in the course of the expedition their various characteristics, under the influence of champagne, expanded so freely as greatly to facilitate the process. We were a society of exotics—Spaniards, Frenchmen, Germans. There were only two Britons, and these, according to my theory, were Australians—an antipodal bride and groom on a centripetal wedding-tour.

The drive to Epsom, when you get well out of London, is sufficiently pretty; but the part of it which most took my fancy was a district pre-eminently suburban—the classic community of Clapham. The vision of Clapham had been a part of the furniture of one's milder historic consciousness—the vision of its respectable common, its evangelical society, its rich drab humanity, its goodly brick mansions of the Georgian era. I now seemed really to focus these elements for the first time, and I thought them very charming. This epithet indeed scarcely applies to the evangelical society, which naturally, on the morning of the Derby day and during the desecrating progress of the Epsom revellers, was not much in the foreground. But all around the verdant if cockneyfied common are ranged commodious houses of a sober red complexion, from under whose neo-classic pediments you expect to see a mild-faced lady emerge—a lady in a cottage-bonnet and mittens, distributing tracts from a green silk satchel. It would take, however, the very ardour of the missionary among cannibals to stem the current of heterogeneous vehicles which at about this point takes up its metropolitan affluents and bears them in its rumbling, rattling tide. The concourse of wheeled conveyances of every possible order here becomes dense, and the spectacle from the top of the coach proportionately absorbing. You begin to perceive that the brilliancy of the road has in truth departed, and that a sustained high tone of appearance is not the note of the conditions. But when once you have grasped this fact your entertainment is continuous. You perceive that you are "in" for the vulgar on an unsurpassable scale, something blatantly, unimaginably, heroically shocking to timid "taste"; all that is necessary is to accept this situation and look out for illustrations. Beside you, before

you, behind you, is the mighty London populace taking its
ébats. You get for the first time a notion of the London population at large. It has piled itself into carts, into omnibuses,
into every possible and impossible species of "trap." A large
proportion of it is of course on foot, trudging along the perilous margin of the middle way in such comfort as may be
gathered from fifteen miles' dodging of broken shins. The
smaller the vehicle, the more rat-like the animal that drags it,
the more numerous and ponderous its human freight; and as
every one is nursing in his lap a parcel of provender as big as
himself, wrapped in ragged newspaper, it is not surprising
that roadside halts are frequent and that the taverns all the
way to Epsom (it is wonderful how many there are) are encompassed by dense groups of dusty pilgrims, indulging liberally in refreshment for man and beast. And when I say man
I must by no means be understood to exclude woman. The
female contingent on the Derby day is not the least remarkable part of the London outpouring. Every one is prepared
for "larks," but the women are even more brilliantly and res-
olutely prepared than the men; there is no better chance to
follow the range of type   not that it is to be called large—of
the British female of the lower orders. The lady in question
is usually not ornamental. She is useful, robust, prolific, excellently fitted to play the somewhat arduous part allotted to
her in the great scheme of English civilisation, but she has
not those graces which enable her to lend herself easily to
the decoration of life. On smaller holidays—or on simple
working-days—in London crowds, I have often thought she
had points to contribute to the primary fine drawing, as to
head and shoulders, of the Briton of the two sexes as the race
at large sketches them. But at Epsom she is too stout, too
hot, too red, too thirsty, too boisterous, too strangely accou-
tred. And yet I wish to do her justice; so I must add that if
there is something to which an American cannot refuse a tribute of admiration in the gross plebeian jollity of the Derby
day, it is not evident why these dowdy Bacchantes should not
get part of the credit of it. The striking thing, the interesting
thing, both on the outward drive and on the return, was that
the holiday was so frankly, heartily, good-humouredly taken.
The people that of all peoples is habitually the most governed

by decencies, proprieties, rigidities of conduct, was for one happy day unbuttoning its respectable straight-jacket and affirming its large and simple sense of the joy of life. In such a spectacle there was inevitably much that was unlucky and unprofitable; these things came uppermost chiefly on the return, when demoralisation was supreme, when the temperament of the people had begun really to take the air. For the rest, to be dressed with a kind of brutal gaudiness, to be very thirsty and violently flushed, to laugh perpetually at everything and at nothing, thoroughly to enjoy, in short, a momentous occasion—all this is not, in simple persons of the more susceptible sex, an unpardonable crime.

The course at Epsom is in itself very pretty, and disposed by nature herself in sympathetic prevision of the sporting passion. It is something like the crater of a volcano without the mountain. The outer rim is the course proper; the space within it is a vast, shallow, grassy concavity in which vehicles are drawn up and beasts tethered and in which the greater part of the multitude—the mountebanks, the betting-men and the myriad hangers-on of the scene—are congregated. The outer margin of the uplifted rim in question is occupied by the grand stand, the small stands, the paddock. The day was exceptionally beautiful; the charming sky was spotted over with little idle-looking, loafing, irresponsible clouds; the Epsom Downs went swelling away as greenly as in a coloured sporting-print, and the wooded uplands, in the middle distance, looked as innocent and pastoral as if they had never seen a policeman or a rowdy. The crowd that spread itself over this immense expanse was as rich representation of human life off its guard as one need see. One's first fate after arriving, if one is perched upon a coach, is to see the coach guided, by means best known to the coachman himself, through the tremendous press of vehicles and pedestrians, introduced into a precinct roped off and guarded from intrusion save under payment of a fee, and then drawn up alongside of the course, as nearly as possible opposite the grand stand and the winning-post. Here you have only to stand up in your place—on tiptoe, it is true, and with a good deal of stretching—to see the race fairly well. But I hasten to add that seeing the race is indifferent entertainment. In the

The Start for the Derby

first place you *don't* see it, and in the second—to be Irish on
the occasion of a frolic—you perceive it to be not much
worth the seeing. It may be fine in quality, but in quantity it
is inappreciable. The horses and their jockeys first go dandling
and cantering along the course to the starting-point, looking
as insubstantial as sifted sunbeams. Then there is a long wait,
during which, of the sixty thousand people present (my figures are imaginary), thirty thousand declare positively that
they have started, and thirty thousand as positively deny it.
Then the whole sixty thousand are suddenly resolved into
unanimity by the sight of a dozen small jockey-heads whiz-
zing along a very distant sky-line. In a shorter space of time
than it takes me to write it, the whole thing is before you, and
for the instant it is anything but beautiful. A dozen furiously
revolving arms—pink, green, orange, scarlet, white—whack-
ing the flanks of as many straining steeds; a glimpse of this,
and the spectacle is over. The spectacle, however, is of course
an infinitesimally small part of the purpose of Epsom and the
interest of the Derby. The finer vibration resides presumably
in having money on the affair.

When the Derby Stakes had been carried off by a horse of
which I confess I am barbarous enough to have forgotten the
name, I turned my back to the running, for all the world as if
I too were largely "interested," and sought entertainment in
looking at the crowd. The crowd was very animated; that is
the most succinct description I can give of it. The horses of
course had been removed from the vehicles, so that the pedestrians were free to surge against the wheels and even to a
certain extent to scale and overrun the carriages. This tendency became most pronounced when, as the mid-period of
the day was reached, the process of lunching began to unfold
itself and every coach-top to become the scene of a picnic.
From this moment, at the Derby, demoralisation begins. I
was in a position to observe it, all around me, in the most
characteristic forms. The whole affair, as regards the conventional rigidities I spoke of a while since, becomes a real *dé-
gringolade*. The shabbier pedestrians bustle about the vehicles,
staring up at the lucky mortals who are perched in a kind of
tormentingly near empyrean—a region in which dishes of
lobster-salad are passed about and champagne-corks cleave
the air like celestial meteors. There are nigger-minstrels and
beggars and mountebanks and spangled persons on stilts and
gipsy matrons, as genuine as possible, with glowing Oriental
eyes and dropping their *h*'s; these last offer you for sixpence
the promise of everything genteel in life except the aspirate.
On a coach drawn up beside the one on which I had a place, a
party of opulent young men were passing from stage to stage
of the higher beatitude with a zeal which excited my admiration. They were accompanied by two or three young ladies of
the kind that usually shares the choicest pleasures of youthful
British opulence—young ladies in whom nothing has been
neglected that can make a complexion superlative. The whole
party had been drinking deep, and one of the young men, a
pretty lad of twenty, had in an indiscreet moment staggered
down as best he could to the ground. Here his cups proved
too many for him, and he collapsed and rolled over. In plain
English he was beastly drunk. It was the scene that followed
that arrested my observation. His companions on the top of
the coach called down to the people herding under the wheels
to pick him up and put him away inside. These people were

The Finish of the Derby

the grimiest of the rabble, and a couple of men who looked
like coal-heavers out of work undertook to handle this hapless
youth. But their task was difficult; it was impossible to imagine a young man more drunk. He was a mere bag of liquor—at once too ponderous and too flaccid to be lifted. He
lay in a helpless heap under the feet of the crowd—the best
intoxicated young man in England. His extemporised cham-
berlains took him first in one way and then in another; but he
was like water in a sieve. The crowd hustled over him; every
one wanted to see; he was pulled and shoved and fumbled.
The spectacle had a grotesque side, and this it was that
seemed to strike the fancy of the young man's comrades. They
had not done lunching, so they were unable to bestow upon
the incident the whole of that consideration which its high
comicality deserved. But they did what they could. They
looked down very often, glass in hand, during the half-hour
that it went on, and they stinted neither their generous, joy-
ous laughter nor their appreciative comments. Women are
said to have no sense of humour; but the young ladies with

the complexions did liberal justice to the pleasantry of the scene. Toward the last indeed their attention rather flagged; for even the best joke suffers by reiteration, and when you have seen a stupefied young man, infinitely bedusted, slip out of the embrace of a couple of clumsy roughs for the twentieth time, you may very properly suppose that you have arrived at the furthest limits of the ludicrous.

After the great race had been run I quitted my perch and spent the rest of the afternoon in wandering about the grassy concave I have mentioned. It was amusing and picturesque; it was just a huge Bohemian encampment. Here also a great number of carriages were stationed, freighted in like manner with free-handed youths and young ladies with gilded hair. These young ladies were almost the only representatives of their sex with pretensions to elegance; they were often pretty and always exhilarated. Gentlemen in pairs, mounted on stools, habited in fantastic sporting garments and offering bets to whomsoever listed, were a conspicuous feature of the scene. It was equally striking that they were not preaching in the desert and that they found plenty of patrons among the baser sort. I returned to my place in time to assist at the rather complicated operation of starting for the drive back to London. Putting in horses and getting vehicles into line seemed in the midst of the general crush and entanglement a process not to be facilitated even by the most liberal swearing on the part of those engaged in it. But little by little we came to the end of it; and as by this time a kind of mellow cheerfulness pervaded the upper atmosphere—the region of the perpendicular whip—even those interruptions most trying to patience were somehow made to minister to jollity. It was for people below not to get trampled to death or crunched between opposing wheel-hubs, but it was all for *them* to manage it. Above, the carnival of "chaff" had set in, and it deepened as the lock of vehicles grew denser. As they were all locked together (with a comfortable padding of pedestrians at points of acutest contact), they contrived somehow to move together; so that we gradually got away and into the road. The four or five hours consumed on the road were simply an exchange of repartee, the profusely good-humoured savour of which, on the whole, was certainly striking. The chaff was not brilliant nor subtle nor especially graceful; and here and there it was quite too tipsy to be even articulate. But as an expression of that unbuttoning of the popular straight-jacket of which I spoke a while since, it had its wholesome and even innocent side. It took indeed frequently an importunate physical form; it sought emphasis in the use of pea-shooters and water-squirts. At its best, too, it was extremely low and rowdyish. But a stranger even of the most refined tastes might be glad to have a glimpse of this popular revel, for it would make him feel that he was learning something more about the English people. It would give a meaning to the old description of England as merry. It would remind him that the natives of that country are subject to some of the lighter of the human impulses, and that the decent, dusky vistas of the London residential streets—those discreet creations of which Thackeray's Baker Street is the type—are not a complete symbol of the complicated race that erected them.

II

It seemed to me such a piece of good fortune to have been asked down to Oxford at Commemoration by a gentleman implicated in the remarkable ceremony which goes on under that name, who kindly offered me the hospitality of his college, that I scarcely stayed even to thank him—I simply went and awaited him. I had had a glimpse of Oxford in former years, but I had never slept in a low-browed room looking out on a grassy quadrangle and opposite a mediæval clock-tower. This satisfaction was vouchsafed me on the night of my arrival; I was made free of the rooms of an absent undergraduate. I sat in his deep armchairs; I burned his candles and read his books, and I hereby thank him as effusively as possible. Before going to bed I took a turn through the streets and renewed in the silent darkness that impression of the charm imparted to them by the quiet college-fronts which I had gathered in former years. The college-fronts were now quieter than ever, the streets were empty, and the old scholastic city was sleeping in the warm starlight. The undergraduates had retired in large numbers, encouraged in this impulse by the

collegiate authorities, who deprecate their presence at Commemoration. However many young gownsmen may be sent
away, there yet always remain a collection sufficient to represent the sound of many voices. There can be no better indication of the resources of Oxford in a spectacular way than this
fact that the first step toward preparing an impressive ceremony is to get rid of as many as possible of the actors.

In the morning I breakfasted with a young American who,
in common with a number of his countrymen, had come
hither to seek stimulus for a finer strain of study. I know not
whether he would have reckoned as such stimulus the conversation of a couple of those ingenuous youths, sons of the soil,
whose society I always find charming; but it added, from my
own point of view, in respect to the place, to the element of
intensity of character. After the entertainment was over I repaired, in company with a crowd of ladies and elderly people,
interspersed with gownsmen, to the hoary rotunda of the
Sheldonian theatre, which every visitor to Oxford will remember from its curious cincture of clumsily carven heads of
warriors and sages perched upon stone posts. The interior of
this edifice is the scene of the classic hooting, stamping, and
cat-calling by which the undergraduates confer the last consecration upon the distinguished gentlemen who come up for
the honorary degree of D.C.L. It is with the design of atten-
uating as much as possible this volume of sound that the
heads of colleges, on the close of the term, a few days before
Commemoration, speed their too demonstrative disciples
upon the homeward way. As I have already hinted, however,
the contingent of irreverence was on this occasion quite large
enough to preserve the type of the racket. This made the
scene a very singular one. An American of course, with his
fondness for antiquity, his relish for picturesqueness, his
"emotional" attitude at historic shrines, takes Oxford much
more seriously than its sometimes unwilling familiars can be
expected to do. These people are not always upon the high
horse; they are not always in a state of fine vibration. Nevertheless, there is a certain maximum of disaccord with their
beautiful circumstances which the ecstatic outsider vaguely expects them not to transcend. No effort of the intellect beforehand would enable him to imagine one of those silver-gray

The Sheldonian Theatre, Oxford

temples of learning converted into a semblance of the Bowery
Theatre when the Bowery Theatre is being trifled with.

The Sheldonian edifice, like everything at Oxford, is more
or less monumental. There is a double tier of galleries, with
sculptured pulpits protruding from them; there are full-length
portraits of kings and worthies; there is a general air of antiquity and dignity, which, on the occasion of which I speak,
was enhanced by the presence of certain ancient scholars
seated in crimson robes in high-backed chairs. Formerly, I
believe, the undergraduates were placed apart—packed together in a corner of one of the galleries. But now they are
scattered among the general spectators, a large number of
whom are ladies. They muster in especial force, however, on
the floor of the theatre, which has been cleared of its benches.
Here the dense mass is at last severed in twain by the entrance
of the prospective D.C.L.'s walking in single file, clad in crimson gowns, preceded by mace-bearers and accompanied by
the Regius Professor of Civil Law, who presents them individually to the Vice-Chancellor of the University, in a Latin
speech which is of course a glowing eulogy. The five gentlemen to whom this distinction had been offered in 1877 were
not among those whom fame has trumpeted most loudly; but
there was something "as pretty as a picture" in their standing
in their honourable robes, with heads modestly bent, while
the orator, as effectively draped, recited their titles sonorously
to the venerable dignitary in the high-backed chair. Each of
them, when the little speech is ended, ascends the steps leading to the chair; the Vice-Chancellor bends forward and
shakes his hand, and the new D.C.L. goes and sits in the
blushing row of his fellow doctors. The impressiveness of all
this is much diminished by the boisterous conduct of the
"students," who superabound in extravagant applause, in impertinent interrogation and in lively disparagement of the orator's Latinity. Of the scene that precedes the episode I have
just described I have given no account; vivid portrayal of it is
not easy. Like the return from the Derby it is a carnival of
"chaff"; and it is a singular fact that the scholastic festival
should have forcibly reminded me of the great popular "lark."
In each case it is the same race enjoying a certain definitely
chartered licence; in the young votaries of a liberal education

Magdalen Bridge and Tower

and the London rabble on the Epsom road it is the same
perfect good-humour, the same muscular jocosity.

After the presentation of the doctors came a series of those
collegiate exercises which have a generic resemblance all the
world over: a reading of Latin verses and English essays, a
spouting of prize poems and Greek paraphrases. The prize
poem alone was somewhat attentively listened to; the other
things were received with an infinite variety of critical ejacula-
tion. But after all, I reflected as the ceremony drew to a close,
the romping element is more characteristic than it seems; it is
at bottom only another expression of the venerable and historic side of Oxford. It is tolerated because it is traditional; it
is possible because it is classical. Looked at in this light it
became romantically continuous with the human past that
everything else referred to.

I was not obliged to find ingenious pretexts for thinking
well of another ceremony of which I was witness after we

adjourned from the Sheldonian theatre. This was a lunch-party at the particular college in which I should find it the highest privilege to reside and which I may not further specify. Perhaps indeed I may go so far as to say that the reason for my dreaming of this privilege is that it is deemed by persons of a reforming turn the best-appointed abuse in a nest of abuses. A commission for the expurgation of the universities has lately been appointed by Parliament to look into it—a commission armed with a gigantic broom, which is to sweep away all the fine old ivied and cobwebbed improprieties. Pending these righteous changes, one would like while one is about it—about, that is, this business of admiring Oxford—to attach one's self to the abuse, to bury one's nostrils in the rose before it is plucked. At the college in question there are no undergraduates. I found it agreeable to reflect that those gray-green cloisters had sent no delegates to the slangy congregation I had just quitted. This delightful spot exists for the satisfaction of a small society of Fellows who, having no dreary instruction to administer, no noisy hobble-dehoys to govern, no obligations but toward their own culture, no care save for learning as learning and truth as truth, are presumably the happiest and most charming people in the world. The party invited to lunch assembled first in the library of the college, a cool, gray hall, of very great length and height, with vast wall-spaces of rich-looking book-titles and statues of noble scholars set in the midst. Had the charming Fellows ever anything more disagreeable to do than to finger these precious volumes and then to stroll about together in the grassy courts, in learned comradeship, discussing their precious contents? Nothing, apparently, unless it were to give a lunch at Commemoration in the dining-hall of the college. When lunch was ready there was a very pretty procession to go to it. Learned gentlemen in crimson gowns, ladies in bright finery, paired slowly off and marched in a stately diagonal across the fine, smooth lawn of the quadrangle, in a corner of which they passed through a hospitable door. But here we cross the threshold of privacy; I remained on the further side of it during the rest of the day. But I brought back with me certain memories of which, if I were not at the end of my space, I should attempt a discreet adumbration: memories of

The High Street, Oxford

a *fête champêtre* in the beautiful gardens of one of the other colleges—charming lawns and spreading trees, music of Grenadier Guards, ices in striped marquees, mild flirtation of youthful gownsmen and bemuslined maidens: memories, too, of quiet dinner in common-room, a decorous, excellent repast; old portraits on the walls and great windows open upon the ancient court, where the afternoon light was fading in the stillness; superior talk upon current topics, and over all the peculiar air of Oxford—the air of liberty to care for the things of the mind assured and secured by machinery which is in itself a satisfaction to sense.

Kenilworth

In Warwickshire

THERE is no better way to plunge *in medias res*, for the stranger who wishes to know something of England, than to spend a fortnight in Warwickshire. It is the core and centre of the English world; midmost England, unmitigated England. The place has taught me a great many English secrets; I have been interviewing the genius of pastoral Britain. From a charming lawn—a lawn delicious to one's sentient boot-sole—I looked without obstruction at a sombre, soft, romantic mass whose outline was blurred by mantling ivy. It made a perfect picture, and in the foreground the great trees overarched their boughs, from right and left, so as to give it a majestic frame. This interesting object was the castle of Kenilworth. It was within distance of an easy walk, but one hardly thought of walking to it, any more than one would have thought of walking to a purple-shadowed tower in the background of a Berghem or a Claude. Here were purple shadows and slowly shifting lights, with a soft-hued, bosky country for the middle distance.

Of course, however, I did walk over to the castle; and of course the walk led me through leafy lanes and beside the hedgerows that make a tangled screen for large lawn-like meadows. Of course too, I am bound to add, there was a row of ancient pedlars outside the castle-wall, hawking twopenny pamphlets and photographs. Of course, equally, at the foot of the grassy mound on which the ruin stands were half a dozen public-houses and, always of course, half a dozen beery vagrants sprawling on the grass in the moist sunshine. There was the usual respectable young woman to open the castle-gate and to receive the usual sixpenny fee. There were the usual squares of printed cardboard, suspended upon venerable surfaces, with further enumeration of twopence, threepence, fourpence. I do not allude to these things querulously, for Kenilworth is a very tame lion—a lion that, in former years, I had stroked more than once. I remember perfectly my first visit to this romantic spot; how I chanced upon a picnic; how I stumbled over beer-bottles; how the very echoes of the beautiful ruin seemed to have dropped all their *h*'s. That was a sultry afternoon; I allowed my spirits to sink and I came away hanging my head. This was a beautiful fresh morning, and in the interval I had grown philosophic. I had learned that, with regard to most romantic sites in England, there is a constant cockneyfication with which you must make your account. There are always people on the field before you, and there is generally something being drunk on the premises.

I hoped, on the occasion of which I am now speaking, that the attack would not be acute, and indeed for the first five minutes I flattered myself that this was the case. In the beautiful grassy court of the castle, on my entrance, there were not more than eight or ten fellow intruders. There were a couple of old ladies on a bench, eating something out of a newspaper; there was a dissenting minister, also on a bench, reading the guide-book aloud to his wife and sister-in-law; there were three or four children pushing each other up and down the turfy hillocks. This was sweet seclusion indeed; and I got a capital start with the various noble square-windowed fragments of the stately pile. They are extremely majestic, with their even, pale-red colour, their deep-green drapery, their princely vastness of scale. But presently the tranquil ruin began to swarm like a startled hive. There were plenty of people, if they chose to show themselves. They emerged from crumbling doorways and gaping chambers with the best conscience in the world; but I know not, after all, why I should bear them a grudge, for they gave me a pretext for wandering about in search of a quiet point of view. I cannot say that I found my point of view, but in looking for it I saw the castle, which is certainly an admirable ruin. And when the respectable young woman had let me out of the gate again, and I had shaken my head at the civil-spoken pedlars who form a little avenue for the arriving and departing visitor, I found it in my good-nature to linger a moment on the trodden, grassy slope, and to think that in spite of the hawkers, the paupers and the beer-shops, there was still a good deal of old England in the scene. I say in spite of these things, but it may have been, in some degree, because of them. Who shall resolve into its component parts any impression of this richly complex English world, where the present is always seen, as it were, in profile, and the past presents a full face? At all events the solid red castle rose behind me, towering above its small old ladies and its investigating parsons; before me, across the patch of common, was a row of ancient cottages, black-timbered, red-gabled, pictorial, which evidently had a memory of the castle in its better days. A quaintish village straggled away on the right, and on the left the dark, fat meadows were lighted up with misty sun-spots and browsing sheep. I looked about for the village stocks; I was ready to take the modern vagrants for Shakespearean clowns; and I was on the point of going into one of the ale-houses to ask Mrs. Quickly for a cup of sack.

I began these remarks, however, with no intention of talking about the celebrated curiosities in which this region abounds, but with a design rather of noting a few impressions of some of the shyer and more elusive ornaments of the show. Stratford of course is a very sacred place, but I prefer to say a word, for instance, about a charming old rectory a good many miles distant, and to mention the pleasant picture it made, of a summer afternoon, during a domestic festival.

These are the happiest of a stranger's memories of English life, and he feels that he need make no apology for lifting the corner of the curtain. I drove through the leafy lanes I spoke of just now, and peeped over the hedges into fields where the yellow harvest stood waiting. In some places they were already shorn, and, while the light began to redden in the west and to make a horizontal glow behind the dense wayside foliage, the gleaners here and there came brushing through gaps in the hedges with enormous sheaves upon their shoulders. The rectory was an ancient, gabled building, of pale red brick, with facings of white stone and creepers that wrapped it up. It dates, I imagine, from the early Hanoverian time; and as it stood there upon its cushiony lawn and among its ordered gardens, cheek to cheek with its little Norman church, it seemed to me the model of a quiet, spacious, easy English home. The cushiony lawn, as I have called it, stretched away to the edge of a brook, and afforded to a number of very amiable people an opportunity of playing lawn-tennis. There were half a dozen games going forward at once, and at each of them a great many "nice girls," as they say in England, were distinguishing themselves. These young ladies kept the ball going with an agility worthy of the sisters and sweethearts of a race of cricketers, and gave me a chance to admire their flexibility of figure and their freedom of action. When they came back to the house, after the games, flushed a little and a little dishevelled, they might have passed for the attendant nymphs of Diana flocking in from the chase. There had, indeed, been a chance for them to wear the quiver, a target for archery being erected on the lawn. I remembered George Eliot's Gwendolen, and waited to see her step out of the muslin group; but she was not forthcoming, and it was plain that if lawn-tennis had been invented in Gwendolen's day this young lady would have captivated Mr. Grandcourt by her exploits with the racket. She certainly would have been a mistress of the game; and, if the suggestion be not too gross, the alertness she would have learned from it might have proved an inducement to her boxing the ears of the insupportable Deronda.

After a while it grew too dark for lawn-tennis; but while the twilight was still mildly brilliant I wandered away, out of the grounds of the charming parsonage, and turned into the little churchyard beside it. The small weather-worn, rust-coloured church had an appearance of high antiquity; there were some curious Norman windows in the apse. Unfortunately I could not get inside; I could only glance into the open door across the interval of an old-timbered, heavy-hooded, padlocked porch. But the sweetest evening stillness hung over the place, and the sunset was red behind a dark row of rook-haunted elms. The stillness seemed the greater because three or four rustic children were playing, with little soft cries, among the crooked, deep-buried grave-stones. One poor little girl, who seemed deformed, had climbed some steps that served as a pedestal for a tall, mediæval-looking cross. She sat perched there and stared at me through the gloaming. This was the heart of England, unmistakably; it might have been the very pivot of the wheel on which her fortune revolves. One need not be a rabid Anglican to be extremely sensible of the charm of an English country church— and indeed of some of the features of an English rural Sunday. In London there is a certain flatness in the observance of this festival; but in the country some of the ceremonies that accompany it have an indefinable harmony with an ancient, pastoral landscape. I made this reflection on an occasion that is still very fresh in my memory. I said to myself that the walk to church from a beautiful country-house, of a lovely summer afternoon, may be the prettiest possible adventure. The house stands perched upon a pedestal of rock and looks down from its windows and terraces upon a shadier spot in the wooded meadows, of which the blunted tip of a spire explains the character. A little company of people, whose costume denotes the highest pitch of civilisation, winds down through the blooming gardens, passes out of a couple of small gates and reaches the footpath in the fields. This is especially what takes the fancy of the sympathetic stranger; the level, deep-green meadows, studded here and there with a sturdy oak; the denser grassiness of the footpath, the lily-sheeted pool beside which it passes, the rustic stiles, where he stops and looks back at the great house and its wooded background. It is in the highest degree probable that he has the privilege of walking with a pretty girl, and it is morally certain

Stratford Church

that he thinks a pretty English girl the very type of the maddening magic of youth. He knows that she doesn't know how
lovely is this walk of theirs; she has been taking it—or taking
another quite as good—any time these twenty years. But her
want of immediate intelligence only makes her the more a
part of his delicate entertainment. The latter continues unbroken while they reach the little churchyard and pass up to the
ancient porch, round which the rosy rustics are standing, decently and deferentially, to watch the arrival of the smarter
contingent. This party takes its place in a great square pew, as
large as a small room, and with seats all round, and while he
listens to the respectable intonings the sympathetic stranger
reads over the inscriptions on the mural tablets before him, all
to the honour of the earlier bearers of a name which is, for
himself, a symbol of hospitality.

When I came back to the parsonage the entertainment had
been transferred to the interior, and I had occasion to admire
the maidenly vigour of all the nice girls who, after playing
lawn-tennis all the afternoon, were modestly expecting to
dance all the evening. And in regard to this it is not impertinent to say that from almost any group of young English
creatures of this order—though preferably from such as have
passed their lives in quiet country homes—an American receives a delightful impression of something that he may describe as an intimate salubrity. He notices face after face in
which this rosy absence of a morbid strain—this simple, natural, affectionate development—amounts to positive beauty.
If the young lady have no other beauty the air I speak of is a
charm in itself; but when it is united, as it so often is, to real
perfection of feature and colour the result is the most delightful thing in nature. It makes the highest type of English
beauty, and to my sense there is nothing so satisfyingly high
as that. Not long since I heard a clever foreigner indulge, in
conversation with an English lady—a very wise and liberal
woman—in a little lightly restrictive criticism of her countrywomen. "It is possible," she answered, in regard to one of his
objections; "but such as they are, they are inexpressibly dear
to their husbands." This is doubtless true of good wives all
over the world; but I felt, as I listened to these words of my
friend, that there is often something in an English girl-face

which gives it an extra touch of *justesse*. Such as the woman is, she has here, more than elsewhere, the look of being completely and profoundly, without reservations for other uses, at the service of the man she loves. This look, after one has been a while in England, comes to seem so much a proper and indispensable part of a "nice" face, that the absence of it appears a sign of irritability or of shallowness. Latent responsiveness to the manly appeal—that is what it means; which one must take as a very comfortable meaning.

As for the prettiness, I cannot forbear, in the face of a fresh reminiscence, to give it another word. And yet in regard to prettiness what do words avail? This was what I asked myself the other day as I looked at a young girl who stood in an old oaken parlour, the rugged panels of which made a background for her lovely head, in simple conversation with a handsome lad. I said to myself that the faces of the English young have often a perfect charm, but that this same charm is too soft and shy a thing to talk about. The face of this fair creature had a pure oval, and her clear brown eyes a quiet warmth. Her complexion was as bright as a sunbeam after rain, and she smiled in a way that made any other way of smiling than that seem a shallow grimace—a mere creaking of the facial muscles. The young man stood facing her, slowly scratching his thigh and shifting from one foot to the other. He was tall and straight, and so sun-burned that his fair hair was lighter than his complexion. He had honest, stupid blue eyes, and a simple smile that showed handsome teeth. He had the look of a gentleman. Presently I heard what they were saying. "I suppose it's pretty big," said the beautiful young girl. "Yes; it's pretty big," said the handsome young man. "It's nicer when they are big," said his interlocutress. The young man looked at her, and at everything in general, with his slowly apprehending blue eye, and for some time no further remark was made. "It draws ten feet of water," he at last went on. "How much water is there?" said the young girl. She spoke in a charming voice. "There are thirty feet of water," said the young man. "Oh, that's enough," rejoined the damsel. I had had an idea they were flirting, and perhaps indeed that is the way it is done. It was an ancient room and extremely delightful; everything was polished over with the

brownness of centuries. The chimney-piece was carved a foot
thick, and the windows bore, in coloured glass, the quarter-
ings of ancestral couples. These had stopped two hundred
years before; there was nothing newer than that date. Outside
the windows was a deep, broad moat, which washed the base
of gray walls—gray walls spotted over with the most delicate
yellow lichens.

In such a region as this mellow conservative Warwickshire
an appreciative American finds the small things quite as suggestive as the great. Everything indeed is suggestive, and impressions are constantly melting into each other and doing
their work before he has had time to ask them whence they
came. He can scarce go into a cottage muffled in plants, to see
a genial gentlewoman and a "nice girl," without being reminded forsooth of "The Small House at Allington." Why of
"The Small House at Allington"? There is a larger house to
which the ladies come up to dine; but that is surely an insufficient reason. That the ladies are charming—even that is not
reason enough; for there have been other nice girls in the
world than Lily Dale and other mild matrons than her
mamma. Reminded, however, he is—especially when he goes
out upon the lawn. Of course there is lawn-tennis, and it
seems all ready for Mr. Crosbie to come and take a racket.
This is a small example of the way in which in the presence of
English life the imagination must be constantly at play on the
part of members of a race in whom it has necessarily been
trained to do extra service. In driving and walking, in looking
and listening, everything affected one as in some degree or
other characteristic of a rich, powerful, old-fashioned society.
One had no need of being told that this is a conservative
county; the fact seemed written in the hedgerows and in the
verdant acres behind them. Of course the owners of these
things were conservative; of course they were stubbornly unwilling to see the harmonious edifice of their constituted, convenient world the least bit shaken. I had a feeling, as I went
about, that I should find some very ancient and curious opinions still comfortably domiciled in the fine old houses whose
clustered gables and chimneys appeared here and there, at a
distance, above their ornamental woods. Imperturbable British Toryism, viewed in this vague and conjectural fashion—

Leicester's Hospital, Warwick

across the fields and behind the oaks and beeches—is by no means a thing the irresponsible stranger would wish away; it deepens the very colour of the air; it may be said to be the style of the landscape. I got a sort of constructive sense of its presence in the picturesque old towns of Coventry and Warwick, which appear to be filled with those institutions— chiefly of an eleemosynary order—that make the undoubting more undoubting still. There are ancient charities in these places—hospitals, almshouses, asylums, infant-schools—so quaint and venerable that they almost make the existence of respectful dependence a delectable and satisfying thought. In Coventry in especial, I believe, these pious foundations are so numerous as fairly to place a premium upon personal woe. Invidious reflections apart, however, there are few things that speak more quaintly and suggestively of the old England that an American loves than these clumsy little monuments of ancient benevolence. Such an institution as Leicester's Hospital at Warwick seems indeed to exist primarily for the sake of its spectacular effect upon the American tourists, who, with the dozen rheumatic old soldiers maintained in affluence there, constitute its principal *clientèle*.

The American tourist usually comes straight to this quarter of England—chiefly for the purpose of paying his respects to the birthplace of Shakespeare. Being here, he comes to Warwick to see the castle; and being at Warwick, he comes to see the odd little theatrical-looking refuge for superannuated warriors which lurks in the shadow of one of the old gate-towers. Every one will remember Hawthorne's account of the place, which has left no touch of charming taste to be added to any reference to it. The hospital struck me as a little museum kept up for the amusement and confusion of those inquiring Occidentals who are used to seeing charity more dryly and practically administered. The old hospitallers—I am not sure, after all, whether they are necessarily soldiers, but some of them happen to be—are at once the curiosities and the keepers. They sit on benches outside of their door, at the receipt of custom, all neatly brushed and darned and ready to do you the honours. They are only twelve in number, but their picturesque dwelling, perched upon the old city rampart and full of dusky little courts, cross-timbered gable-ends and deeply sunken lattices, seems a wonderfully elaborate piece of machinery for its humble purpose. Each of the old gentlemen must be provided with a wife or "housekeeper"; each of them has a dusky parlour of his own; and they pass their latter days in their scoured and polished little refuge as softly and honourably as a company of retired lawgivers or pensioned soothsayers.

At Coventry I went to see a couple of old charities of a similar pattern—places with black-timbered fronts, little clean-swept courts and Elizabethan windows. One of them was a romantic residence for a handful of old women, who sat, each of them, in a cosy little bower, in a sort of mediæval darkness; the other was a school for little boys of humble origin, and this last establishment was charming. I found the little boys playing at "top" in a gravelled court, in front of the prettiest old building of tender-coloured stucco and painted timber, ornamented with two delicate little galleries and a fantastic porch. They were dressed in small blue tunics and odd caps, like those worn by sailors, but, if I remember rightly, with little yellow tags affixed. I was able to wander at my pleasure all over the establishment; there was no sign of pastor or master anywhere; nothing but the little yellow-headed boys playing before the ancient house and practising most correctly the Warwickshire accent. I went indoors and looked at a fine old oaken staircase; I even ascended it and walked along a gallery and peeped into a dormitory at a row of very short beds; and then I came down and sat for five minutes on a bench hardly wider than the top rail of a fence, in a little, cold, dim refectory where there was not a crumb to be seen, nor any lingering odour of bygone repasts to be perceived. And yet I wondered how it was that the sense of many generations of boyish feeders seemed to abide there. It came, I suppose, from the very bareness and, if I may be allowed the expression, the clean-licked aspect of the place, which wore the appearance of the famous platter of Jack Sprat and his wife.

Inevitably, of course, the sentimental tourist has a great deal to say to himself about this being Shakespeare's county —about these densely grassed meadows and parks having been, to his musing eyes, the normal landscape, the green picture of the world. In Shakespeare's day, doubtless, the coat of nature was far from being so prettily trimmed as it is now; but there is one place, nevertheless, which, as he passes it in the summer twilight, the traveller does his best to believe unaltered. I allude, of course, to Charlecote Park, whose venerable verdure seems a survival from an earlier England and whose innumerable acres, stretching away, in the early evening, to vaguely seen Tudor walls, lie there like the backward years receding to the age of Elizabeth. It was, however, no part of my design in these remarks to pause before so thickly besieged a shrine as this; and if I were to allude to Stratford it would not be in connection with the fact that Shakespeare planted there, to grow for ever, the torment of his unguessed riddle. It would be rather to speak of a delightful old house, near the Avon, which struck me as the ideal home for a Shakespearean scholar, or indeed for any passion-

ate lover of the poet. Here, with books and memories and the
recurring reflection that he had taken his daily walk across the
bridge at which you look from your windows straight down
an avenue of fine old trees, with an ever-closed gate at the end
of them and a carpet of turf stretched over the decent drive—
here, I say, with old brown wainscotted chambers to live in,
old polished doorsteps to lead you from one to the other,
deep window-seats to sit in, with a play in your lap, here a
person for whom the cares of life should have resolved themselves into a care for the greatest genius who has represented
and ornamented life might find a very congruous asylum. Or,
speaking a little wider of the mark, the charming, rambling,
low-gabled, many-staired, much-panelled mansion would be a
very agreeable home for any person of taste who should prefer an old house to a new. I find I am talking about it quite
like an auctioneer; but what I chiefly had at heart was to commemorate the fact that I had lunched there and, while I
lunched, kept saying to myself that there is nothing in the
world so delightful as the happy accidents of old English
houses.

   And yet that same day, on the edge of the Avon, I found it
in me to say that a new house too may be a very charming
affair. But I must add that the new house I speak of had really
such exceptional advantages that it could not fairly be placed
in the scale. Besides, was it new after all? It must have been,
and yet one's impression there was all of a kind of silvered
antiquity. The place stood upon a decent Stratford road, from
which it looked usual enough; but when, after sitting a while
in a charming modern drawing-room, one stepped thought-
lessly through an open window upon a verandah, one found
that the horizon of the morning call had been wonderfully
widened. I will not pretend to detail all I saw after I stepped
off the verandah; suffice it that the spire and chancel of the
beautiful old church in which Shakespeare is buried, with the
Avon sweeping its base, were one of the elements of the
vision. Then there were the smoothest lawns in the world
stretching down to the edge of this liquid slowness and making, where the water touched them, a line as even as the rim
of a champagne-glass—a verge near which you inevitably lingered to see the spire and the chancel (the church was close at

Charlecote Park

hand) among the well-grouped trees, and look for their reflection in the river. The place was a garden of delight; it was a
stage set for one of Shakespeare's comedies—for *Twelfth
Night* or *Much Ado*. Just across the river was a level meadow,
which rivalled the lawn on which I stood, and this meadow
seemed only the more essentially a part of the scene by reason
of the voluminous sheep that were grazing on it. These sheep
were by no means mere edible mutton; they were poetic, historic, romantic sheep; they were not there for their weight or
their wool, they were there for their presence and their com-
positional value, and they visibly knew it. And yet, knowing
as they were, I doubt whether the wisest old ram of the flock
could have told me how to explain why it was that this happy
mixture of lawn and river and mirrored spire and blooming
garden seemed to me for a quarter of an hour the richest
corner of England.

If Warwickshire is Shakespeare's country, I found myself
not dodging the consciousness that it is also George Eliot's.
The author of "Adam Bede" and "Middlemarch" has called
the rural background of those admirable fictions by another
name, but I believe it long ago ceased to be a secret that her
native Warwickshire had been in her intention. The stranger
who treads its eternal stretched velvet recognises at every turn
the elements of George Eliot's novels—especially when he
carries himself back in imagination to the Warwickshire of
forty years ago. He says to himself that it would be impossible to conceive anything—anything equally rural—more
sturdily central, more densely definite. It was in one of the
old nestling farmhouses, beyond a hundred hedgerows, that
Hetty Sorrel smiled into her milk-pans as if she were looking
for a reflection of her pretty face; it was at the end of one of
the leafy-pillared avenues that poor Mrs. Casaubon paced up
and down with her many questions. The country suggests in
especial both the social and the natural scenery of "Middlemarch." There must be many a genially perverse old Mr.
Brooke there yet, and whether there are many Dorotheas or
not, there must be many a well-featured and well-acred young
country gentleman, of the pattern of Sir James Chettam, who,
as he rides along the leafy lanes, softly cudgels his brain to
know why a clever girl shouldn't wish to marry him. But I

doubt whether there be many Dorotheas, and I suspect that the Sir James Chettams of the county are not often pushed to that intensity of meditation. You feel, however, that George Eliot could not have placed her heroine in a local medium better fitted to throw her fine impatience into relief—a community more likely to be startled and perplexed by a questioning attitude on the part of a well-housed and well-fed young gentlewoman.

Among the edifying days that I spent in these neighbourhoods there is one in especial of which I should like to give a detailed account. But I find on consulting my memory that the details have melted away into the single deep impression of a perfect ripeness of civilisation. It was a long excursion, by rail and by carriage, for the purpose of seeing three extremely interesting old country-houses. Our errand led us, in the first place, into Oxfordshire, through the ancient market-town of Banbury, where of course we made a point of looking out for the Cross referred to in the famous nursery-rhyme. It stood there in the most natural manner—though I am afraid it has been "done up"—with various antique gables around it, from one of whose exiguous windows the young person appealed to in the rhyme may have looked at the old woman as she rode and heard the music of her bells. The houses we went to see have not a national reputation; they are simply interwoven figures in the rich pattern of the Midlands. They have indeed a local renown but they are not thought of as unexampled, still less as abnormal, and the stranger has a feeling that his surprises and ecstasies are held to betray the existence, on his part, of a blank background. Such places, to a Warwickshire mind of good habits, must appear the pillars and props of a heaven-appointed order of things; and accordingly, in a land on which heaven smiles, they are as natural as the geology of the county or the supply of mutton. But nothing could well give a stranger a stronger impression of the wealth of England in such matters—of the interminable list of her territorial homes—than this fact that the so eminent specimens I speak of should have but a limited fame, should not be lions of the first magnitude. Of one of them, the finest in the group, one of my companions, who lived but twenty miles away, had never even heard. Such a place was not thought a

subject for local swagger. Its peers and mates are scattered all
over the country; half of them are not even mentioned in the
county guide-books. You stumble upon them in a drive or a
walk. You catch a glimpse of an ivied front at some midmost
point of wide acres, and taking your way, by leave of a serious
old woman at a lodge-gate, along an overarching avenue, you
find yourself introduced to an edifice so human-looking in its
beauty that it seems for the occasion fairly to reconcile art and
morality.

To Broughton Castle, the first seen in this beautiful group,
I must do no more than allude; but this is not because I failed
to think it, as I think every house I see, the most delightful
habitation in England. It lies rather low, and its woods and
pastures slope down to it; it has a deep, clear moat all round
it, spanned by a bridge that passes under a charming old gate-
tower, and nothing can be sweeter than to see its clustered
walls of yellow-brown stone so sharply islanded while its gardens bloom on the other side of the water. Like several other
houses in this part of the country, Broughton Castle played a
part (on the Parliamentary side) in the civil wars, and not the
least interesting features of its beautiful interior are the several
mementoes of Cromwell's station there. It was within a moderate drive of this place that in 1642 the battle of Edgehill was
fought—the first great battle of the war—and gained by neither party. We went to see the battlefield, where an ancient
tower and an artificial ruin (of all things in the world) have
been erected for the entertainment of convivial visitors. These
ornaments are perched upon the edge of a slope which commands a view of the exact scene of the contest, upwards of a
mile away. I looked in the direction indicated and saw misty
meadows a little greener perhaps than usual and colonnades
of elms a trifle denser. After this we paid our respects to another old house which is full of memories and suggestions of
that most dramatic period of English history. But of Compton Wyniates (the name of this seat of enchantment) I despair
of giving any coherent or adequate account. It belongs to the
Marquis of Northampton, and it stands empty all the year
round. It sits on the grass at the bottom of a wooded hollow,
and the glades of a superb old park go wandering upward
away from it. When I came out in front of the house from a

short and steep but stately avenue I said to myself that here surely we had arrived at the farthest limits of what ivy-smothered brick-work and weather-beaten gables, conscious old windows and clustered mossy roofs can accomplish for the eye. It is impossible to imagine a more finished picture. And its air of solitude and delicate decay—of having been dropped into its grassy hollow as an ancient jewel is deposited upon a cushion, and being shut in from the world and back into the past by its circling woods—all this drives the impression well home. The house is not large, as great houses go, and it sits, as I have said, upon the grass, without even a flagging or a footpath to conduct you from the point where the avenue stops to the beautiful sculptured doorway which admits you into the small, quaint inner court. From this court you are at liberty to pass through the crookedest series of oaken halls and chambers, adorned with treasures of old wainscotting and elaborate doors and chimneypieces. Outside, you may walk all round the house on a grassy bank, which is raised above the level on which it stands, and find it from every point of view a more charming composition. I should not omit to mention that Compton Wyniates is supposed to have been in Scott's eye when he described the dwelling of the old royalist knight in "Woodstock." In this case he simply transferred the house to the other side of the county. He has indeed given several of the features of the place, but he has not given what one may call its colour. I must add that if Sir Walter could not give the colour of Compton Wyniates, it is useless for any other writer to try. It is a matter for the brush and not for the pen.

And what shall I say of the colour of Wroxton Abbey, which we visited last in order and which in the thickening twilight, as we approached its great ivy-muffled face, laid on the mind the burden of its felicity? Wroxton Abbey, as it stands, is a house of about the same period as Compton Wyniates—the latter years, I suppose, of the sixteenth century. But it is quite another affair. The place is inhabited, "kept up," full of the most interesting and most splendid detail. Its happy occupants, however, were fortunately not in the act of staying there (happy occupants, in England, are almost always absent), and the house was exhibited with a civility worthy of its merit. Everything that in the material line can render life noble and charming has been gathered into it with a profusion which makes the whole place a monument to past opportunity. As I wandered from one rich room to another and looked at these things that intimate appeal to the romantic sense which I just mentioned was mercilessly emphasised. But who can tell the story of the romantic sense when that adventurer really rises to the occasion—takes its ease in an old English country-house while the twilight darkens the corners of expressive rooms and the victim of the scene, pausing at the window, turns his glance from the observing portrait of a handsome ancestral face and sees the great soft billows of the lawn melt away into the park?

Abbeys and Castles

IT IS a frequent perception with the stranger in England that the beauty and interest of the country are private property and that to get access to them a key is always needed. The key may be large or it may be small, but it must be something that will turn a lock. Of the things that contribute to the happiness of an American observer in these tantalising conditions, I can think of very few that do not come under this definition of private property. When I have mentioned the hedgerows and the churches I have almost exhausted the list. You can enjoy a hedgerow from the public road, and I suppose that even if you are a Dissenter you may enjoy a Norman abbey from the street. If therefore you talk of anything beautiful in England, the presumption will be that it is private; and indeed such is my admiration of this delightful country that I feel inclined to say that if you talk of anything private the presumption will be that it is beautiful. This is something of a dilemma. When the observer permits himself to commemorate charming impressions he is in danger of giving to the world the fruits of friendship and hospitality. When on the other hand he withholds his impression he lets something admirable slip away without having marked its passage, without having done it proper honour. He ends by mingling discretion with enthusiasm, and he says to himself that it is not treating a country ill to talk of its treasures when the mention of each has tacit reference to some kindness conferred.

The impressions I have in mind in writing these lines were gathered in a part of England of which I had not before had even a traveller's glimpse; but as to which, after a day or two, I found myself quite ready to agree with a friend who lived there and who knew and loved it well, when he said very frankly "I do believe it is the loveliest corner of the world!" This was not a dictum to quarrel about, and while I was in the neighbourhood I was quite of his opinion. I felt I might easily come to care for it very much as he cared for it; I had a glimpse of the kind of romantic passion such a country may inspire. It is a capital example of that density of feature which

is the great characteristic of English scenery. There are no
waste details; everything in the landscape is something particular—has a history, has played a part, has a value to the
imagination. It is a region of hills and blue undulations, and,
though none of the hills are high, all of them are interesting—interesting as such things are interesting in an old, small
country, by a kind of exquisite modulation, something suggesting that outline and colouring have been retouched and
refined by the hand of time. Independently of its castles and
abbeys, the definite relics of the ages, such a landscape seems
charged and interfused. It has, has always had, human relations and is intimately conscious of them. That little speech
about the loveliness of his county, or of his own part of his
county, was made to me by my companion as we walked up
the grassy slope of a hill, or "edge," as it is called there, from
the crest of which we seemed in an instant to look away over
most of the remainder of England. Certainly one would have
grown to love such a view as that quite in the same way as
to love some magnificent yet sensitive friend. The "edge"
plunged down suddenly, as if the corresponding slope on the
other side had been excavated, and you might follow the long
ridge for the space of an afternoon's walk with this vast,
charming prospect before your eyes. Looking across an English county into the next but one is a very pretty entertainment, the county seeming by no means so small as might be
supposed. How can a county seem small in which, from such
a vantage-point as the one I speak of, you see, as a darker
patch across the lighter green, the great territory of one of the
greatest representatives of territorial greatness? These things
constitute immensities, and beyond them are blue undulations
of varying tone, and then another bosky province which fur-
nishes forth, as you are told, the residential and other umbrage of another magnate. And to right and left of these, in
wooded expanses, lie other domains of equal consequence. It
was therefore not the smallness but the vastness of the country that struck me, and I was not at all in the mood of a
certain American who once, in my hearing, burst out laugh-
ing at an English answer to my inquiry as to whether my
interlocutor often saw Mr. B——. "Oh no," the answer had
been, "we never see him: he lives away off in the West." It

was the western part of his county our friend meant, and my American humorist found matter for infinite jest in his meaning. "I should as soon think," he remarked, "of talking of my own west or east foot."

I do not think, even, that my sensibility to the charm of this delightful region—for its hillside prospect of old red farmhouses lighting up the dark-green bottoms, of gables and chimney-tops of great houses peeping above miles of woodland, and, in the vague places of the horizon, of far away towns and sites that one had always heard of—was conditioned upon having "property" in the neighbourhood, so that the little girls in the town should suddenly drop curtsies to me in the street; though that too would certainly have been pleasant. At the same time having a little property would without doubt have made the attachment stronger. People who wander about the world without money in their pockets indulge in dreams—dreams of the things they would buy if their pockets were workable. These dreams are very apt to have relation to a good estate in any neighbourhood in which the wanderer may happen to find himself. For myself, I have never been in a country so unattractive that I didn't find myself "drawn" to its most exemplary mansion. In New England and other portions of the United States I have felt my heart go out to the Greek temple, the small Parthenon, in white-painted wood; in Italy I have made imaginary proposals for the yellow-walled villa with statues on the roof. My fancy, in England, has seldom fluttered so high as the very best house, but it has again and again hovered about one of the quiet places, unknown to fame, which are locally spoken of as merely "good." There was one in especial, in the neighbourhood I allude to, as to which the dream of having impossibly acquired it from an embarrassed owner kept melting into the vision of "moving in" on the morrow. I saw this place unfortunately, to small advantage; I saw it in the rain, but I am glad fine weather didn't meddle with the affair, for the irritation of envy might in this case have poisoned the impression. It was a long, wet Sunday, and the waters were deep. I had been in the house all day, for the weather can best be described by my saying that it had been deemed to exonerate us from church. But in the afternoon, the prospective interval between lunch and tea assuming formidable proportions, my host took me a walk, and in the course of our walk he led me into a park which he described as "the paradise of a small English country-gentleman." It was indeed a modern Eden, and the trees might have been trees of knowledge. They were of high antiquity and magnificent girth and stature; they were strewn over the grassy levels in extraordinary profusion, and scattered upon and down the slopes in a fashion than which I have seen nothing more felicitous since I last looked at the chestnuts above the Lake of Como. The point was that the property was small, but that one could perceive nowhere any limit. Shortly before we turned into the park the rain had renewed itself, so that we were awkwardly wet and muddy; but, being near the house, my companion proposed to leave his card in a neighbourly way. The house was most agreeable: it stood on a kind of terrace, in the middle of a lawn and garden, and the terrace overhung one of the most copious rivers in England, as well as looking across to those blue undulations of which I have already spoken. On the terrace also was a piece of ornamental water, and there was a small iron paling to divide the lawn from the park. All this I beheld in the rain. My companion gave his card to the butler with the remark that we were too much bespattered to come in, and we turned away to complete our circuit. As we turned away I became acutely conscious of what I should have been tempted to call the cruelty of this proceeding. My imagination gauged the whole position. It was a blank, a blighted Sunday afternoon—no one could come. The house was charming, the terrace delightful, the oaks magnificent, the view most interesting. But the whole thing confessed to the blankness if not to the dulness. In the house was a drawing-room, and in the drawing-room was—by which I meant *must be*—an English lady, a perfectly harmonious figure. There was nothing fatuous in believing that on this rainy Sunday afternoon it would not please her to be told that two gentlemen had walked across the country to her door only to go through the ceremony of leaving a card. Therefore, when, before we had gone many yards, I heard the butler hurrying after us, I felt how just my sentiment of the situation had been. Of course we went back, and I carried my muddy boots into the drawing-room—just the drawing-room I had imagined—where I found—I will not say just the lady I had imagined, but a lady even more in keeping. Indeed there were two ladies, one of whom was staying in the house. In whatever company you find yourself in England, you may always be sure that some one present is "staying," and you come in due time to feel the abysses within the word. The large windows of the drawing-room I speak of looked away over the river to the blurred and blotted hills, where the rain was drizzling and drifting. It was very quiet, as I say; there was an air of large leisure. If one wanted to do anything here, there was evidently plenty of time—and indeed of every other appliance—to do it. The two ladies talked about "town": that is what people talk about in the country. If I were disposed I might represent them as talking with a positive pathos of yearning. At all events I asked myself how it could be that one should live in this charming place and trouble one's head about what was going on in London in July. Then we had fine strong tea and bread and butter.

I returned to the habitation of my friend—for I too was guilty of "staying"—through an old Norman portal, massively arched and quaintly sculptured, across whose hollow threshold the eye of fancy might see the ghosts of monks and the shadows of abbots pass noiselessly to and fro. This aperture admits you to a beautiful ambulatory of the thirteenth century—a long stone gallery or cloister, repeated in two stories, with the interstices of its traceries now glazed, but with its long, low, narrow, charming vista still perfect and picturesque, with its flags worn away by monkish sandals and with huge round-arched doorways opening from its inner side into great rooms roofed like cathedrals. These rooms are furnished with narrow windows, of almost defensive aspect, set in embrasures three feet deep and ornamented with little grotesque mediæval faces. To see one of the small monkish masks grinning at you while you dress and undress, or while you look up in the intervals of inspiration from your letter-writing, is a mere detail in the entertainment of living in a *ci-devant* priory. This entertainment is inexhaustible; for every step you take in such a house confronts you in one way or another with the remote past. You devour the documentary, you inhale the his-

toric. Adjoining the house is a beautiful ruin, part of the walls
and windows and bases of the piers of the magnificent church
administered by the predecessor of your host, the mitred abbot. These relics are very desultory, but they are still abundant, and they testify to the great scale and the stately beauty
of the abbey. You may lie upon the grass at the base of an
ivied fragment, measure the girth of the great stumps of the
central columns, half smothered in soft creepers, and think
how strange it is that in this quiet hollow, in the midst of
lonely hills, so exquisite and elaborate a work of art should
have risen. It is but an hour's walk to another great ruin,
which has held together more completely. There the central
tower stands erect to half its altitude and the round arches
and massive pillars of the nave make a perfect vista on the
unencumbered turf. You get an impression that when catholic
England was in her prime great abbeys were as thick as mile-
stones. By native amateurs even now the region is called
"wild," though to American eyes it seems almost suburban in
its smoothness and finish. There is a noiseless little railway
running through the valley, and there is an ancient little town
at the abbey-gates—a town indeed with no great din of vehicles, but with goodly brick houses, with a dozen "publics,"
with tidy, whitewashed cottages, and with little girls, as I
have said, bobbing curtsies in the street. Yet even now, if one
had wound one's way into the valley by the railroad, it would
be rather a surprise to find a great architectural display in a
setting so peaceful and pastoral. How impressive then must
the beautiful church have been in the days of its prosperity,
when the pilgrim came down to it from the grassy hillside
and its bells made the stillness sensible! The abbey was in
those days a great affair; it sprawled, as my companion said,
all over the place. As you walk away from it you think you
have got to the end of its geography, but you encounter it
still in the shape of a rugged outhouse enriched with an early-
English arch, of an ancient well hidden in a kind of sculptured
cavern. It is noticeable that even if you are a traveller from a
land where there are no early-English—and indeed few late-
English—arches, and where the well-covers are, at their hoar-
iest, of fresh-looking shingles, you grow used with little delay
to all this antiquity. Anything very old seems extremely natural;

Stokesay

there is nothing we suffer to get so near us as the tokens of the remote. It is not too much to say that after spending twenty-four hours in a house that is six hundred years old you seem yourself to have lived in it six hundred years. You seem yourself to have hollowed the flags with your tread and to have polished the oak with your touch. You walk along the little stone gallery where the monks used to pace, looking out of the Gothic window-places at their beautiful church, and you pause at the big, round, rugged doorway that admits you to what is now the drawing-room. The massive step by which you ascend to the threshold is a trifle crooked, as it should be; the lintels are cracked and worn by the myriad-fingered years. This strikes your casual glance. You look up and down the miniature cloister before you pass in; it seems wonderfully old and queer. Then you turn into the drawing-room, where you find modern conversation and late publications and the prospect of dinner. The new life and the old have melted together; there is no dividing-line. In the drawing-room wall is a queer funnel-shaped hole, with the broad end inward, like a small casemate. You ask what it is, but people have forgotten. It is something of the monks; it is a mere detail. After dinner you are told that there is of course a ghost—a gray friar who is seen in the dusky hours at the end of passages. Sometimes the servants see him; they afterwards go surreptitiously to sleep in the village. Then, when you take your chamber-candle and go wandering bedward by a short cut through empty rooms, you are conscious of an attitude toward the gray friar which you hardly know whether to read as a fond hope or as a great fear.

A friend of mine, an American, who knew this country, had told me not to fail, while I was in the neighbourhood, to go to Stokesay and two or three other places. "Edward IV. and Elizabeth," he said, "are still hanging about there." So admonished, I made a point of going at least to Stokesay, and I saw quite what my friend meant. Edward IV. and Elizabeth indeed are still to be met almost anywhere in the county; as regards domestic architecture few parts of England are still more vividly old-English. I have rarely had, for a couple of hours, the sensation of dropping back personally into the past so straight as while I lay on the grass beside the well in the little sunny court of this small castle and lazily appreciated the

Ludlow Castle

still definite details of mediæval life. The place is a capital example of a small *gentilhommière* of the thirteenth century. It
has a good deep moat, now filled with wild verdure, and a
curious gatehouse of a much later period—the period when
the defensive attitude had been well-nigh abandoned. This
gatehouse, which is not in the least in the style of the habitation, but gabled and heavily timbered, with quaint cross-
beams protruding from surfaces of coarse white plaster, is a
very effective anomaly in regard to the little gray fortress on
the other side of the court. I call this a fortress, but it is a
fortress which might easily have been taken, and it must have
assumed its present shape at a time when people had ceased
to peer through narrow slits at possible besiegers. There are
slits in the outer walls for such peering, but they are noticeably broad and not particularly oblique, and might easily have
been applied to the uses of a peaceful parley. This is part of
the charm of the place; human life there must have lost an
earlier grimness; it was lived in by people who were beginning to believe in good intentions. They must have lived very
much together; that is one of the most obvious reflections in
the court of a mediæval dwelling. The court was not always
grassy and empty, as it is now, with only a couple of gentlemen in search of impressions lying at their length, one of
them handling a wine-flask that colours the clear water drawn
from the well into a couple of tumblers by a decent, rosy,
smiling, talking old woman who has come bustling out of the
gatehouse and who has a large, dropsical, innocent husband
standing about on crutches in the sun and making no sign
when you ask after his health. This poor man has reached that
ultimate depth of human simplicity at which even a chance to
talk about one's ailments is not appreciated. But the civil old
woman talks for every one, even for an artist who has come
out of one of the rooms, where I see him afterward reproduc-
ing its mouldering repose. The rooms are all unoccupied and
in a state of extreme decay, though the castle is, as yet, far
from being a ruin. From one of the windows I see a young
lady sitting under a tree, across a meadow, with her knees up,
dipping something into her mouth. It is indubitably a camel's
hair paint-brush; the young lady is inevitably sketching. These
are the only besiegers to which the place is exposed now, and

Ludlow Castle

they can do no great harm, as I doubt whether the young lady's aim is very good. We wandered about the empty interior, thinking it a pity such things should fall to pieces. There is a beautiful great hall—great, that is, for a small castle (it would be extremely handsome in a modern house)—with tall, ecclesiastical-looking windows and a long staircase at one end, which climbs against the wall into a spacious bedroom. You may still apprehend very well the main lines of that simpler life; and it must be said that, simpler though it was, it was apparently by no means destitute of many of our own conveniences. The chamber at the top of the staircase ascending from the hall is charming still, with its irregular shape, its low-browed ceiling, its cupboards in the walls, its deep bay window formed of a series of small lattices. You can fancy people stepping out from it upon the platform of the staircase, whose rugged wooden logs, by way of steps, and solid, deeply guttered hand-rail, still remain. They looked down into the hall, where, I take it, there was always a congregation of retainers, much lounging and waiting and passing to and

fro, with a door open into the court. The court, as I said just
now, was not the grassy, æsthetic spot which you may find it
at present of a summer's day; there were beasts tethered in it,
and hustling men at arms, and the earth was trampled into
puddles. But my lord or my lady, looking down from the
chamber-door, commanded the position and, no doubt, issued their orders accordingly. The sight of the groups on the
floor beneath, the calling up and down, the oaken tables
spread and the brazier in the middle—all this seemed present
again; and it was not difficult to pursue the historic vision
through the rest of the building—through the portion which
connected the great hall with the tower (where the confederate of the sketching young lady without had set up the peaceful three-legged engine of his craft); through the dusky,
roughly circular rooms of the tower itself, and up the cork-
screw staircase of the same to that most charming part of
every old castle, where visions must leap away off the
battlements to elude you—the bright, dizzy platform at the
tower-top, the place where the castle-standard hung and the
vigilant inmates surveyed the approaches. Here, always, you
really overtake the impression of the place—here, in the
sunny stillness, it seems to pause, panting a little, and give
itself up.

It was not only at Stokesay that I lingered a while on the
summit of the keep to enjoy the complete impression so overtaken. I spent such another half-hour at Ludlow, which is a
much grander and more famous monument. Ludlow, however, is a ruin—the most impressive and magnificent of ruins.
The charming old town and the admirable castle form a capital object of pilgrimage. Ludlow is an excellent example of a
small English provincial town that has not been soiled and
disfigured by industry; it exhibits no tall chimneys and smoke-
streamers, no attendant purlieus and slums. The little city is
perched upon a hill near which the goodly Severn wanders,
and it has a remarkable air of civic dignity. Its streets are wide
and clean, empty and a little grass-grown, and bordered with
spacious, mildly ornamental brick houses which look as if
there had been more going on in them in the first decade of
the century than there is in the present, but which can still
nevertheless hold up their heads and keep their window-panes

Ludlow

clear, their knockers brilliant and their door-steps whitened. The place seems to say that some hundred years ago it was the centre of a large provincial society and that this society was very "good" of its kind. It must have transported itself to Ludlow for the season—in rumbling coaches and heavy curricles—and there entertained itself in decent emulation of that more majestic capital which a choice of railway lines had not as yet placed within its immediate reach. It had balls at the assembly rooms; it had Mrs. Siddons to play; it had Catalani to sing. Miss Burney's and Miss Austen's heroines might perfectly well have had their first love-affair there; a journey to Ludlow would certainly have been a great event to Fanny Price or Emma Woodhouse, or even to those more romantically connected young ladies Evelina and Cecilia. It is a place on which a provincial aristocracy has left so sensible a stamp as to enable you to measure both the grand manners and the small ways. It is a very interesting array of houses of

the period after the poetry of domestic architecture had begun to wane and before the vulgarity had come—a fine familiar classic prose. Such places, such houses, such relics and
intimations, carry us back to the near antiquity of that pre-
Victorian England which it is still easy for a stranger to picture with a certain vividness, thanks to the partial survival of
many of its characteristics. It is still easier for a stranger who
has dwelt a time in England to form an idea of the tone, the
habits, the aspect of the social life before its classic insularity
had begun to wane, as all observers agree that it did about
thirty years ago. It is true that the mental operation in this
matter reduces itself to our imaging some of the things which
form the peculiar national notes as infinitely exaggerated: the
rigidly aristocratic constitution of society, the unæsthetic temper of the people, the small public fund of convenience, of
elegance. Let an old gentleman of conservative tastes, who
can remember the century's youth, talk to you at a club *temporis acti*—tell you wherein it is that from his own point of
view London, as a residence for a gentleman, has done nothing but fall off for the last forty years. You will listen, of
course, with an air of decent sympathy, but privately you will
say to yourself how difficult a place of sojourn London must
have been in those days for the traveller from other countries—how little cosmopolitan, how bound, in a thousand
ways, with narrowness of custom. What was true of the great
city at that time was of course doubly true of the provinces;
and a community of the type of Ludlow must have been a
kind of focus of insular propriety. Even then, however, the
irritated alien would have had the magnificent ruins of the
castle to dream himself back into good humour in. They
would effectually have transported him beyond all waning or
waxing Philistinisms.

English Vignettes

Toward the last of April, in Monmouthshire, the primroses were as big as your fist. I say in Monmouthshire,
because I believe that a certain grassy mountain which I gave
myself the pleasure of climbing and to which I took my way
across the charming country, through lanes where the hedges
were perched upon blooming banks, lay within the borders of
this ancient province. It was the festive Eastertide, and a pretext for leaving London had not been wanting. Of course it
rained—it rained a good deal—for man and the weather are
usually at cross-purposes. But there were intervals of light and
warmth, and in England a couple of hours of brightness islanded in moisture assert their independence and leave an uncompromised memory. These reprieves were even of longer
duration; that whole morning for instance on which, with a
companion, I scrambled up the little Skirrid. One had a feeling that one was very far from London; as in fact one was,
after six or seven hours in a swift, straight train. In England
this is a long span; it seemed to justify the half-reluctant confession, which I heard constantly made, that the country was
extremely "wild." There is wildness and wildness, I thought;
and though I had not been a great explorer I compared this
rough district with several neighbourhoods in another part of
the world that passed for tame. I went even so far as to wish
that some of its ruder features might be transplanted to that
relatively unregulated landscape and commingled with its suburban savagery. We were close to the Welsh border, and a
dozen little mountains in the distance were peeping over each
other's shoulders, but nature was open to the charge of no
worse disorder than this. The Skirrid (I like to repeat the
name) wore, it is true, at a distance, the aspect of a magnified
extinguisher; but when, after a bright, breezy walk through
lane and meadow, we had scrambled over the last of the
thickly flowering hedges which lay around its shoulders like
loosened strings of coral and begun to ascend the grassy cone

(very much in the attitude of Nebuchadnezzar), it proved as
smooth-faced as a garden-mound. Hard by, on the flanks of
other hills, were troops of browsing sheep, and the only thing
that confessed in the least to a point or an edge was the
strong, damp wind. But even the high breeze was good-
humoured and only wanted something to play with, blowing
about the pearly morning mists that were airing themselves
upon neighbouring ridges and shaking the vaporous veil that
fluttered down in the valley over the picturesque little town
of Abergavenny. A breezy, grassy English hill-top, looking
down on a country full of suggestive names and ancient memories and implied stories (especially if you are exhilarated by a
beautiful walk and have a flask in your pocket), shows you the
world as a very smooth place, fairly rubbed so by human use.

I was warned away from church, on Sunday, by my mistrust of its mediæval chill—lumbago there was so clearly
catching. In the still hours, when the roads and lanes were
empty, I simply walked to the churchyard and sat upon one
of the sun-warmed gravestones. I say the roads were empty,
but they were peopled with the big primroses I just now
spoke of—primroses of the size of ripe apples and yet, in
spite of their rank growth, of as pale and tender a yellow as if
their gold had been diluted with silver. It was indeed a mixture of gold and silver, for there was a wealth of the white
wood-anemone as well, and these delicate flowers, each of so
perfect a coinage, were tumbled along the green wayside as if
a prince had been scattering largess. The outside of an old
English country church in service-time is a very pleasant
place; and this is as near as I often dare approach the celebration of the Anglican mysteries. A just sufficient sense of their
august character may be gathered from that vague sound of
village-music which makes its way out into the stillness and
from the perusal of those portions of the Prayer-Book which
are inscribed upon mouldering slabs and dislocated head-
stones. The church I speak of was a beautiful specimen of its
kind—intensely aged, variously patched, but still solid and
useful and with no touch of restoration. It was very big and
massive and, hidden away in the fields, had a kind of lonely
grandeur; there was nothing in particular near it but its
out-of-the-world little parsonage. It was only one of ten

The Cliff at Ventnor

thousand; I had seen a hundred such before. But I watched the watery sunshine upon the rugosities of its ancient masonry; I stood a while in the shade of two or three spreading yews which stretched their black arms over graves decorated for Easter, according to the custom of that country, with garlands of primrose and dog-violet; and I reflected that in a "wild" region it was a blessing to have so quiet a place of refuge as that.

Later I chanced upon a couple of other asylums which were more spacious and no less tranquil. Both of them were old country-houses, and each in its way was charming. One was a half-modernised feudal dwelling, lying in a wooded hollow —a large concavity filled with a delightful old park. The house had a long gray façade and half a dozen towers, and the usual supply of ivy and of clustered chimneys relieved against a background of rook-haunted elms. But the windows were all closed and the avenue was untrodden; the house was the property of a lady who could not afford to live in it in becoming state and who had let it, furnished, to a rich young man, "for the shooting." The rich young man occupied it but for three weeks in the year and for the rest of the time left it a prey to the hungry gaze of the passing stranger, the would-be redresser of æsthetic wrongs. It seemed a great æsthetic wrong that so charming a place should not be a conscious, sentient home. In England all this is very common. It takes a great many plain people to keep a "perfect" gentleman going; it takes a great deal of wasted sweetness to make up a saved property. It is true that, in the other case I speak of, the sweetness, which here was even greater, was less sensibly squandered. If there was no one else in the house at least there were ghosts. It had a dark red front and grim-looking gables; it was perched upon a vague terrace, quite high in the air, which was reached by steep, crooked, mossy steps. Beneath these steps was an ancient bit of garden, and from the hither side of the garden stretched a great expanse of turf. Out of the midst of the turf sprang a magnificent avenue of Scotch firs—a perfect imitation of the Italian stone-pine. It looked like the Villa Borghese transplanted to the Welsh hills. The huge, smooth stems, in their double row, were crowned with dark parasols. In the Scotch fir or the Italian pine there is always an element of oddity; the open umbrella in a rainy country is not a poetical analogy, and the case is not better if you compare the tree to a colossal mushroom. But, without analogies, there was something very striking in the effect of this enormous, rigid vista, and in the grassy carpet of the avenue, with the dusky, lonely, high-featured house looking down upon it. There was something solemn and tragical; the place was made to the hand of a story-seeker, who might have found his characters within, as, the leaden lattices being open, the actors seemed ready for the stage.

II

The Isle of Wight is at first disappointing. I wondered why it should be, and then I found the reason in the influence of the detestable little railway. There can be no doubt that a railway in the Isle of Wight is a gross impertinence, is in evident contravention to the natural style of the place. The place is pure picture or is nothing at all. It is ornamental only—it

Ventnor

exists for exclamation and the water-colour brush. It is separated by nature from the dense railway-system of the less diminutive island, and is the corner of the world where a good
carriage-road is most in keeping. Never was a clearer opportunity for sacrificing to prettiness; never was a better chance
for not making a railway. But now there are twenty trains a
day, so that the prettiness is twenty times less. The island is so
small that the hideous embankments and tunnels are obtrusive; the sight of them is as painful as it would be to see a
pedlar's pack on the shoulders of a lovely woman. This is
your first impression as you travel (naturally by the objectionable conveyance) from Ryde to Ventnor; and the fact that the
train rumbles along very smoothly and stops at half a dozen
little stations, where the groups on the platform enable you to
perceive that the population consists almost exclusively of
gentlemen in costumes suggestive of unlimited leisure for attention to cravats and trousers (an immensely large class in
England), of old ladies of the species denominated in France
rentières, of young ladies of the highly educated and sketching

variety, this circumstance fails to reconcile you to the chartered cicatrix which forms your course. At Ventnor, however,
face to face with the sea, and with the blooming shoulder of
the Undercliff close behind you, you lose sight to a certain
extent of the superfluities of civilisation. Not indeed that
Ventnor has not been diligently civilised. It is a formed and
finished watering-place, it has been reduced to a due degree
of cockneyfication. But the glittering ocean remains, shimmering at moments with blue and silver, and the large gorse-
covered downs rise superbly above it. Ventnor hangs upon
the side of a steep hill, and here and there it clings and scram-
bles, is propped up and terraced, like one of the bright-faced
little towns that look down upon the Mediterranean. To add
to the Italian effect the houses are all denominated villas,
though it must be added that nothing is less like an Italian
villa than an English. Those which ornament the successive
ledges at Ventnor are for the most part small semi-detached
boxes, predestined, even before they have fairly come into the
world, to the entertainment of lodgers. They stand in serried
rows all over the place, with the finest names in the Peerage
painted upon their gate-posts. Their severe similarity of
aspect, however, is such that even the difference between
Plantagenet and Percival, between Montgomery and Montmorency, is hardly sufficient to enlighten the puzzled visitor.
An English place of recreation is more comfortable than an
American; in a Plantagenet villa the art of receiving "summer
guests" has usually been brought to a higher perfection than
in an American rural hotel. But what strikes an American,
with regard to even so charmingly nestled a little town as
Ventnor, is that it is far less natural, less pastoral and bosky
than his own fond image of a summer retreat. There is too
much brick and mortar; there are too many smoking chimneys and shops and public-houses; there are no woods nor
brooks nor lonely headlands; there is none of the virginal stillness of Nature. Instead of these things there is an esplanade
mostly paved with asphalt, bordered with benches and little
shops and provided with a German band. To be just to Ventnor, however, I must hasten to add that once you get away
from the asphalt there is a great deal of vegetation. The little
village of Bonchurch, which closely adjoins it, is buried in

Shanklin

the most elaborate verdure, muffled in the smoothest lawns and the densest shrubbery. Bonchurch is simply delicious and indeed in a manner quite absurd. It is like a model village in imitative substances, kept in a big glass case; the turf might be of green velvet and the foliage of cut paper. The villagers are all happy gentlefolk, the cottages have plate-glass windows, and the rose-trees on their walls looked as if tied up with ribbon "to match." Passing from Ventnor through the elegant umbrage of Bonchurch, and keeping along the coast toward Shanklin, you come to the prettiest part of the Undercliff, or in other words to the prettiest place in the world. The immense grassy cliffs which form the coast of the island make what the French would call a "false descent" to the sea. At a certain point the descent is broken, so that a wide natural terrace, all overtangled with wild shrubs and flowers, hangs there in mid-air, half-way above salt water. It is impossible to imagine anything more charming than this long, blooming platform, protected from the north by huge green bluffs and plunging on the other side into the murmuring tides. This delightful arrangement constitutes for a distance of some fifteen miles the south shore of the Isle of Wight; but the best of it, as I have said, is to be found in the four or five that separate Ventnor from Shanklin. Of a lovely afternoon in April these four or five miles are an admirable walk.

Of course you must first catch your lovely afternoon. I caught one; in fact I caught two. On the second I climbed up the downs and perceived that it was possible to put their gorse-covered stretches to still other than pedestrian uses—to devote them to sedentary pleasures. A long lounge in the lee of a stone wall, the lingering, fading afternoon light, the reddening sky, the band of blue sea above the level-topped bunches of gorse—these things, enjoyed as an undertone to the conversation of an amiable compatriot, seemed indeed a very sufficient substitute for that primitive stillness of the absence of which I ventured just now to complain.

III

It was probably a mistake to stop at Portsmouth. I had done so, however, in obedience to a familiar theory that seaport towns abound in local colour, in curious types, in the quaint and the strange. But these charms, it must be confessed, were signally wanting to Portsmouth, along whose sordid streets I strolled for an hour, vainly glancing about me for an overhanging façade or a group of Maltese sailors. I was distressed to perceive that a famous seaport could be at once untidy and prosaic. Portsmouth is dirty, but it is also dull. It may be roughly divided into the dockyard and the public-houses. The dockyard, into which I was unable to penetrate, is a colossal enclosure, signalised externally by a grim brick wall, as featureless as an empty black-board. The dockyard eats up the town, as it were, and there is nothing left over but the gin-shops, which the town drinks up. There is not even a crooked old quay of any consequence, with brightly patched houses looking out upon a forest of masts. To begin with, there are no masts; and then there are no polyglot sign-

Chichester Cross

boards, no overhanging upper stories, no outlandish parrots and macaws perched in open lattices. I had another hour or so before my train departed, and it would have gone hard with me if I had not bethought myself of hiring a boat and being pulled about in the harbour. Here a certain amount of entertainment was to be found. There were great ironclads and white troopships that looked vague and spectral, like the floating home of the Flying Dutchman, and small, devilish vessels whose mission was to project the infernal torpedo. I coasted about these metallic islets, and then, to eke out my entertainment, I boarded the *Victory*. The *Victory* is an ancient frigate of enormous size, which in the days of her glory carried I know not how many hundred guns, but whose only function now is to stand year after year in Portsmouth waters and exhibit herself to the festive cockney. Bank-holiday is now her great date; once upon a time it was Trafalgar. The *Victory*, in short, was Nelson's ship; it was on her huge deck that he was struck, and in her deep bowels he breathed his last. The venerable shell is provided with a company of ushers, like the Tower of London or Westminster Abbey, and is hardly less solid and spacious than either of the land-vessels. A good man in uniform did me the honours of the ship with a terrible displacement of *h*'s, and there seemed something strange in the way it had lapsed from its heroic part. It had carried two hundred guns and a mighty warrior, and boomed against the enemies of England; it had been the scene of one of the most thrilling and touching events in English history. Now, it was hardly more than a mere source of income to the Portsmouth watermen, an objective point for Whitsuntide excursionists, a thing a pilgrim from afar must allude to very casually, for fear of seeming vulgar or even quite serious.

IV

But I recouped myself, as they say, by stopping afterwards at Chichester. In this dense and various old England two places may be very near together and yet strike a very different note. I knew in a general way that this one had for its main sign a cathedral, and indeed had caught the sign, in the form of a beautiful spire, from the window of the train. I had

The "Victory"

always regarded an afternoon in a small cathedral-town as a high order of entertainment, and a morning at Portsmouth had left me in the mood for not missing such an exhibition. The spire of Chichester at a little distance greatly resembles that of Salisbury. It is on a smaller scale, but it tapers upward with a delicate slimness which, like that of its famous rival, makes a picture of the level landscape in which it stands. Unlike the spire of Salisbury, however, it has not at present the charm of antiquity. A few years ago the old steeple collapsed and tumbled into the church, and the present structure is but a modern facsimile. The cathedral is not of the highest interest; it is rather inexpressive, and, except for a curious old detached bell-tower which stands beside it, has no particular element of unexpectedness. But an English cathedral of restricted grandeur may yet be a very charming affair; and I spent an hour or so circling round this highly respectable edifice, with the spell of contemplation unbroken by satiety. I approached it, from the station, by the usual quiet red-brick street of the usual cathedral town—a street of small, excellent shops, before which, here and there, one of the vehicles of the neighbouring gentry was drawn up beside the curbstone while the grocer or the bookseller, who had hurried out obsequiously, was waiting upon the comfortable occupant. I went into a bookseller's to buy a Chichester guide, which I perceived in the window; I found the shopkeeper talking to a young curate in a soft hat. The guide seemed very desirable, though it appeared to have been but scantily desired; it had been published in the year 1841, and a very large remnant of the edition, with a muslin back and a little white label and paper-covered boards, was piled up on the counter. It was dedicated, with terrible humility, to the Duke of Richmond, and ornamented with primitive woodcuts and steel plates; the ink had turned brown and the page musty; and the style itself—that of a provincial antiquary of upwards of forty years ago penetrated with the grandeur of the aristocracy—had grown rather sallow and stale. Nothing could have been more mellifluous and urbane than the young curate: he was arranging to have the *Times* newspaper sent him every morning for perusal. "So it will be a penny if it is fetched away at noon?" he said, smiling very sweetly and with the most gentlemanly voice possible; "and it will be three halfpence if it is fetched away at four o'clock?" At the top of the street, into which, with my guide-book, I relapsed, was an old market-cross of the fifteenth century—a florid, romantic little structure. It consists of a stone pavilion, with open sides and a number of pinnacles and crockets and buttresses, besides a goodly medallion of the high-nosed visage of Charles I., which was placed above one of the arches, at the Restoration, in compensation for the violent havoc wrought upon the little town by the Parliamentary soldiers, who had wrested the place from the Royalists and who amused themselves, in their grim fashion, with infinite hacking and hewing in the cathedral. Here, to the left, the cathedral discloses itself, lifting its smart gray steeple out of a pleasant garden. Opposite to the garden was the Dolphin or the Dragon—in fine the most eligible inn. I must confess that for a time it divided my attention with the cathedral, in virtue of an ancient, musty parlour on the second floor, with hunting-pictures hung above haircloth sofas; of a red-faced waiter, in evening dress; of a big round of cold beef

Cambridge

and a tankard of ale. The prettiest thing at Chichester is a charming little three-sided cloister, attached to the cathedral, where, as is usual in such places, you may sit upon a gravestone amid the deep grass in the middle and measure the great central mass of the church—the large gray sides, the high foundations of the spire, the parting of the nave and transept. From this point the greatness of a cathedral seems more complex and impressive. You watch the big shadows slowly change their relations; you listen to the cawing of rooks and the twittering of swallows; you hear a slow footstep echoing in the cloisters.

V

If Oxford were not the finest thing in England the case would be clearer for Cambridge. It was clear enough there, for that matter, to my imagination, for thirty-six hours. To the barbaric mind, ambitious of culture, Oxford is the usual image of the happy reconciliation between research and acceptance. It typifies to an American the union of science and sense—of aspiration and ease. A German university gives a greater impression of science and an English country-house or an Italian villa a greater impression of idle enjoyment; but in these cases, on one side, knowledge is too rugged, and on the other satisfaction is too trivial. Oxford lends sweetness to labour and dignity to leisure. When I say Oxford I mean Cambridge, for a stray savage is not the least obliged to know the difference, and it suddenly strikes me as being both very pedantic and very good-natured in him to pretend to know it. What institution is more majestic than Trinity College? what can affect more a stray savage than the hospitality of such an institution? The first quadrangle is of immense extent, and the buildings that surround it, with their long, rich fronts of time-deepened gray, are the stateliest in the world. In the centre of the court are two or three acres of close-shaven lawn, out of the midst of which rises a grand Gothic fountain, where the serving-men fill up their buckets. There are towers and battlements and statues, and besides these things there are cloisters and gardens and bridges. There are charming rooms in a kind of stately gate-tower, and the rooms, occupying the

Gateway, Cambridge

thickness of the building, have windows looking out on one side over the magnificent quadrangle, with half a mile or so of Decorated architecture, and on the other into deep-bosomed trees. And in the rooms is the best company conceivable — distinguished men who are thoroughly conversible, intimately affable. I spent a beautiful Sunday morning walking about the place with one of these gentlemen and attempting to *débrouiller* its charms. These are a very complicated tangle, and I do not pretend, in memory, to keep the colleges apart. There are none the less half a dozen points that make ineffaceable pictures. Six or eight of the colleges stand in a row, turning their backs to the river; and hereupon ensues the loveliest confusion of Gothic windows and ancient trees, of grassy banks and mossy balustrades, of sun-chequered avenues and groves, of lawns and gardens and terraces, of single-arched bridges spanning the little stream, which is small and shallow and looks as if it had been turned on for ornamental purposes. The thin-flowing Cam appears to exist simply as an occasion for these brave little bridges — the beautiful covered gallery of John's or the slightly collapsing arch of Clare. In the way of college-courts and quiet scholastic porticoes, of gray-walled gardens and ivied nooks of study, in all the pictorial accidents of a great English university, Cambridge is delightfully and inexhaustibly rich. I looked at these one by one and said to myself always that the last was the best. If I were called upon, however, to mention the prettiest corner of the world, I should draw out a thoughtful sigh and point the way to the garden of Trinity Hall. My companion, who was very competent to judge (but who spoke indeed with the partiality of a son of the house), declared, as he ushered me into it, that it was, to his mind, the most beautiful *small* garden in Europe. I freely accepted, and I promptly repeat, an affirmation so magnanimously conditioned. The little garden at Trinity Hall is narrow and crooked; it leans upon the river, from which a low parapet, all muffled in ivy, divides it; it has an ancient wall adorned with a thousand matted creepers on one side, and on the other a group of extraordinary horse-chestnuts. The trees are of prodigious size; they occupy half the garden, and are remarkable for the fact that their giant limbs strike down into the earth, take root again and emulate, as they rise,

Peterhouse, Cambridge

the majesty of the parent stem. The manner in which this magnificent group of horse-chestnuts sprawls about over the grass, out into the middle of the lawn, is one of the most heart-shaking features of the garden of Trinity Hall. Of course the single object at Cambridge that makes the most abiding impression is the famous chapel of King's College—the most beautiful chapel in England. The effect it attempts to produce within is all in the sphere of the sublime. The attempt succeeds, and the success is attained by a design so light and elegant that at first it almost defeats itself. The sublime usually has more of a frown and straddle, and it is not until after you have looked about you for ten minutes that you perceive the chapel to be saved from being the prettiest church in England by the accident of its being one of the noblest. It is a cathedral without aisles or columns or transepts, but (as a compensation) with such a beautiful slimness of clustered tracery soaring along the walls and spreading, bending and commingling in the roof, that its simplicity seems only a richness the more. I stood there for a quarter of an hour on a Sunday morning; there was no service, but in the choir behind the great screen which divides the chapel in half the young choristers were rehearsing for the afternoon. The beautiful boy-voices rose together and touched the splendid vault; they hung there, expanding and resounding, and then, like a rocket that spends itself, they faded and melted toward the end of the building. It was positively a choir of angels.

VI

Cambridgeshire is one of the so-called ugly counties; which means that it is observably flat. It is for this reason that the absence of terrestrial accent which culminates at Newmarket constitutes so perfect a means to an end. The country is like a board of green cloth; the turf presents itself as a friendly provision of nature. Nature offers her gentle bosom as a gaming-table; card-tables, billiard-tables are but a humble imitation of Newmarket Heath. It was odd to think that amid so much of the appearance of the humility of real virtue, there is more profane betting than anywhere else in the world. The large, neat English meadows roll away to a humid-looking sky, the

The Backs, Cambridge

young partridges jump about in the hedges, and nature looks not in the least as if she were offering you odds. The gentlemen look it, though, the gentlemen whom you meet on the roads and in the railway-carriage; they have that marked air—it pervades a man from the cut of his whisker to the shape of his boot-toe—as of the sublimated stable. It is brought home to you that to an immense number of people in England the events in the *Racing Calendar* constitute the most important portion of contemporary history. The very breeze has an equine snort, if it doesn't breathe as hard as a hostler; the blue and white of the sky, dappled and spotty, recalls the figure of the necktie of "spring meetings"; and the landscape is coloured as a sporting-print is coloured—with the same gloss, the same that seems to say a thousand grooms have rubbed it down.

The destruction of partridges is, if an equally classical, a less licentious pursuit, for which, I believe, Cambridgeshire offers peculiar facilities. Among these is a particular shooting-box which is a triumph of the familiar, the accidental style and a temple of clear hospitality. The shooting belongs to the autumn, not to this vernal period; but as I have spoken of echoes I suppose that if I had listened attentively I might have heard the ghostly crack of some of the famous shots that have been discharged there. The air, notedly, had vibrated to several august rifles, but all that I happened to hear by listening was some excellent talk.

In England, at any rate, as I said just now, a couple of places may be very near together and yet have what the philosophers call a connotation strangely different. Only a few miles beyond Newmarket lies Bury St. Edmunds, a town whose tranquil antiquity turns its broad gray back straight upon the sporting papers. I confess that I went to Bury simply on the strength of its name, which I had often encountered and which had always seemed to me to have a high value for the picture-seeker. I knew that St. Edmund had been an Anglo-Saxon worthy, but my conviction that the little town that bore his name would move me to rapture between trains had nothing definite to rest upon. The event, however, rewarded my faith—rewarded it with the sight of a magnificent old gatehouse of the thirteenth century, the most

Gateway, Bury St. Edmunds

On the Cam

substantial of many relics of the great abbey which once flourished there. There are many others; they are scattered about
the old precinct of the abbey, a large portion of which has
been converted into a rambling botanic garden, the resort at
Whitsuntide of a thousand very modern merry-makers. The
monument I speak of has the proportions of a triumphal arch;
it is at once a gateway and a fortress; it is covered with beautiful ornament, and is altogether the lion of Bury.

An English New Year

IT WILL hardly be pretended this year that the English Christmas has been a merry one, or that the New Year has the promise of being particularly happy. The winter is proving very cold and vicious—as if Nature herself were loath to be left out of the general conspiracy against the comfort and self-complacency of man. The country at large has a sense of embarrassment and depression, which is brought home more or less to every class in the closely graduated social hierarchy, and the light of Christmas firesides has by no means dispelled the gloom. Not that I mean to overstate the gloom. It is difficult to imagine any combination of adverse circumstances powerful enough to infringe very sensibly upon the appearance of activity and prosperity, social stability and luxury, which English life must always present to a stranger. Nevertheless the times are distinctly of the kind synthetically spoken of as hard—there is plenty of evidence of it—and the spirits of the public are not high. The depression of business is extreme and universal; I am ignorant whether it has reached so calamitous a point as that almost hopeless prostration of every industry which it is assured us you have lately witnessed in America, and I believe the sound of lamentation is by no means so loud as it has been on two or three occasions within the present century. The possibility of distress among the lower classes has been minimised by the gigantic poor-relief system which is so characteristic a feature of English civilisation and which, under especial stress, is supplemented (as is the case at present) by private charity proportionately huge. I notice too that in some parts of the country discriminating groups of workpeople have selected these dismal days as a happy time for striking. When the labouring classes rise to the recreation of a strike I suppose the situation may be said to have its cheerful side. There is, however, great distress in the North, and there is a general feeling of scant money to play with throughout the country. The *Daily News* has sent a correspondent to the great industrial regions, and almost every morning for the last three weeks a very cleverly executed

The Workhouse

picture of the misery of certain parts of Yorkshire and Lancashire has been served up with the matutinal tea and toast. The work is a good one, and, I take it, eminently worth doing, as it appears to have had a visible effect upon the pursestrings of the well-to-do. There is nothing more striking in England than the success with which an "appeal" is always made. Whatever the season or whatever the cause, there always appears to be enough money and enough benevolence in the country to respond to it in sufficient measure—a remarkable fact when one remembers that there is never a moment of the year when the custom of "appealing" intermits. Equally striking perhaps is the perfection to which the science of distributing charity has been raised—the way it has been analysed and organised and made one of the exact sciences. You perceive that it has occupied for a long time a foremost place among administrative questions, and has received all the light that experience and practice can throw upon it. Is there in this perception more of a lightened or more of an added weight for the brooding consciousness?

The Factory Town

Truly there are aspects of England at which one can but darkly stare.

I left town a short time before Christmas and went to spend the festive season in the North, in a part of the country with which I was unacquainted. It was quite possible to absent one's self from London without a sense of sacrifice, for the charms of the capital during the last several weeks have been obscured by peculiarly vile weather. It is of course a very old story that London is foggy, and this simple statement raises no blush on the face of Nature as we see it here. But there are fogs and fogs, and the folds of the black mantle have been during the present winter intolerably thick. The thickness that draws down and absorbs the smoke of the housetops, causes it to hang about the streets in impenetrable density, forces it into one's eyes and down one's throat, so that one is half blinded and quite sickened—this form of the particular plague has been much more frequent than usual. Just before Christmas, too, there was a heavy snowstorm, and even a tolerably light fall of snow has London quite at its mercy. The emblem of purity is almost immediately converted into a sticky, lead-coloured mush, the cabs skulk out of sight or take up their stations before the lurid windows of a public-house, which glares through the sleety darkness at the desperate wayfarer with an air of vulgar bravado. For recovery of one's nervous balance the only course was flight—flight to the country and the confinement of one's vision to the large area of one of those admirable homes which at this season overflow with hospitality and good cheer. By this means the readjustment is effectually brought about—these are conditions that you cordially appreciate. Of all the great things that the English have invented and made a part of the credit of the national character, the most perfect, the most characteristic, the one they have mastered most completely in all its details, so that it has become a compendious illustration of their social genius and their manners, is the well-appointed, well-administered, well-filled country-house. The grateful stranger makes these reflections—and others besides—as he wanders about in the beautiful library of such a dwelling, of an inclement winter afternoon, just at the hour when six o'clock tea is impending. Such a place and such a time abound in agreeable

The Factory Town

episodes; but I suspect that the episode from which, a fortnight ago, I received the most ineffaceable impression was but
indirectly connected with the charms of a luxurious fireside.
The country I speak of was a populous manufacturing region,
full of tall chimneys and of an air that is gray and gritty. A
lady had made a present of a Christmas-tree to the children of
a workhouse, and she invited me to go with her and assist at
the distribution of the toys. There was a drive through the
early dusk of a very cold Christmas eve, followed by the drawing up of a lamp-lit brougham in the snowy quadrangle of a
grim-looking charitable institution. I had never been in an
English workhouse before, and this one transported me, with
the aid of memory, to the early pages of "Oliver Twist." We
passed through cold, bleak passages, to which an odour of
suet-pudding, the aroma of Christmas cheer, failed to impart
an air of hospitality; and then, after waiting a while in a little
parlour appertaining to the superintendent, where the remainder of a dinner of by no means eleemosynary simplicity
and the attitude of a gentleman asleep with a flushed face on

the sofa seemed to effect a tacit exchange of references, we were ushered into a large frigid refectory, chiefly illumined by the twinkling tapers of the Christmas-tree. Here entered to us some hundred and fifty little children of charity, who had been making a copious dinner and who brought with them an atmosphere of hunger memorably satisfied—together with other traces of the occasion upon their pinafores and their small red faces. I have said that the place reminded me of "Oliver Twist," and I glanced through this little herd for an infant figure that should look as if it were cut out for romantic adventures. But they were all very prosaic little mortals. They were made of very common clay indeed, and a certain number of them were idiotic. They filed up and received their little offerings, and then they compressed themselves into a tight infantine bunch and, lifting up their small hoarse voices, directed a melancholy hymn toward their benefactress. The scene was a picture I shall not forget, with its curious mixture of poetry and sordid prose—the dying wintry light in the big bare, stale room; the beautiful Lady Bountiful, standing in the twinkling glory of the Christmas-tree; the little multitude of staring and wondering, yet perfectly expressionless, faces.

An English Winter
Watering-place

I HAVE just been spending a couple of days at a well-known resort upon the Kentish coast, and though such an exploit is by no means unprecedented, yet, as to the truly observing mind no opportunity is altogether void and no impressions are wholly valueless, I have it on my conscience to make a note of my excursion. Superficially speaking, it was wanting in originality; but I am afraid that it afforded me as much entertainment as if the idea of paying a visit to Hastings had been an invention of my own. This is so far from being the case that the most striking feature of the town in question is the immense provision made there for the entertainment of visitors. Hastings and St. Leonards, standing side by side, present a united sea-front of more miles in length than I shall venture to compute. It is sufficient that in going from one end of the place to the other I had a greater sense of having taken a long, straight walk through street scenery than I had done since I last measured the populated length of Broadway. This is not an image that evokes any one of the graces, and it must be confessed that the beauty of Hastings does not reside in a soft irregularity or a rural exuberance. Like all the larger English watering-places it is simply a little London *super mare*. The graceful, or at least the pictorial, is always to be found in England if one will take the trouble of looking for it; but it must be conceded that at Hastings this element is less obtrusive than it might be. I had heard it described as a "dull Brighton," and this description had been intended to dispose of the place. In fact, however—such is the perversity of the inquiring mind—it had rather quickened than quenched my interest. It occurred to me that it might be as entertaining to follow out the variations of Brighton, the possible embroideries of the theme, as it is often found to listen to those with which some expressed musical idea is over-scored by another composer. Four or five miles of lodging-houses and hotels staring at the sea across a "parade" adorned with iron benches, with hand-organs and German bands, with nurse-

maids and British babies, with ladies and gentlemen of leisure—looking rather embarrassed with it and trying rather
unsuccessfully to get rid of it—this is the great feature which
Brighton and Hastings have in common. At Brighton there is
a certain variety and gaiety of colour—something suggesting
crookedness and yellow paint—which gives the scene a kind
of cheerful, easy, more or less vulgar, foreign air. But Hastings is very gray and sober and English, and indeed it is because it seemed to me so English that I gave my best attention
to it. If one is attempting to gather impressions of a people
and to learn to know them, everything is interesting that is
characteristic, quite apart from its being beautiful. English
manners are made up of such a multitude of small details that
the portrait a stranger has privately sketched in is always liable
to receive new touches. And this indeed is the explanation of
his noting a great many small points, on the spot, with a degree of relish and appreciation which must often, to persons
who are not in his position, appear exaggerated, if not absurd. He has formed a mental picture of the civilisation of the
people he lives among, and whom, when he has a great deal
of courage, he makes bold to say he is studying; he has drawn
up a kind of tabular view of their manners and customs, their
idiosyncrasies, their social institutions, their general features
and properties; and when once he has suspended this rough
cartoon in the chambers of his imagination he finds a great
deal of occupation in touching it up and filling it in. Wherever he goes, whatever he sees, he adds a few strokes. That is
how I spent my time at Hastings.

I found it, for instance, a question more interesting than it
might superficially appear to choose between the inns—between the Royal Hotel upon the Parade and an ancient hostel,
a survival of the posting-days, in a side-street. A friend had
described the latter establishment to me as "mellow," and this
epithet complicated the problem. The term mellow, as applied
to an inn, is the comparative degree of a state of things of
which (say) "musty" would be the superlative. If you can
seize this tendency in its comparative stage you may do very
well indeed; the trouble is that, like all tendencies, it contains,
even in its earlier phases, the germs of excess. I thought it
very possible that the Swan would be over-ripe; but I thought

The Crescent, Hastings

it equally probable that the Royal would be crude. I could claim a certain acquaintance with "royal" hotels—I knew just how they were constituted. I foresaw the superior young woman sitting at a ledger, in a kind of glass cage, at the bottom of the stairs, and expressing by refined intonations her contempt for a gentleman who should decline to "require" a sitting-room. The functionary whom in America we know and dread as an hotel-clerk belongs in England to the sex which, at need, is able to look over your head to a still further point. Large hotels here are almost always owned and carried on by companies, and the company is represented by a well-shaped female figure belonging to the class whose members are more particularly known as "persons." The chambermaid is a young woman, and the female tourist is a lady; but the occupant of the glass cage, who hands you your key and assigns you your apartment, is designated in the manner I have mentioned. The "person" has various methods of revenging herself for her shadowy position in the social scale, and I think it was from a vague recollection of having on former occasions felt the weight of her embittered spirit that I determined to seek the hospitality of the humbler inn, where it was probable that one who was himself humble would enjoy a certain consideration. In the event, I was rather oppressed by the feather-bed quality of the welcome extended to me at the Swan. Once established there, in a sitting-room (after all), the whole affair had all the local colour I could desire.

I have sometimes had occasion to repine at the meagreness and mustiness of the old-fashioned English inn, and to feel that in poetry and in fiction these defects had been culpably glossed over. But I said to myself the other evening that there is a kind of venerable decency even in some of its dingiest consistencies, and that in an age in which the conception of good manners is losing most of its ancient firmness one should do justice to an institution that is still more or less of a stronghold of the faded amenities. It is a satisfaction in moving about the world to be treated as a gentleman, and this gratification appears to be more than, in the light of modern science, a Company can profitably undertake to bestow. I have an old friend, a person of admirably conservative instincts, from whom, a short time since, I borrowed a hint of this kind. This lady had been staying at a small inn in the country with her daughter; the daughter, whom we shall call Mrs. B., had left the house a few days before the mother. "Did you like the place?" I asked of my friend; "was it comfortable?" "No, it was not comfortable; but I liked it. It was shabby, and I was much overcharged; but it pleased me." "What was the mysterious charm?" "Well, when I was coming away, the landlady—she had cheated me horribly—came to my carriage, and dropped a curtsey, and said: 'My duty to Mrs. B., ma'am.' Que voulez-vous? That pleased me." There was an old waiter at Hastings who would have been capable of that—an old waiter who had been in the house for forty years and who was not so much an individual waiter as the very spirit and genius, the incarnation and tradition of waiterhood. He was faded and weary and rheumatic, but he had a sort of mixture of the paternal and the deferential, the philosophic and the punctilious, which seemed but grossly requited by a present of a small coin. I am not fond of jugged hare for dinner, either as a light *entrée* or as a *pièce de résistance*;

Brighton

but this accomplished attendant had the art of presenting you such a dish in a manner that persuaded you, for the time, that it was worthy of your serious consideration. The hare, by the way, before being subjected to the mysterious operation of jugging, might have been seen dangling from a hook in the bar of the inn, together with a choice collection of other viands. You might peruse the bill of fare in an elementary form as you passed in and out of the house, and make up your *menu* for the day by poking with your stick at a juicy-looking steak or a promising fowl. The landlord and his spouse were always on the threshold of the bar, polishing a brass candlestick and paying you their respects; the place was pervaded by an aroma of rum-and-water and of commercial travellers' jokes.

This description, however, is lacking in the element of gentility, and I will not pursue it farther, for I should give a very false impression of Hastings if I were to omit so characteristic a feature. It was, I think, the element of gentility that most impressed me. I know that the word I have just ventured to use is under the ban of contemporary taste; so I may as well say outright that I regard it as indispensable in almost any attempt at portraiture of English manners. It is vain for an observer of such things to pretend to get on without it. One may talk of foreign life indefinitely—of the manners and customs of France, Germany, and Italy—and never feel the need of this suggestive, yet mysteriously discredited, epithet. One may survey the remarkable face of American civilisation without finding occasion to strike this particular note. But in England no circumlocution will serve—the note must be definitely struck. To attempt to speak of an English watering-place in winter and yet pass it over in silence would be to forfeit all claims to the analytic spirit. For a stranger, at any rate, the term is invaluable—it is more convenient than I should find easy to say. It is instantly evoked in my mind by long rows of smuttily plastered houses, with a card inscribed "Apartments" suspended in the window of the ground-floor sitting-room—that portion of the dwelling which is known in lodging-house parlance as "the parlours." Everything, indeed, suggests it—the bath-chairs, drawn up for hire in a melancholy row; the innumerable and excellent shops,

The Hastings Parade

adorned with the latest photographs of the royal family and of Mrs. Langtry; the little reading-room and circulating library on the Parade, where the daily papers, neatly arranged, may be perused for a trifling fee, and the novels of the season are stacked away like the honeycombs in an apiary; the long pier, stretching out into the sea, to which you are admitted by the payment of a penny at a wicket, and where you may enjoy the music of an indefatigable band, the enticements of several little stalls for the sale of fancy-work, and the personal presence of good local society. It is only the winking, twinkling, easily rippling sea that is not genteel. But, really, I was disposed to say at Hastings that if the sea was not genteel, so much the worse for Neptune; for it was the favourable aspect of the great British properties and solemnities that struck me. Hastings and St. Leonards, with their long, warm sea-front and their multitude of small, cheap comforts and conveniences, offer a kind of *résumé* of middle-class English civilisation and of advantages of which it would ill become an American to make light. I don't suppose that life at Hastings is the most exciting or the most gratifying in the world, but it must certainly have its advantages. If I were a quiet old lady of modest income and nice habits—or even a quiet old gentleman of the same pattern—I should certainly go to Hastings. There, amid the little shops and the little libraries, the bath-chairs and the German bands, the Parade and the long Pier, with a mild climate, a moderate scale of prices and the consciousness of a high civilisation, I should enjoy a seclusion which would have nothing primitive or crude.

Old Timbered Houses, Rye

Winchelsea, Rye, and "Denis Duval"

I HAVE recently had a literary adventure which, though not followed by the prostration that sometimes ensues on adventures, has nevertheless induced meditation. The adventure itself indeed was not astounding, and I mention it, to be frank, only in the interest of its sequel. It consisted merely, on taking up an old book again for the sake of a certain desired and particular light, of my having found that the light was in fact not there to shine, but was, on the contrary, directly projected *upon* the book from the very subject itself as to which I had invoked assistance. The case, in short, to put it simply, was that Thackeray's charming fragment of "Denis Duval" proved to have much less than I had supposed to say about the two little old towns with which the few chapters left to us are mainly concerned, but that the two little old towns, on the other hand, unexpectedly quickened reflection on "Denis Duval." Reading over Thackeray to help me further to Winchelsea, I became conscious, of a sudden, that Winchelsea—which I already in a manner knew—was only helping me further to Thackeray. Reinforced, in this service, by its little sister-city of Rye, it caused a whole question to open, and the question, in turn, added a savour to a sense already, by good-fortune, sharp. Winchelsea and Rye form together a very curious small corner, and the measure, candidly undertaken, of what the unfinished book had done with them, brought me to a nearer view of them—perhaps even to a more jealous one; as well as to some consideration of what books in general, even when finished, may do with curious small corners.

I dare say I speak of "Denis Duval" as "old" mainly to make an impression on readers whose age is less. I remember, after all, perfectly, the poetry of its original appearance—there was such a thrill, in those days, even after "Lovel the Widower" and "Philip," at any new Thackeray—in the cherished *Cornhill* of the early time, with a drawing of Frederick Walker to its every number and a possibility of its being like "Esmond" in its embroidered breast. If, moreover, it after a few months broke short off, that really gave it something as well as took something away. It might have been as true of works of art as of men and women, that if the gods loved them they died young. "Denis Duval" was at any rate beautiful, and was beautiful again on reperusal at a later time. It is all beautiful once more to a final reading, only it is remarkably different: and this is precisely where my story lies. The beauty is particularly the beauty of its being its author's—which is very much, with book after book, what we find ourselves coming to in general, I think, at fifty years. Our appreciation changes—how in the world, with experience always battering away, shouldn't it?—but our feeling, more happily, doesn't. There *are* books, of course, that criticism, when we are fit for it, only consecrates, and then, with association fiddling for the dance, we are in possession of a literary pleasure that is the highest of raptures. But in many a case we drag along a fond

indifference, an element of condonation, which is by no
means of necessity without its strain of esteem, but which,
obviously, is not founded on one of our deeper satisfactions.
Each can but speak, at all events, on such a matter, for himself. It is a matter also, doubtless, that belongs to the age of
the loss—so far as they quite depart—of illusions at large.
The reason for liking a particular book becomes thus a better,
or at least a more generous, one than the particular book
seems in a position itself at last to supply. Woe to the mere
official critic, the critic who has never felt the *man*. You go on
liking "The Antiquary" because it is Scott. You go on liking
"David Copperfield"—I don't say you go on reading it,
which is a very different matter—because it is Dickens. So
you go on liking "Denis Duval" because it is Thackeray—
which, in this last case, is the logic of the charm I alluded to.

The recital here, as every one remembers, is autobio-
graphic; the old battered, but considerably enriched, world-
worn, but finely sharpened Denis looks back upon a troubled
life from the winter fireside and places you, in his talkative
and contagious way—he is a practised literary artist—in possession of the story. We see him in a placid port after many
voyages, and have that amount of evidence—the most, after
all, that the most artless reader needs—as to the "happy" side
of the business. The evidence indeed is, for curiosity, almost
excessive, or at least premature; as he again and again puts it
before us that the companion of his later time, the admirable
wife seated there beside him, is nobody else at all, any hopes
of a more tangled skein notwithstanding, than the object of
his infant passion, the little French orphan, slightly younger
than himself, who is brought so promptly on the scene. The
way in which this affects us as undermining the "love-
interest" bears remarkably on the specific question of the subject of the book as the author would have expressed this
subject to his own mind. We get, to the moment the work
drops, not a glimpse of his central idea; nothing, if such had
been his intention, was in fact ever more triumphantly concealed. The darkness therefore is intensified by our seeming
to gather that, like the love-interest, at all events, the "female interest" was not to have been largely invoked. The
narrator is in general, from the first, full of friendly hints, in

Thackeray's way, of what is to come; but the chapters completed deal only with his childish years, his wondrous boy-life at Winchelsea and Rye, the public and private conditions of which—practically, in the last century, the same for the two places—form the background for this exposition. The south-eastern counties, comparatively at hand, were enriched at that period by a considerable French immigration, the accession of Huguenot fugitives too firm in their faith to have bent their necks to the dire rigours with which the revocation of the Edict of Nantes was followed up. This corner of Sussex received—as it had received in previous centuries—its forlorn contingent; to the interesting origin of which many Sussex family names—losing, as it were, their drawing but not their colour—still sufficiently testify. Portions of the stranger race suffered, struggled, sank; other portions resisted, took root and put forth branches, and Thackeray, clearly, had found his rough material in some sketchy vision of one of these obscure cases of troubled adjustment, which must often have been, for difficulty and complexity, of the stuff of dramas. Such a case, for the informed fancy, might indeed overflow with possibilities of character, character reinforced, in especial, by the impression, gathered and matured on the spot, of the two small ghosts of the Cinque Ports family, the pair of blighted hill-towns that were once sea-towns and that now draw out their days in the dim after-sense of a mere indulged and encouraged picturesqueness. "Denis Duval" could only, it would seem, have been conceived as a "picturesque" affair; but that may serve exactly as a reason for the attempt to refigure it.

Little hilltop communities sensibly even yet, with the memory of their tight walls and stiff gates not wholly extinct, Rye and Winchelsea hold fast to the faint identity which remains their least fragile support, their estate as "Antient Towns" involved (with the distincter Five and raising the number to seven), in that nominal, though still occasionally pompous, Wardenship the image—for our time—of the most famous assignment of which is preserved in Longfellow's fine verses on the death of the Duke of Wellington. The sea, in previous times half friend, half foe, began long since to fight, in each character, shy of them, and now, in wrinkled wistfulness, they look across at the straight blue band, two miles or so away, that tells of the services they rendered, the illusions they cherished—illusions in the case of poor Winchelsea especially absurd—and the extreme inconvenience they repeatedly suffered. They were again and again harried and hacked by the French, and might have had, it would seem, small appetite for the company, however reduced and disarmed, of these immemorial neighbours. The retreating waters, however, had even two centuries ago already placed such dangers on a very different footing, and the recovery and evocation of some of the old processes of actual absorption may well have presented themselves to Thackeray as a problem of the sort that tempts the lover of human histories. Happy and enviable always the first trepidation of the artist who lights on a setting that "meets" his subject or on a subject that meets his setting. The editorial notes to "Denis Duval" yield unfortunately no indication of whether Winchelsea put into his head the idea of this study, or of whether he carried it about till he happened judiciously to drop it there. Appearances point, in truth, to a connection of the latter kind, for the fragment itself contains no positive evidence that Thackeray ever, with the mere eye of sense, beheld the place; which is precisely one of the ambiguities that challenge the critic and an item in the unexpectedness that I spoke of at the beginning of these remarks. What—in the light, at least, of later fashions—the place has to offer the actual observer is the effect of an object seen, a thing of aspect and suggestion, situation and colour; but what had it to offer Thackeray—or the taste of forty years ago—that he so oddly forbore to give us a tangled clue to? The impression of to-day's reader is that the chapters we possess might really have been written without the author's having stood on the spot; and that is just why they have, as I began by saying, so much less to contribute to our personal vision than this influence, for its part, has to suggest in respect to the book itself.

Evidently, none the less, the setting, little as it has got itself "rendered," did somehow come into the painter's ken; we know this, moreover, independently, and we make out that he had his inner mysteries and his reasons. The little house of Duval, faring forth from the stress of the Alsatian fatherland, seeks safety and finds business in the shrunken city, scarce at last more than a hamlet, of Edward the First's defeated design, where, in three generations, well on into the century, it grinds and sleeps, smuggles and spends, according to the fashions of the place and time. These communities appear to have had, in their long decline, little industry but their clandestine traffic with other coasts, in the course of which they quite mastered the art of going, as we say, "one better" than the officers of the revenue. It is to this hour a part of the small romance of Rye that you may fondly fancy such scant opulence as rears its head to have had its roots in the malpractice of forefathers not too rude for much cunning—in nightly plots and snares and flurries, a hurrying, shuffling, hiding, that might at any time have put a noose about most necks. Some of those of the small gentry who were not smugglers were recorded highwaymen, flourishing about in masks and with pistols; and indeed in the general scene, as rendered by the supposed chronicler, these appear the principal features. The only others are those of his personal and private situation, which in fact, however, strikes me as best expressed in the fact that the extremely talkative, discursive, ejaculatory and moralising Denis was possessed in perfection of his master's maturest style. He writes, almost to the life, the language of "The Roundabout Papers"; so that if the third person had been exchanged, throughout, for his first, and his occasional present tense been superseded by the past, the rest of the text would have needed little rearrangement. This imperfect unity was more or less inevitable—the difficulty of projecting yourself as somebody else is never so great as when you retain the *form* of being yourself; but another of the many reflections suggested by reperusal is as to whether the speaker is not guilty of a slight abuse. Of course it may be said that what really has happened was that Thackeray had, on his side, anticipated his hero in the use of his hero's natural idiom. It may thus have been less that Denis had come to write highly "evolved" nineteenth-century English than that his creator had arrived, in "The Roundabout Papers" and elsewhere, at writing excellent reconstructed eighteenth. It would not, however, were the inquiry to be pushed, be only on the autobiographer's personal and grammatical, but on his moral and sentimental accent, as it were, that criticism would probably

The Road to Rye

most bear. His manner of thinking and feeling is quite as "Roundabout" as his manner of saying.

A dozen wonderments rise here, and a dozen curiosities and speculations; as to which, in truth, I am painfully divided between the attraction of such appeals and a certain other aspect of my subject to which I shall attempt presently to do justice. The superior stroke, I remind myself—possibly not in vain—would be to deal handsomely with both solicitations. The almost irresistible fascination, critically speaking, of the questions thus abruptly, after long years, thrust forth by the book, lies in their having reference to this very opposition of times and tastes. The thing is not forty years old, but it points already—and that is above all the amusement of it—to a general *poetic* that, both on its positive and its negative sides, we have left well behind. Can the author perhaps have had in mind, misguidedly, some idea of what his public "wanted" or didn't want? The public is really, to a straight vision, I think, not a capacity for wanting, at all, but only an unlimited capacity for *taking*—taking that (whatever it is) which will, in effect, make it open its mouth. It goes to the expense of few preconceptions, and even on the question of opening its mouth has a consciousness limited to the suspicion that in a given case this orifice *has*—or has not—gaped. We are therefore to imagine Thackeray as perfectly conscious that he himself, working by his own fine light, constituted the public he had most to reckon with. On the other hand, his time, in its degree, had helped to shape him, and a part of the consequence of this shaping, apparently, was his extraordinary avoidance of picture. This is the mystery that drives us to the hypothesis of his having tried to pay, in some uncanny quarter, some deluded deference. Was he under the fear that, even as *he* could do it, "description" would not, in the early sixties, be welcome? It is impossible to stand to-day in the high, loose, sunny, haunted square of Winchelsea without wondering what he could have been thinking of. There are ladies in view with easels, sun-bonnets, and white umbrellas—often perceptibly, too, with nothing else that makes for successful representation; but I doubt if it were these apparitions that took the bloom from his vision, for they were much less frequent in those looser days, and moreover would have formed much more a reason for not touching the place at all than for taking it up indifferently. Of any impulse to make the reader see it with seeing eyes his page, at all events, gives no sign. We must presently look at it for ourselves, even at the cost, or with the consequence, of a certain loyal resentment. For Winchelsea is strange, individual, charming. What *could* he — yes — have been thinking of? We are wound up for saying that he has given his subject away, until we suddenly remember that, to this hour, we have never really made out what his subject was to have been.

Never was a secret more impenetrably kept. Read over the fragment itself — which reaches, after all, to some two hundred and fifty pages; read over, at the end of the volume, the interesting editorial notes; address yourself, above all, in the charming series of introductions lately prepared by Mrs. Richmond Ritchie for a new and, so far as possible, biographical edition of her father's works, to the reminiscences briefly bearing on Denis, and you will remain in each case equally distant from a clue. It is the most puzzling thing in the world, but there *is* no clue. There are indications, in respect to the book, from Thackeray's hand, memoranda on matters of detail, and there is in especial a highly curious letter to his publisher; yet the clue that his own mind must have held never shows the tip of its tail. The letter to his publisher, in which, according to the editor of the fragment, he "sketches his plot for the information of" that gentleman, reads like a mystification by which the gentleman was to be temporarily kept quiet. With an air of telling him a good deal, Thackeray really tells him nothing — nothing, I mean, by which he himself would have been committed to (any more than deterred from) any idea kept up his sleeve. If he were holding this card back, to be played at his own time, he could not have proceeded in the least differently; and one can construct to-day, with a free hand, one's picture of his private amusement at the success of his diplomacy. All the while, what *was* the card? The production of a novel finds perhaps its nearest analogy in the ride across country; the competent novelist — that is, the novelist with the real seat — presses his subject, in spite of hedges and ditches, as hard as the keen fox-hunter presses the game that has been started for his day with the hounds. The fox is the novelist's idea, and when he rides straight he rides, regardless of danger, in whatever direction that animal takes. As we lay down "Denis Duval," however, we feel not only that we are off the scent, but that we never really have been, with the author, on it. The fox has got quite away. For it carries us no further, surely, to say—as may possibly be objected—that the author's subject was to have been neither more or less than the adventures of his hero; inasmuch as, turn the thing as we will, these "adventures" could at the best have constituted nothing more than its *form*. It is an affront to the memory of a great writer to pretend that they were to have been arbitrary and unselected, that there was nothing in his mind to determine them. The book was, obviously, to have been, as boys say, "about" them. But what were *they* to have been about? Thackeray carried the mystery to his grave.

II

If I spoke just now of Winchelsea as haunted, let this somewhat overworked word stand as an ineffectual tribute to the small, sad, civic history that the place appeals to us to reconstruct as we gaze vaguely about. I have a little ancient and most decorative map of Sussex—testifying remarkably to the changes of relation between sea and land in this corner of the coast—in which "Old Winchelsey Drowned" figures as the melancholy indication of a small circular spot quite out at sea. If new Winchelsea is old, the earlier town is to-day but the dim ghost of a tradition, with its very site—distant several miles from that of its successor—rendered uncertain by the endless mutation of the shore. After suffering, all through the thirteenth century, much stress of wind and weather, it was practically destroyed in 1287 by a great storm which cast up masses of beach, altered the course of a river and roughly handled the face of many things. The reconstruction of the town in another place was thereupon decreed by a great English king, and we need but a little fuller chronicle to help us to assist at one of those migrations of a whole city of which antiquity so often gives us the picture. The survivors of Winchelsea were colonised, and colonised in much state. The "new" community, whose life was also to be so brief, sits on

Gateway, Rye

the pleasant table of a great cliff-like hill which, in the days
of the Plantagenets, was an admirable promontory washed by
the waves. The sea surrounded its base, came up past it to the
east and north in a long inlet, and stretched away, across the
level where the sheep now graze, to stout little neighbouring
Rye, perched—in doubtless not quite equal pride—on an
eminence more humble, but which must have counted then
even for more than to-day in the pretty figure made, as you
stand off, by the small, compact, pyramidal port. The "Antient Towns" looked at each other then across the water,
which made almost an island of the rock of huddled, church-
crowned Rye—which had too much to say to them alike, on
evil days, at their best time, but which was too soon to begin
to have too little. If the early Winchelsea was to suffer by
"drowning," its successor was to bear the stroke of remaining
high and dry. The haven on the hill-top—a bold and extraordinary conception—had hardly had time to get, as we should
now say, "started," before it began to see its days numbered.
The sea and the shore were never at peace together, and it
was, most remarkably, not the sea that got the best of it.
Winchelsea had only time to dream a great dream—the
dream of a scant pair of centuries—before its hopes were
turned to bitterness and its boasts to lamentation. It had literally, during its short career, put in a claim to rivalship with
the port of London. The irony of fate now sits in its empty
lap; but the port of London has never suggested even a frus-
trate "Denis Duval."

While Winchelsea dreamed, at any rate, she worked, and
the noble fragment of her great church, rising solid from the
abortive symmetry of her great square, helps us to put our
hand on her deep good faith. She built at least as she believed—she planned as she fondly imagined. The huge ivy-
covered choir and transepts of St. Thomas of Canterbury—to
whom the structure was addressed—represent to us a great
intention. They are not so mighty, but they are almost as
brave, as the wondrous fragment of Beauvais. Walled and
closed on their unfinished side, they form at present all the
church, and, with its grand lines of arch and window, its
beautiful Gothic tombs and general hugeness and height, the
church—mercifully exempt as yet from restoration—is won-

derful for the place. You may at this hour—if you are given
to such emotions—feel a mild thrill, not be unaware even of
the approach of tears, as you measure the scale on which the
building had been planned and the ground that the nave and
aisles would have covered. You murmur, in the summer twilight, a soft "Bravo!" across the ages—to the ears of heaven
knows what poor nameless ghosts. The square—apparently
one of many—was to have been worthy of New York or of
Turin; for the queerest, quaintest, most touching thing of all
is that the reinstated city was to have been laid out on the
most approved modern lines. Nothing is more interesting—to the mooning, sketching spectator—than this evidence that the great Edward had anticipated us all in the
convenient chess-board pattern. It is true—attention has been
called to the fact—that Pompeii had anticipated *him*; but I
doubt if he knew much about Pompeii. His abstract avenues
and cross-streets straggle away, through the summer twilight,
into mere legend and mystery. In speaking awhile since of the
gates of these shattered strongholds as "stiff," I also spoke of
their walls as "tight"; but the scheme of Winchelsea must
have involved, after all, a certain looseness of cincture. The
old vague girdle is lost to-day in the fields where the sheep
browse, in the parkish acres where the great trees cluster. The
Sussex oak is mighty—it was of the Sussex oak that, in the
old time, the king's ships were built; it was, in particular, to
her command of this material that Rye owed the burdensome
honour of supplying vessels, on constant call, to the royal
navy. Strange is this record, in Holloway's History of that
town, and in presence of the small things of to-day; so perpetual, under stress, appears to have been the demand and so free
the supply and the service.

Rye continued indeed, under her old brown south cliff, to
build big boats till this industry was smitten by the adoption
of iron. That was the last stroke; though even now you may
see things as you stand on the edge of the cliff: best of all on
the open, sunny terrace of a dear little old garden—a garden
brown-walled, red-walled, rose-covered on its other sides, divided by the width of a quiet street of grass-grown cobbles
from the house of its master, and possessed of a little old
glass-fronted, panelled pavilion which I hold to be the special

spot in the world where Thackeray might most fitly have figured out his story. There is not much room in the pavilion,
but there is room for the hard-pressed table and the tilted
chair—there is room for a novelist and his friends. The panels
have a queer paint and a venerable slant; the small chimney-
place is at your back; the south window is perfect, the privacy
bright and open. How can I tell what old—what young—
visions of visions and memories of images come back to me
under the influence of this quaint receptacle, into which, by
kind permission, I occasionally peep, and still more under the
charm of the air and the view that, as I just said, you may
enjoy, close at hand, from the small terrace? How can I tell
why I always keep remembering and losing there the particular passages of some far-away foolish fiction, absorbed in extreme youth, which haunt me, yet escape me, like the echo of
an old premonition? I seem to myself to have lain on the grass
somewhere, as a boy, poring over an English novel of the
period, presumably quite bad—for they were pretty bad then
too—and losing myself in the idea of just such another scene
as this. But even could I rediscover the novel I wouldn't go
back to it. It couldn't have been so good as this; for this—all
concrete and doomed and minimised as it is—is the real
thing. The other little gardens, other little odds and ends of
crooked brown wall and supported terrace and glazed winter
sun-trap, lean over the cliff that still, after centuries, keeps its
rude drop; they have beneath them the river, a tide that
comes and goes, and the mile or more of grudging desert
level, beyond it, which now throws the sea to the near horizon, where, on summer days, with a depth of blue and a scattered gleam of sails, it looks forgiving and resigned. The little
old shipyards at the base of the rock are for the most part
quite empty, with only vague piles of brown timber and the
deposit of generations of chips; yet a fishing-boat or two are
still on the stocks—an "output" of three or four a year!—
and the ring of the hammer on the wood, a sound, in such
places, rare to the contemporary ear, comes up, through the
sunny stillness, to your meditative perch.

The tidal river, on the left, wanders away to Rye Harbour
and its bar, where the black fishing-boats, half the time at
lop-sided rest in the mud, make a cluster of slanting spears

against the sky. When the river is full we are proud of its wide light and many curves; when it is empty we call it, for vague reasons, "rather Dutch"; and empty or full we sketch it in the fine weather as hard as ever we can. When I say "we" I mean *they* do—it is to speak with hospitality. They mostly wear, as I have hinted, large sun-bonnets, and they crouch on low camp-stools; they put in, as they would say, a bit of white, in places often the least likely. Rye is in truth a rudimentary drawing-lesson, and you quite embrace the question when you have fairly seized the formula. Nothing so "quaint" was ever so easy—nothing so easy was ever so quaint. Much more to be loved than feared, she has not, alas, a scrap of "style," and she may be effectively rendered without the obligation of subtlety. At favoured seasons there appear within her precinct sundry slouch-hatted gentlemen who study her humble charms through a small telescope formed by their curved fingers and thumb, and who are not unliable to define themselves as French artists leading a train of English and American lady pupils. They distribute their disciples over the place, at selected points, where the master, going his round from hour to hour, reminds you of nothing so much as a busy *chef* with many saucepans on the stove and periodically lifting their covers for a sniff and a stir. There are ancient doorsteps that are fairly haunted, for their convenience of view, by the "class," and where the fond proprietor, going and coming, has to pick his way among paraphernalia or to take flying leaps over genius and industry. If Winchelsea is, as I gather, less beset, it is simply that Winchelsea enjoys the immunity of her greater distinction. She is full of that and must be even more difficult than she at first appears. But I forsook her and her distinction, just now, and I must return to them; though the right moment would quite have been as we stood, at Rye, on the terrace of the little old south-garden, to which she presents herself, beyond two or three miles of flat Dutch-looking interval, from the extreme right, her few red roofs almost lost on her wooded hill and her general presence masking, for this view, the headland of Hastings, ten miles, by the coast, westward.

It was about her spacious solitude that we had already begun to stroll; for the purpose, however, mainly, of measuring the stretch, south and north, to the two more crumbled of her three old gates. They are very far gone, each but the ruin of a ruin; but it is their actual countrified state that speaks of the circuit—one hundred and fifty acres—they were supposed to defend. Under one of them you may pass, much round about, by high-seated villages and in constant sight of the sea, toward Hastings; from the other, slightly the less dilapidated, you may gather, if much so minded, the suggestion of some illustration or tail-piece in a volume of Italian travel. The steep white road plunges crookedly down to where the poor arches that once were massive straddle across it, while a spreading chestnut, beside them, plays exactly the part desired—prepares you, that is, for the crack of the whip of the *vetturino* trudging up beside his travelling-carriage. With a bare-legged urchin and a browsing goat the whole thing would be there. But we turn, at that point, to mount again and cross the idle square and come back to the east gate, which is the aspect of Winchelsea that presents itself most— and in fact quite admirably—as the front. Yet by what is it that, at the end of summer afternoons, my sense of an obliterated history is fed? There is little but the church really to testify, for the extraordinary groined vaults and crypts that are part of the actual pride of the place—treasure-houses of old merchants, foundations of upper solidities that now are dust—count for nothing, naturally, in the immediate effect. The early houses passed away long ago, and the present ones speak, in broken accents and scant and shabby signs, but of the last hundred, the last couple of hundred, years. Everything that ever happened is gone, and, for that matter, nothing very eminent, only a dim mediocrity of life, ever did happen. Rye has Fletcher the dramatist, the Fletcher of Beaumont, whom it brought to birth; but Winchelsea has only the last preachment, under a tree still shown, of John Wesley. The third Edward and the Black Prince, in 1350, overcame the Spaniards in a stout sea-fight within sight of the walls; but I am bound to confess that I do not at all focus that performance, am unable, in the changed conditions, to "place" anything so pompous. In the same way I fail to "visualise," thank goodness, either of the several French inroads that left their mark of massacre and ruin. What I do see, on the other hand,

East Gate, Winchelsea

very comfortably, is the little undistinguished picture of a nearer antiquity, the antiquity for a glimpse of which I re-opened "Denis Duval." Where please, was the barber's shop of the family of that hero, and where the apartments, where the preferred resorts, the particular scenes of occupation and diversion of the dark Chevalier de la Motte? Where did this subtle son of another civilisation, with whom Madame de Saverne had eloped from France, *en plein ancien régime*, with-out the occurrence between them of the least impropriety, spend his time for so long a period; where had he his little habits and his numerous indispensable conveniences? What was the general geography, to express it synthetically, of the state of life of the orphaned Clarisse, quartered with a family of which one of the sons, furiously desirous of the girl, was, at his lost moments, a highwayman stopping coaches in the dead of night? Over nothing in the whole fragment does such vagueness hover as over the domestic situation, in her tender years, of the future Madame Denis. Yet these are just the things I should have liked to know—the things, above all, I should have liked most to tell. Into a vision of *them*, at least, we can work ourselves; it is exactly the sort of vision into which Rye and Winchelsea, and all the land about, full of lurking hints and modest memories, most throws us back. I should, in truth, have liked to lock up our novelist in our little pavilion of inspiration, the gazebo at Rye, not letting him out till he should quite have satisfied us.

Close beside the east gate, so close that one of its battered towers leans heavily on the little garden, is a wonderfully perched cottage, of which the mistress is a very celebrated lady who resorts to the place in the intervals of an exacting profession—the scene of her renown, I may go so far as to mention, is the theatre—for refreshment and rest. The small grounds of this refuge, supported by the old town-wall and the steep plunge of the great hill, have a rare position and view. The narrow garden stretches away in the manner of a terrace to which the top of the wall forms a low parapet; and here it is that, when the summer days are long, the sweet old soul of all the land seems most to hang in the air. It is almost a question indeed whether this fine Winchelsea front, all silver-gray and ivy-green, is not even better when making a picture itself from below than when giving you one, with much immensity, from its brow. This picture is always your great effect, artfully prepared by an absence of prediction, when you take a friend over from Rye; and it would appear quite to settle the small discussion—that may be said to come up among us so often—of which is the happier abode. The great thing is that if you live at Rye you have Winchelsea to show; whereas if you live at Winchelsea you have nothing but Rye. This latter privilege I should be sorry to cry down; but nothing can alter the fact that, to begin with, the pedestal of Winchelsea has twice the height, by a rough measure, of that of its neighbour; and we all know the value of an inch at the end of a nose. Almost directly under the Winchelsea hill, crossing the little bridge of the Brede, you pass beyond a screen of trees and take in, at the top of the ascent, the two round towers and arch, ivied and mutilated, but still erect, of the old main gate. The road either way is long and abrupt, so that people kind to their beasts alight at the foot, and cyclists careful of their necks alight at the head. The brooding spectator, moreover, who forms a class by himself, pauses, infallibly, as he goes, to admire the way the great trees cluster and compose on the high slope, always striking, for him, as day gathers in and the whole thing melts together, a classic, academic note, the note of Turner and Claude. From the garden of the distinguished cottage, at any rate, it is a large, melancholy view—a view that an occasional perverse person whom it fails to touch finds easy, I admit, to speak of as dreary; so that those who love it and are well advised will ever, at the outset, carry the war into the enemy's country by announcing it, with glee, as sad. Just this it must be that nourishes the sense of obliterated history as to which I a moment ago wondered. The air is like that of a room through which something has been carried that you are aware of without having seen it. There is a vast deal of level in the prospect, but, though much depends on the day and still more on the hour, it is, at the worst, all too delicate to be ugly. The best hour is that at which the compact little pyramid of Rye, crowned with its big but stunted church and quite covered by the westering sun, gives out the full measure of its old browns that turn to red and its old reds that turn to purple. These tones of

evening are now pretty much all that Rye has left to give, but
there are truly, sometimes, conditions of atmosphere in which
I have seen the effect as fantastic. I sigh when I think, however, what it might have been if, perfectly placed as it is, the
church tower—which in its more perverse moods only resembles a big central button, a knob on a pin-cushion—had had
the grace of a few more feet of stature. But that way depression lies, and the humiliation of those moments at which the
brooding spectator says to himself that both tower and hill
would have been higher if the place had only been French or
Italian. Its whole pleasant little pathos, in point of fact, is just
that it is homely English. And even with this, after all, the
imagination can play. The wide, ambiguous flat that stretches
eastward from Winchelsea hill, and on the monotone of
whose bosom, seen at sunset from a friendly eminence that
stands nearer, Rye takes the form of a huge floating boat, its
water-line sharp and its bulk defined from stem to stern—this
dim expanse is the great Romney Marsh, no longer a marsh
to-day, but, at the end of long years, drained and ordered, a
wide pastoral of grazing, with "new" Romney town, a Port
no more—not the least of the shrunken Five—mellowed to
mere russet at the far end, and other obscure charms, revealed
best to the slow cyclist, scattered over its breast: little old
"bits" that are not to be described, yet are known, with a
small thrill, when seen; little lonely farms, red and gray; little
mouse-coloured churches; little villages that seem made only
for long shadows and summer afternoons. Brookland, Old
Romney, Ivychurch, Dymchurch, Lydd—they have positively the prettiest names. But the point to be made is that,
comparing small things with great—which may always be
done when the small things are amiable—if Rye and its rock
and its church are a miniature Mont-Saint-Michel, so, when
the summer deepens, the shadows fall, and the mounted shepherds and their dogs pass before you in the grassy desert,
you find in the mild English "marsh" a recall of the Roman
Campagna.

A Suffolk Common

Old Suffolk

I AM not sure that before entering the county of Suffolk in the early part of August, I had been conscious of any personal relation to it save my share in what we all inevitably feel for a province enshrining the birthplace of a Copperfield. The opening lines of David's history offered in this particular an easy perch to my young imagination; and to recall them to-day, though with a memory long unrefreshed, is to wonder once more at the depth to which early impressions strike down. This one in especial indeed has been the privilege of those millions of readers who owe to Dickens the glow of the prime response to the romantic, that first bite of the apple of knowledge which leaves a taste for ever on the tongue. The great initiators give such a colour to mere names that the things they represent have often, before contact, been a lively part of experience. It is hard therefore for an undefended victim of this kind of emotion to measure, when contact arrives, the quantity of picture already stored up, to point to the nucleus of the gallery or trace the history of the acquaintance. It is true that for the divine plant of sensibility in youth the watering need never have been lavish. It flowered, at all events, at the right moment, in a certain case, into the branching image of Blunderstone—which, by the way, I am sorry to see figure as "Blunderston" in gazetteers of recent date and more than questionable tact. Dickens took his Rookery exactly where he found it, and simply fixed it for ever; he left the cradle of the Copperfields the benefit of its delightful name; or I should say better, perhaps, left the delightful name and the obscure nook the benefit of an association ineffaceable: all of which makes me the more ashamed not as yet to have found the right afternoon—it would have in truth to be abnormally long—for a pious pilgrimage to the distracting little church where, on David's sleepy Sundays, one used to lose one's self with the sketchy Phiz. One of the reasons of this omission, so profane on a prior view, is doubtless that everything, in England, in old-time corners, has the connecting touch and the quality of illustration, and that, in a particularly golden August, with an impression in every bush, the immediate vision, wherever one meets it, easily attaches and suffices. Another must have been, I confess, the somewhat depressed memory of a visit paid a few years since to the ancient home of the Peggottys, supposedly so "sympathetic," but with little left, to-day, as the event then proved, of the glamour it had worn to the fancy. Great Yarmouth, it will be remembered, was a convenient drive from Blunderstone; but Great Yarmouth, with its mile of cockneyfied sea-front and its overflow of nigger minstrelsy, now strikes the wrong note so continuously that I, for my part, became conscious, on the spot, of a chill to the spirit of research.

This time, therefore, I have allowed that spirit its ease; and I may perhaps intelligibly make the point I desire if I contrive to express somehow that I have found myself, most of the month, none the less abundantly occupied in reading a fuller sense into the lingering sound given out, for a candid mind, by my superscription and watching whatever it may stand for gradually flush with a stronger infusion. It takes, in England, for that matter, no wonderful corner of the land to make the fiddle-string vibrate. The old usual rural things do this enough, and a part of the charm of one's exposure to them is that they ask one to rise to no heroics. What is the charm, after all, but just the abyss of the familiar? The peopled fancy, the haunted memory are themselves what pay the bill. The game can accordingly be played with delightful economy, a thrift involving the cost of little more than a good bicycle. The bicycle indeed, since I fall back on that admission, may perhaps, without difficulty, be too good for the roads. Those of the more devious kind often engender hereabouts, like the Aristotelian tragedy, pity and terror; but almost equally with others they lead, on many a chance, to the ruddiest, greenest hamlets. What this comes to is saying that I have had, for many a day, the sweet sense of living, æsthetically, at really high pressure without, as it were, drawing on the great fund. By the great fund I mean the public show, the show for ad-mission to which you are charged and overcharged, made to taste of the tree of possible disappointment. The beauty of old Suffolk in general, and above all of the desperate depth of it from which I write, is that these things whisk you straight out of conceivable relation to that last danger.

I defy any one, at desolate, exquisite Dunwich, to be dis-appointed in anything. The minor key is struck here with a felicity that leaves no sigh to be breathed, no loss to be suffered; a month of the place is a real education to the pa-tient, the inner vision. The explanation of this is, appreciably, that the conditions give you to deal with not, in the manner of some quiet countries, what is meagre and thin, but what has literally, in a large degree, ceased to be at all. Dunwich is not even the ghost of its dead self; almost all you can say of it is that it consists of the mere letters of its old name. The coast, up and down, for miles, has been, for more centuries than I presume to count, gnawed away by the sea. All the grossness of its positive life is now at the bottom of the Ger-man Ocean, which moves for ever, like a ruminating beast, an insatiable, indefatigable lip. Few things are so melancholy— and so redeemed from mere ugliness by sadness—as this long, artificial straightness that the monster has impartially maintained. If at low tide you walk on the shore, the cliffs, of little height, show you a defence picked as bare as a bone; and you can say nothing kinder of the general humility and general sweetness of the land than that this sawlike action gives it, for the fancy, an interest, a sort of mystery, that more than makes up for what it may have surrendered. It stretched, within historic times, out into towns and promontories for which there is now no more to show than the empty eyeholes of a skull; and half the effect of the whole thing, half the secret of the impression, and what I may really call, I think, the source of the distinction, is this very visibility of the mutilation. Such at any rate is the case for a mind that can properly brood. There is a presence in what is missing—there is history in there being so little. It is so little, to-day, that every item of the handful counts.

The biggest items are of course the two ruins, the great church and its tall tower, now quite on the verge of the cliff, and the crumbled, ivied wall of the immense cincture of the Priory. These things have parted with almost every grace, but they still keep up the work that they have been engaged in for centuries and that cannot better be described than as the adding of mystery to mystery. This accumulation, at present prodigious, is, to the brooding mind, unconscious as the shrunken little Dunwich of to-day may be of it, the beginning and the end of the matter. I hasten to add that it is to the brooding mind only, and from it, that I speak. The mystery sounds for ever in the hard, straight tide, and hangs, through the long, still summer days and over the low, diked fields, in the soft, thick light. We play with it as with the answerless question, the question of the spirit and attitude, never again to be recovered, of the little city submerged. For it *was* a city, the main port of Suffolk, as even its poor relics show; with a fleet of its own on the North Sea, and a big religious house on the hill. We wonder what were then the apparent conditions of security, and on what rough calculation a community could so build itself out to meet its fate. It keeps one easy company here to-day to think of the whole business as a magnificent mistake. But Mr. Swinburne, in verses of an extraordinary poetic eloquence, quite brave enough for whatever there may have been, glances in the right direction much further than I can do. Read moreover, for other glances, the "Letters of Edward Fitzgerald," Suffolk worthy and whimsical

On the Marshes

subject, who, living hard by at Woodbridge, haunted these regions during most of his life, and has left, in delightful pages, at the service of the emulous visitor, the echo of every odd, quaint air they could draw from his cracked, sweet instrument. He has paid his tribute, I seem to remember, to the particular delicate flower—the pale Dunwich rose—that blooms on the walls of the Priory. The emulous visitor, only yesterday, on the most vulgar of vehicles—which, however, he is quite aware he must choose between using and abusing—followed, in the mellow afternoon, one of these faint hints across the land and as far as the old, old town of Aldeburgh, the birthplace and the commemorated "Borough" of the poet Crabbe.

Fitzgerald, devoted to Crabbe, was apparently not less so to this small break in the wide, low, heathery bareness that brings the sweet Suffolk commons—rare purple and gold when I arrived—nearly to the edge of the sea. We don't, none the less, always gather the particular impression we bravely go forth to seek. We doubtless gather another indeed that will serve as well any such turn as here may wait for it; so that if it was somehow not easy to work Fitzgerald into the small gentility of the sea-front, the little "marina," as of a fourth-rate watering-place, that has elbowed away, evidently in recent years, the old handful of character, one could at least, to make up for that, fall back either on the general sense of the happy trickery of genius or on the special beauty of the mixture, in the singer of Omar Kháyyám, that, giving him such a place for a setting, could yet feed his fancy so full. Crabbe, at Aldeburgh, for that matter, is perhaps even more wonderful—in the light, I mean, of what is left of the place by one's conjuring away the little modern vulgar accumulation. What is left is just the stony beach and the big gales and the cluster of fishermen's huts and the small, wide, short street of decent, homely, shoppy houses. These are the private emotions of the historic sense—glimpses in which we recover for an hour, or rather perhaps, with an intensity, but for the glimmer of a minute, the conditions that, grimly enough, could engender masterpieces, or at all events classics. What a mere pinch of manners and customs in the midst of winds and waves! Yet if it was a feature of these to return a member to Parliament,

Dunwich

what wonder that, up to the Reform Bill, dead Dunwich should have returned two?

The glimpses I speak of are, in all directions, the constant company of the afternoon "spin." Beginning, modestly enough, at Dunwich itself, they end, for intensity, as far inland as you have time to go; far enough—this is the great point—to have shown you, in their quiet vividness of type, a placid series of the things into which you may most read the old story of what is softest in the English complexity. I scarce know what murmur has been for weeks in my ears if it be not that of the constant word that, as a recall of the story, may serve to be put under the vignette. And yet this word is in its last form nothing more eloquent than the mere admonition to be pleased. Well, so you are, even as I was yesterday at Wesselton with the characteristic "value" that expressed itself, however shyly, in the dear old red inn at which I halted for the queer restorative—I thus discharge my debt to it—of a bottle of lemonade with a "dash." The dash was only of beer, but the refreshment was immense. So even was that of the sight of a dim, draped, sphinx-like figure that loomed, at the end of a polished passage, out of a little dusky back parlour which had a windowful of the choked light of a small green garden—a figure proving to be an old woman desirous to dilate on all the years she had sat there with rheumatism "most cruel." So, inveterately—and in these cases without the after-taste—is that of the pretty little park gates you pass to skirt the walls and hedges beyond which the great affair, the greatest of all, the deep, still home, sits in the midst of its acres and strikes you all the more for being, precisely, so un-renowned. It is the charming repeated lesson that the amenity of the famous seats in this country is nothing to that of the lost and buried ones. This impression in particular may bring you round again harmoniously to Dunwich and above all per-haps to where the Priory, laid, as I may say flat on its back, rests its large outline on what was once the high ground, with the inevitable "big" house, beyond and a little above, folded, for privacy, in a neat, impenetrable wood. Here as elsewhere the cluster offers without complication just the signs of the type. At the base of the hill are the dozen cottages to which the village has been reduced, and one of which contains, to my hearing, though by no means, alas, to his own, a very ancient man who will count for you on his fingers, till they fail, the grand acres that, in his day, he has seen go the way of the rest. He likes to figure that he ploughed of old where only the sea ploughs now. Dunwich, however, will still last his time; and that of as many other as—to repeat my hint—may yet be drawn here (though not, I hope, on the instance of these prudent lines) to judge for themselves into how many meanings a few elements can compose. One never need be bored, after all, when "composition" really rules. It rules in the way the brown hamlet disposes itself, and the gray square tower of the church, in just the right relation, peeps out of trees that remind me exactly of those which, in the frontis-pieces of Birket Foster, offered to my childish credulity the very essence of England. Let me put it directly for old Suffolk that this credulity finds itself here, at the end of time, more than ever justified. Let me put it perhaps also that the very essence of England has a way of presenting itself with com-pleteness in almost any fortuitous combination of rural ob-

Fitzgerald's Home

jects at all, so that, wherever you may be, you get, reduced and simplified, the whole of the scale. The big house and its woods are always at hand; with a "party" always, in the intervals of shooting, to bring down to the rustic sports that keep up the tradition of the village green. The russet, low-browed inn, the "ale-house" of Shakespeare, the immemorial fountain of beer, looking over that expanse, swings, with an old-time story-telling creak, the sign of the Marquis of Carabas. The pretty girls, within sight of it, alight from the Marquis's wagonette; the young men with the one eye-glass and the new hat sit beside them on the benches supplied for their sole accommodation, and thanks to which the meditator on manners has, a little, the image, gathered from faded fictions by female hands, of the company brought over, for the triumph of the heroine, to the hunt or the county ball. And it is always Hodge and Gaffer that, at bottom, *font les frais*—always the mild children of the glebe on whom, in the last resort, the complex superstructure rests.

The discovery, in the twilight of time, of the merits, as a

building-site, of Hodge's broad bent back remains surely one of the most sagacious strokes of the race from which the squire and the parson were to be evolved. He is there in force—at the rustic sports—in force or in feebleness, with Mrs. Hodge and the Miss Hodges, who participate with a silent glee in the chase, over fields where their shadows are long, of a pig with a greased tail. He pulls his forelock in the tent in which, after the pig is caught, the rewards of valour are dispensed by the squire's lady, and if he be in favour for respectability and not behind with rent, he penetrates later to the lawn within the wood, where he is awaited by a band of music and a collation of beer, buns, and tobacco.

I mention these things as some of the light notes, but the picture is never too empty for a stronger one not to sound. The strongest, at Dunwich, is indeed one that, without in the least falsifying the scale, counts immensely for filling in. The palm in the rustic sports is for the bluejackets; as, in England, of course, nothing is easier than for the village green to alternate with the element that Britannia still more admirably rules. I had often dreamed that the ideal refuge for a man of letters was a cottage so placed on the coast as to be circled, as it were, by the protecting arm of the Admiralty. I remember to have heard it said in the old country—in New York and Boston—that the best place to live in is next to an engine-house, and it is on this analogy that, at Dunwich, I have looked for ministering peace in near neighbourhood to one of those stations of the coastguard that, round all the edge of England, at short intervals, on rock and sand and heath, make, with shining whitewash and tar, clean as a great State is at least theoretically clean, each its own little image of the reach of the empire. It is in each case an image that, for one reason and another, you respond to with a sort of thrill; and the thing becomes as concrete as you can wish on your discovering in the three or four individual members of the simple staff of the establishment all sorts of educated decency and many sorts of beguilement to intercourse. Prime among the latter, in truth, is the great yarn-spinning gift. It differs from man to man, but here and there it glows like a cut ruby. May the last darkness close before I cease to care for sea-folk!— though this, I hasten to add, is not the private predilection at

A Suffolk Mill

which, in these incoherent notes, I proposed most to glance.
Let me have mentioned it merely as a sign that the fault is all
my own if, this summer, the arm of the Admiralty has not, in
the full measure of my theory, represented the protection under which the long literary morning may know—abyss of delusion!—nothing but itself.

GREAT BRITAIN:
UNCOLLECTED
TRAVEL WRITINGS

Contents

London Sights

LONDON, NOV. 10, 1875.

WHEN the Albert Memorial was completed and uncovered in London more than a year since, and displayed through the smoky air its treasures of florid architecture, there was much almost ribald jesting at the way the local atmosphere was destined to blight its gilding and its precious stones. The thing seemed like a sort of magnificent satire upon the London climate. Some five years ago the beautiful new structure of the Royal Academy was brilliant with its carved white stone and its gleaming statues; to-day it is of a dusky, smutty gray, and to-morrow it will be as black and hoary as Westminster Abbey and St. Paul's. Having seen the Albert Memorial just after its erection, I was lately curious to observe whether its splendor had as yet begun perceptibly to wane. It must be confessed that up to this moment it has made a very successful resistance. It will have the best wishes of all lovers of the picturesque for its continued success; for whatever may be thought of its artistic merit or of the moral necessity for having erected it, it at least may be valued by the London wayfarers as the sole specimen of vivid color in the metropolis. Its position of course helps to preserve its purity, with the vast open spaces of Kensington Gardens beside it and behind it in one quarter, and the mitigated contaminations of the far-spreading terraces and crescents of Prince's Gate, Queen's Gate, etc., facing it on the other. Readers interested in these matters may be reminded that the Memorial stands on the edge of Kensington Gardens, opposite the great red-and-yellow rotunda of Albert Hall—a sort of utilitarian Coliseum, which, I believe, has not been found very useful. The Memorial is a wonderful combination of British sculpture and architecture, gilding, mosaic, and the work of the lapidary. It consists of an immense gilt canopy of Gothic design, under which an image of the Prince-Consort is destined to repose. It rises colossally from a huge embankment, as it were, of steps, at each corner of which is a group in marble representing one of the four great continents. The "motive" of these groups is sufficiently picturesque, a great local beast, of heroic proportions—the bull, the bison, the camel, and the elephant—being in each case the central figure; but the sculpture, like all the sculpture, is second-rate and common. It is the work, of course, of the highest English skill—of Messrs. Macdowell, Bell, Foley, and Theed. At each angle of the upper platform where the shafts of the canopy rise is another group—"Manufactures," by Mr. Weekes; "Commerce," by Mr. Thorneycroft; "Agriculture," by Mr. Marshall; and "Engineering," by Mr. Lawlor. Round this outer base of the canopy runs an immense frieze in white marble, executed half by Mr. Philip and half by Mr. Armstead, representing, a trifle below life-size, the array of the world's great artists—poets, painters, sculptors, musicians, and architects. They have been sagaciously chosen and cleverly combined, and the most expressive and original portion of the sculpture is here, we should say, especially on Mr. Armstead's side. As for the canopy itself, with its flamboyant Gothic, its columns of porphyry, its statues and statuettes of bronze and gold (or seeming gold), its chased and chiselled jeweller's-work, its radiant mosaics, its thick-strewn gems of malachite and lapis and jasper and onyx and more rare stones than we know the names of, its gables and spires and pinnacles and crockets, its general gleaming and flashing and climbing and soaring, its great jewelled cross at the summit—all this quite beggars description. We should say in general that the workmanship throughout has been of a finer sort than the original taste, and that if the Memorial preserves in the future the memory of our present knowingness in architecture, it will also perpetuate the modern weakness of that art which once unfolded the friezes along the Parthenon and suspended the tombs in the Italian cathedrals.

The exhibition of paintings by Gustave Doré now on view in London ceased a good while since to demand notice as a novelty, but has become one of the regular sights of the great city, and it suggests some reflections that are always pertinent. The general air of the establishment is not so much that of a temple of the arts as of an enterprising place of business. The pictures seem to be placed on view chiefly with the design of securing subscribers to certain projected engravings. The agents for subscriptions are liberally diffused through the rooms, and, as they mingle "quite promiscuous" (as the London vernacular has it) with the visitors, the latter are liable to be buttonholed in the midst of such attentive contemplation as Doré's canvases may have provoked. The engravings are to be executed in England, in the finest and smoothest style of the old-fashioned "line." It may very well be that the pictures will gain on being reduced to small dimensions and to simple black and white, for they look, as a general thing, like "illustrations" hugely magnified and rather crudely colored. The exhibition is of course an interesting one, and gives an extraordinary impression of imagination, vigor, and facility. On the whole, doubtless, one ought not to be afraid of enjoying it. We may be tolerably sure that, where his pictures are wanting, M. Doré knows it, that he has deliberately chosen to do only what he conveniently could, and that he has settled it in his mind that a magnificent effect, however obtained, is its own justification. The artist's "convenience," we are at liberty to infer, has been to cover an immense quantity of canvas and make a great deal of money. As for his effects, the best of them are certainly magnificent. The only valid criticism of Gustave Doré must rest, it seems to me, on the admission that in the degree to which he possesses the temperament of the designer—in energy, and force, and consistency of talent—he ranks with the few greatest names. He has a touch of Michael Angelo about him; the fact that he is an enterprising Parisian of the nineteenth century ought not to make this inconceivable to us. In the power to compose an immense combination of figures at short notice he recalls two of his greatest predecessors—Rubens and Tintoretto. We may prefer Rubens and Tintoretto, and yet do justice to other members of the family. It is Doré's own fault if so often we find it very easy to prefer them. He has chosen to work by wholesale, and so very often did they, who, however, had the advantage that wholesale painting in their times, owing to the essential tone of men's thoughts, could not of necessity be so superficial as it may be to-day. Their merit is that, whatever they did, they always achieved something that may be called painting; and Doré's fault is that half the time his work is not painting at all. It is a rapid, superficial application of turbid and meaningless color—an imitation of painting not always particularly skilful. The two great things in London—the "Christ coming down from Judgment" and the "Tapis Vert"—are full of examples of this. The latter of these—a very cleverly imaginative representation of the gaming-table at Baden-Baden—is well known by photography, and known very favorably. The photograph flatters it, and so probably will the engraving, in giving it a charm of detail which the original lacks. The other picture—one of the largest ever painted—is full of imagination, skill, and power, and looks, as we intimated, like one of Doré's most successful drawings shown by a magic-lantern. It is a most extraordinary performance. The other pictures are full of cleverness and invention, especially certain "Christian Martyrs in the Coliseum," a heap of corpses lying in the empty arena, with wild beasts prowling over them in the blue starlight, and cold, phantasmal angels hovering above. The landscapes are singularly bad, many of them looking for all the world like second-rate American work. The best things have a merit which the way Doré has cheapened himself has made at last to seem trivial, but which would seem quite incomparable if it had been more abruptly presented. Their great fault is that they have no agreeable passages of painting—nothing exquisite, nothing that looks not only as if the artist had lingered over it, but as if he had even paused at it.

The Oxford-Cambridge Boat-Race

T HE ANNUAL boat-race between the two universities," writes a correspondent from London, under date of March 25, "has had this year an unprecedented result— namely, a 'dead heat.' The closeness of the struggle made the race a particularly beautiful one, the prettiest, I am told, that has been rowed for many years. This was my consolation for getting up in the gray dawn of a particularly acrid March morning, and journeying forth to stand for an hour in the fierce, raw wind that sweeps over Barnes Bridge. The race, this year, took place at an unusually early hour—nominally, at a quarter to eight. This fact, together with the prospect of a rainy morning, thinned out the customary crowd; but the concourse of people seemed to me very vast, and in a certain way very impressive. It was a great proof of the 'muscularity' of the English race, and of the touch of nature which makes all classes akin here being admiration for the power of doing something wonderful with one's legs or arms. When one re-flected that the closely-pressed thousands that lined the river-bank, and encumbered the stream in barges and wherries, were assembled to witness twenty minutes' boyish sport on the part of a few young gentlemen engaged in book-learning at college, one hardly knew whether to laugh or to feel very solemn. I suppose, certainly, that it is the thing in the modern world which gives one most of a hint of what the Olympic games may have been. It is very true that certain elements in the scene are but slenderly Olympic—the dingy, British mob, with coal-smoke ground into its pores, the dank suburban landscape, the low and dusky sky, the taverns, the railway bridges, and the Thames mud. But when the two boats came shooting down the stream, spreading their simultaneous oars like great white, water-skimming birds, with eight-feathered wings, and followed closely by the three densely-laden steam-ers—the umpires, the universities, and the press—which are allowed to attend them, I suspect the sight is as stirring as any that Greece had to show. Next to being on one of these steamers—a privilege inaccessible to the vulgar—the best position for the spectators is on the railway bridge at Barnes, for admission to which, by special train from Waterloo, you pay a sovereign. Of course but a moderate portion of a four-mile course is visible from any one point; but the spot in question is the one point from which most can be seen. For a long time yesterday morning we breakfastless hundreds stood there cooling our heels, with nothing but the shoving and shifting barges and the crowd on the towing-path to see, and nothing to swallow but the bitter March wind. The start of the crews was delayed more than half an hour, and we had a great many false alarms; but at last we knew they were off, though for a good while we could make out nothing but the shining upper reaches of the stream itself. Little by little, however, the two boats became visible, vaguely gleaming in the grey light, and becoming rapidly distincter and larger. After they had once come well into sight, Oxford leading and Cambridge three-quarters of a boat's length behind, our own admiration for the splendid pace at which they were going (the tide was dead, but the wind was against them and the water not smooth) was tempered with regret. It was provoking to be losing so fast so beautiful a sight. For some moments, however, from the bridge, we had it directly under our noses. Nearly three miles of the course had been rowed and Cambridge was, although not losing ground, not recovering ground already lost. The uproar from the shore and the bridge—the shouts, and howls, and conflicting adjurations—swelled and deepened, and (along the shore) was caught up as the boats advanced. As they passed under the bridge they were, from side to side, wonderfully close together, but Cambridge was still behind. Then it was that, seen from high above and much foreshortened, they looked, as I have said, like great birds grazing the water with their bellies. There was something very picturesque in the way the three low, black steamers, abreast, looking ugly and hungry, came crowding on their quivering wake. It looked much less like a race than like a chase. The Oxford crew seemed magnificent—eight shining young giants. They were larger men than their rivals, and, so far as I could see in so short a space of time, they seemed to be pulling a grander, smoother stroke. They passed under the bridge, and we all surged with an inarticulate roar to the further parapet. It was between here and the finish that the fortune of the race changed. So long as the two boats kept in sight the advantage was still with Oxford. Cambridge seemed extremely plucky, but decidedly overmatched. She splashed more or less, which her rival didn't. The boats rounded the turn towards Mortlake, and we lost sight of them, taking for granted that Oxford had kept ahead to the end. At the end of a quarter of an hour the dark-blue streamer was hoisted from the bridge on top of the light one, and we were presently despatched back to London in the faith that there would be lamentation, a few minutes later, at Trinity and Jesus. But on arriving in London we learned that an accident, inappreciable from the bridge, had damaged the advance of Oxford. Her bow had split or in some way injured his oar, and had been unable for the last half-mile to feather it, or, indeed, practically use it. The Cambridge boat had caught up, though Oxford, with but seven oars, had kept her from doing more, and the two boats had touched goal together. It was a beautiful race—very powerful for Oxford, very plucky for Cambridge."

1877

The Suburbs of London

THE TERM "suburban" has always seemed to me to have a peculiarly English meaning. It suggests images that are not apt to present themselves in America. American cities have suburbs, but they have to a very limited extent what may be called suburban scenery. The essence of suburban scenery in the western world is to be straggling, shabby, inexpensive; to consist of rail fences and loose planks, vacant, dusty lots in which carpet-beating goes forward, Irish cabins, lumber yards, and rudely bedaubed advertisements of quack medicines. The peculiar function of the neighborhood of most foreign towns, on the other hand, is to be verdant and residential, thickly inhabited, and replete with devices for making habitation agreeable. Some of the prettiest things in England and France are to be found in the immediate vicinity of the capitals of those countries. There is nothing more charming in Europe than the great terrace at Saint Germain; there are few things so picturesque as Richmond bridge and the view thence along either bank of the Thames. There are certainly ugly things enough in the neighborhood of London, and there is much agreeable detail to be found within an hour's drive of several American towns; but the suburban quality, the mingling of density and rurality, the ivy-covered brick walls, the riverside holiday-making, the old royal seats at an easy drive, the little open-windowed inns, where the charm of rural seclusion seems to merge itself in that of proximity to the city market—these things must be caught in neighborhoods that have been longer a-growing.

Murray (of the Hand-Books) has lately put forward a work which I have found very full of entertaining reading: a couple of well-sized volumes treating of every place of the smallest individuality within a circuit of twenty miles round London. The number of such places is surprising; so large an amount of English history has gone on almost within sight of the tower of the Abbey. From time to time, as the days grow long, the contemplative stranger finds a charm in the idea of letting himself loose in this interesting circle. Even to a tolerably inveterate walker London itself will not appear in the long run a very delightful field for pedestrian exercise. London is too monotonous and, in plain English, too ugly to supply that wayside entertainment which the observant pedestrian demands. The shabby quarters are too dusky, too depressing, English low life is too unrelieved by out-of-door picturesqueness, to be treated as a daily spectacle. There are too many gin shops, and too many miserable women at their doors; too many, far too many dirty-faced children sprawling between one's legs; the young ladies of the neighborhood are too much addicted to violent forms of coquetry. On the other hand, the Squares and Crescents, the Roads and Gardens, are too rigidly, too blankly genteel. They are enlivened by groups of charming children, coming out to walk with their governesses or nursemaids, and by the figures of superior flunkies, lingering, in the consciousness of elegant leisure, on the doorstep. But, although these groups—the children and the flunkies—are the most beautiful specimens in the world of their respective classes, they hardly avail to impart a lively interest to miles of smoke-darkened stucco, subdivided into porticoes and windows. The most entertaining walk, therefore, is a suburban walk, which will introduce you to fewer butlers and footmen, but to children as numerous and as rosy, and to something more unexpected in the way of architecture.

There is a charming place of refuge from the London streets of which I fain would speak, although it hardly belongs to my modest programme. There was a time when Kensington was a suburb, but the suburban phase of its history has pretty well passed away. Nothing can well be conceived less suburban than the vast expanses of residential house frontage of which this region now chiefly consists; and yet to go thither is the shortest way of getting out of London. Step into Kensington Gardens, and a ten minutes' walk will carry you practically fifty miles from the murky Babylon on the other side of the railing. It may really be said that Kensington Gardens contain some of the finest rural scenery in England. If they were not a huge city square, they would be an admirable nobleman's park. To sit down for an hour at the base of one of the great elms and see them studding the grass around you in vistas, which, as you do not perceive their limits, may be as long-drawn as you choose to suppose them, is one of the most accessible as well as one of the most agreeable methods of spending a June afternoon.

Whenever, toward six o'clock, I have mustered the spirit to go to Hyde park, I have ended, after a duly dazzled gaze at the wonderful throng that assembles there, by slinking away into the comparative wilderness of the neighboring enclosure. I use the expression "slinking," because I have usually taken this course with a bad conscience. In Hyde park you see fine people; in Kensington Gardens you see only fine trees; and the observant stranger feels that it is upon eminent specimens of the human rather than of the vegetable race that he should bestow his attention. Every one in London, as the phrase is, goes to Hyde park of a fine afternoon; and the spectacle, therefore, may be presumed to have no small impressiveness.

It is certainly a very brilliant mob, and the copper coin which you pay for the use of your little chair is a small equivalent for the greatness of the privilege. Before you is the Drive, with its serried ranks of carriages; behind you is the Row, with its misty, red-earthed vista, and its pacing and bounding equestrians; between the two is the broad walk in which your fellow starers are gathered together lolling back in the tightly-packed chairs or shuffling along with wistful looks at them. The first time the observant stranger betakes himself to the park, he certainly is struck with the splendor of the show. There seems to be so much of everything; there are so many carriages, so many horses, so many servants, so many policemen, so many people in the carriages, on horseback, in the chairs, on foot. The observant stranger is again reminded of those constant factors in every more distinctively "social" spectacle in England—the boundless wealth and the boundless leisure. Leisure is suggested even more forcibly if he goes to the park of a fine summer morning. In the afternoon people may be supposed to have brought the day's labors to a close, to have done their usual stint of work and earned the right to *flâner*. But American eyes do not easily accustom themselves to the sight of a great multitude in a busy metropolis, beginning the day's entertainment, a couple of hours after breakfast, by going to sit in a public garden and watch several hundred ladies and gentlemen gallop past them on horseback. To the great commercial *bourgeoisie*, which constitutes "American society," this free disposal of the precious morning hours is an unattainable luxury. The men are attending to business; they are immersed in offices, counting-houses, and "stores." The ladies are ordering the dinner, setting the machinery of the household in motion for the day, finding occupation among their children. To people brought up in these traditions there is, therefore, something very—what shall I call it?—very picturesque, in these elegant matutinal groups, for whom the work of life is done to order, and who lose so little time of a morning in beginning the play.

They seem to have time enough, in all conscience; why should they be in such a hurry to begin? Here you catch that "leisured class" the absence of which is so often pointed out to you as the distinguishing feature of our awkward civilization, and the existence of which in England is, to many good Americans, a source of envy, admiration, and despair—here you catch it in the very act, as it were; and you may stroll about and envy and admire it as much as you find warrant for. It is very good looking, very well dressed; it sits very quietly, looking without eagerness at passing things, and talking about them without striking animation. Women, all over the world, have less to do than men; and these unmortgaged hours are, on the ladies' parts, comparatively natural. What an American particularly notices is the number of disengaged men; well dressed, gentlemanly, agreeable fellows, who have nothing more urgent to do, at twelve o'clock in the morning, than to stroll about under green trees, with a stick and a pair of gloves in their hands, or to sit with their legs crossed and murmur soft nothings to a lady in a Gainsborough hat. And in all this I am speaking only of the spectators; I am not including the show itself—the fine folks in the carriages and the happy folks on horseback.

If the spectators testify to English leisure, the carriages testify more particularly to English incomes. To keep a carriage and pair in London costs, I believe, about five hundred pounds a year; the number of people driving about at this expense defies any powers of calculation at the command of the contemplative stranger. The carriages flock into the park in thousands; they roll along in dense, far-stretching masses;

they stand locked together in a wilderness of wheels and cock-
ades. In the morning, however, they are few in number, and
you may bestow your attention upon the Row, which is at
any time, indeed, a much prettier sight. It is the prettiest sight
possible, and it shows you the finest side of English idleness.
There is every kind of horse save the ugly one, and if it is not
quite equally true that there is every kind of rider save the bad
one, at least the bad ones are few and far between. The good
Homer sometimes nods, and the good Englishman has sometimes a slippery saddle. I have heard American ladies say that
they were "disappointed" in Rotten Row; but for myself, I
was never disappointed. I don't exactly know what my countrywomen expected; but they have in everything, I know, a
high standard. A young English girl, in a habit without a
wrinkle, mounted upon a beautiful English horse, with health
in her cheek and modesty in her eye, pulling up, flushed and
out of breath, at the end of a long gallop, is a picture in which
I can pretend to pick no flaws. "Ah, pulling up," my disappointed countrywoman will say; "when they have pulled up
they are doubtless very well; it is their rapid motion that is
not what we have been taught to believe it." And she will go
on to say that these disappointments are an old story, and
that there is nothing like coming to Europe and seeing for
one's self.

However few my own disappointments, I have, as I said
just now, usually brought my sessions in Hyde park to a premature close, and wandered away to the shady precinct of the
old red palace which stares across the pond, and which has, I
believe, a respectable collection of historical associations. It
was, I believe, in Kensington Palace that the present Queen
passed a large part of her youth; it was there that the news of
her accession was brought to her. It is a modest, homely, but
delightful old residence, and so much more agreeable of aspect than the villanous pile which overlooks St. James's park,
that the privilege of living there might reconcile one to being
on the steps of the throne rather than on the throne itself
(Buckingham Palace being habitable, I believe, only by the
sovereign, and Kensington being allotted to the sovereign's
near relations). London—apropos of this matter—is, compared with continental capitals, singularly destitute of royal

residences. Buckingham Palace is lamentably ugly; St. James's Palace is less shabby only because it is less pretentious; Marlborough House is hidden away in a courtyard, and presents no face whatever to the world. Marlborough House is, indeed, completely effaced, as the French say, by the neighboring clubs in Pall Mall. You have to go but a short distance out of London, however, to see two of the most beautiful of all royal seats. One of the first of your excursions in the lengthening days is, as a matter of course, to Windsor. Windsor Castle, as you see it from the train, while you are yet at some distance from the station, massing its long cluster of towers and battlements against the sky, is quite as impressive as the one considerable residence of English sovereigns should be.

If these sovereigns have fewer dwelling places than most other members of the royal fraternity, they may at least claim that their single castle is the most magnificent of castles. Nothing can well be more royal than the tremendous mass of Windsor, looking down from its height over the valley of the Thames, and the vast expanse of its park and forest. As you turn into the town, out of the station, you find yourself confronted with the foundations of the castle, along whose rugged base, and the steep on which it is perched, the little High street wanders in pygmy fashion. It has been my misfortune that at the time of each of my visits to Windsor the interior of the palace was not being shown; this is the case whenever the Queen is living there. But I must add that I use the term "misfortune" here in a great measure for form's sake. The rooms at Windsor are, I believe, numerous and interesting; they contain, among other treasures, some very fine pictures. But when I reflect that I should have had to go through them in the company of a large assemblage of fellow starers, "personally conducted," like Mr. Cook's tourists, by a droning custodian, and shuffling in dull, gregarious fashion over the miles of polished floor and through the vistas of gilded chambers in which they are requested not to "touch"—when the memory of this ordeal, frequently repeated in earlier years, comes back to me, I cannot help feeling a diminution of regret.

The "observant stranger" ought perhaps to be ashamed to confess to such levity, but a couple of years of indoor sight-seeing will have done a good deal toward making him ask himself whether the most beautiful rooms in the world are worth visiting in one of these bands of centripetal stragglers. The thing is disagreeable; one is not bound to say how or why. It is disagreeable to wander about any house—be it even Windsor Castle—without entering into relation with the master; and at Windsor and some other great houses the casual visitor is not only referred to the servants, but actually denied entrance unless the proprietor be absent. It is, however, one's fellow starers, one's fellow shufflers, that make the shoe pinch. It appears to be a fundamental rule of human nature, lying lower than the plummet of analysis will drop, that one shall, for the time, despise such people. On the continent, perhaps, you can keep better terms with them; they are usually, like yourself, foreigners in the country, and this gives them a cosmopolitan, independent air which tempers their subjection to the housekeeper or the beadle. But in England, wherever you go, there are usually fifty English people there before you; and the class which, in England, indulges in the inspection of native monuments, appears to be for the most part the class for which the housekeeper and the beadle have irresistible terrors.

Even when the apartments at Windsor are closed, the great terrace behind the castle is open, and this lordly platform is one of the finest things in the world. I talk of its being "behind" the castle, but I have no warrant for attempting to distinguish between back and front in an edifice of such irregular magnificence. The terrace, at any rate, looks over a beautiful country, and straight down at the playing fields of Eton, which are bordered by the sinuous Thames. It is not beneath the dignity of this line of observation to relate that the last time I was at Windsor I strolled along the terrace—it has a magnificent length—toward a point at which a portion of it is marked off by an iron railing for the use of the inhabitants of the castle. Here a gentleman was standing, with his back against the parapet, looking up intently at the wall. At the narrow window of a tower was placed the face of a housemaid, which was removed a moment after I had perceived it. The gentleman carried, slung over his shoulder, an opera glass, of which he appeared not to have made use.

Turning to me very solemnly—"I think it was the Queen," he said.

"Do you mean that person at the window?" I inquired.

"Yes; she looked at me a long time, and I looked at her."

"I thought it was a housemaid," I rejoined.

He shook his head. "She looked very much like the Queen. She looked just like her photographs."

"Possibly," I said. "But she had on a housemaid's cap."

Once more he shook his head and lifted his eyes to the empty window. "She looked at me a long time," he murmured, "and I looked at her. I am sure it was the Queen." And I left him in the happy faith that he had sustained the awful gaze of royalty out of a back staircase window.

I left him in order to walk back under the castle arches and through the triple courts, through the town and across the bridge to Eton; and then come up into the town again, hire a vehicle at the stand beneath the granite walls, and take a long drive in the park. Eton college is on the other side of the Thames; you approach it by a long, dull, provincial street, consisting apparently chiefly of print shops, filled with portraits of the pretty women of the period. I approached it with a certain sentimental agitation, for I had always had a theory that the great English schools are delightful places to have been to. A few weeks before this I had paid a short visit to Winchester, and in the grounds of the venerable college which adjoins that ancient town I had seen a hundred rosy lads playing cricket (I am counting the lookers-on), with as business-like a jollity as if the ball were rebounding from the maternal bosom of Britannia herself. The courts of the old college, empty and silent in the eventide; the mellow light on the battered walls; the great green meadows, where the little clear-voiced boys made gigantic shadows; the neighborhood of the old cathedral city, with its admirable church, where early kings are buried—all this seemed to make a charming background for boyish lives, and to offer a provision of tender, picturesque memories to the grown man who has passed through it. Eton, of a clear June evening, must be quite as good, or indeed a great deal better.

The day I speak of was a half-holiday, and the college itself was pretty well deserted. It consists of a couple of not particularly ornamental quadrangles, a good deal the worse for wear, a fine old chapel, and a queer bronze statue of Henry II., the founder of the school. All this stands near the river, among goodly trees, and hard by are the masters' houses, in which the boys are lodged. A good many of the boys were strolling about, in their little man's hats and broad collars; this was apparently a holiday costume. Some of them were buying tarts from a wheedling Jew, who had rested his basket on the parapet of the schoolhouse green; some were looking at the types of female beauty in the print-sellers' windows; one was very carefully carrying a jug full of some foaming liquid home from the pastry cook's. Beyond the houses, toward the river, some of them were playing at their eternal cricket. The river, just here, is very pretty; the great elms, in the meadows beside it, are magnificent; there is a bosky-looking little island in the middle, and silvery reaches up and down; and from the further side the castle looks down with a kind of maternal majesty. This is the extent of my knowledge of Eton. I had a letter of introduction to an excellent little boy—it was from his mamma; but I had not the heart to spoil his half-holiday by making him play *cicerone* to my dismal seniority.

So, as I said, I drove away through Windsor park; through the Long Walk, which stretches from the castle gates for the space of three miles, bordered with trees as old, very nearly, as the English monarchy, and quite as solid, to a great grassy mound on which a rather ridiculous statue of George III. is perched. The statue stares across the interval at the castle, and the great avenue—thanks to its very perfection—looks like a much smaller affair than it is. But nothing in Windsor park is small. I drove for some fifteen miles, and everywhere the great trees were scattered over the slopes and lawns; everywhere there was a glimpse of browsing deer; everywhere, at the end of cross-roads, the same wooded horizon. It is the perfection of park scenery, the noblest of all parks. I drove to Virginia Water, and left my carriage to come and meet me at some unknown point, to which my driver directed my steps. The walk proved charming; it led me over the grass and under the trees—and such trees, always—for a couple of miles, beside an agreeable lake. It was all delightfully sylvan, and almost solitary; and yet it retained the comfortable park character.

There was no losing of one's way nor scratching away under-brush; and there was at the end a little inn, as pretty as a tavern in a comic opera, at which it was not impossible to lunch. I drove back through other avenues and over other slopes, with an occasional view of the long-outlined castle above the tree tops. There had been a great deal of it, and yet I had seen nothing of the forest.

Hampton Court Palace is always open, and you are free to wander through the apartments as you list. They form indeed a museum of second and third-rate works of art—a kind of pictorial hospital. Most of the pictures are doubtful specimens of the great masters whose names are affixed to their frames; there are a few very good ones, however, of a more modest attribution. The long row of great drawings in tempera by Andrea Mantegna, representing the triumph of Julius Cæsar, are alone worth a moderate pilgrimage; and the collection of meretricious countesses of the Restoration, by Lely, is very brilliant in its own peculiar way. The great charm of Hampton Court is not, however, in the pictures; it would not be even if these were a great deal better. It is the old red palace itself that is chiefly delightful; its great round-windowed, stone-embossed courts; its long, warm-colored front and sides; its brown old chambers with their dusky canvases, their fireplaces, and their tapestry; its beautiful formal garden, with its close-clipt lawns, its shaded walks, its curious yews, and its Dutch-looking canal.

Of all the suburban lions Hampton Court is the most cockneyfied; London holiday-makers flock down there in hundreds, and spread themselves over the place, which is especially dedicated to that form of popular entertainment known as "school feasts." These simple festivals are celebrated within the enclosure of Bushey park, just beyond the palace gardens. There would be something inhuman in saying that they spoil the place for the solitary, selfish stroller; inasmuch as they are a source of entertainment to crowds of underfed little Londoners, who make a juvenile uproar under the great horse-chestnuts. I hasten, therefore, to say that on the three or four occasions when I have spent the afternoon at Hampton Court, the presence of the London contingent has never been fatal to my enjoyment. The place has such an honest, friendly charm, that it seems good-naturedly to refuse to be vulgarized; and your fellow cockneys become, as it were, a part of the homely animation of the landscape, like the greedy swans in the canal or the very tame deer in the park. The school children, moreover, with their dusky pinafores and clumsy gambols, their tea tables and omnibuses, all, for reasons best known to themselves, herd together near the park gates. Ten minutes' walk will carry you out of sight or sound of them; and you may stroll down the great vistas of horse-chestnut without the fear of encountering any object more displeasing than a young man on an occasional bench, encircling the waist of his sweetheart, or a young person sketching difficult foliage at the base of one of the trees.

Bushey park consists of a single long avenue of trees in a double row; that is, there are four lines of trees. At about a quarter of its length this avenue is crossed by another, which puts out two arms—two high green corridors—of almost equal magnitude. All this foliage is magnificent; and we know what the horse-chestnut is capable of. One afternoon it was very warm—warm enough (far too rare a blessing in England) to fling one's self on the grass at the base of one of the giant trunks. I made a point of doing so, and spent a couple of hours in this attitude, in the faintly stirred shade, watching the soft, still evening close in. You must do something of this kind, to feel the charm of an old English park. It has more to say to you, a great deal more, than it can ever say as you pass by in the most neatly appointed "fly," or even as you stroll along in company the most exempt from a vulgar sense of unexpectedness. During an idle lounge in the mellowing, fading light, the beautiful quality of the place steals irresistibly over your spirit, the air seems charged with serene antiquity and accumulated peace, and the rustle of the leaves strikes you as the continuous sound made in their passage by the hours and years which have given all this its quiet chance to grow. To the contemplative stranger who permits himself not only to talk sentimental nonsense, but to think it, it seems as if, somehow, all England had been gathered up into such a place—as if nothing less than her glorious past, her wealth, her power, her honor, her uninvaded centuries, had been needed to produce it.

Another charm of Hampton Court is its being directly upon the river, which flows beside the long, ivy-muffled brick wall of the gardens. Nothing can be prettier than the walk on the further side of this wall, whose charming old mottled red extent you have on one hand, as you have the grassy bank of the Thames on the other. After a while the wall stops and a tall iron paling begins. Its interstices are choked with shrubbery, but they permit you to look into the great, peaceful, private expanse of the Home park. Its timbered acres stretch away with a very grand air, and it seems to be simply a park for a park's sake. There- [   ] duced gentlewomen who occupy apartments in the palace, at the Queen's pleasure, are free to take their exercise there; and for picturesqueness's sake I ought certainly to have seen a couple of them, in eventide gossip, dragging a scanty train over the soft grass. I must add that you see more of the Home park from within the gardens. The limit of these is marked by a sort of semicircular canal, of the quaintest aspect, ornamented with shaven banks, and with huge water-lilies and swans. Directly opposite the centre of the palace this artificial pool puts forth a long, straight arm, which stretches away into the Home park to a great distance, and makes one of those geometrical vistas that old-fashioned monarchs used to like to look at from their palace windows. This one is bordered with tall, stiff trees, and is a model of its kind. Round about it the park expands immensely, and you may look at it all across the canal, over a little fence.

As for the river, in talking about London suburbs we should have come to that first of all. The Thames is the great feature of suburban London; and these neighborhoods are, for the most part, worth describing only as they bear some relation to it. Londoners appreciate their river in the highest degree; and they manifest their regard in a thoroughly practical fashion. They use the Thames: it might almost be said they abuse it. They use it, I mean, for pleasure; for above Chelsea bridge there are happily few traces of polluting traffic. When once indeed, going up the stream, you fairly emerge from the region of the London bridges, the Thames turns rural with surprising quickness. At every bend and reach it throws off something of its metropolitan degradation; with each successive mile it takes on another prettiness. By the time you reach Richmond, which is only nine miles from London, this suburban prettiness touches its maximum. Higher in its course the Thames is extremely pretty; but nothing can well be so charming as what you see of it from Richmond bridge and just above. The bridge itself is a very happy piece of picturesqueness. Sketches and photographs have, I believe, made it more or less classical. The banks are lined compactly with villas embowered in walled gardens, which lie on the slope of Richmond hill, whose crest, as seen from below, is formed by the long, bosky mass of Richmond park.

To speak of Richmond park is to speak of one of the loveliest spots in England. It has not the vast extent of Windsor, but in other respects it is quite as fine. It is poor work talking of English parks, for one is reduced to ringing the changes on a few lamentably vague epithets of praise. One talks of giant oaks and grassy downs, of browsing deer and glades of bracken; and yet nine-tenths of what one would say remains unsaid. I will therefore content myself with observing that, to take a walk in Richmond park and afterward repair to the Star and Garter inn to satisfy the appetite you have honestly stimulated, is as complete an entertainment as you are likely to find. It is rounded off by your appreciation of the famous view of the Thames from the windows of the inn—the view which Turner has painted and poets have versified, and which certainly is as charming as possible, though to an American eye it just grazes, a trifle painfully, the peril of over-tameness. But the river makes a graceful, conscious bend, and wanders away into that thick detail of distance characteristic of the English landscape.

Richmond is in every way the most beautiful of the environs of London. I had a sense of it during a couple of visits that I lately paid to a delightful old house on the outskirts of the town. This was such an old house as we should go barefoot to see in America, though in this happy land of domiciles with antecedents it enjoys no particular distinction. It stands close to the river; it dates from the reign of Queen Anne; it has a red brick front and elaborate cornices and copings; it is guarded by a high brick wall and tall iron gates. Within, it is rich in wainscoted parlors, with rococo mouldings and carvings, to which you ascend by a great square staircase that is panelled and embellished in proportion. Opposite, on the other side of the river, are the villas and lawns of Twickenham. Close at hand, among converging, overshadowing elms, is a strange, haunted-looking mansion, with weedy gardens and foreign medallions set in its face. Beyond this are the great botanical gardens of Kew; behind is Sudbrook park and the greater extent of Richmond park. Staying there, one need not be at loss for a walk.

And then you have the river. When I said just now that Londoners and suburbans use their river, I meant in the first place that they dwell upon its edges as closely as possible, and in the second place that they set themselves afloat upon it in tremendous force. From early spring to the last of the autumn, the river is given up to boating. Wherever you approach it the symptoms of this pastime are in the foreground; there are always a dozen young men with bare legs and jerseys pulling themselves up and down in cigar-shaped boats. There are boats, indeed, of every form and dimension: sharp-cutting wherries, in which the occupant seems to be sitting on the back of a knife-blade; uncomfortable canoes, in which he paddles with an awkward movement, as if he were bailing out a sinking craft; capacious barges, containing a party in which a lady usually reclines in the stern and plays coxswain. Of a summer afternoon these innumerable water parties make a very pretty bustle. I took a boat at Richmond on such an afternoon, and rowed up to Teddington, whence I walked along the towing path to Hampton Court. Between Richmond and Teddington the riverside is an unbroken succession of small country houses, each perched upon a lawn as smooth as a billiard table and dipping its border into the water. The prettiness, smoothness, trimness, cottage-of-gentility look of all this is quite inexpressible.

I said just now that the view from Richmond was "overtame," and I hardly know how to qualify the impression it produces when looked at in detail. It seems like a country that is over-ripe; that cannot afford any more mellowing. The innumerable boats, the little green carpet-patches on the banks, the perfectly appointed cottages, the people sitting on the painted-looking lawns, with whom you can almost converse from across the stream—these things suggest a kind of imminent repletion, a climax of maturity. And yet I don't suppose that another season's sunshine will begin to bruise the mellow earth, or that the boats will crowd the water out of its channel. The villas and cottages will go on being let as eligible residences, and young men in white flannel will feather their oars for all generations to come. It has lately become greatly the fashion to row down from Oxford, devoting a week to the voyage, and sleeping at the riverside inns. I can imagine nothing more charming, if—to measure the matter rather grossly—you carry a week's dinner in the boat.

If I had not almost exhausted my space I should here devote a parenthesis to the singular meagreness of the British larder as exemplified at the village inn whose scented porch and latticed windows the poets and story-tellers have taught us in America to venerate. During a series of suburban afternoons it often happens that one applies for the evening meal at a tavern of prepossessing aspect, but usually with no greater profit than the right to register one's experience in that list of strange anomalies in which the tradition of English "comfort" is so prolific. One day I came down the river to Teddington, which I reached at half-past seven in the evening. As I had the prospect of not arriving in London till nearly ten o'clock, I went in quest of a house of entertainment. I found one on the river bank, standing in a garden, the perfection apparently of a rural hostelry, and adorned with the sign of the "Angler." I enter the establishment and am met on the threshold, with every manifestation of hospitality, by a prosperous-looking host and hostess who have emerged from a snug and shining bar. I ask if I can be provided with dinner, and I receive an affirmative answer. It seems, however, to lack a certain savory downrightness, and I further inquire of what the dinner will be composed. I am informed that it will be composed of *cold 'am*, and I can prevail upon my entertainers to add nothing else to the *menu*. This is apparently considered by an English innkeeper a very handsome offer; the *ultima ratio* of the frigid joint is thrust at you with a stolid complacency which in the anguish of a disappointed stomach you pardonably qualify as barbaric. But the phase of disappointment passes away, and you permit yourself to decide, once for all, that the English innkeeper lacks the culinary sense. Public opinion asks too little of him.

One evening I came back late from the country; it was a quarter past nine when I arrived in London. My dinner had been too long deferred, and I determined to obtain it without further delay. The station at which I had alighted was adorned, like most of the London stations, with a huge railway hotel. I entered this establishment, and, being directed to the coffee room, ascended a monumental staircase and passed along a corridor remarkable for its sober-colored massiveness and elegance. Everything here was a pledge of comfort, abundance, succulence. The coffee room was as vast and impressive as a cathedral; and the high priest and his acolyte—the waiter and a little page—approached me with a solemnity which seemed to promise a formal initiation into its most savory mysteries. The usual request for dinner was followed by the usual offer of cold meat, to which, being faint from inanition, I reluctantly assented. This attractive repast was set before me, flanked on either side by a chunk of bread and a mustard pot. It made a pitiful figure beneath the gilded vault of the coffee room, and I succumbed to a pardonable desire to give it an harmonious accessory. A simple expedient to this end seemed to be to ask for some potatoes. Hereupon followed this dialogue:

"We have no potatoes, sir."

"You have no potatoes?"

"No, sir. We have no potatoes, sir."

"Isn't that very extraordinary?"

"Yes, sir. We have no potatoes, sir."

"You never have potatoes, perhaps. The absence of potatoes is perhaps a specialty of this hotel?"

"Yes, sir. We have no potatoes after nine o'clock, sir."

The waiter was a very "fine man"; he was in evening dress. Near him stood the little page, with a hundred polished buttons on his jacket. I looked from one to the other, and then I looked up at the gilded dome and the stately pilasters of the room. This operation concluded, I addressed myself to what I have called the frigid—and I may now add the rigid—joint. But I am sorry to conclude in this plaintive key. If I had not exhausted my space, I should speak of the satisfaction of going down to Greenwich, at the duskier end of the Thames, and eating at the Ship hotel the best of all possible dinners.

1877

London in the Dead Season

THERE ARE moments when it seems to savor of affectation to talk of London at any time as "empty"—to declare, in the language of the locality, that there is not a creature in town. But everything is relative, and it is not to be denied that at this time of the year the noisiest city in the world is apt to become peculiarly quiet. Bond Street is tranquil and Picca- dilly is soundless; the knocker is dumb in genteel neighbor- hoods, the little double-tap of the postman even becomes unfamiliar, and the ear is conscious only of the creaking boots of the lonely policeman as he slowly marches through a vista of darkened windows. I don't know how the policeman likes his solitude and his leisure; but there is something about London in its interlunar swoon, as Shelley says, which an occasional survivor of the fashionable period finds decidedly agreeable. It may be that as an adoptive rather than a native cockney I exaggerate its charms at the present moment, ac- cording to the rule that converts are always apt to be fanatics. If you like London for itself, as the phrase is, you get more of London itself at this time than at any other. You enjoy a kind of monopoly of certain parts of it, and you appreciate some of those great features which, at any time from January to July, are thrown into the background by the crowd and the bustle. I will not attempt to enumerate the features in question, or suffer myself to be beguiled into an attempt to demonstrate that among the gentle influences of September the British me- tropolis takes on an unsuspected loveliness. One's enjoyment here at such a time must after all be mainly, as the metaphysi- cians say, subjective. It comes from the sense of boundless leisure—of the absence of interruptions. This operates as a kindly revelation of the crowded quality of existence during the lively portion of the year. For a person leading, in how- ever small a degree, what is called a "London life," a fair, smooth, open stretch of time—without visits or notes or so- cial obligations—becomes the ideal of felicity.

If this ideal is realized at present, there are of course losses in the matter as well as gains. The London clubs, in the early autumn, betake themselves to house-cleaning; the familiar portal of your favorite resort is shut in your face, with the imperfect compensation of an announcement that for the next few weeks you are at liberty to make use of another establishment. At the other establishment you feel a good deal like an intruder; you are unfamiliar with the customs of the place—you imagine that the servants and members glower at you, as you go and come—you feel that there is a want of confidence in your deportment, that you are not welcomed, but only tolerated. In so far, however, as a club is a place for reading the papers, that at the present time is soon done; and if a gentleman should happen to want the copy of the *Times* which you have in hand you will not deprive him of it for many minutes. The morning journals are distinctly dull; in the absence of stirring intelligence the smallest contributions are thankfully received. That ingenious species of composition and product of our time, known as the "social article," receives particular attention; it is usually of a jocular cast and—once a text, or a pretext, is secured—is remarkable for the facility of its transitions. That characteristic of English manners which is supposed by strangers to be the leading one—the passion for "writing to the *Times*"—is at present a great godsend to that journal. I am ignorant whether the *Times* receives during the months of August and September a greater number of confidential epistles from the injured or the gratified, the disappointed, the swindled, the inquisitive, or the communicative Briton, but it certainly prints a great many more. One class of communications comes to it, of course, in especial abundance—the complaints of English travellers who are taking a holiday upon the Continent. There is a daily outpouring of grievances into the maternal bosom of the great newspaper; and I think there are few spectacles more striking and suggestive to a stranger. A stranger makes all kinds of reflections upon it, but he ends on the whole, decidedly, with admiring it. It is ridiculous, in many ways—sordid, egotistical, obtrusive; but it throws an interesting light upon that feature of the English character which is so intimately connected with the greatness of England—the stubborn sense of the rights of the individual. The English individual has not only a stronger, but a much more definite, conception of his rights than any other; he has a more definite and more cultivated notion of justice. It is this definiteness that is the striking point. Theoretically, an American has quite as lively a sense of his dues; but practically, politics apart, his notion of what these dues consist of is exceedingly vague and amateurish. An Englishman never hesitates; he has them at his fingers' ends. The magnitude of the infraction matters little; his comfort is as sensitive as his honor; the principle is sacred that the *other* part of the bargain—the part complementary to his own (which he has discharged by paying a certain sum of money or taking a certain course)—shall be performed rigidly and to the letter. No American who has known many Englishmen can have failed to be struck with the trouble his friends have often been willing to take for the redress of grievances which have seemed to him trifling and not worth time and temper; and many Englishmen, on the other hand, who have been acquainted with Americans, must often have been amazed at the good humor of the latter—the blank serenity, akin to the Mussulman's assent to fate—under imposition, delay, incivility. What is meant by "English comfort" is at bottom but this fixed standard of punctuality and of deference to the expectations of the consumer; and it is very certain that life is very comfortable—for consumers, of course—in a country where no offence against this standard is accounted venial.

I should give a very false impression of the current hour in London if I failed to say that for the last three days the newspapers have contained something very different from the usual complaints of leaking lamps in railway carriages and of the heavy boots worn at night in the corridors of Swiss hotels. A very terrible accident occurred on the 3d ult. on the Thames—an accident which has added a peculiar gloom to the actual soberness of London. A small, overcrowded steamer, returning from an excursion to Gravesend, was run down by a big collier and sunk in an instant, with seven hundred persons on board. This huge calamity will, of course, long since have been made known in America, and you will have been spared those horrible details in which the voluminous reports published here abound. The collision took place just above Woolwich, and the latest computation appears to be that six hundred persons have perished. I have, at various idle moments, found entertainment in a sixpenny steamer, and may almost claim familiarity with that dusky stretch of the Thames which lies between Woolwich and London. The adoptive cockney, of whom I spoke just now, feels a curiosity to sound the depths of metropolitan amusement, and he has been known, under the guidance of this feeling, to push his researches even as far as Gravesend—a very shabby resort of pleasure, now for some time to be associated with the hideous disaster of three days since. The Thames scenery between London and Gravesend is anything but beautiful, but it has always seemed to me to have a certain sordid picturesqueness. There was entertainment to the eye in the dusky, irregular waterside, which seemed to stand begging to be "etched," and in the large, turbid, crowded river, with the slow-moving vessels almost fixed in it, as if it were liquid glue. The place seemed dingy and dreary, but it never seemed tragical—any more than the participants in a Gravesend excursion looked like actors in a tragedy.

I can speak of such an assemblage from observation, for on a certain hot Sunday, some time ago, I found myself in the midst of one. Partly as an enquiring stranger and partly as the victim of a misconception of the attractions of Gravesend I went to the latter place by train, to take the air. After taking as much of it as seemed agreeable, I returned to London with a very big crowd on a very small boat—the same rotten little steamer, possibly, which collapsed at a touch the other night. In so far as my expedition served as a study of the manners of the British populace it was highly successful, and the objects of that study have remained vividly imprinted on my memory. Gravesend itself can best be described by an expression borrowed from the feminine vocabulary: it is simply too dreadful. It is an extremely dirty and most ingeniously vulgar little place, close upon the river, whose bank is adorned with a row of small establishments, half cottage and half shop, devoted to traffic in shrimps and tea. The doors of these little tea-houses are garnished with terrible maidens—very stout and robust, high-colored and loud-voiced—who dart forth at the wayfarer, tea-pot in hand, and, vociferating in his ears certain local formulas, almost hustle him into their unappetizing bowers. Behind the town is a place of entertainment known as the Rosherville Gardens, where there are more conveniences of the kind I have described, together with a hundred others in the way of rock-work and plaster statues and convivial grottoes. The British populace, returning from what the advertisements call a "happy day" at Rosherville, struck me, on the steamer, rather less favorably than an adoptive cockney could have wished. I had nothing to do for a couple of hours but to sit upon the paddle-box and watch it; but there was no great charm in the spectacle. The "people" in certain foreign countries, notably in France and Italy, is a decidedly more remunerative spectacle than the moneyed class. It strikes one as containing more than half the vivacity and originality of the nation. But this is far from being the case here. There is something particularly coarse and dusky about an English mob, something which is not redeemed even by its great good-nature, and which comes, I think, in a great measure from the absence of the look of taste and thrift in the women. I don't know, however, that this reflection is at all pertinent to the horrible disaster which occurred last Tuesday, and which has made, for the week, a kind of charnel-house of all the Woolwich shore. With all its imperfections on its head, a very considerable group of the London populace was cruelly submerged. There will be an enquiry and a good deal of sensational reporting, and then the whole episode will sink beneath the surface as the boatload of excursionists sank. Meanwhile the grouse-shooting and the destruction of pheasants and partridges will proceed apace. A very large number of Englishmen are just now engaged in this pastime, and in the great stillness of London you can almost hear the crack of the fowling-pieces on the northern moors. A great many legislators are within earshot of this delightful sound; a few others are listening to the even sweeter music of their own voices. The *Times* has a regular corner devoted to Parliament out of session, which has lately contained several long speeches from honorable members to their constituents. But for the moment the public mind—or, at any rate, the private mind—is not political.

In Scotland

EDINBURGH, September 25, 1878.

Now THAT the metropolis is so inanimate I hardly need apologize to you for writing from a livelier place than London. It is not making an exorbitant claim for Edinburgh to say that at present it deserves this description, for it has simply gained by the departed life of its sister capital. This afternoon, with a military band playing in the long green garden below Princes Street, in the shadow of the magnificent mass of the Castle Rock, with a host of well-dressed people collected to listen to the music; with the brilliant terrace above adorned with prosperous hotels and besprinkled with tourists divided between the attractions of shop-fronts and the striking picture formed by the Old Town and its high-perched citadel—this admirable Edinburgh looked like a very merry place. Scotland is a highly convenient play-ground for English idlers, and Edinburgh, during the early autumn, comes in for a great deal of the bustle produced by the ebb of the southern tide. For the last six weeks this annual current has been irrigating (not to say irritating) the Scottish moors and mountains; and it is hardly too much to say that at this period you must come to Scotland to see what England is about.

When I came hither myself, a little more than a fortnight ago, there were still plenty of members of the large class which has autumnal leisure to spare, hurrying northward. The railway-carriages were occupied, and the platforms of the stations ornamented, by ladies and gentlemen in shooting-jackets of every pattern and hue. I say "ladies" advisedly, for the fairer members of these groups had every appearance of being sporting characters. I do not know what may be the feminine costume of this particular period in America, but here it consists of a billycock hat with a very small brim, a standing collar of a striped or figured linen, like that belonging to a "fancy" shirt, a scarf in a sailor's knot, a coachman's overcoat, made of some cross-barred material like the nether integuments of a "nigger-minstrel," and a petticoat clinging as closely as a pair of tight trousers and effectually completing the illusion. The proper accessories of such a figure are a gentleman draped rather more redundantly, and an aggregation of luggage consisting of a good many baskets and bath tubs, of several *fasces* of fishing-rods, and divers gun-cases that look like carpet-bags flattened and elongated by steam-pressure; the whole set off by a couple of delightful setters or retrievers fastened to the handle of a trunk, and, amid the bustle of the railway-platform, turning themselves about and sniffing at this and that in touching bewilderment. A friend of mine, an American, was once asked to mention the two features of English life which had made most impression on him. He hesitated a moment, and then he said, "The dogs and the children." The children apart, it is worth coming to Scotland simply to encounter the very flower of the canine race—the beautiful silken-eared animals that follow in the train of the happy Englishmen who have hired a moor at a thousand pounds for six weeks' grouse-shooting. England is certainly the paradise of dogs; nowhere are they better appreciated and understood. But Scotland is their seventh heaven. Of course all the Englishmen who cross the Tweed have not paid a thousand pounds down as the basis of their entertainment, though the number of gentlemen who have permitted themselves this fancy appears to be astonishing. Tourists of the more vulgar pattern, who have simply come to enjoy the beauties of nature and to read the quotations, in the guide-books, from Sir Walter Scott, are extremely numerous, and Scotland, as regards some of the provisions that she makes for them, takes on the air of a humbler Switzerland. One must admit, however, that though the Scotch inns are much better than the English, they do not push their easy triumph very far; they bear the same relation to the Swiss hotels that the scenery of the Highlands does to that of the Alps. But if their merits are not unalloyed, it is not for want of resolution—as, for instance, in the matter of the table d'hôte. The table d'hôte in the British Islands is essentially an importation, an exotic, a drooping and insalubrious flame. But like all new converts the Scotch innkeepers are immoderate; they are of the opinion that of a good thing there can never be too much. A couple of days since, at Stirling, I was invited to be present at a table d'hôte at half-past eight A.M. The idea was sufficient to make the bodies of Meurice and Francatelli turn over in their graves. I am bound to admit, however, that I countenanced this matutinal heresy by my presence; and I again had occasion to reflect upon the extreme punctuality with which, in the British organism, the desire for copious supplies of animal food asserts itself. A week ago, at a table d'hôte at Ballater, just after the company had seated itself, there came a great thump at the head of the table—a rap which caused me to start with the apprehension that I had inadvertently introduced myself into a spiritualistic *séance*. I was speedily reassured—a gentleman growled out a "grace." Nothing, in effect, could have been less spiritual than this performance; but I wondered what, even from a material point of view, the shades of Francatelli and Meurice thought of it.

"This admirable Edinburgh," I said just now; and I must venture to emphasize the fresh approbation of a susceptible stranger. The night of my arrival here was a superb one; the full moon had possession of a cloudless sky. I saw, on my way from the station, that it was working wonders on some very remunerative material; so that after a very brief delay I came forth into the street, and presently wandered all over the place. There is no street in Europe more spectacular than Princes Street, where all the hotels stand in a row, looking off, across the long green gulf that divides the New Town from the Old, at the dark, rugged mass of the latter section. But on the evening of which I speak Princes Street was absolutely operatic. The radiant moon hung right above the Castle and the ancient houses that keep it company on its rocky pedestal, and painted them over with a thousand silvery, ghostly touches. They looked fantastic and ethereal, like the battlements of a magician's palace. I had not gone many steps from my hotel before I encountered the big gothic monument to Scott, which rises on the edge of the terrace into which Princes Street practically resolves itself. Viewing it in the broad daylight of good taste, I am not sure that I greatly care for this architectural effort, which, as all the world knows, consists of a colossal canopy erected above a small seated image of the great romancer. It looks a little too much like a steeple without a church, or like a hat a great deal too big for the head it covers. But the other night, in the flattering moonlight, it presented itself in all respects so favorably that I found myself distinctly what the French call *ému*, and said to myself that it was a grand thing to have deserved so well of one's native town that she should build a towering temple in one's honor. Sir Walter's great canopy is certainly an object which a member of the scribbling fraternity may contemplate with a sort of reflex complacency. I carried my reflex compla-cency—a rather awkward load—up the Calton Hill, whose queer jumble of monuments and colonnades looked really sublime in the luminous night, and then I descended into the valley and watched the low, black mass of Holyrood Palace sleeping in its lonely outlying corner, where Salisbury Crags and Arthur's Seat seemed rather to lose than to define them-selves in the clarified dusk. The sight of all this really splendid picturesqueness suggested something that has occurred to me more than once since I have been in Scotland—the idea, namely, that if that fine quality of Scotch conceit which, if I mistake not, all the world recognizes, is, as I take it to be, the most robust thing of its kind in the world, the wonder after all is not great. I have said to myself during the last fortnight that if I were a Scotchman I too should be conceited, and that I should especially avail myself of this privilege if I were a native of Edinburgh. I should be proud of a great many things. I should be proud of belonging to a country whose capital is one of the most romantic and picturesque in Eu-rope. I should be proud of Scott and Burns, of Wallace and Bruce, of Mary Stuart and John Knox, of the tremendously long list of Scotch battles and heroic deeds. I should brag about the purple of the heather and the colors of the moors, and I should borrow a confidence (which indeed I should be far from needing) from the bold, masculine beauty of my na-tive mountains. Above all, I should take comfort in belonging to a country in which natural beauty and historical association are blended only less perfectly than they are blended in Italy and Greece; whose physiognomy is so intensely individual and homogeneous, and, as the artists say, has so much style.

I am afraid, however, that I am sketching here a fancy pic-ture of Scottish conceit; the chief characteristic of this great gift being its extreme independence—the fact that it is much more personal than national. An Englishman believes in England and a Frenchman in France, but a Scotchman believes in—a Scotchman. The acute Scotch intellect—the *perfervidum ingenium*—believes in itself. Of the frankness with which it can acknowledge national shortcomings I find an interesting example in a speech which Principal Shairp, of St. Andrew's, who was lately the successful candidate for the chair of Poetry at Oxford, has just had occasion to deliver at Edinburgh. The main subject of his remarks was the existing defects in some portions of the present Scotch educational system; but before he had done he devoted some observations to a cognate topic—the tone of Scotch manners. These he described as rather rough and rude, dry and wanting in urbanity; and he attributed the defect to the influence of those two principles which he declared to be paramount on this side of the Tweed—sectarianism and the love of money. "Mr. Matthew Arnold had spoken of the uncivilizedness of Glasgow. That was strong language; but he dared not deny it when he remembered what he himself had seen in walking down the High Street of Glasgow on a Saturday night—a spectacle of human hideousness of which, he believed, no other civilized country could produce a parallel." Among various remedies for this state of things Principal Shairp, as befits a professor of poetry, recommends the perusal of the great bards and the cultivation of music. I am afraid the poets and singers would quite lose their way in Glasgow High Street. It is not for a visitor who has received none but delightful impressions to pretend to agree with Principal Shairp; but there is nothing invidious in saying that an American coming into Scotland after a residence in England cannot fail to be struck with the democratic tone of the common people. They address you as from equal to equal, they are not in the least cap-in-hand, and they are frugal—almost miserly—in the use of the "sir." This is as good a basis of good manners as any other, though of course one can't answer for it when Principal Shairp's "sectarianism" comes in. But I have really no business even to quote such expressions. I have encountered in Scotland but a single sect—the sect whose religion is hospitality.

*   *   *

EDINBURGH, September 30, 1878.

There are two things in England in regard to which I think it safe to say that a stranger, however familiar he may become with English life, remains always a stranger—always uninitiated, profane, and even more or less indifferent. One of these matters is—with all respect be it written—the internal dissensions and perplexities of the Anglican Church. This remarkable body strikes the pure outsider so much more as a social than as a religious institution that he feels inclined to say to himself that these are purely local and national mysteries, and that, so far as he is concerned, they may be left to take care of themselves. The other point is the great British passion for sport—the deepest and most general of all British passions. This, in England, is the touch of nature that makes the whole world kin. A person from another country may have a lively enjoyment of riding, shooting, rowing; but in face of the tremendous cohesiveness of the sporting interest in England he feels that to care for such things as these people do, one must be to the manner born. It will seem to him at times that they care too much, and he will, perhaps, embark upon that interesting line of enquiry, at what particular point the love of physical exercise becomes stultifying. It behooves him to remember, however, that there is one particular way in which the sporting interest in England is humanizing. It is the subject on which the greatest number of Englishmen, at a given moment, can feel together; it is the thing which, as M. Thiers said of the French Republic, divides them least. It serves as a bond of union, as a patch of common ground, in a country extraordinarily cut up by social distinctions; it introduces the leaven of democracy into the most aristocratically constituted society in the world. On the receipt of the latest intelligence from Newmarket a "cad" may feel very much like a lord; I won't, indeed, go so far as to say that a lord may feel like a cad.

What I intended especially to say was that a fortnight spent in Scotland is to the alien mind a kind of revelation of the part allotted to physical recreation in a well-arranged English life. It is very true that I am unable to add that in this particular case the democratic bearings of the fact are noticeable. Scotland, for the late summer and autumn, becomes an immense "shooting." It is excellently arranged for the purpose, and its purple moors and heathery hillsides resolve themselves into the last luxury of a supremely luxurious class. This is the real identity of the various elements of the beautiful Scottish scenery. The uninitiated eye sees nothing but a lovely purple mountain or a blushing moor, adorned with the advantages of aerial perspective. But in its essential and individual character such a piece of landscape is Mr. So-and-So's deer-forest (a deer-forest by no means implies trees) or Lord Such-a-One's provision of grouse. There is something very singular in the part played by Scotland nowadays—the small number of proprietors of the territory, the immense extent of the estates, and the fact that these exist almost wholly for purposes of recreation. I spoke the other day of a Scotchman's just grounds for national pride; but it is fair to add that just here this tendency might perhaps encounter an obstacle. It seems to me that if I were a fervid Caledonian I should find something irritating, and even mortifying, in the sight of my beautiful little country parcelled out, on so immense a scale, into playgrounds for English millionaires. Was it for this that my ancestors bled with Wallace or flocked about Bruce? Doubtless, however, this is an idle line of speculation, for the moors and hillsides are apparently better for playgrounds than for anything else, and if the Sassenach has money to pay for them it is hard to see how he is to be prevented. In the south of Scotland (in Dumfriesshire) a friend with whom I was walking led me up to a hilltop and showed me a remarkable view. The country seemed of immense extent—it consisted of innumerable grassy sheepdowns—and the blue horizon looked ever so far away. The afternoon light was slanting over the long undulations and dying away in the distance; the whole region looked like a little kingdom. "It's all the Duke's," said my friend—"this, twenty miles away, and ever so much besides." In every Scotch or English county there is a personage known as "the Duke" *par excellence*. This fortunate mortal, in the present case, was the Duke of Buccleuch, upon whose remarkable merits as a landlord my companion proceeded to expatiate. What I saw of the Duke's kingdom seemed an admirable grazing country; but elsewhere my observation was confined to picturesque expanses of rock-scattered heath.

Even if they were keeping a superior sort of exploitation at bay, it would be hard, from their own point of view, to blame the deer-stalking and grouse-shooting gentry. I speak not even from the point of view of a sportsman, but simply from that of an unarmed promenader stepping across the elastic heather on a brilliant September morning. On such an occasion the admirable freshness of the Scotch air, the glory of the light and color, the absence from the landscape of economical suggestions, appear to be equal parts of one's entertainment.

This absence of economical suggestions does not in the least mean, however, that the happy residents on a Scotch moor are obliged to rough it. The English, who arrange their lives everywhere so well, arrange them nowhere better than in Scotland. It is indeed, in many cases, simply Mayfair among the heather. From the point of view of a purely Wordsworthian love of nature, a shooting-lodge with ball-room may appear an anomaly; but I encountered this phenomenon in the midst of a Scotch deer-forest. The ball-room, too, was in full operation, and the national dance—the Highland reel—in course of performance. The ladies and gentlemen engaged in this choregraphic revel were by no means all, or even preponderantly, native—a fact which may account for the vivacity of their movements, inasmuch as we know that proselytes are always more violent than the natural heirs of a tradition. Apart, however, from its suggesting that the Highland kilt is an odd sort of garment for ceremonial purposes and the sanctity of the English after-dinner period, the Scotch reel, with its leapings and hootings, its liftings of the leg and brandishings of the arm, is a very pretty country-house frolic. A stranger, looking for local color in everything, finds a great deal of it here; and he pays a compliment, moreover, to the muscular resources and good spirits of those young Englishmen who can dance till three o'clock in the morning after tramping over the moors all day with a gun. Like a good many other things, the reel has doubtless suffered by the conversion of the Highlanders into an adjunct of Piccadilly. Among the things that have suffered, I believe, are the old Highland sports, from which it was intimated to me that the good faith and the ancient cunning had departed. Though it was further intimated to me that one must be a deplorable cockney to be still taken in by them, I ventured to find a great deal of entertainment in what I saw of them. There was certainly one occasion with which it was impossible not to be charmed, including as it did a capital collation under a graceful marquee, not at all crowded, on the edge of a great green meadow that was circled about with hills. Through the front of the tent, largely looped up, one saw the bright-colored little crowd sitting about on the grass, and in the midst, on a platform, a series of Highlanders, one by one, with their great tartans flying, jumping about in the figures of the sword-dance. And then there were leaping and tugging and hurdle-racing and a little tournament of bag-pipes. The lively drone of this instrument came in from the distance with the summer breeze; far away, as an undertone to agreeable talk, it was not unpleasant. I was annoyed at being told the Highlanders were "cads"; and indeed, on a nearer view, they had a rather jaded and histrionic look. But if the play was a comedy, it was a very successful one.

There are some other old Scottish institutions which have retained their vitality and are apparently in very good repair. The Caledonian "Sawbath," I believe, still flourishes, and I am told that in Edinburgh and Aberdeen it may be observed in high perfection. I had a glimpse of it only in the country, where it was mitigated by the charming scenery, which remained persistently and profanely bright. But it was very ugly; it was grotesquely ugly. There was a horrible little kirk on a windy hillside, equally naked without and within—except, indeed, as regards such internal warmth as was supplied by the deportment of a rustic congregation listening in almost voracious silence and immobility to a doctrine addressed to violent theological appetites. My host had recommended me to attend this service (which was an excellent example of grim Presbyterianism) for local color's sake; and certainly the little exhibition was very complete. The strange compound produced in the sermon by the profusion of Jewish names and of Scotch accents; the air of doctrinal vigilance on the part of the cautious, dry-faced auditory; the crude, nasal singing; the rapid dispersal afterwards, over the stony hillsides to their rugged little cottages, of a congregation for which this occasion represented the imaginative side of life, as if the native granite had given it out and had immediately reabsorbed it—all this had at least a character of its own.

Old Scotland survives, however, fortunately, in more graceful forms than this. There is one advantage which European life will long have over American—the opportunity that it affords for going to picnic in the shadow of ancient castles. Given one of those Franco-Scottish fortified dwellings which sprang up so thickly under the influence of that long union between Scotland and France which was produced by their having an enemy in common; given, moreover, one of those admirable English lunch-hampers which, as it exposes its ingenious receptacles to view, the passing stranger pauses to admire in the shop-windows of Piccadilly; given in connection with this instrument a British butler's punctual performance of familiar duties; given, finally, a stretch of greensward, a group of bushes, a peeping above them of grey old towers and battlements, a charming company, and you have the elements of one of the most agreeable episodes of a sojourn beyond the Tweed. Some of the old foreign-looking Scotch castles are admirable; there are very few of them that would not seem very much more in their proper place in France or Germany than in Scotland. The Scotch nobility, before the son of Mary Stuart came to the English throne, must have been intensely Gallicized; the taste for French forms is visible in every detail of their domestic architecture. The old *poivrière*—the "pepper-pot" turret—is almost universal, and the very material of the edifice is Continental. In England it is a very rare thing to find an old manor-house covered with stucco or untimbered plaster; it is almost invariably of honest brick or stone. There is plenty of stucco in English street-architecture, but our own ingenious period must have the credit of it. In Scotland it abounds on the tall sides of the old domiciliary fortresses. One of these interesting monuments struck me as more than French—it was absolutely Italian. On its roof, in the midst of its gables and turrets, it had a couple of balustraded loggias, such as you see in very old Italian villas; and the resemblance was carried out by the large, windowless expanses of grey, rugged, sun-baked plaster on the walls. There is something decidedly Continental, too, in the older portions of the Scotch towns. I except the granitic Aberdeen and the industrial Glasgow; but nothing is less recognizably British than the high-piled, unconventional Edinburgh. The other evening, at Stirling, taking a stroll at hazard, I encountered a *porte-cochère*.

The Question of the Mind

GREAT public convulsions are an upheaval of many things, and are only too apt to destroy more treasure than they collect, to agitate, even fatally to deform, more questions than they settle; so that among the elements let loose and the bewilderments multiplied confusion overtakes inward values no less than outward, matters of knowledge and experience, appreciation, conviction, faith, as one has held them and as one has more or less comfortably lived by so doing. To take a thousand things for granted is to live comfortably, but the very first effect of great world-shocks is to blight that condition by laying bare all our grounds and our supposed roots. We had been believing them very deep down, but of a sudden they are tossed about on the surface, when not tossed high in the air. They are thus exposed to view at least; which, I hasten to add, is a very good thing for many of them, or may become so, and not a bad thing for any.

The difference made, however, meanwhile, by our having to face them as comparative strangers, to introduce ourselves to them afresh and then introduce them afresh to others, dealing with them on new terms and picking them over as people are sometimes figured to pick over their visiting lists with a rise in the world, this difference is perhaps like nothing so much as the obligation, under some strange and violent law, to perform in public and the garish light of day those rites of the toilet or whatever, those common preparations of personal state and appearance, which usually go on behind our most closed doors. Thus springs up a condition still more perturbed than that either of not knowing what to do or of having to do the impossible; predicaments these that may often depend but on indications from without and be relieved by such indications.

The recovery of a straight current of feeling has to come of itself; scattered abroad and so dislodged from the conduit of experience, it affects us with the possibility and the sharp fear of its losing itself before it re-enters a channel. Such an accident may mean waste at the very time when our yearning is most for force; but the difficulty is not that we ourselves are wasteful: that may come much rather while presumption remains unchecked and may in fact often have occurred through the absence of an account to be rendered.

What has perhaps at the very first stage come upon us in such a shaken world as the present is the sense of the huge break in experience, our most intimate and as who should say our most secret; which accordingly leaves us to stare at the separating chasm before we somehow get over to that other side on which we may, or possibly alas, may not, again find life. The dreadful thing seems that experience of so fine an order, the heart's and the soul's experience, the deepest-striking we are capable of, *should* suddenly split after such a fashion and make us feel that we must, by some art never yet practised, tinker it up, patch it together, bridge it over, in order to go on at all.

Happy then if we have not to descend into the abyss, implements in hand, and climb out again to where the opposite ground will bear us, happy if some flight of the imagination, some boldly applied hypothesis, some blest even if casual refreshment of sense, carries us across into air once more breathable; for that does mean experience again, and if the new flows into the vessel that has long contained and been scented by the old, who will say that after all we shall not recognise the savour and the tang?

All of which may perhaps figure too obscurely the fact that the social characteristics, the elements of race and history, the native and acquired values, the whole "psychological" mystery marking the people of Great Britain, were so abruptly thrust into the critical smelting-pot for a citizen of another country, a country up to the present speaking formally neutral, who had spent long years of his life on English soil and in English air, that he at first saw the case in the light in which he has just generalised it. He to-day feels no image too extravagant, none the less, for report of the drama that began so sharply, even if all subjectively, to enact itself on the stage of his anxious spirit; a drama in which the protagonist was to be simply the question of the true worth of his forty years of observation and interest, and the dénouement to crown it, through whatever ups and downs, those quite proper to the stage, with the happy critical climax. I say "simply" because the decision in suspense mattered to this fond observer himself, thrown back upon half his spiritual history, so much more than it could possibly matter to persons either not agitated at all or agitated to more demonstrable and more immediate purpose.

Yet complications really and thrillingly attended, since where would have been the suspense, which I think I must have positively cultivated in the interest of the rapture of final relief, if the fortune of my exposed and imperilled, and hence so ideally recoverable, or in other words positively ponderable, stake didn't seem at moments to sway this way and that? What did one after all, oh what *did* one, as the upshot of experience, "think of the English mind"? I should perhaps blush to translate my figure of the wavering issue, launched on scenic and heroic adventures, into such a pale and lean abstraction; blush, that is, so to translate it for others. To my own view it at once invested itself with every appearance and attribute of life; to that degree in fact as to make dependent upon it my personal consciousness, my own life and reality, all my care for what might happen to anything. I must have intimately known thus that if the action exhibited, the entanglement of my question in its dangers, with the retarded issue, was not, as we say at the play, to end happily, I should feel that I myself had declined into misery.

The great thing, however, was not to let that apprehension interfere; I was no *deus ex machina*, and would have been ashamed to be one; the question was just of the impassioned critic, impassioned because surmounting of a sudden old habits of detachment and ease and springing to his freshly-wiped fieldglass much as the summoned soldier might spring to his rifle, yet of the critic incorruptible withal and prepared to bow to fate even if fate should demolish his subject. My state became, to the exclusion of every other, since none was of comparable *portée*, the state of sought certitude, a certitude difficult but not impossible, and carrying everything with it if it should come.

The situation was of course that what you had supposed or presumed you thought was not now of the smallest consequence: to sleep at night, to hold up your head, or, otherwise expressed, your heart, to go and come save as one of the merely mechanic and bewildered, you had to *know*, and to know with that competence which would rest on your having again and more thoroughly learnt. It was true that to learn was to study, and that the pitch of the public agitation left no spacious air for *that*; every impression one had ever suffered, all impatiences and all submissions, stupefactions and recognitions alike, stale perplexities and sublime conclusions, trooped together into view and, claiming in a vague mixed manner some of them justice and some generosity, still insisted that each represented a truth and had thereby its point to make.

Great the responsibility, surely, when the British intelligence was to be on exhibition on that scale and under such a strain; the eyes of the world having now more attention for it, and of a more searching kind, than at any moment in the whole course of the appeal it had ever made to them. They had indeed, these eyes, an immense call to their different, their very own vast masses of interest; but wouldn't the effect of that be at the same time to quicken rather than restrict for them their awareness of the English affirmation, whether as hostile or as helpful, and so to make the degree and the mode of our display of genius signify, that is count all round, as it had not in all the ages had to?

Well, prodigiously to one's help, at a given moment, and quite simultaneously, turned up these two ideas of our "genius"—for it would, of course, be impossible to doubt that we *had* one—and of our being unprecedentedly in evidence and in peril; by which one meant in peril more particularly of the uncertainties of appreciation. These last would inevitably, and probably very soon, strain themselves clear; so far as to care so much meant to be so much in suspense, this clutch of the formula, this idea of a genius only waiting to be identified, gave relief to the tension and saw me as by a sudden jump ever so much further on the way.

I recognised that what I began these remarks by calling the spirit of experience had yet left undestroyed its main acquisition; which was neither more nor less than that our very genius was what made us—made our intelligence, as I have termed it, our contributive, our exhibitable, virtue, our capacity in fine for *being* on our best behaviour—so consistently worth worrying about. Our best behaviour on every face and in every relation of course—*that* was the impending need; but again, as I say, vagueness waned, or at least began to, from the moment one saw, or at any rate reasoned, that with genius there couldn't not be a light.

So what, when it came to this, had been the former, the ancient light? that of the time, too prolonged perhaps, when for the attached and familiarised individual mind to which I impute these refinements of ponderation almost any behaviour had seemed good enough on the part of so goodnatured, so incorrigibly goodnatured, a people? One thought of tests, the suddenly swarming, the unparalleled, those with which the air fairly darkened, till it struck one that after all one had done little else during the long years that represented experience but apply one's own most intimate of tests. There was the genius, in other words the nature (the good nature, and the incorrigible, again!) of the people, and if one wasn't possessed of it, if one didn't know what to think of it, after living with it on such terms, where could the fault be but in one's own infirmity of wit?

Vaguely recurred in this connection the old anecdote of the member of the *comité de lecture* of the Théâtre Français and his reply to the author of a disapproved play who had remarked to him that as he was asleep while the thing was read he had no right to an opinion. "My dear sir, what was my sleep but an opinion?" were the classic words in consonance with which I asked what a relation so established could be but an affection, and what an affection so successfully tried but an estimate. And yet if it was the collective mind withal that (exactly as in the case of the other belligerents) was to be supremely on exhibition, with the fierce light of history beating on it to the unspeakable pitch, it helped little to call that resource the English genius unless one could express to one's private satisfaction one's resultant measure of the same. What did the article supremely consist of, what had one found it in long converse to consist more of on the whole than of anything else?

The British intellect—how extraordinarily one had passed from the facetious to the earnest use of that prior term!—had done in its out-in-the-world way all the splendid things we knew, which were there, piled up behind, and yet the tradition of which didn't in familiar intercourse testify so directly, so intensely, so measurably or so showily, one might almost say, as one's previous, and indeed one's constant, profit of the general achievement would have led one to expect. There was I in presence of the curious fact that while the actual acute demand for display had pounced on the nation's understanding, had challenged its "mentality," clamouring for attestations, the great note of one's observational experience might really be described as that of the completest incapacity for show, for the current and casual play of the imagination to the impressive or attractive end, that had perhaps ever been seen on earth.

Hadn't it been much like a presentation of the mind, of the intellect, from *behind*, so to speak, and with its face turned precisely the other way from the way at present required? Hadn't the impression been as of an averted or muffled or even reluctant exercise of the faculty, exercise of free energy, free fancy, free curiosity, free wit, however one might name the blest thing—the blest thing that had at the same time been so tremendously recorded, and that was more or less continuing to be, in the documentary evidence of libraries and courts? How could one have lived in the society of so many such matters, in the presence verily of all of them, with those consequences of interest and affection, those visions of illumination and education, if, in spite of the fact that one had so almost inveterately to walk for satisfaction of curiosity, for extraction of value, round from the presented face to the quarter of the averted, the total result of acquaintance hadn't been a peculiar faith?

The answer to all of which, I saw, would meanwhile be no answer if it didn't properly provide for that truth of the genius—the genius that had somehow kept acting and impressing just in proportion as so few pains were taken about it. What was happening, accordingly, that the critic could wonder about the "display"—by which he meant about the absence of it—and yet not wonder in the least about the apparently all so sufficing force? The puzzle might have lasted goodness knows how long hadn't it been for that consciousness of the good nature, incorrigibility and all, felt as fundamental from far back, which one had been looking to right and left of, and to top and bottom of, without discovering that in the very centre of it sat one's sublime solution.

To grasp even in so absurdly delayed a manner the perception that *there* was one's golden key made the whole certitude come on with a rush. It was incredible and impossible that a people should be so incorrigible unless they were strong—no people without a great margin could for any period at all afford to be; and with that *constatation* everything was clear. It didn't matter if they were strong because good-natured, or good-natured because strong: the point was to that extraordinary tune in what they could afford.

This affording became then, to one's infinite recreation, the drama, the picture, and, to repeat the term that was the actual essence of the case, the exhibition, of their life. They were at their ease (there it was!) for their favourite amusement of putting the cart before the horse and the idea out of sight—that is behind, miles behind, everything else. They *kept* the idea in that situation, where one would find it, with one's mistrust fairly unlearnt, if one walked far enough round outside to— well, I won't say its prison, but, by way of a better image, its secret garden. Here it grew with a stoutness that spoke doubtless not so much of cultivation as of the happy patches of parent earth, and here it could be gathered, after the fashion of the savoury seasoning herb, "as required."

If such then was the case for the background by what art did the foreground not only hold together but form to the extent I have noted the place of frequentation the most attaching, not to say even the most edifying, one could have desired? By the art not anywhere else in the world so subtly practised, assuredly—that of so mixing up character, personal or, as who should say, moral, yes, positively, the dear old moral, the instinctively individual, with every other sign of understanding and every other reward of intercourse, in fact with every other condition of it. What it came to in the last fine analysis thus seemed to be that whereas in association with other people you for the most part knew by their conversability what you had got hold of, or whether this were at a given moment their reflective or their active, their cerebral or their practical part, so in the association I had happened most to enjoy there was no such clear and perhaps I should say convenient distinction, convenient in especial for the demonstration of one's grounds. This might certainly represent in regard to the others that conversability worked better, but could it represent that association did?

To put this last question, I quickly recognised, was to find it answered, and with other attendant ones disposed of really by the same stroke; not least that one of the drawback of the usual confusion. Not knowing what one had got hold of might certainly appear at the best and in no matter what connection but a muddled form of appreciation—which appearance was doubtless directly signified by your comfort in the fact that when a Frenchman or an Italian talked he really told you so much about his mind that there seemed little left to tell you about anything else.

Only, if that was satisfactory, so far as it went, and was, so far as the Frenchman and the Italian were concerned, exhaustive, there was then nevertheless no mystery more, nothing of the unexplored and, as you could put it, more eventually and shyly, call it even rather proudly, producible.

The part you had got hold of left you comparatively incurious about the other part. This exhibited, most exhibited part informed you about itself entirely, and tasted of itself, yielding by this reason whatever sharpest or sweetest savour; so that it was upon that luxury one threw one's self and fed, to the full appeasement of one's critical impulse.

If on the other hand you went by the information the Englishman gave you about his mind—the Scotsman's and the Irishman's information about *his* remains, I confess, a matter apart—you didn't by any means go such lengths; if you depended on the taste of that article alone for your sense of his power to nourish or beguile you would find a vast tract of the recorded history of your relation with him unaccounted for; you would have yourself to account for the circumstance, superficially inscrutable but nevertheless so substantial, that in no general intercourse whatever could you as a final result be left less consciously starved. You might be left hungry, beyond doubt; yet wasn't this only that you were left curious, in other words unsatisfied, but because your meal, copious though it should keep on proving, was never all served at one sitting?

The reason of that might well be, no doubt, that it wasn't ready, hadn't been prepared with the punctuality and presentability of those other, those exotic repasts, those from which one got up with the wondrous sense of appetite, properly the sense of curiosity, gratified or gorged.

Such, I made out, was my inevitable figure for that dissipation of mystery in these connections which I had been feeling as an interest and even as a sensation the less at the very time of feeling it as a happy convenience and a lively social exercise the more. This pointed with the last sharpness, you were at any rate all the while conscious, that noted moral of your knowing what you had hold of. But were you then on the side of your experience of the British, roughly taken together, simply to resign yourself to the correspondingly baffled state? Well, yes, verily yes, at last, and for the very best of reasons, a reason quite magnificent, as it could only appear to me, when once I had at least got hold of that affirmative.

There was the savour, the desideratum, the force and quantity, that we have been talking of—a savour immense and extraordinary, in relation to which the muddlement that I have called subjective came directly from the fact that it is not, like the savours to which I just paid tribute, "dished," served, administered after the fashion of precious things in general, isn't perhaps in any degree the result of what passes in other societies for preparation. It grows wild, and I had doubtless partaken of it crude—with the marvellous effect of its not disagreeing with me. Crude things, we know, mostly do disagree: there accordingly and exactly was the mystery that kept imagination on the stretch. Why hadn't it disagreed, why didn't it, why doesn't it? Why above all does it not only at last purge bewilderment of any shade of impatience, but make it a condition, not to say an adventure, romantic and agreeable? If the reply to this just at first hangs fire it floods the subject when it does come with the clearest light in the world.

The wildness, the crudity, the undressed and uneconomised state are themselves the unidentified force, or the force to the identification of which we come nearest when we catch it in its supreme act of good-nature. What a blessing to work round again to the consciousness of *that* clue, the clue of the incorrigibility, in the hand! For the good-nature was the light—the light, ever so vividly, on the character; just as the character was the light, ever so richly and blurringly, but none the less ever so extensively and perspectively, on the mind. So then I stood with my feet on the ground: the case was sole and single, and quite as splendid, yes, as one could have wished it to be. The mind was so drenched with the character, in opposition to the examples in which the character was drenched with the mind, that all one could at the very best feel (though goodness knew indeed it quite sufficed!) was that the value finally run to earth was a value which would do for everything.

1915

Refugees in England

THIS is not a report on our so interesting and inspiring Chelsea work since November last, in aid of the Belgians driven thither from their country by a violence of unprovoked invasion and ravage more appalling than has ever before overtaken a peaceful and industrious people; it is the simple statement of a neighbor and an observer deeply affected by the most tragic exhibition of national and civil prosperity and felicity suddenly subjected to bewildering outrage that it would have been possible to conceive. The case, as the generous American communities have shown they well understand, has had no analogue in the experience of our modern generations, no matter how far back we go; it has been recognized, in surpassing practical ways, as virtually the greatest public horror of our age, or of all the preceding, and one gratefully feels, in presence of so much done in direct mitigation of it, that its appeal to the pity and the indignation of the civilized world anticipated and transcended from the first all superfluity of argument. We live into, that is we learn to cultivate, possibilities of sympathy and reaches of beneficence very much as the stricken and suffering themselves live into their dreadful history and explore and reveal its extent; and this admirable truth it is that unceasingly pleads with the intelligent, the fortunate, and the exempt not to consent in advance to any dull limitation of the helpful idea. The American people have surely a genius, of the most eminent kind, for withholding any such consent and despising all such limits; and there is doubtless no remarked connection in which they have so shown the sympathetic imagination in free and fearless activity, that is, in high originality, as under the suggestion of the tragedy of Belgium.

The happy fact in this order is that the genius commits itself, always does so, by the mere act of self-betrayal; so that just to assume its infinite exercise is but to see how it must live above all on happy terms with itself. That is the impulse and the need which operate most fully, to our recognition, in any form of the American overflow of the excited social instinct; which circumstance, as I make these remarks, seems to place under my feet a great firmness of confidence. That confidence rests on this clear suggestibility, to the American apprehension of any and every aspect of the particular moving truth; when these aspects are really presented, the response becomes but a matter of calculable spiritual health. Very wonderful, I think, that with a real presentation, as I call it, inevitably affected by the obstructive element of distance, of so considerable a social and personal disconnection, of the very violence done, for that matter, to credibility as well, the sense of relatedness to the awful story should so have emerged and so lucidly insisted on it rights. To make that reflection indeed might well be to feel even here on our most congested ground no great apparatus of demonstration or evocation called for; in spite of which, however, I remind myself that as Reports and Tables are of the essence of our anxious duty, so they are rather more than less efficient when not altogether denuded of the atmosphere and the human motive that have conduced to their birth.

I have small warrant perhaps to say that atmospheres are communicable, but I can testify at least that they are breathable on the spot, to whatever effect of depression or of cheer, and I should go far, I feel, were I to attempt to register the full bittersweet taste, by our Chelsea waterside, all these months, of the refugee element in our vital medium. (The sweet, as I strain a point perhaps to call it, inheres, to whatever distinguishability, in our hope of having really done something, verily done much: the bitter ineradicably seasons the consciousness, hopes and demonstrations and fond presumptions and all.) I need go no further, none the less, than the makeshift provisional gates of Crosby Hall, marvelous monument transplanted a few years since from the Bishopgate quarter of the city to a part of the ancient suburban site of the garden of Sir Thomas More, and now serving with extraordinary beneficence as the most splendid of shelters for the homeless. This great private structure, though of the grandest civic character, dating from the fifteenth century and one of the noblest relics of the past that London could show, was held a few years back so to cumber the precious acre or more on which it stood that it was taken to pieces in the candid commercial interest and in order that the site it had so long sanctified should be converted to such uses as would stuff out still further the ideal number of private pockets. Dismay and disgust were unable to save it: the most that could be done was to gather in with tenderness of care its innumerable constituent parts and convey them into safer conditions, where a sad defeated piety has been able to re-edify them into some semblance of the original majesty.

Strange withal some of the turns of the whirligig of time; the priceless structure came down to the sound of lamentation, not to say of execration, and of the gnashing of teeth, and went up again before cold and disbelieving, quite despairing eyes; in spite of which history appears to have decided once more to cherish it and give a new consecration. It is in truth still magnificent; it lives again for our gratitude in its noblest particulars and the almost incomparable roof has arched all this Winter and Spring over a scene probably more interesting and certainly more pathetic than any that have ever drawn down its ancient far-off blessing.

The place has formed then the headquarters of the Chelsea circle of hospitality to the exiled, the broken and the bewildered, and if I may speak of having taken home the lesson of their state and the sense of their story it is by meeting them in the finest club conditions conceivable that I have been able to do so. Hither, month after month and day after day the unfortunates have flocked, each afternoon, and here the comparatively exempt, almost ashamed of their exemption in presence of so much woe, have made them welcome to every form of succor and reassurance. Certain afternoons, each week, have worn the character of the huge comprehensive tea party, a fresh well-wisher discharging the social and financial cost of the fresh occasion—which has always festally profited, in addition, by the extraordinary command of musical accomplishment, the high standard of execution, that is the mark of the Belgian people. This exhibition of our splendid local resource has rested, of course, on a multitude of other resources, still local, but of a more intimate hospitality, little by little worked out and applied; and into the detail of which I may not here pretend to go beyond noting that they have been accountable for the large housed and fed and clothed and generally protected and administered numbers, all provided for in Chelsea and its outer fringe, on which our scheme of sociability at Crosby Hall itself has up to now been able to draw. To have seen this scheme so long in operation has been to find it suggest many reflections, all of the most poignant and moving order; the foremost of which has, perhaps, had for its subject that never before can the wanton hand of history have descended upon a group of communities less expectant of public violence from without or less prepared for it and attuned to it.

The bewildered and amazed passivity of the Flemish civil population, the state as of people surprised by sudden ruffians, murderers, and thieves in the dead of night and hurled out, terrified and half clad, snatching at the few scant household goods nearest at hand, into a darkness mitigated but by flaring incendiary torches, this has been the experience stamped on our scores and scores of thousands, whose testimony to suffered dismay and despoilment, silence alone, the silence of vain uncontributive wonderment, has for the most part been able to express. Never was such a revelation of a deeply domestic, a rootedly domiciled and instinctively and separately clustered people, a mass of communities for which the sight of the home violated, the objects helping to form it profaned and the cohesive family, the Belgian ideal of the constituted life, dismembered, disemboweled and shattered, had so supremely to represent the crack of doom and the end of everything. There have been days and days when under this particular impression the mere aspect and manner of our serried recipients of relief, something vague and inarticulate as in persons who have given up everything but patience and are living, from hour to hour, but in the immediate and the unexplained, has put on such a pathos as to make the heart sick. One has had just to translate any seated row of figures, thankful for warmth and light and covering, for sustenance and human words and human looks, into terms that would exemplify some like exiled and huddled and charity-fed predicament for our superior selves, to feel our exposure to such a fate, our submission to it, our holding in the least together under it, darkly unthinkable.

Dim imaginations would at such moments interpose, a

confused theory that even at the worst our adventurous habits, our imperial traditions, our general defiance of the superstition of domesticity would dash from our lips the cup of bitterness; from these it was at all events impossible not to come back to the consciousness that almost every creature there collected was indebted to our good offices for the means to come at all. I thought of our parents and children, our brothers and sisters, aligned in borrowed garments and settled to an as yet undetermined future of eleemosynary tea and buns, and I ask myself, doubtless to little purpose, either what grace of resignation or what clamor of protest we should, beneath the same star, be noted as substituting for the inveterate Belgian decency.

I can only profess at once that the sense of this last, round about one, was at certain hours, when the music and the chant of consolation rose in the stillness from our improvised stage at the end of the great hall, a thing to cloud with tears any pair of eyes lifted to our sublime saved roof in thanks for its vast comprehension. Questions of exhibited type, questions as to a range of form and tradition, a measure of sensibility and activity, not our own, dwindled and died before the gross fact of our having here an example of such a world tragedy as we supposed Europe had outlived, and that nothing at all therefore mattered but that we should bravely and handsomely hold up our quite heavy enough end of it.

It is because we have responded in this degree to the call unprecedented that we are, in common with a vast number of organizations scattered through these islands, qualified to claim that no small part of the inspiration to our enormous act of welcome resides in the moral interest it yields. One can indeed be certain of such a source of profit but in the degree in which one has found one's self personally drawing upon it; yet it is obvious that we are not treated every day to the disclosure of a national character, a national temperament and type, confined for the time to their plainest and stoutest features and set, on a prodigious scale, in all the relief that the strongest alien air and alien conditions can give them. Great salience, in such a case, do all collective idiosyncrasies acquire—upon the fullest enumeration of which, however, as the Belgian instance and the British atmosphere combine to represent them, I may not now embark, prepossessed wholly as I am with the more generally significant social stamp and human aspect so revealed, and with the quality derived from these things by the multiplied examples that help us to take them in. This feeling that our visitors illustrate above all the close and comfortable household life, with every implication of a seated and saturated practice of it, practice of the intimate and private and personal, the securely sensual and genial arts that flow from it, has been by itself the key to a plenitude of observation and in particular to as much friendly searching insight as one could desire to enjoy.

The moving, the lacerating thing is the fashion after which such a reading of the native elements, once adopted, has been as a light flaring into every obscurest retreat, as well as upon any puzzling ambiguity, of the state of shock of the national character under the infamy of the outrage put upon it. That they of all people the most given over to local and patriarchal beatitude among the admirable and the cherished objects handed down to them by their so interesting history on every spot where its action has been thickest—that is on every inch, so to speak, of their teeming territory—should find themselves identified with the most shamelessly cynical public act of which the civilized world at this hour retains the memory, is a fact truly representing the exquisite in the horrible; so peculiarly addressed has been their fate to the desecration of ideals that had fairly become breath of their lungs and flesh of their flesh. Oh! The installed and ensconced, the immemorially edified and arranged, the thoroughly furnished and provided and nourished people!—not in the least besotted or relaxed in their security and density, like the self smothered society of the ancient world upon which the earlier Huns and Vandals poured down, but candidly complacent and admirably intelligent in their care for their living tradition, and only so off their guard as to have consciously set the example of this care to all such as had once smoked with them their wondrous pipe of peace. Almost any posture of stupefaction would have been conceivable in the shaken victims of this delusion; I can speak best, however, but of what I have already glanced at, that temperamental weight of their fall which has again and again, at sight of many of them gathered together, made the considering heart as heavy for them as if it too had for the time been worsted.

However, it would take me far to tell of half the penetrating admonitions, whether of the dazed or of the roused appearance, that have for so long almost in like degree made our attention ache. I think of particular faces, in the whole connection, when I want most to remember—since to remember always, and never, never to forget, is a prescription shining before us like a possible light of dawn; faces saying such things in their silence, or in their speech of quite different matters, as to make the only thinkable comment or response some word or some gesture of reprieve to dumb or to dissimulated anguish. Blessed be the power that has given to civilized men the appreciation of the face—such an immeasurable sphere of exercise—for it has this monstrous trial of the peoples come to supply. Such histories, such a record of moral experience, of emotion convulsively suppressed, as one meets in some of them, and this even if on the whole one has been able to think of these special allies, all sustainingly, much rather as the sturdiest than as the most demonstrative of sufferers. I have in these rapid remarks to reduce my many impressions to the fewest, but must even thus spare one of them for commemoration of the admirable cast of working countenance we are rewarded by the sight of wherever we turn amid the quantity of helpful service and all the fruitful industries that we have been able to start and that keep themselves going.

These are the lights in the picture, and who indeed would wish that the lights themselves should be anything less than tragic? The strong young men (no young men are familiarly stronger,) mutilated, amputated, dismembered in penalty for their defense of their soil against the horde and now engaged at Crosby Hall in the making of handloom socks, to whom I pay an occasional visit much more for my own cheer, I apprehend, than for theirs, express so in their honest concentration under difficulties the actual and general value of their people that just to be in their presence is a blest renewal of faith. Excellent, exemplary, is this manly, homely, handy type, grave in its somewhat strained attention, but at once lighted to the briefest, sincerest humor of protest by any direct reference to the general cruelty of its misfortune. Anything but unsuggestive, the range of the "quiet" physiognomy when one feels the consciousness behind it not to have run thin. Thick and strong is the good Flemish sense of life and all its functions—which fact is responsible for no empty and really unmodeled "mug."

I am afraid at the same time that if the various ways of being bad are beyond our reckoning, the condition and the action of exemplary goodness tend rather to reduce to a certain rich unity of appearance those marked by them, however dissociated from each other such persons may have been by race and education. Otherwise what tribute shouldn't I be moved to pay to the gentleman of Flanders to whom the specially improvised craftsmen I have just mentioned owe their training and their inspiration?—through *his* having, in his proscribed and denuded state, mastered the craft in order to recruit them to it and, in fine, so far as my observation has been concerned, exhibit clear human virtue, courage and patience and the humility of sought fellowship in privation, with an unconscious beauty that I should be ashamed in this connection not to have noted publicly. I scarce know what such a "personality" as his suggests to me if not that we had all, on our good Chelsea ground, best take up and cherish as directly and intimately as possible every scrap of our community with our gentlemen of Flanders. I make such a point as this, at the same time, only to remember how, almost wherever I have tried sustainingly to turn, my imagination and my intelligence have been quickened, and to recognize in particular, for that matter, that this couldn't possibly be more the case for them than in visiting a certain hostel in one of our comparatively contracted but amply decent local Squares—riverside Chelsea having, of course, its own urban identity in the multitudinous County of London; which, in itself as happy an example, doubtless, of the hostel smoothly working as one need cite, placed me in grateful relation with a lady, one of the victims of her country's convulsion and in charge of the establishment I allude to, whom simply to "meet," as we say, is to learn how singular a dignity, how clear a distinction, may shine in active fortitude and economic self-effacement under an all but crushing catastrophe.

"Talk about faces—!" I could but privately ejaculate as I gathered the senses of all that this one represented in the way of natural nobleness and sweetness, a whole past acquaintance with letters and art and taste, insisting on their present restrictedness to bare sisterly service.

The proud rigor of association with pressing service alone, with absolutely nothing else, the bare commodious house, so otherwise known to me of old and now, like most of our hostels if I am not mistaken, the most unconditioned of loans from its relinquishing owner; the lingering look of ancient peace in the precincts, an element I had already as I passed and repassed, at the afternoon hour, found somehow not at all dispelled by the presence in the central green garden itself of sundry maimed and hobbling and smiling convalescents from an extemporized small hospital close at hand, their battered khaki replaced by a like uniformity of the loose light blue, and friendly talk with them through the rails of their inclosure as blessed to one participant at least as friendly talk with them always and everywhere is; such were the hovering elements of an impression in which the mind had yet mainly to yield to that haunting force on the part of our waiting proscripts which never consent to be long denied. The proof of which universally recognized power of their spell amid us is indeed that they have led me so far with a whole side of my plea for them still unspoken.

This, however, I hope on another occasion to come back to; and I am caught meanwhile by my memory of how the note of this conviction was struck for me, with extraordinary force, many months ago and in the first flush of recognition of what the fate that had overtaken our earliest tides of arrival and appeal really meant—meant so that all fuller acquaintance, since pursued, has but piled one congruous reality after another upon the horror. It was in September, in a tiny Sussex town which I had not quitted since the outbreak of the war, and here the advent of our first handful of fugitives before the warning of Louvain and Aerschott and Termonde and Dinant had just been announced. Our small hilltop city, covering the steep sides of the compact pedestal crowned by its great church, had reserved a refuge at its highest point, and we had waited all day, from occasional train to train, for the moment at which we should attest our hospitality. It came at last, but late in the evening, when a vague outside rumor called me to my doorstep, where the unforgettable impression at once assaulted me. Up the precipitous little street that led from the station, over the old grass-grown cobbles, where vehicles rarely pass, came the panting procession of the homeless and their comforting, their almost clinging entertainers, who seemed to hurry them on as in a sort of overflow of expression of fever of charity. It was swift and eager, in the Autumn darkness and under the flare of a single lamp—with no vociferation and but for a woman's voice scarce a sound save the shuffle of mounting feet and the thick-drawn breath of emotion.

The note I except, however, was that of a young mother carrying her small child and surrounded by those who bore her on and on, almost lifting her as they went together. The resonance through our immemorial old street of her sobbing and sobbing cry was the voice itself of history; it brought home to me more things than I could then quite take the measure of, and these just because it expressed for her not direct anguish, but the incredibility, as who should say, of honest assured protection. Months have elapsed, and from having been then one of a few hundred she is now one of scores and scores of thousands; yet her cry is still in my ears, whether to speak most of what she had lately or what she actually felt, and it plays to my own sense, as a great fitful tragic light over the dark exposure of her people.

1915

Within the Rim

THE FIRST sense of it all to me after the first shock and
horror was that of a sudden leap back into life of the
violence with which the American Civil War broke upon us,
at the North, fifty-four years ago, when I had a consciousness
of youth which perhaps equalled in vivacity my present consciousness of age. The illusion was complete, in its immediate
rush; everything quite exactly matched in the two cases; the
tension of the hours after the flag of the Union had been fired
upon in South Carolina living again, with a tragic strangeness
of recurrence, in the interval during which the fate of Belgium
hung in the scales and the possibilities of that of France
looked this country harder in the face, one recognised, than
any possibility, even that of the England of the Armada, even
that of the long Napoleonic menace, could be imagined to
have looked her. The analogy quickened and deepened with
every elapsing hour; the drop of the balance under the invasion of Belgium reproduced with intensity the agitation of the
New England air by Mr. Lincoln's call to arms, and I went
about for a short space as with the queer secret locked in my
breast of at least already knowing how such occasions helped
and what a big war was going to mean. That this was literally
a light in the darkness, or that it materially helped the prospect to be considered, is perhaps more than I can say; but it at
least added the strangest of savours, an inexpressible romantic
thrill, to the harsh taste of the crisis: I found myself literally
knowing "by experience" what immensities, what monstrosities, what revelations of what immeasurabilities, our affair
would carry in its bosom—a knowledge that flattered me by
its hint of immunity from illusion. The sudden new tang in
the atmosphere, the flagrant difference, as one noted, in the
look of everything, especially in that of people's faces, the
expressions, the hushes, the clustered groups, the detached
wonderers, and slow-paced public meditators, were so many
impressions long before received and in which the stretch of
more than half a century had still left a sharpness. So I took
the case in and drew a vague comfort, I can scarce say why,

from recognition; so, while recognition lasted, I found it come home to me that we, we of the ancient day, had known, had tremendously learnt, what the awful business is when it is "long," when it remains for months and months bitter and arid, void even of any great honour. In consequence of which, under the rapid rise of presumptions of difficulty, to whatever effect of dismay or of excitement, my possession of something like a standard of difficulty, and, as I might perhaps feel too, of success, became in its way a private luxury.

My point is, however, that upon this luxury I was allowed after all but ever so scantly to feed. I am unable to say when exactly it was that the rich analogy, the fine and sharp identity between the faded and the vivid case broke down, with the support obscurely derived from them; the moment anyhow came soon enough at which experience felt the ground give way and that one swung off into space, into history, into darkness, with every lamp extinguished and every abyss gaping. It ceased quite to matter for reassurance that the victory of the North had been so delayed and yet so complete, that our struggle had worn upon the world of the time, and quite to exasperation, as could well be remembered, by its length; if the present complication should but begin to be as long as it was broad no term of comparison borrowed from the past would so much as begin to fit it. I might have found it humiliating; in fact, however, I found it of the most commanding interest, whether at certain hours of dire apprehension or at certain others of the finer probability, that the biggest like convulsion our generations had known was still but too clearly to be left far behind for exaltations and terrors, for effort and result, as a general exhibition of the perversity of nations and of the energy of man. Such at least was the turn the comparison took at a given moment in a remembering mind that had been steeped, so far as its restricted contact went, but in the Northern story; I did, I confess, cling awhile to the fancy that what loomed perhaps for England, what already did so much more than loom for crucified Belgium, what was let loose in a torrent upon indestructible France, might correspond more or less with the pressure of the old terrible time as the fighting South had had to know it, and with the grim conditions under which she had at last given way. For the rest of the matter, as I say, the difference of aspect produced by the difference of intensity cut short very soon my vision of similitude. The intensity swallowed up everything; the rate and the scale and the speed, the unprecedented engines, the vast incalculable connections, the immediate presence, as it were, of France and Belgium, whom one could hear pant, through the summer air, in their effort and their alarm, these things, with the prodigious might of the enemy added, made me say, dropping into humility in a manner that resembled not a little a drop into still greater depths, "Oh no, that surely can't have been 'a patch' on this!" Which conclusion made accordingly for a new experience altogether, such as I gratefully embrace here an occasion not to leave unrecorded.

It was in the first place, after the strangest fashion, a sense of the extraordinary way in which the most benign conditions of light and air, of sky and sea, the most beautiful English summer conceivable, mixed themselves with all the violence of action and passion, the other so hideous and piteous, so heroic and tragic facts, and flouted them as with the example of something far superior. Never were desperate doings so blandly lighted up as by the two unforgettable months that I was to spend so much of in looking over from the old rampart of a little high-perched Sussex town at the bright blue streak of the Channel, within a mile or two of us at its nearest point, the point to which it had receded after washing our rock-base in its earlier ages, and staring at the bright mystery beyond the rim of the furthest opaline reach. Just on the other side of that finest of horizon-lines history was raging at a pitch new under the sun; thinly masked by that shameless smile the Belgian horror grew; the curve of the globe toward these things was of the scantest, and yet the hither spaces of the purest, the interval representing only charm and calm and ease. One grew to feel that the nearer elements, those of land and water and sky at their loveliest, were making thus, day after day, a particular prodigious point, insisting in their manner on a sense and a wondrous story which it would be the restless watcher's fault if he didn't take in. Not that these were hints or arts against which he was in the least degree proof; they penetrated with every hour deeper into the soul, and, the contemplations I speak of aiding, irresistibly worked out an endless volume of references. It was all somehow the history of the hour addressing itself to the individual mind—or to that in any case of the person, at once so appalled and so beguiled, of whose response to the whole appeal I attempt this brief account. Roundabout him stretched the scene of his fondest frequentation as time had determined the habit; but it was as if every reason and every sentiment conducing to the connection had, under the shock of events, entered into solution with every other, so that the only thinkable approach to rest, that is to the recovery of an inward order, would be in restoring them each, or to as many as would serve the purpose, some individual dignity and some form.

It came indeed largely of itself, my main help to the reparatory, the re-identifying process; came by this very chance that in the splendour of the season there was no mistaking the case or the plea. "This, as you can see better than ever before," the elements kept conspiring to say, "is the rare, the sole, the exquisite England whose weight now hangs in the balance, and your appreciation of whose value, much as in the easy years you may have taken it for granted, seems exposed to some fresh and strange and strong determinant, something that breaks in like a character of high colour in a play." Nothing could have thrilled me more, I recognise, than the threat of this irruption or than the dramatic pitch; yet a degree of pain attached to the ploughed-up state it implied—so that, with an elderly dread of a waste of emotion, I fear I almost pusillanimously asked myself why a sentiment from so far back recorded as lively should need to become any livelier, and in fact should hesitate to beg off from the higher diapason. I felt as the quiet dweller in a tenement so often feels when the question of "structural improvements" is thrust upon him; my house of the spirit, amid everything about me, had become more and more the inhabited, adjusted, familiar home, quite big enough and sound enough for the spirit's uses and with any intrinsic inconvenience corrected long since by that principle's having cultivated and formed, at whatever personal cost (since my spirit was essentially a person), the right habits, and so settled into the right attitude for practical, for con-

tented occupation. If, however, such was my vulgar apprehension, as I put it, the case was taken out of my hands by the
fate that so often deals with these accidents, and I found myself before long building on additions and upper storeys,
throwing out extensions and protrusions, indulging even, all
recklessly, in gables and pinnacles and battlements—things
that had presently transformed the unpretending place into I
scarce know what to call it, a fortress of the faith, a palace of
the soul, an extravagant, bristling, flag-flying structure which
had quite as much to do with the air as with the earth. And
all this, when one came to return upon it in a considering or
curious way, because to and fro one kept going on the old
rampart, the town "look-out," to spend one's aching wonder
again and again on the bright sky-line that at once held and
mocked it. Just over that line were unutterable things, massacre and ravage and anguish, all but irresistible assault and cruelty, bewilderment and heroism all but overwhelmed; from
the sense of which one had but to turn one's head to take in
something unspeakably different and that yet produced, as by
some extraordinary paradox, a pang almost as sharp.

It was of course by the imagination that this latter was
quickened to an intensity thus akin to pain—but the imagination had doubtless at every turn, without exception, more to
say to one's state of mind, and dealt more with the whole
unfolding scene, than any other contributive force. Never in
all my life, probably, had I been so glad to have opened betimes an account with this faculty and to be able to feel for
the most part something to my credit there; so vivid I mean
had to be one's prevision of the rate at which drafts on that
source would require cashing. All of which is a manner of
saying that in face of what during those horrible days seemed
exactly over the way the old inviolate England, as to whom
the fact that she *was* inviolate, in every valid sense of the term,
had become, with long acquaintance, so common and dull,
suddenly shone in a light never caught before and which was
for the next weeks, all the magnificence of August and September, to reduce a thousand things to a sort of merciless
distinctness. It was not so much that they leaped forth, these
things, under the particular recognition, as that they multiplied without end and abounded, always in some association

at least that caught the eye, all together overscoring the image as a whole or causing the old accepted synthesis to bristle with accents. The image as a whole, thus richly made up of them—or of the numberless testifying touches to the effect that we were not there on our sea defence as the other, the harried, countries were behind such bulwarks as they could throw up—was the central fact of consciousness and the one to which every impression and every apprehension more or less promptly related themselves; it made of itself the company in which for the time the mind most naturally and yet most importunately lived. One walked of course in the shade of the ambiguous contrast—ambiguous because of the dark question of whether it was the liabilities of Belgium and France, to say nothing of their awful actualities, that made England's state so rare, or England's state that showed her tragic sisters for doubly outraged; the action of the matter was at least that of one's feeling in one's hand and weighing it there with the last tenderness, for fullest value, the golden key that unlocked every compartment of the English character.

Clearly this general mystery or mixture was to be laid open under stress of fortune as never yet—the unprecedentedness was above all what came over us again and again, armaments unknown to human experience looming all the while larger and larger; but whatever face or succession of faces the genius of the race should most turn up the main mark of them all would be in the difference that, taken together, couldn't fail to keep them more unlike the peoples off there beyond than any pair even of the most approved of these peoples are unlike each other. "Insularity!"—one had spent no small part of one's past time in mocking or in otherwise fingering the sense out of that word; yet here it was in the air wherever one looked and as stuffed with meaning as if nothing had ever worn away from it, as if its full force on the contrary amounted to inward congestion. What the term essentially signified was in the oddest way a question at once enormous and irrelevant; what it might *show* as signifying, what it was in the circumstances actively and most probably going to, seemed rather the true consideration, indicated with all the weight of the evidence scattered about. Just the fixed *look* of England under the August sky, what was this but the most

vivid exhibition of character conceivable and the face turned
up, to repeat my expression, with a frankness that really left
no further inquiry to be made? That appearance was of the
exempt state, the record of the long safe centuries, in its happiest form, and even if any shade of happiness at such an hour
might well seem a sign of profanity or perversity. To *that*
there were all sorts of things to say, I could at once reflect,
however; wouldn't it be the thing supremely in character that
England should look most complacently herself, irradiating all
her reasons for it, at the very crisis of the question of the true
toughness, in other words the further duration, of her identity? I might observe, as for that matter I repeatedly and unspeakably did while the two months lasted, that she was
pouring forth this identity, as atmosphere and aspect and picture, in the very measure and to the very top of her consciousness of how it hung in the balance. Thus one arrived, through
the succession of shining days, at the finest sense of the case—
the interesting truth that her consciously not being as her
tragic sisters were in the great particular was virtually just her
genius, and that the very straightest thing she could do would
naturally be not to flinch at the dark hour from any profession
of her genius. Looking myself more askance at the dark hour
(politically speaking I mean) than I after my fashion figured
her as doing in her mass, I found it of an extreme, of quite an
endless fascination to trace as many as possible of her felt idiosyncrasies back to her settled sea-confidence, and to see this
now in turn account for so many other things, the smallest as
well as the biggest, that, to give the fewest hints of illustration, the mere spread of the great trees, the mere gathers in
the little bluey-white curtains of the cottage windows, the
mere curl of the tinted smoke from the old chimneys matching that note, became a sort of exquisite evidence.

Exquisite evidence of a like general class, it was true, didn't
on the other side of the Channel prevent the awful liability to
the reach of attack—its having borne fruit and been corrected
or averted again was in fact what half the foreign picture
meant; but the foreign genius was other, other at almost
every point; it had always in the past and on the spot, one remembered, expressed things, confessed things, with a difference, and part of that difference was of course the difference

of history, the fact of exemption, as I have called it, the fact that a blest inviolacy was almost exactly what had least flourished. France and Belgium, to refer only to them, became dear accordingly, in the light I speak of, because, having suffered and suffered, they were suffering yet again, while precisely the opposite process worked for the scene directly beneath my eyes. England was interesting, to put it mildly—which is but a shy evasion of putting it passionately—because she hadn't suffered, because there were passages of that sort she had publicly declined and defied; at the same time that one wouldn't have the case so simple as to set it down wholly to her luck. France and Belgium, for the past, confessed, to repeat my term; while England, so consistently harmonised, with all her long unbrokenness thick and rich upon her, seemed never to do that, nor to need it, in order to practise on a certain fine critical, not to mention a certain fine prejudiced, sensibility. It was the season of sensibility now, at any rate for just those days and just that poor place of yearning, of merely yearning, vigil; and I may add with all emphasis that never had I had occasion so to learn how far sensibility may go when once well wound up. It was saying little to say I did justice easiest at once and promptest to the most advertised proposal of the enemy, his rank intention of clapping down the spiked helmet, than which no form of headgear, by the way, had ever struck one as of a more graceless, a more telltale platitude, upon the priceless genius of France; far from new, after all, was that measure of the final death in him of the saving sense of proportion which only gross dementia can abolish. Those of my generation who could remember the detected and frustrated purpose of a renewed Germanic pounce upon the country which, all but bled to death in 1871, had become capable within five years of the most penetrating irony of revival ever recorded, were well aware of how in that at once sinister and grotesque connection they had felt notified in time. It was the extension of the programme and its still more prodigious publication during the quarter of a century of interval, it was the announced application of the extinguisher to the quite other, the really so contrasted genius the expression of which surrounded me in the manner I have glanced at, it was the extraordinary fact of a declared non-sufferance any longer, on Germany's part, of either of the obnoxious national forms disfiguring her westward horizon, and even though by her own allowance they had nothing intellectually or socially in common save that they were objectionable and, as an incident, crushable—it was this, I say, that gave one furiously to think, or rather, while one thanked one's stars for the luxury, furiously and all but unutterably to feel.

The beauty and the interest, the now more than ever copious and welcome expression, of the aspects nearest me found their value in their being so resistingly, just to that very degree of eccentricity, with that very density of home-grownness, what they were; in the same way as the character of the sister-land lately joined in sisterhood showed for exquisite because so ingrained and incorrigible, so beautifully all her own and inimitable on other ground. If it would have been hard really to give the measure of one's dismay at the awful proposition of a world squeezed together in the huge Prussian fist and with the variety and spontaneity of its parts oozing in a steady trickle, like the sacred blood of sacrifice, between those hideous knuckly fingers, so, none the less, every reason with which our preference for a better condition and a nobler fate could possibly bristle kept battering at my heart, kept, in fact, pushing into it, after the fashion of a crowd of the alarmed faithful at the door of a church. The effect was literally, yes, as of the occasion of some great religious service, with prostrations and exaltations, the light of a thousand candles and the sound of soaring choirs—all of which figured one's individual inward state as determined by the menace. One could still note at the same time, however, that this high pitch of private emotion was by itself far from meeting the case as the enemy presented it; what I wanted, of course, to do was to meet it with the last lucidity, the fullest support for particular defensive pleas or claims—and this even if what most underlay all such without exception came back to my actual vision, that and no more, of the general sense of the land. The vision was fed, and fed to such a tune that in the quest for reasons—that is, for the particulars of one's affection, the more detailed the better—the blades of grass, the outlines of leaves, the drift of clouds, the streaks of mortar between old bricks, not to speak of the call of child-voices muffled in the comforting air, became, as I have noted, with a hundred other like touches, casually felt, extraordinary admonitions and symbols, close links of a tangible chain. When once the question fairly hung there of the possibility, more showily set forth than it had up to then presumed to be, of a world without use for the tradition so embodied, an order substituting for this, by an unmannerly thrust, quite another and really, it would seem, quite a ridiculous, a crudely and clumsily improvised story, we might all have resembled together a group of children at their nurse's knee disconcerted by some tale that it isn't their habit to hear. We loved the old tale, or at least I did, exactly because I knew it; which leaves me keen to make the point, none the less, that my appreciation of the case for world-variety found the deeply and blessedly familiar perfectly consistent with it. This came of what I "read into" the familiar; and of what I did so read, of what I kept reading through that uplifted time, these remarks were to have attempted a record that has reached its limit sooner than I had hoped.

I was not then to the manner born, but my apprehension of what it was on the part of others to be so had been confirmed and enriched by the long years, and I gave myself up to the general, the native image I thus circled around as to the dearest and most precious of all native images. That verily became at the crisis an occupation sublime; which was not, after all, so much an earnest study or fond arrangement of the mixed aspects as a positive, a fairly sensual bask in their light, too kindled and too rich not to pour out by its own force. The strength and the copious play of the appearances acting in this collective fashion carried everything before them; no dark discrimination, no stiff little reserve that one might ever have made, stood up in the diffused day for a moment. It was in the opposite way, the most opposite possible, that one's intelligence worked, all along the line; so that with the warmth of the mere sensation that "they" were about as good, above all when it came to the stress, as could well be expected of people, there was the acute interest of the successive points at which one recognised why. This last, the satisfaction of the deepened intelligence, turned, I may frankly say, to a prolonged revel—"they" being the people about me and every comfort I had ever had of them smiling its individual smile straight at me and conducing to an effect of candour that is beyond any close notation. They didn't know how good they were, and their candour had a peculiar lovability of unconsciousness; one had more imagination at their service in this cause than they had in almost any cause of their own; it was wonderful, it was beautiful, it was inscrutable, that they could make one feel this and yet not feel with it that it at all practically diminished them. Of course, if a shade should come on occasion to fall across the picture, that shade would perhaps be the question whether the most restless of the faculties mightn't on the whole too much fail them. It beautified life, I duly remembered, it promoted art, it inspired faith, it crowned conversation, but hadn't it—always again under stress—still finer applications than these, and mightn't it in a word, taking the right direction, peculiarly conduce to virtue? Wouldn't it, indeed, be indispensable to virtue of the highest strain? Never mind, at any rate—so my emotion replied; with it or without it we seemed to *be* taking the right direction; moreover, the next best thing to the imagination people may have, if they can, is the quantity of it they may set going in others, and which, imperfectly aware, they are just exposed to from such others, and must make the best of: their advantage becoming simply that it works, for the connection, all in their favour. That of the associated outsider, the order of whose feelings, for the occasion, I have doubtless not given a wholly lucid sketch of, cultivated its opportunity week after week at such a rate that, technical alien as he was, the privilege of the great partaking, of shared instincts and ideals, of a communion of race and tongue, temper and tradition, put on before all the blest appearances a splendour to which I hoped that so long as I might yet live my eyes would never grow dim. And the great intensity, the melting together of the spiritual sources so loosed in a really intoxicating draught, was when I shifted my watch from near east to far west and caught the enemy, who seemed ubiquitous, in the long-observed effort that most fastened on him the insolence of his dream and the depth of his delusion. There in the west were those of my own fond fellowship, the other, the ready and rallying partakers, and it was on the treasure of our whole unquenchable association that in the riot of his ignorance—this at least apparently armour-proof—he had laid his unholy hands.

1915

The Long Wards

THERE comes back to me out of the distant past an impression of the citizen soldier at once in his collective grouping and in his impaired, his more or less war-worn state, which was to serve me for long years as the most intimate vision of him that my span of life was likely to disclose. This was a limited affair indeed, I recognise as I try to recover it, but I mention it because I was to find at the end of time that I had kept it in reserve, left it lurking deep down in my sense of things, however shyly and dimly, however confusedly even, as a term of comparison, a glimpse of something by the loss of which I should have been the poorer; such a residuary possession of the spirit, in fine, as only needed darkness to close round it a little from without in order to give forth a vague phosphorescent light. It was early, it must have been very early, in our Civil War, yet not so early but that a large number of those who had answered President Lincoln's first call for an army had had time to put in their short period (the first term was so short then, as was likewise the first number,) and reappear again in camp, one of those of their small New England State, under what seemed to me at the hour, that of a splendid autumn afternoon, the thickest mantle of heroic history. If I speak of the impression as confused I certainly justify that mark of it by my failure to be clear at this moment as to how much they were in general the worse for wear—since they can't have been exhibited to me, through their waterside settlement of tents and improvised shanties, in anything like hospital conditions. However, I cherish the rich ambiguity, and have always cherished it, for the sake alone of the general note exhaled, the thing that has most kept remembrance unbroken. I carried away from the place *the* impression, the one that not only was never to fade, but was to show itself susceptible of extraordinary eventual enrichment. I may not pretend now to refer it to the more particular sources it drew upon at that summer's end of 1861, or to say why my repatriated warriors were, if not somehow definitely stricken, so largely either lying in apparent helplessness or moving about in confessed languor: it suffices me that I have always thought of them as expressing themselves at almost every point in the minor key, and that this has been the reason of their interest. What I call the note therefore is the characteristic the most of the essence and the most inspiring—inspiring I mean for consideration of the admirable sincerity that we thus catch in the act: the note of the quite abysmal softness, the exemplary genius for accommodation, that forms the alternative aspect, the passive as distinguished from the active, of the fighting man whose business is in the first instance formidably to bristle. This aspect has been produced, I of course recognise, amid the horrors that the German powers had, up to a twelvemonth ago, been for years conspiring to let loose upon the world by such appalling engines and agencies as mankind had never before dreamed of; but just that is the lively interest of the fact unfolded to us now on a scale beside which, and though save indeed for a single restriction, the whole previous illustration of history turns pale. Even if I catch but in a generalising blur that exhibition of the first American levies as a measure of experience had stamped and harrowed them, the signally attaching mark that I refer to is what I most recall; so that if I did n't fear, for the connection, to appear to compare the slighter things with the so much greater, the diminished shadow with the far-spread substance, I should speak of my small old scrap of truth, miserably small in contrast with the immense evidence even then to have been gathered, but in respect to which latter occasion did n't come to me, as having contained possibilities of development that I must have languished well-nigh during a lifetime to crown it with.

One had during the long interval not lacked opportunity for a vision of the soldier at peace, moving to and fro with a professional eye on the horizon, but not fished out of the bloody welter and laid down to pant, as we actually see him among the Allies, almost on the very bank and within sound and sight of his deepest element. The effect of many of the elapsing years, the time in England and France and Italy, had indeed been to work his collective presence so closely and familiarly into any human scene pretending to a full illustration of our most generally approved conditions that I confess to

having missed him rather distressfully from the picture of
things offered me during a series of months spent not long
ago in a few American cities after years of disconnection. I
can scarce say why I missed him sadly rather than gladly—I
might so easily have prefigured one's delight in his absence;
but certain it is that my almost outraged consciousness of
our practically doing without him amid American conditions
was a revelation of the degree in which his great imaging,
his great reminding and enhancing function is rooted in the
European basis. I felt his non-existence on the American
positively produce a void which nothing else, as a vivifying
substitute, hurried forward to fill; this being indeed the case
with many of the other voids, the most aching, which left
the habituated eye to cast about as for something to nibble
in a state of dearth. We never know, I think, how much
these wanting elements have to suggest to the pampered
mind till we feel it living in view of the community from
which they have been simplified away. On these occasions
they conspire with the effect of certain other, certain similar
expressions, examples of social life proceeding as by the
serene, the possibly too serene, process of mere ignorance, to
bring to a head for the fond observer the wonder of what is
supposed to strike, for the projection of a furnished world,
the note that they are not there to strike. However, as I
quite grant the hypothesis of an observer still fond and yet
remarking the lapse of the purple patch of militarism but
with a joy unclouded, I limit myself to the merely personal
point that the fancy of a particular brooding analyst *could* so
sharply suffer from a vagueness of privation, something like
an unseasoned observational diet, and then, rather to his relief, find the mystery cleared up. And the strict relevancy of
the bewilderment I glance at, moreover, becomes questionable, further, by reason of my having, with the outbreak of
the horrors in which we are actually steeped, caught myself
staring at the exhibited militarism of the general British
scene not much less ruefully than I could remember to have
stared, a little before, at the utter American deficit. Which
proves after all that the rigour of the case had begun at a
bound to defy the largest luxury of thought; so that the
presence of the military in the picture on the mere moderate

insular scale struck one as "furnishing" a menaced order but in a pitiful and pathetic degree.

The degree was to alter, however, by swift shades, just as one's comprehension of the change grew and grew with it; and thus it was that, to cut short the record of our steps and stages, we have left immeasurably behind us here the question of what might or what should have been. That belonged, with whatever beguiled or amused ways of looking at it, to the abyss of our past delusion, a collective state of mind in which it had literally been possible to certain sophists to argue that, so far from not having soldiers enough, we had more than we were likely to know any respectable public call for. It was in the very fewest weeks that we replaced a pettifogging consciousness by the most splendidly liberal, and, having swept through all the first phases of anxiety and suspense, found no small part of our measure of the matter settle down to an almost luxurious study of our multiplied defenders after the fact, as I may call it, or in the light of that acquaintance with them as products supremely tried and tested which I began by speaking of. We were up to our necks in this relation before we could turn round, and what upwards of a year's experience of it has done in the contributive and enriching way may now well be imagined. I might feel that my marked generalisation, the main hospital impression, steeps the case in too strong or too stupid a synthesis, were it not that to consult my memory, a recollection of countless associative contacts, is to see the emphasis almost absurdly thrown on my quasi-paradox. Just so it is of singular interest for the witnessing mind itself to feel the happy truth stoutly resist any qualifying hint—since I *am* so struck with the charm, as I can only call it, of the tone and temper of the man of action, the creature appointed to advance and explode and destroy, and elaborately instructed as to how to do these things, reduced to helplessness in the innumerable instances now surrounding us. It does n't in the least take the edge from my impression that his sweet reasonableness, representing the opposite end of his wondrous scale, is probably the very oldest story of the touching kind in the world; so far indeed from my claiming the least originality for the appealing appearance as it has lately reached me from so many sides, I find its suggestion of vast communities, communities of patience and placidity, acceptance and submission pushed to the last point, to be just what makes the whole show most illuminating.

"Wonderful that, from east to west, they must *all* be like this," one says to one's self in presence of certain consistencies, certain positive monotonies of aspect; "wonderful that if joy of battle (for the classic term, in spite of new horrors, seems clearly still to keep its old sense,) has, to so attested a pitch, animated these forms, the disconnection of spirit should be so prompt and complete, should hand the creature over as by the easiest turn to the last refinements of accommodation. The disconnection of the flesh, of physical function in whatever ravaged area, *that* may well be measureless; but how interesting, if the futility of such praise does n't too much dishonour the subject, the exquisite anomaly of the intimate readjustment of the really more inflamed and exasperated part, or in other words of the imagination, the captured, the haunted vision, to life at its most innocent and most ordered!" To that point one's unvarying thought of the matter; which yet, though but a meditation without a conclusion, becomes the very air in which fond attention spends itself. So far as commerce of the acceptable, the tentatively helpful kind goes, one looks for the key to success then, among the victims, exactly on that ground of the apprehension pacified and almost, so to call it, trivialised. The attaching thing becomes thus one's intercourse with the imagination of the particular patient subject, the individual himself, in the measure in which this interest bears us up and carries us along; which name for the life of his spirit has to cover, by a considerable stretch, all the ground. By the stretch of the name, moreover, I am far from meaning any stretch of the faculty itself— which remains for the most part a considerably contracted or inert force, a force in fact often so undeveloped as to be insusceptible of measurement at all, so that one has to resort, in face of the happy fact that communion still does hold good, to some other descriptive sign for it. That sign, however, fortunately presents itself with inordinate promptitude and fits to its innocent head with the last perfection the cap, in fact the very crown, of an office that we can only appraise as predetermined goodnature. We after this fashion score our very highest on behalf of a conclusion, I think, in feeling that whether or no the British warrior's goodnature has much range of fancy, his imagination, whatever there may be of it, is at least so goodnatured as to show absolutely everything it touches, everything without exception, even the worst machinations of the enemy, in that colour. Variety and diversity of exhibition, in a world virtually divided as now into hospitals and the preparation of subjects for them, are, I accordingly conceive, to be looked for quite away from the question of physical patience, of the general consent to suffering and mutilation, and, instead of that, in this connection of the sort of mind and thought, the sort of moral attitude, that are born of the sufferer's other relations; which I like to think of as being different from country to country, from class to class, and as having their fullest national and circumstantial play.

It would be of the essence of these remarks, could I give them within my space all the particular applications naturally awaiting them, that they pretend to refer here to the British private soldier only—generalisation about his officers would take us so considerably further and so much enlarge our view. The high average of the beauty and modesty of these, in the stricken state, causes them to affect me, I frankly confess, as probably the very flower of the human race. One's apprehension of "Tommy"—and I scarce know whether more to dislike the liberty this mode of reference takes with him, or to incline to retain it for the tenderness really latent in it—is in itself a theme for fine notation, but it has brought me thus only to the door of the boundless hospital ward in which, these many months, I have seen the successive and the so strangely quiet tides of his presence ebb and flow, and it stays me there before the incalculable vista. The perspective stretches away, in its mild order, after the fashion of a tunnel boring into the very character of the people, and so going on forever—never arriving or coming out, that is, at anything in the nature of a station, a junction or a terminus. So it draws off through the infinite of the common personal life, but planted and bordered, all along its passage, with the thick-growing flower of the individual illustration, this sometimes vivid enough and sometimes pathetically pale. The great fact, to my now so informed vision, is that it undiscourageably continues and that an unceasing repetition of its testifying particulars seems never either to exhaust its sense or to satisfy that of the beholder. Its sense indeed, if I may so far simplify, is pretty well always the same, that of the jolly fatalism abovementioned, a state of moral hospitality to the practices of fortune, however outrageous, that may at times fairly be felt as providing amusement, providing a new and thereby a refreshing turn of the personal situation, for the most interested party. It is true that one may be sometimes moved to wonder which *is* the most interested party, the stricken subject in his numbered bed or the friendly, the unsated inquirer who has tried to forearm himself against such a measure of the "criticism of life" as might well be expected to break upon him from the couch in question, and who yet, a thousand occasions for it having been, all round him, inevitably neglected, finds this ingenious provision quite left on his hands. He may well ask himself what he is to do with people who so consistently and so comfortably content themselves with *being* —being for the most part incuriously and instinctively admirable—that nothing whatever is left of them for reflection as distinguished from their own practice; but the only answer that comes is the reproduction of the note. He may, in the interest of appreciation, try the experiment of lending them some scrap of a complaint or a curse in order that they shall meet him on congruous ground, the ground of encouragement to his own participating impulse. They are imaged, under that possibility, after the manner of those unfortunates, the very poor, the victims of a fire or shipwreck, to whom you have to lend something to wear before they can come to thank you for helping them. The inmates of the long wards, however, have no use for any imputed or derivative sentiments or reasons; they feel in their own way, they feel a great deal, they don't at all conceal from you that to have seen what they have seen is to have seen things horrible and monstrous—but there is no estimate of them for which they seek to be indebted to you, and nothing they less invite from you than to show them that such visions must have poisoned their world. Their world isn't in the least poisoned: they have assimilated their experience by a process scarce at all to be distinguished from their having healthily got rid of it.

The case thus becomes for you that they consist wholly of their applied virtue, which is accompanied with no waste of consciousness whatever. The virtue may strike you as having been, and as still being, greater in some examples than others, but it has throughout the same sign of differing at almost no point from a supreme amiability. How can creatures so amiable, you allow yourself vaguely to wonder, have welcomed even for five minutes the stress of carnage? and how can the stress of carnage, the murderous impulse at the highest pitch, have left so little distortion of the moral nature? It has left none at all that one has at the end of many months been able to discover; so that perhaps the most steadying and refreshing effect of intercourse with these hospital friends is through the almost complete rest from the facing of generalisations to which it treats you. One would even like perhaps, as a stimulus to talk, more generalisation; but one gets enough of that out in the world, and one does n't get there nearly so much of what one gets in this perspective, the particular perfect sufficiency of the extraordinary principle, whatever it is, which makes the practical answer so supersede any question or any argument that it seems fairly to have acted by chronic instinctive anticipation, the habit of freely throwing the personal weight into any obvious opening. The personal weight, in its various forms and degrees, is what lies there with a head on the pillow and whatever wise bandages thereabout or elsewhere, and it becomes interesting in itself, and just in proportion, I think, to its having had all its history after the fact. All its history is that of the particular application which has brought it to the pass at which you find it, and is a stream roundabout which you have to press a little hard to make it flow clear. Then, in many a case, it does flow, certainly, as clear as one could wish, and with the strain that it is always somehow English history and illustrates afresh the English way of doing things and regarding them, of feeling and naming them. The sketch extracted is apt to be least coloured when the prostrate historian, as I may call him, is an Englishman of the English; it has more point, though not perhaps more essential tone, when he is a Scot of the Scots, and has most when he is an Irishman of the Irish; but there is absolutely no difference, in the light of race and save as by inevitable variation from individual to individual, about the really constant and precious matter, the attested possession on the part of the contributor of a free loose undisciplined quantity of being to contribute.

This is the palpable and ponderable, the admirably appreciable, residuum—as to which if I be asked just how it is that I pluck the flower of amiability from the bramble of an individualism so bristling with accents, I am afraid I can only say that the accents would seem by the mercy of chance to fall together in the very sense that permits us to detach the rose with the fewest scratches. The rose of active goodnature, irreducible, incurable, or in other words all irreflective, *that* is the variety which the individualistic tradition happens, up and down these islands, to wear upon its ample breast—even it may be with a considerable effect of monotony. There it is, for what it is, and the very simplest summary of one's poor bedside practice is perhaps to confess that one has most of all kept one's nose buried in it. There hangs about the poor practitioner by that fact, I profess, an aroma not doubtless at all mixed or in the least mystical, but so unpervertedly wholesome that what can I pronounce it with any sort of conscience but sweet? That is the rough, unless I rather say the smooth, report of it; which covers of course, I hasten to add, a constant shift of impression within the happy limits. Did I not, by way of introduction to these awaiters of articulate acknowledgment, find myself first of all, early in the autumn, in presence of the first aligned rows of lacerated Belgians?—the eloquence of whose mere mute expression of their state, and thereby of their cause, remains to me a vision unforgettable forever, and this even though I may not here stretch my scale to make them, Flemings of Flanders though they were, fit into my remarks with the English of the English and the Scotch of the Scotch. If other witnesses might indeed here fit in they would decidedly come nearest, for there were aspects under which one might almost have taken them simply for Britons comparatively starved of sport and, to make up for that, on straighter and homelier terms with their other senses and appetites. But their effect, thanks to their being so seated in everything that their ripe and rounded temperament had done for them, was to make their English entertainers, and their successors in the long wards especially, seem ever so much more complicated—besides making of what had happened to themselves, for that matter, an enormity of outrage beyond all thought and all pity. Their fate had cut into their spirit to a peculiar degree through their flesh, as if they had had an unusual thickness of this, so to speak—which up to that time had protected while it now but the more exposed and, collectively, entrapped them; so that the ravaged and plundered domesticity that one felt in them, which was mainly what they had to oppose, made the terms of their exile and their suffering an extension of the possible and the dreadful. But all that vision is a chapter by itself—the essence of which is perhaps that it has been the privilege of this placid and sturdy people to show the world a new shade and measure of the tragic and the horrific. The first wash of the great Flemish tide ebbed at any rate from the hospitals—creating moreover the vast needs that were to be so unprecedentedly met, and the native procession which has prompted these remarks set steadily in. I have played too uncertain a light, I am well aware, not arresting it at half the possible points, yet with one aspect of the case staring out so straight as to form the vivid moral that asks to be drawn. The deepest impression from the sore human stuff with which such observation deals is that of its being strong and sound in an extraordinary degree for the conditions producing it. These conditions represent, one feels at the best, the crude and the waste, the ignored and neglected state; and under the sense of the small care and scant provision that have attended such hearty and happy growths, struggling into life and air with no furtherance to speak of, the question comes pressingly home of what a better economy might, or verily might n't, result in. If this abundance all slighted and unencouraged can still comfort us, what would n't it do for us tended and fostered and cultivated? That is my moral, for I believe in Culture—speaking strictly now of the honest and of our own congruous kind.

1916

THE AMERICAN SCENE

Preface

The following pages duly explain themselves, I judge, as to the Author's point of view and his relation to his subject; but I prefix this word on the chance of any suspected or perceived failure of such references. My visit to America had been the first possible to me for nearly a quarter of a century, and I had before my last previous one, brief and distant to memory, spent other years in continuous absence; so that I was to return with much of the freshness of eye, outward and inward, which, with the further contribution of a state of desire, is commonly held a precious agent of perception. I felt no doubt, I confess, of my great advantage on that score; since if I had had time to become almost as "fresh" as an inquiring stranger, I had not on the other hand had enough to cease to be, or at least to feel, as acute as an initiated native. I made no scruple of my conviction that I should understand and should care better and more than the most earnest of visitors, and yet that I should vibrate with more curiosity—on the extent of ground, that is, on which I might aspire to intimate intelligence at all—than the pilgrim with the longest list of questions, the sharpest appetite for explanations and the largest exposure to mistakes.

I felt myself then, all serenely, not exposed to grave mistakes—though there were also doubtless explanations which would find me, and quite as contentedly, impenetrable. I would take my stand on my gathered impressions, since it was all for them, for them only, that I returned; I would in fact go to the stake for them—which is a sign of the value that I both in particular and in general attach to them and that I have endeavoured to preserve for them in this transcription. My cultivated sense of aspects and prospects affected me absolutely as an enrichment of my subject, and I was prepared to abide by the law of that sense—the appearance that it would react promptly in some presences only to remain imperturbably inert in others. There would be a thousand matters—matters already the theme of prodigious reports and statistics—as to which I should have no sense whatever, and as to information about which my record would accordingly stand naked and unashamed. It should unfailingly be proved against me that my opportunity had found me incapable of information, incapable alike of receiving and of imparting it; for then, and then only, would it be clearly enough attested that I *had* cared and understood.

There are features of the human scene, there are properties of the social air, that the newspapers, reports, surveys and blue-books would seem to confess themselves powerless to "handle," and that yet represented to me a greater array of items, a heavier expression of character, than my own pair of scales would ever weigh, keep them as clear for it as I might. I became aware soon enough, on the spot, that these elements of the human subject, the results of these attempted apprecia-tions of life itself, would prove much too numerous even for a capacity all given to them for some ten months; but at least therefore, artistically concerned as I had been all my days with the human subject, with the appreciation of life itself, and with the consequent question of literary representation, I should not find such matters scant or simple. I was not in fact to do so, and they but led me on and on. How far this might have been my several chapters show; and yet even here I fall short. I shall have to take a few others for the rest of my story.

H. J.

Contents

I

New England:
An Autumn Impression

I

ONSCIOUS that the impressions of the very first hours have always the value of their intensity, I shrink from wasting those that attended my arrival, my return after long years, even though they be out of order with the others that were promptly to follow and that I here gather in, as best I may, under a single head. They referred partly, these instant vibrations, to a past recalled from very far back; fell into a train of association that receded, for its beginning, to the dimness of extreme youth. One's extremest youth had been full of New York, and one was absurdly finding it again, meeting it at every turn, in sights, sounds, smells, even in the chaos of confusion and change; a process under which, verily, recognition became more interesting and more amusing in proportion as it became more difficult, like the spelling-out of foreign sentences of which one knows but half the words. It was not, indeed, at Hoboken, on emerging from the comparatively assured order of the great berth of the ship, that recognition *was* difficult: there, only too confoundingly familiar and too serenely exempt from change, the waterside squalor of the great city put forth again its most inimitable notes, showed so true to the barbarisms it had not outlived that one could only fall to wondering what obscure inward virtue had preserved it. There was virtue evident enough in the crossing of the water, that brave sense of the big, bright, breezy bay; of light and space and multitudinous movement; of the serried, bristling city, held in the easy embrace of its great good-natured rivers very much as a battered and accommodating beauty may sometimes be "distinguished" by a gallant less fastidious, with his open arms, than his type would seem to imply. But what was it that was still holding together, for observation, on the hither shore, the same old sordid facts, all the ugly items that had seemed destined so long ago to fall apart from their very cynicism?—the rude cavities, the loose cobbles, the dislodged supports, the unreclaimed pools, of the roadway; the unregulated traffic, as of innumerable desperate drays charging upon each other with tragic long-necked, sharp-ribbed horses (a length and a sharpness all emphasized by the anguish of effort); the corpulent constables, with helmets askew, swinging their legs, in high detachment, from coigns of contemplation; the huddled houses of the other time, red-faced, off their balance, almost prone, as from too conscious an affinity with "saloon" civilization.

It was, doubtless, open to the repentant absentee to feel these things sweetened by some shy principle of picturesqueness; and I admit that I asked myself, while I considered and bumped, why what was "sauce for the goose" should *not* be in this case sauce for the gander; and why antique shabbiness shouldn't plead on this particular waterside the cause it more or less successfully pleads on so many others. The light of the September day was lovely, and the sun of New York rests mostly, with a laziness all its own, on that dull glaze of crimson paint, as thick as on the cheek of the cruder coquetry, which is, in general, beneath its range, the sign of the old-fashioned. Yes; I could remind myself, as I went, that Naples, that Tangiers or Constantinople has probably nothing braver to flaunt, and mingle with excited recognition the still finer throb of seeing in advance, seeing even to alarm, many of the responsibilities lying in wait for the habit of headlong critical or fanciful reaction, many of the inconsistencies in which it would probably have, at the best, more or less defiantly to drape itself. Such meditations, at all events, bridged over alike the weak places of criticism and some of the rougher ones of my material passage. Nothing was left, for the rest of the episode, but a kind of fluidity of appreciation—a mild, warm wave that broke over the succession of aspects and objects according to some odd inward rhythm, and often, no doubt, with a violence that there was little in the phenomena themselves flagrantly to justify. It floated me, my wave, all that day and the next; so that I still think tenderly—for the short backward view is already a distance with "tone"—of the service it rendered me and of the various perceptive penetrations, charming coves of still blue water, that carried me up into the subject, so to speak, and enabled me to step ashore. The subject was everywhere—that was the beauty, that the advantage: it was thrilling, really, to find one's self in presence of a theme to which everything directly contributed, leaving no touch of experience irrelevant. That, at any rate, so far as feeling it went; treating it, evidently, was going to be a matter of prodigious difficulty and selection—in consequence of which, indeed, there might even be a certain recklessness in the largest surrender to impressions. Clearly, however, these were not for the present—and such as they were—to be kept at bay; the hour of reckoning, obviously, would come, with more of them heaped up than would prove usable, a greater quantity of vision, possibly, than might fit into decent form: whereby, assuredly, the part of wisdom was to put in as much as possible of one's recklessness while it was fresh.

It was fairly droll, for instance, the quantity of vision that began to press during a wayside rest in a house of genial but discriminating hospitality that opened its doors just where the fiddle-string of association could most intensely vibrate, just where the sense of "old New York," of the earlier stages of the picture now so violently overpainted, found most of its occasions—found them, to extravagance, within and without. The good easy Square, known in childhood, and as if the light were yellower there from that small accident, bristled with reminders as vague as they were sweet; within, especially, the place was a cool backwater, for time as well as for space; out of the slightly dim depths of which, at the turn of staircases and from the walls of communicating rooms, portraits and relics and records, faintly, quaintly æsthetic, in intention at least, and discreetly—yet bravely, too, and all so archaically and pathetically—Bohemian, laid traps, of a pleasantly primitive order, for memory, for sentiment, for relenting irony; gross little devices, on the part of the circumscribed past, which appealed with scarce more emphasis than so many tail-pieces of closed chapters. The whole impression had fairly a rococo tone; and it was in this perceptibly golden air, the air of old empty New York afternoons of the waning summertime, when the long, the perpendicular rattle, as of buckets, forever thirsty, in the bottomless well of fortune, almost dies

out in the merciful cross-streets, that the ample rearward
loggia of the Club seemed serenely to hang; the glazed, dis-
glazed, gallery dedicated to the array of small spread tables for
which blank "backs," right and left and opposite, made a privacy; backs blank with the bold crimson of the New York
house-painter, and playing upon the chord of remembrance,
all so absurdly, with the scarcely less simplified green of their
great cascades of Virginia creeper, as yet unturned: an admonition, this, for piety, as well as a reminder—since one had
somehow failed to treasure it up—that the rather pettifogging plan of the city, the fruit, on the spot, of an artless age,
happened to leave even so much margin as that for consoling
chances. There were plenty of these—which I perhaps seem
unduly to patronize in speaking of them as only "consoling"—for many hours to come and while the easy wave that
I have mentioned continued to float me: so abysmal are the
resources of the foredoomed student of manners, or so helpless, at least, his case when once adrift in that tide.

If in Gramercy Park already, three hours after his arrival, he
had felt himself, this victim, up to his neck in what I have
called his "subject," the matter was quite beyond calculation
by the time he had tumbled, in such a glorified "four-
wheeler," and with such an odd consciousness of roughness
superimposed upon smoothness, far down-town again, and,
on the deck of a shining steamer bound for the Jersey shore,
was taking all the breeze of the Bay. The note of manners, the
note that begins to sound, everywhere, for the spirit newly
disembarked, with the first word exchanged, seemed, on the
great clean deck, fairly to vociferate in the breeze—and not at
all, so far, as was pleasant to remark, to the harshening of that
element. Nothing could have been more to the spectator's
purpose, moreover, than the fact he was ready to hail as the
most characteristic in the world, the fact that what surrounded him was a rare collection of young men of business
returning, as the phrase is, and in the pride of their youth and
their might, to their "homes," and that, if treasures of "type"
were not here to be disengaged, the fault would be all his
own. It was perhaps this simple sense of treasure to be gathered in, it was doubtless this very confidence in the objective
reality of impressions, so that they could deliciously be left to

ripen, like golden apples, on the tree—it was all this that gave a charm to one's sitting in the orchard, gave a strange and inordinate charm both to the prospect of the Jersey shore and to every inch of the entertainment, so divinely inexpensive, by the way. The immense liberality of the Bay, the noble amplitude of the boat, the great unlocked and tumbled-out city on one hand, and the low, accessible mystery of the opposite State on the other, watching any approach, to all appearance, with so gentle and patient an eye; the gaiety of the light, the gladness of the air, and, above all (for it most came back to that), the unconscious affluence, the variety in identity, of the young men of business: these things somehow left speculation, left curiosity exciting, yet kept it beguilingly safe. And what shall I say more of all that presently followed than that it sharpened to the last pleasantness—quite draining it of fears of fatuity—that consciousness of strolling in the orchard that was all one's own to pluck, and counting, overhead, the apples of gold? I figure, I repeat, under this name those thick-growing items of the characteristic that were surely going to drop into one's hand, for vivid illustration, as soon as one could begin to hold it out.

Heavy with fruit, in particular, was the whole spreading bough that rustled above me during an afternoon, a very wonderful afternoon, that I spent in being ever so wisely driven, driven further and further, into the large lucidity of—well, of what else shall I call it but a New Jersey condition? That, no doubt, is a loose label for the picture; but impressions had to range themselves, for the hour, as they could. I had come forth for a view of such parts of the condition as might peep out at the hour and on the spot, and it was clearly not going to be the restless analyst's own fault if conditions in general, everywhere, should strike him as peculiarly, as almost affectingly, at the mercy of observation. They came out to meet us, in their actuality, in the soft afternoon; they stood, artless, unconscious, unshamed, at the very gates of Appearance; they might, verily, have been there, in their plenitude, at the call of some procession of drums and banners—the principal facts of the case being collected along our passage, to my fancy, quite as if they had been principal citizens. And then there was the further fact of the case, one's own ridiculous property and sign—the romantic, if not the pathetic, circumstance of one's having had to wait till now to read even such meagre meanings as this into a page at which one's geography might so easily have opened. It might have threatened, for twenty minutes, to be almost complicating, but the truth was recorded: it was an adventure, unmistakably, to have a revelation made so convenient—to be learning at last, in the maturity of one's powers, what New Jersey might "connote." This was nearer than I had ever come to any such experience; and it was now as if, all my life, my curiosity had been greater than I knew. Such, for an excited sensibility, are the refinements of personal contact. These influences then were present, as a source of glamour, at every turn of our drive, and especially present, I imagined, during that longest perspective when the road took no turn, but showed us, with a large, calm consistency, the straight blue band of summer sea, between the sandy shore and the reclaimed margin of which the chain of big villas was stretched tight, or at least kept straight, almost as for the close stringing of more or less monstrous pearls. The association of the monstrous thrusts itself somehow into my retrospect, for all the decent humility of the low, quiet coast, where the shadows of the waning afternoon could lengthen at their will and the chariots of Israel, on the wide and admirable road, could advance, in the glittering eye of each array of extraordinarily exposed windows, as through an harmonious golden haze.

There was gold-dust in the air, no doubt—which would have been again an element of glamour if it had not rather lighted the scene with too crude a confidence. It was one of the phases, full of its own marks and signs, of New York, the immense, in *villeggiatura*—and, presently, with little room left for doubt of what particular phase it might be. The huge new houses, up and down, looked over their smart, short lawns as with a certain familiar prominence in their profiles, which was borne out by the accent, loud, assertive, yet benevolent withal, with which they confessed to their extreme expensiveness. "Oh, yes; we were awfully dear, for what we are and for what we do"—it was proud, but it was rather rueful; with the odd appearance everywhere as of florid creations waiting, a little bewilderingly, for their justification, waiting for the next clause in the sequence, waiting in short for life, for time, for interest, for character, for identity itself to come to them, quite as large spread tables or superfluous shops may wait for guests and customers. The scene overflowed with curious suggestion; it comes back to me with the afternoon air and the amiable flatness, the note of the sea in a drowsy mood; and I thus somehow think of the great white boxes as standing there with the silvered ghostliness (for all the silver involved) of a series of candid new moons. It could only be the occupants, moreover, who were driving on the vast, featureless highway, to and fro in front of their ingenuous palaces and as if pretending not to recognize them when they passed; German Jewry—wasn't it conceivable?—tending to the stout, the simple, the kind, quite visibly to the patriarchal, and with the old superseded shabbiness of Long Branch partly for the goal of their course; the big brown wooden barracks of the hotels, the bold rotunda of the gaming-room—monuments already these, in truth, of a more artless age, and yet with too little history about them for dignity of ruin. Dignity, if not of ruin at least of reverence, was what, at other points, doubtless, we failed considerably less to read into the cottage where Grant lived and the cottage where Garfield died; though they had, for all the world, those modest structures, exactly the effect of objects diminished by recession into space—as if to symbolize the rapidity of their recession into time. They have been left so far behind by the expensive, as the expensive is now practised; in spite of having apparently been originally a sufficient expression of it.

This could pass, it seemed, for the greatest vividness of the picture—that the expensive, for New York in *villeggiatura*, even on such subordinate showing, is like a train covering ground at maximum speed and pushing on, at present, into regions unmeasurable. It included, however, other lights, some of which glimmered, to my eyes, as with the promise of great future intensity—hanging themselves as directly over the question of manners as if they had been a row of lustres reflected in the polished floor of a ball-room. Here was the expensive as a power by itself, a power unguided, undirected, practically unapplied, really exerting itself in a void that could make it no response, that had nothing—poor gentle, patient, rueful, but altogether helpless, void!—to offer in return. The game was that of its doing, each party to the whole combination, what it could, but with the result of the common effort's falling so short. Nothing could be of a livelier interest—with the question of manners always in view—than to note that the most as yet accomplished at such a cost was the air of unmitigated publicity, publicity as a condition, as a doom, from which there could be no appeal; just as in all the topsy-turvy order, the defeated scheme, the misplaced confidence, or whatever one may call it, there was no achieved protection, no constituted mystery of retreat, no saving complexity, not so much as might be represented by a foot of garden wall or a preliminary sketch of interposing shade. The homely principle under which the picture held at all together was that of the famous freedom of the cat to look at the king; that seemed, so clearly, throughout, the only motto that would work. The ample villas, in their full dress, planted each on its little square of brightly-green carpet, and as with their stiff skirts pulled well down, eyed each other, at short range, from head to foot; while the open road, the chariots, the buggies, the motors, the pedestrians—which last number, indeed, was remarkably small—regarded at their ease both this reciprocity and the parties to it. It was in fact all *one* participation, with an effect deterrent to those ingenuities, or perhaps indeed rather to those commonplaces, of conjecture produced in general by the outward show of the fortunate life. That, precisely, appeared the answer to the question of manners: the fact that in such conditions there couldn't *be* any manners to speak of; that the basis of privacy was somehow wanting for them; and that nothing, accordingly, no image, no presumption of constituted relations, possibilities, amenities, in the social, the domestic order, was inwardly projected. It was as if the projection had been so completely outward that one could but find one's self almost uneasy about the mere perspective required for the common acts of the personal life, that minimum of vagueness as to what takes place in it for which the complete "home" aspires to provide.

What had it been their idea to *do*, the good people—do, exactly, *for* their manners, their habits, their intercourse, their relations, their pleasures, their general advantage and justification? Do, that is, in affirming their wealth with such innocent emphasis and yet not at the same time affirming anything else. It would have rested on the cold-blooded critic, doubtless, to explain why the crudity of wealth did strike him with so direct a force; accompanied after all with no paraphernalia, no visible redundancies of possession, not so much as a lodge at any gate, nothing but the scale of many of the houses and their candid look of having cost as much as they knew how. Unmistakably they all proclaimed it—they would have cost still more had the way but been shown them; and, meanwhile, they added as with one voice, they would take a fresh start as soon as ever it should be. "We are only instalments, symbols, stop-gaps," they practically admitted, and with no shade of embarrassment; "expensive as we are, we have nothing to do with continuity, responsibility, transmission, and don't in the least care what becomes of us after we have served our present purpose." On the detail of this impression, however, I needn't insist; the essence of it, which was all that was worth catching, was one's recognition of the odd treachery that may practically lie in wait for isolated opulence. The highest luxury of all, the supremely expensive thing, is constituted privacy—and yet it was the supremely expensive thing that the good people had supposed themselves to be getting: all of which, I repeat, enriched the case, for the restless analyst, with an illustrative importance. For what did it offer but the sharp interest of the match everywhere and everlastingly played between the short-cut and the long road?—an interest never so sharp as since the short-cut has been able to find itself so endlessly backed by money. Money in fact *is* the short-cut—or the short-cut money; and the long road having, in the instance before me, so little operated, operated for the effect, as we may say, of the cumulative, the game remained all in the hands of its adversary.

The example went straight to the point, and thus was the drama presented: what turn, on the larger, the general stage, was the game going to take? The whole spectacle, with the question, opened out, diffusing positively a multitudinous murmur that was in my ears, for some of the more subtly-romantic parts of the drive, as who should say (the sweet American vaguenesses, hailed again, the dear old nameless, promiscuous lengths of woodside and waterside), like the collective afternoon hum of invisible insects. Yes; it was all actually going to be drama, and *that* drama; than which nothing could be more to the occult purpose of the confirmed, the systematic story-seeker, or to that even of the mere ancient contemplative person curious of character. The very *donnée* of the piece could be given, the subject formulated: the great adventure of a society reaching out into the apparent void for the amenities, the consummations, after having earnestly gathered in so many of the preparations and necessities. "Into the apparent void"—I had to insist on that, since without it there would be neither comedy nor tragedy; besides which so little was wanting, in the way of vacancy, to the completeness of the appearance. What would lurk beneath this—or indeed what wouldn't, what mightn't—to thicken the plot from stage to stage and to intensify the action? The story-seeker would be present, quite intimately present, at the general effort—showing, doubtless, as quite heroic in many a case—to gouge an interest *out* of the vacancy, gouge it with tools of price, even as copper and gold and diamonds are extracted, by elaborate processes, from earth-sections of small superficial expression. What was such an effort, on its associated side, for the attentive mind, but a more or less adventurous fight, carried on from scene to scene, with fluctuations and variations, the shifting quantity of success and failure? Never would be such a chance to see how the short-cut works, and if there be really any substitute for roundabout experience, for troublesome history, for the long, the immitigable process of time. It was a promise, clearly, of the highest entertainment.

II

It was presently to come back to me, however, that there were other sorts, too—so many sorts, in fact, for the ancient contemplative person, that selection and omission, in face of them, become almost a pain, and the sacrifice of even the least of these immediate sequences of impression in its freshness a lively regret. But without much foreshortening is no representation, and I was promptly to become conscious, at all events, of quite a different part of the picture, and of personal perceptions, to match it, of a different order. I woke up, by a quick transition, in the New Hampshire mountains, in the deep valleys and the wide woodlands, on the forest-fringed slopes, the far-seeing crests of the high places, and by the side of the liberal streams and the lonely lakes; things full, at first, of the sweetness of belated recognition, that of the sense of some bedimmed summer of the distant prime flushing back into life and asking to give again as much as possible of what it had given before—all in spite, too, of much unacquaintedness, of the newness, to my eyes, through the mild September glow, of the particular rich region. I call it rich without compunction, despite its several poverties, caring little that half the charm, or half the response to it, may have been shamelessly "subjective"; since that but slightly shifts the ground of the beauty of the impression. When you wander about in Arcadia you ask as few questions as possible. That *is* Arcadia in fact, and questions drop, or at least get themselves deferred and shiftlessly shirked; in conformity with which truth the New England hills and woods—since they were not all, for the weeks to come, of mere New Hampshire—the mild September glow and even the clear October blaze were things to play on the chords of memory and association, to say nothing of those of surprise, with an admirable art of their own. The tune may have dropped at last, but it succeeded for a month in being strangely sweet, and in producing, quite with intensity, the fine illusion. Here, moreover, was "interest" of the sort that could come easily, and therefore not of the sort— quite the contrary—that involved a consideration of the millions spent; a fact none the fainter, into the bargain, for having its curious, unexpected, inscrutable side.

Why was the whole connotation so *delicately* Arcadian, like that of the Arcadia of an old tapestry, an old legend, an old love-story in fifteen volumes, one of those of Mademoiselle de Scudéri? Why, in default of other elements of the higher finish, did all the woodwalks and nestled nooks and shallow, carpeted dells, why did most of the larger views themselves, the outlooks to purple crag and blue horizon, insist on referring themselves to the idyllic *type* in its purity?—as if the higher finish, even at the hand of nature, were in some sort a perversion, and hillsides and rocky eminences and wild orchards, in short any common sequestered spot, could strike one as the more exquisitely and ideally Sicilian, Theocritan, poetic, romantic, academic, from their not bearing the burden of too much history. The history was there in its degree, and one came upon it, on sunny afternoons, in the form of the classic abandoned farm of the rude forefather who had lost patience with his fate. These scenes of old, hard New England effort, defeated by the soil and the climate and reclaimed by nature and time—the crumbled, lonely chimney-stack, the overgrown threshold, the dried-up well, the cart-track vague and lost—these seemed the only notes to interfere, in their meagreness, with the queer *other*, the larger, eloquence that one kept reading into the picture. Even the wild legend, immediately local, of the Indian who, having, a hundred years ago, murdered a husbandman, was pursued, by roused avengers, to the topmost peak of Chocorua Mountain, and thence, to escape, took his leap into the abyss—even so sharp an echo of a definite far-off past, enriching the effect of an admirable silvered summit (for Chocorua Mountain carries its grey head quite with the grandest air), spent itself in the mere idleness of the undiscriminated, tangled actual. There was one thinkable reason, of course, for everything, which hung there as a possible answer to any question, should any question insist. Did one by chance exaggerate, did one rhapsodize amiss, and was the apparent superior charm of the whole thing mainly but an accident of one's own situation, the state of having happened to be deprived to excess—that is for too long—of naturalism in *quantity*? Here it was in such quantity as one hadn't for years had to deal with; and that might by itself be a luxury corrupting the judgment.

It was absurd, perhaps, to have one's head so easily turned; but there was perfect convenience, at least, in the way the parts of the impression fell together and took a particular light. This light, from whatever source proceeding, cast an irresistible spell, bathed the picture in the confessed resignation of early autumn, the charming sadness that resigned itself with a silent smile. I say "silent" because the voice of the air had dropped as forever, dropped to a stillness exquisite, day by day, for a pilgrim from a land of stertorous breathing, one of the windiest corners of the world; the leaves of the forest turned, one by one, to crimson and to gold, but never broke off: all to the enhancement of this strange conscious hush of the landscape, which kept one in presence as of a world created, a stage set, a sort of ample capacity constituted, for— well, for things that wouldn't, after all, happen: more the pity for them, and for me and for you. This view of so many of the high places of the hills and deep places of the woods, the lost trails and wasted bowers, the vague, empty, rock-roughened pastures, the lonely intervals where the afternoon lingered and the hidden ponds over which the season itself seemed to bend as a young bedizened, a slightly melodramatic mother, before taking some guilty flight, hangs over the crib of her sleeping child—these things put you, so far as you were preoccupied with the human history of places, into a mood in which appreciation became a positive wantonness and the sense of quality, plucking up unexpectedly a spirit, fairly threatened to take the game into its hands. You discovered, when once it was stirred, an elegance in the commonest objects, and a mystery even in accidents that really represented, perhaps, mere plainness unashamed. Why otherwise, for instance, the inveterate charm of the silver-grey rock cropping through thinly-grassed acres with a placed and "composed" felicity that suggested the furniture of a drawing-room? The great boulders in the woods, the pulpit-stones, the couchant and rampant beasts, the isolated cliffs and lichened cathedrals, had all, seen, as one passed, through their drizzle of forest light, a special New Hampshire beauty; but I never tired of finding myself of a sudden in some lonely confined place, that was yet at the same time both wide and bright, where I could recognize, after the fashion of the old New Hampshire sociability, every facility for spending the day. There was the oddity—the place was furnished by its own good taste; its bosky ring shut it in, the two or three gaps of the old forgotten enclosure made symmetrical doors, the sweet old stones had the surface of grey velvet, and the scattered wild apples were like figures in the carpet.

It might be an ado about trifles—and half the poetry, roundabout, the poetry in solution in the air, was doubtless but the alertness of the touch of autumn, the imprisoned painter, the Bohemian with a rusty jacket, who had already broken out with palette and brush; yet the way the colour begins in those days to be dabbed, the way, here and there, for a start, a solitary maple on a woodside flames in single scarlet, recalls nothing so much as the daughter of a noble house dressed for a fancy-ball, with the whole family gathered round to admire her before she goes. One speaks, at the same time, of the orchards; but there are properly no orchards where half the countryside shows, all September, the easiest, most familiar sacrifice to Pomona. The apple-tree, in New England, plays the part of the olive in Italy, charges itself with the effect of detail, for the most part otherwise too scantly produced, and, engaged in this charming care, becomes infinitely decorative and delicate. What it must do for the too under-dressed land in May and June is easily supposable; but its office in the early autumn is to scatter coral and gold. The apples are everywhere and every interval, every old clearing, an orchard; they have "run down" from neglect and shrunken from cheapness—you pick them up from under your feet but to bite into them, for fellowship, and throw them away; but as you catch their young brightness in the blue air, where they suggest strings of strange-coloured pearls tangled in the knotted boughs, as you note their manner of swarming for a brief and wasted gaiety, they seem to ask to be praised only by the cheerful shepherd and the oaten pipe. The question of the encircled waters too, larger and smaller—that again was perhaps an ado about trifles; but you can't, in such conditions, and especially at first, resist the appeal of their extraordinarily mild faces and wooded brims, with the various choice spots where the great straight pines, interspaced beside them, and yielding to small strands as finely curved as the eyebrows of beauty, make the sacred grove and the American classic temple, the temple for the worship of the evening sky, the cult of the Indian canoe, of Fenimore Cooper, of W. C. Bryant, of the immortalizable water-fowl. They look too much alike, the lakes and the ponds, and this is, indeed, all over the world, too much a reproach to lakes and ponds—to all save the pick of the family, say, like George and Champlain; the American idea, moreover, is too inveterately that woods shall grow thick to the water. Yet there is no feature of grace the landscape could so ill spare—let alone one's not knowing what other, what baser, promiscuity mightn't oppress the banks if that of the free overgrowth didn't. Each surface of this sort is a breathing-space in the large monotony; the rich recurrence of water gives a polish to the manner itself, so to speak, of nature; thanks to which, in any case, the memory of a characteristic perfection attaches, I find, to certain hours of declining day spent, in a shallow cove, on a fallen log, by the scarce-heard plash of the largest liquid expanse under Chocorua; a situation interfused with every properest item of sunset and evening star, of darkening circle of forest, of boat that, across the water, put noiselessly out—of analogy, in short, with every typical triumph of the American landscape "school," now as rococo as so many squares of ingenious wool-work, but the remembered delight of our childhood. On *terra firma*, in New England, too often dusty or scrubby, the guarantee is small that some object at variance, cruelly at variance, with the glamour of the landscape school may not "put out." But that boat across the water is safe, is sustaining as far as it goes; it puts out from the cove of romance, from the inlet of poetry, and glides straight over, with muffled oar, to the—well, to the right place.

The consciousness of quantity, rather, as opposed to quality, to which I just alluded, quantity inordinate, quantity duly impressive and duly, if need be, overwhelming, had been the form of vigilance posting itself at the window—whence, incontestably, after a little, yielding to the so marked agitation of its sister-sense, it stepped back into the shadow of the room. If memory, at any rate, with its message so far to carry, had played one a trick, imagination, or some finer faculty still, could play another to match it. If it had settled to a convenience of the mind that "New England scenery" was hard and dry and thin, scrubby and meagre and "plain," here was that comfort routed by every plea of fancy—though of a fancy indeed perhaps open to the charge of the morbid—and by every refinement of appeal. The oddest thing in the world would delightfully have happened—and happened just there—in case one had really found the right word for the anomaly of one's surprise. What would the right word be but that nature, in these lights, was no single one of the horrid things I have named, but was, instead of them all, that quite

other happy and charming thing, *feminine?*—feminine from
head to foot, in expression, tone and touch, mistress throughout of the feminine attitude and effect. That had by no means
the figure recalled from far back, but when once it had fully
glimmered out it fitted to perfection, it became the case like a
crown of flowers and provided completely for one's relation
to the subject.

"Oh Italy, thou woman-land!" breaks out Browning, more
than once, straight at *that* mark, and with a force of example
that, for this other collocation, served much more as an incite-
ment than as a warning. Reminded vividly of the identities of
latitude and living so much in the same relation to the sun,
you never really in New Hampshire—nor in Massachusetts, I
was soon able to observe—look out at certain hours for the
violet spur of an Apennine or venture to speak, in your admiration, of Tuscan or Umbrian forms, without feeling that the
ground has quite gratefully borne you. The matter, however,
the matter of the insidious grace, is not at all only a question
of amusing coincidence; something intrinsically lovable everywhere lurks—which most comes out indeed, no doubt, under
the consummate art of autumn. How shall one lightly enough
express it, how describe it or to what compare it?—since,
unmistakably, after all, the numbered items, the few flagrant
facts, fail perfectly to account for it. It is like some diffused,
some slightly confounding, sweetness of voice, charm of tone
and accent, on the part of some enormous family of rugged,
of almost ragged, rustics—a tribe of sons and daughters too
numerous to be counted and homogeneous perhaps to monotony. There was a voice in the air, from week to week, a
spiritual voice: "Oh, the *land's* all right!"—it took on fairly a
fondness of emphasis, it rebounded from other aspects, at
times, with such a tenderness. Thus it sounded, the blessed
note, under many promptings, but always in the same form
and to the effect that the poor dear land itself—if that was all
that was the matter—would beautifully "do." It seemed to
plead, the pathetic presence, to be liked, to be loved, to be
stayed with, lived with, handled with some kindness, shown
even some courtesy of admiration. What was that but the
feminine attitude?—not the actual, current, impeachable, but
the old ideal and classic; the air of meeting you everywhere,

standing in wait everywhere, yet always without conscious defiance, only in mild submission to your doing what you would with it. The mildness was of the very essence, the essence of all the forms and lines, all the postures and surfaces, all the slimness and thinness and elegance, all the consent, on the part of trees and rocks and streams, even of vague happy valleys and fine undistinguished hills, to be viewed, to their humiliation, in the mass, instead of being viewed in the piece.

It is perhaps absurd to have to hasten to add that doing what you would with it, in these irresponsible senses, simply left out of account, for the country in general, the proved, the notorious fact that nothing useful, nothing profitable, nothing directly economic, *could* be done at all. Written over the great New Hampshire region at least, and stamped, in particular, in the shadow of the admirable high-perched cone of Chocorua, which rears itself, all granite, over a huge interposing shoulder, quite with the *allure* of a minor Matterhorn— everywhere legible was the hard little historic record of agricultural failure and defeat. It had to pass for the historic background, that traceable truth that a stout human experiment had been tried, had broken down. One was in presence, everywhere, of the refusal to consent to history, and of the consciousness, on the part of every site, that this precious compound is in no small degree being insolently made, on the other side of the continent, at the expense of such sites. The touching appeal of nature, as I have called it therefore, the "Do something kind for me," is not so much a "Live upon me and thrive by me" as a "Live *with* me, somehow, and let us make out together what we may do for each other—something that is not merely estimable in more or less greasy greenbacks. See how 'sympathetic' I am," the still voice seemed everywhere to proceed, "and how I am therefore better than my fate; see how I lend myself to poetry and sociability—positively to æsthetic use: give me that consolation." The appeal was thus not only from the rude absence of the company that had gone, and the still ruder presence of the company left, the scattered families, of poor spirit and loose habits, who had feared the risk of change; it was to a listening ear, directly—that of the "summer people," to whom, in general, one soon began to figure so much of the country, in

New England, as looking for its future; with the consequence in fact that, from place to place, the summer people themselves almost promised to glow with a reflected light. It was a clue, at any rate, in the maze of contemplation, for this vision of the relation so established, the disinherited, the impracticable land throwing itself, as for a finer argument, on the non-rural, the intensely urban class, and the class in question throwing itself upon the land for reasons of its own. What would come of such an *entente*, on the great scale, for both parties?—that special wonderment was to strike me everywhere as in order. How populations with money to spare may extract a vulgar joy from "show" sections of the earth, like Switzerland and Scotland, we have seen abundantly proved, so that this particular lesson has little more to teach us; in America, however, evidently, the difference in the conditions, and above all in the scale of demonstration, is apt to make lessons new and larger.

Once the whole question had ranged itself under that head—what would the "summer people," as a highly comprehensive term, do with the aspects (perhaps as a highly comprehensive term also), and what would the aspects do with the summer people?—it became conveniently portable and recurrently interesting. Perhaps one of the best reasons I can give for this last side of it was that it kept again and again presenting the idea of that responsibility for *appearances* which, in such an association as loomed thus large, was certain to have to fix itself somewhere. What was one to say of appearances as they actually prevailed—from the moment, I mean, they were not of the charming order that nature herself could care for? The appearances of man, the appearances of woman, and of their conjoined life, the general latent spectacle of their arrangements, appurtenances, manners, devices, opened up a different chapter, the leaves of which one could but musingly turn. A better expression of the effect of most of this imagery on the mind should really be sought, I think, in its seeming, through its sad consistency, a mere complete negation of appearances—using the term in the sense of any familiar and customary "care for looks." Even the recognition that, the scattered summer people apart, the thin population was poor and bare had its bewilderment, on which I shall presently touch; but the poverty and the bareness were, as we seemed to measure them, a straight admonition of all we had, from far back, so easily and comfortably taken for granted, in the rural picture, on the other side of the world. There was a particular thing that, more than any other, had been pulled out of the view and that left the whole show, humanly and socially, a collapse. This particular thing was exactly the fact of the *importance*, the significance, imputable, in a degree, to appearances. In the region in which these observations first languished into life that importance simply didn't exist at all, and its absence was everywhere forlornly, almost tragically, attested. There was the little white wooden village, of course, with its houses in queer alignment and its rudely-emphasized meeting-house, in particular, very nearly as unconsecrated as the store or the town pump; but this represented, throughout, the highest tribute to the amenities. A sordid ugliness and shabbiness hung, inveterately, about the wayside "farms," and all their appurtenances and incidents—above all, about their inmates; when the idea of appearance was anywhere expressed (and its highest flights were but in the matter of fresh paint or a swept dooryard), a summer person was usually the author of the boon. The teams, the carts, the conveyances in their kinds, the sallow, saturnine natives in charge of them, the enclosures, the fences, the gates, the wayside "bits," of whatever sort, so far as these were referable to human attention or human neglect, kept telling the tale of the difference made, in a land of long winters, by the suppression of the two great factors of the familiar English landscape, the squire and the parson.

What the squire and the parson do, between them, for appearances (which is what I am talking of) in scenes, predominantly Anglo-Saxon, subject to their sway, is brought home, as in an ineffable glow, when the elements are reduced to "composing," in the still larger Anglo-Saxon light, without them. Here was no church, to begin with; and the shrill effect of the New England meeting-house, in general, so merely continuous and congruous, as to type and tone, with the common objects about it, the single straight breath with which it seems to blow the ground clear of the seated solidity of religion, is an impression that responds to the renewed sight of one of these structures as promptly as the sharp ring to the pressure of the electric button. One lives among English ancientries, for instance, as in a world toward the furnishing of which religion has done a large part. And here, immediately, was a room vast and vacant, with a vacancy especially reducible, for most of the senses, to the fact of that elimination. Perpetually, inevitably, moreover, as the restless analyst wandered, the eliminated thing *par excellence* was the thing most absent to sight—and for which, oh! a thousand times, the small substitutes, the mere multiplication of the signs of theological enterprise, in the tradition and on the scale of commercial and industrial enterprise, had no attenuation worth mentioning. The case, in the New Hampshire hills at least, was quite the same for the pervasive Patron, whose absence made such a hole. We went on counting up all the blessings we had, too unthankfully, elsewhere owed to him; we lost ourselves in the intensity of the truth that to compare a simplified social order with a social order in which feudalism had once struck deep was the right way to measure the penetration of feudalism. If there was no point here at which they had perceptibly begun, there was on the other side of the world no point at which they had perceptibly ceased. One's philosophy, one's logic might perhaps be muddled, but one clung to them for the convenience of their explanation of so much of the ugliness. The ugliness—one pounced, indeed, on this as on a talisman for the future—was the so complete abolition of *forms*; if, with so little reference to their past, present or future possibility, they could be said to have been even so much honoured as to be abolished.

The pounce at any rate was, for a guiding light, effectual; the guiding light worked to the degree of seeming at times positively to save the restless analyst from madness. He could make the absence of forms responsible, and he could thus react without bitterness—react absolutely with pity; he could judge without cruelty and condemn without despair; he could think of the case as perfectly definite and say to himself that, could forms only *be*, as a recognized accessory to manners, introduced and developed, the ugliness might begin scarcely to know itself. He could play with the fancy that the people might at last grow fairly to like them—far better, at any rate, than the class in question may in its actual ignorance suppose: the necessity would be to give it, on an adequate scale and in some lucid way, a taste of the revelation. What "form," meanwhile, *could* there be in the almost sophisticated dinginess of the present destitution? One thoughtfully asked that, though at the cost of being occasionally pulled up by odd glimpses of the underlying existence of a standard. There was the wage-standard, to begin with; the well-nigh awestruck view of the high rate of remuneration open to the most abysmally formless of "hired" men, indeed to field or house labour, expert or inexpert, on the part of either sex, in any connection: the ascertainment of which was one of the "bewilderments" I just now spoke of, one of the failures of consistency in the grey revelation. After this there was the standard, ah! the very high standard, of sensibility and propriety, so far as tribute on this ground was not owed by the parties themselves, but owed *to* them, not to be rendered, but to be received, and with a stiff, a warningly stiff, account kept of it. Didn't it appear at moments a theme for endless study, this queer range of the finer irritability in the breasts of those whose fastidiousness was compatible with the violation of almost every grace in life *but* that one? "Are you the woman of the house?" a rustic cynically squalid, and who makes it a condition of *any* intercourse that he be received at the front door of the house, not at the back, asks of a *maîtresse de maison*, a summer person trained to resignation, as preliminary to a message brought, as he then mentions, from the "washerlady." These are the phenomena, of course, that prompt the woman of the house, and perhaps still more the man, to throw herself, as I say, on the land, for what it may give her of balm and beauty—a character to which, as I also say, the land may affect these unfortunates as so consciously and tenderly playing up. The lesson had perhaps to be taught; if the Patron is at every point so out of the picture, the end is none the less not yet of the demonstration, on the part of the figures peopling it, that they are not to be patronized. Once to see this, however, was again to focus the possible evolution of manners, the latent drama to come: the æsthetic enrichment of the summer people, so far as they should be capable or worthy of it, by contact with the consoling background, so full of charming secrets, and the forces thus conjoined for the production and the imposition of forms. Thrown back again almost altogether, as by the Jersey shore, on the excitement of the speculative, one could extend unlimitedly—by which I mean one could apply to a thousand phases of the waiting spectacle—the idea of the possible drama. So everything worked round, afresh, to the promise of the large interest.

III

If the interest then was large, this particular interest of the "social" side of the general scene, more and more likely to emerge, what better proof could I want again than the differences of angle at which it continued to present itself? The differences of angle—as obvious most immediately, for instance, "north of the mountains," and first of all in the valley of the Saco—gathered into their train a hundred happy variations. I kept tight hold of my temporary clue, the plea of the country's amiability, as I have called it, its insinuating appeal from too rigorous a doom; but there was a certain strain in this, from day to day, and relief was apparent as soon as the conditions changed. They changed, notably, by the rapid and complete drop of the sordid element from the picture; it was, for all the world, of a sudden, as if Appearance, precious principle, had again asserted its rights. That confidence, clearly, at North Conway, had come to it in the course of the long years, too many to reckon over, that separated my late from my early vision—though I recognized as disconcerting, toward the close of the autumn day, to have to owe this perception, in part, to the great straddling, bellowing railway, the high, heavy, dominant American train that so reverses the relation of the parties concerned, suggesting somehow that the country exists for the "cars," which overhang it like a conquering army, and not the cars for the country. This presence had learned to penetrate the high valleys and had altered, unmistakably, the old felicity of proportion. The old informal earthy coach-road was a firm highway, wide and white—and ground to dust, for all its firmness, by the whirling motor; without which I might have followed it, back and back a little, into the near, into the far, country of youth—left lying,

however, as the case stood, beyond the crest of a hill. Only
the high rock-walls of the Ledges, the striking sign of the
spot, were there; grey and perpendicular, with their lodged
patches of shrub-like forest growth, and the immense floor,
below them, where the Saco spreads and turns and the elms
of the great general meadow stand about like candelabra
(with their arms reversed) interspaced on a green table. There
hung over these things the insistent hush of a September Sunday morning; nowhere greater than in the tended woods enclosing the admirable country home that I was able to enjoy
as a centre for contemplation; woods with their dignity maintained by a large and artful clearance of undergrowth, and
repaying this attention, as always, by something of the semblance of a sacred grove, a place prepared for high uses, even
if for none rarer than high talk. There was a latent poetry—
old echoes, ever so faint, that *would* come back; it made a
general meaning, lighted the way to the great modern farm,
all so contemporary and exemplary, so replete with beauty of
beasts and convenience of man, with a positive dilettantism of
care, but making one perhaps regret a little the big, dusky,
heterogeneous barns, the more Bohemian bucolics, of the earlier time. I went down into the valley—that was an impression to woo by stages; I walked beside one of those great
fields of standing Indian corn which make, to the eye, so perfect a note for the rest of the American rural picture, throwing the conditions back as far as our past permits, rather than
forward, as so many other things do, into the age to come.
The maker of these reflections betook himself at last, in any
case, to an expanse of rock by a large bend of the Saco, and
lingered there under the infinite charm of the place. The rich,
full lapse of the river, the perfect brownness, clear and deep,
as of liquid agate, in its wide swirl, the large indifferent ease
in its pace and motion, as of some great benevolent institution smoothly working; all this, with the sense of the deepening autumn about, gave I scarce know what pastoral nobleness to the scene, something raising it out of the reach of even
the most restless of analysts. The analyst in fact could scarce
be restless here; the impression, so strong and so final, persuaded him perfectly to peace. This, on September Sunday
mornings, was what American beauty *should* be; it filled to

the brim its idea and its measure—albeit Mount Washington, hazily overhung, happened not to contribute to the effect. It was the great, gay river, singing as it went, like some reckless adventurer, good-humoured for the hour and with his hands in his pockets, that argued the whole case and carried everything assentingly before it.

Who, for that matter, shall speak, who shall begin to speak, of the alacrity with which, in the New England scene (to confine ourselves for the moment only to that), the eye and the fancy take to the water?—take to it often for relief and security, the corrective it supplies to the danger of the common. The case is rare when it is not better than the other elements of the picture, even if these be at their best; and its strength is in the fact that the common has, for the most part, to stop short at its brink; no water being intrinsically less distinguished—save when it is dirty—than any other. By a fortunate circumstance, moreover, are not the objects usually afloat on American lakes and rivers, to say nothing of bays and sounds, almost always white and wonderful, high-piled, characteristic, fantastic things, begotten of the native conditions and shining in the native light? Let my question, however, not embroider too extravagantly my mere sense of driving presently, though after nightfall, and in the public conveyance, into a village that gave out, through the dusk, something of the sense of a flourishing Swiss village of the tourist season, as one recalls old Alpine associations: the swing of the coach, the cold, high air, the scattered hotels and their lighted windows, the loitering people who might be celebrated climbers or celebrated guides, the resonance of the bridge as one crossed, the gleam of the swift river under the lamps. My village had no happy name; it was, crudely speaking, but Jackson, N. H., just as the swift river that, later on, in the morning light, to the immediate vision, easily surpassed everything else, was only the river of the Wildcat—a superiority strictly comparative. The note of this superiority was in any case already there, for the first, for the nocturnal impression; scarce seen, only heard as yet, it could still give the gloom a larger lift than any derived from a tour of the piazzas of the hotels. This tour, undertaken while supper was preparing, in the interest of a study of manners, left room, all the same, for much support to the conviction I just expressed, the conviction that, name for name, the stream had got off better than the village, that streams *couldn't*, at the worst, have such cruel names as villages, and that this too, after all, was an intimation of their relative value. That inference was, for the actual case, to be highly confirmed; the Wildcat River, on the autumn morning, in its deep valley and its precipitous bed, was as headlong and romantic as one could desire; though, indeed, I am not, in frankness, prepared to say better things of it than of the great picture, the feature of the place, to a view of which I mounted an hour or two after breakfast.

Here, at least, where a small and charming country-house had seated itself very much as the best box, on the most expensive tier, rakes the prospect for grand opera—here might manners too be happily studied, save perhaps for their being enjoyed at too short range. Here, verily, were verandahs of contemplation, but admitting to such images of furnished peace, within, as could but illustrate a rare personal history. This was a felicity apart; whereas down in the valley, the night before, the story told at the lighted windows of the inns was precisely, was above all, of advantages impartially diffused and shared. That, at any rate, would seem in each instance the most direct message of the life displayed to the observer, on the fresher evenings, in the halls and parlours, the large, clean, bare spaces (almost penally clean and bare), where plain, respectable families seemed to sit and study in silence, with a kind of awe indeed, as from a sense of inevitable doom, their reflected resemblances, from group to group, their baffling identities of type and tone, their inability to escape from participations and communities. My figure of the opera-box, for the other, the removed, case, is justified meanwhile by the memory of the happy vision that was to make up to me for having missed Mount Washington at Intervale; the something splendidly scenic in the composition of the "Presidential range," hung in the air, across the valley, with its most eminent object holding exactly the middle of the stage and the grand effect stretching without a break to either wing. Mount Washington, seen from such a point of vantage, a kind of noble equality of intercourse, looks admirably, solidly *seated*, as with the other Presidential peaks standing at his chair; and the picture is especially sublime far off to the right, with the grand style of Carter's Dome, a masterly piece of drawing against the sky, and the romantic dip of Carter's Notch, the very ideal of the pass (other than Alpine) that announces itself to the winding wayfarer, for beauty and interest, from a distance. The names, "Presidential" and other, minister little to the poetry of association; but that, throughout the American scene, is a source of irritation with which the restless analyst has had, from far back, to count. Charming places, charming objects, languish, all round him, under designations that seem to leave on them the smudge of a great vulgar thumb—which is precisely a part of what the pleading land appears to hint to you when it murmurs, in autumn, its intelligent refrain. If it feels itself better than so many of the phases of its fate, so there are spots where you see it turn up at you, under some familiar tasteless infliction of this order, the plaintive eye of a creature wounded with a poisoned arrow.

You learn, after a little, not to insist on names—that is not to inquire of them; and are happiest perchance when the answer is made you as it was made me by a neighbour, in a railway train, on the occasion of my greatly admiring, right and left of us, a tortuous brawling river. I had supposed it for a moment, in my innocence, the Connecticut—which it decidedly was not; it was only, as appeared, a stream *quelconque*, a stream without an identity. That was better, somehow, than the adventure of a little later—my learning, too definitely, that another stream, ample, admirable, in every way distinguished, a stream worthy of Ruysdael or Salvator Rosa, was known but as the Farmington River. This I could in no manner put up with—this taking by the greater of the comparatively common little names of the less. Farmington, as I was presently to learn, is a delightful, a model village; but villages, fords, bridges are not the godparents of the element that makes them possible, they are much rather the godchildren. So far as such reflections might be idle, however, in an order so differently determined, they easily lost themselves, on the morrow of Jackson, N. H., in an impression of sharper intensity; that of a drive away, on the top of the coach, in the wondrous, lustrous early morning and in company that positively gave what it had to give quite as if it had had my curiosity on its conscience. That curiosity held its breath, in truth, for fear of breaking the spell—the spell of the large liberty with which a pair of summer girls and a summer youth, from the hotel, took all nature and all society (so far as society was present on the top of the coach) into the confidence of their personal relation. Their personal relation—that of the young man was with the two summer girls, whose own was all with *him*; any other, with their mother, for instance, who sat speechless and serene beside me, with the other passengers, with the coachman, the guard, the quick-eared four-in-hand, being for the time completely suspended. The freedoms of the young three—who were, by the way, not in their earliest bloom either—were thus bandied in the void of the gorgeous valley without even a consciousness of its shriller, its recording echoes. The whole phenomenon was documentary; it started, for the restless analyst, innumerable questions, amid which he felt himself sink beyond his depth. The immodesty was too colossal to be anything but innocence—yet the innocence, on the other hand, was too colossal to be anything but inane. And they were alive, the slightly stale three: they talked, they laughed, they sang, they shrieked, they romped, they scaled the pinnacle of publicity and perched on it flapping their wings; whereby they were shown in possession of many of the movements of life. Life, however, involved in some degree experience—if only the experience, for instance, of the summer apparently just spent, at a great cost, in the gorgeous valley. How was *that*, how was the perception of any concurrent presence, how was the human or social function at all, compatible with the *degree* of the inanity? There was, as against this, the possibility that the inanity was feigned, if not the immodesty; and the fact that there would have been more immodesty in feigning it than in letting it flow clear. These were maddening mystifications, and the puzzle fortunately dropped with the arrival of the coach at the station.

IV

Clearly, none the less, there were puzzles and puzzles, and I had almost immediately the amusement of waking up to another—this one of a different order altogether. The point was that if the bewilderments I have just mentioned had dropped, most other things had dropped too: the challenge to curiosity here was in the extreme simplification of the picture, a simplification on original lines. Not that there was not still much to think of—if only because one had to stare at the very wonder of a picture so simplified. The thing now was to catch this note, to keep it in the ear and see, really, how far and how long it would sound. The simplification, for that immediate vision, was to a broad band of deep and clear blue sea, a blue of the deepest and clearest conceivable, limited in one quarter by its far and sharp horizon of sky, and in the other by its near and sharp horizon of yellow sand overfringed with a low woody shore; the whole seen through the contorted cross-pieces of stunted, wind-twisted, far-spreading, quite fantastic old pines and cedars, whose bunched bristles, at the ends of long limbs, produced, against the light, the most vivid of all reminders. Cape Cod, on this showing, was exactly a pendent, pictured Japanese screen or banner; a delightful little triumph of "impressionism," which, during my short visit at least, never departed, under any provocation, from its type. Its type, so easily formulated, so completely filled, was there the last thing at night and the first thing in the morning; there was rest for the mind—for that, certainly, of the restless analyst—in having it so exactly under one's hand. After that one could read into it other meanings without straining or disturbing it. There was a couchant promontory in particular, half bosky with the evergreen boskage of the elegant kakemono, half bare with the bareness of refined, the *most* refined, New England decoration—a low, hospitable headland projected, as by some water-colourist master of the trick, into a mere brave wash of cobalt. It interfered, the sweet promontory, with its generous Boston bungalow, its verandahs still haunted with old summer-times, and so wide that the present could elbow and yet not jostle the past—it interfered no whit, for all its purity of style, with the human, the social question always dogging the steps of the ancient contemplative person and making him, before each scene, wish really to get *into* the picture, to cross, as it were, the threshold of the frame. It never lifts, verily, this obsession of the story-seeker, however often it may flutter its wings, it may bruise its breast, against surfaces either too hard or too blank. "The *manners*, the manners: where and what are they, and what have they to tell?"—that haunting curiosity, essential to the honour of his office, yet making it much of a burden, fairly buzzes about his head the more pressingly in proportion as the social mystery, the lurking human secret, seems more shy.

Then it is that, as he says to himself, the secret must be most queer—and it might therefore well have had, so insidiously sounded, a supreme queerness on Cape Cod. For not the faintest echo of it trembled out of the blankness; there were always the little white houses of the village, there were always the elegant elms, feebler and more feathery here than further inland; but the life of the little community was practically locked up as tight as if it had *all* been a question of painted Japanese silk. And that was doubtless, for the story-seeker, absolutely the little story: the constituted blankness was the whole business, and one's opportunity was all, thereby, for a study of exquisite emptiness. This was stuff, in its own way, of a beautiful quality; that impression came to me with a special sweetness that I have not forgotten. The help in the matter was that I had not forgotten, either, a small pilgrimage or two of far-away earlier years—the sense as of absent things in other summer-times, golden afternoons that referred themselves for their character simply to sandy roads and primitive "farms," crooked inlets of mild sea and, at the richest, large possibilities of worked cranberry-swamp. I re-membered, in fine, Mattapoisett, I remembered Marion, as admirable examples of that frequent New England phenome-non, the case the consummate example of which I was soon again to recognize in Newport—the presence of an *unrea-soned* appeal, in nature, to the sense of beauty, the appeal on a basis of items that failed somehow, count and recount them as one would, to justify the effect and make up the precious sum. The sum, at Newport above all, as I was soon again to see, is the exquisite, the irresistible; but you falter before be-ginning to name the parts of the explanation, conscious how short the list may appear. Thus everything, in the whole range of imagery, affirms itself and interposes; you will, you in-wardly determine, arrive at some notation of manners even if you perish in the attempt. Thus, as I jogged southward, from Boston, in a train that stopped and stopped again, for my fuller enlightenment, and that insisted, the good old promiscuous American car itself, on having as much of its native character as possible for my benefit, I already knew I must fall back on old props of association, some revival of the process of seeing the land grow mild and vague and interchangeably familiar with the sea, all under the spell of the reported "gulf-stream," those mystic words that breathe a softness wherever they sound.

It was imperative here that they should do what they could for me, and they must have been in full operation when, on my arrival at the small station from which I was to drive across to Cotuit—"across the Cape," as who should say, romantic thought, though I strain a point geographically for the romance—I found initiation awaiting me in the form of minimized horse-and-buggy and minimized man. The man was a little boy in tight knickerbockers, the horse barely an animal at all, a mere ambling spirit in shafts on the scale of a hairpin, the buggy disembodied save for its wheels, the whole thing the barest infraction of the road, of the void: circumstances, altogether, that struck the note, the right, the persistent one—that of my baffled endeavour, while in the neighbourhood, to catch life in the fact, and of my then having to recognize it as present *without* facts, or with only the few (the little white houses, the feathery elms, the band of ocean blue, the stripe of sandy yellow, the tufted pines in angular silhouette, the cranberry-swamps stringed across, for the picking, like the ruled pages of ledgers), that fell, incorruptibly silent, into the picture. We were still far from our goal, that first hour, when I had recognized the full pictorial and other "value" of my little boy and his little accessories; had seen, in the amiable waste that we continued to plough till we struck, almost with a shock, the inconsistency of a long stretch of new "stone" road, that, socially, economically, every contributive scrap of this detail was required. I drained my small companion, by gentle pressure, of such side-lights as he could project, consisting almost wholly, as they did, of a prompt and shrill, an oddly-emphasized "Yes, *sir!*" to each interrogative attempt to break ground. The summer people had already departed—with, as it seemed to me, undue precipitation; the very hotel offered, in its many-windowed bulk, the semblance of a mere huge brittle sea-shell that children tired of playing with it have cast again upon the beach; the alignments of white cottages were, once more, as if the children had taken, for a change, to building houses of cards and then had deserted *them*. I remember the sense that something *must* be done for penetration, for discovery; I remember an earnest stroll, undertaken for a view of waterside life, which resulted in the perception of a young man, in a spacious but otherwise unpeopled nook, a clear, straightforward young man to converse with, for a grand opportunity, across the water, waist-high in the quiet tide and prodding the sea-bottom for oysters; also in the discovery of an animated centre of industry of which oysters again were the motive: a mute citizen or two packing them in boxes, on the beach, for the Boston market, the hammer of some vague carpentry hard by, and, filling the air more than anything else, the unabashed discourse of three or four school-children at leisure, visibly "prominent" and apparently in charge of the life of the place. I remember not less a longish walk, and a longer drive, into low extensions of woody, piney, pondy landscape, veined with blue inlets and trimmed, on opportunity, with blond beaches— through all of which I pursued in vain the shy spectre of a revelation. The only revelation seemed really to be that, quite as in New Hampshire, so many people had "left" that the remaining characters, on the sketchy page, were too few to form a word. With this, accordingly, of what, in the bright air, for the charmed visitor, were the softness and sweetness of impression *made*? I had again to take it for a mystery.

V

This was really, for that matter, but the first phase of a resumed, or rather of a greatly-enlarged, acquaintance with the New England village in its most exemplary state: the state of being both sunned and shaded; of exhibiting more fresh white paint than can be found elsewhere in equal areas, and yet of correcting that conscious, that doubtless often somewhat embarrassed, hardness of countenance with an art of its

own. The descriptive term is of the simplest, the term that
suffices for the whole family when at its best: having spoken
of them as "elm-shaded," you have said so much about them
that little else remains. It is but a question, throughout, of the
quantity, the density, of their shade; often so thick and ample,
from May to November, that their function, in the social, in
the economic, order would seem on occasion to consist solely
of their being passive to that effect. To note the latter, accordingly, to praise it, to respond to its appeal for admiration,
practically represents, as you pass beneath the great feathery
arches, the only comment that may be addressed to the scene.
The charming thing—if that be the best way to take it—is
that the scene is everywhere the same; whereby tribute is always ready and easy, and you are spared all shocks of surprise
and saved any extravagance of discrimination. These communities stray so little from the type, that you often ask yourself
by what sign or difference you know one from the other. The
goodly elms, on either side of the large straight "street," rise
from their grassy margin in double, ever and anon in triple,
file; the white paint, on wooden walls, amid open dooryards,
reaffirms itself eternally behind them—though hanging back,
during the best of the season, with a sun-checkered, "amusing" vagueness; while the great verdurous vista, the high canopy of meeting branches, has the air of consciously playing
the trick and carrying off the picture. "See with how little we
do it; count over the elements and judge how few they are: in
other words come back in winter, in the months of the naked
glare, when the white paint looks dead and dingy against the
snow, the poor dear old white paint—immemorial, ubiquitous, save as venturing into brown or yellow—which is really
all we have to build on!" Some such sense as that you may
catch from the murmur of the amiable elms—if you are a
very restless analyst indeed, that is a very indiscreet listener.
      As you wouldn't, however, go back in winter on any ac-
count whatever, and least of all for any such dire discovery,
the picture hangs undisturbed in your gallery, and you even,
with extended study of it, class it among your best mementos
of the great autumnal harmony. The truth is that, for six or
seven weeks after the mid-September, among the mountains
of Massachusetts and Connecticut, the mere *fusion* of earth

and air and water, of light and shade and colour, the almost shameless tolerance of nature for the poor human experiment, are so happily effective that you lose all reckoning of the items of the sum, that you in short find in your draught, contentedly, a single strong savour. By all of which I don't mean to say that this sweetness of the waning year has not more taste in the presence of certain objects than in the presence of certain others. Objects remarkable enough, objects rich and rare perhaps, objects at any rate curious and interesting, emerge, for genial reference, from the gorgeous blur, and would commit me, should I give them their way, to excesses of specification. So I throw myself back upon the fusion, as I have called it—with the rich light hanging on but half-a-dozen spots. This renews the vision of the Massachusetts Berkshire—land beyond any other, in America, to-day, as one was much reminded, of leisure on the way to legitimation, of the social idyll, of the workable, the expensively workable, American form of country life; and, in especial, of a perfect consistency of surrender to the argument of the verdurous vista. This is practically the last word of such communities as Stockbridge, Pittsfield, Lenox, or of such villages as Salisbury and Farmington, over the Connecticut border. I speak of consistency in spite of the fact that it has doubtless here and there, under the planted elms, suffered some injury at the hands of the summer people; for really, beneath the wide mantle of particoloured Nature, nothing matters but the accidental liability of the mantle here and there to fall thickest. Thus it is then that you do, after a little, differentiate, from place to place, and compare and even prefer; thus it is that you recognize a scale and a range of amplitude—nay, more, wonderful to say, on occasion an emergence of detail; thus it is, in fine, that, while accepting the just eminence of Stockbridge and Pittsfield, for instance, you treat yourself on behalf of Farmington to something like a luxury of discrimination.

I may perhaps not go the length of asserting that Farmington might brave undismayed the absolute removal of the mantle of charity; since the great elm-gallery there struck me as not less than elsewhere essentially mistress of the scene. Only there were particular felicities there within the general— and anything very particular, in the land at large, always gave the case an appearance of rarity. When the great elm-gallery happens to be garnished with old houses, and the old houses happen to show style and form and proportion, and the hand of time, further, has been so good as to rest on them with all the pressure of protection and none of that of interference, then it is that the New England village may placidly await any comer. Farmington sits with this confidence on the top of a ridge that presents itself in its fringed length—a straight avenue seen in profile—to the visitor taking his way from the station across a couple of miles of level bottom that speak, for New England, of a luxury of culture; and nothing could be more fastidious and exceptional, and thereby more impressive in advance, than such upliftedness of posture. What is it but the note of the aristocratic in an air that so often affects us as drained precisely, and well-nigh to our gasping, of any exception to the common? The indication I here glance at secures for the place in advance, as you measure its detachment across the valley, a positively thrilled attention. Then comes, under the canopy of autumn, your vision of the grounds of this mild haughtiness, every one of which you gratefully allow. Stay as many hours as you will—and my stay was but of hours— they don't break down; you trace them into fifty minor titles and dignities, all charming aspects and high refinements of the older New England domestic architecture. Not only, moreover, are the best houses so "good"—the good ones are so surprisingly numerous. That is all they seem together to say. "We are good, yes—we are excellent; though, if we know it very well, we make no vulgar noise about it: we only just stand here, in our long double line, in the manner of mature and just slightly-reduced gentlewomen seated against the wall at an evening party (some party where mature gentle-women unusually abound), and neither too boldly affront the light nor shrink from the favouring shade." That again, on the spot, is the discreet voice of the air—which quavered away, for me, into still other admissions.

It takes but the barest semitone to start the story-seeker curious of manners—the story-seeker impenitent and uncor-rected, as happened in this case, by a lesson unmistakably re-ceived, or at least intended, a short time before. He had put a question, on that occasion, with an expectancy doubtless too crude; he had asked a resident of a large city of the middle West what might be, credibly, the conditions of the life "socially" led there. He had not, at Farmington, forgotten the ominous pause that had preceded the reply: "The conditions of the life? Why, the same conditions as everywhere else." He had not forgotten, either, the thrill of his sense of this collapse of his interlocutor: the case being, obviously, that it is of the very nature of conditions, as reported on by the expert—and it was to the expert he had appealed—to vary from place to place, so that they fall into as many groups, and constitute as many stamps, as there are different congregations of men. His interlocutor was not of the expert—*that* had really been the lesson; and it was with a far different poetry, the sweet shyness of veracity, that Farmington confessed to idiosyncrasies. I have too little space, however, as I had then too little time, to pretend to have lifted more than the smallest corner of this particular veil; besides which, if it is of the essence of the land, in these regions, to throw you back, after a little, upon the possible humanities, so it often results from the social study, too baffling in many a case, that you are thrown back upon the land. That agreeable, if sometimes bewildering, see-saw is perhaps the best figure, in such conditions, for the restless analyst's tenor of life. It was an effect of the fusion he has endeavoured to suggest; it is certainly true, at least, that, among the craggy hills, among little mountains that turned so easily, at any opening, to clearness of violet and blue, among the wood-circled dells that seemed to wait as for afternoon dances, among the horizons that recalled at their will the Umbrian note and the finer drawing, every ugliness melted and dropped, any wonderment at the other face of the medal seemed more trouble than it was worth. It was enough that the white village or the painted farm could gleam from afar, on the faintly purple slope, like a thing of mystery or of history; it was enough that the charming hill-mass, happily presented and foreshortened, should lie there like some beast, almost heraldic, resting his nose on his paws.

Those images, for retrospect, insistently supplant the others; though I have notes enough, I find, about the others too—about the inscrutability of the village street in general, for instance, in any relation but its relation to its elms. What *they* seemed to say is what I have mentioned; but what se-crets, meanwhile, did the rest of the scene keep? *Were* there any secrets at all, or had the outward blankness, the quantity of absence, as it were, in the air, its inward equivalent as well? There was the high, thin church, made higher, made highest, and sometimes, as at Farmington, made as pretty as a mon-strous Dutch toy, by its steeple of quaint and classic carpen-try; but this monument appeared to *testify* scarce more than some large white card, embellished with a stencilled border, on which a message or a sentence, an invitation or a revela-tion, might be still to be inscribed. The present, the positive, was mainly represented, ever, by the level railway-crossing, gaining expression from its localization of possible death and destruction, where the great stilted, strident, yet so almost comically impersonal train, which, with its so often undesig-nated and so always unservanted stations, and its general air of "bossing" the neighbourhoods it warns, for climax of its characteristic curtness, to "look out" for its rush, is every-where a large contribution to one's impression of a kind of monotony of acquiescence. This look as of universal acquies-cence plays somehow through the visible vacancy—seems a part of the thinness, the passivity, of that absence of the set-tled standard which contains, as I more and more felt, from day to day, the germ of the most final of all my generaliza-tions. I needn't be too prompt with it—so much higher may it hold its head, I foresee, when it flowers, perfectly, as a con-clusion, than when it merely struggles through the side of the subject as a tuft for provisional clutching. It sprouts in that soil, none the less, betimes, this apprehension that the "common man" and the common woman have here their appointed paradise and sphere, and that the sign of it is the abeyance, on many a scene, of any wants, any tastes, any hab-its, any traditions but theirs. The bullying railway orders them off their own decent avenue without a fear that they will "stand up" to it; the tone of the picture is the pitch of their lives, and when you listen to what the village street seems to say, marking it, at the end, with your "Is that *all*?" it is as if you had had your account of a scheme fashioned preponder-antly in their image.

I mean in *theirs* exactly, with as little provision for what is too foul for them as for what is too fair: the very middle, the golden mean, of the note of the common, to which the two extremes of condition are equally wanting; though with the mark strongest, if anywhere, against dusky misfortune and precarious dependence. The romance of costume, for better or worse, the implication of vices, accomplishments, manners, accents, attitudes, is as absent for evil as for good, for a low connection as for a high: which is why the simplification covers so much ground, that of public houses, that of kinds of people, that of suggestions, however faint, of discernible opportunity, of any deviation, in other words, into the *un*-common. There are no "kinds" of people; there are simply people, very, very few, and all of one kind, the kind who thus simply invest themselves for you in the grey truth that they don't go to the public house. It's a negative garment, but it must serve you; which it makes shift to do while you keep on asking, from the force of acquired habit, what may be behind, what beneath, what within, what may represent, in such con-ditions, the appeal of the senses or the tribute to them; what, in such a show of life, may take the place (to put it as simply as possible) of amusement, of social and sensual margin, over-flow and by-play. Of course there *is* by-play here and there; here and there, of course, extremes *are* touched: otherwise, the whole concretion, in its thinness, would crack, and the fact is that two or three of these strong patches of surface-embroidery remain with me as curious and interesting. Never was such by-play as in a great new house on a hilltop that overlooked the most composed of communities; a house ap-parently conceived—and with great felicity—on the lines of a magnified Mount Vernon, and in which an array of modern "impressionistic" pictures, mainly French, wondrous examples of Manet, of Degas, of Claude Monet, of Whistler, of other rare recent hands, treated us to the momentary effect of a large slippery sweet inserted, without a warning, between the compressed lips of half-conscious inanition. One hadn't quite known one was starved, but the morsel went down by the mere authority of the thing consummately *prepared*. Nothing else had been, in all the circle, prepared to anything like the same extent; and though the consequent taste, as a mixture with the other tastes, was of the queerest, no proof of the sovereign power of art could have been, for the moment, sharper. It happened to be that particular art—it might as well, no doubt, have been another; it made everything else shrivel and fade: it was like the sudden trill of a nightingale, lord of the hushed evening.

These appeared to be, over the land, always possible adventures; obviously I should have others of the same kind; I could let them, in all confidence, accumulate and wait. But, if that was one kind of extreme, what meanwhile was the other kind, the kind portentously alluded to by those of the sagacious who had occasionally put it before me that the village street, the arched umbrageous vista, half so candid and half so cool, is too frequently, in respect to "morals," but a whited sepulchre? They had so put it before me, these advisers, but they had as well, absolutely and all tormentingly, so left it: partly as if the facts were too abysmal for a permitted distinctness, and partly, no doubt, as from the general American habit of indirectness, of positive primness, of allusion to those matters that are sometimes collectively spoken of as "the great facts of life." It had been intimated to me that the great facts of life are in high fermentation on the other side of the ground glass that never for a moment flushes, to the casual eye, with the hint of a lurid light: so much, at least, one had no alternative, under pressure, but to infer. The inference, however, still left the question a prey to vagueness—it being obvious that vice requires forms not less than virtue, or perhaps even more, and that forms, up and down the prospect, were exactly what one waited in vain for. The theory that no community *can* live wholly without by-play, and the confirmatory word, for the particular case, of more initiated reporters, these things were all very well; but before a scene peeled as bare of palpable pretext as the American sky is often peeled of clouds (in the interest of the slightly acid juice of its light), where and how was the application to be made? It came at last, the application—that, I mean, of the portentous hint; and under it, after a fashion, the elements fell together. Why the picture *shouldn't* bristle with the truth—that was all conceivable; that the truth could only strike inward, horribly inward, not playing up to the surface—this too needed no insistence; what was sharpest for reflection being, meanwhile, a couple of minor appearances, which one gathered as one went. That our little arts of pathetic, of humorous, portrayal may, for all their claim to an edifying "realism," have on occasion small veracity and courage—that again was a remark pertinent to the matter. But the strangest link in the chain, and quite the horridest, was this other, of high value to the restless analyst—that, as the "interesting" puts in its note but where it can and where it will, so the village street and the lonely farm and the hillside cabin became positively richer objects under the smutch of imputation; twitched with a grim effect the thinness of their mantle, shook out of its folds such crudity and levity as they might, and borrowed, for dignity, a shade of the darkness of Cenci-drama, of monstrous legend, of old Greek tragedy, and thus helped themselves out for the story-seeker more patient almost of anything than of flatness.

There was not flatness, accordingly, though there might be dire dreariness, in some of those impressions gathered, for a climax, in the Berkshire country of Massachusetts, which forced it upon the fancy that here at last, in far, deep mountain valleys, where the winter is fierce and the summer irresponsible, was that heart of New England which makes so pretty a phrase for print and so stern a fact, as yet, for feeling. During the great loops thrown out by the lasso of observation from the wonder-working motor-car that defied the shrinkage of autumn days, this remained constantly the best formula of the impression and even of the emotion; it sat in the vehicle with us, but spreading its wings to the magnificence of movement, and gathering under them indeed most of the meanings of the picture. The heart of New England, at this rate, was an ample, a generous, heart, the largest demands on which, as to extent and variety, seemed not to overstrain its capacity. But it was where the mountain-walls rose straight and made the valleys happiest or saddest—one couldn't tell which, as to the felicity of the image, and it didn't much matter—that penetration was, for the poetry of it, deepest; just as generalization, for an opposite sort of beauty, was grandest on those several occasions when we perched for a moment on the summit of a "pass," a real little pass, slowly climbed to and keeping its other side, with an art all but Alpine, for a complete revelation, and hung there over the full vertiginous effect of the long and steep descent, the clinging road, the precipitous fall, the spreading, shimmering land bounded by blue horizons. We liked the very vocabulary, reduced to whatever minimum, of these romanticisms of aspect; again and again the land would do beautifully, if that were all that was wanted, and it deserved, the dear thing, thoroughly, any verbal caress, any tenderness of term, any share in a claim to the grand manner, to which we could responsively treat it. The grand manner was in the winding ascent, the rocky defile, the sudden rest for wonder, and all the splendid reverse of the medal, the world belted afresh as with purple sewn with pearls—melting, in other words, into violet hills with vague white towns on their breasts.

That was, at the worst, for October afternoons, the motor helping, our frequent fare; the habit of confidence in which was, perhaps, on no occasion so rewarded as on that of a particular plunge, from one of the highest places, through an ebbing golden light, into the great Lebanon "bowl," the vast, scooped hollow in one of the hither depths of which (given the quarter of our approach) we found the Shaker settlement once more or less, I believe, known to fame, ever so grimly planted. The grimness, even, was all right, when once we had admiringly dropped down and down and down; it would have done for that of a Buddhist monastery in the Himalayas—though more savagely clean and more economically impersonal, we seemed to make out, than the communities of older faiths are apt to show themselves. I remember the mere chill of contiguity, like the breath of the sepulchre, as we skirted, on the wide, hard floor of the valley, the rows of gaunt windows polished for no whitest, stillest, meanest face, even, to look out; so that they resembled the parallelograms of black paint criss-crossed with white lines that represent transparency in Nuremberg dolls'-houses. It wore, the whole settlement, as seen from without, the strangest air of active, operative death; as if the state of extinction were somehow, obscurely, administered and applied—the final hush of passions, desires, dangers, converted into a sort of huge stiff brush for sweeping away rubbish, or still more, perhaps, into a monstrous comb for raking in profit. The whole thing had the oddest appearance of mortification made to "pay." This

was really, however, sounding the heart of New England beyond its depth, for I am not sure that the New York boundary
had not been, just there, overpassed; there flowered out of
that impression, at any rate, another adventure, the very bravest possible for a shortened day, of which the motive, whether
formulated or not, had doubtless virtually been to feel, with a
far-stretched arm, for the heart of New York. *Had* New York,
the miscellaneous monster, a heart at all? — this inquiry, amid
so much encouraged and rewarded curiosity, might have been
well on the way to become sincere, and we kept groping,
between a prompt start and an extremely retarded return, for
any stray sign of an answer.

The answer, perhaps, in the event, still eluded us, but the
pursuit itself, away across State lines, through zones of other
manners, through images of other ideals, through densities of
other values, into a separate sovereign civilization in short—
this, with "a view of the autumnal Hudson" for an added
incentive, became, in all the conditions, one of the finer flowers of experience. To be on the lookout for differences was,
not unnaturally, to begin to meet them just over the border
and see them increase and multiply; was, indeed, with a mild
consistency, to feel it steal over us that we were, as we advanced, in a looser, shabbier, perhaps even rowdier world,
where the roads were of an easier virtue and the "farms" of a
scantier pride, where the absence of the ubiquitous sign-post
of New England, joy of lonely corners, left the great spaces
with an accent the less; where, in fine, the wayside bravery of
the commonwealth of Massachusetts settled itself, for memory, all serenely, to suffer by no comparison whatever. And
yet it wasn't, either, that this other was not also a big, bold
country, with ridge upon ridge and horizon by horizon to
deal with, insistently, pantingly, puffingly, pausingly, before
the great river showed signs of taking up the tale with its
higher hand; it wasn't, above all, that the most striking signs
by which the nearness of the river was first announced, three
or four fine old houses overlooking the long road, reputedly
Dutch manors, seats of patriarchs and patroons, and unmistakably rich "values" in the vast, vague scene, had not a nobler
archaic note than even the best of the New England colonial;
it wasn't that, finally, the Hudson, when we reached the town

that repeats in so minor a key the name of the stream, was not autumnal indeed, with majestic impenetrable mists that veiled the waters almost from sight, showing only the dim Catskills, off in space, as perfunctory graces, cheaply thrown in, and leaving us to roam the length of a large straight street which was, yes, decidedly, for comparison, for curiosity, not as the streets of Massachusetts.

The best here, to speak of, was that the motor underwent repair and that its occupants foraged for dinner—finding it indeed excellently at a quiet cook-shop, about the middle of the long-drawn way, after we had encountered coldness at the door of the main hotel by reason of our French poodle. This personage had made our group, admirably composed to our own sense as it was, only the more illustrious; but minds indifferent to an opportunity of intercourse, if but the intercourse of mere vision, with fine French poodles, may be taken always as suffering where they have sinned. The hospitality of the cook-shop was meanwhile touchingly, winningly unconditioned, yet full of character, of local, of national truth, as we liked to think: documentary, in a high degree—we talked it over—for American life. Wasn't it interesting that with American life so personally, so freely affirmed, the superstition of cookery should yet be so little denied? It was the queer old complexion of the long straight street, however, that most came home to me: Hudson, in the afternoon quiet, seemed to stretch back, with fumbling friendly hand, to the earliest outlook of my consciousness. Many matters had come and gone, innumerable impressions had supervened; yet here, in the stir of the senses, a whole range of small forgotten things revived, things intensely Hudsonian, more than Hudsonian; small echoes and tones and sleeping lights, small sights and sounds and smells that made one, for an hour, *as* small—carried one up the rest of the river, the very river of life indeed, as a thrilled, roundabouted pilgrim, by primitive steamboat, to a mellow, mediæval Albany.

VI

It is a convenience to be free to confess that the play of perception during those first weeks was quickened, in the oddest way, by the wonderment (which was partly also the amusement) of my finding how many corners of the general, of the local, picture had anciently never been unveiled for me at all, and how many unveiled too briefly and too scantly, with quite insufficient bravery of gesture. That might make one ask by what strange law one had lived in the other time, with gaps, to that number, in one's experience, in one's consciousness, with so many muffled spots in one's general vibration—and the answer indeed to such a question might carry with it an infinite penetration of retrospect, a penetration productive of ghostly echoes as sharp sometimes as aches or pangs. So many had been the easy things, the contiguous places, the conspicuous objects, to right or to left of the path, that had been either unaccountably or all too inevitably left undiscovered, and which were to live on, to the inner vision, through the long years, as mere blank faces, round, empty, metallic, senseless disks dangling from familiar and reiterated names. Why, at the same time, one might ask, had the consciousness of irritation from these vain forms not grown greater? why had the inconvenience, or the disgrace, of early privation become an accepted memory? All, doubtless, in the very interest, precisely, of this eventual belated romance, and so that adventures, even of minor type, so preposterously postponed should be able to deck themselves at last with a kind of accumulation of freshness.

So the freshness, all the autumn, kept breaking through the staleness—when the staleness, so agreeably flavoured with hospitality, and indeed with new ingredients, was a felt element at all. There was after all no moment perhaps at which one element stood out so very sharply from the other—the hundred emendations and retouches of the old picture, its greater depth of tone, greater show of detail, greater size and scale, tending by themselves to confound and mislead, in a manner, the lights and shades of remembrance. Very promptly, in the Boston neighbourhoods, the work of time loomed large, and the difference made by it, as one might say, for the general richness. The richness might have its poverties still and the larger complexity its crudities; but, all the same, to look back was to seem to have been present at an extraordinary general process, that of the rapid, that of the ceaseless relegation of the *previous* (on the part of the whole visible order) to one of the wan categories of misery. What was taking place was a perpetual repudiation of the past, so far as there had been a past to repudiate, so far as the past was a positive rather than a negative quantity. There had been plenty in it, assuredly, of the negative, and that was but a shabbiness to disown or a deception to expose; yet there had been an old conscious commemorated life too, and it was this that had become the victim of supersession. The pathos, so to call it, of the impression was somehow that it didn't, the earlier, simpler condition, still resist or protest, or at all expressively flush through; it was consenting to become a past with all the fine candour with which it had tried to affirm itself, in its day, as a present—and very much, for that matter, as with a due ironic forecast of the fate in store for the hungry, triumphant actual.

This savors perhaps of distorted reflection, but there was really a light over it in which the whole spectacle was to shine. *The will to grow* was everywhere written large, and to grow at no matter what or whose expense. I had naturally seen it before, I had seen it, on the other side of the world, in a thousand places and forms, a thousand hits and misses: these things are the very screeches of the pipe to which humanity is actually dancing. But here, clearly, it was a question of scale and space and chance, margin and elbow-room, the quantity of floor and loudness of the dance-music; a question of the ambient air, above all, the permitting medium, which had at once, for the visitor's personal inhalation, a dry taste in the mouth. Thin and clear and colourless, what would it ever say "no" to? or what would it ever paint thick, indeed, with sympathy and sanction? With so little, accordingly, within the great frame of the picture, to prevent or to prescribe, it was as if anything might be done there that any sufficient number of subscribers to any sufficient number of sufficiently noisy newspapers might want. That, moreover, was but another name for the largest and straightest perception the restless analyst had yet risen to—the perception that awaits the returning absentee from this great country, on the wharf of disembarkation, with an embodied intensity that no superficial confusion, no extremity of chaos any more than any brief mercy of accident, avails to mitigate. The waiting observer need be little enough of an analyst, in truth, to arrive at that consciousness, for the phenomenon is vivid in direct proportion as the ship draws near. The great presence that bristles for him on the sounding dock, and that shakes the planks, the loose boards of its theatric stage to an inordinate unprecedented rumble, is the monstrous form of Democracy, which is thereafter to project its shifting angular shadow, at one time and another, across every inch of the field of his vision. It is the huge democratic broom that has made the clearance and that one seems to see brandished in the empty sky.

That is of course on one side no great discovery, for what does even the simplest soul ever sail westward for, at this time of day, if not to profit, so far as possible, by "the working of democratic institutions"? The political, the civic, the economic view of them is a study that may be followed, more or less, at a distance; but the way in which they determine and qualify manners, feelings, communications, modes of contact and conceptions of life—this is a revelation that has its full force and its lively interest only on the spot, where, when once caught, it becomes the only clue worth mentioning in the labyrinth. The condition, notoriously, represents an immense boon, but what does the enjoyment of the boon represent? The clue is never out of your hands, whatever other objects, extremely disconnected from it, may appear at the moment to fill them. The democratic consistency, consummately and immitigably complete, shines through with its hard light, whatever equivocal gloss may happen momentarily to prevail. You may talk of other things, and you do, as much as possible; but you are really thinking of that one, which has everything else at its mercy. What indeed is this circumstance that the condition is thus magnified but the commanding value of the picture, its message and challenge to intelligent curiosity? Curiosity is fairly fascinated by the sense of the immensity of the chance, and by the sense that the whole of the chance has been taken. It is rarely given to us to see a great game played as to the very end—and that was where, with his impression of nothing to prevent, of nothing, anywhere around him, to prevent anything, the ancient contemplative person, floating serenely in his medium, had yet occasionally to gasp before the assault of the quantity of illustration. The illustration might be, enormously, of something deficient, absent—in which case it was for the aching void to be (as an aching void) striking and interesting. As an explication or an implication the democratic intensity could always figure.

VII

There was little need, for that matter, to drag it into the foreground on the evening of my renewed introduction to the particular Boston neighbourhood—the only one of them all—with which I had been formerly somewhat acquainted. I had alighted in New York but three days before, and my senses were all so full of it that as I look back I can again feel it, under the immediate Cambridge impression, assert itself by turning quite to insidious softness, to confused and surprised recognition. I had driven out from Boston through the warm September night and through a town-picture as of extraordinary virtuous vacancy (without so much as the figure of a policeman in sight from the South Station to the region of Harvard Square), and I remember how the odorous hour —charged with the old distinctively American earth-smell, which in the darkness fairly poetized the suburbs, and with the queer, far, wild throb of shrilling insects—prescribed to me the exact form of the response to the question as to one's sense of a "great change" already so often sounded. "A great change? No change at all. Where then would the 'intensity' be? But *changes*—ever so many and so amusing and so agreeable. The intensity is compatible with *them*—nothing, clearly, is going to be so interesting as to make out, with plenty of good-will, how compatible!" There was unmistakably everywhere a more embroidered surface—the new free figures played over the canvas; so that at this rate, in the time to come, how far might the embroidery not go, what silk and gold mightn't it weave into the pattern? It wasn't of course a question of rhapsodizing—Cambridge was Cambridge still, and all faithful to its type; but the rustle of the trees in the summer night had a larger tone, the more frequent lamplight slept on ampler walls, the body of impression was greater and the University, above all, seemed in more confident possession. It massed there in multiplied forms, with new and strange architectures looming through the dark; it appeared to have wandered wide and to be stretching forth, in many directions, long, acquisitive arms.

This vision, for the moment, of a great dim, clustered but restlessly expansive Harvard, hushed to vacation stillness as to a deep ambitious dream, was, for the impressible story-seeker, practically the germ of the most engaging of the generalized images of reassurance, the furniture, so to speak, of the *other* scale, that the extension of his view was to cause him to cultivate. Reassurance is required, before the spectacle of American manners at large, whenever one most acutely perceives how little honour they tend to heap on the art of discrimination, and it is at such hours that, turning in his frequent stupefaction, the restless analyst reaches out for support to the nearest faint ghost of a constituted Faculty. It takes no exceptional exposure to the promiscuous life to show almost any institution pretending to university form as stamped here with the character and function of the life-saving monasteries of the dark ages. They glow, the humblest of them, to the imagination—the imagination that fixes the surrounding scene as a huge Rappacini-garden, rank with each variety of the poison-plant of the money-passion—they glow with all the vividness of the defined alternative, the possible antidote, and seem to call on us to blow upon the flame till it is made inextinguishable. So little time had it taken, at any rate, to suggest to me that a new and higher price, in American conditions, is attaching to the cloister, literally—the place inaccessible (to put it most pertinently) to the shout of the newspaper, the place to perambulate, the place to think, apart from the crowd. Doubtless indeed I was not all aware of it at the time, but the image I touch upon in connection with those first moments was to remain with me, the figure of the rich old Harvard organism brooding, exactly, through the long vacation, brooding through the summer night, on discriminations, on insistences, on sublime and exquisite heresies to come.

After that arrived daylight recognitions, but they were really for the most part offered me, as in a full cup, by the accident of a couple of hours that were to leave me the pure essence, the finer sense of them. These were a matter of a fortnight later, as I had had immediately to make an absence, and the waning September afternoon of the second occasion took on a particular quality for this deferred surrender of a dozen stored secrets. "Secrets" I call them because the total impression was of the production of some handful of odds and ends that had lurked, for long, in a locked drawer, and which, being brought out, might promote, by their blinking consciousness, either derision or respect. They excited, as befell, an extraordinary tenderness—on which conclusion it was fortunate to be able afterwards to rest. I wandered, for the day's end, with a young modern for whom the past had not been and who was admirably unconscious of the haunting moral of the whole mutation—the tune to which the pampered present made the other time look comparatively grim. Each item of the pampered state contributed to this effect— the finer *mise en scène*, the multiplied resources, halls, faculties, museums, undergraduate and postgraduate habitations (these last of so large a luxury); the pompous little club-houses, visited, all vacant, in the serious tell-tale twilight that seemed to give them, intellectually, "away"; the beautiful new Union, with its great grave noble hall, of which there would be so much more to be said; and above all, doubtless, the later majesties of the Law School, in the near presence of which the tiny old disinherited seat of that subject, outfaced and bedimmed, seemed unable to make even a futile plea for quaintness. I went into the new Law Library, immense and supreme—in the shadow of which I caught myself sniffing the very dust, prehistoric but still pungent, of the old. I saw in the distance a distinguished friend, all alone, belatedly working there, but to go to him I should have had to cross the bridge that spans the gulf of time, and, with a suspicion of weak places, I was nervous about its bearing me.

What such delicacies came to, then and afterwards, for the whole impression, was the instinct not to press, not to push on, till forced, through any half-open door of the real. The real was there, certainly enough, outside and all round, but there was standing-ground, more immediately, for a brief idyll, and one would walk in the idyll, if only from hour to hour, while one could. This could but mean that one would cultivate the idyllic, for the social, for the pictorial illusion, by every invoking and caressing art; and in fact, as a consequence, the reflection of our observer's experience for the next few weeks—that is so long as the spell of the autumn lasted—would be but the history of his more or less ingenious arts. With the breaking of the autumn, later on, everything broke, everything went—everything was transposed at least into another key. But for the time so much had been gained—the happy trick had been played.

VIII

It was after all in the great hall of the Union perhaps (to come back to that delicate day's end) that the actual vibration of response seemed most to turn to audible music—repeated, with all its suggestiveness, on another occasion or two. For the case was unmistakably that just there, more than anywhere, by a magnificent stroke, an inspiration working perhaps even beyond its consciousness, the right provision had been made for the remembering mind. The place was addressed in truth so largely to an enjoying and producing future that it might seem to frown on mere commemoration, on the backward vision; and yet, at the moment I speak of, its very finest meaning might have been that of a liberal monument to those who had come and gone, to the company of the lurking ghosts. The air there was full of them, and this was its service, that it cared for them *all*, and so eased off the intensity of their appeal. And yet it appeared to play that part for a reason more interesting than reducible to words—a reason that mainly came out for me while, in the admirable hall aforesaid, I stood before Sargent's high portrait of Major Henry Lee Higginson, *donatorio* of the house (as well as author, all round about, of innumerable other civil gifts); a representation of life and character, a projection of genius, which even that great painter has never outdone. Innumerable, ever, are the functions performed and the blessings wrought by the supreme work of art, but I know of no case in which it has been so given to such a work to make the human statement with a great effect, to interfuse a group of public acts with the personality, with the characteristics, of the actor. The acts would still have had all their value if the portrait had had less, but they would not assuredly have been able to become so interesting, would not have grown to affect each beneficiary, however obscure, as proceeding, for him, from a possible relation, a possible intimacy. It is to the question of intimacy with somebody or other that all great practical public recognition is finally carried back—but carried only by the magic carpet, when the magic carpet happens to be there. Mr. Sargent's portrait of Henry Higginson is exactly the magic carpet.

That was the "pull" (one kept on feeling) that this happy commemorative creation of the Union had over the great official, the great bristling brick Valhalla of the early "seventies," that house of honour and of hospitality which, under the name of the Alumni Hall, dispenses (apart from its containing a noble auditorium) laurels to the dead and dinners to the living. The recording tablets of the members of the University sacrificed, on the Northern side, in the Civil War, are too impressive not to retain here always their collective beauty; but the monumental office and character suffer throughout from the too scant presence of the massive and the mature. The great structure spreads and soars with the best will in the world, but succeeds in resembling rather some high-masted ship at sea, in slightly prosaic equilibrium, than a thing of builded foundations and embrasured walls. To which it is impossible not immediately to add that these distinctions are relative and these comparisons almost odious, in face of the recent generations, gathered in from beneath emptier skies, who must have found in the big building as it stands an admonition and an ideal. So much the better for the big building, assuredly, and none so calculably the worse for the generations themselves. The reflection follows close moreover that, tactfully speaking, criticism has no close concern with Alumni Hall; it is as if that grim visitor found the approaches closed to him—had to enter, to the loss of all his identity, some relaxing air of mere sentimental, mere shameless association. He turns his back, a trifle ruefully whistling, and wanders wide; so at least I seemed to see him do, all September, all October, and hereabouts in particular: I felt him resignedly reduced, for the time, to looking over, to looking through, the fence—all the more that at Cambridge there was at last something in the nature of a fence so to be dealt with.

The smaller aspects, the sight of mere material arrears made up, may seem unduly to have held me when I say that few fresh circumstances struck me as falling more happily into the picture than this especial decency of the definite, the palpable affirmation and belated delimitation of College Yard. The high, decorated, recurrent gates and the still insufficiently high iron palings—representing a vast ring and even now incomplete—may appear, in spots, extemporized and thin; but that signifies little in presence of the precious idea on the side of which, in the land of the "open door," the all-abstract outline, the timid term and the general concession, they bravely range themselves. The open door—as it figures here in respect to everything but trade—may make a magnificent place, but it makes poor places; and in places, despite our large mistrust of privacy, and until the national ingenuity shall have invented a substitute for them, we must content ourselves with living. This especial drawing of the belt at Harvard is an admirably interesting example of the way in which the formal enclosure of objects at all interesting immediately refines upon their interest, immediately establishes values. The enclosure may be impressive from without, but from within it is sovereign; nothing is more curious than to trace in the aspects so controlled the effect of their established relation to it. This resembles, in the human or social order, the improved situation of the foundling who has discovered his family or of the actor who has mastered his part.

The older buildings, in the Yard, profit indeed, on the spot, to the story-seeking mind, by the fact of their comparative exhibition of the tone of time—so prompt an ecstasy and so deep a relief reward, in America, everywhere, any suggested source of interest that is not the interest of importunate newness. That source overflows, all others run thin; but the wonder and the satisfaction are that in College Yard more than one of these should have finally been set to running thick. The best pieces of the earlier cluster, from Massachusetts to Stoughton, emerge from their elongation of history with a paler archaic pink in their brickwork; their scant primitive details, small "quaintnesses" of form, have turned, each, to the

expressive accent that no short-cut of "style" can ever successfully imitate, and from their many-paned windows, where, on
the ensconced benches, so many generations have looked out,
they fall, in their minor key, into the great main current of
ghostly gossip. "See, see, we are getting on, we are getting
almost ripe, ripe enough to justify the question of taste about
us. We are growing a complexion—which takes almost as
long, and is in fact pretty well the same thing, as growing a
philosophy; but we are putting it on and entering into the
dignity of time, the beauty of life. We are in a word beginning
to begin, and we have the best sign of it, haven't we? that we
make the vulgar, the very vulgar, think we are beginning to
end."

   That moreover was not the only relation thus richly promoted; there could be no unrest of analysis worthy of the
name that failed to perceive how, after term had opened, the
type of the young men coming and going in the Yard gained,
for vivacity of appeal, through this more marked constitution
of a *milieu* for it. Here, verily, questions could swarm; for
there was scarce an impression of the local life at large that
didn't play into them. One thing I had not yet done—I had
not been, under the best guidance, out to Ellis Island, the seat
of the Commissioner of Immigration, in the bay of New
York, to catch in the fact, as I was to catch later on, a couple
of hours of the ceaseless process of the recruiting of our race,
of the plenishing of our huge national *pot au feu*, of the introduction of fresh—of perpetually fresh so far it isn't perpetually stale—foreign matter into our heterogeneous system. But
even without that a haunting wonder as to what might be
becoming of us all, "typically," ethnically, and thereby physiognomically, linguistically, *personally*, was always in order.
The young men in their degree, as they flocked candidly up to
college, struck me as having much to say about it, and there
was always the sense of light on the subject, for comparison
and reference, that a long experience of other types and other
manners could supply. Swarming ingenuous youths, *whom did
they look like the sons of?*—that inquiry, as to any group, any
couple, any case, represented a game that it was positively
thrilling to play out. There was plenty to make it so, for there
was, to begin with, both the forecast of the thing that might

easily settle the issue and the forecast of the thing that might easily complicate it.

No impression so promptly assaults the arriving visitor of the United States as that of the overwhelming preponderance, wherever he turns and twists, of the unmitigated "business man" face, ranging through its various possibilities, its extraordinary actualities, of intensity. And I speak here of facial cast and expression alone, leaving out of account the questions of voice, tone, utterance and attitude, the chorus of which would vastly swell the testimony and in which I seem to discern, for these remarks at large, a treasure of illustration to come. Nothing, meanwhile, is more concomitantly striking than the fact that the women, over the land—allowing for every element of exception—appear to be of a markedly finer texture than the men, and that one of the liveliest signs of this difference is precisely in their less narrowly specialized, their less commercialized, distinctly more generalized, physiognomic character. The superiority thus noted, and which is quite another matter from the universal fact of the mere usual female femininity, is far from constituting absolute distinction, but it constitutes relative, and it is a circumstance at which interested observation snatches, from the first, with an immense sense of its *portée*. There are, with all the qualifications it is yet open to, fifty reflections to be made upon the truth it seems to represent, the appearance of a queer deep split or chasm between the two stages of personal polish, the two levels of the conversible state, at which the sexes have arrived. It is at all events no exaggeration to say that the imagination at once embraces it as *the* feature of the social scene, recognizing it as a subject fruitful beyond the common, and wondering even if for pure drama, the drama of manners, anything anywhere else touches it. If it be a "subject," verily—with the big vision of the intersexual relation as, at such an increasing rate, a prey to it—the right measure for it would seem to be offered in the art of the painter of life by the concrete example, the art of the dramatist or the novelist, rather than in that of the talker, the reporter at large. The only thing is that, from the moment the painter begins to look at American life brush in hand, he is in danger of seeing, in comparison, almost nothing else in it—nothing, that is, so characteristic as this apparent privation, for the man, of his right kind of woman, and this apparent privation, for the woman, of her right kind of man.

The right kind of woman for the American man may really be, of course, as things are turning out with him, the woman as to whom his most workable relation is to support her and bear with her—just as the right kind of man for the American woman may really be the man who intervenes in her life only by occult, by barely divinable, by practically disavowed courses. But the ascertainment and illustration of these truths would be, exactly, very conceivably high sport for the ironic poet—who has surely hitherto neglected one of his greatest current opportunities. It in any case remains vivid that American life may, as regards much of its manifestation, fall upon the earnest view as a society of women "located" in a world of men, which is so different a matter from a collection of men of the world; the men supplying, as it were, all the canvas, and the women all the embroidery. Just this vividness it was that held up the torch, through the Cambridge autumn, to that question of the affiliation of the encountered Harvard undergraduate which I may not abandon. In what proportion of instances would it stick out that the canvas, rather than the embroidery, was what he had to show? In what proportion would he wear the stamp of the unredeemed commercialism that should betray his paternity? In what proportion, in his appearance, would the different social "value" imputable to his mother have succeeded in interposing? The discerned answer to these inquiries is really, after all, too precious (in its character of contribution to one's total gathered wisdom) to be given away prematurely; but there was at least always the sense, to which the imagination reverted, that in the collegiate cloisters and academic shades of other countries this absence of a possible *range* of origin and breeding in a young type had not been so felt. The question of origin, the question of breeding, had been large—never settled in advance; there had been fifty *sorts* of persons, fifty representatives of careers, to whom the English, the French, the German universitarian of tender years might refer you for a preliminary account of him.

I speak of my keeping back, for the present, many of my ultimate perceptions, but I may none the less recall my having had, all the season, from early, the ring in my ears of a reply I had heard made, on the spot, to a generous lady offering entertainment to a guest, a stranger to the scene, whose good impression she had had at heart. "What kind of people should I like to meet? Why, my dear madam, have you more than *one* kind?" At the same time that I could remember this, however, I could also remember that the consistently *bourgeois* fathers must themselves in many cases have had mothers whose invitation to their male offspring to clutch at their relatively finer type had not succeeded in getting itself accepted. That constituted a fatal precedent, and it would have to be in the female offspring, probably, that one should look for evidences of the clutching—an extension of the inquiry for which there was plenty of time. What did escape from submersion, meanwhile, as is worth mentioning, was the golden state of being reminded at moments that there are no such pleasure-giving accidents, for the mind, as violations of the usual in conditions that make them really precarious and rare. As the usual, in our vast crude democracy of trade, is the new, the simple, the cheap, the common, the commercial, the immediate, and, all too often, the ugly, so any human product that those elements fail conspicuously to involve or to explain, any creature, or even any feature, not turned out to pattern, any form of suggested rarity, subtlety, ancientry, or other pleasant perversity, prepares for us a recognition akin to rapture. These lonely ecstasies of the truly open sense make up often, in the hustling, bustling desert, for such "sinkings" of the starved stomach as have led one too often to have to tighten one's æsthetic waistband.

IX

All of which is sufficiently to imply, again, that for adventurous contemplation, at any of the beguiled hours of which I pretend here but to give the general happier drift, there was scarce such a thing as a variation of insistence. As every fact was convertible into a fancy, there was only an encouraged fusion of possible felicities and possible mistakes, stop-gaps before the awful advent of a "serious sense of critical responsibility." Or say perhaps rather, to alter the image, that there was only a builded breakwater against the assault of matters demanding a *literal* notation. I walked, at the best, but on the breakwater—looking down, if one would, over the flood of the real, but much more occupied with the sight of the old Cambridge ghosts, who seemed to advance one by one, even at that precarious eminence, to meet me. My small story would gain infinitely in richness if I were able to name them, but they swarmed all the while too thick, and of but two or three of them alone is it true that they push their way, of themselves, through any silence. It was thus at any rate a question—as I have indeed already sufficiently shown—of what one read *into* anything, not of what one read out of it; and the occasions that operated for that mild magic resolve themselves now into three or four of an intrinsic colour so dim as to be otherwise well-nigh indistinguishable. Why, if one could tell it, would it be so wonderful, for instance, to have stood on the low cliff that hangs over the Charles, by the nearer side of Mount Auburn, and felt the whole place bristle with merciless memories? It was late in the autumn and in the day—almost evening; with a wintry pink light in the west, the special shade, fading into a heartless prettiness of grey, that shows with a polar chill through the grim tracery of November. Just opposite, at a distance, beyond the river and its meadows, the white face of the great empty Stadium stared at me, as blank as a rising moon —with Soldiers' Field squaring itself like some flat memorial slab that waits to be inscribed. I had seen it inscribed a week or two before in the fantastic lettering of a great intercollegiate game of football, and that impression had been so documentary, as to the capacity of the American public for momentary gregarious emphasis, that I regret having to omit here all the reflections it prompted.

They were not, however, what was now relevant, save in so far as the many-mouthed uproar they recalled was a voice in the more multitudinous modern hum through which one listened almost in vain for the sound of the old names. One of these in particular rose to my lips—it was impossible to stand there and not reach out a hand to J. R. L. as to a responsive personal presence, the very genius of the spot, who had given it from so early the direct literary consecration without which even the most charming seats of civilization go through life awkwardly and ruefully, after the manner of unchristened children. They lack thus, for the great occasions, the great formal necessities, their "papers." It was thanks to Lowell even more immediately than to Longfellow that Cambridge *had* its papers—though if I find myself putting that word into the past tense it is perhaps because of the irresistible admonition, too (proceeding so from a thousand local symptoms), that titles embodied in literary form are less and less likely, in the Harvard air, to be asked for. That is clearly not the way the wind sets: we see the great University sit and look very hard, at blue horizons of possibility, across the high table-land of her future; but the light of literary desire is not perceptibly in her eye (nothing is more striking than the recent drop in her of any outward sign of literary curiosity); precisely for which reason it was, doubtless, in part, that the changed world seemed reflected with a certain tragic intensity even in faces ever so turned to cheerful lights as those of my two constructive companions.

I had passed high, square, sad old Elmwood on the way to my cliff over the Charles, and had wonderingly lingered a little about it. I had passed Mr. Longfellow's immemorial, historical, admired residence, still ample and symmetrical and visibly tourist-haunted (the only detected ruffle of its noble calm); elements of the picture that had rekindled for an hour the finer sensibility, the finer continuity and piety. It was because of these things, again, that I felt the invoked pair beside me presently turn away, as under a chill, from that too spectral (in its own turn) stare of the Stadium—perceived as a portent of the more *roaring*, more reported and excursionized scene; and in particular seemed to see J. R. L.'s robust humour yield to the recognition of the irony of fate, dear to every poet, in one of its most pointed forms. That humour had played of old, charmingly, over the thesis that Cambridge, Mass., was, taken altogether, the most inwardly civilized, most intimately humane, among the haunts of men; whereby it had committed itself, this honest adventurer, to a patient joy in the development of the *genius loci*, and was therefore without provision, either of poetry or of prose, against the picture of proportions and relations overwhelmingly readjusted. If the little old place, with its accessible ear, had been so brave, what was the matter with the big new one, going in, as it would itself say, for greater braveries still? Nothing, no doubt, but that the possession of an ear would be ceasing to count as an advantage. In what produced form, for instance, if he had been right, was now represented the love of letters of which he had been so distinguished an example? If he had on the other hand *not* been right—well, it would all be rather dreadful. Such, at all events, may be the disconcertments of a revisiting spirit—when he has happened to revisit too ingenious an old friend.

The old friend moreover had meanwhile had, and in relation to this large loose fringe of the town, there so freely disposed, one of his very own disconcertments; he had turned his steps, for the pleasure of memory, to Fresh Pond, dear to the muses of youth, the Sunday afternoons of spring, and had to accept there his clearest vision perhaps of the new differences and indifferences. The little nestling lake of other days had ceased to nestle; there was practically no Fresh Pond any more, and I seemed somehow to see why the muses had fled even as from the place at large. The light flutter of their robes had surrounded far-away walks and talks: one could at this day, on printed, on almost faded pages, give chapter and verse for the effect, audible on the Sunday afternoons, of their habit of murmurous hinted approval. Other things had come by makeweight; the charming Country Club on toward Watertown, all verandahs and golf-links and tennis-lawns, all tea and ices and self-consciousness; and there had come, thereabouts too, the large extension of the "Park System," the admirable commissioners' roads that reach across the ruder countryside like the arms of carnivorous giants stretching over a tea-table of blackberries and buns. But these things were in the eternal American note, the note of the gregarious, the concentric, and pervaded moreover by the rustle of petticoats too distinguishable from any garment-hem of the sacred nine. The desecrated, the destroyed resort had favoured, save on rare feast-days, the single stroll, or at the worst the double, dedicated to shared literary secrets; which was why I almost

angrily missed, among the ruins, what I had mainly gone back
to recover—some echo of the dreams of youth, the titles of
tales, the communities of friendship, the sympathies and patiences, in fine, of dear W. D. H.

II

New York Revisited

I

T HE SINGLE impression or particular vision most answering to the greatness of the subject would have been, I think, a certain hour of large circumnavigation that I found prescribed, in the fulness of the spring, as the almost immediate crown of a return from the Far West. I had arrived at one of the transpontine stations of the Pennsylvania Railroad; the question was of proceeding to Boston, for the occasion, without pushing through the terrible town—why "terrible," to my sense, in many ways, I shall presently explain—and the easy and agreeable attainment of this great advantage was to embark on one of the mightiest (as appeared to me) of train-bearing barges and, descending the western waters, pass round the bottom of the city and remount the other current to Harlem; all without "losing touch" of the Pullman that had brought me from Washington. This absence of the need of losing touch, this breadth of effect, as to the whole process, involved in the prompt floating of the huge concatenated cars not only without arrest or confusion, but as for positive prodigal beguilement of the artless traveller, had doubtless much to say to the ensuing state of mind, the happily-excited and amused view of the great face of New York. The extent, the ease, the energy, the quantity and number, all notes scattered about as if, in the whole business and in the splendid light, nature and science were joyously romping together, might have been taking on again, for their symbol, some collective presence of great circling and plunging, hovering and perching sea-birds, white-winged images of the spirit, of the restless freedom of the Bay. The Bay had always, on other opportunities, seemed to blow its immense character straight into one's face—coming "at" you, so to speak, bearing down on you, with the full force of a thousand prows of steamers seen exactly on the line of their longitudinal axis; but I had never before been so conscious of its boundless cool assurance

416

or seemed to see its genius so grandly at play. This was presumably indeed because I had never before enjoyed the remarkable adventure of taking in so much of the vast bristling promontory from the water, of ascending the East River, in especial, to its upper diminishing expanses.

Something of the air of the occasion and of the mood of the moment caused the whole picture to speak with its largest suggestion; which suggestion is irresistible when once it is sounded clear. It is all, absolutely, an expression of things lately and currently *done*, done on a large impersonal stage and on the basis of inordinate gain—it is not an expression of any other matters whatever; and yet the sense of the scene (which had at several previous junctures, as well, put forth to my imagination its power) was commanding and thrilling, was in certain lights almost charming. So it befell, exactly, that an element of mystery and wonder entered into the impression—the interest of trying to make out, in the absence of features of the sort usually supposed indispensable, the reason of the beauty and the joy. It is indubitably a "great" bay, a great harbour, but no one item of the romantic, or even of the picturesque, as commonly understood, contributes to its effect. The shores are low and for the most part depressingly furnished and prosaically peopled; the islands, though numerous, have not a grace to exhibit, and one thinks of the other, the real flowers of geography in this order, of Naples, of Capetown, of Sydney, of Seattle, of San Francisco, of Rio, asking how if *they* justify a reputation, New York should seem to justify one. Then, after all, we remember that there are reputations and reputations; we remember above all that the imaginative response to the conditions here presented may just happen to proceed from the intellectual extravagance of the given observer. When this personage is open to corruption by almost any large view of an intensity of life, his vibrations tend to become a matter difficult even for *him* to explain. He may have to confess that the group of evident facts fails to account by itself for the complacency of his appreciation. Therefore it is that I find myself rather backward with a perceived sanction, of an at all proportionate kind, for the fine exhilaration with which, in this free wayfaring relation to them, the wide waters of New York inspire me. There is the beauty of light and air, the great scale of space, and, seen far away to the west, the open gates of the Hudson, majestic in their degree, even at a distance, and announcing still nobler things. But the real appeal, unmistakably, is in that note of vehemence in the local life of which I have spoken, for it is the appeal of a particular type of dauntless power.

The aspect the power wears then is indescribable; it is the power of the most extravagant of cities, rejoicing, as with the voice of the morning, in its might, its fortune, its unsurpassable conditions, and imparting to every object and element, to the motion and expression of every floating, hurrying, panting thing, to the throb of ferries and tugs, to the plash of waves and the play of winds and the glint of lights and the shrill of whistles and the quality and authority of breeze-borne cries—all, practically, a diffused, wasted clamour of *detonations*—something of its sharp free accent and, above all, of its sovereign sense of being "backed" and able to back. The universal *applied* passion struck me as shining unprecedentedly out of the composition; in the bigness and bravery and insolence, especially, of everything that rushed and shrieked; in the air as of a great intricate frenzied dance, half merry, half desperate, or at least half defiant, performed on the huge watery floor. This appearance of the bold lacing-together, across the waters, of the scattered members of the monstrous organism—lacing as by the ceaseless play of an enormous system of steam-shuttles or electric bobbins (I scarce know what to call them), commensurate in form with their infinite work—does perhaps more than anything else to give the pitch of the vision of energy. One has the sense that the monster grows and grows, flinging abroad its loose limbs even as some unmannered young giant at his "larks," and that the binding stitches must for ever fly further and faster and draw harder; the future complexity of the web, all under the sky and over the sea, becoming thus that of some colossal set of clockworks, some steel-souled machine-room of brandished arms and hammering fists and opening and closing jaws. The immeasurable bridges are but as the horizontal sheaths of pistons working at high pressure, day and night, and subject, one apprehends with perhaps inconsistent gloom, to certain, to fantastic, to merciless multiplication. In the light of this apprehension indeed the breezy brightness of the Bay puts on the semblance of the vast white page that awaits beyond any other perhaps the black overscoring of science.

Let me hasten to add that its present whiteness is precisely its charming note, the frankest of the signs you recognize and remember it by. That is the distinction I was just feeling my way to name as the main ground of its doing so well, for effect, without technical scenery. There are great imposing ports Glasgow and Liverpool and London—that have already their page blackened almost beyond redemption from any such light of the picturesque as can hope to irradiate fog and grime, and there are others, Marseilles and Constantinople say, or, for all I know to the contrary, New Orleans, that contrive to abound before everything else in colour, and so to make a rich and instant and obvious show. But memory and the actual impression keep investing New York with the tone, predominantly, of summer dawns and winter frosts, of sea-foam, of bleached sails and stretched awnings, of blanched hulls, of scoured decks, of new ropes, of polished brasses, of streamers clear in the blue air; and it is by this harmony, doubtless, that the projection of the individual character of the place, of the candour of its avidity and the freshness of its audacity, is most conveyed. The "tall buildings," which have so promptly usurped a glory that affects you as rather surprised, as yet, at itself, the multitudinous sky-scrapers standing up to the view, from the water, like extravagant pins in a cushion already overplanted, and stuck in as in the dark, anywhere and anyhow, have at least the felicity of carrying out the fairness of tone, of taking the sun and the shade in the manner of towers of marble. They are not all of marble, I believe, by any means, even if some may be, but they are impudently new and still more impudently "novel"—this in common with so many other terrible things in America—and they are triumphant payers of dividends; all of which uncontested and unabashed pride, with flash of innumerable windows and flicker of subordinate gilt attributions, is like the flare, up and down their long, narrow faces, of the lamps of some general permanent "celebration."

You see the pin-cushion in profile, so to speak, on passing between Jersey City and Twenty-third Street, but you get it broadside on, this loose nosegay of architectural flowers, if you skirt the Battery, well out, and embrace the whole plantation. Then the "American beauty," the rose of interminable stem, becomes the token of the cluster at large—to that degree that, positively, this is all that is wanted for emphasis of your final impression. Such growths, you feel, have confessedly arisen but to be "picked," in time, with a shears; nipped short off, by waiting fate, as soon as "science," applied to gain, has put upon the table, from far up its sleeve, some more winning card. Crowned not only with no history, but with no credible possibility of time for history, and consecrated by no uses save the commercial at any cost, they are simply the most piercing notes in that concert of the expensively provisional into which your supreme sense of New York resolves itself. They never begin to speak to you, in the manner of the builded majesties of the world as we have heretofore known such—towers or temples or fortresses or palaces—with the authority of things of permanence or even of things of long duration. One story is good only till another is told, and sky-scrapers are the last word of economic ingenuity only till another word be written. This shall be possibly a word of still uglier meaning, but the vocabulary of thrift at any price shows boundless resources, and the consciousness of that truth, the consciousness of the finite, the menaced, the essentially *invented* state, twinkles ever, to my perception, in the thousand glassy eyes of these giants of the mere market. Such a structure as the comparatively windowless bell-tower of Giotto, in Florence, looks supremely serene in its beauty. You don't feel it to have risen by the breath of an interested passion that, restless beyond all passions, is for ever seeking more pliable forms. Beauty has been the object of its creator's idea, and, having found beauty, it has found the form in which it splendidly rests.

Beauty indeed was the aim of the creator of the spire of Trinity Church, so cruelly overtopped and so barely distinguishable, from your train-bearing barge, as you stand off, in its abject helpless humility; and it may of course be asked how much of this superstition finds voice in the actual shrunken presence of that laudable effort. Where, for the eye, is the felicity of simplified Gothic, of noble pre-eminence, that once made of this highly-pleasing edifice the pride of the town and the feature of Broadway? The answer is, as obviously, that these charming elements are still there, just where they ever were, but that they have been mercilessly deprived of their visibility. It aches and throbs, this smothered visibility, we easily feel, in its caged and dishonoured condition, supported only by the consciousness that the dishonour is no fault of its own. We commune with it, in tenderness and pity, through the encumbered air; our eyes, made, however unwillingly, at home in strange vertiginous upper atmospheres, look down on it as on a poor ineffectual thing, an architectural object addressed, even in its prime aspiration, to the patient pedestrian sense and permitting thereby a relation of intimacy. It was to speak to me audibly enough on two or three other occasions—even through the thick of that frenzy of Broadway just where Broadway receives from Wall Street the fiercest application of the maddening lash; it was to put its tragic case there with irresistible lucidity. "Yes, the wretched figure I am making is as little as you see my fault—it is the fault of the buildings whose very first care is to deprive churches of their visibility. There are but two or three—two or three outward and visible churches—left in New York 'anyway,' as you must have noticed, and even they are hideously threatened: a fact at which no one, indeed, appears to be shocked, from which no one draws the least of the inferences that stick straight out of it, which every one seems in short to take for granted either with remarkable stupidity or with remarkable cynicism." So, at any rate, they may still effectively communicate, ruddy-brown (where not browny-black) old Trinity and any pausing, any attending survivor of the clearer age—and there is yet more of the bitterness of history to be tasted in such a tacit passage, as I shall presently show.

Was it not the bitterness of history, meanwhile, that on that day of circumnavigation, that day of highest intensity of impression, of which I began by speaking, the ancient rotunda of Castle Garden, viewed from just opposite, should have lurked there as a vague nonentity? One had known it from far, far back and with the indelibility of the childish vision—from the time when it was the commodious concert-hall of New York, the firmament of long-extinguished stars; in spite

of which extinction there outlives for me the image of the
infant phenomenon Adelina Patti, whom (another large-eyed
infant) I had been benevolently taken to hear: Adelina Patti,
in a fan-like little white frock and "pantalettes" and a hussar-
like red jacket, mounted on an armchair, its back supporting
her, wheeled to the front of the stage and warbling like a tiny
thrush even in the nest. Shabby, shrunken, barely discernible
to-day, the ancient rotunda, adjusted to other uses, had afterwards, for many decades, carried on a conspicuous life—and
it was the present remoteness, the repudiated barbarism of all
this, foreshortened by one's own experience, that dropped the
acid into the cup. The sky-scrapers and the league-long
bridges, present and to come, marked the point where the
age—the age for which Castle Garden could have been, in its
day, a "value"—had come out. That in itself was nothing—
ages do come out, as a matter of course, so far from where
they have gone in. But it had done so, the latter half of the
nineteenth century, in one's own more or less immediate presence; the difference, from pole to pole, was so vivid and concrete that no single shade of any one of its aspects was lost.
This impact of the whole condensed past at once produced a
horrible, hateful sense of personal antiquity.

Yet was it after all that those monsters of the mere market,
as I have called them, had more to say, on the question of
"effect," than I had at first allowed?—since they are the element that looms largest for me through a particular impression, with remembered parts and pieces melting together
rather richly now, of "down-town" seen and felt from the inside. "Felt"—I use that word, I dare say, all presumptuously,
for a relation to matters of magnitude and mystery that I
could begin neither to measure nor to penetrate, hovering
about them only in magnanimous wonder, staring at them as
at a world of immovably-closed doors behind which immense
"material" lurked, material for the artist, the painter of life, as
we say, who shouldn't have begun so early and so fatally to
fall away from possible initiations. This sense of a baffled
curiosity, an intellectual adventure forever renounced, was
surely enough a state of feeling, and indeed in presence of the
different half-hours, as memory presents them, at which I
gave myself up both to the thrill of Wall Street (by which I

mean that of the whole wide edge of the whirlpool), and the too accepted, too irredeemable ignorance, I am at a loss to see what intensity of response was wanting. The imagination might have responded more if there had been a slightly less settled inability to understand what every one, what any one, was really doing; but the picture, as it comes back to me, is, for all this foolish subjective poverty, so crowded with its features that I rejoice, I confess, in not having more of them to handle. No open apprehension, even if it be as open as a public vehicle plying for hire, can carry more than a certain amount of life, of a kind; and there was nothing at play in the outer air, at least, of the scene, during these glimpses, that didn't scramble for admission into mine very much as I had seen the mob seeking entrance to an up-town or a down-town electric car fight for life at one of the apertures. If it had been the final function of the Bay to make one feel one's age, so, assuredly, the mouth of Wall Street proclaimed it, for one's private ear, distinctly enough; the breath of existence being taken, wherever one turned, as that of youth on the run and with the prize of the race in sight, and the new landmarks crushing the old quite as violent children stamp on snails and caterpillars.

The hour I first recall was a morning of winter drizzle and mist, of dense fog in the Bay, one of the strangest sights of which I was on my way to enjoy; and I had stopped in the heart of the business quarter to pick up a friend who was to be my companion. The weather, such as it was, worked wonders for the upper reaches of the buildings, round which it drifted and hung very much as about the flanks and summits of emergent mountain-masses—for, to be just all round, there *was* some evidence of their having a message for the eyes. Let me parenthesize, once for all, that there are other glimpses of this message, up and down the city, frequently to be caught; lights and shades of winter and summer air, of the literally "finishing" afternoon in particular, when refinement of modelling descends from the skies and lends the white towers, all new and crude and commercial and over-windowed as they are, a fleeting distinction. The morning I speak of offered me my first chance of seeing one of them from the inside—which was an opportunity I sought again, repeatedly, in respect to others; and I became conscious of the force with which this vision of their prodigious working, and of the multitudinous life, as if each were a swarming city in itself, that they are capable of housing, may beget, on the part of the free observer, in other words of the restless analyst, the impulse to describe and present the facts and express the sense of them. Each of these huge constructed and compressed communities, throbbing, through its myriad arteries and pores, with a single passion, even as a complicated watch throbs with the one purpose of telling you the hour and the minute, testified overwhelmingly to the *character* of New York—and the passion of the restless analyst, on his side, is for the extraction of character. But there would be too much to say, just here, were this incurable eccentric to let himself go; the impression in question, fed by however brief an experience, kept overflowing the cup and spreading in a wide waste of speculation. I must dip into these depths, if it prove possible, later on; let me content myself for the moment with remembering how from the first, on all such ground, my thought went straight to poor great wonder-working Émile Zola and *his* love of the human aggregation, the artificial microcosm, which had to spend itself on great shops, great businesses, great "apartment-houses," of inferior, of mere Parisian scale. His image, it seemed to me, really asked for compassion—in the presence of this material that his energy of evocation, his alone, would have been of a stature to meddle with. What if *Le Ventre de Paris*, what if *Au Bonheur des Dames*, what if *Pot-Bouille* and *L'Argent*, could but have come into being under the New York inspiration?

The answer to that, however, for the hour, was that, in all probability, New York was not going (as it turns such remarks) to produce both the maximum of "business" spectacle and the maximum of ironic reflection of it. Zola's huge reflector got itself formed, after all, in a far other air; it had hung there, in essence, awaiting the scene that was to play over it, long before the scene really approached it in scale. The reflecting surfaces, of the ironic, of the epic order, suspended in the New York atmosphere, have yet to show symptoms of shining out, and the monstrous phenomena themselves, meanwhile, strike me as having, with their im-

mense momentum, got the start, got ahead of, in proper parlance, any possibility of poetic, of dramatic capture. That
conviction came to me most perhaps while I gazed across at
the special sky-scraper that overhangs poor old Trinity to the
north—a south face as high and wide as the mountain-wall
that drops the Alpine avalanche, from time to time, upon the
village, and the village spire, at its foot; the interest of this
case being above all, as I learned, to my stupefaction, in the
fact that the very creators of the extinguisher are the church-
wardens themselves, or at least the trustees of the church
property. What was the case but magnificent for pitiless fe-
rocity?—that inexorable law of the growing invisibility of
churches, their everywhere reduced or abolished *presence*,
which is nine-tenths of their virtue, receiving thus, at such
hands, its supreme consecration. This consecration was positively the greater that just then, as I have said, the vast
money-making structure quite horribly, quite romantically
justified itself, looming through the weather with an insolent
cliff-like sublimity. The weather, for all that experience, mixes
intimately with the fulness of my impression; speaking not
least, for instance, of the way "the state of the streets" and the
assault of the turbid air seemed all one with the look, the
tramp, the whole quality and *allure*, the consummate monotonous commonness, of the pushing male crowd, moving in
its dense mass—with the confusion carried to chaos for any
intelligence, any perception; a welter of objects and sounds in
which relief, detachment, dignity, meaning, perished utterly
and lost all rights. It appeared, the muddy medium, all one
with every other element and note as well, all the signs of the
heaped industrial battle-field, all the sounds and silences,
grim, pushing, trudging silences too, of the universal will to
move—to move, move, move, as an end in itself, an appetite
at any price.

In the Bay, the rest of the morning, the dense raw fog that
delayed the big boat, allowing sight but of the immediate ice-
masses through which it thumped its way, was not less of the
essence. Anything blander, as a medium, would have seemed
a mockery of the facts of the terrible little Ellis Island, the first
harbour of refuge and stage of patience for the million or so
of immigrants annually knocking at our official door. Before

this door, which opens to them there only with a hundred forms and ceremonies, grindings and grumblings of the key, they stand appealing and waiting, marshalled, herded, divided, subdivided, sorted, sifted, searched, fumigated, for longer or shorter periods—the effect of all which prodigious process, an intendedly "scientific" feeding of the mill, is again to give the earnest observer a thousand more things to think of than he can pretend to retail. The impression of Ellis Island, in fine, would be—as I was to find throughout that so many of my impressions would be—a chapter by itself; and with a particular page for recognition of the degree in which the liberal hospitality of the eminent Commissioner of this wonderful service, to whom I had been introduced, helped to make the interest of the whole watched drama poignant and unforgettable. It is a drama that goes on, without a pause, day by day and year by year, this visible act of ingurgitation on the part of our body politic and social, and constituting really an appeal to amazement beyond that of any sword-swallowing or fire-swallowing of the circus. The wonder that one couldn't keep down was the thought that these two or three hours of one's own chance vision of the business were but as a tick or two of the mighty clock, the clock that never, never stops—least of all when it strikes, for a sign of so much winding-up, some louder hour of our national fate than usual. I think indeed that the simplest account of the action of Ellis Island on the spirit of any sensitive citizen who may have happened to "look in" is that he comes back from his visit not at all the same person that he went. He has eaten of the tree of knowledge, and the taste will be for ever in his mouth. He had thought he knew before, thought he had the sense of the degree in which it is his American fate to share the sanctity of his American consciousness, the intimacy of his American patriotism, with the inconceivable alien; but the truth had never come home to him with any such force. In the lurid light projected upon it by those courts of dismay it shakes him—or I like at least to imagine it shakes him—to the depths of his being; I like to think of him, I positively *have* to think of him, as going about ever afterwards with a new look, for those who can see it, in his face, the outward sign of the new chill in his heart. So is stamped, for detection, the questionably privileged person who has had an apparition, seen a ghost in his supposedly safe old house. Let not the unwary, therefore, visit Ellis Island.

The after-sense of that acute experience, however, I myself found, was by no means to be brushed away; I felt it grow and grow, on the contrary, wherever I turned: other impressions might come and go, but this affirmed claim of the alien, however immeasurably alien, to share in one's supreme relation was everywhere the fixed element, the reminder not to be dodged. One's supreme relation, as one had always put it, was one's relation to one's country—a conception made up so largely of one's countrymen and one's countrywomen. Thus it was as if, all the while, with such a fond tradition of what these products predominantly were, the idea of the country itself underwent something of that profane overhauling through which it appears to suffer the indignity of change. Is not our instinct in this matter, in general, essentially the safe one—that of keeping the idea simple and strong and continuous, so that it shall be perfectly sound? To touch it overmuch, to pull it about, is to put it in peril of weakening; yet on this free assault upon it, this readjustment of it in *their* monstrous, presumptuous interest, the aliens, in New York, seemed perpetually to insist. The combination there of their quantity and their quality—that loud primary stage of alienism which New York most offers to sight—operates, for the native, as their note of settled possession, something they have nobody to thank for; so that *un*settled possession is what we, on our side, seem reduced to—the implication of which, in its turn, is that, to recover confidence and regain lost ground, we, not they, must make the surrender and accept the orientation. We must go, in other words, *more* than half-way to meet them; which is all the difference, for us, between possession and dispossession. This sense of dispossession, to be brief about it, haunted me so, I was to feel, in the New York streets and in the packed trajectiles to which one clingingly appeals from the streets, just as one tumbles back into the streets in appalled reaction from *them*, that the art of beguiling or duping it became an art to be cultivated—though the fond alternative vision was never long to be obscured, the imagination, exasperated to envy, of the ideal, in the order in question; of the luxury of some such close and sweet and *whole* national consciousness as that of the Switzer and the Scot.

II

My recovery of impressions, after a short interval, yet with their flush a little faded, may have been judged to involve itself with excursions of memory—memory directed to the antecedent time—reckless almost to extravagance. But I recall them to-day, none the less, for that value in them which ministered, at happy moments, to an artful evasion of the actual. There was no escape from the ubiquitous alien into the future, or even into the present; there was an escape but into the past. I count as quite a triumph in this interest an unbroken ease of frequentation of that ancient end of Fifth Avenue to the whole neighbourhood of which one's earlier vibrations, a very far-away matter now, were attuned. The precious stretch of space between Washington Square and Fourteenth Street had a value, had even a charm, for the revisiting spirit—a mild and melancholy glamour which I am conscious of the difficulty of "rendering" for new and heedless generations. Here again the assault of suggestion is too great; too large, I mean, the number of hares started, before the pursuing imagination, the quickened memory, by this fact of the felt moral and social value of this comparatively unimpaired morsel of the Fifth Avenue heritage. Its reference to a pleasanter, easier, hazier past is absolutely comparative, just as the past in question itself enjoys as such the merest courtesy-title. It is all recent history enough, by the measure of the whole, and there are flaws and defacements enough, surely, even in its appearance of decency of duration. The tall building, grossly tall and grossly ugly, has failed of an admirable chance of distinguished consideration for it, and the dignity of many of its peaceful fronts has succumbed to the presence of those industries whose foremost need is to make "a good thing" of them. The good thing is doubtless being made, and yet this lower end of the once agreeable street still just escapes being a wholly bad thing. What held the fancy in thrall, however, as I say, was the admonition, proceeding from all the facts, that values of this romantic order are at best, anywhere, strangely relative. It was an extraordinary statement on the subject of New York that the space between Fourteenth Street and Washington Square *should* count for "tone," figure as the old ivory of an overscored tablet.

True wisdom, I found, was to let it, to make it, so count and figure as much as it would, and charming assistance came for this, I also found, from the young good-nature of May and June. There had been neither assistance nor good-nature during the grim weeks of mid-winter; there had been but the meagre fact of a discomfort and an ugliness less formidable here than elsewhere. When, toward the top of the town, circulation, alimentation, recreation, every art of existence, gave way before the full onset of winter, when the upper avenues had become as so many congested bottle-necks, through which the wine of life simply refused to be decanted, getting back to these latitudes resembled really a return from the North Pole to the Temperate Zone: it was as if the wine of life had been poured for you, in advance, into some pleasant old punch-bowl that would support you through the temporary stress. Your condition was not reduced to the endless vista of a clogged tube, of a thoroughfare occupied as to the narrow central ridge with trolley-cars stuffed to suffocation, and as to the mere margin, on either side, with snow-banks resulting from the cleared rails and offering themselves as a field for all remaining action. Free existence and good manners, in New York, are too much brought down to a bare rigour of marginal relation to the endless electric coil, the monstrous chain that winds round the general neck and body, the general middle and legs, very much as the boa-constrictor winds round the group of the Laocoon. It struck me that when these folds are tightened in the terrible stricture of the snow-smothered months of the year, the New York predicament leaves far behind the anguish represented in the Vatican figures. To come and go where East Eleventh Street, where West Tenth, opened their kind short arms was at least to keep clear of the awful hug of the serpent. And this was a grace that grew large, as I have hinted, with the approach of summer, and that made in the afternoons of May and of the first half of June, above all, an insidious appeal. There, I repeat, was the delicacy, there

the mystery, there the wonder, in especial, of the unquenchable intensity of the impressions received in childhood. They
are made then once for all, be their intrinsic beauty, interest,
importance, small or great; the stamp is indelible and never
wholly fades. This in fact gives it an importance when a lifetime has intervened. I found myself intimately recognizing
every house my officious tenth year had, in the way of imagined adventure, introduced to me—incomparable master of
ceremonies after all; the privilege had been offered since to
millions of other objects that had made nothing of it, that had
gone as they came; so that here were Fifth Avenue corners
with which one's connection was fairly exquisite. The lowered
light of the days' ends of early summer became them, moreover, exceedingly, and they fell, for the quiet northward perspective, into a dozen delicacies of composition and tone.

One could talk of "quietness" now, for the shrinkage of life
so marked, in the higher latitudes of the town, after Easter,
the visible early flight of that "society" which, by the old custom, used never to budge before June or July, had almost the
effect of clearing some of the streets, and indeed of suggesting
that a truly clear New York might have an unsuspected charm
or two to put forth. An approach to peace and harmony
might have been, in a manner, promised, and the sense of
other days took advantage of it to steal abroad with a ghostly
tread. It kept meeting, half the time, to its discomfiture, the
lamentable little Arch of Triumph which bestrides these beginnings of Washington Square—lamentable because of its
poor and lonely and unsupported and unaffiliated state. With
this melancholy monument it could make no terms at all, but
turned its back to the strange sight as often as possible, helping itself thereby, moreover, to do a little of the pretending
required, no doubt, by the fond theory that nothing hereabouts was changed. Nothing *was*, it could occasionally appear to me—there was no new note in the picture, not one,
for instance, when I paused before a low house in a small row
on the south side of Waverley Place and lived again into the
queer mediæval costume (preserved by the daguerreotypist's
art) of the very little boy for whom the scene had once
embodied the pangs and pleasures of a dame's small school.
The dame must have been Irish, by her name, and the Irish

tradition, only intensified and coarsened, seemed still to possess the place, the fact of the survival, the sturdy sameness, of
which arrested me, again and again, to fascination. The
shabby red house, with its mere two storeys, its lowly
"stoop," its dislocated ironwork of the forties, the early fifties,
the record, in its face, of blistering summers and of the long
stages of the loss of self-respect, made it as consummate a
morsel of the old liquor-scented, heated-looking city, the city
of no pavements, but of such a plenty of politics, as I could
have desired. And neighbouring Sixth Avenue, overstraddled
though it might be with feats of engineering unknown to the
primitive age that otherwise so persisted, wanted only, to
carry off the illusion, the warm smell of the bakery on the
corner of Eighth Street, a blessed repository of doughnuts,
cookies, cream-cakes and pies, the slow passing by which, on
returns from school, must have had much in common with
the experience of the shipmen of old who came, in long
voyages, while they tacked and hung back, upon those belts
of ocean that are haunted with the balm and spice of tropic
islands.

These were the felicities of the backward reach, which,
however, had also its melancholy checks and snubs; nowhere
quite so sharp as in presence, so to speak, of the rudely, the
ruthlessly suppressed birth-house on the other side of the
Square. That was where the pretence that nearly nothing was
changed had most to come in; for a high, square, impersonal
structure, proclaiming its lack of interest with a crudity all its
own, so blocks, at the right moment for its own success, the
view of the past, that the effect for me, in Washington Place,
was of having been amputated of half my history. The grey
and more or less "hallowed" University building—wasn't it
somehow, with a desperate bravery, both castellated and
gabled?—has vanished from the earth, and vanished with it
the two or three adjacent houses, of which the birthplace was
one. This was the snub, for the complacency of retrospect,
that, whereas the inner sense had positively erected there for
its private contemplation a commemorative mural tablet, the
very wall that should have borne this inscription had been
smashed as for demonstration that tablets, in New York, are
unthinkable. And I have had indeed to permit myself this free

fantasy of the hypothetic rescued identity of a given house—
taking the vanished number in Washington Place as most pertinent—in order to invite the reader to gasp properly with
me before the fact that we not only fail to remember, in the
whole length of the city, one of these frontal records of birth,
sojourn, or death, under a celebrated name, but that we have
only to reflect an instant to see any such form of civic piety
inevitably and for ever absent. The form is cultivated, to the
greatly quickened interest of street-scenery, in many of the
cities of Europe; and is it not verily bitter, for those who feel
a poetry in the noted passage, longer or shorter, here and
there, of great lost spirits, that the institution, the profit, the
glory of any such association is denied in advance to communities tending, as the phrase is, to "run" preponderantly to the
sky-scraper? Where, in fact, is the point of inserting a mural
tablet, at any legible height, in a building certain to be destroyed to make room for a sky-scraper? And from where, on
the other hand, in a façade of fifty floors, does one "see" the
pious plate recording the honour attached to one of the apartments look down on a responsive people? We have but to ask
the question to recognize our necessary failure to answer it as
a supremely characteristic local note—a note in the light of
which the great city is projected into its future as, practically,
a huge, continuous fifty-floored conspiracy against the very
idea of the ancient graces, those that strike us as having flourished just in proportion as the parts of life and the signs
of character have *not* been lumped together, not been indis-
tinguishably sunk in the common fund of mere economic
convenience. So interesting, as object-lessons, may the developments of the American gregarious ideal become; so traceable, at every turn, to the restless analyst at least, are the heavy
footprints, in the finer texture of life, of a great commercial
democracy seeking to abound supremely in its own sense and
having none to gainsay it.

Let me not, however, forget, amid such contemplations,
what may serve here as a much more relevant instance of the
operation of values, the price of the as yet undiminished dignity of the two most southward of the Fifth Avenue churches.
Half the charm of the prospect, at that extremity, is in their
still being there, and being as they are; this charm, this se-

renity of escape and survival positively works as a blind on the side of the question of their architectural importance. The last shade of pedantry or priggishness drops from your view of that element; they illustrate again supremely your grasped truth of the *comparative* character, in such conditions, of beauty and of interest. The special standard they may or may not square with signifies, you feel, not a jot: all you know, and want to know, is that they are probably menaced—some horrible voice of the air has murmured it—and that with them will go, if fate overtakes them, the last cases worth mentioning (with a single exception), of the modest felicity that sometimes used to be. Remarkable certainly the state of things in which mere exemption from the "squashed" condition can shed such a glamour; but we may accept the state of things if only we can keep the glamour undispelled. It reached its maximum for me, I hasten to add, on my penetrating into the Ascension, at chosen noon, and standing for the first time in presence of that noble work of John La Farge, the representation, on the west wall, in the grand manner, of the theological event from which the church takes its title. Wonderful enough, in New York, to find one's self, in a charming and considerably dim "old" church, hushed to admiration before a great religious picture; the sensation, for the moment, upset so all the facts. The hot light, outside, might have been that of an Italian *piazzetta*; the cool shade, within, with the important work of art shining through it, seemed part of some other-world pilgrimage—all the more that the important work of art itself, a thing of the highest distinction, spoke, as soon as one had taken it in, with that authority which makes the difference, ever afterwards, between the remembered and the forgotten quest. A rich note of interference came, I admit, through the splendid window-glass, the finest of which, unsurpassably fine, to my sense, is the work of the same artist; so that the church, as it stands, is very nearly as commemorative a monument as a great reputation need wish. The deeply pictorial windows, in which clearness of picture and fulness of expression consort so successfully with a tone as of magnified gems, did not strike one as looking into a yellow little square of the south—they put forth a different implication; but the flaw in the harmony was, more than anything else, that sinister voice of the air of which I have spoken, the fact that one *could* stand there, vibrating to such impressions, only to remember the suspended danger, the possibility of the doom. Here was the loveliest cluster of images, begotten on the spot, that the preoccupied city had ever taken thought to offer itself; and here, to match them, like some black shadow they had been condemned to cast, was this particular prepared honour of "removal" that appeared to hover about them.

One's fear, I repeat, was perhaps misplaced—but what an air to live in, the shuddering pilgrim mused, the air in which such fears are not misplaced only when we are conscious of very special reassurances! The vision of the doom that does descend, that had descended all round, was at all events, for the half-hour, all that was wanted to charge with the last tenderness one's memory of the transfigured interior. Afterwards, outside, again and again, the powers of removal struck me as looming, awfully, in the newest mass of multiplied floors and windows visible at this point. *They*, ranged in this terrible recent erection, were going to bring in money—and was not money the only thing a self-respecting structure could be thought of as bringing in? Hadn't one heard, just before, in Boston, that the security, that the sweet serenity of the Park Street Church, charmingest, there, of aboriginal notes, the very light, with its perfect position and its dear old delightful Wren-like spire, of the starved city's eyes, had been artfully practised against, and that the question of saving it might become, in the near future, acute? Nothing, fortunately, I think, is so much the "making" of New York, at its central point, for the visual, almost for the romantic, sense, as the Park Street Church is the making, by its happy coming-in, of Boston; and, therefore, if it were thinkable that the peculiar rectitude of Boston might be laid in the dust, what mightn't easily come about for the reputedly less austere conscience of New York? Once such questions had obtained lodgment, to take one's walks was verily to look at almost everything in their light; and to commune with the skyscraper under this influence was really to feel worsted, more and more, in any magnanimous attempt to adopt the æsthetic view of it. I may appear to make too much of these invidious presences, but it must be remembered that they represent, for our time, the only claim to any consideration other than merely statistical established by the resounding growth of New York. The attempt to take the æsthetic view is invariably blighted sooner or later by their most salient characteristic, *the* feature that speaks loudest for the economic idea. Window upon window, at any cost, is a condition never to be reconciled with any grace of building, and the logic of the matter here happens to put on a particularly fatal front. If quiet interspaces, always half the architectural battle, exist no more in such a structural scheme than quiet tones, blest breathing-spaces, occur, for the most part, in New York conversation, so the reason is, demonstrably, that the building can't afford them. (It is by very much the same law, one supposes, that New York conversation cannot afford stops.) The building can only afford lights, each light having a superlative value as an aid to the transaction of business and the conclusion of sharp bargains. Doesn't it take in fact acres of window-glass to help even an expert New Yorker to get the better of another expert one, or to see that the other expert one doesn't get the better of *him*? It is easy to conceive that, after all, with this origin and nature stamped upon their foreheads, the last word of the mercenary monsters should not be their address to our sense of formal beauty.

Still, as I have already hinted, there was always the case of the one other rescued identity and preserved felicity, the happy accident of the elder day still ungrudged and finally legitimated. When I say ungrudged, indeed, I seem to remember how I had heard that the divine little City Hall had *been* grudged, at a critical moment, to within an inch of its life; had but just escaped, in the event, the extremity of grudging. It lives on securely, by the mercy of fate—lives on in the delicacy of its beauty, speaking volumes again (more volumes, distinctly, than are anywhere else spoken) for the exquisite truth of the *conferred* value of interesting objects, the value derived from the social, the civilizing function for which they have happened to find their opportunity. It is the opportunity that gives them their price, and the luck of there being, round about them, nothing greater than themselves to steal it away from them. They strike thus, virtually, the supreme note, and—such is the mysterious play of our finer sensibility!—one takes this note, one is glad to work it, as the phrase goes, for all it is worth. I so work the note of the City Hall, no doubt, in speaking of the spectacle there constituted as "divine"; but I do it precisely by reason of the spectacle taken *with* the delightful small facts of the building: largely by reason, in other words, of the elegant, the gallant little structure's situation and history, the way it has played, artistically, ornamentally, its part, has held out for the good cause, through the long years, alone and unprotected. The fact is it has been the very centre of that assault of vulgarity of which the innumerable mementos rise within view of it and tower, at a certain distance, over it; and yet it has never parted with a square inch of its character, it has forced them, in a manner, to stand off. I hasten to add that in expressing thus its uncompromised state I speak of its outward, its æsthetic character only. So, at all events, it has discharged the civilizing function I just named as inherent in such cases—that of representing, to the community possessed of it, all the Style the community is likely to get, and of making itself responsible for the same.

The consistency of this effort, under difficulties, has been the story that brings tears to the eyes of the hovering kindly critic, and it is through his tears, no doubt, that such a personage reads the best passages of the tale and makes out the proportions of the object. Mine, I recognize, didn't prevent my seeing that the pale yellow marble (or whatever it may be) of the City Hall has lost, by some late excoriation, the remembered charm of its old surface, the pleasant promiscuous patina of time; but the perfect taste and finish, the reduced yet ample scale, the harmony of parts, the just proportions, the modest classic grace, the living look of the type aimed at, these things, with gaiety of detail undiminished and "quaintness" of effect augmented, are all there; and I see them, as I write, in that glow of appreciation which made it necessary, of a fine June morning, that I should somehow pay the whole place my respects. The simplest, in fact the only way, was, obviously, to pass under the charming portico and brave the consequences: this impunity of such audacities being, in America, one of the last of the lessons the repatriated absentee finds himself learning. The crushed spirit he brings back from

European discipline never quite rises to the height of the native argument, the brave sense that the public, the civic building is his very own, for any honest use, so that he may tread even its most expensive pavements and staircases (and very expensive, for the American citizen, these have lately become,) without a question asked. This further and further unchallenged penetration begets in the perverted person I speak of a really romantic thrill: it is like some assault of the dim scraglio, with the guards bribed, the eunuchs drugged and one's life carried in one's hand. The only drawback to such freedom is that penetralia it is so easy to penetrate fail a little of a due impressiveness, and that if stationed sentinels are bad for the temper of the freeman they are good for the "prestige" of the building.

Never, in any case, it seemed to me, had any freeman made so free with the majesty of things as I was to make on this occasion with the mysteries of the City Hall—even to the point of coming out into the presence of the Representative of the highest office with which City Halls are associated, and whose thoroughly gracious condonation of my act set the seal of success upon the whole adventure. Its dizziest intensity in fact sprang precisely from the unexpected view opened into the old official, the old so thick-peopled local, municipal world: upper chambers of council and state, delightfully of their nineteenth-century time, as to design and ornament, in spite of rank restoration; but replete, above all, with portraits of past worthies, past celebrities and city fathers, Mayors, Bosses, Presidents, Governors, Statesmen at large, Generals and Commodores at large, florid ghosts, looking so unsophisticated now, of years not remarkable, municipally, for the absence of sophistication. Here were types, running mainly to ugliness and all bristling with the taste of their day and the quite touching provincialism of their conditions, as to many of which nothing would be more interesting than a study of New York annals in the light of their personal look, their very noses and mouths and complexions and heads of hair—to say nothing of their waistcoats and neckties; with such colour, such sound and movement would the thick stream of local history then be interfused. Wouldn't its thickness fairly become transparent? since to walk through the collection was not only to see and feel so much that had happened, but to understand, with the truth again and again inimitably pointed, why nothing could have happened otherwise; the whole array thus presenting itself as an unsurpassed demonstration of the real reasons of things. The florid ghosts look out from their exceedingly gilded frames—all that *that* can do is bravely done for them—with the frankest responsibility for everything; their collective presence becomes a kind of copious tell-tale document signed with a hundred names. There are few of these that at this hour, I think, we particularly desire to repeat; but the place where they may be read is, all the way from river to river and from the Battery to Harlem, the place in which there is most of the terrible town.

III

If the Bay had seemed to me, as I have noted, most to help the fond observer of New York aspects to a sense, through the eyes, of embracing possession, so the part played there for the outward view found its match for the inward in the portentous impression of one of the great caravansaries administered to me of a winter afternoon. I say with intention "administered": on so assiduous a guide, through the endless labyrinth of the Waldorf-Astoria was I happily to chance after turning out of the early dusk and the January sleet and slosh into permitted, into enlightened contemplation of a pandemonium not less admirably ordered, to all appearance, than rarely intermitted. The seer of great cities is liable to easy error, I know, when he finds this, that or the other caught glimpse the supremely significant one—and I am willing to preface with that remark my confession that New York told me more of her story at once, then and there, than she was again and elsewhere to tell. With this apprehension that she was in fact fairly shrieking it into one's ears came a curiosity, corresponding, as to its kind and its degree of interest; so that there was nought to do, as we picked our tortuous way, but to stare with all our eyes and miss as little as possible of the revelation. That harshness of the essential conditions, the outward, which almost any large attempt at the amenities, in New York, has to take account of and make the best of, has at least

the effect of projecting the visitor with force upon the spectacle prepared for him at this particular point and of marking
the more its sudden high pitch, the character of violence
which all its warmth, its colour and glitter so completely muffle. There is violence outside, mitigating sadly the frontal majesty of the monument, leaving it exposed to the vulgar assault
of the street by the operation of those dire facts of absence of
margin, of meagreness of site, of the brevity of the block, of
the inveteracy of the near thoroughfare, which leave "style,"
in construction, at the mercy of the impertinent cross-streets,
make detachment and independence, save in the rarest cases,
an insoluble problem, preclude without pity any element of
court or garden, and open to the builder in quest of distinction the one alternative, and the great adventure, of seeking
his reward in the sky.

Of their licence to pursue it there to any extent whatever
New Yorkers are, I think, a trifle too assertively proud; no
court of approach, no interspace worth mention, ever forming meanwhile part of the ground-plan or helping to receive
the force of the breaking public wave. New York pays at this
rate the penalty of her primal topographic curse, her old inconceivably bourgeois scheme of composition and distribution, the uncorrected labour of minds with no imagination of
the future and blind before the opportunity given them by
their two magnificent water-fronts. This original sin of the
longitudinal avenues perpetually, yet meanly intersected, and
of the organized sacrifice of the indicated alternative, the great
perspectives from East to West, might still have earned for-
giveness by some occasional departure from its pettifogging
consistency. But, thanks to this consistency, the city is, of all
great cities, the least endowed with any blest item of stately
square or goodly garden, with any happy accident or surprise,
any fortunate nook or casual corner, any deviation, in fine,
into the liberal or the charming. That way, however, for the
regenerate filial mind, madness may be said to lie—the way
of imagining what might have been and putting it all together
in the light of what so helplessly is. One of the things that
helplessly are, for instance, is just this assault of the street, as I
have called it, upon any direct dealing with our caravansary.
The electric cars, with their double track, are everywhere

almost as tight a fit in the narrow channel of the roadway as the projectile in the bore of a gun; so that the Waldorf-Astoria, sitting by this absent margin for life with her open lap and arms, is reduced to confessing, with a strained smile, across the traffic and the danger, how little, outside her mere swing-door, she can do for you. She seems to admit that the attempt to get at her may cost you your safety, but reminds you at the same time that any good American, and even any good inquiring stranger, is supposed willing to risk that boon for her. "*Un bon mouvement*, therefore: you must make a dash for it, but you'll see I'm worth it." If such a claim as this last be ever justified, it would indubitably be justified here; the survivor scrambling out of the current and up the bank finds in the amplitude of the entertainment awaiting him an instant sense as of applied restoratives. The amazing hotel-world quickly closes round him; with the process of transition reduced to its minimum he is transported to conditions of extraordinary complexity and brilliancy, operating—and with proportionate perfection—by laws of their own and expressing after their fashion a complete scheme of life. The air swarms, to intensity, with the *characteristic*, the characteristic condensed and accumulated as he rarely elsewhere has had the luck to find it. It jumps out to meet his every glance, and this unanimity of its spring, of all its aspects and voices, is what I just now referred to as the essence of the loud New York story. That effect of violence in the whole communication, at which I thus hint, results from the inordinate mass, the quantity of presence, as it were, of the testimony heaped together for emphasis of the wondrous moral.

The moral in question, the high interest of the tale, is that you are in presence of a revelation of the possibilities of the hotel—for which the American spirit has found so unprecedented a use and a value; leading it on to express so a social, indeed positively an æsthetic ideal, and making it so, at this supreme pitch, a synonym for civilization, for the capture of conceived manners themselves, that one is verily tempted to ask if the hotel-spirit may not just *be* the American spirit most seeking and most finding itself. That truth—the truth that the present is more and more the day of the hotel—had not waited to burst on the mind at the view of this particular establishment; we have all more or less been educated to it, the world over, by the fruit-bearing action of the American example: in consequence of which it has been opened to us to see still other societies moved by the same irresistible spring and trying, with whatever grace and ease they may bring to the business, to unlearn as many as possible of their old social canons, and in especial their old discrimination in favour of the private life. The business for them—for communities to which the American ease in such matters is not native—goes much less of itself and produces as yet a scantier show; the great difference with the American show being that in the United States every one is, for the lubrication of the general machinery, practically in everything, whereas in Europe, mostly, it is only certain people who are in anything; so that the machinery, so much less generalized, works in a smaller, stiffer way. This one caravansary makes the American case vivid, gives it, you feel, that quantity of illustration which renders the place a new thing under the sun. It is an expression of the gregarious state breaking down every barrier but two—one of which, the barrier consisting of the high pecuniary tax, is the immediately obvious. The other, the rather more subtle, is the condition, for any member of the flock, that he or she—in other words especially she—be presumably "respectable," be, that is, not discoverably anything else. The rigour with which any appearance of pursued or desired adventure is kept down—adventure in the florid sense of the word, the sense in which it remains an euphemism—is not the least interesting note of the whole immense promiscuity. Protected at those two points the promiscuity carries, through the rest of the range, everything before it.

It sat there, it walked and talked, and ate and drank, and listened and danced to music, and otherwise revelled and roamed, and bought and sold, and came and went there, all on its own splendid terms and with an encompassing material splendour, a wealth and variety of constituted picture and background, that might well feed it with the finest illusions about itself. It paraded through halls and saloons in which art and history, in masquerading dress, muffled almost to suffocation as in the gold brocade of their pretended majesties and their conciliatory graces, stood smirking on its passage with the last cynicism of hypocrisy. The exhibition is wonderful for that, for the suggested sense of a promiscuity which manages to be at the same time an inordinate untempered monotony; manages to be so, on such ground as this, by an extraordinary trick of its own, wherever one finds it. The combination forms, I think, largely, the very interest, such as it is, of these phases of the human scene in the United States—if only for the pleasant puzzle of our wondering how, when types, aspects, conditions, have so much in common, they should seem at all to make up a conscious miscellany. That question, however, the question of the play and range, the practical elasticity, of the social sameness, in America, will meet us else-where on our path, and I confess that all questions gave way, in my mind, to a single irresistible obsession. This was just the ache of envy of the spirit of a society which had found there, in its prodigious public setting, so exactly what it wanted. One was in presence, as never before, of a realized ideal and of that childlike rush of surrender to it and clutch at it which one was so repeatedly to recognize, in America, as the note of the supremely gregarious state. It made the whole vision unforgettable, and I am now carried back to it, I con-fess, in musing hours, as to one of my few glimpses of perfect human felicity. It had the admirable sign that it was, precisely, so comprehensively collective—that it made so vividly, in the old phrase, for the greatest happiness of the greatest number. Its rare beauty, one felt with instant clarity of perception, was that it was, for a "mixed" social manifestation, blissfully ex-empt from any principle or possibility of disaccord with itself. It was absolutely a fit to its conditions, those conditions which were both its earth and its heaven, and every part of the picture, every item of the immense sum, every wheel of the wondrous complexity, was on the best terms with all the rest.

The sense of these things became for the hour as the golden glow in which one's envy burned, and through which, while the sleet and the slosh, and the clangorous charge of cars, and the hustling, hustled crowds held the outer world, one carried one's charmed attention from one chamber of the temple to another. For that is how the place speaks, as great constructed and achieved harmonies mostly speak—as a temple builded, with clustering chapels and shrines, to an idea. The hundreds and hundreds of people in circulation, the innumerable huge-hatted ladies in especial, with their air of finding in the gilded and storied labyrinth the very firesides and pathways of home, became thus the serene faithful, whose rites one would no more have sceptically brushed than one would doff one's disguise in a Mohammedan mosque. The question of who they all might be, seated under palms and by fountains, or communing, to some inimitable New York tune, with the shade of Marie Antoinette in the queer recaptured actuality of an easy Versailles or an intimate Trianon—such questions as that, interesting in other societies and at other times, insisted on yielding here to the mere eloquence of the general truth. Here was a social order in positively stable equilibrium. Here was a world whose relation to its form and medium was practically imperturbable; here was a conception of publicity *as* the vital medium organized with the authority with which the American genius for organization, put on its mettle, alone could organize it. The whole thing remains for me, however, I repeat, a gorgeous golden blur, a paradise peopled with unmistakable American shapes, yet in which, the general and the particular, the organized and the extemporized, the element of ingenuous joy below and of consummate management above, melted together and left one uncertain which of them one was, at a given turn of the maze, most admiring. When I reflect indeed that without my clue I should not have even known the maze—should not have known, at the given turn, whether I was engulfed, for instance, in the *vente de charité* of the theatrical profession and the onset of persuasive peddling actresses, or in the annual tea-party of German lady-patronesses (of I know not what) filling with their Oriental opulence and their strange idiom a playhouse of the richest rococo, where some other expensive anniversary, the ball of a guild or the carouse of a club, was to tread on their heels and instantly mobilize away their paraphernalia—when I so reflect I see the sharpest dazzle of the eyes as precisely the play of the genius for organization.

There are a thousand forms of this ubiquitous American force, the most ubiquitous of all, that I was in no position to measure; but there was often no resisting a vivid view of the form it may take, on occasion, under pressure of the native conception of the hotel. Encountered embodiments of the gift, in this connection, master-spirits of management whose influence was as the very air, the very expensive air, one breathed, abide with me as the intensest examples of American character; indeed as the very interesting supreme examples of a type which has even on the American ground, doubtless, not said its last word, but which has at least treated itself there to a luxury of development. It gives the impression, when at all directly met, of having at its service something of that fine flame that makes up personal greatness; so that, again and again, as I found, one would have liked to see it more intimately at work. Such failures of opportunity and of penetration, however, are but the daily bread of the visionary tourist. Whenever I dip back, in fond memory, none the less, into the vision I have here attempted once more to call up, I see the whole thing overswept as by the colossal extended arms, waving the magical bâton, of some high-stationed orchestral leader, the absolute presiding power, conscious of every note of every instrument, controlling and commanding the whole volume of sound, keeping the whole effect together and making it what it is. What may one say of such a spirit if not that he understands, so to speak, the forces he sways, understands his boundless American material and plays with it like a master indeed? One sees it thus, in its crude plasticity, almost in the likeness of an army of puppets whose strings the wealth of his technical imagination teaches him innumerable ways of pulling, and yet whose innocent, whose always ingenuous agitation of their members he has found means to make them think of themselves as delightfully free and easy. Such was my impression of the perfection of the concert that, for fear of its being spoiled by some chance false note, I never went into the place again.

It might meanwhile seem no great adventure merely to walk the streets; but (beside the fact that there is, in general, never a better way of taking in life), this pursuit irresistibly solicited, on the least pretext, the observer whose impressions I note—accustomed as he had ever been conscientiously to yield to it: more particularly with the relenting year, when the breath of spring, mildness being really installed, appeared the one vague and disinterested presence in the place, the one presence not vociferous and clamorous. Any definite presence that doesn't bellow and bang takes on in New York by that simple fact a distinction practically exquisite; so that one goes forth to meet it as a guest of honour, and that, for my own experience, I remember certain aimless strolls as snatches of intimate communion with the spirit of May and June—as abounding, almost to enchantment, in the comparatively *still* condition. Two secrets, at this time, seemed to profit by that influence to tremble out; one of these to the effect that New York would really have been "meant" to be charming, and the other to the effect that the restless analyst, willing at the lightest persuasion to let so much of its ugliness edge away un scathed from his analysis, must have had for it, from far back, one of those loyalties that are beyond any reason.

"It's all very well," the voice of the air seemed to say, if I may so take it up; "it's all very well to 'criticize,' but you distinctly take an interest and are the victim of your interest, be the grounds of your perversity what they will. You can't escape from it, and don't you see that this, precisely, is what *makes* an adventure for you (an adventure, I admit, as with some strident, battered, questionable beauty, truly some 'bold bad' charmer), of almost any odd stroll, or waste half-hour, or other promiscuous passage, that results for you in an impression? There is always your bad habit of receiving through almost any accident of vision more impressions than you know what to do with; but that, for common convenience, is your eternal handicap and may not be allowed to plead here against your special responsibility. You *care* for the terrible town, yea even for the 'horrible,' as I have overheard you call it, or at least think it, when you supposed no one would know; and you see now how, if you fly such fancies as that it was conceivably meant to be charming, you are tangled by that weakness in some underhand imagination of its possibly, one of these days, as a riper fruit of time, becoming so. To do that, you indeed sneakingly provide, it must get away from itself; but you are ready to follow its hypothetic dance even to the mainland and to the very end of its tether. What makes the general relation of your adventure with it is that, at bottom, you are all the while wondering, in presence of the aspects of its genius and its shame, what elements or parts, if any, would be worth its saving, worth carrying off for the fresh embodiment and the better life, and which of them would have, on the other hand, to face the notoriety of going *first* by the board. I have literally heard you qualify the monster as 'shameless'—though that was wrung from you, I admit, by the worst of the winter conditions, when circulation, in any fashion consistent with personal decency or dignity, was merely mocked at, when the stony-hearted 'trolleys,' cars of Juggernaut in their power to squash, triumphed all along the line, when the February blasts became as cyclones in the darkened gorges of masonry (which down-town, in particular, put on, at their mouths, the semblance of black rat-holes, holes of gigantic rats, inhabited by whirlwinds;) when all the pretences and impunities and infirmities, in fine, had massed themselves to be hurled at you in the fury of the elements, in the character of the traffic, in the unadapted state of the place to almost *any* dense movement, and, beyond everything, in that pitch of all the noises which acted on your nerves as so much wanton provocation, so much conscious cynicism. The fury of sound took the form of derision of the rest of your woe, and thus it *might*, I admit, have struck you as brazen that the horrible place should, in such confessed collapse, still be swaggering and shouting. It might have struck you that great cities, with the eyes of the world on them, as the phrase is, should be capable either of a proper form or (failing this) of a proper compunction; which tributes to propriety were, on the part of New York, equally wanting. This made you remark, precisely, that nothing was wanting, on the other hand, to that analogy with the character of the bad bold beauty, the creature the most blatant of whose pretensions is that she is one of those to whom everything is always forgiven. On what ground 'forgiven'? of course you ask; but note that you ask it while you're in the very act of forgiving. Oh yes, you are; you've as much as said so yourself. So there it all is; arrange it as you can. Poor dear bad bold beauty; there must indeed be something about her——!"

Let me grant then, to get on, that there *was* doubtless, in the better time, something about her; there was enough about her, at all events, to conduce to that distinct cultivation of her company for which the contemplative stroll, when there was time for it, was but another name. The analogy was in truth complete; since the repetition of such walks, and the admission of the beguiled state contained in them, resembled nothing so much as the visits so often still incorrigibly made to compromised charmers. I defy even a master of morbid observation to perambulate New York unless he be interested; so that in a case of memories so gathered the interest must be taken as a final fact. Let me figure it, to this end, as lively in every connection—and so indeed no more lively at one mild crisis than at another. The crisis—even of observation at the morbid pitch—is inevitably mild in cities intensely new; and it was with the quite peculiarly insistent newness of the upper reaches of the town that the spirit of romantic inquiry had always, at the best, to reckon. There are new cities enough about the world, goodness knows, and there are new parts enough of old cities—for examples of which we need go no farther than London, Paris and Rome, all of late so mercilessly renovated. But the newness of New York—unlike even that of Boston, I seemed to discern—had this mark of its very own, that it affects one, in every case, as having treated itself as still more provisional, if possible, than any poor dear little interest of antiquity it may have annihilated. The very sign of its energy is that it doesn't believe in itself; it fails to succeed, even at a cost of millions, in persuading you that it does. Its mission would appear to be, exactly, to gild the temporary, with its gold, as many inches thick as may be, and then, with a fresh shrug, a shrug of its splendid cynicism for its freshly detected inability to convince, give up its actual work, however exorbitant, as the merest of stop-gaps. The difficulty with the compromised charmer is just this constant inability to convince; to convince ever, I mean, that she is serious, serious about any form whatever, or about anything but that perpetual passionate pecuniary purpose which plays with all forms, which derides and devours them, though it may pile up the cost of them in order to rest a while, spent and haggard, in the illusion of their finality.

The perception of this truth grows for you by your simply walking up Fifth Avenue and pausing a little in presence of certain forms, certain exorbitant structures, in other words, the elegant domiciliary, as to which the illusion of finality was within one's memory magnificent and complete, but as to which one feels to-day that their life wouldn't be, as against any whisper of a higher interest, worth an hour's purchase. They sit there in the florid majesty of the taste of their time—a light now, alas, generally clouded; and I pretend of course to speak, in alluding to them, of no individual case of danger or doom. It is only a question of that unintending and unconvincing expression of New York everywhere, as yet, on the matter of the *maintenance* of a given effect—which comes back to the general insincerity of effects, and truly even (as I have already noted) to the insincerity of the effect of the skyscrapers themselves. There results from all this—and as much where the place most smells of its millions as elsewhere—that unmistakable New York admission of unattempted, impossible maturity. The new Paris and the new Rome do at least propose, I think, to be old—one of these days; the new London even, erect as she is on leaseholds destitute of dignity, yet does, for the period, appear to believe in herself. The vice I glance at is, however, when showing, in our flagrant example, on the forehead of its victims, much more a cause for pitying than for decrying them. Again and again, in the upper reaches, you pause with that pity; you learn, on the occasion of a kindly glance up and down a quiet cross-street (there being objects and aspects in many of them appealing to kindness), that such and such a house, or a row, is "coming down"; and you gasp, in presence of the elements involved, at the strangeness of the moral so pointed. It rings out like the crack of that lash in the sky, the play of some mighty teamster's whip, which ends by affecting you as the poor New Yorker's one association with the idea of "powers above." "No"—this is the tune to which the whip seems flourished— "there's no step at which you shall rest, no form, as I'm constantly showing you, to which, consistently with my interests, you *can*. I build you up but to tear you down, for if I were to let sentiment and sincerity once take root, were to let any tenderness of association once accumulate, or any 'love of the old' once pass unsnubbed, what would become of *us*, who have our hands on the whipstock, please? Fortunately we've learned the secret for keeping association at bay. We've learned that the great thing is not to suffer it to so much as begin. Wherever it does begin we find we're lost; but as that takes some time we get in ahead. It's the reason, if you must know, why you shall 'run,' all, without exception, to the fifty floors. We defy you even to aspire to venerate shapes so grossly constructed as the arrangement in fifty floors. You may have a feeling for keeping on with an old staircase, consecrated by the tread of generations—especially when it's 'good,' and old staircases are often so lovely; but how can you have a feeling for keeping on with an old elevator, how can you have it any more than for keeping on with an old omnibus? You'd be ashamed to venerate the arrangement in fifty floors, accordingly, even if you could; whereby, saving you any moral trouble or struggle, they are conceived and constructed—and you must do us the justice of this care for your sensibility—in a manner to put the thing out of the question. In such a manner, moreover, as that there shall be immeasurably more of them, in quantity, to tear down than of the actual past that we are now sweeping away. Wherefore we shall be kept in precious practice. The word will perhaps be then—who knows?—for building from the earth-surface downwards; in which case it will be a question of tearing, so to speak, 'up.' It little matters, so long as we blight the superstition of rest."

Yet even in the midst of this vision of eternal waste, of conscious, sentient-looking houses and rows, full sections of streets, to which the rich taste of history is forbidden even while their fresh young lips are just touching the cup, something charmingly done, here and there, some bid for the ampler permanence, seems to say to you that the particular place only asks, as a human home, to lead the life it has begun, only asks to enfold generations and gather in traditions, to show itself capable of growing up to character and authority. Houses of the best taste are like clothes of the best tailors—it takes their age to show us how good they are; and I frequently recognized, in the region of the upper reaches, this direct appeal of the individual case of happy construction. Construction at large abounds in the upper reaches, construction indescribably precipitate and elaborate—the latter fact about it always so oddly hand in hand with the former; and we should exceed in saying that felicity is always its mark. But some highly liberal, some extravagant intention almost always is, and we meet here even that happy accident, already encountered and acclaimed, in its few examples, down-town, of the object shining almost absurdly in the light of its merely comparative distinction. All but lost in the welter of instances of sham refinement, the shy little case of real refinement detaches itself ridiculously, as being (like the saved City Hall, or like the pleasant old garden-walled house on the north-west corner of Washington Square and Fifth Avenue) of so beneficent an admonition as to show, relatively speaking, for priceless. These things, which I may not take time to pick out, are the salt that saves, and it is enough to say for their delicacy that they are the direct counterpart of those other dreadful presences, looming round them, which embody the imagination of new kinds and new clustered, emphasized quantities of vulgarity. To recall these fine notes and these loud ones, the whole play of wealth and energy and untutored liberty, of the movement of a breathless civilization reflected, as brick and stone and marble may reflect, through all the contrasts of prodigious flight and portentous stumble, is to acknowledge, positively, that one's rambles were delightful, and that the district abutting on the east side of the Park, in particular, never engaged my attention without, by the same stroke, making the social question dance before it in a hundred interesting forms.

The social question quite fills the air, in New York, for any spectator whose impressions at all follow themselves up; it wears, at any rate, in what I have called the upper reaches, the perpetual strange appearance as of Property perched high aloft and yet itself looking about, all ruefully, in the wonder of what it is exactly doing there. We see it perched, assuredly, in other and older cities, other and older social orders; but it strikes us in those situations as knowing a little more where it is. It strikes us as knowing how it has got up and why it must, infallibly, stay up; it has not the frightened look, measuring the spaces around, of a small child set on a mantel-shelf and about to cry out. If old societies are interesting, however, I am far from thinking that young ones may not be more so — with their collective countenance so much more presented,

precisely, to observation, as by their artless need to get themselves explained. The American world produces almost everywhere the impression of appealing to any attested interest for
the word, the *fin mot*, of what it may mean; but I somehow
see those parts of it most at a loss that are already explained
not a little by the ample possession of money. This is the
amiable side there of the large developments of private ease in
general—the amiable side of those numerous groups that are
rich enough and, in the happy vulgar phrase, bloated enough,
to be candidates for the classic imputation of haughtiness.
The amiability proceeds from an essential vagueness; whereas
real haughtiness is never vague about itself—it is only vague
about others. That is the human note in the huge American
rattle of gold—so far as the "social" field is the scene of the
rattle. The "business" field is a different matter—as to which
the determination of the audibility in it of the human note (so
interesting to try for if one had but the warrant) is a line of
research closed to me, alas, by my fatally uninitiated state. My
point is, at all events, that you cannot be "hard," really, with
any society that affects you as ready to learn from you, and
from this resource for it of your detachment combining with
your proximity, what in the name of all its possessions and all
its destitutions it would honestly be "at."

III

New York and the Hudson: A Spring Impression

I

I<small>T WAS</small> a concomitant, always, of the down-town hour that it could be felt as *most* playing into the surrendered consciousness and making the sharpest impression; yet, since the up-town hour was apt, in its turn, to claim the same distinction, I could only let each of them take its way with me as it would. The oddity was that they seemed not at all to speak of different things—by so quick a process does any one aspect, in the United States, in general, I was to note, connect itself with the rest; so little does any link in the huge looseness of New York, in especial, appear to come as a whole, or as final, out of the fusion. The fusion, as of elements in solution in a vast hot pot, is always going on, and one stage of the process is as typical or as vivid as another. Whatever I might be looking at, or be struck with, the object or the phase was an item in the pressing conditions of the place, and as such had more in common with its sister items than it had in difference from them. It mattered little, moreover, whether this might be a proof that New York, among cities, most deeply languishes and palpitates, or vibrates and flourishes (whichever way one may put it) under the breath of her conditions, or whether, simply, this habit of finding a little of *all* my impressions reflected in any one of them testified to the enjoyment of a real relation with the subject. I like indeed to think of my relation to New York as, in that manner, almost inexpressibly intimate, and as hence making, for daily sensation, a keyboard as continuous, and as free from hard transitions, as if swept by the fingers of a master-pianist. You cannot, surely, say more for your sense of the underlying unity of an occasion than that the taste of each dish in the banquet recalls the taste of most of the others; which is what I mean by the "continuity," not to say the affinity, on the island of Manhattan, between the fish and the sweets, between the soup and the game. The whole feast affects one as eaten—that is the point—with the general queer sauce of New York; a preparation as freely diffused, somehow, on the East side as on the West, in the quarter of Grand Street as in the quarter of Murray Hill. No fact, I hasten to add, would appear to make the place more amenable to delineations of the order that may be spoken of as hanging together.

I must confess, notwithstanding, to not being quite ready to point directly to the common element in the dense Italian neighbourhoods of the lower East side, and in the upper reaches of Fifth and of Madison Avenues; though indeed I wonder at this inability in recollecting two or three of those charming afternoons of early summer, in Central Park, which showed the fruit of the foreign tree as shaken down there with a force that smothered everything else. The long residential vistas I have named were within a quarter of an hour's walk, but the alien was as truly in possession, under the high "aristocratic" nose, as if he had had but three steps to come. If it be asked why, the alien still striking you so as an alien, the singleness of impression, throughout the place, should still be so marked, the answer, close at hand, would seem to be that the alien himself fairly *makes* the singleness of impression. Is not the universal sauce essentially *his* sauce, and do we not feel ourselves feeding, half the time, from the ladle, as greasy as he chooses to leave it for us, that he holds out? Such questions were in my ears, at all events, with the cheerful hum of that babel of tongues established in the vernal Park, and they supplied, beyond doubt, the livelier interest of any hour of contemplation there. I hate to drift into dealing with them at the expense of a proper tribute, kept distinct and vivid, to the charming bosky precinct itself, the great field of recreation with which they swarmed; but it could not be the fault of the brooding visitor, and still less that of the restored absentee, if he was conscious of the need of mental adjustment to phenomena absolutely fresh. He could remember still how, months before, a day or two after his restoration, a noted element of one of his first impressions had been this particular revealed anomaly. He had been, on the Jersey shore, walking with a couple of friends through the grounds of a large new rural residence, where groups of diggers and ditchers were working, on those lines of breathless haste which seem always, in the United States, of the essence of any question, toward an expensive effect of landscape gardening. To pause before them, for interest in their labour, was, and would have been everywhere, instinctive; but what came home to me on the spot was that whatever *more* would have been anywhere else involved had here inevitably to lapse.

What lapsed, on the spot, was the element of communication with the workers, as I may call it for want of a better name; that element which, in a European country, would have operated, from side to side, as the play of mutual recognition, founded on old familiarities and heredities, and involving, for the moment, some impalpable exchange. The men, in the case I speak of, were Italians, of superlatively southern type, and any impalpable exchange struck me as absent from the air to positive intensity, to mere unthinkability. It was as if contact were out of the question and the sterility of the passage between us recorded, with due dryness, in our staring silence. This impression was for one of the party a shock—a member of the party for whom, on the other side of the world, the imagination of the main furniture, as it might be called, of any rural excursion, of *the* rural in particular, had been, during years, the easy sense, for the excursionist, of a social relation with any encountered type, from whichever end of the scale proceeding. Had that not ever been, exactly, a part of the vague warmth, the intrinsic colour, of any honest man's rural walk in his England or his Italy, his Germany or his France, and was not the effect of its so suddenly dropping out, in the land of universal brotherhood—for I was to find it drop out again and again—rather a chill, straightway, for the heart, and rather a puzzle, not less, for the head? Shortly after the spring of this question was first touched for me I found it ring out again with a sharper stroke. Happening to have lost my way, during a long ramble among the New Hampshire hills, I appealed, for information, at a parting of the roads, to a young man whom, at the moment of my need, I happily saw emerge from a neighbouring wood. But his stare was blank, in answer to my inquiry, and, seeing that he failed to understand me and that he had a dark-eyed "Latin" look, I jumped to the inference of his being a French Canadian. My repetition of my query in French, however, forwarded the case as little, and my trying him with Italian had no better effect. "What *are* you then?" I wonderingly asked—on which my accent loosened in him the faculty of speech. "I'm an Armenian," he replied, as if it were the most natural thing in the world for a wage-earning youth in the heart of New England to be—so that all I could do was to try and make my profit of the lesson. I could have made it better, for the occasion, if, even on the Armenian basis, he had appeared to expect brotherhood; but this had been as little his seeming as it had been that of the diggers by the Jersey shore.

To inquire of these things on the spot, to betray, that is, one's sense of the "chill" of which I have spoken, is of course to hear it admitted, promptly enough, that there is no claim to brotherhood with aliens in the first grossness of their alienism. The material of which they consist is being dressed and prepared, at this stage, for brotherhood, and the consummation, in respect to many of them, will not be, can not from the nature of the case be, in any lifetime of their own. Their children are another matter—as in fact the children throughout the United States, are an immense matter, are almost the greatest matter of all; it is the younger generation who will fully profit, rise to the occasion and enter into the privilege. The machinery is colossal—nothing is more characteristic of the country than the development of this machinery, in the form of the political and social habit, the common school and the newspaper; so that there are always millions of little transformed strangers growing up in regard to whom the idea of intimacy of relation may be as freely cherished as you like. *They* are the stuff of whom brothers and sisters are made, and the making proceeds on a scale that really need leave nothing to desire. All this you take in, with a wondering mind, and in the light of it the great "ethnic" question rises before you on a corresponding scale and with a corresponding majesty. Once it has set your observation, to say nothing of your imagination, working, it becomes for you, as you go and come, the wonderment to which everything ministers and that is quickened well-nigh to madness, in some places and on some occasions, by every face and every accent that meet your eyes and ears. The sense of the elements in the cauldron—the cauldron of the "American" character—becomes thus about as vivid a thing as you can at all quietly manage, and the question settles into a form which makes the intelligible answer further and further recede. "What meaning, in the presence of such impressions, can continue to attach to such a term as the 'American' character?—what type, as the result of such a prodigious amalgam, such a hotch-potch of racial ingredients, is to be conceived as shaping itself?" The challenge to speculation, fed thus by a thousand sources, is so intense as to be, as I say, irritating; but practically, beyond doubt, I should also say, you take refuge from it—since your case would otherwise be hard; and you find your relief not in the least in any direct satisfaction or solution, but absolutely in that blest general drop of the immediate need of conclusions, or rather in that blest general feeling for the impossibility of them, to which the philosophy of any really fine observation of the American spectacle must reduce itself, and the large intellectual, quite even the large æsthetic, margin supplied by which accompanies the spectator as his one positively complete comfort.

It is more than a comfort to him, truly, in all the conditions, this accepted vision of the too-defiant scale of numerosity and quantity—the effect of which is so to multiply the possibilities, so to open, by the million, contingent doors and windows: he rests in it at last as an absolute luxury, converting it even into a substitute, into *the* constant substitute, for many luxuries that are absent. He doesn't *know*, he can't *say*, before the facts, and he doesn't even want to know or to say; the facts themselves loom, before the understanding, in too large a mass for a mere mouthful: it is as if the syllables were too numerous to make a legible word. The *il*legible word, accordingly, the great inscrutable answer to questions, hangs in the vast American sky, to his imagination, as something fantastic and *abracadabrant*, belonging to no known language, and it is under this convenient ensign that he travels and considers and contemplates, and, to the best of his ability, enjoys. The interesting point, in the connection, is moreover that this particular effect of the scale of things is the only effect that, throughout the land, is not directly adverse to joy. Extent and reduplication, the multiplication of cognate items and the continuity of motion, are elements that count, there, in general, for fatigue and satiety, prompting the earnest observer, overburdened perhaps already a little by his earnestness, to the reflection that the country is too large for any human convenience, that it can scarce, in the scheme of Providence, have been meant to be dealt with as we are trying, perhaps all in vain, to deal with it, and that its very possibilities of population themselves cause one to wince in the light of the question of intercourse and contact. That relation to its superficies and content—the relation of flat fatigue—is, with the traveller, a constant quantity; so that he feels himself justified of the inward, the philosophic, escape into the immensity. And as it is the restored absentee, with his acquired habit of nearer limits and shorter journeys and more muffled concussions, who is doubtless most subject to flat fatigue, so it is this same personage who most avails himself of the liberty of waiting to see. It is an advantage—acting often in the way of a compensation, or of an appeal from the immediate—that he becomes, early in his period of inquiry, conscious of intimately invoking, in whatever apparent inconsistency it may lodge him. There is too much of the whole thing, he sighs, for the personal relation with it; and yet he would desire no inch less for the relation that he describes to himself best perhaps either as the provisionally-imaginative or as the distantly-respectful. Diminution of quantity, even by that inch, might mark the difference of his having to begin to recognize from afar, as through a rift in the obscurity, the gleam of some propriety of opinion. What would a man make, many things still being as they are, he finds himself asking, of a *small* America?—and what may a big one, on the other hand, still not make of itself? Goodness be thanked, accordingly, for the bigness. The state of flat fatigue, obviously, is not an opinion, save in the sense attributed to the slumber of the gentleman of the anecdote who had lost consciousness during the reading of the play —it belongs to the order of mere sensation and impression;

and as to these the case is quite different: he may have as many of each as he can carry.

II

The process of the mitigation and, still more, of the conversion of the alien goes on, meanwhile, obviously, not by leaps and bounds or any form of easy magic, but under its own mystic laws and with an outward air of quite declining to be unduly precipitated. How little it may be thought of in New York as a quick business we readily perceive as the effect of merely remembering the vast numbers of their kind that the arriving reinforcements, from whatever ends of the earth, find already in possession of the field. There awaits the disembarked Armenian, for instance, so warm and furnished an Armenian corner that the need of hurrying to get rid of the sense of it must become less and less a pressing preliminary. The corner growing warmer and warmer, it is to be supposed, by rich accretions, he may take his time, more and more, for becoming absorbed in the surrounding element, and he may in fact feel more and more that he can do so on his own conditions. I seem to find indeed in this latter truth a hint for the best expression of a whole side of New York— the best expression of much of the medium in which one consciously moves. It is formed by this fact that the alien is taking his time, and that you go about with him meanwhile, sharing, all respectfully, in his deliberation, waiting on his convenience, watching him at his interesting work. The vast foreign quarters of the city present him as thus engaged in it, and they are curious and portentous and "picturesque" just by reason of their doing so. You recognize in them, freely, those elements that are not elements of swift convertibility, and you lose yourself in the wonder of what becomes, as it were, of the obstinate, the unconverted residuum. The country at large, as you cross it in different senses, keeps up its character for you as the hugest thinkable organism for successful "assimilation"; but the assimilative force itself has the residuum still to count with. The operation of the immense machine, identical after all with the total of American life, trembles away into mysteries that are beyond our present notation and that reduce us in many a mood to renouncing analysis.

Who and what is an alien, when it comes to that, in a country peopled from the first under the jealous eye of history? —peopled, that is, by migrations at once extremely recent, perfectly traceable and urgently required. They are still, it would appear, urgently required—if we look about far enough for the urgency; though of that truth such a scene as New York may well make one doubt. Which is the American, by these scant measures?—which is *not* the alien, over a large part of the country at least, and where does one put a finger on the dividing line, or, for that matter, "spot" and identify any particular phase of the conversion, any one of its successive moments? The sense of the interest of so doing is doubtless half the interest of the general question—the possibility of our seeing lucidly presented some such phenomenon, in a given group of persons, or even in a felicitous individual, as the dawn of the American spirit while the declining rays of the Croatian, say, or of the Calabrian, or of the Lusitanian, still linger more or less pensively in the sky. Fifty doubts and queries come up, in regard to any such possibility, as one circulates in New York, with the so ambiguous element in the *launched* foreign personality always in one's eyes; the wonder, above all, of whether there be, comparatively, in the vastly greater number of the representatives of the fresh contingent, any spirit that the American does not find an easy prey. Repeatedly, in the electric cars, one seemed invited to take that for granted—there being occasions, days and weeks together, when the electric cars offer you nothing else to think of. The carful, again and again, is a foreign carful; a row of faces, up and down, testifying, without exception, to alienism unmistakable, alienism undisguised and unashamed. You do here, in a manner perhaps, discriminate; the launched condition, as I have called it, is more developed in some types than in others; but I remember observing how, in the Broadway and the Bowery conveyances in especial, they tended, almost alike, to make the observer gasp with the sense of isolation. It was not for this that the observer on whose behalf I more particularly write had sought to take up again the sweet sense of the natal air.

The great fact about his companions was that, foreign as they might be, newly inducted as they might be, they were *at home*, really more at home, at the end of their few weeks or months or their year or two, than they had ever in their lives been before; and that *he* was at home too, quite with the same intensity: and yet that it was this very equality of condition that, from side to side, made the whole medium so strange. Here again, however, relief may be sought and found —and I say this at the risk of perhaps picturing the restored absentee as too constantly requiring it; for there is fascination in the study of the innumerable ways in which this sense of being at home, on the part of all the types, may show forth. New York offers to such a study a well-nigh unlimited field, but I seem to recall winter days, harsh, dusky, sloshy winter afternoons, in the densely-packed East-side street-cars, as an especially intimate surrender to it. It took its place thus, I think, under the general American law of *all* relief from the great equalizing pressure: it took on that last disinterestedness which consists of one's getting away from one's subject by plunging into it, for sweet truth's sake, still deeper. If I speak, moreover, of this general first grossness of alienism as presented in "types," I use that word for easy convenience and not in respect to its indicating marked variety. There are many different ways, certainly, in which obscure fighters of the battle of life may look, under new high lights, queer and crude and unwrought; but the striking thing, precisely, in the crepuscular, tunnel-like avenues that the "Elevated" over-arches—yet without quenching, either, that constant power of any American exhibition rather luridly to light itself—the striking thing, and the beguiling, was always the manner in which figure after figure and face after face already betrayed the common consequence and action of their whereabouts. Face after face, unmistakably, was "low"—particularly in the men, squared all solidly in their new security and portability, their vague but growing sense of many unprecedented things; and as signs of the reinforcing of a large local conception of manners and relations it was difficult to say if they most affected one as promising or as portentous.

The great thing, at any rate, was that they were all together so visibly on the new, the lifted level—that of consciously not being what they *had* been, and that this immediately glazed them over as with some mixture, of indescribable hue and consistency, the wholesale varnish of consecration, that might have been applied, out of a bottomless receptacle, by a huge white-washing brush. Here, perhaps, was the nearest approach to a seizable step in the evolution of the oncoming citizen, the stage of his no longer being for you—for any complacency of the romantic, or even verily of the fraternizing, sense in you—the foreigner of the quality, of the kind, that he might have been *chez lui.* Whatever he might see himself becoming, he was never to see himself that again, any more than you were ever to see him. He became then, to my vision (which I have called fascinated for want of a better description of it), a creature promptly despoiled of those "manners" which were the grace (as I am again reduced to calling it) by which one had best known and, on opportunity, best liked him. He presents himself thus, most of all, to be plain—and not only in New York, but throughout the country—as wonderingly conscious that his manners of the other world, that everything you have there known and praised him for, have been a huge mistake: to that degree that the sense of this luminous discovery is what we mainly imagine his weighted communications to those he has left behind charged with; those rich letters home as to the number and content of which the Post Office gives us so remarkable a statistic. If there are several lights in which the great assimilative organism itself may be looked at, does it not still perhaps loom largest as an agent for revealing to the citizen-to-be the error in question? He hears it, under this ægis, proclaimed in a thousand voices, and it is as listening to these and as, according to the individual, more or less swiftly, but always infallibly, penetrated and convinced by them, that I felt myself see him go about his business, see him above all, for some odd reason, sit there in the street-car, and with a slow, brooding gravity, a dim calculation of bearings, which yet never takes a backward step, expand to the full measure of it.

So, in New York, largely, the "American" value of the immigrant who arrives at all mature is restricted to the enjoyment (all prepared to increase) of that important preliminary truth; which makes him for us, we must own, till more comes of it, a tolerably neutral and colourless image. He resembles for the time the dog who sniffs round the freshly-acquired bone, giving it a push and a lick, betraying a sense of its possibilities, but not—and quite as from a positive deep tremor of consciousness—directly attacking it. There are categories of foreigners, truly, meanwhile, of whom we are moved to say that only a mechanism working with scientific force could have performed this feat of making them colourless. The Italians, who, over the whole land, strike us, I am afraid, as, after the Negro and the Chinaman, the human value most easily produced, the Italians meet us, at every turn, only to make us ask what has become of that element of the agreeable address in *them* which has, from far back, so enhanced for the stranger the interest and pleasure of a visit to their beautiful country. They shed it utterly, I couldn't but observe, on their advent, after a deep inhalation or two of the clear native air; shed it with a conscientious completeness which leaves one looking for any faint trace of it. "Colour," of that pleasant sort, was what they had appeared, among the races of the European family, most to have; so that the effect I speak of, the rapid action of the ambient air, is like that of the tub of hot water that reduces a piece of bright-hued stuff, on immersion, to the proved state of not "washing": the only fault of my image indeed being that if the stuff loses its brightness the water of the tub at least is more or less agreeably dyed with it. That is doubtless not the case for the ambient air operating after the fashion I here note—since we surely fail to observe that the property washed out of the new subject begins to tint with its pink or its azure his fellow-soakers in the terrible tank. If this property that has quitted him—the general amenity of attitude in the absence of provocation to its opposite—could be accounted for by its having rubbed off on any number of surrounding persons, the whole process would be easier and perhaps more comforting to follow. It will not have been his first occasion of taking leave of short-sighted comfort in the United States, however, if the patient inquirer postpones that ideal to the real solicitation of the question I here touch on.

What *does* become of the various positive properties, on the part of certain of the installed tribes, the good manners, say, among them, as to which the process of shedding and the fact of eclipse come so promptly into play? It has taken long ages of history, in the other world, to produce them, and you ask yourself, with independent curiosity, if they may really be thus extinguished in an hour. And if they are not extinguished, into what pathless tracts of the native atmosphere do they virtually, do they provisionally, and so all undiscoverably, melt? Do they burrow underground, to await their day again?—or in what strange secret places are they held in deposit and in trust? The "American" identity that has profited by their sacrifice has meanwhile acquired (in the happiest cases) all apparent confidence and consistency; but may not the doubt remain of whether the extinction of qualities ingrained in generations is to be taken for quite complete? Isn't it conceivable that, for something like a final efflorescence, the business of slow comminglings and makings-over at last ended, they may rise again to the surface, affirming their vitality and value and playing their part? It would be for them, of course, in this event, to attest that they had been worth waiting so long for; but the speculation, at any rate, irresistibly forced upon us, is a sign of the interest, in the American world, of what I have called the "ethnic" outlook. The cauldron, for the great stew, has such circumference and such depth that we can only deal here with ultimate syntheses, ultimate combinations and possibilities. Yet I am well aware that if these vague evocations of them, in their nebulous remoteness, may charm the ingenuity of the student of the scene, there are matters of the foreground that they have no call to supplant. Any temptation to let them do so is meanwhile, no doubt, but a proof of that impulse irresponsibly to escape from the formidable foreground which so often, in the American world, lies in wait for the spirit of intellectual dalliance.

III

New York really, I think, is all formidable foreground; or, if it be not, there is more than enough of this pressure of the present and the immediate to cut out the close sketcher's work for him. These things are a thick growth all round him, and when I recall the intensity of the material picture in the dense Yiddish quarter, for instance, I wonder at its not having forestalled, on my page, mere musings and, as they will doubtless be called, moonings. There abides with me, ineffaceably, the memory of a summer evening spent there by invitation of a high public functionary domiciled on the spot—to the extreme enhancement of the romantic interest his visitor found him foredoomed to inspire—who was to prove one of the most liberal of hosts and most luminous of guides. I can scarce help it if this brilliant personality, on that occasion the very medium itself through which the whole spectacle showed, so colours my impressions that if I speak, by intention, of the facts that played into them I may really but reflect the rich talk and the general privilege of the hour. That accident moreover must take its place simply as the highest value and the strongest note in the total show—so much did it testify to the quality of appealing, surrounding life. The sense of this quality was already strong in my drive, with a companion, through the long, warm June twilight, from a comparatively conventional neighbourhood; it was the sense, after all, of a great swarming, a swarming that had begun to thicken, infinitely, as soon as we had crossed to the East side and long before we had got to Rutgers Street. There is no swarming like that of Israel when once Israel has got a start, and the scene here bristled, at every step, with the signs and sounds, immitigable, unmistakable, of a Jewry that had burst all bounds. That it has burst all bounds in New York, almost any combination of figures or of objects taken at hazard sufficiently proclaims; but I remember how the rising waters, on this summer night, rose, to the imagination, even above the housetops and seemed to sound their murmur to the pale distant stars. It was as if we had been thus, in the crowded, hustled roadway, where multiplication, multiplication of everything, was the dominant note, at the bottom of some vast sallow aquarium in which innumerable fish, of over-developed proboscis, were to bump together, for ever, amid heaped spoils of the sea.

The children swarmed above all—here was multiplication with a vengeance; and the number of very old persons, of either sex, was almost equally remarkable; the very old persons being in equal vague occupation of the doorstep, pavement, curbstone, gutter, roadway, and every one alike using the street for overflow. As overflow, in the whole quarter, is the main fact of life—I was to learn later on that, with the exception of some shy corner of Asia, no district in the world known to the statistician has so many inhabitants to the yard—the scene hummed with the human presence beyond any I had ever faced in quest even of refreshment; producing part of the impression, moreover, no doubt, as a direct consequence of the intensity of the Jewish aspect. This, I think, makes the individual Jew more of a concentrated person, savingly possessed of everything that is in him, than any other human, noted at random—or is it simply, rather, that the unsurpassed strength of the race permits of the chopping into myriads of fine fragments without loss of race-quality? There are small strange animals, known to natural history, snakes or worms, I believe, who, when cut into pieces, wriggle away contentedly and live in the snippet as completely as in the whole. So the denizens of the New York Ghetto, heaped as thick as the splinters on the table of a glass-blower, had each, like the fine glass particle, his or her individual share of the whole hard glitter of Israel. This diffused intensity, as I have called it, causes any array of Jews to resemble (if I may be allowed another image) some long nocturnal street where every window in every house shows a maintained light. The advanced age of so many of the figures, the ubiquity of the children, carried out in fact this analogy; they were all there for race, and not, as it were, for reason: that excess of lurid meaning, in some of the old men's and old women's faces in particular, would have been absurd, in the conditions, as a really directed attention—it could only be the gathered past of Israel mechanically pushing through. The way, at the same time, this chapter of history did, all that evening, seem to push, was a matter that made the "ethnic" apparition again sit like a skeleton at the feast. It was fairly as if I could see the spectre grin while the talk of the hour gave me, across the board, facts and figures, chapter and verse, for the extent of the Hebrew conquest of New York. With a reverence for intellect, one should doubtless have drunk in tribute to an intellectual people; but I remember being at no time more conscious of that merely portentous element, in the aspects of American growth, which reduces to inanity any marked dismay quite as much as any high elation. The portent is one of too many—you always come back, as I have hinted, with your easier gasp, to *that*: it will be time enough to sigh or to shout when the relation of the particular appearance to all the other relations shall have cleared itself up. Phantasmagoric for me, accordingly, in a high degree, are the interesting hours I here glance at content to remain—setting in this respect, I recognize, an excellent example to all the rest of the New York phantasmagoria. Let me speak of the remainder only as phantasmagoric too, so that I may both the more kindly recall it and the sooner have done with it.

I have not done, however, with the impression of that large evening in the Ghetto; there was too much in the vision, and it has left too much the sense of a rare experience. For what did it all really come to but that one had seen with one's eyes the New Jerusalem on earth? What less than that could it all have been, in its far-spreading light and its celestial serenity of multiplication? There it was, there it is, and when I think of the dark, foul, stifling Ghettos of other remembered cities, I shall think by the same stroke of the city of redemption, and evoke in particular the rich Rutgers Street perspective—rich, so peculiarly, for the eye, in that complexity of fire-escapes with which each house-front bristles and which gives the whole vista so modernized and appointed a look. Omnipresent in the "poor" regions, this neat applied machinery has, for the stranger, a common side with the electric light and the telephone, suggests the distance achieved from the old Jerusalem. (These frontal iron ladders and platforms, by the way, so numerous throughout New York, strike more New York notes than can be parenthetically named—and among them perhaps most sharply the note of the ease with which, in the terrible town, on opportunity, "architecture" goes by the board; but the appearance to which they often most conduce is that of the spaciously organized cage for the nimbler class of animals in some great zoological garden. This general analogy is irresistible—it seems to offer, in each district, a little world of bars and perches and swings for human squirrels and monkeys. The very name of architecture perishes, for the fire-escapes look like abashed afterthoughts, staircases and communications forgotten in the construction; but the inhabitants lead, like the squirrels and monkeys, all the merrier life.) It was while I hung over the prospect from the windows of my friend, however, the presiding genius of the district, and it was while, at a later hour, I proceeded in his company, and in that of a trio of contributive fellow-pilgrims, from one "characteristic" place of public entertainment to another: it was during this rich climax, I say, that the city of redemption was least to be taken for anything less than it was. The windows, while we sat at meat, looked out on a swarming little square in which an ant-like population darted to and fro; the square consisted in part of a "district" public garden, or public lounge rather, one of those small backwaters or refuges, artfully economized for rest, here and there, in the very heart of the New York whirlpool, and which spoke louder than anything else of a Jerusalem disinfected. What spoke loudest, no doubt, was the great overtowering School which formed a main boundary and in the shadow of which we all comparatively crouched.

But the School must not lead me on just yet—so colossally has its presence still to loom for us; that presence which profits so, for predominance, in America, by the failure of con-current and competitive presences, the failure of any others looming at all on the same scale save that of Business, those in particular of a visible Church, a visible State, a visible Society, a visible Past; those of the many visibilities, in short, that warmly cumber the ground in older countries. Yet it also spoke loud that my friend was quartered, for the interest of the thing (from his so interesting point of view), in a "tenement-house"; the New Jerusalem would so have tri-umphed, had it triumphed nowhere else, in the fact that this charming little structure *could* be ranged, on the wonderful little square, under that invidious head. On my asking to what latent vice it owed its stigma, I was asked in return if it didn't sufficiently pay for its name by harbouring some five-and-twenty families. But this, exactly, was the way it testified—this circumstance of the simultaneous enjoyment by five-and-twenty families, on "tenement" lines, of conditions so little

sordid, so highly "evolved." I remember the evolved fire-
proof staircase, a thing of scientific surfaces, impenetrable to
the microbe, and above all plated, against side friction, with
white marble of a goodly grain. The white marble was surely
the New Jerusalem note, and we followed that note, up and
down the district, the rest of the evening, through more
happy changes than I may take time to count. What struck me
in the flaring streets (over and beyond the everywhere insistent, defiant, unhumorous, exotic face) was the blaze of the
shops addressed to the New Jerusalem wants and the splendour with which these were taken for granted; the only thing
indeed a little ambiguous was just this look of the trap too
brilliantly, too candidly baited for the wary side of Israel itself. It is not *for* Israel, in general, that Israel so artfully
shines—yet its being moved to do so, at last, in that luxurious style, might be precisely the grand side of the city of redemption. Who can ever tell, moreover, in any conditions and
in presence of any apparent anomaly, what the genius of
Israel may, or may not, really be "up to"?

The grateful way to take it all, at any rate, was with the
sense of its coming back again to the inveterate rise, in the
American air, of every value, and especially of the lower ones,
those most subject to multiplication; such a wealth of meaning did this keep appearing to pour into the value and function of the country at large. Importances are all strikingly
shifted and reconstituted, in the United States, for the visitor
attuned, from far back, to "European" importances; but I
think of no other moment of my total impression as so
sharply working over my own benighted vision of them. The
scale, in this light of the New Jerusalem, seemed completely
rearranged; or, to put it more simply, the wants, the gratifica-
tions, the aspirations of the "poor," as expressed in the shops
(which were the shops of the "poor"), denoted a new style of
poverty; and this new style of poverty, from street to street,
stuck out of the possible purchasers, one's jostling fellow-
pedestrians, and made them, to every man and woman, individual throbs in the larger harmony. One can speak only of
what one has seen, and there were grosser elements of the
sordid and the squalid that I doubtless never saw. That, with
a good deal of observation and of curiosity, I should have

failed of this, the country over, affected me as by itself something of an indication. To miss that part of the spectacle, or to know it only by its having so unfamiliar a pitch, was an indication that made up for a great many others. It is when this one in particular is forced home to you—this immense, vivid *general* lift of poverty and general appreciation of the living unit's paying property in himself—that the picture seems most to clear and the way to jubilation most to open. For it meets you there, at every turn, as the result most definitely attested. You are as constantly reminded, no doubt, that these rises in enjoyed value shrink and dwindle under the icy breath of Trusts and the weight of the new remorseless monopolies that operate as no madnesses of ancient personal power thrilling us on the historic page ever operated; the living unit's property in himself becoming more and more merely such a property as may consist with a relation to properties overwhelmingly greater and that allow the asking of no questions and the making, for co-existence with them, of no conditions. But that, in the fortunate phrase, is another story, and will be altogether, evidently, a new and different drama. There is such a thing, in the United States, it is hence to be inferred, as freedom to grow up to be blighted, and it may be the only freedom in store for the smaller fry of future generations. If it is accordingly of the smaller fry I speak, and of how large they massed on that evening of endless admonitions, this will be because I caught them thus in their comparative humility and at an early stage of their American growth. The life-thread has, I suppose, to be of a certain thickness for the great shears of Fate to feel for it. Put it, at the worst, that the Ogres were to devour them, they were but the more certainly to fatten into food for the Ogres.

Their dream, at all events, as I noted it, was meanwhile sweet and undisguised—nowhere sweeter than in the half-dozen picked beer-houses and cafés in which our ingenuous *enquête*, that of my fellow-pilgrims and I, wound up. These establishments had each been selected for its playing off some facet of the jewel, and they wondrously testified, by their range and their individual colour, to the spread of that lustre. It was a pious rosary of which I should like to tell each bead, but I must let the general sense of the adventure serve. Our successive stations were in no case of the "seamy" order, an inquiry into seaminess having been unanimously pronounced futile, but each had its separate social connotation, and it was for the number and variety of these connotations, and their individual plenitude and prosperity, to set one thinking. Truly the Yiddish world was a vast world, with its own deeps and complexities, and what struck one above all was that it sat there at its cups (and in no instance vulgarly the worse for them) with a sublimity of good conscience that took away the breath, a protrusion of elbow never aggressive, but absolutely proof against jostling. It was the incurable man of letters under the skin of one of the party who gasped, I confess; for it was in the light of letters, that is in the light of our language as literature has hitherto known it, that one stared at this all-unconscious impudence of the agency of future ravage. The man of letters, in the United States, has his own difficulties to face and his own current to stem—for dealing with which his liveliest inspiration may be, I think, that they are still very much his own, even in an Americanized world, and that more than elsewhere they press him to intimate communion with his honour. For that honour, the honour that sits astride of the consecrated English tradition, to his mind, quite as old knighthood astride of its caparisoned charger, the dragon most rousing, over the land, the proper spirit of St. George, is just this immensity of the alien presence climbing higher and higher, climbing itself into the very light of publicity.

I scarce know why, but I saw it that evening as in some dim dawn of that promise to its own consciousness, and perhaps this was precisely what made it a little exasperating. Under the impression of the mere mob the question doesn't come up, but in these haunts of comparative civility we saw the mob sifted and strained, and the exasperation was the sharper, no doubt, because what the process had left most visible was just the various possibilities of the waiting spring of intelligence. Such elements constituted the germ of a "public," and it was impossible (possessed of a sensibility worth speaking of) to be exposed to them without feeling how new a thing under the sun the resulting public would be. That was where one's "lettered" anguish came in—in the turn of one's eye from face to face for some betrayal of a prehensile hook for the linguistic tradition as one had known it. Each warm lighted and supplied circle, each group of served tables and smoked pipes and fostered decencies and unprecedented accents, beneath the extravagant lamps, took on thus, for the brooding critic, a likeness to that terrible modernized and civilized room in the Tower of London, haunted by the shade of Guy Fawkes, which had more than once formed part of the scene of the critic's taking tea there. In this chamber of the present urbanities the wretched man had been stretched on the rack, and the critic's ear (how else should it have been a critic's?) could still always catch, in pauses of talk, the faint groan of his ghost. Just so the East side cafés—and increasingly as their place in the scale was higher—showed to my inner sense, beneath their bedizenment, as torture-rooms of the living idiom; the piteous gasp of which at the portent of lacerations to come could reach me in any drop of the surrounding Accent of the Future. The accent of the very ultimate future, in the States, may be destined to become the most beautiful on the globe and the very music of humanity (here the "ethnic" synthesis shrouds itself thicker than ever); but whatever we shall know it for, certainly, we shall not know it for English—in any sense for which there is an existing literary measure.

IV

The huge jagged city, it must be nevertheless said, has always at the worst, for propitiation, the resource of its easy reference to its almost incomparable river. New York may indeed be jagged, in her long leanness, where she lies looking at the sky in the manner of some colossal hair-comb turned upward and so deprived of half its teeth that the others, at their uneven intervals, count doubly as sharp spikes; but, unmistakably, you can bear with some of her aspects and her airs better when you have really taken in that reference—which I speak of as easy because she has in this latter time begun to make it with an appearance of some intention. She has come at last, far up on the West side, into possession of her birthright, into the roused consciousness that some possibility of a river-front may still remain to her; though, obviously, a justified pride in this property has yet to await the birth of a more responsible sense of style in her dealings with it, the dawn of some adequate plan or controlling idea. Splendid the elements of position, on the part of the new Riverside Drive (over the small suburbanizing name of which, as at the effect of a second-rate shop-worn article, we sigh as we pass); yet not less irresistible the pang of our seeing it settle itself on meagre, bourgeois, happy-go-lucky lines. The pity of this is sharp in proportion as the "chance" has been magnificent, and the soreness of perception of what merely might have been is as constant as the flippancy of the little vulgar "private houses" or the big vulgar "apartment hotels" that are having their own way, so unchallenged, with the whole question of composition and picture. The fatal "tall" pecuniary enterprise rises where it will, in the candid glee of new worlds to conquer; the intervals between take whatever foolish little form they like; the sky-line, eternal victim of the artless jumble, submits again to the type of the broken hair-comb turned up; the streets that abut from the East condescend at their corners to any crudity or poverty that may suit their convenience. And all this in presence of an occasion for noble congruity such as one scarce knows where to seek in the case of another great city.

A sense of the waste of criticism, however, a sense that is almost in itself consoling, descends upon the fond critic after his vision has fixed the scene awhile in this light of its lost accessibility to some informed and benevolent despot, some power working in one great way and so that the interest of beauty should have been better saved. Is not criticism wasted, in other words, just by the reason of the constant remembrance, on New York soil, that one is almost impudently cheated by any part of the show that pretends to prolong its actuality or to rest on its present basis? Since every part, however blazingly new, fails to affect us as doing more than hold the ground for something else, some conceit of the bigger dividend, that is still to come, so we may bind up the æsthetic wound, I think, quite as promptly as we feel it open. The particular ugliness, or combination of uglinesses, is no more final than the particular felicity (since there are several even of these up and down the town to be noted), and whatever crudely-extemporized look the Riverside heights may wear to-day, the spectator of fifty years hence will find his sorrow, if not his joy, in a different extemporization. The whole thing is the vividest of lectures on the subject of individualism, and on the strange truth, no doubt, that this principle may in the field of art—at least if the art be architecture—often conjure away just that mystery of distinction which it sometimes so markedly promotes in the field of life. It is also quite as suggestive perhaps on the ever-interesting question, for the artist, of the entirely relative nature and value of "treatment." A manner so right in one relation may be so wrong in another, and a house-front so "amusing" for its personal note, or its perversity, in a short perspective, may amid larger elements merely dishonour the harmony. And yet why *should* the charm ever fall out of the "personal," which is so often the very condition of the exquisite? Why should conformity and subordination, that acceptance of control and assent to collectivism in the name of which our age has seen such dreary things done, become on a given occasion the one *not* vulgar way of meeting a problem?

Inquiries these, evidently, that are answerable only in presence of the particular cases provoking them; when indeed they may hold us as under a spell. Endless for instance the æsthetic nobleness of such a question as that of the authority with which the spreading Hudson, at the opening of its gates, would have imposed on the constructive powers, if listened to, some proportionate order—would, in other words, have admirably given us collectivism at its highest. One has only to stand there and *see*—of such value are lessons in "authority." But the great vista of the stream alone speaks of it—save in so far at least as the voice is shared, and to so different, to so dreadful a tune, by the grossly-defacing railway that clings to the bank. The authority of railways, in the United States, sits enthroned as none other, and has always, of course, in any vision of aspects, to be taken into account. Here, at any rate, it is the rule that has prevailed; the other, the high interest of the possible picture, is one that lapses; so that the cliffs overhang the water, and at various points descend to it in green slopes and hollows (where the landscape-gardener does what he can), only to find a wealth of visible baseness installed there before them. That so familiar circumstance, in America, of the completion of the good thing ironically and, as would often seem for the time, insuperably baffled, meets here one of its liveliest illustrations. It at all events helps to give meanwhile the mingled pitch of the whole concert that Columbia College (to sound the old and easier name) should have "moved up"—moved up twice, if I am not mistaken—to adorn with an ampler presence this very neighbourhood. It has taken New York to invent, for the thickening of classic shades, the "moving" University; and does not that quite mark the tune of the dance, of the local unwritten law that forbids almost *any* planted object to gather in a history where it stands, forbids in fact any accumulation that may not be recorded in the mere bank-book? This last became long ago *the* historic page.

It is, however, just because the beauty of the Hudson seems to speak of other matters, and because the sordid city has the honour, after all, of sitting there at the Beautiful Gate, that I alluded above to her profiting in a manner, even from the point of view of "taste," by this close and fortunate connection. The place puts on thus, not a little, the likeness of a large loose family which has had queer adventures and fallen into vulgar ways, but for which a glorious cousinship never quite repudiated by the indifferent princely cousin—*bon prince* in this as in other matters—may still be pleaded. At the rate New York is growing, in fine, she will more and more "command," in familiar intercourse, the great perspective of the River; so that here, a certain point reached, her whole case must change and her general opportunity, swallowing up the mainland, become a new question altogether. Let me hasten to add that in the light of this opportunity even the most restless analyst can but take the hopeful view of her. I fear I am finding too many personal comparisons for her—than which indeed there can be no greater sign of a confessed preoccupation; but she figures, once again, as an heir whose expectations are so vast and so certain that no temporary sowing of wild oats need be felt to endanger them. As soon as the place begins to spread at ease real responsibility of all sorts will begin, and the good-natured feeling must surely be that the civic conscience in her, at such a stage, will fall into step. Of the spreading woods and waters amid which the future in question appears still half to lurk, that mainland region of the Bronx, vast above all in possibilities of Park, out of which it already appears half to emerge, I unluckily failed of occasion to take the adequate measure. But my confused impression was of a kind of waiting abundance, an extraordinary quantity of "nature," for the reformed rake, that is the sobered heir, to play with. It is the fashion in the East to speak of New York as poor of environment, unpossessed of the agreeable, accessible countryside that crowns the convenience not only of London and of Paris, but even, with more humiliating promptitude, that of Boston, of Philadelphia, of Baltimore. In spite, however, of the memory, from far back, of a hundred marginal Mahattanese miseries, an immediate belt of the most sordid character, I cannot but think of this invidious legend as attempting to prove too much.

The countryside is there, on the most liberal of scales—it is the townside, only, that, having the great waters and the greater distances generally to deal with, has worn so rude and demoralized a face as to frighten the country away. And if the townside is now making after the countryside fast, as I say, and with a little less of the mere roughness of the satyr pursuing the nymph, what finer warrant could be desired than such felicities of position as those enjoyed, on the Riverside heights, by the monument erected to the soldiers and sailors of the Civil War and, even in a greater degree, by the tomb of General Grant? These are verily monumental sites of the first order, and I confess that, though introduced to them on a bleak winter morning, with no ingratiation in any element, I felt the critical question, as to the structures themselves, as to taste or intention, as to the amount of involved or achieved consecration or profanation, carried off in the general greatness of the effect. I shall in fact always remember that icy hour, with the temple-crowned headlands, the wide Hudson vista white with the cold, all nature armour-plated and grim, as an extraordinarily strong and simple composition; made stern and kept simple as for some visit of the God of Battles to his chosen. He might have been riding there, on the north wind, to look down at them, and one caught for the moment, the true hard light in which military greatness should be seen. It shone over the miles of ice with its lustre of steel, and if

what, thus attested, it makes one think of was its incomparable, indestructible "prestige," so that association affected me
both then and on a later occasion as with a strange indefinable
consequence—an influence in which the æsthetic consideration, the artistic value of either memorial, melted away and
became irrelevant. For here, if ever, was a great democratic
demonstration caught in the fact, the nakedest possible effort
to strike the note of the august. The tomb of the single hero
in particular presents itself in a manner so opposed to our
common ideas of the impressive, to any past vision of sepul-
chral state, that we can only wonder if a new kind and degree
of solemnity may not have been arrived at in this complete
rupture with old consecrating forms.

The tabernacle of Grant's ashes stands there by the
pleasure-drive, unguarded and unenclosed, the feature of the
prospect and the property of the people, as open as an hotel
or a railway-station to any coming and going, and as dedicated to the public use as builded things in America (when
not mere closed churches) only can be. Unmistakable its air of
having had, all consciously, from the first, to raise its head
and play its part without pomp and circumstance to "back" it,
without mystery or ceremony to protect it, without Church
or State to intervene on its behalf, with only its immediacy,
its familiarity of interest to circle it about, and only its proud
outlook to preserve, so far as possible, its character. The tomb
of Napoleon at the Invalides is a great national property, and
the play of democratic manners sufficiently surrounds it; but
as compared to the small pavilion on the Riverside bluff it is a
holy of holies, a great temple jealously guarded and formally
approached. And yet one doesn't conclude, strange to say,
that the Riverside pavilion fails of its expression a whit more
than the Paris dome; one perhaps even feels it triumph by its
use of its want of reserve as a very last word. The admonition
of all of which possibly is—I confess I but grope for it—that
when there has been in such cases a certain other happy combination, an original sincerity of intention, an original propriety of site, and above all an original high value of name and
fame, something in this line really supreme, publicity, familiarity, immediacy, as I have called them, *carried far enough*,
may stalk in and out of the shrine with their hands in their

pockets and their hats on their heads, and yet not dispel the Presence. The question at any rate puts itself—as new questions in America are always putting themselves: Do certain impressions there represent the absolute extinction of old sensibilities, or do they represent only new forms of them? The inquiry would be doubtless easier to answer if so many of these feelings were not mainly known to us just *by* their attendant forms. At this rate, or on such a showing, in the United States, attendant forms being, in every quarter, remarkably scarce, it would indeed seem that the sentiments implied *are* extinct; for it would be an abuse of ingenuity, I fear, to try to read mere freshness of form into some of the more rank failures of observance. There are failures of observance that stand, at the best, for failures of sense—whereby, however, the question grows too great. One must leave the tomb of Grant to its conditions and its future with the simple note for it that if it be not in fact one of the most effective of commemorations it is one of the most missed. On the whole I distinctly "liked" it.

V

It is still vivid to me that, returning in the spring-time from a few weeks in the Far West, I re-entered New York State with the absurdest sense of meeting again a ripe old civilization and travelling through a country that showed the mark of established manners. It will seem, I fear, one's perpetual refrain, but the moral was yet once more that values of a certain order are, in such conditions, all relative, and that, as some wants of the spirit *must* somehow be met, one knocks together any substitute that will fairly stay the appetite. We had passed great smoky Buffalo in the raw vernal dawn—with a vision, for me, of curiosity, character, charm, whatever it might be, too needfully sacrificed, opportunity perhaps forever missed, yet at the same time a vision in which the lost object failed to mock at me with the last concentration of shape; and history, as we moved Eastward, appeared to meet us, in the look of the land, in its more overwrought surface and thicker detail, quite as if she had ever consciously declined to cross the border and were aware, precisely, of the queer feast we should find in her. The recognition, I profess, was a preposterous ecstasy: one couldn't have felt more if one had passed into the presence of some seated, placid, rich-voiced gentlewoman after leaving that of an honest but bois-terous hoyden. It was doubtless a matter only of degrees and shades, but never was such a pointing of the lesson that a sign of any sort may count double if it be but artfully placed. I spent that day, literally, in the company of the rich-voiced gentlewoman, making my profit of it even in spite of a second privation, the doom I was under of having only, all wistfully, all ruefully, to avert my lips from the quaint silver bowl, as I here quite definitely figured it, in which she offered me the entertainment of antique Albany. At antique Albany, to a cer-tainty, the mature matron involved in my metaphor would have put on a particular grace, and as our train crossed the river for further progress I almost seemed to see her stand at some gable-window of Dutch association, one of the two or three impressed there on my infantile imagination, to ask me why then I had come so far at all.

I could have replied but in troubled tones, and I looked at the rest of the scene for some time, no doubt, as through the glaze of all-but filial tears. Thus it was, possibly, that I saw the River shine, from that moment on, as a great romantic stream, such as could throw not a little of its glamour, for the mood of that particular hour, over the city at its mouth. I had not even known, in my untravelled state, that we were to "strike" it on our way from Chicago, so that it represented, all that afternoon, so much beauty thrown in, so much benefit beyond the bargain—the so hard bargain, for the traveller, of the American railway-journey at its best. That ordeal was in any case at its best here, and the perpetually interesting river kept its course, by my right elbow, with such splendid consis-tency that, as I recall the impression, I repent a little of having just now reflected with acrimony on the cost of the obtrusion of track and stations to the Riverside view. One must of course choose between dispensing with the ugly presence and enjoying the scenery by the aid of the same—which but means, really, that to use the train at all had been to put one's self, for any proper justice to the scenery, in a false position. That, however, takes us too far back, and one can only save one's dignity by laying all such blames on our detestable age. A decent respect for the Hudson would confine us to the use of the boat—all the more that American river-steamers have had, from the earliest time, for the true *raffiné*, their peculiar note of romance. A possible commerce, on the other hand, with one's time—which is always also the time of so many other busy people—has long since made mincemeat of the rights of contemplation; rights as reduced, in the United States, to-day, and by quite the same argument, as those of the noble savage whom we have banished to his narrowing reservation. Letting that pass, at all events, I still remember that I was able to put, from the car-window, as many questions to the scene as it could have answered in the time even had its face been clearer to read.

Its face was veiled, for the most part, in a mist of premature spring heat, an atmosphere draping it indeed in luminous mystery, hanging it about with sun-shot silver and minimizing any happy detail, any element of the definite, from which the romantic effect might here and there have gained an accent. There was not an accent in the picture from the beginning of the run to Albany to the end—for which thank goodness! one is tempted to say on remembering how often, over the land in general, the accents are wrong. Yet if the romantic effect as we know it elsewhere mostly depends on them, why *should* that glamour have so shimmered before me in their absence?—how should the picture have managed to be a constant combination of felicities? Was it just *because* the felicities were all vaguenesses, and the "beauties," even the most celebrated, all blurs?—was it perchance on that very account that I could meet my wonder so promptly with the inference that what I had in my eyes on so magnificent a scale was simply, was famously, "style"? I was landed by that conclusion in the odd further proposition that style could then exist without accents—a quandary soon after to be quenched, however, in the mere blinding radiance of a visit to West Point. I was to make that memorable pilgrimage a fortnight later—and I was to find my question, when it in fact took place, shivered by it to mere silver atoms. The very powers of the air seemed to have taken the case in hand and positively to have been interested in making it transcend all argument. Our

Sunday of mid-May, wet and windy, let loose, over the vast stage, the whole procession of storm-effects; the raw green of wooded heights and hollows was only everywhere rain-brightened, the weather playing over it all day as with some great grey water-colour brush. The essential character of West Point and its native nobleness of position can have been but intensified, I think, by this artful process; yet what was mainly unmistakable was the fact again of the suppression of detail as in the positive interest of the grand style. One had therefore only to take detail as another name for accent, the accent that might prove compromising, in order to see it made good that style *could* do without them, and that the grand style in fact almost always must. How on this occasion the trick was played is more than I shall attempt to say; it is enough to have been conscious of our being, from hour to hour, literally bathed in that high element, with the very face of nature washed, so to speak, the more clearly to express and utter it.

Such accordingly is the strong silver light, all simplifying and ennobling, in which I see West Point; see it as a cluster of high promontories, of the last classic elegance, overhanging vast receding reaches of river, mountain-guarded and dim, which took their place in the geography of the ideal, in the long perspective of the poetry of association, rather than in those of the State of New York. It was as if the genius of the scene had said: "No, you *shan't* have accent, because accent is, at the best, local and special, and might here by some perversity—how do I know after all?—interfere. I want you to have something unforgettable, and therefore you shall have *type*—yes, absolutely have type, and even tone, without accent; an impossibility, you may hitherto have supposed, but which you have only to look about you now really to see expressed. And type and tone of the very finest and rarest; type and tone good enough for Claude or Turner, if they could have walked by these rivers instead of by their thin rivers of France and Italy; type and tone, in short, that gather in shy detail under wings as wide as those with which a motherly hen covers her endangered brood. So there you are—deprived of all 'accent' as a peg for criticism, and reduced thereby, you see, to asking me no more questions." I was able so to take home, I may add, this formula of the matter, that even the interesting facts of the School of the Soldier which have carried the name of the place about the world almost put on the shyness, the air of conscious evasion and escape, noted in the above allocution: they struck me as forsaking the foreground of the picture. It was part of the play again, no doubt, of the grey water-colour brush: there was to be no consent of the elements, that day, to anything but a generalized elegance—in which effect certainly the clustered, the scattered Academy played, on its high green stage, its part. But, of all things in the world, it massed, to my vision, more mildly than I had somehow expected; and I take that for a feature, precisely, of the pure poetry of the impression. It lurked there with grace, it insisted without swagger—and I could have hailed it just for this reason indeed as a presence of the last distinction. It is doubtless too much to say, in fine, that the Institution, at West Point, "suffers" comparatively, for vulgar individual emphasis, from the overwhelming liberality of its setting—and I perhaps chanced to see it in the very conditions that most invest it with poetry. The fact remains that, both as to essence and as to quantity, its prose seemed washed away, and I shall recall it in the future much less as the sternest, the world over, of all the seats of Discipline, than as some great Corot-composition of young, vague, wandering figures in splendidly-classic shades.

VI

I make that point, for what it is worth, only to remind myself of another occasion on which the romantic note sounded for me with the last intensity, and yet on which the picture swarmed with accents—as, absent or present, I must again call them—that contributed alike to its interest and to its dignity. The proof was complete, on this second Sunday, with the glow of early summer already in possession, that affirmed detail was not always affirmed infelicity—since the scene here bristled with detail (and detail of the importance that frankly *constitutes* accent) only to the enhancement of its charm. It was a matter once more of hanging over the Hudson on the side opposite West Point, but further down; the situation was founded, as at West Point, on the presence of

the great feature and on the consequent general lift of foreground and distance alike, and yet infinitely sweet was it to
gather that style, in such conditions and for the success of
such effects, had not really to depend on mere kind vaguenesses, on any anxious deprecation of distinctness. There was
no vagueness now; a wealth of distinctness, in the splendid
light, met the eyes—but with the very result of showing them
how happily it could play. What it came back to was that the
accents, in the delightful old pillared and porticoed house that
crowned the cliff and commanded the stream, were as right
as they were numerous; so that there immediately followed
again on this observation a lively recognition of the ground of
the rightness. To wonder what this was could be but to see,
straightway, that, though many reasons had worked together
for them, mere time had done more than all; that beneficence
of time enjoying in general, in the United States, so little even
of the chance that so admirably justifies itself, for the most
part, when interference happens to have spared it. Cases of
this rare mercy yet exist, as I had had occasion to note, and
their consequent appeal to the touched sense within us comes,
as I have also hinted, with a force out of all proportion,
comes with a kind of accepted insolence of authority. The
things that have lasted, in short, whatever they may be, "succeed" as no newness, try as it will, succeeds, inasmuch as their
success is a created interest.

There we catch the golden truth which so much of the
American world strikes us as positively organized to gainsay,
the truth that production takes time, and that the production
of interest, in particular, takes *most* time. Desperate again and
again the ingenuity of the offered, the obtruded substitute,
and pathetic in many an instance its confessed failure; this
remark being meanwhile relevant to the fact that my charming old historic house of the golden Sunday put me off,
among its great trees, its goodly gardens, its acquired signs
and gathered memories, with no substitute whatever, even the
most specious, but just paid cash down, so to speak, ripe ringing gold, over the counter, for all the attention it invited. It
had character, as one might say, and character is scarce less
precious on the part of the homes of men in a raw medium
than on the part of responsible persons at a difficult crisis.

This virtue was there within and without and on every face; but perhaps nowhere so present, I thought, as in the ideal refuge for summer days formed by the wide north porch, if porch that disposition may be called—happiest disposition of the old American country-house—which sets tall columns in a row, under a pediment suitably severe, to present them as the "making" of a high, deep gallery. I know not what dignity of old afternoons suffused with what languor seems to me always, under the murmur of American trees and by the lap of American streams, to abide in these mild shades; there are combinations with depths of congruity beyond the plummet, it would seem, even of the most restless of analysts, and rather than try to say why my whole impression here melted into the general iridescence of a past of Indian summers hanging about mild ghosts half asleep, in hammocks, over still milder novels, I would renounce altogether the art of refining. For the iridescence consists, in this connection, of a shimmer of association that still more refuses to be reduced to terms; some sense of legend, of aboriginal mystery, with a still earlier past for its dim background and the insistent idea of the River as above all romantic for its warrant. Helplessly analyzed, perhaps, this amounts to no more than the very childish experience of a galleried house or two round about which the views and the trees and the peaches and the pony seemed prodigious, and to the remembrance of which the wonder of Rip Van Winkle and that of the "Hudson River School" of landscape art were, a little later on, to contribute their glamour.

If Rip Van Winkle had been really at the bottom of it all, nothing could have furthered the whole case more, on the occasion I speak of, than the happy nearness of the home of Washington Irving, the impression of which I was thus able, in the course of an hour, to work in—with the effect of intensifying more than I can say the old-time charm and the general legendary fusion. These are beautiful, delicate, modest matters, and how can one touch them with a light enough hand? How can I give the comparatively coarse reasons for my finding at Sunnyside, which contrives, by some grace of its own, to be at once all ensconced and embowered in relation to the world, and all frank and uplifted in relation to the river, a perfect treasure of mild moralities? The highway, the old State road to Albany, bristling now with the cloud-compelling motor, passes at the head of a deep, long lane, winding, embanked, overarched, such an old-world lane as one scarce ever meets in America; but if you embrace this chance to plunge away to the left you come out for your reward into the quite indefinable air of the little American literary past. The place is inevitably, to-day, but a qualified Sleepy Hollow—the Sleepy Hollow of the author's charming imagination was, as I take it, off somewhere in the hills, or in some dreamland of old autumns, happily unprofanable now; for "modernity," with its terrible power of working its will, of abounding in its sense, of gilding its toy—modernity, with its pockets full of money and its conscience full of virtue, its heart really full of tenderness, has seated itself there under pretext of guarding the shrine. What has happened, in a word, is very much what has happened in the case of other shy retreats of anchorites doomed to celebrity—the primitive cell has seen itself encompassed, in time, by a temple of many chambers, all dedicated to the history of the hermit. The cell is still there at Sunnyside, and there is even yet so much charm that one doesn't attempt to say where the parts of it, all kept together in a rich conciliatory way, begin or end— though indeed, I hasten to add, the identity of the original modest house, the shrine within the gilded shell, has been religiously preserved.

One has, in fact, I think, no quarrel whatever with the amplified state of the place, for it is the manner and the effect of this amplification that enable us to read into the scene its very most interesting message. The "little" American literary past, I just now said—using that word—(whatever the real size of the subject) because the caressing diminutive, at Sunnyside, is what rises of itself to the lips; the small uncommodious study, the limited library, the "dear" old portrait-prints of the first half of the century—very dear to-day when properly signed and properly sallow—these things, with the beauty of the site, with the sense that the man of letters of the unimproved age, the age of processes still comparatively slow, could have wanted no deeper, softer dell for mulling material over, represent the conditions that encounter now on the spot the sharp reflection of our own increase of arrangement and loss of leisure. This is the admirable interest of the exhibition of which Wolfert's Roost had been, a hundred years before the date of Irving's purchase, the rudimentary principle—that it throws the facts of our earlier "intellectual activity" into a vague golden perspective, a haze as of some unbroken spell of the same Indian summer I a moment ago had occasion to help myself out with; a fond appearance than which nothing could minister more to envy. If we envy the spinners of prose and tellers of tales to whom our American air anciently either administered or refused sustenance, this is all, and quite the best thing, it would seem, that we need do for them: it exhausts, or rather it forestalls, the futilities of discrimination. Strictly critical, mooning about Wolfert's Roost of a summer Sunday, I defy even the hungriest of analysts to be: his predecessors, the whole connected company, profit so there, to his rueful vision, by the splendour of their possession of better conditions than his. It has taken *our* ugly era to thrust in the railroad at the foot of the slope, among the masking trees; the railroad that is part, exactly, of the pomp and circumstance, the quickened pace, the heightened fever, the narrowed margin expressed within the very frame of the present picture, as I say, and all in the perfect good faith of collateral piety. I had hoped not to have to name the railroad—it seems so to give away my case. There was no railroad, however, till long after Irving's settlement—he survived the railroad but by a few years, and my case is simply that, disengaging *his* Sunnyside from its beautiful extensions and arriving thus at the sense of his easy elements, easy for everything but rushing about and being rushed at, the sense of his "command" of the admirable river and the admirable country, his command of all the mildness of his life, of his pleasant powers and his ample hours, of his friends and his contemporaries and his fame and his honour and his temper and, above all, of his delightful fund of reminiscence and material, I seemed to hear, in the summer sounds and in the very urbanity of my entertainers, the last faint echo of a felicity forever gone. That is the true voice of such places, and not the imputed challenge to the chronicler or the critic.

IV

New York: Social Notes

WERE I not afraid of appearing to strike to excess the so-called pessimistic note, I should really make much of the interesting, appealing, touching vision of waste—I know not how else to name it—that flung its odd melancholy mantle even over one's walks through the parts of the town supposedly noblest and fairest. For it proceeded, the vision, I think, from a source or two still deeper than the most obvious, the constant shocked sense of houses and rows, of recent expensive construction (that had cost thought as well as money, that had taken birth presumably as a *serious* demonstration, and that were thereby just beginning to live into history) marked for removal, for extinction, in their prime, and awaiting it with their handsome faces so fresh and yet so wan and so anxious. The most tragic element in the French Revolution, and thence surely the most tragic in human annals, was the so frequent case of the very young sent to the scaffold—the youths and maidens, all bewildered and stainless, lately born into a world decked for them socially with flowers, and for whom, none the less suddenly, the horror of horrors uprose. They were literally the victims I thought of, absurd as it may seem, under the shock in question; in spite of which, however, even this is not what I mean by my impression of the squandered effort. I have had occasion to speak—and one can only speak with sympathy—of the really human, the communicative, side of that vivid show of a society trying to build itself, with every elaboration, into some coherent sense *of* itself, and literally putting forth interrogative feelers, as it goes, into the ambient air; literally reaching out (to the charmed beholder, say) for some measure and some test of its success. This effect of certain of the manifestations of wealth in New York is, so far as I know, unique; nowhere else does pecuniary power so beat its wings in the void, and so look

round it for the charity of some hint as to the possible awk-
wardness or possible grace of its motion, some sign of
whether it be flying, for good taste, too high or too low. In
the other American cities, on the one hand, the flights are as
yet less numerous—though already promising no small diversion; and amid the older congregations of men, in the proportionately rich cities of Europe, on the other hand, good
taste is present, for reference and comparison, in a hundred
embodied and consecrated forms. Which is why, to repeat, I
found myself recognizing in the New York predicament a particular character and a particular pathos. The whole costly up
town demonstration was a record, in the last analysis, of
individual loneliness; whence came, precisely, its insistent testimony to waste—waste of the still wider sort than the mere
game of rebuilding.

That quite different admonition of the general European
spectacle, the effect, in the picture of things, as of a large,
consummate economy, traditionally practised, springs from
the fact that old societies, old, and even new, aristocracies, are
arranged exactly to supply functions, forms, the whole element of custom and perpetuity, to any massiveness of private
ease, however great. Massive private ease attended with no
force of assertion beyond the hour is an anomaly rarely encountered, therefore, in countries where the social arrangements strike one as undertaking, by their very nature and
pretension, to make the future as interesting as the past.
These conditions, the romantic ones for the picture-seeker,
are generally menaced, one is reminded; they tend to alter
everywhere, partly by the very force of the American example,
and it may be said that in France, for instance, they have done
nothing but alter for a hundred years. It none the less remains
true that for once that we ask ourselves in "Europe" what is
going to become of a given piece of property, whether family
"situation," or else palace, castle, picture, *parure*, other attribute of wealth, we indulge in the question twenty times in
the United States—so scant an engagement does the visible
order strike us as taking to provide for it. *There* comes in the
note of loneliness on the part of these loose values—deep as
the look in the eyes of dogs who plead against a change of
masters. The visible order among ourselves undertakes at the

most that they shall change hands, and the meagreness and indignity of this doom affect them as a betrayal just in proportion as they have grown great. Uppermost Fifth Avenue, for example, is lined with dwellings the very intention both of the spread and of the finish of which would seem to be to imply that they are "entailed" as majestically as red tape can entail them. But we know how little they enjoy any such courtesy or security; and, but for our tender heart and our charming imagination, we would blight them in their bloom with our restless analysis. "It's all very well for you to look as if, since you've had no past, you're going in, as the next best thing, for a magnificent compensatory future. What are you going to make your future *of*, for all your airs, we want to know?—what elements of a future, as futures have gone in the great world, are at all assured to you? Do what you will, you sit here only in the lurid light of 'business,' and you know, without our reminding you, what guarantees, what majestic continuity and heredity, that represents. Where are not only your eldest son and *his* eldest son, those prime indispensables for any real projection of your estate, unable as they would be to get rid of you even if they should wish; but where even is the old family stocking, properly stuffed and hanging so heavy as not to stir, some dreadful day, in the cold breath of Wall Street? No, what you are reduced to for 'importance' is the present, pure and simple, squaring itself between an absent future and an absent past as solidly as it can. You overdo it for what you are—you overdo it still more for what you may be; and don't pretend, above all, with the object-lesson supplied you, close at hand, by the queer case of Newport, don't pretend, we say, not to know what we mean."

"We say," I put it, but the point is that we say nothing, and it is that very small matter of Newport exactly that keeps us compassionately silent. The present state of Newport shall be a chapter by itself, which I long to take in hand, but which must wait its turn; so that I may mention it here only for the supreme support it gives to this reading of the conditions of New York opulence. The show of the case to-day—oh, so vividly and pathetically!—is that New York and other opulence, creating the place, for a series of years, as part of the effort of "American society" to find out, by experiment, what it would be at, now has no further use for it—has only learned from it, at an immense expenditure, how to get rid of an illusion. "We've found out, after all (since it's a question of what we would be 'at'), that we wouldn't be at Newport—if we can possibly be anywhere else; which, with our means, we indubitably *can* be: so that we leave poor dear Newport just ruefully to show it." That remark is written now over the face of the scene, and I can think nowhere of a mistake confessed to so promptly, yet in terms so exquisite, so charmingly cynical; the terms of beautiful houses and delicate grounds closed, condemned and forsaken, yet so "kept up," at the same time, as to cover the retreat of their projectors. The very air and light, soft and discreet, seem to speak, in tactful fashion, for people who would be embarrassed to be there—as if it might shame them to see it proved against them that they could once have been so artless and so bourgeois. The point is that they have learned not to be by the rather terrible process of exhausting the list of mistakes. Newport, for them—or for us others—is only one of these mistakes; and we feel no confidence that the pompous New York houses, most of them so flagrantly tentative, and tentative only, bristling with friezes and pinnacles, but discernibly deficient in reasons, shall not collectively form another. It is the hard fate of new aristocracies that the element of error, with them, has to be contemporary—not relegated to the dimness of the past, but receiving the full modern glare, a light fatal to the fond theory that the best society, everywhere, has grown, in all sorts of ways, in spite of itself. We see it in New York trying, trying its very hardest, to grow, not yet knowing (by so many indications) what to grow *on*.

There comes back to me again and again, for many reasons, a particular impression of this interesting struggle in the void—a constituted image of the upper social organism floundering there all helplessly, more or less floated by its immense good-will and the splendour of its immediate environment, but betrayed by its paucity of real resource. The occasion I allude to was simply a dinner-party, of the most genial intention, but at which the note of high ornament, of the general uplifted situation, was so consistently struck that it presented itself, on the page of New York life, as a purple patch without a possible context—as consciously, almost painfully, unaccompanied by passages in anything like the same key. The scene of our feast was a palace and the perfection of setting and service absolute; the ladies, beautiful, gracious and glittering with gems, were in tiaras and a semblance of court-trains, a sort of prescribed official magnificence; but it was impossible not to ask one's self with what, in the wide American frame, such great matters might be supposed to consort or to rhyme. The material pitch was so high that it carried with it really no social sequence, no application, and that, as a tribute to the ideal, to the exquisite, it wanted company, support, some sort of consecration. The difficulty, the irony, of the hour was that so many of the implications of completeness, that is, of a sustaining social order, were absent. There was nothing for us to do at eleven o'clock—or for the ladies at least—but to scatter and go to bed. There was nothing, as in London or in Paris, to go "on" to; the going "on" is, for the New York aspiration, always the stumbling-block. A great court-function would alone have met the strain, met the terms of the case—would alone properly have crowned the hour. When I speak of the terms of the case I must remind myself indeed that they were not all of one complexion; which is but another sign, however, of the inevitable jaggedness of the purple patch in great commercial democracies. The high colour required could be drawn in abundance from the ladies, but in a very minor degree, one easily perceived, from the men. The impression was singular, but it was there: had there been a court-function the ladies must have gone on to it alone, trusting to have the proper partners and mates supplied them on the premises—supplied, say, with the checks for recovery of their cloaks. The high pitch, all the exalted reference, was of the palatial house, the would-be harmonious women, the tiaras and the trains; it was not of the amiable gentlemen, delightful in their way, in whose so often quaint presence, yet without whose immediate aid, the effort of American society to arrive at the "best" consciousness still goes forward.

This failure of the sexes to keep step socially is to be noted, in the United States, at every turn, and is perhaps more suggestive of interesting "drama," as I have already hinted, than anything else in the country. But it illustrates further that foredoomed *grope* of wealth, in the conquest of the ameni- ties—the strange necessity under which the social interest labours of finding out for itself, as a preliminary, what civili- zation really *is*. If the men are not to be taken as contribut- ing to it, but only the women, what new case is *that*, under the sun, and under what strange aggravations of difficulty therefore is the problem not presented? We should call any such treatment of a different order of question the empirical treatment—the limitations and aberrations of which crop up, for the restless analyst, in the most illustrative way. Its presence is felt unmistakably, for instance, in the general ex- travagant insistence on the Opera, which plays its part as the great vessel of social salvation, the comprehensive substitute for all other conceivable vessels; the *whole* social conscious- ness thus clambering into it, under stress, as the whole com- munity crams into the other public receptacles, the desperate cars of the Subway or the vast elevators of the tall buildings. The Opera, indeed, as New York enjoys it, one promptly perceives, is worthy, musically and picturesquely, of its im- mense function; the effect of it is splendid, but one has none the less the oddest sense of hearing it, as an institution, groan and creak, positively almost split and crack, with the extra weight thrown upon it—the weight that in worlds otherwise arranged is artfully scattered, distributed over all the ground. In default of a court-function our ladies of the tiaras and court-trains might have gone on to the opera- function, these occasions offering the only approach to the implication of the tiara known, so to speak, to the American law. Yet even here there would have been no one for them, in congruity and consistency, to curtsey to—their only pos- sible course becoming thus, it would seem, to make obei- sance, clingingly, to each other. This truth points again the effect of a picture poor in the male presence; for to what male presence of native growth is it thinkable that the wearer of an American tiara *should* curtsey? Such a vision gives the measure of the degree in which we see the social empiricism in question putting, perforce, the cart before the horse. In worlds otherwise arranged, besides there being always plenty of subjects for genuflection, the occasion itself, with its character fully turned on, produces the tiara. In New York this symbol has, by an arduous extension of its virtue, to produce the occasion.

II

I found it interesting to note, furthermore, that the very Clubs, on whose behalf, if anywhere, expert tradition might have operated, betrayed with a *bonhomie* touching in the midst of their magnificence the empirical character. Was not their admirable, their unique, hospitality, for that matter, an empirical note—a departure from the consecrated collective egoism governing such institutions in worlds, as I have said, otherwise arranged? Let the hospitality in this case at least stand for the prospective discovery of a new and better law, under which the consecrated egoism itself will have become the "provincial" sign. Endless, at all events, the power of one or two of these splendid structures to testify to the state of manners—of manners undiscourageably seeking the superior stable equilibrium. There had remained with me as illuminating, from years before, the confidential word of a friend on whom, after a long absence from New York, the privilege of one of the largest clubs had been conferred. "The place is a palace, for scale and decoration, but there is only one kind of letter-paper." There would be more kinds of letter-paper now, I take it—though the American club struck me everywhere, oddly, considering the busy people who employ it, as much less an institution for attending to one's correspondence than others I had had knowledge of; generally destitute, in fact, of copious and various appliances for that purpose. There is such a thing as the imagination of the writing-table, and I nowhere, save in a few private houses, came upon its fruits; to which I must add that this is the one connection in which the provision for ease has not an extraordinary amplitude, an amplitude unequalled anywhere else. One emphatic reservation, throughout the country, the restored absentee finds himself continually making, but the universal custom of the house with almost no one of its indoor parts distinguishable from any other is an affliction against which he has to learn betimes to brace himself. This diffused vagueness of separation between apartments, between hall and room, between one room and another, between the one you are in and the one you are not in, between place of passage and place of privacy, is a provocation to despair which the public institution shares impartially with the luxurious "home." To the spirit attuned to a different practice these dispositions can only appear a strange perversity, an extravagant aberration of taste; but I may here touch on them scarce further than to mark their value for the characterization of manners.

They testify at every turn, then, to those of the American people, to the prevailing "conception of life"; they correspond, within doors, to the as inveterate suppression of almost every outward exclusory arrangement. The instinct is throughout, as we catch it at play, that of minimizing, for any "interior," the guilt or odium or responsibility, whatever these may appear, of its *being* an interior. The custom rages like a conspiracy for nipping the interior in the bud, for denying its right to exist, for ignoring and defeating it in every possible way, for wiping out successively each sign by which it may be known from an exterior. The effacement of the difference has been marvellously, triumphantly brought about; and, with all the ingenuity of young, fresh, frolicsome architecture aiding and abetting, has been made to flourish, alike in the small structure and the great, as the very law of the structural fact. Thus we have the law fulfilled that every part of every house shall be, as nearly as may be, visible, visitable, penetrable, not only from every other part, but from as many parts of as many other houses as possible, if they only be near enough. Thus we see systematized the indefinite extension of all spaces and the definite merging of all functions; the enlargement of every opening, the exaggeration of every passage, the substitution of gaping arches and far perspectives and resounding voids for enclosing walls, for practicable doors, for controllable windows, for all the rest of the essence of the room-character, that room-suggestion which is so indispensable not only to occupation and concentration, but to conversation itself, to the play of the social relation at any other pitch than the pitch of a shriek or a shout. This comprehensive canon has so succeeded in imposing itself that it strikes you as reflecting inordinately, as positively serving you up for convenient inspection, under a clear glass cover, the social tone that has dictated it. But I must confine myself to recording, for the moment, that it takes a whole new discipline to put the visitor at his ease in so merciless a medium; he finds himself looking round for a background or a limit, some localizing fact or two, in the interest of talk, of that "good" talk which always falters before the complete proscription of privacy. He sees only doorless apertures, vainly festooned, which decline to tell him where he is, which make him still a homeless wanderer, which show him other apertures, corridors, staircases, yawning, expanding, ascending, descending, and all as for the purpose of giving his presence "away," of reminding him that what he says must be said for the house. He is beguiled in a measure by reading into these phenomena, ever so sharply, the reason of many another impression; he is beguiled by remembering how many of the things said in America *are* said for the house; so that if all that he wants is to keep catching the finer harmony of effect and cause, of explanation and implication, the cup of his perception is full to overflowing.

That satisfaction does represent, certainly, much of his quest; all the more that what he misses, in the place—the comfort and support, for instance, of windows, porches, verandahs, lawns, gardens, "grounds," that, by not taking the whole world into their confidence, have not the whole world's confidence to take in return—ranges itself for him in that large mass of American idiosyncrasy which contains, unmistakably, a precious principle of future reaction. The desire to rake and be raked has doubtless, he makes out, a long day before it still; but there are too many reasons why it should not be the last word of *any* social evolution. The social idea has too inevitably secrets in store, quite other constructive principles, quite other refinements on the idea of intercourse, with which it must eventually reckon. It will be certain at a given moment, I think, to head in a different direction altogether; though obviously many other remarkable things, changes of ideal, of habit, of key, will have to take place first. The conception of the home, and *a fortiori* of the club,

as a combination of the hall of echoes and the toy "transparency" held against the light, will meanwhile sufficiently
prevail to have made my reference to it not quite futile. Yet I
must after all remember that the reservation on the ground
of comfort to which I just alluded applies with its smallest
force to the interchangeability of club compartments, to the
omnipresence of the majestic open arch in club conditions.
Such conditions more or less prescribe that feature, and criticism begins only when private houses emulate the form of
clubs. What I had mainly in mind was another of these so
inexhaustible values of my subject; with which the question
of rigour of comfort has nothing to do. I cherish certain
remembered aspects for their general vivid eloquence—for
the sake of my impression of the type of great generous
club-establishments in which the "empiricism" of that
already-observed idea of the conquest of splendour could
richly and irresponsibly flower. It is of extreme interest to be
reminded, at many a turn of such an exhibition, that it takes
an endless amount of history to make even a little tradition,
and an endless amount of tradition to make even a little
taste, and an endless amount of taste, by the same token, to
make even a little tranquillity. Tranquillity results largely
from taste tactfully applied, taste lighted above all by experience and possessed of a clue for its labyrinth. There is no
such clue, for club-felicity, as some view of congruities and
harmonies, completeness of correspondence between aspects
and uses. A sense for that completeness is a thing of slow
growth, one of the flowers of tradition precisely; of the
good conservative tradition that walks apart from the extravagant use of money and the unregulated appeal to "style"—
passes in fact, at its best, quite on the other side of the way.
This discrimination occurs when the ground has the good
fortune to be already held by some definite, some transmit-
ted conception of the adornments and enhancements that
consort, and that do not consort, with the presence, the
habits, the tone, of lounging, gossiping, smoking, newspaper-
reading, bridge-playing, cocktail-imbibing men. The club-
developments of New York read here and there the lesson
of the strange deserts in which the appeal to style may lose

itself, may wildly and wantonly stray, without a certain light of the fine old gentlemanly prejudice to guide it.

III

But I should omit half my small story were I not meanwhile to make due record of the numerous hours at which one ceased consciously to discriminate, just suffering one's sense to be flooded with the large clean light and with that suggestion of a crowded "party" of young persons which lurked in the general aspect of the handsomer regions—a great circle of brilliant and dowered *débutantes* and impatient youths, expert in the cotillon, waiting together for the first bars of some wonderful imminent dance-music, something "wilder" than any ever yet. It is such a wait for something more, these innocents scarce know what, it is this, distinctly, that the upper New York picture seems to cause to play before us; but the wait is just that collective alertness of bright-eyed, light-limbed, clear-voiced youth, without a doubt in the world and without a conviction; which last, however, always, may perfectly be absent without prejudice to confidence. The confidence and the innocence are those of children whose world has ever been practically a safe one, and the party so imaged is thus really even a child's party, enormously attended, but in which the united ages of the company make up no formidable sum. In the light of that analogy the New York social movement of the day, I think, always shines—as the whole show of the so-called social life of the country does, for that matter; since it comes home to the restless analyst everywhere that this "childish" explanation is the one that meets the greatest number of the social appearances. To arrive—and with tolerable promptitude—at that generalization is to find it, right and left, immensely convenient, and thereby quite to cling to it: the newspapers alone, for instance, doing so much to feed it, from day to day, as with their huge playfully brandished wooden spoon. We seem at moments to see the incoherence and volatility of childhood, its living but in the sense of its hour and in the immediacy of its want, its instinctive refusal to be brought to book, its boundless liability to contagion and boundless incapacity for attention, its ingenuous blankness to-day over the appetites and clamours of yesterday, its chronic state of besprinklement with the sawdust of its ripped-up dolls, which it scarce goes even through the form of shaking out of its hair—we seem at moments to see these things, I say, twinkle in the very air, as by reflection of the movement of a great, sunny playroom floor. The immensity of the native accommodation, socially speaking, for the child-ish life, is not that exactly the key of much of the spectacle?— the safety of the vast flat expanse where every margin abounds and nothing too untoward need happen. The question is in-teresting, but I remember quickly that I am concerned with it only so far as it is part of the light of New York.

It appeared at all events, on the late days of spring, just a response to the facility of things, and to much of their juve-nile pleasantry, to find one's self "liking," without more ado, and very much even at the risk of one's life, the heteroge-neous, miscellaneous apology for a Square marking the spot at which the main entrance, as I suppose it may be called, to the Park opens toward Fifth Avenue; opens toward the glitter-ing monument to Sherman, toward the most death-dealing, perhaps, of all the climaxes of electric car cross-currents, to-ward the loosest of all the loose distributions of the overtop-ping "apartment" and other hotel, toward the most jovial of all the sacrifices of preconsidered composition, toward the finest of all the reckless revelations, in short, of the brave New York humour. The best thing in the picture, obviously, is Saint-Gaudens's great group, splendid in its golden elegance and doing more for the scene (by thus giving the beholder a point of such dignity for his orientation) than all its other elements together. Strange and seductive for any lover of the reasons of things this inordinate value, on the spot, of the dauntless refinement of the Sherman image; the comparative vulgarity of the environment drinking it up, on one side, like an insatiable sponge, and yet failing at the same time sensibly to impair its virtue. The refinement prevails and, as it were, succeeds; holds its own in the medley of accidents, where nothing else is refined unless it be the amplitude of the "quiet" note in the front of the Metropolitan Club; amuses itself in short with being as extravagantly "intellectual" as it likes. Why, therefore, given the surrounding medium, does it so triumphantly impose itself, and impose itself not insidiously and gradually, but immediately and with force? Why does it not pay the penalty of expressing an idea and being founded on one?—such scant impunity seeming usually to be enjoyed among us, at this hour, by any artistic intention of the finer strain? But I put these questions only to give them up—for what I feel beyond anything else is that Mr. Saint-Gaudens somehow takes care of himself.

To what measureless extent he does this on occasion one was to learn, in due course, from his magnificent Lincoln at Chicago—the lesson there being simply that of a mystery exquisite, the absolute inscrutable; one of the happiest cases known to our time, known doubtless to any time, of the combination of intensity of effect with dissimulation, with deep disavowal, of process. After seeing the Lincoln one consents, for its author, to the drop of questions—that is the lame truth; a truth in the absence of which I should have risked another word or two, have addressed perhaps even a brief challenge to a certain ambiguity in the Sherman. Its idea, to which I have alluded, strikes me as equivocal, or more exactly as double; the image being, on the one side, and splendidly rendered, that of an overwhelming military advance, an irresistible march into an enemy's country—the strain forward, the very inflation of drapery with the rush, symbolizing the very breath of the Destroyer. But the idea is at the same time—which part of it is also admirably expressed—that the Destroyer is a messenger of peace, with the olive branch too waved in the blast and with embodied grace, in the form of a beautiful American girl, attending his business. And I confess to a lapse of satisfaction in the presence of this interweaving—the result doubtless of a sharp suspicion of all attempts, however glittering and golden, to confound destroyers with benefactors. The military monument in the City Square responds evidently, wherever a pretext can be found for it, to a desire of men's hearts; but I would have it always as military as possible, and I would have the Destroyer, in intention at least, not docked of one of his bristles. I would have him deadly and terrible, and, if he be wanted beautiful, beautiful only as a war-god and crested not with peace, but with snakes. Peace is a long way round from him, and blood and ashes in between. So, with a less intimate perversity, I think, than that of Mr. Saint-Gaudens's brilliant scheme, I would have had a Sherman of the terrible march (the "immortal" march, in all abundance, if that be the needed note), not irradiating benevolence, but signifying, by every ingenious device, the misery, the ruin and the vengeance of his track. It is not one's affair to attempt to teach an artist how such horrors may be monumentally signified; it is enough that their having been perpetrated is the very ground of the monument. And monuments should always have a clean, clear meaning.

IV

I must positively get into the gate of the Park, however— even at the risk of appearing to have marched round through Georgia to do so. I found myself, in May and June, getting into it whenever I could, and if I spoke just now of the loud and inexpensive charm (inexpensive in the æsthetic sense) of the precinct of approach to it, that must positively have been because the Park diffuses its grace. One grasped at every pretext for finding it inordinately amiable, and nothing was more noteworthy than that one felt, in doing so, how this was the only way to play the game in fairness. The perception comes quickly, in New York, of the singular and beautiful but almost crushing mission that has been laid, as an effect of time, upon this limited territory, which has risen to the occasion, from the first, so consistently and bravely. It is a case, distinctly, in which appreciation and gratitude for a public function admirably performed are twice the duty, on the visitor's part, that they may be in other such cases. We may even say, putting it simply and strongly, that if he doesn't here, in his thought, keep patting the Park on the back, he is guilty not alone of a failure of natural tenderness, but of a real deviation from social morality. For this mere narrow oblong, much *too* narrow and very much too short, had directly prescribed to it, from its origin, to "do," officially, on behalf of the City, the publicly amiable, and *all* the publicly amiable—all there could be any question of in the conditions: incurring thus a heavier charge, I respectfully submit, than one has ever before seen so gallantly carried. Such places, the municipally-instituted pleasure-grounds of the greater and the smaller cities, abound about the world and everywhere, no doubt, agreeably enough play their part; but is the part anywhere else as heroically played in proportion to the difficulty? The difficulty in New York, *that* is the point for the restless analyst; conscious as he is that other cities even in spite of themselves lighten the strain and beguile the task—a burden which here on the contrary makes every inch of its weight felt. This means a good deal, for the space comprised in the original New York scheme represents in truth a wonderful economy and intensity of effort. It would go hard with us not to satisfy ourselves, in other quarters (and it is of the political and commercial capitals we speak), of some such amount of "general" outside amenity, of charm in the town at large, as may here and there, even at widely-scattered points, relieve the o'erfraught heart. The sense of the picturesque often finds its account in strange and unlikely matters, but has none the less a way of finding it, and so, in the coming and going, takes the chance. But the New York problem has always resided in the absence of any chance to take, however one might come and go—come and go, that is, before reaching the Park.

To the Park, accordingly, and to the Park only, hitherto, the æsthetic appetite has had to address itself, and the place has therefore borne the brunt of many a peremptory call, acting out year after year the character of the cheerful, capable, bustling, even if overworked, hostess of the one inn, somewhere, who has to take all the travel, who is often at her wits' end to know how to deal with it, but who, none the less, has, for the honour of the house, never once failed of hospitality. That is how we see Central Park, utterly overdone by the "run" on its resources, yet also never having had to make an excuse. When once we have taken in thus its remarkable little history, there is no endearment of appreciation that we are not ready to lay, as a tribute, on its breast; with the interesting effect, besides, of our recognizing in this light how the place has had to be, in detail and feature, exactly what it is. It has had to have something for everybody, since everybody arrives famished; it has had to multiply itself to extravagance, to pathetic little efforts of exaggeration and deception, to be, breathlessly, everywhere and everything at once, and produce on the spot the particular romantic object demanded, lake or river or cataract, wild woodland or teeming garden, boundless vista or bosky nook, noble eminence or smiling valley. It has had to have feature at any price, the clamour of its customers being inevitably *for* feature; which accounts, as we forgivingly see, for the general rather eruptive and agitated effect, the effect of those old quaint prints which give in a single view the classic, gothic and other architectural wonders of the world. That is its sole defect—its being inevitably too self-conscious, being afraid to be just vague and frank and quiet. I should compare her again—and the propriety is proved by this instinctively feminine pronoun—to an actress in a company destitute, through an epidemic or some other stress, of all other feminine talent; so that she assumes on successive nights the most dissimilar parts and ranges in the course of a week from the tragedy queen to the singing chambermaid. That valour by itself wins the public and brings down the house—it being really a marvel that she should in no part fail of a hit. Which is what I mean, in short, by the sweet *ingratiation* of the Park. You are perfectly aware, as you hang about her in May and June, that you *have*, as a travelled person, beheld more remarkable scenery and communed with nature in ampler or fairer forms; but it is quite equally definite to you that none of those adventures have counted more to you for experience, for stirred sensibility—inasmuch as you can be, at the best, and in the showiest countries, only thrilled by the pastoral or the awful, and as to pass, in New York, from the discipline of the streets to this so different many-smiling presence is to be thrilled at every turn.

The strange thing, moreover, is that the crowd, in the happiest seasons, at favouring hours, the polyglot Hebraic crowd of pedestrians in particular, has, for what it is, none but the mildest action on the nerves. The nerves are too grateful, the intention of beauty everywhere too insistent; it "places" the superfluous figures with an art of its own, even when placing them in heavy masses, and they become for you practically as your fellow-spectators of the theatre, whose proximity you take for granted, while the little overworked *cabotine* we have hypothesized, the darling of the public, is vocalizing or capering. I recall as singularly contributive in all this sense the impression of a splendid Sunday afternoon of early summer, when, during a couple of hours spent in the mingled medium, the variety of accents with which the air swarmed seemed to make it a question whether the Park itself or its visitors were most polyglot. The condensed geographical range, the number of kinds of scenery in a given space, competed with the number of languages heard, and the whole impression was of one's having had but to turn in from the Plaza to make, in the most agreeable manner possible, the tour of the little globe. And that, frankly, I think, was the best of all impressions— was seeing New York at its best; for if ever one could feel at one's ease about the "social question," it would be surely, somehow, on such an occasion. The number of persons in circulation was enormous—so great that the question of how they had got there, from their distances, and would get away again, in the so formidable public conveyances, loomed, in the background, rather like a skeleton at the feast; but the general note was thereby, intensely, the "popular," and the brilliancy of the show proportionately striking. That is the great and only brilliancy worth speaking of, to my sense, in the general American scene—the air of hard prosperity, the ruthlessly pushed-up and promoted look worn by men, women and children alike. I remember taking that appearance, of the hour or two, for a climax to the sense that had most remained with me after a considerable previous moving about over the land, the sense of the small quantity of mere human sordidness of state to be observed.

One is liable to observe it in *any* best of all possible worlds, and I had not, in truth, gone out of my way either to avoid it or to look for it; only I had met it enough, in other climes, without doing so, and had, to be veracious, not absolutely and utterly missed it in the American. Images of confirmed (though, strangely, of active, occupied and above all "sensitive") squalor had I encountered in New Hampshire hills; also, below the Southern line, certain special, certain awful examples, in Black and White alike, of the last crudity of condition. These spots on the picture had, however, lost themselves in the general attestation of the truth most forced home, the vision of the country as, supremely, a field for the unhampered revel, the unchecked *essor*, material and moral, of the "common man" and the common woman. How splendidly they were making it all answer, for the most part, or to the extent of the so rare public collapse of the individual, had been an observation confirmed for me by a rapid journey to the Pacific coast and back; yet I had doubtless not before seen it so answer as in this very concrete case of the swarming New York afternoon. It was little to say, in that particular light, that such grossnesses as want or tatters or gin, as the unwashed face or the ill-shod, and still less the unshod, foot, or the mendicant hand, became strange, unhappy, far-off things—it would even have been an insult to allude to them or to be explicitly complacent about their absence. The case was, unmistakably, universally, of the common, the very common man, the very common woman and the very common child; but all enjoying what I have called their promotion, their rise in the social scale, with that absence of acknowledging flutter, that serenity of assurance, which marks, for the impressed class, the school-boy or the school-girl who is accustomed, and who always quite expects, to "move up." The children at play, more particularly the little girls, formed the characters, as it were, in which the story was written largest; frisking about over the greenswards, grouping together in the vistas, with an effect of the exquisite in attire, of delicacies of dress and personal "keep-up," as through the shimmer of silk, the gloss of beribboned hair, the gleam of cared-for teeth, the pride of varnished shoe, that might well have created a doubt as to their "popular" affiliation. This affiliation was yet established by sufficiencies of context, and might well have been, for that matter, by every accompanying vocal or linguistic note, the swarm of queer sounds, mostly not to be interpreted, that circled round their pretty heads as if they had been tamers of odd, outlandish, perching little birds. They fell moreover into the vast category of those ubiquitous children of the public schools who occupy everywhere, in the United States, so much of the forefront of the stage, and at the sight of whose so remarkably clad and shod condition the brooding analyst, with the social question never, after all, too much in abeyance, could clap, in private, the most reactionary hands.

The brooding analyst had in fact, from the first of his return, recognized in the mere detail of the testimony every-

where offered to the high pitch of the American shoe-
industry, a lively incentive to cheerful views; the population
showing so promptly, in this connection, as the best equipped
in the world. The impression at first had been irresistible: two
industries, at the most, seemed to rule the American scene.
The dentist and the shoe-dealer divided it between them; to
that degree, positively, that in public places, in the perpetual
electric cars which seem to one's desperation at times (so condemned is one to live in them) all there measurably *is* of the
American scene, almost any other typical, any other personal
fact might be neglected, for consideration, in the interest of
the presentable foot and the far-shining dental gold. It was a
world in which every one, without exception, no matter how
"low" in the social scale, wore the best and the newest, the
neatest and the smartest, boots; to be added to which (always
for the brooding analyst) was the fascination, so to speak, of
noting how much more than any other single thing this may
do for a possibly compromised appearance. And if my claim
for the interest of this exhibition seems excessive, I refer the
objector without hesitation to a course of equivalent observation in other countries, taking an equally miscellaneous show
for his basis. Nothing was more curious than to trace, on a
great ferry-boat, for instance, the effect of letting one's eyes
work up, as in speculation, from the lower to the higher ex-
tremities of some seated row of one's fellow passengers. The
testimony of the lower might preponderantly have been, always, to their comparative conquest of affluence and ease; but
this presumption gave way, at successive points, with the
mounting vision, and was apt to break down entirely under
the evidence of face and head. When I say "head," I mean
more particularly, where the men were concerned, hat; this
feature of the equipment being almost always at pains, and
with the oddest, most inveterate perversity, to defeat and discredit whatever might be best in the others. Such are the
problems in which a restless analysis may land us.

Why should the general "feeling" for the boot, in the
United States, be so mature, so evolved, and the feeling for
the hat lag at such a distance behind it? The standard as to
that article of dress struck me as, everywhere, of the lowest;
governed by no consensus of view, custom or instinct, no

sense of its "vital importance" in the manly aspect. And yet
the wearer of any loose improvisation in the way of a head-
cover will testify as frankly, in his degree, to the extreme
consideration given by the community at large, as I have intimated, to the dental question. The terms in which this evidence is presented are often, among the people, strikingly
artless, but they are a marked advance on the omnipresent
opposite signs, those of a systematic detachment from the
chair of anguish, with which any promiscuous "European"
exhibition is apt to bristle. I remember to have heard it remarked by a French friend, of a young woman who had returned to her native land after some years of domestic service
in America, that she had acquired there, with other advantages, *le sourire Californien*, and the "Californian" smile, indeed, expressed, more or less copiously, in undissimulated
cubes of the precious metal, plays between lips that render
scant other tribute to civilization. The greater interest, in this
connection, however, is that impression of the state and
appearance of the teeth viewed among the "refined" as
supremely important, which the restored absentee, long surrounded elsewhere with the strangest cynicisms of indifference on this article, makes the subject of one of his very first
notes. Every one, in "society," has good, handsome, pretty,
has above all cherished and tended, teeth; so that the offered
spectacle, frequent in other societies, of strange irregularities,
protrusions, deficiencies, fangs and tusks and cavities, is quite
refreshingly and consolingly absent. The consequences of care
and forethought, from an early age, thus write themselves on
the facial page distinctly and happily, and it is not too much
to say that the total show is, among American aspects, cumulatively charming. One sees it sometimes balance, for charm,
against a greater number of less fortunate items, in that totality, than one would quite know how to begin estimating.

But I have strayed again far from my starting-point and
have again, I fear, succumbed to the danger of embroidering
my small original proposition with too many, and scarce
larger, derivatives. I left the Plaza, I left the Park steeped in
the rose-colour of such a brightness of Sunday and of summer
as had given me, on a couple of occasions, exactly what I
desired—a simplified attention, namely, and the power to

rest for the time in the appearance that the awful aliens were flourishing there in perfections of costume and contentment. One had only to take them in as more completely, conveniently and expensively *endimanchés* than one had ever, on the whole, seen any other people, in order to feel that one was calling down upon all the elements involved the benediction of the future—and calling it down most of all on one's embraced permission not to worry any more. It was by way of not worrying, accordingly, that I found in another presentment of the general scene, chanced upon at a subsequent hour, all sorts of interesting and harmonious suggestions. These adventures of the critical spirit were such mere mild walks and talks as I almost blush to offer, on this reduced scale, as matter of history; but I draw courage from the remembrance that history is never, in any rich sense, the immediate crudity of what "happens," but the much finer complexity of what we read into it and think of in connection with it. If a walk across the Park, with a responsive friend, late on the golden afternoon of a warm week-day, and if a consequent desultory stroll, for speculation's sake, through certain northward and eastward streets and avenues, of an identity a little vague to me now, save as a blur of builded evidence as to proprietary incomes—if such an incident ministered, on the spot, to a boundless evocation, it then became history of a splendid order: though I perhaps must add that it became so for the two participants alone, and with an effect after all not easy to communicate. The season was over, the recipients of income had retired for the summer, and the large clear vistas were peopled mainly with that conscious hush and that spectral animation characteristic of places kept, as with all command of time and space, for the indifferent, the all but insolent, absentee. It was a vast, costly, empty newness, redeemed by the rare quiet and coloured by the pretty light, and I scare know, I confess, why it should have had anything murmurous or solicitous to say at all, why its eloquence was not over when it had thus defined itself as intensely rich and intensely modern.

If I have spoken, with some emphasis, of what it "evoked," I might easily be left, it would appear, with that emphasis on my hands—did I not catch, indeed, for my explanation, the very key to the anomaly. Ransacking my brain for the sources of the impressiveness, I see them, of a sudden, locked up in that word "modern"; the mystery clears in the light of the fact that one was perhaps, for that half-hour, more intimately than ever before in touch with the sense of the term. It was exactly because I seemed, with the ear of the spirit, to hear the whole quarter bid, as with one penetrating voice, for the boon of the future, for some guarantee, or even mere hinted promise, of history and opportunity, that the attitude affected me as the last revelation of modernity. What made the revelation was the collective sharpness, so to speak, of this vocal note, offering any price, offering everything, wanting only to outbid and prevail, at the great auction of life. "See how ready we are"—one caught the tone: "ready to buy, to pay, to promise; ready to place, to honour, our purchase. We have everything, don't you see? every capacity and appetite, every advantage of education and every susceptibility of sense; no 'tip' in the world, none that our time is capable of giving, has been lost on us: so that all we now desire is what you, Mr. Auctioneer, have to dispose of, the great 'going' chance of a time to come." That was the sound unprecedentedly evoked for me, and in a form that made sound somehow overflow into sight. It was as if, in their high gallery, the bidders, New Yorkers every one, were before one's eyes; pressing to the front, hanging over the balustrade, holding out clamorous importunate hands. It was not, certainly, for general style, pride and colour, a Paul Veronese company; even the women, in spite of pearls and brocade and golden hair, failed of that type, and still more inevitably the men, without doublet, mantle, ruff or sword; the nearest approach might have been in the great hounds and the little blackamoors. But my vision had a kind of analogy; for what were the Venetians, after all, but the children of a Republic and of trade? It was, however, mainly, no doubt, an affair of the supporting marble terrace, the platform of my crowd, with as many columns of onyx and curtains of velvet as any great picture could need. About these there would be no difficulty whatever; though this luxury of vision of the matter had meanwhile no excuse but the fact that the hour was charming, the waning light still lucid, the air admirable, the neighbourhood a great empty stage, expen-

sively, extravagantly set, and the detail in frontage and cornice
and architrave, in every feature of every edifice, as sharp as the
uttered words of the plea I have just imagined.

V

The American air, I take advantage of this connection to
remember, lends a felicity to all the exactitudes of architecture
and sculpture, favours sharp effects, disengages differences,
preserves lights, defines projected shadows. Sculpture, in it,
never either loses a value or conceals a loss, and it is everywhere full of help to discriminated masses. This remark was
to be emphatically made, I found myself observing, in presence of so distinct an appeal to high clearness as the great
Palladian pile just erected by Messrs. Tiffany on one of the
upper corners of Fifth Avenue, where it presents itself to the
friendly sky with a great nobleness of white marble. One is so
thankful to it, I recognize, for not having twenty-five stories,
which it might easily have had, I suppose, in the wantonness
of wealth or of greed, that one gives it a double greeting,
rejoicing to excess perhaps at its merely remaining, with the
three fine arched and columned stages above its high basement, within the conditions of sociable symmetry. One may
break one's heart, certainly, over its only being, for "interest,"
a great miscellaneous shop—if one has any heart left in New
York for such adventures. One may also reflect, if any similar
spring of reflection will still serve, on its being, to the very
great limitation of its dignity, but a more or less pious *pastiche*
or reproduction, the copy of a model that sits where Venetian
water-steps keep—or used to keep!—vulgar invasion at bay.
But I hasten to add that one will do these things only at the
cost of not "putting in" wherever one can the patch of opti-
mism, the sigh of relief, the glow of satisfaction, or whatever
else the pardonably factitious emotion may be called—which
in New York is very bad economy. Look for interest where
you may, cultivate a working felicity, press the spring hard,
and you will see that, to whatever air Palladian piles may have
been native, they can nowhere tell their great cold calculated
story, in measured chapter and verse, better than to the strong
sea-light of New York. This medium has the abundance of

some ample childless mother who consoles herself for her sterility by an unbridled course of adoption—as I seemed again
to make out in presence of the tiers of white marble that are
now on their way to replace the granitic mass of the old Reservoir, *ultima Thule* of the northward walk of one's early
time.

The reservoir of learning here taking form above great terraces—which my mind's eye makes as great as it would like—
lifts, once more, from the heart the weight of the "tall"
building it apparently doesn't propose to become. I could admire, in the unfinished state of the work, but the lower
courses of this inestimable structure, the Public Library that is
to gather into rich alliance and splendid ease the great minor
Libraries of the town; it was enough for my delight, however,
that the conditions engage for a covering of the earth rather
than an invasion of the air—of so supreme an effect, at the
pitch things have reached, is this single element of a generous
area. It offers the best of reasons for speaking of the project as
inestimable. Any building that, being beautiful, presents itself
as seated rather than as standing, can do with your imagination what it will; you ask it no question, you give it a free
field, content only if it will sit and sit and sit. And if you
interrogate your joy, in the connection, you will find it largely
founded, I think, on all the implications thus conveyed of a
proportionately smaller quantity of the great religion of the
Elevator. The lateral development of great buildings is as yet,
in the United States, but an opportunity for the legs, is in fact
almost their sole opportunity—a circumstance that, taken
alone, should eloquently plead; but it has another blest value,
for the imagination, for the nerves, as a check on the constant
obsession of one's living, of every one's living, by the packed
and hoisted basket. The sempiternal lift, for one's comings
and goings, affects one at last as an almost intolerable symbol
of the herded and driven state and of that malady of preference for gregarious ways, of insistence on gregarious ways
only, by which the people about one seem ridden. To wait,
perpetually, in a human bunch, in order to be hustled, under
military drill, the imperative order to "step lively," into some
tight mechanic receptacle, fearfully and wonderfully working,
is conceivable, no doubt, as a sad liability of our nature, but

represents surely, when cherished and sacrificed to, a strange perversion of sympathies and ideals. Anything that breaks the gregarious spell, that relieves one of one's share, however insignificant, of the abject collective consciousness of being pushed and pressed in, with something that one's shoulders and one's heels must dodge at their peril, something that slides or slams or bangs, operating, in your rear, as ruthlessly as the guillotine—anything that performs this office puts a price on the lonely sweetness of a step or two taken by one's self, of deviating into some sense of independent motive power, of climbing even some grass-grown staircase, with a dream perhaps of the thrill of fellow-feeling *then* taking, then finding, place—something like Robinson Crusoe's famous thrill before Friday's footprint in the sand.

However these things might be, I recall further, as an incident of that hour of "evocation," the goodly glow, under this same illumination, of an immense red building, off in the clear north-east quarter, which had hung back, with all success, from the perpendicular form, and which actually covered ground with its extensions of base, its wide terrestrial wings. It had, I remember, in the early evening light, a homely kindness of diffused red brick, and to make out then that it was a great exemplary Hospital, one of the many marvels of New York in this general order, was to admire the exquisite art with which, in such a medium, it had so managed to invest itself with stillness. It was as quiet there, on its ample interspace, as if the clamorous city, roundabout, as if the passion of the Elevated and of the Elevator in especial, were forever at rest and no one were stepping lively for miles and miles away; so that visibly, it had a spell to cast and a character to declare—things I was won over, on the spot, to desire a nearer view of. Fortune presently favoured this purpose, and almost my last impression of New York was gathered, on a very hot June morning, in the long, cool corridors of the Presbyterian Hospital, and in those "halls of pain," the high, quiet, active wards, silvery-dim with their whiteness and their shade, where the genius of the terrible city seemed to filter in with its energy sifted and softened, with its huge good-nature refined. There were reasons beyond the scope of these remarks for the interest of that hour, but it is at least within the scope that I recall noting there, all responsively, as not before, that if the *direct* pressure of New York is too often to ends that strike us as vulgar, the indirect is capable, and perhaps to an unlimited degree, of these lurking effects of delicacy. The immediate expression is the expression of violence, but you may find there is something left, something kept back for you, if that has not from the first fatally deafened you. It carries with it an after-sense which put on for me, under several happy intimations, the image of some garden of the finest flowers —or of such as might be on the way to become the finest— masked by an enormous bristling hedge of defensive and aggressive vegetation, lacerating, defiant, not to be touched without blood. One saw the garden itself, behind its hedge and approachable only by those in the secret—one divined it to contain treasures of delicacy, many of them perhaps still to be developed, but attesting the possibilities of the soil. My Presbyterian Hospital was somehow in the garden, just where the soil, the very human soil itself, was richest, and— though this may appear an odd tribute to an institution founded on the principle of instant decision and action—it affected me, amid its summer airs and its boundless, soundless business, as surpassingly delicate. *There*, if nowhere else, was adjustment of tone; there was the note of mildness and the sense of manners; under the impression of which I am not sure of not having made up my mind that, were I merely alone and disconcerted, merely unprepared and unwarned, in the vast, dreadful place, as must happen to so many a helpless mortal, I should positively desire or "elect," as they say, to become the victim of some such mischance as would put me into relation again, the ambulance or the police aiding, with these precious saving presences. They might re-establish for me, before the final extinction or dismissal, some belief in manners and in tone.

Was it in the garden also, as I say, that the Metropolitan Museum had meanwhile struck me as standing?—the impression of a quite other hazard of *flânerie* this, and one of those memories, once more, that I find myself standing off from, as under the shadow of their too numerous suggestion. That institution *is*, decidedly, to-day, part of the inner New York harmony that I have described as a touched after-sense; so that if there were, scattered about the place, elements prompting rich, if vague, evocations, this was recognizably one of the spots over which such elements would have most freedom to play. The original Museum was a thing of the far past; hadn't I the vision of it, from ancient days, installed, stately though scrappy, in a large eccentric house in West Fourteenth Street, a house the prior period, even the early, impressive construction of which one recalled from days still more ancient, days so far away that to be able to travel back to them was almost as good, or as bad, as being a centenarian? This superfluous consciousness of the original seat of the Museum, of where and what it had been, was one of those terrible traps to memory, about the town, which baited themselves with the cheese of association, so to speak, in order to exhibit one afterwards as "caught," or, otherwise expressed, as old; such being the convicted state of the unfortunate who knows the *whole* of so many of his stories. The case is never really disguisable; we get off perhaps when we only know the ends of things, but beyond that our historic sense betrays us. We have known the beginnings, we have been present, in the various connections, at the birth, the life and the death, and it is wonderful how traceably, in such a place as New York, careers of importance may run their course and great institutions, while you are just watching, rise, prosper and fall. I had had my shudder, in that same Fourteenth Street, for the complete disappearance of a large church, as massive as brown stone could make it, at the engaging construction of which one's tender years had "assisted" (it exactly faced the parental home, and nefarious, perilous play was found possible in the works), but which, after passing from youth to middle age and from middle age to antiquity, has vanished as utterly as the Assyrian Empire.

So, it was to be noted, had the parental home, and so the first home of the Museum, by what I made out, beyond Sixth Avenue—after which, for the last-named, had there not been a second seat, long since superseded too, a more prolonged *étape* on the glorious road? This also gave out a shimmer from the middle time, but with the present favouring stage of the journey the glorious road seems to stretch away. It is a palace of art, truly, that sits there on the edge of the Park, rearing itself with a radiance, yet offering you expanses to tread; but I found it invite me to a matter of much more interest than any mere judging of its dispositions. It spoke with a hundred voices of that huge process of historic waste that the place in general keeps putting before you; but showing it in a light that drew out the harshness or the sadness, the pang, whatever it had seemed elsewhere, of the reiterated sacrifice to pecuniary profit. For the question here was to be of the advantage to the spirit, not to the pocket; to be of the æsthetic advantage involved in the wonderful clearance to come. From the moment the visitor takes in two or three things—first, perhaps, the scale on which, in the past, bewildering tribute has flowed in; second, the scale on which it must absolutely now flow out; and, third, the presumption created by the vivacity of these two movements for a really fertilizing stir of the ground—he sees the whole place as the field of a drama the nearer view of the future course of which he shall be sorry to lose. One never winces after the first little shock, when Education is expensive—one winces only at the expense which, like so much of the expense of New York, doesn't educate; and Education, clearly, was going to seat herself in these marble halls—admirably prepared for her, to all appearance—and issue her instructions without regard to cost. The obvious, the beautiful, the thrilling thing was that, without regard to cost either, they were going to be obeyed: that inference was somehow irresistible, the disembodied voices I have spoken of quite forcing it home and the palace roof arching to protect it as the dome of the theatre protects the performance. I know not if all past purchase, in these annals (putting the Cesnola Collection aside), has been without reproach, but it struck me as safe to gather that (putting aside again Mr. Marquand's rare munificence) almost no past acceptance of gifts and bequests "in kind" had been without weakness. In the light of Sargent's splendid portrait, simply, there would have been little enough weakness to associate with Mr. Marquand's collection; but the gifts and bequests in general, even when speciously pleasing or interesting, constitute an object-lesson in the large presence of which the New York mind will perform its evolution—an evolution traceable, and with sharpness, in advance. I shall nevertheless not attempt to foretell it; for sufficient to the situation, surely, is the ap-

pearance, represented by its announcing shadow, that Acquisition—acquisition if need be on the highest terms—may,
during the years to come, bask here as in a climate it has never
before enjoyed. There was money in the air, ever so much
money—that was, grossly expressed, the sense of the whole
intimation. And the money was to be all for the most exquisite things—for *all* the most exquisite except creation, which
was to be off the scene altogether; for art, selection, criticism,
for knowledge, piety, taste. The intimation—which was
somehow, after all, so pointed—would have been detestable
if interests other, and smaller, than these had been in question. The Education, however, was to be exclusively that of
the sense of beauty; this defined, romantically, for my evoked
drama, the central situation. What left me wondering a little,
all the same, was the contradiction involved in one's not
thinking of some of its prospective passages as harsh. Here it
is, no doubt, that one catches the charm of rigours that take
place all in the æsthetic and the critical world. They would be
invidious, would be cruel, if applied to personal interests, but
they take on a high benignity as soon as the values concerned
become values mainly for the mind. (If they happen to have
also a trade-value this is pure superfluity and excess.) The
thought of the acres of canvas and the tons of marble to be
turned out into the cold world as the penalty of old error and
the warrant for a clean slate ought to have drawn tears from
the eyes. But these impending incidents affected me, in fact,
on the spot, as quite radiant demonstrations. The Museum, in
short, was going to be great, and in the geniality of the life to
come such sacrifices, though resembling those of the funeral-
pile of Sardanapalus, dwindled to nothing.

V

The Bowery and Thereabouts

I

I SCARCE know, once more, if such a matter be a sign of the city itself, or only another perversity on the part of a visitor apt to press a little too hard, everywhere, on the spring of the show; but wherever I turned, I confess, wherever any aspect seemed to put forth a freshness, there I found myself saying that this aspect was one's strongest impression. It is impossible, as I now recollect, not to be amused at the great immediate differences of scene and occasion that could produce such a judgment, and this remark directly applies, no doubt, to the accident of a visit, one afternoon of the dire midwinter, to a theatre in the Bowery at which a young actor in whom I was interested had found for the moment a fine melodramatic opportunity. This small adventure—if the adventures of rash observation be ever small—was to remain embalmed for me in all its odd, sharp notes, and perhaps in none more than in its element of contrast with an image antediluvian, the memory of the conditions of a Bowery theatre, *the* Bowery Theatre in fact, contemporary with my more or less gaping youth. Was that vast dingy edifice, with its illustrious past, still standing?—a point on which I was to remain vague while I electrically travelled through a strange, a sinister over-roofed clangorous darkness, a wide thoroughfare beset, for all its width, with sound and fury, and bristling, amid the traffic, with posts and piles that were as the supporting columns of a vast cold, yet also uncannily-animated, sepulchre. It was like moving the length of an interminable cage, beyond the remoter of whose bars lighted shops, struggling dimly under other pent-house effects, offered their Hebrew faces and Hebrew names to a human movement that affected one even then as a breaking of waves that had rolled, for their welter on this very strand, from the other side of the globe. I was on my way to enjoy, no doubt, some peculiarly "American" form of the theatric mystery, but my way led me, apparently, through depths of the Orient, and I should clearly take my place with an Oriental public.

I took it in fact in such a curtained corner of a private box as might have appeared to commit me to the most intimate interest possible—might have done so, that is, if all old signs had not seemed visibly to fail and new questions, mockingly insoluble, to rise. The old signs would have been those of some "historic" community, so to speak, between the play and the public, between those opposed reciprocal quantities: such a consciousness of the same general terms of intercourse for instance, as I seemed to have seen prevail, long years ago, under the great dim, bleak, sonorous dome of the old Bowery. Nothing so much imposed itself at first as this suggestive contrast—the vision of the other big bare ranting stupid stage, the grey void, smelling of dust and tobacco-juice, of a scene on which realism was yet to dawn, but which addressed itself, on the other hand, to an audience at one with it. Audience and "production" had been then of the same stripe and the same "tradition"; the pitch, that is, had been of our own domestic and romantic tradition (to apply large words to a loose matter, a matter rich in our very own æsthetic idiosyncrasy). I should say, in short, if it didn't savour of pedantry, that if this ancient "poetic" had been purely a home-grown thing, nursed in the English intellectual cradle, and in the American of a time when the American resembled the English closely enough, so the instincts from which it sprang were instincts familiar to the whole body of spectators, whose dim sense of art (to use again the big word) was only not thoroughly English because it must have been always so abundantly Irish. The foreign note, in that thinner air, was, at the most, the Irish, and I think of the elements of the "Jack Sheppard" and "Claude Duval" Bowery, including the peanuts and the orange-peel, as quite harmoniously Irish. From the corner of the box of my so improved playhouse further down, the very name of which moreover had the cosmopolite lack of point, I made out, in the audience, the usual mere monotony of the richer exoticism. No single face, beginning with those close beside me (for my box was a shared luxury), but referred itself, by my interpretation, to some such strange outland form as we had not dreamed of in my day. There they all sat, the representatives of the races we have nothing "in common" with, as naturally, as comfortably, as munchingly, as if the theatre were their constant practice—and, as regards the munching, I may add, I was struck with the appearance of quality and cost in the various confections pressed from moment to moment upon our notice by the little playhouse peddlers.

It comes over me under this branch of my reminiscence, that these almost "high-class" luxuries, circulating in such a company, were a sort of supreme symbol of the *promoted* state of the aspirant to American conditions. He, or more particularly she, had been promoted, and, more or less at a bound, to the habitual use of chocolate-creams, and indeed of other dainties, refined and ingenious, compared with which these are quite *vieux jeu*. This last remark might in fact open up for us, had I space, a view, interesting to hold a moment, or to follow as far as it might take us, of the wondrous consumption by the "people," over the land, of the most elaborate solid and liquid sweets, such products as form in other countries an expensive and select dietary. The whole phenomenon of this omnipresent and essentially "popular" appeal of the confectioner and pastry-cook, I can take time but to note, is more significant of the economic, and even of the social situation of the masses than many a circumstance honoured with more attention. I found myself again and again—in presence, for example, of the great glittering temples, the bristling pagodas, erected to the worship in question wherever men and women, perhaps particularly women, most congregate, and above all under the high domes of the great modern railway stations—I found myself wondering, I say, what such facts represented, what light they might throw upon manners and wages. Wages, in the country at large, *are* largely manners—the only manners, I think it fair to say, one mostly encounters; the market and the home therefore look alike dazzling, at first, in this reflected, many-coloured lustre. It speaks somehow, beyond anything else, of the diffused sense of material ease—since the solicitation of sugar couldn't be so hugely and artfully organized if the response were not clearly proportionate. But how is the response itself organized, and what are the other items of that general budget of labour, what in especial are the attenuations of that general state of fatigue, in which so much purchasing-power can flow to the supposedly superfluous? The wage-earners, the toilers of old, notably in other climes, were known by the wealth of their songs; and has it, on these lines, been given to the American people to be known by the number of their "candies"?

I must not let the question, however, carry me too far— quite away from the point I was about to make of my sense of the queer chasm over which, on the Saturday afternoon at the Windsor Theatre, I seemed to see the so domestic drama reach out to the so exotic audience and the so exotic audience reach out to the so domestic drama. The play (a masterpiece of its type, if I may so far strain a point, in such a case, and in the interest of my young friend's excellent performance, as to predicate "type") was American, to intensity, in its blank con formity to convention, the particular implanted convention of the place. This convention, simply expressed, was that there should never be anything different in a play (the most conservative of human institutions) from what there had always been before; that *that place*, in a word, should always know the very same theatric thing, any deviation from which might be phrenology, or freemasonry, or ironmongery, or anything else in the world, but would never be drama, especially drama addressed to the heart of the people. The tricks and the traps, the *trucs*, the whole stage-carpentry, might freely renew them selves, to create for artless minds the illusion of a difference; but the sense of the business would still have to reside in our ineradicable Anglo-Saxon policy, or our seemingly deep seated necessity, of keeping, where "representation" is concerned, so far away from the truth and the facts of life as really to betray a fear in us of possibly doing something like them should we be caught nearer. "Foreigners," in general, unmistakably, in any attempt to render life, obey the instinct of keeping closer, positively recognize the presence and the solicitation of the deep waters; yet here was my houseful of foreigners, physiognomically branded as such, confronted with our pale poetic—fairly caught for schooling in our art of making the best of it. Nothing (in the texture of the occasion) could have had a sharper interest than this demonstration that, since what we most pretend to do with them is thoroughly to school them, the schooling, by our system, cannot begin too soon nor pervade their experience too much. Were they going to rise to it, or rather to fall to it—to *our* instinct, as distinguished from their own, for picturing life? Were they to take our lesson, submissively, in order to get with it our smarter traps and tricks, our superior Yankee machinery (illustrated in the case before them, for instance, by a wonderful folding bed in which the villain of the piece, pursuing the virtuous heroine round and round the room and trying to leap over it after her, is, at the young lady's touch of a hidden spring, engulfed as in the jaws of a crocodile?) Or would it be their dim intellectual resistance, a vague stir in them of some unwitting heritage—of the finer irony, that I should make out, on the contrary, as withstanding the effort to corrupt them, and thus perhaps really promising to react, over the head of our offered mechanic bribes, on our ingrained intellectual platitude?

One had only to formulate that question to seem to see the issue hang there, for the excitement of the matter, quite as if the determination were to be taken on the spot. For the opposition over the chasm of the footlights, as I have called it, grew intense truly, as I took in on one side the hue of the Galician cheek, the light of the Moldavian eye, the whole pervasive facial mystery, swaying, at the best, for the moment, over the gulf, on the vertiginous bridge of American confectionery—and took in on the other the perfect "Yankee" quality of the challenge which stared back at them as in the white light of its hereditary thinness. I needn't say that when I departed—perhaps from excess of suspense—it was without seeing the balance drop to either quarter, and I am afraid I think of the odd scene as still enacted in many places and many ways, the inevitable rough union in discord of the two groups of instincts, the fusion of the two camps by a queer, clumsy, wasteful social chemistry. Such at all events are the roundabout processes of peaceful history, the very history that succeeds, for our edification, in *not* consisting of battles and blood and tears.

II

I was happily to find, at all events, that I had not, on that occasion, done with the Bowery, or with its neighbourhood—as how could one not rejoice to return to an air in which such infinite suggestion might flower? The season had advanced, though the summer night was no more than genial, and the question, for this second visit, was of a "look-in," with two or three friends, at three or four of the most "characteristic" evening resorts (for reflection and conversation) of the dwellers on the East side. It was definitely not, the question, of any gaping view of the policed underworld—unanimously pronounced an imposture, in general, at the best, and essentially less interesting than the exhibition of public manners. I found on the spot, in harmony with this preference, that nothing better could have been desired, in the way of pure presentable picture, subject always to the swinging lantern-light of the individual imagination, than the first (as I think it was, for the roaming hour) of our penetrated "haunts"—a large semi-subterranean establishment, a beer-cellar rich in the sporting note, adorned with images of strong men and lovely women, prize-fighters and *ballerine*, and finding space in its deep bosom for a billiard-room and a bowling-alley, all sociably squeezed together; finding space, above all, for a collection of extraordinarily equivocal types of consumers: an intensity of equivocation indeed planted, just as if to await direct and convenient study, in the most typical face of the collection, a face which happened, by good fortune, to be that of the most officious presence. When the element of the equivocal in personal character and history takes on, in New York, an addition from all the rest of the swarming ambiguity and fugacity of race and tongue, the result becomes, for the picture-seeker, indescribably, luridly strong. There always comes up, at view of the "low" physiognomy shown in conditions that denote a measure of impunity and ease, the question—than which few, I think, are more interesting to the psychologist—of the forms of ability *consistent* with lowness; the question of the quality of intellect, the subtlety of character, the mastery of the art of life, with which the extremity of baseness may yet be associated. That question held me, I confess, so under its spell during those almost first steps of our ingenuous *enquête*, that I would gladly have prolonged, just there, my opportunity to sound it.

The fascination was of course in the perfection of the baseness, and the puzzle in the fact that it could be subject, without fatally muddling, without tearing and rending them, to those arts of life, those quantities of conformity, the numerous involved accommodations and patiences, that are *not* in the repertory of the wolf and the snake. Extraordinary, we say to ourselves on such occasions, the amount of formal tribute that civilization is after all able to gouge out of apparently hopeless stuff; extraordinary that it can make a presentable sheath for such fangs and such claws. The mystery is in the *how* of the process, in the wonderful little wavering borderland between nature and art, the place of the crooked seam where, if psychology had the adequate lens, the white stitches would show. All this played through one's thought, to the infinite extension of the sufficiently close and thoroughly *banal* beer-cellar. There happened to be reasons, not to be shaded over, why one of my companions should cause a particular chord of recognition to vibrate, and the very convergence of hushed looks, in the so "loud" general medium, seemed to lay bare, from table to table, the secret of the common countenance (common to that place) put off its guard by curiosity, almost by amiability. The secret was doubtless in many cases but the poor familiar human secret of the vulgar mind, of the soul unfurnished, so to speak, in respect to delicacy, probity, pity, with a social decoration of the mere bleak walls of instinct; but it was the unforgettable little personality that I have referred to as the presiding spirit, it was the spokesman of our welcome, the master of the scene himself, who struck me as presenting my question in its finest terms. To conduct a successful establishment, to *be* a spokesman, an administrator, an employer of labour and converser on subjects, let alone a citizen and a tax-payer, was to have an existence abounding in relations and to be subject to the law that a relation, however imperfectly human or social, is at the worst a matter that can only be described as delicate. Well, in presence of the abysmal obliquity of such a face, of the abysmal absence of traceability or coherency in such antecedents,

where did the different delicacies involved come in at all?—
how did intercourse emerge at all, and, much more, emerge
so brilliantly, as it were, from its dangers? The answer had to
be, for the moment, no doubt, that if there be such a state as
that of misrepresenting your value and use, there is also the
rare condition of being so sunk beneath the level of appearance as not to be able to represent them at all. Appearance, in
you, has thus not only no notes, no language, no authority,
but is literally condemned to operate *as* the treacherous sum
of your poverties.

The jump was straight, after this, to a medium so different
that I seem to see, as the one drawback to evoking it again,
however briefly, the circumstance that it started the speculative hare for even a longer and straighter run. This irrepressible animal covered here, however, a much goodlier country,
covered it in the interest of a happy generalization—the bold
truth that even when apparently done to death by that property of the American air which reduces so many aspects to a
common denominator, certain finer shades of saliency and
consistency do often, by means known to themselves, recover
their rights. They are like swimmers who have had to plunge,
to come round and under water, but who pop out a panting
head and shine for a moment in the sun. My image is perhaps
extravagant, for the question is only of the kept recollection
of a café pure and simple, particularly pure and particularly
simple in fact, inasmuch as it dispensed none but "soft"
drinks and presented itself thus in the light, the quiet, tempered, intensely individual light, of a beerhouse innocent of
beer. I have indeed no other excuse for calling it a beerhouse
than the fact that it offered to every sense such a deep Germanic peace as abides, for the most part (though not always
even then), where the deep-lidded tankard balances with the
scarce shallower bowl of the meditative pipe. This modest
asylum had its tone, which I found myself, after a few minutes, ready to take for exquisite, if on no other ground than
its almost touching suggestion of discriminations made and
preserved in the face of no small difficulty. That is what
I meant just now by my tribute to the occasional patience
of unquenched individualism—the practical subtlety of the
spirit unashamed of its preference for the minor key, clinging,

through thick and thin, to its conception of decency and dignity, and finding means to make it good even to the exact true shade. These are the real triumphs of art—the discriminations in favour of taste produced not by the gilded and guarded "private room," but by making publicity itself delicate, making your barrier against vulgarity consist but in a few tables and chairs, a few coffee-cups and boxes of dominoes. Money in quantities enough can always create tone, but it had been created here by mere unbuyable instinct. The charm of the place in short was that its note of the exclusive had been arrived at with such a beautifully fine economy. I try, in memory, and for the value of the lesson, to analyze, as it were, the elements, and seem to recall as the most obvious the contemplative stillness in which the faint click of the moved domino could be heard, and into which the placid attention of the quiet, honest men who were thus testifying for the exquisite could be read. The exquisite, yes, *was* the triumph of their tiny temple, with all the loud surrounding triumphs, those of the coarse and the common, making it but stick the faster, like a well-inserted wedge. And fully to catch this was to catch by the same stroke the main ground of the effect, to see that it came most of all from felicity of suppression and omission. There was so visibly too much everywhere else of everything vulgar, that there reigned here, for the difference, the learnt lesson that there could scarce be in such an air of infection little enough, in quantity and mass, of anything. The felicity had its climax in the type, or rather in the individual character, of our host, who, officiating alone, had apparently suppressed all aids to service and succeeded, as by an inspiration of genius, in omitting, for all his years, to learn the current American. He spoke but a dozen words of it, and that was doubtless how he best kept the key of the old Germanic peace—of the friendly stillness in which, while the East side roared, a new metaphysic might have been thought out or the scheme of a new war intellectualized.

III

After this there were other places, mostly higher in the scale, and but a couple of which my memory recovers. There was also, as I recall, a snatched interlude—an associated dash into a small crammed convivial theatre, an oblong hall, bristling with pipe and glass, at the end of which glowed for a moment, a little dingily, some broad passage of a Yiddish comedy of manners. It hovered there, briefly, as if seen through a spy-glass reaching, across the world, to some far-off dowdy Jewry; then our sense of it became too mixed a matter—it was a scent, literally, not further to be followed. There remained with me none the less the patch of alien comedy, with all it implied of esoteric vision on the part of the public. Something of that admonition had indeed, earlier in the season, been sharp—so much had one heard of a brilliant Yiddish actress who was drawing the town to the East side by the promise of a new note. This lady, however, had disconcerted my own purpose by suddenly appearing, in the orthodox quarter, in a language only definable as not in *intention* Yiddish—not otherwise definable; and I also missed, through a like alarm, the opportunity of hearing an admired actor of the same school. He was Yiddish on the East side, but he cropped up, with a wild growth, in Broadway as well, and his auditors seemed to know as little as care to what idiom they supposed themselves to be listening. Marked in New York, by many indications, this vagueness of ear as to differences, as to identities, of idiom.

I must not, however, under that interference, lose the echo of a couple of other of the impressions of my crowded summer night—and all the less that they kept working it, as I seem to remember, up to a higher and higher pitch. It had been intimated to me that one of these scenes of our climax had entered the sophisticated phase, that of sacrificing to a self-consciousness that was to be regretted—that of making eyes, so to speak, at the larger, the up-town public; that pestilent favour of "society" which is fatal to everything it touches and which so quickly leaves the places of its passage unfit for its own use and uninteresting for any other. This establishment had learned to lay on local colour with malice prepense—the local colour of its "Slav" origin—and was the haunt, on certain evenings of the week, of yearning groups from Fifth Avenue sated with familiar horizons. Yet there were no yearning groups—none, that is, save our own—at

the time of our visit; there was only, very amply and pleasantly presented, another aspect of the perpetual process of the
New York intermarriage. As the Venetian Republic, in the
person of the Doge, used to go forth, on occasion, to espouse
the Adriatic, so it is quite as if the American, incarnate in its
greatest port, were for ever throwing the nuptial ring to the
still more richly-dowered Atlantic. I speak again less of the
nuptial rites themselves than of those immediate fruits that
struck me everywhere as so characteristic—so equally characteristic, I mean, of each party to the union. The flourishing
establishment of my present reference offered distinctly its
outland picture, but showed it in an American frame, and the
features of frame and picture arranged themselves shrewdly
together. Quiet couples, elderly bourgeois husbands and
wives, sat there over belated sausage and cheese, potato-salad
and Hungarian wine, the wife with her knitting produced
while the husband finished his cigar; and the indication, for
the moment, might have been of some evening note of
Dantzig or of Buda-Pesth. But the conditioning foreign, and
the visibility of their quite so happily conjugal give-and-take,
in New York, is my reason for this image of the repeated es-
pousals. Why were the quiet easy couples, with their homely
café habit (kept in the best relation to the growth, under the
clicking needles, of the marital stocking), such remote and indirect results of our local anecdotic past, our famous escape,
at our psychological moment, from King George and his
works, with all sorts of inevitable lapses and hitches in any
grateful consciousness they might ever have of that prime
cause of their new birth? Yet why, on the other hand, could
they affect one, even with the Fatherland planked under them
in the manner of the praying-carpet spread beneath the good
Mahometan, as still more disconnected from the historic
consciousness implied in their own type, and with the mere
moral identity of German or Slav, or whatever it might be,
too extinct in them for any possibility of renewal? The exotic
boss here did speak, I remember, fluent East-side New
Yorkese, and it was in this wonderful tongue that he expressed
to us his superior policy, his refined philosophy, announced
his plans for the future and presented himself, to my vision, as
a possibly far-reaching master-spirit. What remains with me is

this expression, and the colour and the quality of it, and the free familiarity and the "damned foreign impudence," with so much taken for granted, and all the hitches and lapses, all the solutions of continuity, in *his* inward assimilation of our heritage and point of view, matched as these were, on our own side, by such signs of large and comparatively witless concession. What, oh, what again, were he and his going to make of us?

Well, there was the impression, and that was a question on which, for a certain intensity in it, our adventure might have closed; but it was so far from closing that, late though the hour, it presently opened out into a vast and complicated picture which I find myself thinking of, after an interval, as the splendid crown of the evening. Here were we still on the East side, but we had moved up, by stages artfully inspired, into the higher walks, into a pavilion of light and sound and savoury science that struck one as vaguely vast, as possibly gardened about, and that, blazing into the stillness of the small hours, dazzled one with the show of its copious and various activity. The whole vision was less intimate than elsewhere, but it was a world of custom quite away from any mere Delmonico tradition of one's earlier time, and rich, as one might reckon it, in its own queer marks, marks probably never yet reduced—inspiring thought!—to literary notation; with which it would seem better to form a point of departure for fresh exploration than serve as tail-piece to the end of a chapter. Who were all the people, and whence and whither and why, in the good New York small hours? Where *was* the place after all, and what might it, or might it not, truly, represent to slightly-fatigued feasters who, in a recess like a privileged opera-box at a *bal masqué*, and still communing with polyglot waiters, looked down from their gallery at a multitudinous supper, a booming orchestra, an elegance of disposed plants and flowers, a perfect organization and an abyss of mystery? Was it "on" Third Avenue, on Second, on fabulous unattempted First? Nothing would induce me to cut down the romance of it, in remembrance, to a mere address, least of all to an awful New York one; New York addresses falling so below the grace of a city where the very restaurants may on occasion, under restless analysis, flash back the likeness of

Venetian palaces flaring with the old carnival. The ambiguity is the element in which the whole thing swims for me—so nocturnal, so bacchanal, so hugely hatted and feathered and flounced, yet apparently so innocent, almost so patriarchal again, and matching, in its mixture, with nothing one had elsewhere known. It breathed its simple "New York! New York!" at every impulse of inquiry; so that I can only echo contentedly, with analysis for once quite agreeably baffled, "Remarkable, unspeakable New York!"

VI

The Sense of Newport

I

NEWPORT, on my finding myself back there, threatened me sharply, quite at first, with that predicament at which I have glanced in another connection or two—the felt condition of having known it too well and loved it too much for description or definition. What was one to say about it except that one *had* been so affected, so distraught, and that discriminations and reasons were buried under the dust of use? There was a chance indeed that the breath of the long years (of the interval of absence, I mean) would have blown away this dust—and that, precisely, was what one was eager to see. To go out, to look about, to recover the sense, was accordingly to put the question, without delay, to the proof —and with the happy consequence, I think, of an escape from a grave discomfiture. The charm was there again, unmistakably, the little old strange, very simple charm—to be expressed, as a fine proposition, or to be given up; but the answer came in the fact that to have walked about for half-an-hour was to have felt the question clear away. It cleared away so conveniently, so blissfully, in the light of the benign little truth that nothing had been less possible, even in the early, ingenuous, infatuated days, than to describe or define Newport. It had clearly had nothing about it *to* describe or define, so that one's fondness had fairly rested on this sweet oddity in it. One had only to look back to recognize that it had never condescended to give a scrap of reasoned account of itself (as a favourite of fortune and the haunt of the *raffiné*); it had simply lain there like a little bare, white, open hand, with slightly-parted fingers, for the observer with a presumed sense for hands to take or to leave. The observer with a real sense never failed to pay this image the tribute of quite tenderly grasping the hand, and even of raising it, delicately, to his lips; having no less, at the same time, the instinct of not shaking it too hard, and that above all of never putting it to any rough work.

Such had been from the first, under a chastened light and in a purple sea, the dainty isle of Aquidneck; which might have avoided the weak mistake of giving up its pretty native name and of becoming thereby as good as nameless—with an existence as Rhode Island practically monopolized by the State and a Newport identity borrowed at the best and applicable but to a corner. Does not this vagueness of condition, however, fitly symbolize the small virtual promontory, of which, superficially, nothing could be predicated but its sky and its sea and its sunsets? One views it as placed there, by some refinement in the scheme of nature, just as a touchstone of taste—with a beautiful little sense to be read into it by a few persons, and nothing at all to be made of it, as to its essence, by most others. I come back, for its essence, to that figure of the little white hand, with the gracefully-spread fingers and the fine grain of skin, even the dimples at the joints and the shell-like delicacy of the pink nails—all the charms in short that a little white hand may have. I see all the applications of the image—I see a special truth in each. It is the back of the hand, rising to the swell of the wrist, that is exposed—which is the way, I think, the true lover takes and admires it. He makes out in it, bending over it—or he used to in the old days—innumerable shy and subtle beauties, almost requiring, for justice, a magnifying-glass; and he winces at the sight of certain other obtruded ways of dealing with it. The touchstone of taste was indeed to operate, for the critical, the tender spirit, from the moment the pink palm was turned up on the chance of what might be "in" it. For nine persons out of ten, among its visitors, its purchasers of sites and builders of (in the old parlance) cottages, there had never been anything in it at all—except of course an opportunity: an opportunity for escaping the summer heat of other places, for bathing, for boating, for riding and driving, and for many sorts of more or less expensive riot. The pink palm being empty, in other words, to their vision, they had begun, from far back, to put things into it, things of their own, and of all sorts, and of many ugly, and of more and more expensive, sorts; to fill it substantially, that is, with gold, the gold that they have ended by heaping up there to an amount so oddly out of proportion to the scale of nature and of space.

This process, one was immediately to perceive with that renewal of impression, this process of injection and elaboration, of creating the palpable pile, had been going on for years to such a tune that the face of nature was now as much obliterated as possible, and the original shy sweetness as much as possible bedizened and bedevilled: all of which, moreover, might also at present be taken as having led, in turn, to the most unexpected climax, a matter of which I shall presently speak. The original shy sweetness, however, that range of effect which I have referred to as practically too latent and too modest for notation, had meanwhile had its votaries, the fond pedestrian minority, for whom the little white hand (to return for an instant to my figure, with which, as you see, I am charmed) had always been so full of treasures of its own as to discredit, from the point of view of taste, any attempt, from without, to stuff it fuller. Such attempts had, in the nature of the case, and from far back, been condemned to show for violations; violations of taste and discretion, to begin with— violations, more intimately, as the whole business became brisker, of a thousand delicate secret places, dear to the disinterested rambler, small, mild "points" and promontories, far away little lonely, sandy coves, rock-set, lily-sheeted ponds, almost hidden, and shallow Arcadian summer-haunted valleys, with the sea just over some stony shoulder: a whole world that called out to the long afternoons of youth, a world with its scale so measured and intended and happy, its detail so finished and pencilled and stippled (certainly for American detail!) that there comes back to me, across the many years, no better analogy for it than that of some fine foreground in an old "line" engraving. There remained always a sense, of course, in which the superimpositions, the multiplied excrescences, were a tribute to the value of the place; where no such liberty was ever taken save exactly *because* (as even the most blundering builder would have claimed) it was all so beautiful, so solitary and so "sympathetic." And that indeed has been, thanks to the "pilers-on" of gold, the fortune, the history of its beauty: that it now bristles with the villas and palaces into which the cottages have all turned, and that these monuments of pecuniary power rise thick and close, precisely, in order that their occupants may constantly remark to each other, from the windows to the "grounds," and from house to house, that it *is* beautiful, it *is* solitary and sympathetic. The thing has been done, it is impossible not to perceive, with the best faith in the world—though not altogether with the best light, which is always so different a matter; and it is with the general consequence only, at the end of the story, that I find myself to-day concerned.

So much concerned I found myself, I profess, after I had taken in this fact of a very distinct general consequence, that the whole interest of the vision was quickened by it; and that when, in particular, on one of the last days of June, among the densely-arrayed villas, I had followed the beautiful "ocean drive" to its uttermost reach and back without meeting either another vehicle or a single rider, let alone a single pedestrian, I recognized matter for the intellectual thrill that attests a social revolution foreseen and completed. The term I use may appear extravagant, but it was a fact, none the less, that I seemed to take full in my face, on this occasion, the cold stir of air produced when the whirligig of time has made one of its liveliest turns. It is always going, the whirligig, but its effect is so to blow up the dust that we must wait for it to stop a moment, as it now and then does with a pant of triumph, in order to see what it has been at. I saw, beyond all doubt, on the spot—and *there* came in, exactly, the thrill; I could remember far back enough to have seen it begin to blow all the artless buyers and builders and blunderers into their places, leaving them there for half a century or so of fond security, and then to see it, of a sudden, blow them quite out again, as with the happy consciousness of some new amusing use for them, some other game still to play with them. This acquaintance, as it practically had been, with the whole rounding of the circle (even though much of it from a distance), was tantamount to the sense of having sat out the drama, the social, the local, that of a real American period, from the rise to the fall of the curtain—always assuming that truth of the reached catastrophe or *dénouement*. *How* this climax or solution had been arrived at—that, clearly, for the spectator, would have been worth taking note of; but what he made of it I shall not glance at till I have shown him as first of all, on the spot, quite modestly giving in to mere primary beguilement. It had been certain in advance that he would find the whole picture overpainted, and the question could only be, at the best, of how much of the ancient surface would here and there glimmer through. The ancient surface had been the concern, as I have hinted, of the small fond minority, the comparatively few people for whom the lurking shy charm, all there, but all to be felt rather than published, did in fact constitute a surface. The question, as soon as one arrived, was of whether some ghost of that were recoverable.

II

There was always, to begin with, the Old Town—we used, before we had become Old ourselves, to speak of it that way, in the manner of an allusion to Nuremberg or to Carcassonne, since it had been leading its little historic life for centuries (as we implied) before "cottages" and house-agents were dreamed of. It was not that we had great illusions about it or great pretensions for it; we only thought it, without interference, very "good of its kind," and we had as to its *being* of that kind no doubt whatever. Would it still be of that kind, and what had the kind itself been?—these questions made one's heart beat faster as one went forth in search of it. Distinctly, if it had been of a kind it *would* still be of it; for the kind wouldn't at the worst or at the best (one scarce knew how to put it) have been worth changing: so that the question for the restored absentee, who so palpitated with the sense of it, all hung, absolutely, on the validity of the past. One might well hold one's breath if the past, with the dear little blue distances in it, were in danger now of being given away. One might well pause before the possible indication that a cherished impression of youth had been but a figment of the mind. Fortunately, however, at Newport, and especially where the antiquities cluster, distances are short, and the note of reassurance awaited me almost round the first corner. One had been a hundred times right—for how *was* one to think of it all, as one went on, if one didn't think of it as Old? There played before one's eyes again, in fine, in that unmistakable silvery shimmer, a particular property of the local air, the exquisite law of the relative—the application of which, on the spot, is required to make even such places as Viterbo and Bagdad not seem new. One may sometimes be tired of the word, but anything that has succeeded in living long enough to become conscious of its *note*, is capable on occasion of making that note effectively sound. It *will* sound, we gather, if we listen for it, and the small silver whistle of the past, with its charming quaver of weak gaiety, quite played the tune I asked of it up and down the tiny, sunny, empty Newport vistas, perspectives coming to a stop like the very short walks of very old ladies. What indeed but little very old ladies did they resemble, the little very old streets? with the same suggestion of present timidity and frugality of life, the same implication in their few folds of drab, of mourning, of muslin still mysteriously starched, the implication of no adventure at any time, however far back, that mightn't have been suitable to a lady.

The whole low promontory, in its wider and remoter measurements, is a region of jutting tide-troubled "points," but we had admired the Old Town too for the emphasis of its peculiar point, *the* Point; a quarter distinguished, we considered, by a really refined interest. Here would have been my misadventure, if I was to have any—that of missing, on the grey page of to-day, the suggestive passages I remembered; but I was to find, to my satisfaction, that there was still no more mistaking their pleasant sense than there had ever been: a quiet, mild waterside sense, not that of the bold, bluff outer sea, but one in which shores and strands and small coast things played the greater part; with overhanging back verandahs, with little private wooden piers, with painted boathouses and boats laid up, with still-water bathing (the very words, with their old slightly prim discrimination, as of ladies and children jumping up and down, reach me across the years), with a wide-curving Bay and dim landward distances that melted into a mysterious, rich, superior, but quite disconnected and not at all permittedly patronizing Providence. There were stories, anciently, for the Point— so prescribed a feature of it that one made them up, freely and handsomely, when they were not otherwise to be come by; though one

was never quite sure if they ought most to apply to the rather
blankly and grimly Colonial houses, fadedly drab at their richest and mainly, as the legend ran, appurtenant to that Quaker
race whom Massachusetts and Connecticut had prehistorically
cast forth and the great Roger Williams had handsomely welcomed, or to the other habitations, the felicitous cottages,
with their galleries on the Bay and toward the sunset, their
pleasure-boats at their little wharves, and the supposition,
that clung to them, of their harbouring the less fashionable of
the outer Great, but also the more cultivated and the more
artistic. Everything was there still, as I say, and quite as much
as anything the prolonged echo of that ingenuous old-time
distinction. It was a marvel, no doubt, that the handful of
light elements I have named should add up to any total de-
serving the name of *picture*, and if I must produce an explanation I seek it with a certain confidence in the sense of the
secret enjoyed by that air for bathing or, as one figures, for
dipping, the objects it deals with. It takes them uninteresting,
but feels immediately what submersion can do for them; tips
them in, keeps them down, holds them under, just for the
proper length of time: after which they come up, as I say,
irradiating vague silver—the reflection of which I have perhaps here been trying to catch even to extravagance.

  I did nothing, at any rate, all an autumn morning, but
discover again how "good" everything had been—positively
better than one had ventured to suppose in one's care to make
the allowance for one's young simplicity. Some things indeed,
clearly, had been better than one knew, and now seemed to
surpass any fair probability: else why, for instance, should I
have been quite awestruck by the ancient State House that
overlooks the ancient Parade?—an edifice ample, majestic,
archaic, of the finest proportions and full of a certain
public Dutch dignity, having brave, broad, high windows, in
especial, the distinctness of whose innumerable square white-
framed panes is the recall of some street view of Haarlem or
Leyden. Here was the charming impression of a treasure of
antiquity to the vague image of which, through the years, one
hadn't done justice—any more than one had done it, positively, to three or four of the other old-time ornaments of the
Parade (which, with its wide, cobbly, sleepy space, of those

years, in the shadow of the State House, must have been much more of a Van der Heyden, or somebody of that sort, than one could have dreamed). There was a treasure of modernity to reckon with, in the form of one of the Commodores Perry (they are somehow much multiplied at Newport, and quite monumentally ubiquitous) engaged in his great naval act; but this was swept away in the general flood of justice to be done. I continued to do it all over the place, and I remember doing it next at a certain ample old-time house which used to unite with the still prettier and archaic Vernon, near it, to form an honourable pair. In this mild town-corner, where it was so indicated that the grass should be growing between the primitive paving-stones, and where indeed I honestly think it mainly is, amid whatever remains of them, ancient peace had appeared formerly to reign—though attended by the ghost of ancient war, inasmuch as these had indubitably been the haunts of our auxiliary French officers during the Revolution, and no self-respecting legend could fail to report that it was in the Vernon house Washington would have visited Rochambeau. There had hung about this structure, which is, architecturally speaking, all "rusticated" and indefinable decency, the implication of an inward charm that refined even on its outward, and this was the tantalizing message its clean, serious windows, never yet debased, struck me as still giving. But it was still (something told me) a question of not putting, anywhere, too many presumptions to the touch; so that my hand quitted the knocker when I was on the point of a tentative tap, and I fell back on the neighbour and mate, as to which there was unforgotten acquaintance to teach me certainty. Here, alas, cold change was installed; the place had become a public office—none of the "artistic" super-civilized, no *raffiné* of them all, among the passing fanciers or collectors, having, strangely enough, marked it for his own. This mental appropriation it is, or it was a few months ago, really impossible not to make, at sight of its delightful hall and almost "grand" staircase, its charming recessed, cupboarded, window-seated parlours, its general panelled amplitude and dignity: the due taster of such things putting himself straight into possession on the spot, and, though wondering at the indifference and neglect, breathing thanks for the absence of positive ravage. For me there were special ghosts on the stair-case, known voices in the brown old rooms—presences that one would have liked, however, to call a little to account. "People don't do those things"; people didn't let so clear a case—clear for sound curiosity—go like that; they didn't, somehow, even if they were only ghosts. But I thought too, as I turned away, of all the others of the foolish, or at least of the responsible, those who for so long have swarmed in the modern quarter and who make profession of the finer sense.

This impression had been disturbing, but it had served its purpose in reconstituting, with a touch, a link—in laying down again every inch of the train of association with the human, the social, personal Newport of what I may call the middle years. To go further afield, to measure the length of the little old Avenue and tread again the little old cliff-walk, to hang over, from above, the little old white crescent of the principal bathing-sands, with the big pond, behind them, set in its stone-walled featureless fields; to do these things and many others, every one of them thus accompanied by the ad-mission that all that *had* been had been little, was to feel dead and buried generations push off even the transparence of their shroud and get into motion for the peopling of a scene that a present posterity has outgrown. The company of the middle years, the so considerably prolonged formative, tentative, imaginative Newport time, hadn't outgrown it—this catas-trophe was still to come, as it constitutes, precisely, the strik-ing dramatic *dénouement* I have already referred to. American society—so far as that free mixture was to have arrived at cohesion—had for half a century taken its whole relation with the place seriously (which was by intention very gaily); it long remained, for its happiness, quite at one with this most favoured resort of its comparative innocence. In the attesting presence of all the constant elements, of natural conditions that have, after all, persisted more than changed, a hundred far-away passages of the extinct life and joy, and of the com-parative innocence, came back to me with an inevitable grace. A glamour as of the flushed ends of beautiful old summers, making a quite rich medium, a red sunset haze, as it were, for a processional throng of charioteers and riders, fortunate folk, fortunate above all in their untouched good faith, adjourning from the pleasures of the day to those of the evening—this benignity in particular overspread the picture, hanging it there as the Newport aspect that most lived again. Those good people all could make discoveries within the frame itself—beginning of course to push it out, in all directions, so as sufficiently to enlarge it, as they fondly fancied, even for the experience of a sophisticated world. They danced and they drove and they rode, they dined and wined and dressed and flirted and yachted and polo'd and Casino'd, responding to the subtlest inventions of their age; on the old lawns and verandahs I saw them gather, on the old shining sands I saw them gallop, past the low headlands I saw their white sails verily flash, and through the dusky old shrubberies came the light and sound of their feasts.

It had all been in truth a history—for the imagination that could take it so; and when once that kindly stage was offered them it was a wonder how many figures and faces, how many names and voices, images and embodiments of youth mainly, and often of Beauty, and of felicity and fortune almost always, or of what then passed for such, pushed, under my eyes, in blurred gaiety, to the front. Hadn't it been above all, in its good faith, the Age of Beauties—the blessed age when it was so easy to *be*, "on the Avenue," a Beauty, and when it was so easy, not less, not to doubt of the unsurpassability of such as appeared there? It was through the fact that the whole scheme and opportunity satisfied them, the fact that the place was, as I say, good enough for them—it was through this that, with ingenuities and audacities and refinements of their own (some of the more primitive of which are still touching to think of) they extended the boundaries of civilization, and fairly taught themselves to believe they were doing it in the interest of nature. Beautiful the time when the Ocean Drive had been hailed at once as a triumph of civilization and as a proof of the possible appeal of Scenery even to the dissipated. It was spoken of as of almost boundless extent—as one of the wonders of the world; as indeed it does turn often, in the gloaming, to purple and gold, and as the small sea-coves then gleam on its edge like barbaric gems on a mantle. Yet if it was a question of waving the wand and of breathing again, till it stirred, on the quaintness of the old manners—I refer to those of the fifties, sixties, seventies, and don't exclude those of the eighties—it was most touching of all to go back to dimmest days, days, such as now appear antediluvian, when ocean-drives, engineered by landscape artists and literally macadamized all the way, were still in the lap of time; when there was only an afternoon for the Fort, and another for the Beach, and another for the "Boat-house"—inconceivable innocence!—and even the shortness of the Avenue seemed very long, and even its narrowness very wide, and even its shabbiness very promising for the future, and when, in fine, chariots and cavaliers took their course, across country, to Bateman's, by inelegant precarious tracts and returned, through the darkling void, with a sense of adventure and fatigue. That, I can't but think, was the *pure* Newport time, the most perfectly guarded by a sense of margin and of mystery.

It was the time of settled possession, and yet furthest removed from these blank days in which margin has been consumed and the palaces, on the sites but the other day beyond price, stare silently seaward, monuments to the *blasé* state of their absent proprietors. Purer still, however, I remind myself, was that stretch of years which I have reasons for thinking sacred, when the custom of seeking hibernation on the spot partly prevailed, when the local winter inherited something of the best social grace (as it liked at least to think) of the splendid summer, and when the strange sight might be seen of a considerable company of Americans, not gathered at a mere rest-cure, who confessed brazenly to not being in business. Do I grossly exaggerate in saying that this company, candidly, quite excitedly self-conscious, as all companies not commercial, in America, may be pleasantly noted as being, formed, for the time of its persistence, an almost unprecedented small body—unprecedented in American conditions; a collection of the detached, the slightly disenchanted and casually disqualified, and yet of the resigned and contented, of the socially orthodox: a handful of mild, oh delightfully mild, cosmopolites, united by three common circumstances, that of their having for the most part more or less lived in Europe, that of their sacrificing openly to the ivory idol whose name is leisure, and that, not least, of a formed critical habit. These things had been felt as making them excrescences on the

American surface, where nobody ever criticized, especially after the grand tour, and where the great black ebony god of business was the only one recognized. So I see them, at all events, in fond memory, lasting as long as they could and finding no successors; and they are most embalmed for me, I confess, in that scented, somewhat tattered, but faintly spiced, wrapper of their various "European" antecedents. I see them move about in the light of these, and I understand how it was this that made them ask what would have become of them, and where in the world, the hard American world, they *could* have hibernated, how they could even, in the Season, have bowed their economic heads and lurked, if it hadn't been for Newport. I think of that question as, in their reduced establishments, over their winter whist, under their private theatricals, and pending, constantly, their loan and their return of the *Revue des Deux Mondes*, their main conversational note. I find myself in fact tenderly evoking them as special instances of the great—or perhaps I have a right only to say of the small—American complication; the state of one's having been so pierced, betimes, by the sharp outland dart as to be able ever afterwards but to move about, vaguely and helplessly, with the shaft still in one's side.

Their nostalgia, however exquisite, was, I none the less gather, sterile, for they appear to have left no seed. They must have died, some of them, in order to "go back"—to go back, that is, to Paris. If I make, at all events, too much of them, it is for their propriety as a delicate subjective value matching with the intrinsic Newport delicacy. They must have felt that they, obviously, notably, notoriously, did match—the proof of which was in the fact that to them alone, of the customary thousands, was the beauty of the good walk, over the lovely little land, revealed. The customary thousands here, as throughout the United States, never set foot to earth—yet this had happened so, of old, to be the particular corner of *their* earth that made that adventure most possible. At Newport, as the phrase was, in autumnal, in vernal hibernation, you *could* walk—failing which, in fact, you failed of impressions the most consolatory; and it is mainly to the far ends of the low, densely shrubbed and perfectly finished little headlands that I see our friends ramble as if to stretch fond arms

across the sea. There used to be distant places beyond Bateman's, or better still on the opposite isle of Conanicut, now
blighted with ugly uses, where nursing a nostalgia on the sun-
warmed rocks was almost as good as having none at all. So it
was not only not our friends who had overloaded and overcrowded, but it was they at last, I infer, who gave way before
that grossness. How should they have wished to leave seed
only to be trampled by the white elephants?

The white elephants, as one may best call them, all cry and
no wool, all house and no garden, make now, for three or
four miles, a barely interrupted chain, and I dare say I think
of them best, and of the distressful, inevitable waste they represent, as I recall the impression of a divine little drive, roundabout them and pretty well everywhere, taken, for renewal of
acquaintance, while November was still mild. I sought another renewal, as I have intimated, in the vacant splendour of
June, but the interesting evidence then only refined on that
already gathered. The place itself, as man—and often, no
doubt, alas, as woman, with her love of the immediate and
contiguous—had taken it over, was more than ever, to the
fancy, like some dim, simplified ghost of a small Greek island,
where the clear walls of some pillared portico or pavilion,
perched afar, looked like those of temples of the gods, and
where Nature, deprived of that ease in merely massing herself
on which "American scenery," as we lump it together, is too
apt to depend for its effect, might have shown a piping shepherd on any hillside or attached a mythic image to any point
of rocks. What an idea, originally, to have seen this miniature
spot of earth, where the sea-nymphs on the curved sands, at
the worst, might have chanted back to the shepherds, as a
mere breeding-ground for white elephants! They look queer
and conscious and lumpish—some of them, as with an air
of the brandished proboscis, really grotesque—while their
averted owners, roused from a witless dream, wonder what in
the world is to be done with them. The answer to which, I
think, can only be that there is absolutely nothing to be done;
nothing but to let them stand there always, vast and blank,
for reminder to those concerned of the prohibited degrees of
witlessness, and of the peculiarly awkward vengeances of af-
fronted proportion and discretion.

VII

Boston

I T SOMETIMES uncomfortably happens for a writer, consulting his remembrance, that he remembers too much and finds himself knowing his subject too well; which is but the case of the bottle too full for the wine to start. There has to be room for the air to circulate between one's impressions, between the parts of one's knowledge, since it is the air, or call it the intervals on the sea of one's ignorance, of one's indifference, that sets these floating fragments into motion. This is more or less what I feel in presence of the invitation — even the invitation written on the very face of the place itself, of its actual aspects and appearances — to register my "impression" of Boston. Can one *have*, in the conditions, an impression of Boston, any that has not been for long years as inappreciable as a "sunk" picture? — that dead state of surface which requires a fresh application of varnish. The situation I speak of is the consciousness of "old" knowledge, knowledge so compacted by the years as to be unable, like the bottled wine, to flow. The answer to such questions as these, no doubt, however, is the practical one of trying a shake of the bottle or a brushful of the varnish. My "sunk" sense of Boston found itself vigorously varnished by mere renewal of vision at the end of long years; though I confess that under this favouring influence I ask myself why I should have had, after all, the notion of overlaid deposits of experience. The experience had anciently been small — so far as smallness may be imputed to any of our prime initiations; yet it had left consequences out of proportion to its limited seeming self. Early contacts had been brief and few, and the slight bridge had long ago collapsed; wherefore the impressed condition that acquired again, on the spot, an intensity, struck me as but half explained by the inordinate power of assimilation of the imaginative young. I should have had none the less to content myself with this evidence of the magic of past sensibilities had not the question suddenly been lighted for me as by a sudden flicker of the torch — and for my special benefit — carried in the hand of history. This light, waving for an instant over the scene, gave me the measure of my relation to it, both as to immense little extent and to quite subjective character.

I

It was in strictness only a matter of noting the harshness of change—since I scarce know what else to call it—on the part of the approaches to a particular spot I had wished to revisit. I made out, after a little, the entrance to Ashburton Place; but I missed on that spacious summit of Beacon Hill more than I can say the pleasant little complexity of the other time, marked with its share of the famous old-world "crookedness" of Boston, that element of the mildly tortuous which did duty, for the story-seeker, as an ancient and romantic note, and was half envied, half derided by the merely rectangular criticism. Didn't one remember the day when New Yorkers, when Philadelphians, when pilgrims from the West, sated with their eternal equidistances, with the quadrilateral scheme of life, "raved" about Cornhill and appeared to find in the rear of the State House a recall of one of the topographical, the architectural jumbles of Europe or Asia? And did not indeed the small happy accidents of the disappearing Boston exhale in a comparatively sensible manner the warm breath of history, the history of something as against the history of nothing?—so that, being gone, or generally going, they enabled one at last to feel and almost to talk about them as one had found one's self feeling and talking about the sacrificed relics of old Paris and old London. In this immediate neighbourhood of the enlarged State House, where a great raw clearance has been made, memory met that pang of loss, knew itself sufficiently bereft to see the vanished objects, a scant but adequate cluster of "nooks," of such odds and ends as parochial schemes of improvement sweep away, positively overgrown, within one's own spirit, by a wealth of legend. There was at least the gain, at any rate, that one was now going to be free to picture them, to embroider them, at one's ease—to tangle them up in retrospect and make the real romantic claim for them. This accordingly is what I am doing, but I am doing it in particular for the sacrificed end of Ashburton Place, the Ashburton Place that I anciently knew. This eminently respectable by-way, on my return to question it, opened its short vista for me honestly enough, though looking rather exposed and undermined, since the mouth of the passage to the west, formerly measured and narrow, had begun to yawn into space, a space peopled in fact, for the eye of appreciation, with the horrific glazed perpendiculars of the future. But the pair of ancient houses I was in quest of kept their tryst; a pleasant individual pair, mated with nothing else in the street, yet looking at that hour as if their old still faces had lengthened, their shuttered, lidded eyes had closed, their brick complexions had paled, above the good granite basements, to a fainter red—all as with the cold consciousness of a possible doom.

That possibility, on the spot, was not present to me, occupied as I was with reading into one of them a short page of history that I had my own reasons for finding of supreme interest, the history of two years of far-away youth spent there at a period—the closing-time of the War—full both of public and of intimate vibrations. The two years had been those of a young man's, a very young man's earliest fond confidence in a "literary career," and the effort of actual attention was to recover on the spot some echo of ghostly footsteps— the sound as of taps on the window-pane heard in the dim dawn. The place itself was meanwhile, at all events, a conscious memento, with old secrets to keep and old stories to witness for, a saturation of life as closed together and preserved in it as the scent lingering in a folded pocket-handkerchief. But when, a month later, I returned again (a justly-rebuked mistake) to see if another whiff of the fragrance were not to be caught, I found but a gaping void, the brutal effacement, at a stroke, of every related object, of the whole precious past. Both the houses had been levelled and the space to the corner cleared; hammer and pickaxe had evidently begun to swing on the very morrow of my previous visit—which had moreover been precisely the imminent doom announced, without my understanding it, in the poor scared faces. I had been present, by the oddest hazard, at the very last moments of the victim in whom I was most interested; the act of obliteration had been breathlessly swift, and if I had often seen how fast history could be made I had doubtless never so felt that it could be unmade still faster. It was as if the bottom had fallen out of one's own biography, and one plunged backward into space without meeting anything. That, however, seemed just to give me, as I have hinted, the whole figure of my connection with everything about, a connection that had been sharp, in spite of brevity, and then had broken short off. Thus it was the sense of the rupture, more than of anything else, that I was, and for a still much briefer time, to carry with me. It seemed to leave me with my early impression of the place on my hands, inapt, as might be, for use; so that I could only try, rather vainly, to fit it to present conditions, among which it tended to shrink and stray.

It was on two or three such loitering occasions, wondering and invoking pauses that had, a little vaguely and helplessly perhaps, the changed crest of Beacon Hill for their field—it was at certain of these moments of charged, yet rather chilled, contemplation that I felt my small cluster of early associations shrivel to a scarce discernible point. I recall a Sunday afternoon in particular when I hung about on the now vaster platform of the State House for a near view of the military monuments erected there, the statues of Generals Hooker and Devens, and for the charm at once and the pang of feeling the whole backward vista, with all its features, fall from that eminence into grey perspective. The top of Beacon Hill quite rakes, with a but slightly shifting range, the old more definite Boston; for there seemed no item, nor any number, of that remarkable sum that it would not anciently have helped one to distinguish or divine. There all these things essentially were at the moment I speak of, but only again as something ghostly and dim, something overlaid and smothered by the mere modern thickness. I lingered half-an-hour, much of the new disposition of the elements here involved being duly impressive, and the old uplifted front of the State House, surely, in its spare and austere, its ruled and pencilled kind, a thing of beauty, more delightful and harmonious even than I had remembered it; one of the inestimable values again, in the eye of the town, for taste and temperance, as the perfectly felicitous "Park Street" Church hard by, was another. The

irresistible spell, however, I think, was something sharper
yet—the coercion, positively, of feeling one's case, the case of
one's deeper discomfiture, completely made out. The day itself,
toward the winter's end, was all benignant, like the immense
majority of the days of the American year, and there went
forward across the top of the hill a continuous passage of men
and women, in couples and talkative companies, who struck
me as labouring wage-earners, of the simpler sort, arrayed, very
comfortably, in their Sunday best and decently enjoying their
leisure. They came up as from over the Common, they passed
or they paused, exchanging remarks on the beauty of the scene,
but rapidly presenting themselves to me as of more interest, for
the moment, than anything it contained.

   For no sound of English, in a single instance, escaped their
lips; the greater number spoke a rude form of Italian, the
others some outland dialect unknown to me—though I
waited and waited to catch an echo of antique refrains. No
note of any shade of American speech struck my ear, save in
so far as the sounds in question represent to-day so much of
the substance of that idiom. The types and faces bore them
out; the people before me were gross aliens to a man, and
they were in serene and triumphant possession. Nothing, as I
say, could have been more effective for figuring the hitherward bars of a grating through which I might make out, far-
off in space, "my" small homogeneous Boston of the more
interesting time. It was not of course that our gross little
aliens were immediate "social" figures in the narrower sense
of the term, or that any personal commerce of which there
might be question could colour itself, to its detriment, from
their presence; but simply that they expressed, as everywhere
and always, the great cost at which every place on my list had
become braver and louder, and that they gave the measure of
the distance by which the general movement was *away*—
away, always and everywhere, from the old presumptions and
conceivabilities. Boston, the bigger, braver, louder Boston,
was "away," and it was quite, at that hour, as if each figure in
my procession were there on purpose to leave me no doubt of
it. Therefore had I the vision, as filling the sky, no longer of
the great Puritan "whip," the whip for the conscience and the
nerves, of the local legend, but that of a huge applied sponge,

a sponge saturated with the foreign mixture and passed over almost everything I remembered and might still have recovered. The detail of this obliteration would take me too far, but I had even then (on a previous day as well as only half-an-hour before) caught at something that might stand for a vivid symbol of the general effect of it. To come up from School Street into Beacon was to approach the Athenæum—exquisite institution, to fond memory, joy of the aspiring prime; yet to approach the Athenæum only to find all disposition to enter it drop as dead as if from quick poison, what did *that* denote but the dreadful chill of change, and of the change in especial that was most completely dreadful? For had not this honoured haunt of all the most civilized—library, gallery, temple of culture, the place that was to Boston at large as Boston at large was to the rest of New England—had it not with peculiar intensity had a "value," the most charming of its kind, no doubt, in all the huge country, and had not this value now, evidently, been brought so low that one shrank, in delicacy, from putting it to the test?

It was a case of the detestable "tall building" again, and of its instant destruction of quality in everything it overtowers. Put completely out of countenance by the mere masses of brute ugliness beside it, the temple of culture looked only rueful and snubbed, hopelessly down in the world; so that, far from being moved to hover or to penetrate, one's instinct was to pass by on the other side, averting one's head from an humiliation one could do nothing to make less. And this indeed though one would have liked to do something; the brute masses, above the comparatively small refined façade (one saw how happy one had always thought it) having for the inner ear the voice of a pair of school-bullies who hustle and pummel some studious little boy. " 'Exquisite' was what they called you, eh? We'll teach you, then, little sneak, to be exquisite! We allow none of that rot round here." It was heart-breaking, this presentation of a Boston practically void of an Athenæum; though perhaps not without interest as showing how much one's own sense of the small city of the earlier time had been dependent on that institution. I found it of no use, at any rate, to think, for a compensatory sign of the new order, of the present Public Library; the present Public

Library, however remarkable in its pomp and circumstance, and of which I had at that hour received my severe impression, being neither exquisite nor on the way to become so—a difficult, an impassable way, no doubt, for Public Libraries. Nor did I cast about, in fact, very earnestly, for consolation—so much more was I held by the vision of the closed order which shaped itself, continually, in the light of the differing present; an order gaining an interest for this backward view precisely as one felt that all the parts and tokens of it, while it lasted, had hung intimately together. Missing those parts and tokens, or as many of them as one could, became thus a constant slightly painful joy: it made them fall so into their place as items of the old character, or proofs, positively, as one might say, of the old distinction. It was impossible not to see Park Street itself, for instance—while I kept looking at the matter from my more "swagger" hilltop as violently vulgarized; and it was incontestable that, whatever might be said, there had anciently not been, on the whole continent, taking everything together, an equal animated space more exempt from vulgarity. There had probably been comparable spaces—impressions, in New York, in Philadelphia, in Baltimore, almost as good; but only almost, by reason of their lacking (which was just the point) the indefinable perfection of Park Street.

It seems odd to have to borrow from the French the right word in this association—or would seem so, rather, had it been less often indicated that that people have better names than ours even for the qualities we are apt to suppose ourselves more in possession of than they. Park Street, in any case, had been magnificently *honnête*—the very type and model, for a pleasant street-view, of the character. The aspects that might elsewhere have competed were *honnêtes* and weak, whereas Park Street was *honnête* and strong—strong as founded on *all* the moral, material, social solidities, instead of on some of them only; which made again all the difference. Personal names, as notes of that large emanation, need scarcely be invoked—they might even have a weakening effect; the force of the statement was in its collective, cumulative look, as if each member of the row, from the church at the Tremont Street angle to the amplest, squarest, most purple presence at the Beacon Street corner (where it always had a little the air of a sturdy proprietor with back to the fire, legs apart and thumbs in the armholes of an expanse of high-coloured plush waistcoat), was but a syllable in the word Respectable several times repeated. One had somehow never heard it uttered with so convincing an emphasis. But the shops, up and down, are making all this as if it had never been, pleasant "premises" as they have themselves acquired; and it was to strike me from city to city, I fear, that the American shop in general pleads but meagrely—whether on its outer face or by any more intimate art—for indulgence to its tendency to swarm, to bristle, to vociferate. The shop-front, observed at random, produced on me from the first, and almost everywhere alike, a singular, a sinister impression, which left me uneasy till I had found a name for it: the sense of an economic law of which one had not for years known the unholy rigour, the vision of "protected" production and of commodities requiring certainly, in many cases, every advantage Protection could give them. They looked to me always, these exhibitions, consciously and defiantly protected—insolently safe, able to be with impunity anything they would; and when once that lurid light had settled on them I could see them, I confess, in none other; so that the objects composing them fell, throughout, into a vicious and villainous category—quite as if audibly saying: "Oh come; don't look among us for what you won't, for what you shan't find, the best quality attainable; but only for that quite other matter, the best value we allow you. You must take us or go without, and if you feel your nose thus held to the grindstone by the hard fiscal hand, it's no more than you deserve for harbouring treasonable thoughts."

So it was, therefore, that while the imagination and the memory strayed—strayed away to other fiscal climates, where the fruits of competition so engagingly ripen and flush—the streets affected one at moments as a prolonged show-case for every arrayed vessel of humiliation. The fact that several classes of the protected products appeared to consist of articles that one might really anywhere have preferred did little, oddly enough, to diminish the sense of severe discipline awaiting the restored absentee on contact with these occasions of traffic. The discipline indeed is general, proceeding as

it does from so many sources, but it earns its name, in particular, from the predicament of the ingenuous inquirer who
asks himself if he can "really bear" the combination of such
general manners and such general prices, of such general
prices and such general manners. He has a helpless bewildered
moment during which he wonders if he mightn't bear the
prices a little better if he were a little better addressed, or bear
the usual form of address a little better if the prices were in
themselves, given the commodity offered, a little less humiliating to the purchaser. Neither of these elements of his dilemma strikes him as likely to abate—the general cost of the
things to drop, or the general grimness of the person he deals
with over the counter to soften; so that he reaches out again
for balm to where he has had to seek it under other wounds,
falls back on the cultivation of patience and regret, on large
international comparison. He is confronted too often, to his
sense, with the question of what may be "borne"; but what
does he see about him if not a vast social order in which the
parties to certain relations are all the while marvellously, inscrutably, desperately "bearing" each other? He may wonder,
at his hours, how, under the strain, social cohesion does not
altogether give way; but that is another question, which belongs to a different plane of speculation. For he asks himself
quite as much as anything else how the shopman or the shop-
lady can bear to be barked at in the manner he constantly
hears used to them by customers—he recognizes that no
agreeable form of intercourse *could* survive a day in such air:
so that what is the only relation finding ground there but a
necessary vicious circle of gross mutual endurance?

These reflections connect themselves moreover with that
most general of his restless hauntings in the United States—
not only with the lapse of all wonderment at the immense
number of absentees unrestored and making their lives as they
may in other countries, but with the preliminary American
postulate or basis for any successful accommodation of life.
This basis is that of active pecuniary gain and of active pecuniary gain only—that of one's making the conditions so
triumphantly pay that the prices, the manners, the other
inconveniences, take their place as a friction it is comparatively easy to salve, wounds directly treatable with the wash of

gold. What prevails, what sets the tune, is the American scale of gain, more magnificent than any other, and the fact that the whole assumption, the whole theory of life, is that of the individual's participation in it, that of his being more or less punctually and more or less effectually "squared." To make so much money that you won't, that you don't "mind," don't mind anything—that is absolutely, I think, the main American formula. Thus your making no money—or so little that it passes there for none—and being thereby distinctly reduced to minding, amounts to your being reduced to the knowledge that America is no place for you. To mind as one minds, for instance, in Europe, under provocation or occasion offered, and yet to have to live under the effect of American pressure, is speedily to perceive that the knot can be untied but by a definite pull of one or the other string. The immense majority of people pull, luckily for the existing order, the string that consecrates their connection with it; the minority (small, however, only in comparison) pull the string that loosens that connection. The existing order is meanwhile safe, inasmuch as the faculty of making money is in America the commonest of all and fairly runs the streets: so simple a matter does it appear there, among vast populations, to make betimes enough *not* to mind. Yet the withdrawal of the considerable group of the pecuniarily disqualified seems no less, for the present, an assured movement; there will always be scattered individuals condemned to mind on a scale beyond any scale of making. The relation of this modest body to the country of their birth, which asks so much, on the whole—so many surrenders and compromises, and the possession above all of such a prodigious head for figures—before it begins, in its wonderful way, to give or to "pay," would appear to us supremely touching, I think, as a case of communion baffled and blighted, if we had time to work it out. It would bathe in something of a tragic light the vivid truth that the "great countries" are all, more and more, happy lands (so far as any can be called such) for any, for every sort of person rather than the middle sort. The upper sort—in the scale of wealth, the only scale now—can to their hearts' content build their own castles and move by their own motors; the lower sort, masters of gain in *their* degree, can profit, also to their hearts' content, by the enormous extension of those material facilities which may be gregariously enjoyed; they are able to rush about, as never under the sun before, in promiscuous packs and hustled herds, while to the act of so rushing about all felicity and prosperity appear for them to have been comfortably reduced. The frustrated American, as I have hinted at him, scraping for *his* poor practical solution in the depleted silver-mine of history, is the American who "makes" too little for the castle and yet "minds" too much for the hustled herd, who can neither achieve such detachment nor surrender to such society, and who most of all accordingly, in the native order, fails of a working basis. The salve, the pecuniary salve, in Europe, is sensibly less, but less on the other hand also the excoriation that makes it necessary, whether from above or below.

II

Let me at all events say for the Park Street Church, while I may still, on my hilltop, keep more or less in line with it, that this edifice persistently "holds the note," as yet, the note of the old felicity, and remains by so doing a precious public servant. Strange enough, doubtless, to find one's self pleading sanctity for a theological structure sanctified only by such a name—as who should say the Park Street Hotel or the Park Street Post-office; so much clearer would the claim seem to come were it the case of another St. Clement Danes or of another St. Mary-le-Strand. But in America we get our sanctity as we can, and we plead it, if we are wise, wherever the conditions suffer the faintest show of colour for it to flush through. Again and again it is a question, on behalf of the memorial object (and especially when preservation is at stake), of an interest and an appeal proceeding exactly *from* the conditions, and thereby not of an absolute, but of a relative force and weight; which is exactly the state of the matter with the Park Street Church. This happy landmark is, in strictness, with its mild recall, by its spire, of Wren's bold London examples, the comparatively thin echo of a far-away song—playing its part, however, for harmonious effect, as perfectly as possible. It is admirably placed, quite peculiarly *present*, on the

Boston scene, and thus, for one reason and another, points its moral as not even the State House does. So we see afresh, under its admonition, that charm is a flower of wild and windblown seed—often not to be counted on when most anxiously planted, but taking its own time and its own place both for enriching and for mocking us. It mocks assuredly, above all, our money and our impatience, elements addressed to buying or "ordering" it, and only asks that when it does come we shall know it and love it. When we fail of this intelligence it simply, for its vengeance, boycotts us—makes us vulgar folk who have no concern with it. Then if we ever miss it we can never get it back—though our deepest depth of punishment of course is to go on fatuously not missing it, the joy of ourselves and of each other and the derision of those who know. These reflections were virtually suggested to me, on the eve of my leaving Boston, by ten words addressed to my dismay; the effect of which was to make Park Street Church, for the hour, the most interesting mass of brick and mortar and (if I may risk the supposition) timber in America.

The words had been spoken, in the bright July air, by a friend encountered in the very presence of the mild monument, on the freshly-perceived value of which, for its position, for its civil function, I had happened irrepressibly to exclaim. Thus I learned that its existence might be spoken of as gravely menaced—menaced by a scheme for the erection of a "business block," a huge square of innumerable tiers and floors, thousands of places of trade, the trade that in such a position couldn't fail to be roaring. In the eye of financial envy the church was but a cumberer of the ground, and where, about us, had we seen financial envy fail when it had once really applied the push of its fat shoulder? Drunk as it was with power, what was to be thought of as resisting it? This was a question, truly, to frighten answers away—until I presently felt the most pertinent of all return as if on tiptoe. The perfect force of the case *as* a case, as an example, that was the answer of answers; the quite ideal pitch of the opportunity for virtue. Ideal opportunities are rare, and this occasion for not sacrificing the high ornament and cynosure of the town to the impudence of private greed just happens to be one, and to have the finest marks of the character. One had but to imagine

a civilized community reading these marks, feeling that character, and then consciously and cynically falling below its
admirable chance, to take in the impossibility of any such blot
on the page of honour, any such keen appetite for the base
alternative. It would be verily the end—the end of the old
distinguished life, of the common intelligence that had flowered formerly, for attesting fame, from so strong a sap and
into so thick and rich a cluster. One had thought of these
things as one came and went—so interesting to-day in Boston are such informal consultations of the oracle (that of the
very air and "tone"), such puttings to it of the question of
what the old New England spirit may have still, intellectually,
æsthetically, or for that matter even morally, to give; of what
may yet remain, for productive scraping, of the formula of the
native Puritanism educated, the formula once capacious
enough for the "literary constellation" of the Age of Emerson.
Is that cornucopia empty, or does some handful of strong or
at least sound fruit lurk to this day, a trifle congested by keeping, up in the point of the horn? What, if so, are, in the
ambient air, the symptoms of this possibility? what are the
signs of intellectual promise, poetic, prosaic, philosophic, in
the current generations, those actually learning their principal
lesson, as one assumes, from the great University hard by?
The old formula, that of Puritanism educated, has it, in fine,
except for "business," anything more to communicate?—or
do we perhaps mistake the case in still speaking, by reason
of the projected shadow of Harvard, of "education" as at all
involved?

Oh, for business, for a commercial, an organizing energy of
the first order, the indications would seem to abound; the air
being full of them as of one loud voice, and nowhere so full
perhaps as at that Park Street corner, precisely, where it was
to be suggested to me that their meaning was capable on
occasion of turning to the sinister. The commercial energy at
least was educated, up to the eyes—Harvard was still caring
for that more than for anything else—but the wonderments,
or perhaps rather the positive impressions I have glanced at,
bore me constant company, keeping the last word, all emphasis of answer, back as if for the creation of a dramatic suspense. I liked the suspense, none the less, for what it had in

common with "intellectual curiosity," and it gave me a light, moreover, which was highly convenient, helping me to look at everything in some related state to this proposition of the value of the Puritan residuum—the question of whether value *is* expressed, for instance, by the little tales, mostly by ladies, and about and for children romping through the ruins of the Language, in the monthly magazines. Some of my perceptions of relation might seem forced, for other minds, but it sufficed me that they were straight and clear for myself— straight and clear again, for example, when (always on my hilltop and raking the prospect over for memories) I quite assented to the tacit intimation that a long æsthetic period had closed with the disappearance of the old Museum Theatre. This had been the theatre of the "great" period—so far as such a description may fit an establishment that never produced during that term a play either by a Bostonian or by any other American; or it had at least, with however unequal steps, kept the great period company, made the Boston of those years quite complacently participate in its genial continuity. This character of its *being* an institution, its really being a theatre, with a repertory and a family of congruous players, not one of them the baleful actor-manager, head and front of all the so rank and so acclaimed vulgarities of our own day— this nature in it of not being the mere empty shell, the indifferent cave of the winds, that yields a few nights' lodging, under stress, to the passing caravan, gave it a dignity of which I seemed to see the ancient city gratefully conscious, fond and jealous, and the thought of which invites me to fling over it now perhaps too free a fold of the mantle of romance. And yet why too free? is what I ask myself as I remember that the Museum had for long years a repertory—the repertory of its age—a company and a cohesion, theatrical trifles of the cultivation of which no present temple of the drama from end to end of the country appears to show a symptom. Therefore I spare a sigh to its memory, and, though I doubtless scarce think of it as the haunt of Emerson, of Hawthorne or of Mr. Ticknor, the common conscience of the mid-century in the New England capital insists on showing, at this distance of time, as the richer for it.

That then was one of the missed elements, but the consequent melancholy, I ought promptly to add, formed the most appropriate soil for stray sprouts of tenderness in respect to the few aspects that had not suffered. The old charm of Mount Vernon Street, for instance, wandering up the hill, almost from the waterside, to the rear of the State House, and fairly hanging about there to rest like some good flushed lady, of more than middle age, a little spent and "blown"—this ancient grace was not only still to be felt, but was charged, for depth of interest, with intenser ghostly presences, the rich growth of time, which might have made the ample slope, as one mounted, appear as beautifully peopled as Jacob's Ladder. That was exactly the kind of impression to be desired and welcomed; since ghosts belong only to places and suffer and perish with them. It was as if they themselves moreover were taking pleasure in this place, fairly indeed commending to me the fine old style of the picture. Nothing less appeared to account for my not having, in the other age, done it, as the phrase is, full justice, recognized in it so excellent a peace, such a clear Boston bravery—all to the end that it should quite strike me, on the whole, as not only, for the minor stretch and the domestic note, the happiest street-scene the country could show, but as pleasant, on those respectable lines, in a degree not surpassed even among outland pomps. Oh, the wide benignity of brick, the goodly, friendly, ruddy fronts, the felicity of scale, the solid *seat* of everything, even to the handful of happy deviations from the regular produced, we may fancy, by one of those "historic" causes which so rarely complicate, for humanization, the blankness of the American street-page, and the occasional occurrence of which, in general, as I am perhaps too repeatedly noting, excites on the part of the starved story-seeker a fantastic insistence. I find myself willing, after all, to let my whole estimate of these mere mild monuments of private worth pass for extravagant if it but leave me a perch for musing on the oddity of our nature which makes us still like the places we have known or loved to grow old, when we can scarcely bear it in the people. To walk down Mount Vernon Street to Charles was to have a brush with that truth, to recognize at least that we like the sense of age to come, locally, when it comes with the right accompaniments, with the preservation of character and the continuity of tradition, merits I had been admiring on the brow of the eminence. From the other vision, the sight of the "decline in the social scale," the lapse into shabbiness and into bad company, we only suffer, for the ghosts in that case either refuse to linger, or linger at the most with faces ashamed and as if appealing against their association.

Such was the condition of the Charles Street ghosts, it seemed to me—shades of a past that had once been so thick and warm and happy; they moved, dimly, through a turbid medium in which the signs of their old life looked soiled and sordid. Each of them was there indeed, from far, far back; they met me on the pavement, yet it was as if we could pass but in conscious silence, and nothing could have helped us, for any courage of communion, if we had not enjoyed the one merciful refuge that remained, where indeed we could breathe again, and with intensity, our own liberal air. Here, behind the effaced anonymous door, was the little ark of the modern deluge, here still the long drawing-room that looks over the water and toward the sunset, with a seat for every visiting shade, from far-away Thackeray down, and relics and tokens so thick on its walls as to make it positively, in all the town, the votive temple to memory. Ah, if it hadn't been for *that* small patch of common ground, with its kept echo of the very accent of the past, the revisiting spirit, at the bottom of the hill, could but have muffled his head, or but have stifled his heart, and turned away for ever. Let me even say that—always now at the bottom of the hill—it was in this practical guise he afterwards, at the best, found himself roaming. It is from about that point southward that the new splendours of Boston spread, and will clearly continue to spread, but it opened out to me as a tract pompous and prosaic, with which the little interesting city, the city of character and genius, exempt as yet from the Irish yoke, had had absolutely nothing to do. This disconnection was complete, and the southward, the westward territory made up, at the most, a platform or stage from which the other, the concentrated Boston of history, the Boston of Emerson, Thoreau, Hawthorne, Longfellow, Lowell, Holmes, Ticknor, Motley, Prescott, Parkman and the rest (in the sense either of birthplace or of central or sacred city) could be seen in as definite, and indeed now in

almost as picturesquely mediæval, a concretion, appear to
make as black and minute and "composed" a little pyramidal
image, as the finished background of a Dürer print. It seemed
to place itself there, in the middle distance, on the sharp salience of its commingled Reforms and Reserves—reformers
and reservists rubbing shoulders in the common distinctness
of their detachment from an inexpressive generation, and the
composition rounding itself about as with the very last of its
loose ends snipped off or tucked in.

III

There are neither loose ends nor stray flutters, whether of
the old prose or the old poetry, to be encountered on the
large lower level, though there are performances of a different
order, in the shadow of which such matters tend to look
merely, and perhaps rather meagrely, subjective. It is all very
rich and prosperous and monotonous, the large lower level,
but oh, so inexpressibly vacant! Where the "new land" corresponds most to its name, rejoices most visibly and complacently in its newness, its dumped and shovelled foundations,
the home till recently of a mere vague marine backwater,
there the long, straight residential avenues, vistas quite documentary, as one finds one's self pronouncing them, testify
with a perfection all their own to a whole vast side of American life. The winter winds and snows, and the eternal dust,
run races in them over the clearest course anywhere provided
for that grim competition; the league-long brick pavements
mirror the expansive void, for many months of the year, in
their smooth, tight ice-coats (and ice over brick can only be
described as heels over head), and the innumerable windows,
up and down, watch each other, all hopelessly, as for revelations, indiscretions, audible, resonant, rebellious or explosive
breakages of the pane from within, that never disturb the
peace. (No one will begin, and the buried hatchet, in spite of
whatever wistful looks to where it lies, is never dug up.) So it
is that these sustained affirmations of one of the smoothest
and the most settled social states "going" excite perversely,
on the part of the restless analyst, questions that would seem
logically the very last involved. We call such aspects "docu-

mentary" because they strike us, more than any others, as speaking volumes for the possible *serenity*, the common decency, the quiet cohesion, of a vast commercial and professional bourgeoisie left to itself. Here was such an order caught in the very fact, the fact of its living maximum. A bourgeoisie without an aristocracy to worry it is of course a very different thing from a bourgeoisie struggling *in* that shade, and nothing could express more than these interminable perspectives of security the condition of a community leading its life in the social sun.

Why, accordingly, of December afternoons, did the restless analyst, pausing at eastward-looking corners, find on his lips the vague refrain of Tennyson's "long, unlovely street"? Why, if Harley Street, if Wimpole, is unlovely, should Marlborough Street, Boston, be so—beyond the mere platitude of its motiveless name? Here is no monotony of black leasehold brick, no patent disavowal, in the interest of stale and strictly subordinate gentilities, of expression, animation, variety, curiosity; here, on the contrary, is often the individual house-front in all its independence and sometimes in all its felicity: this whole region being, like so many such regions in the United States to-day, the home of the free hand, a field for the liveliest architectural experiment. There are interesting, admirable houses—though always too much of the detestable vitreous "bow"—and there is above all what there is everywhere in America for saving, or at least for propping up, the situation, that particular look of the clear course and large opportunity ahead, which, when taken in conjunction with all the will to live, all the money to spend, all the knowledge to acquire and apply, seems to marshal the material possibilities in glittering illimitable ranks. Beacon Street, moreover, used to stretch back like a workable telescope for the focussing, at its higher extremity, in an air of which the positive defect is to be too seldom prejudicial, of the gilded dome of the State House— fresh as a Christmas toy seen across the floor of a large salubrious nursery. This made a civic vignette that furnished a little the desert of cheerful family life. But Marlborough Street, for imperturbable reasons of its own, used periodically to break my heart. It was of no use to make a vow of hanging about till I should have sounded my mystery—learned to say *why* black, stale Harley Street, for instance, in featureless row after row, had character and depth, while what was before me fell upon my sense with the thinness of tone of a precocious child—and still more why this latter effect should have been, as it were, so insistently irritating. If there be strange ways of producing an interest, to the critical mind, there are doubtless still stranger ways of not producing one, and it was important to me, no doubt, to make "my" defunct and compact and expressive little Boston appear to don all the signs of that character that the New Land, and what is built thereon, miss. How could one consider the place at all unless in a light?—so that one had to decide definitely on one's light.

This it was after all easy to do from the moment one had determined to concede to the New Land the fact of possession of everything convenient and handsome under heaven. Peace could always come with this recognition of all the accessories and equipments, a hundred costly things, parks and palaces and institutions, that the earlier community had lacked; and there was an individual connection—only one, presently to be noted—in which the actual city might seem for an hour to have no capacity for the uplifting *idea*, no aptitude for the finer curiosity, to envy the past. But meanwhile it was strange that even so fine a conception, finely embodied, as the new Public Library, magnificently superseding all others, was committed to speak to one's inner perception still more of the power of the purse and of the higher turn for business than of the old intellectual, or even of the old moral, sensibility. Why else then should one have thought of some single, some admirable hour of Emerson, in one of the dusky, primitive lecture-halls that have ceased to be, or of some large insuperable anti-slavery eloquence of Wendell Phillips's, during the same term and especially during the War, as breathing more of the consciousness of literature and of history than all the promiscuous bustle of the Florentine palace by Copley Square? Not that this latter edifice, the fruit of immense considerations, has not its honourable interest too; which it would have if only in the light of the constant truth that almost any American application or practice of a general thought puts on a new and original aspect. Public libraries are a thoroughly general thought, and one has seen plenty of them, one is seeing dreadfully many, in these very days, the world over; yet to be confronted with an American example is to have sight straightway of more difference than community, and to glean on the spot fresh evidence of that democratic way of dealing which it has been the American office to translate from an academic phrase into a bristling fact. The notes of difference of the Florentine palace by Copley Square—more delicately elegant, in truth, if less sublimely rugged, than most Florentine palaces—resolve themselves, like so many such notes everywhere, into our impression here, once more, that every one is "in" everything, whereas in Europe so comparatively few persons are in anything (even as yet in "society," more and more the common refuge or retreat of the masses).

The Boston institution then is a great and complete institution, with this reserve of its striking the restored absentee as practically without *penetralia*. A library without *penetralia* may affect him but as a temple without altars; it will at any rate exemplify the distinction between a benefit given and a benefit taken, a borrowed, a lent, and an owned, an appropriated convenience. The British Museum, the Louvre, the Bibliothèque Nationale, the treasures of South Kensington, are assuredly, under forms, at the disposal of the people; but it is to be observed, I think, that the people walk there more or less under the shadow of the right waited for and conceded. It remains as difficult as it is always interesting, however, to trace the detail (much of it obvious enough, but much more indefinable) of the personal port of a democracy that, unlike the English, is social as well as political. One of these denotements is that social democracies are unfriendly to the preservation of *penetralia*; so that when *penetralia* are of the essence, as in a place of study and meditation, they inevitably go to the wall. The main staircase, in Boston, has, with its amplitude of wing and its splendour of tawny marble, a high and luxurious beauty—bribing the restored absentee to emotion, moreover, by expanding, monumentally, at one of its rests, into admirable commemoration of the Civil War service of the two great Massachusetts Volunteer regiments of *élite*. Such visions, such felicities, such couchant lions and recorded names and stirred memories as these, encountered in the early autumn twilight, *colour* an impression—even though to say so be the limit of breach of the silence in which, for persons of the generation of the author of these pages, appreciation of them can best take refuge: the refuge to which I felt myself anon reduced, for instance, opposite the State House, in presence of Saint-Gaudens's noble and exquisite monument to Robert Gould Shaw and the Fifty-fourth Massachusetts. There are works of memorial art that may suddenly place themselves, by their operation in a given case, outside articulate criticism—which was what happened, I found, in respect to the main feature, the rich staircase of the Library. Another way in which the bribe, as I have called it, of that masterpiece worked on the spot was by prompting one to immediate charmed perception of the character of the deep court and inner arcade of the palace, where a wealth of science and taste has gone to producing a sense, when the afternoon light sadly slants, of one of the myriad gold-coloured courts of the Vatican.

These are the refinements of the present Boston—keeping company as they can with the healthy animation, as it struck me, of the rest of the building, the multitudinous bustle, the coming and going, as in a railway-station, of persons with carpet-bags and other luggage, the simplicity of plan, the open doors and immediate accesses, admirable *for* a railway-station, the ubiquitous children, *most* irrepressible little democrats of the democracy, the vain quest, above all, of the deeper depths aforesaid, some part that should be sufficiently *within* some other part, sufficiently withdrawn and consecrated, not to constitute a thoroughfare. Perhaps I didn't adequately explore; but there was always the visible scale and scheme of the building. It was a shock to find the so brave decorative designs of Puvis de Chavannes, of Sargent and Abbey and John Elliott, hanging over mere chambers of familiarity and resonance; and then, I must quickly add, it was a shock still greater perhaps to find one had no good reason for defending them against such freedoms. What was sauce for the goose was sauce for the gander: had one not in other words, in the public places and under the great loggias of Italy, acclaimed it as just the charm and dignity of these resorts that, in their pictured and embroidered state, they still serve for the graceful common life? It was true that one had not been imprisoned in that consistency in the Laurentian, in the Ambrosian

Library—and at any rate one was here on the edge of abysses. Was it not splendid, for example, to see, in Boston, such large provision made for the amusement of children on rainy afternoons?—so many little heads bent over their story-books that the edifice took on at moments the appearance worn, one was to observe later on, by most other American edifices of the same character, that of a lively distributing-house of the new fiction for the young. The note was bewildering—yet would one, snatching the bread-and-molasses from their lips, cruelly deprive the young of rights in which they have been installed with a majesty nowhere else approaching that of their American installation? I am not wrong, probably, at all events, in qualifying such a question as that as abysmal, and I remember how, more than once, I took refuge from it in craven flight, straight across the Square, to the already so interesting, the so rapidly-expanding Art Museum.

There, for some reason, questions exquisitely dropped; perhaps only for the reason that things sifted and selected have, very visibly, the effect of challenging the confidence even of the rash. It is of the nature of objects doomed to show distinction that they virtually make a desert round them, and peace reigned unbroken, I usually noted, in the two or three Museum rooms that harbour a small but deeply-interesting and steadily-growing collection of fragments of the antique. Here the restless analyst found work to his hand—only too much; and indeed in presence of the gem of the series, of the perhaps just too conscious grace of a certain little wasted and dim-eyed head of Aphrodite, he felt that his function should simply give way, in common decency, to that of the sonneteer. For it is an impression by itself, and I think quite worth the Atlantic voyage, to catch in the American light the very fact of the genius of Greece. There are things we don't know, feelings not to be foretold, till we have had that experience—which I commend to the *raffiné* of almost any other clime. I should say to him that he has not *seen* a fine Greek thing till he has seen it in America. It is of course on the face of it the most merciless case of transplanting—the mere moral of which, none the less, for application, becomes by no means flagrant. The little Aphrodite, with her connections, her antecedents and references exhibiting the maximum of breakage, is no doubt as *lonely* a jewel as ever strayed out of its setting; yet what does one quickly recognize but that the intrinsic lustre will have, so far as that may be possible, doubled? She has lost her background, the divine creature—has lost her company, and is keeping, in a manner, the strangest; but so far from having lost an iota of her power, she has gained unspeakably more, since what she essentially stands for she here stands for alone, rising ineffably to the occasion. She has in short, by her single presence, as yet, annexed an empire, and there are strange glimmers of moments when, as I have spoken of her consciousness, the very knowledge of this seems to lurk in the depth of her beauty. Where was she ever more, where was she ever so much, a goddess—and who knows but that, being thus divine, she foresees the time when, as she has "moved over," the place of her actual whereabouts will have become one of her shrines? Objects doomed to distinction make round them a desert, I have said; but that is only for any gross confidence in other matters. For confidence in *them* they make a garden, and that is why I felt this quarter of the Boston Art Museum bloom, under the indescribable dim eyes, with delicate flowers. The impression swallowed up every other; the place, whatever it was, was supremely justified, and I was left cold by learning that a much bigger and grander and richer place is presently to overtop it.

The present establishment "dates back," back almost to the good Boston of the middle years, and is full of all sorts of accumulated and concentrated pleasantness; which fact precisely gives the signal, by the terrible American law, for its coming to an end and giving a chance to the untried. It is a consistent application of the rotary system—the untried always awaiting its turn, and quite perceptibly stamping and snorting while it waits; all heedless as it is, poor innocent untried, of the certain hour of the impatiences before which it too will have to retreat. It is not indeed that the American laws, so operating, have not almost always their own queer interest; founded as they are, all together, on one of the strongest of the native impulses. We see this characteristic again and again at play, see it in especial wherever we see (which is more than frequently enough) a university or a college "started" or amplified. This process almost always takes the form, primarily, of more lands and houses and halls and rooms, more swimming-baths and football-fields and gymnasia, a greater luxury of brick and mortar, a greater ingenuity, the most artful conceivable, of accommodation and installation. Such is the magic, such the presences, that tend, more than any other, to figure *as* the Institution, thereby perverting not a little, as need scarce be remarked, the finer collegiate idea: the theory being, doubtless, and again most characteristically, that with all the wrought stone and oak and painted glass, the immense provision, the multiplied marbles and tiles and cloisters and acres, "people will come," that is, individuals of value will, and in some manner work some miracle. In the early American time, doubtless, individuals of value had to wait too much for things; but that is now made up by the way things are waiting for individuals of value. To which I must immediately add, however—and it is the ground of my allusion of a moment ago—that no impression of the "new" Boston can feel itself hang together without remembrance of what it owes to that rare exhibition of the living spirit lately achieved, in the interest of the fine arts, and of all that is noblest in them, by the unaided and quite heroic genius of a private citizen. To attempt to tell the story of the wonderfully-gathered and splendidly-lodged Gardner Collection would be to displace a little the line that separates private from public property; and yet to find no discreet word for it is to appear to fail of feeling for the complexity of conditions amid which so undaunted a devotion to a great idea (undaunted by the battle to fight, losing, alas, with State Protection of native art, and with other scarce less uncanny things) has been able consummately to flower. It is in presence of the results magnificently attained, the energy triumphant over everything, that one feels the fine old disinterested tradition of Boston least broken.

VIII

Concord and Salem

I

I FELT myself, on the spot, cast about a little for the right expression of it, and then lost any hesitation to say that, putting the three or four biggest cities aside, Concord, Massachusetts, had an identity more palpable to the mind, had nestled in other words more successfully beneath her narrow fold of the mantle of history, than any other American town. "Compare me with places of my size, you know," one seemed to hear her plead, with the modesty that, under the mild autumn sun, so well became her russet beauty; and this exactly it was that prompted the emphasis of one's reply, or, as it may even be called, of one's declaration.

"Ah, my dear, it isn't a question of places of your 'size,' since among places of your size you're too obviously and easily first: it's a question of places, so many of them, of fifty times your size, and which yet don't begin to have a fraction of your weight, or your character, or your intensity of presence and sweetness of tone, or your moral charm, or your pleasant appreciability, or, in short, of anything that is yours. Your 'size'? Why, you're the biggest little place in America—with only New York and Boston and Chicago, by what I make out, to surpass you; and the country is lucky indeed to have you, in your sole and single felicity, for if it hadn't, where in the world should we go, inane and unappeased, for the particular communication of which you have the secret? The country is colossal, and you but a microscopic speck on the hem of its garment; yet there's nothing else like you, take you all round, for we *see* you complacently, with the naked eye, whereas there are vast sprawling, bristling areas, great grey 'centres of population' that spread, on the map, like irremediable grease-spots, which fail utterly of any appeal to our vision or any control of it, leaving it to pass them by as if they were not. If you are so thoroughly the opposite of one of these I don't say it's all your superlative merit; it's rather, as I have put it, your felicity, your good fortune, the result of the half-dozen happy turns of the wheel in your favour. Half-a-dozen such turns, you see, are, for any mortal career, a handsome allowance; and your merit is that, recognizing this, you have not fallen below your estate. But it's your fortune, above all, that's your charm. One doesn't want to be patronizing, but you didn't, thank goodness, make yours. That's what the other places, the big ones that are as nothing to you, are trying to do, the country over—to make theirs; and, from the point of view of these remarks, all in vain. Your luck is that you didn't have to; yours had been, just as it shows in you to-day, made *for* you, and you at the most but gratefully submitted to it. It must be said for you, however, that you keep it; and it isn't every place that would have been capable——! You keep the look, you keep the feeling, you keep the air. Your great trees arch over these possessions more protectingly, covering them in as a cherished presence; and you have settled to your tone and your type as to treasures that can now never be taken. Show me the other places in America (of the few that have *had* anything) from which the best hasn't mainly been taken, or isn't in imminent danger of being. There is old Salem, there is old Newport, which I am on my way to see again, and which, if you will, are, by what I hear, still comparatively intact; but their having was never a having like yours, and they adorn, precisely, my little tale of your supremacy. No, I don't want to be patronizing, but your only fault is your tendency to improve—I mean just by your duration as you *are*; which indeed is the only sort of improvement that is not questionable."

Such was the drift of the warm flood of appreciation, of reflection, that Concord revisited could set rolling over the field of a prepared sensibility; and I feel as if I had quite made my point, such as it is, in asking what other American village could have done anything of the sort. I should have been at fault perhaps only in speaking of the interest in question as visible, on that large scale, to the "naked eye"; the truth being perhaps that one wouldn't have been so met half-way by one's impression unless one had rather particularly *known*, and that knowledge, in such a case, amounts to a pair of magnifying spectacles. I remember indeed putting it to myself on the November Sunday morning, tepid and bright and perfect for its use, through which I walked from the station under the constant archway of the elms, as yet but indulgently thinned: would one know, for one's self, what had formerly been the matter here, if one hadn't happened to be able to get round behind, in the past, as it were, and more or less understand? Would the operative elements of the past—little old Concord Fight, essentially, and Emerson and Hawthorne and Thoreau, with the rest of the historic animation and the rest of the figured and shifting "transcendental" company, to its last and loosest ramifications—would even these handsome quantities have so lingered to one's intelligent after-sense, if one had not brought with one some sign by which they too would know; dim, shy spectralities as, for themselves, they must, at the best, have become? Idle, however, such questions when, by the chance of the admirable day, everything, in its own way and order, unmistakably came *out*—every string sounded as if, for all the world, the loose New England town (and I apply the expression but to the relations of objects and places), were a lyre swept by the hand of Apollo. Apollo was the spirit of antique piety, looking about, pausing, remembering, as he moved to his music; and there were glimpses and reminders that of course kept him much longer than others.

Seated there at its ease, as if placidly familiar with pilgrims and quite taking their homage for granted, the place had the very aspect of some grave, refined New England matron of the "old school," the widow of a high celebrity, living on and on in possession of all his relics and properties, and, though not personally addicted to gossip or to journalism, having become, where the great company kept by her in the past is concerned, quite cheerful and modern and responsive. From her position, her high-backed chair by the window that commands most of the coming and going, she looks up intelligently, over her knitting, with no vision of any limit on her part as yet, to this attitude, and with nothing indeed to suggest the possibility of a limit save a hint of that loss of temporal perspective in which we recognize the mental effect of a great weight of years. I had formerly the acquaintance of a very interesting lady, of extreme age, whose early friends, in "literary circles," are now regarded as classics, and who, toward the end of her life, always said, "You know Charles Lamb has produced a play at Drury Lane," or "You know William Hazlitt has fallen in love with such a very odd woman." Her facts were perfectly correct; only death had beautifully passed out of her world—since I don't remember her mentioning to me the demise, which she might have made so contemporary, either of Byron or of Scott. When people were ill she admirably forebore to ask about them—she disapproved wholly of such conditions; and there were interesting invalids round about her, near to her, whose existence she for long years consummately ignored. It is some such quiet backward stride as those of my friend that I seem to hear the voice of old Concord take in reference to her annals, and it is not too much to say that where her soil is most sacred, I fairly caught, on the breeze, the mitigated perfect tense. "You know there has been a fight between our men and the King's"—one wouldn't have been surprised, that crystalline Sunday noon, where so little had changed, where the stream and the bridge, and all nature, and the *feeling*, above all, still so directly testify, at any fresh-sounding form of such an announcement.

I had forgotten, in all the years, with what thrilling clearness that supreme site speaks—though anciently, while so much of the course of the century was still to run, the distinctness might have seemed even greater. But to stand there again was to take home this foreshortened view, the gained nearness, to one's sensibility; to look straight over the heads of the "American Weimar" company at the inestimable hour that had so handsomely set up for them their background. The Fight had been the hinge—so one saw it—on which the large revolving future was to turn; or it had been better, perhaps, the large firm nail, ringingly driven in, from which the beautiful portrait-group, as we see it to-day, was to hang. Beautiful exceedingly the local Emerson and Thoreau and Hawthorne and (in a fainter way) *tutti quanti*; but beautiful largely because the fine old incident down in the valley had so seriously prepared their effect. That seriousness gave once for all the pitch, and it was verily as if, under such a value, even with the seed of a "literary circle" so freely scattered by an intervening hand, the vulgar note would in that air never be possible. As I had inevitably, in long absence, let the value, for immediate perception, rather waste itself, so, on the spot, it came back most instantly with the extraordinary sweetness of the river, which, under the autumn sun, like all the American rivers one had seen or was to see, straightway took the whole case straightway into its hands. "Oh, you shall tell me of your impression when you have felt what *I* can do for it: so hang over me well!"—that's what they all seem to say.

I hung over Concord River then as long as I could, and recalled how Thoreau, Hawthorne, Emerson himself, have expressed with due sympathy the sense of this full, slow, sleepy, meadowy flood, which sets its pace and takes its twists like some large obese benevolent person, scarce so frankly unsociable as to pass you at all. It had watched the Fight, it even now confesses, without a quickening of its current, and it draws along the woods and the orchards and the fields with the purr of a mild domesticated cat who rubs against the family and the furniture. Not to be recorded, at best, however, I think, never to emerge from the state of the inexpressible, in respect to the spot, by the bridge, where one most lingers, is the sharpest suggestion of the whole scene—the power diffused in it which makes it, after all these years, or perhaps indeed by reason of their number, so irresistibly touching. All the commemorative objects, the stone marking the burial-place of the three English soldiers, the animated image of the young belted American yeoman by Mr. Daniel French, the intimately associated element in the presence, not far off, of the old manse, interesting theme of Hawthorne's pen, speak to the spirit, no doubt, in one of the subtlest tones of which official history is capable, and yet somehow leave the exquisite melancholy of everything unuttered. It lies too deep, as it always so lies where the ground has borne the weight of the short, simple act, intense and unconscious, that was to determine the event, determine the future in the way we call immortally. For we read into the scene too little of what we may, unless this muffled touch in it somehow reaches us so that we feel the pity and the irony of the *precluded* relation on the part of the fallen defenders. The sense that was theirs and that moved them we know, but we seem to know better still the sense that wasn't and that couldn't, and that forms our luxurious heritage as our eyes, across the gulf, seek to meet their eyes; so that we are almost ashamed of taking so much, such colossal quantity and value, as the equivalent of their dimly-seeing offer. The huge bargain they made for us, in a word, made by the gift of the little all they had—to the modesty of which amount the homely rural facts grouped there together have appeared to go on testifying—this brilliant advantage strikes the imagination that yearns over them as unfairly enjoyed at their cost. Was it delicate, was it decent— that is *would* it have been—to ask the embattled farmers, simple-minded, unwitting folk, to make us so inordinate a present with so little of the conscious credit of it? Which all comes indeed, perhaps, simply to the most poignant of all those effects of disinterested sacrifice that the toil and trouble of our forefathers produce for us. The minute-men at the bridge were of course interested intensely, as they believed— but such, too, was the artful manner in which we see *our* latent, lurking, waiting interest, like a Jew in a dusky back-shop, providentially bait the trap.

Beyond even such broodings as these, and to another purpose, moreover, the communicated spell falls, in its degree, into that pathetic oddity of the small aspect, and the rude and the lowly, the reduced and humiliated above all, that sits on so many nooks and corners, objects and appurtenances, old contemporary things—contemporary with the doings of our race; simplifying our antecedents, our annals, to within an inch of their life, making us ask, in presence of the rude relics even of greatness, mean retreats and receptacles, construction-ally so poor, from what barbarians or from what pigmies we have sprung. There are certain rough black mementos of the early monarchy, in England and Scotland, there are glimpses of the original humble homes of other greatness as well, that strike in perfection this grim little note; which has the interest of our being free to take it, for curiosity, for luxury of thought, as that of the real or that of the romantic, and with which, again, the deep Concord rusticity, momentary medium of our national drama, essentially consorts. We remember the small hard facts of the Shakespeare house at Stratford; we remember the rude closet, in Edinburgh Castle, in which

James VI of Scotland was born, or the other little black hole, at Holyrood, in which Mary Stuart "sat" and in which Rizzio was murdered. These, I confess, are odd memories at Concord; although the manse, near the spot where we last paused, and against the edge of whose acre or two the loitering river seeks friction in the manner I have mentioned, would now seem to have shaken itself a trifle disconcertingly free of the ornamental mosses scattered by Hawthorne's light hand; it stands there, beyond its gate, with every due similitude to the shrunken historic site in general. To which I must hasten to add, however, that I was much more struck with the way these particular places of visitation resist their pressure of reference than with their affecting us as below their fortune. Intrinsically they are as naught—deeply depressing, in fact, to any impulse to reconstitute, the house in which Hawthorne spent what remained to him of life after his return from the Italy of his Donatello and his Miriam. Yet, in common with everything else, this mild monument benefits by that something in the air which makes us tender, keeps us respectful; meets, in the general interest, waving it vaguely away, any closer assault of criticism.

It is odd, and it is also exquisite, that these witnessing ways should be the last ground on which we feel moved to ponderation of the "Concord school"—to use, I admit, a futile expression; or rather, I should doubtless say, it *would* be odd if there were not inevitably something absolute in the fact of Emerson's all but lifelong connection with them. We may smile a little as we "drag in" Weimar, but I confess myself, for my part, much more satisfied than not by our happy equivalent, "in American money," for Goethe and Schiller. The money is a potful in the second case as in the first, and if Goethe, in the one, represents the gold and Schiller the silver, I find (and quite putting aside any bimetallic prejudice) the same good relation in the other between Emerson and Thoreau. I open Emerson for the same benefit for which I open Goethe, the sense of moving in large intellectual space, and that of the gush, here and there, out of the rock, of the crystalline cupful, in wisdom and poetry, in Wahrheit and Dichtung; and whatever I open Thoreau for (I needn't take space here for the good reasons) I open him oftener than I open

Schiller. Which comes back to our feeling that the rarity of Emerson's genius, which has made him so, for the attentive peoples, the first, and the one really rare, American spirit in letters, couldn't have spent his career in a charming woody, watery place, for so long socially and typically and, above all, interestingly homogeneous, without an effect as of the communication to it of something ineffaceable. It was during his long span his immediate concrete, sufficient world; it gave him his nearest vision of life, and he drew half his images, we recognize, from the revolution of its seasons and the play of its manners. I don't speak of the other half, which he drew from elsewhere. It is admirably, to-day, as if we were still seeing these things *in* those images, which stir the air like birds, dim in the eventide, coming home to nest. If one had reached a "time of life" one had thereby at least heard him lecture; and not a russet leaf fell for me, while I was there, but fell with an Emersonian drop.

II

It never failed that if in moving about I made, under stress, an inquiry, I should prove to have made it of a flagrant foreigner. It never happened that, addressing a fellow-citizen, in the street, on one of those hazards of possible communion with the indigenous spirit, I should not draw a blank. So, inevitably, at Salem, when, wandering perhaps astray, I asked my way to the House of the Seven Gables, the young man I had overtaken was true to his nature; he stared at me as a remorseless Italian—as remorseless, at least, as six months of Salem could leave him. On that spot, in that air, I confess, it was a particular shock to me to be once more, with my so good general intention, so "put off"; though, if my young man but glared frank ignorance of the monument I named, he left me at least with the interest of wondering how the native estimate of it as a romantic ruin might strike a taste formed for such features by the landscape of Italy. I will not profess that by the vibration of this note the edifice of my fond fancy—I mean Hawthorne's Salem, and the witches', and that of other eminent historic figures—was not rather essentially shaken; since what had the intention of my pilgrimage been, in all good faith, in artless sympathy and piety, but a search again, precisely, for the New England homogeneous—for the renewal of that impression of it which had lingered with me from a vision snatched too briefly, in a midsummer gloaming, long years ago. I had been staying near, at that far-away time, and, the railroad helping, had got myself dropped there for an hour at just the right moment of the waning day. This memory had been, from far back, a kept felicity altogether; a picture of goodly Colonial habitations, quite the high-water mark of that type of state and ancientry, seen in the clear dusk, and of almost nothing else but a pleasant harbour-side vacancy, the sense of dead marine industries, that finally looked out at me, for a climax, over a grass-grown interval, from the blank windows of the old Customs House of the Introduction to *The Scarlet Letter*.

I could on that occasion have seen, with my eye on my return-train, nothing else; but the image of these things I had not lost, wrapped up as it even was, for the fancy, in some figment of the very patch of old embroidered cloth that Hawthorne's charming prefatory pages unfold for us—pages in which the words are as finely "taken" as the silk and gold stitches of poor Hester Prynne's compunctious needle. It had hung, all the years, closely together, and had served—oh, so conveniently!—as the term of comparison, the rather rich frame, for any suggested vision of New England life unalloyed. The case now was the more marked that, already, on emerging from the station and not knowing quite where to look again for my goodly Georgian and neo-Georgian houses, I had had to permit myself to be directed to them by a civil Englishman, accosted by the way, who, all kindness and sympathy, immediately mentioned that they formed the Grosvenor Square, as might be said, of Salem. We conversed for the moment, and settled, as he told me, in the town, he was most sustaining; but when, a little later on, I stood there in admiration of the noble quarter, I could only feel, even while doing it every justice, that the place was not quite what my imagination had counted on. It was possibly even better, for the famous houses, almost without exception ample and charming, seemed to me to show a grace even beyond my recollection; the only thing was that I had never bargained for

looking at them through a polyglot air. Look at them none
the less, and at the fine old liberal scale, and felt symmetry,
and simple dignity, and solid sincerity of them, I gratefully
did, with due speculation as to their actual chances and
changes, as to what they represent to-day as social "values,"
and with a lively impression, above all, of their preserved and
unsophisticated state. That was a social value—which I found
myself comparing, for instance, with similar aspects, frequent
and excellent, in old English towns.

The Salem houses, the best, were all of the old English
family, and, from picture to picture, all the parts would have
matched; but the moral, the social, the political climate, even
more than the breath of nature, had had in each case a different action, had begotten on either side a different consciousness. Or was it nearer even to say that these things had on
one side begotten a consciousness, and had on the other begotten comparatively none? The approximation would have
been the more interesting as each arrayed group might pass
for a supreme expression of respectability. It would be the
tone and weight, the quantity and quality, of the respectability that make the difference; massive and square-shouldered,
yet rather battered and mottled, chipped and frayed, at last
rather sceptical and cynical, in fine, in the English figure—
thin and clear, consistently sharp, boldly unspotted, blankly
serene, in the American. It was more amusing at any rate to
spin such fancies, in reaction from the alien snub, than simply
to see one's antitheses reduced to a mere question of the effect
of climate. There would be yet more to say for the Salem
picture, many of the "bits" of which remain, as Ruskin might
have put it, entirely delightful; but their desperate clean freshness was what was more to abide with me after the polyglot
air had cleared a little. The spacious, courteous doorways of
the houses, expansively columned, fluted, framed; their large
honest windows, in ample tiers, only here and there dishonoured by the modern pane; their high bland foreheads, in
short, with no musty secrets in the eaves—yes, not one, in
spite of the "speciality," in this respect, of the Seven Gables,
to which I am coming—clarify too much perhaps the expressive mask, the look of experience, depress the balance toward

the type of the expensive toy, shown on its shelf, but too good to be humanly used. It's as if the old witches had been suffered to live again, penally, as public housemaids, using nocturnally, for purposes of almost viciously-thorough purification, the famous broomsticks they used wantonly to ride.

Was it a sacred terror, after this, that stayed me from crossing the threshold of the Witch House? — in spite of the quite definite sturdy stamp of this attraction. I think it was an almost sacred tenderness rather, the instinct of not pressing too hard on my privilege and of not draining the offered cup to the lees. It is always interesting, in America, to see any object, some builded thing in particular, look as old as it possibly can; for the sight of which effort we sometimes hold our breath as if to watch, over the course of the backward years, the straight "track" of the past, the course of some hero of the foot-race on whom we have staked our hopes. How long will he hold out, how far back will he run, and where, heroically blown, will he have to drop? Our suspense is great in proportion to our hope, and if we are nervously constituted we may very well, at the last, turn away for anxiety. It was really in some such manner I was affected, I think, before the Salem Witch House, in presence of the mystery of antiquity. It is a modest wooden structure, consciously primitive, standing, if I remember rightly, in some effective relation to a street-corner and putting no little purpose into its archaism. The pity is, however, that unrelieved wooden houses never very curiously testify — as I was presently to learn, to my cost, from the dreadful anti-climax of the Seven Gables. They look brief and provisional at the best — look, above all, incorrigibly and witlessly innocent. The quite sufficiently sturdy little timbered mass by the Salem street, none the less, with a sidelong crook or twist that we may take as symbolizing ancient perversity, runs the backward race as long-windedly as we may anywhere, over the land, see it run. Had I gone in, as a frank placard invited me, I might have better measured the exploit; yet, on the other hand, fearing frank placards, in general, in these cases, fearing nothing so much as reconstituted antiquity, I might have lost a part of my good little impression — which otherwise, as a small pale flower plucked from a withered tree, I could fold away, intact, between the leaves of my romantic herbarium.

I wanted, moreover, to be honest, not to fail, within the hour, of two other urgent matters, my train away (my sense of Salem was too destined to be train-haunted) and a due visitation of the Seven Gables and of the birth-house of their chronicler. It was in the course of this errand that I was made to feel myself, as I have mentioned, living, rather witlessly, in a world unknown to the active Salemite of to-day—a world embodied, I seemed to make out, in the large untidy indus-trial quarter that had sprung up since my early visit. Did I quite escape from this impression before alighting at last hap-pily upon the small stale structure that had sheltered the ro-mancer's entrance into life and that now appears, according to the preference of fancy, either a strange recipient of the romantic germ or the very spot to cause it, in protest and desperation, to develop? I took the neighbourhood, at all events, for the small original Hawthornesque world, keeping the other, the smoky modernism, at a distance, keeping every-thing, in fact, at a distance—on so spare and bare and lean and mean a face did the bright hard sky strike me as looking down. The way to think of it evidently was in some frank rural light of the past, that of all the ancient New England simplicities, with the lap of wide waters and the stillness of rocky pastures never far off (they seem still indeed close at hand), and with any number of our present worryings and pamperings of the "literary temperament" too little in ques-tion to be missed. It kept at a distance, in fact, so far as my perception was concerned, everything but a little boy, a dear little harsh, intelligent, sympathetic American boy, who dropped straight from the hard sky for my benefit (I hadn't seen him emerge from elsewhere) and turned up at my side with absolute confidence and with the most knowing tips. He might have been a Weimar tout or a Stratford amateur—only he so beautifully wasn't. That is what I mean by my having alighted happily; the little boy was so completely master of his subject, and we formed, on the spot, so close an alliance. He made up to me for my crude Italian—the way they *become* crude over here!—he made up to me a little even for my civil Englishman; he was exactly what I wanted—a presence (and he was the only thing far or near) old enough, native and intimate enough, to reach back and to understand.

He showed me the window of the room in which Hawthorne had been born; wild horses, as the phrase is, wouldn't have dragged me into it, but *he* might have done so if he hadn't, as I say, understood. But he understood everything, and knew when to insist and when not to; knew, for instance, exactly why I said "Dear, dear, are you very sure?" after he had brought me to sight of an object at the end of a lane, by a vague waterside, I think, and looking across to Marblehead, that he invited me to take, if I could, for the Seven Gables. I couldn't take it in the least, as happens, and though he was perfectly sure, our reasons, on either side, were equally clear to him—so that in short I think of him as the very genius of the place, feeding his small shrillness on the cold scraps of Hawthorne's leaving and with the making of his acquaintance alone worth the journey. Yet the fact that, the Seven Gables being in question, the shapeless object by the waterside wouldn't do at all, not the least little bit, troubled us only till we had thrown off together, with a quick, competent gesture and at the breaking of light, the poor illusion of a *necessity* of relation between the accomplished thing, for poetry, for art, and those other quite equivocal things that we inflate our ignorance with seeing it suggested by. The weak, vague domiciliary presence at the end of the lane may have "been" (in our poor parlance) the idea of the admirable book—though even here we take a leap into dense darkness; but the idea that is the inner force of the admirable book so vividly forgets, before our eyes, any such origin or reference, "cutting" it dead as a low acquaintance and outsoaring the shadow of its night, that the connection has turned a somersault into space, repudiated like a ladder kicked back from the top of a wall. Hawthorne's ladder at Salem, in fine, has now quite gone, and we but tread the air if we attempt to set our critical feet on its steps and its rounds, learning thus as we do, and with infinite interest as I think, how merely "subjective" in us are our discoveries about genius. Endless are its ways of besetting and eluding, of meeting and mocking us. When there are appearances that might have nourished it we see it as swallowing them all; yet we see it as equally gorged when there are no appearances at all—*then* most of all, sometimes, quite insolently bloated; and we recognize ruefully that we are forever condemned to know it only after the fact.

IX

Philadelphia

I

To be at all critically, or as we have been fond of calling it, analytically, minded—over and beyond an inherent love of the general many-coloured picture of things—is to be subject to the superstition that objects and places, coherently grouped, disposed for human use and addressed to it, must have a sense of their own, a mystic meaning proper to themselves to give out: to give out, that is, to the participant at once so interested and so detached as to be moved to a report of the matter. That perverse person is obliged to take it for a working theory that the essence of almost any settled aspect of anything may be extracted by the chemistry of criticism, and may give us its right name, its formula, for convenient use. From the moment the critic finds himself sighing, to save trouble in a difficult case, that the cluster of appearances can *have* no sense, from that moment he begins, and quite consciously, to go to pieces; it being the prime business and the high honour of the painter of life always to *make* a sense—and to make it most in proportion as the immediate aspects are loose or confused. The last thing decently permitted him is to recognize incoherence—to recognize it, that is, as baffling; though of course he may present and portray it, in all richness, *for* incoherence. That, I think, was what I had been mainly occupied with in New York; and I quitted so qualified a joy, under extreme stress of winter, with a certain confidence that I should not have moved even a little of the way southward without practical relief: relief which came in fact ever so promptly, at Philadelphia, on my feeling, unmistakably, the change of half the furniture of consciousness. This change put on, immediately, the friendliest, the handsomest aspect—supplied my intelligence on the spot with the clear, the salient note. I mean by this, not that the happy definition or synthesis instantly came—came with the perception that

579

character and sense were there, only waiting to be disengaged; but that the note, as I say, was already, within an hour, the germ of these things, and that the whole flower, assuredly, wouldn't fail to bloom. I was in fact sniffing up its fragrance after I had looked out for three minutes from one of the windows of a particularly wide-fronted house and seen the large residential square that lay before me shine in its native light. This light, remarkably tender, I thought, for that of a winter afternoon, matched with none other I had ever seen, and announced straight off fifty new circumstances—an enormous number, in America, for any prospect to promise you in contradistinction from any other. It was not simply that, beyond a doubt, the outlook was more *méridional*; a still deeper impression had begun to work, and, as I felt it more and more glimmer upon me, I caught myself about to jump, with a single leap, to my synthesis. I of course stayed myself in the act, for there would be too much, really, yet to come; but the perception left me, I even then felt, in possession of half the ground on which later experience would proceed. It was not too much to say, as I afterwards saw, that I had in those few illumined moments put the gist of the matter into my pocket.

Philadelphia, incontestably then, was the American city of the large type, that didn't *bristle*—just as I was afterwards to recognize in St. Louis the nearest approach to companionship with her in this respect; and to recognize in Chicago, I may parenthetically add, the most complete divergence. It was not only, moreover, at the ample, tranquil window there, that Philadelphia *didn't* "bristle" (by the record of my moment) but that she essentially couldn't and wouldn't ever; that no movement or process could be thought of, in fine, as more foreign to her genius. I do not just now go into the question of what the business of bristling, in an American city, may be estimated as consisting of; so infallibly is one aware when the thousand possible quills *are* erect, and when, haply, they are not—such a test does the restored absentee find, at least, in his pricked sensibility. A place may abound in its own sense, as the phrase is, without bristling in the least—it is liable indeed to bristle most, I think, when not too securely possessed of any settled sense to abound in. An imperfect grasp of such a luxury is not the weakness of Philadelphia—just as that admirable comprehensive flatness in her which precludes the image of the porcupine figured to me from the first, precisely, as her positive source of strength. The absence of the note of the perpetual perpendicular, the New York, the Chicago note—and I allude here to the material, the constructional exhibition of it—seemed to symbolize exactly the principle of indefinite level extension and to offer refreshingly, a challenge to horizontal, to lateral, to more or less tangental, to rotary, or, better still, to absolute centrifugal motion. If it was to befall me, during my brief but various acquaintance with the place, not to find myself more than two or three times hoisted or lowered by machinery, my prime illumination had been an absolute forecast of that immunity—a virtue of general premonition in it at which I have already glanced. I should in fact, I repeat, most truly or most artfully repaint my little picture by mixing my colours with the felt amenity of that small crisis, and by showing how this, that and the other impression to come had had, while it lasted, quite the definite prefigurement that the chapters of a book find in its table of contents. The afternoon blandness, for a fugitive from Madison Avenue in January snow, didn't mean nothing; the little marble steps and lintels and cornices and copings, all the so clear, so placed accents in the good prose text of the mildly purple houses across the Square, which seemed to wear them, as all the others did, up and down the streets, in the manner of nice white stockings, neckties, collars, cuffs, didn't mean nothing; and this was somehow an assurance that joined on to the vibration of the view produced, a few hours before, by so merely convenient a circumstance as my taking my place, at Jersey City, in the Pennsylvania train.

I had occasion, repeatedly, to find the Pennsylvania Railroad a beguiling and predisposing influence—in relation to various objectives; and indeed I quite lost myself in the singularity of this effect, which existed for me, certainly, only in that connection, touching me with a strange and most agreeable sense that the great line in question, an institution with a style and *allure* of its own, is not, even the world over, as other railroads are. It absolutely, with a little frequentation, affected me as better and higher than its office or function, and almost as supplying one with a mode of life intrinsically superior; as if it ought really to be on its way to much grander and more charming places than any that happen to mark its course—as if indeed, should one persistently keep one's seat, not getting out anywhere, it would in the end carry one to some such ideal city. One might under this extravagant spell, which always began to work for me at Twenty-third Street, and on the constantly-adorable Ferry, have fancied the train, disvulgarized of passengers, steaming away, in disinterested empty form, to some terminus too noble to be marked in *our* poor schedules. The consciousness of this devotion would have been thus like that of living, all sublimely, up in a balloon. It was not, however—I recover myself—that if I had been put off at Philadelphia I was not, for the hour, contented; finding so immediately, as I have noted, more interest to my hand than I knew at first what to do with. There was the quick light of explanation, following on everything else I have mentioned—the light in which I had only to turn round again and see where I was, and how it was, in order to feel everything "come out" under the large friendliness, the ordered charm and perfect peace of the Club, housing me with that *whole* protection the bestowal of which on occasion is the finest grace of the hospitality of American clubs. Philadelphia, manifestly, was beyond any other American city, a *society*, and was going to show as such, as a thoroughly confirmed and settled one—which fact became the key, precisely, to its extension on one plane, and to its having no pretext for bristling. Human groups that discriminate in their own favour do, one remembers, in general, bristle; but that is only when they have not been really successful, when they have not been able to discriminate enough, when they are not, like Philadelphia, settled and confirmed and content. It would clearly be impossible not to regard the place before me as possessed of this secret of serenity to a degree elsewhere—at least among ourselves—unrivalled. The basis of the advantage, the terms of the secret, would be still to make out—which was precisely the high interest; and I was afterwards to be justified of my conviction by the multiplication of my lights.

New York, in that sense, had appeared to me then not a society at all, and it was rudimentary that Chicago would be one still less; neither of them, as a human group, having been able to discriminate in its own favour with anything like such success. The proof of that would be, obviously, in one's so easily imputing to them alteration, extension, development; a change somehow unimaginable in the case of Philadelphia, which was a fixed quantity and had filled to the brim, one felt—and wasn't that really to be part of the charm?—the measure of her possibility. Boston even was thinkable as subject to mutation; had I not in fact just seemed to myself to catch her in the almost uncanny inconsequence of change? There had been for Boston the old epigram that she wasn't a place, but a state of mind; and that might remain, since we know how frequently states of mind alter. Philadelphia then wasn't a place, but a state of consanguinity, which is an absolute final condition. She had arrived at it, with nothing in the world left to bristle for, or against; whereas New York, and above all Chicago, were only, and most precariously, on the way to it, and indeed, having started too late, would probably never arrive. There were, for them, interferences and complications; they knew, and would yet know, other conditions, perhaps other beatitudes; only the beatitude I speak of—that of being, in the composed sense, a society—was lost to them forever. Philadelphia, without complications or interferences, enjoyed it in particular through having begun to invoke it in time. And now she had nothing more to invoke; she had everything; her *cadres* were all full; her imagination was at peace. This, exactly again, would be the reason of the bristling of the other places: the *cadres* of New York, Chicago, Boston, being as to a third of them empty and as to another third objectionably filled—with much consequent straining, reaching, heaving, both to attain and to eject. What makes a society was thus, more than anything else, the number of organic social relations it represents; by which logic Philadelphia would represent nothing *but* organic social relations. The degrees of consanguinity were the *cadres*; every one of them was full; it was a society in which every individual was as many times over cousin, uncle, aunt, niece, and so on through the list, as poor human nature is susceptible of being. These degrees are, when one reflects, the only really organic social relations, and when they are all there for every one the scheme of security, in a community, has been worked out. Philadelphia, in other words, would not only be a family, she would be a "happy" one, and a probable proof that the happiness comes as a matter of course if the family but be large enough. Consanguinity provides the marks and features, the type and tone and ease, the common knowledge and the common consciousness, but number would be required to make these things social. Number, accordingly, for her perfection, was what Philadelphia would have—it having been clear to me still, in my charming Club and at my illuminating window, that she couldn't *not* be perfect. She would be, of all goodly villages, the very goodliest, probably, in the world; the very largest, and flattest, and smoothest, the most rounded and complete.

II

The simplest account of such success as I was to have in putting my vision to the test will be, I think, to say that the place never for a moment belied to me that forecast of its animated intimacy. Yet it might be just here that a report of my experience would find itself hampered—this learning the lesson, from one vivid page of the picture-book to another, of how perfectly "intimate" Philadelphia is. Such an exhibition would be, prohibitively, the exhibition of private things, of private things only, and of a charmed contact with them, were it not for the great circumstance which, when what I have said has been fully said, remains to be taken into account. The state of infinite cousinship colours the scene, makes the predominant tone; but you get a light upon it that is worth all others from the moment you see it as, ever so savingly, historic. This perception moreover promptly operates; I found it stirred, as soon as I went out or began to circulate, by all immediate aspects and signs. The place "went back"; or, in other words, the social equilibrium, forestalling so that of the other cities, had begun early, had had plenty of time on its side, and thus had its history behind it—the past that looms through it, not at all luridly, but so squarely and substantially, to-day, and gives it, by a mercy, an extension other than the lateral. This, frankly, was required, it struck me, for the full comfort of one's impression—for a certain desirable and imputable richness. The backward extension, in short, is the very making of Philadelphia; one is so uncertain of the value one would attach to her being as she is, if she hadn't been so by prescription and for a couple of centuries. This has established her right and her competence; the fact is the parent, so to speak, of her consistency and serenity; it has made the very law under which her parts and pieces have held so closely together. To walk her streets is to note with all promptness that William Penn *must* have laid them out—no one else could possibly have done it so ill. It was his best, though, with our larger sense for a street, it is far from ours; we at any rate no more complain of them, nor suggest that they might have been more liberally conceived, than we so express ourselves about the form of the chairs in sitting through a morning call.

I found myself liking them, then, as I moved among them, just in proportion as they conformed, in detail, to the early pattern—the figure, for each house, of the red-faced old gentleman whose thick eyebrows and moustache have turned to white; and I found myself detesting them in any instance of a new front or a new fashion. They were narrow, with this aspect as of a double file of grizzled veterans, or they were nothing; the narrowness had been positively the channel or conduit of continuity of character: it made the long pipe on which the tune of the place was played. From the moment it was in any way corrected the special charm broke—the charm, a rare civic possession, as of some immense old ruled and neatly-inked chart, not less carefully than benightedly flattened out, stretching its tough parchment under the very feet of all comings and goings. This was an image with which, as it furthermore seemed to me, everything else consorted—above all the soothing truth that Philadelphia was, yes, beyond cavil, solely and singly Philadelphian. There was an interference absent, or one that I at least never met: that sharp note of the outlandish, in the strict sense of the word, which I had already found almost everywhere so disconcerting. I pretend here of course neither to estimate the numbers in which the grosser aliens may actually have settled on these bland banks of the Delaware, nor to put my finger on the principle of the shock I had felt it, and was still to feel it, in their general power to administer; for I am not now concerned so much with the impression made by one's almost everywhere meeting them, as with the impression made by one's here and there failing of it. They may have been gathered, in their hordes, in some vast quarter unknown to me and of which I was to have no glimpse; but what would this have denoted, exactly, but some virtue in the air for reducing their presence, or their effect, to naught? There precisely was the difference from New York—that they themselves had been in that place half the virtue, or the vice, of the air, and that there were few of its agitations to which they had not something to say.

The logic of the case had been visible to me, for that matter, on my very first drive from the train—from that precious "Pennsylvania" station of Philadelphia which was to strike me as making a nearer approach than elsewhere to the arts of ingratiation. There was an object or two, windowed and chimneyed, in the central sky—but nothing to speak of: I then and there, in a word, took in the admirable flatness. And if it seemed so spacious, by the same token, this was because it was neither eager, nor grasping, nor pushing. It drew its breath at its ease, clearly—never sounding the charge, the awful "Step lively!" of New York. The fury of the pavement had dropped, in fine, as I was to see it drop, later on, between Chicago and St. Louis. This affected me on the spot as symbolic, and I was to have no glimpse of anything that gainsaid the symbol. It was somehow, too, the very note of the homogeneous; though this indeed is not, oddly enough, the head under which at St. Louis my impression was to range itself. I at all events here gave myself up to the vision—that of the vast, firm chess-board, the immeasurable spread of little squares, covered *all* over by perfect Philadelphians. It was an image, in face of some of the other features of the view, dissimilar to any by which one had ever in one's life been assaulted; and this elimination of the foreign element has been what was required to make it consummate. Nothing is more notable, through the States at large, than that hazard of what one may happen, or may not happen, to see; but the only use to be made of either accident is, clearly, to let it stand and to let it serve. This intensity and ubiquity of the local tone, that of the illimitable *town*, serves so successfully for my sense of Philadelphia that I should feel as if a little masterpiece of the creative imagination had been destroyed by the least correction. And there is, further, the point to make that if I knew, all the while, that there was something more, and different, and less beatific, under and behind the happy appearance I grasped, I knew it by no glimmer of direct perception, and should never in the world have guessed it if some sound of it had not, by a discordant voice, been, all superfluously, rather tactlessly, dropped into my ear.

It was not, however, disconcerting at the time, this presentation, as in a flash, of the other side of the medal—the other side being, in a word, as was mentioned to me, one of the most lurid pages in the annals of political corruption. The place, by this revelation, was two distinct things—a Society, from far back, the society I had divined, the most genial and delightful one could think of, and then, parallel to this, and not within it, nor quite altogether above it, but beside it and beneath it, behind it and before it, enclosing it as in a frame of fire in which it still had the secret of keeping cool, a proportionate City, the most incredible that ever was, organized all for plunder and rapine, the gross satisfaction of official appetite, organized for eternal iniquity and impunity. Such were the conditions, it had been hinted to me—from the moment the medal spun round; but I even understate, I think, in speaking of the knowledge as only not disconcerting. It was better than that, for it positively added the last touch of colour to my framed and suspended picture. Here, strikingly then, was an American *case*, and presumably one of the best; one of the best, that is, for some study of the wondrous problem, admiration and amazement of the nations, who yearn over it from far off: the way in which sane Society and pestilent City, in the United States, successfully cohabit, each keeping it up with so little of fear or flutter from the other. The thing presents itself, in its prime unlikelihood, as a thorough good neighbouring of the Happy Family and the Infernal Machine—the machine so rooted as to continue to defy removal, and the family still so indifferent, while it carries on the family business of buying and selling, of chattering and dancing, to the danger of being blown up. It is all puzzled out, from afar, as a matter of the exchange, and in a large decree of the observance, from side to side, of guarantees, and the interesting thing to get at, for the student of manners, will ever be just this mystery of the terms of the bargain. I must add, none the less, that, though one was one's self, inevitably and always and everywhere, that student, my attention happened to be, or rather was obliged to be, confined to one view of the agreement. The arrangement is, obviously, between the great municipalities and the great populations, on the grand scale, and I lacked opportunity to look at it all round. I had but my glimpse of the apparently wide social acceptance of it—that is I saw but the face of the medal most directly turned to the light of day, and could note that nowhere so much as in Philadelphia was any carking care, in the social mind, any uncomfortable consciousness, as of a skeleton at the banquet of life, so gracefully veiled.

This struck me (on my looking back afterwards with more knowledge) as admirable, as heroic, in its way, and as falling in altogether with inherent habits of sociability, gaiety, gallantry, with that felt presence of a "temperament" with which the original Quaker drab seems to flush—giving it, as one might say for the sake of the figure, something of the iridescence of the breast of a well-fed dove. The original Quaker drab is still there, and, ideally, for the picture, up and down the uniform streets, one should see a bland, broad-brimmed, square-toed gentleman, or a bonneted, kerchiefed, mittened lady, on every little flight of white steps; but the very note of the place has been the "worldly" overscoring, for most of the senses, of the primitive monotone, the bestitching of the drab with pink and green and silver. The mixture has been, for a social effect, admirably successful, thanks, one seems to see, to the subtle, the charming absence of pedantry in the Quaker purity. It flushes gracefully, that temperate prejudice (with its predisposition to the universal *tutoiement*), turning first but to the prettiest pink; so that we never quite know where the drab has ended and the colour of the world has begun. The "disfrocked" Catholic is too strange, the paganized Puritan too angular; it is the accommodating Friend who has most the secret of a *modus vivendi*. And if it be asked, I may add, whether, in this case of social Philadelphia, the genius for life,

and what I have called the gallantry of it above all, wouldn't
have been better shown by a scorn of *any* compromise to
which the nefarious City could invite it, I can only reply that,
as a lover, always of romantic phenomena, and an inveterate
seeker for them, I should have been deprived, by the action of
that particular virtue, of the thrilled sense of a society dancing, all consciously, on the thin crust of a volcano. It is the
thinness of the crust that makes, in such examples, the wild
fantasy, the gay bravery, of the dance—just as I admit that a
preliminary, an original extinction of the volcano would have
illustrated another kind of virtue. The crust, for the social
tread, would in this case have been firm, but the spectator's
imagination would have responded less freely, I think, to the
appeal of the scene. If I may indeed speak my whole thought
for him he would so have had to drop again, to his regret, the
treasure of a small analogy picked up on its very threshold.

How shall he confess at once boldly and shyly enough that
the situation had at the end of a very short time begun to
strike him, for all its immeasurably reduced and simplified
form, as a much nearer approach to the representation of an
"old order," an *ancien régime*, socially speaking, than any the
field of American manners had seemed likely to regale him
with? Grotesque the comparison if pushed; yet how had he
encountered the similitude if it hadn't been hanging about?
From the moment he adopted it, at any rate, he found it taking on touch after touch. The essence of old orders, as history
lights them, is just that innocent beatitude of consanguinity,
of the multiplication of the assured felicities, to which I have
already alluded. From this, in Philadelphia, didn't the rest follow?—the sense, for every one, of being in the same boat
with every one else, a closed circle that would find itself happy
enough if only it could remain closed enough. The boat
might considerably pitch, but its occupants would either float
merrily together or (almost as merrily) go down together, and
meanwhile the risk, the vague danger, the jokes to be made
about it, the general quickened sociability and intimacy, were
the very music of the excursion. There are even yet to be observed about the world fragments and ghosts of old social
orders, thin survivals of final cataclysms, and it was not less
positive than beguiling that the common marks by which

these companies are known, and which we still distinguish through their bedimmed condition, cropped up for me in the high American light, making good my odd parallel at almost every point. Yet if these signs of a slightly congested, but still practically self-sufficing, little world were all there, they were perhaps there most, to my ear, in the fact of the little world's proper intimate idiom and accent: a dialect as much its very own, even in drawing-rooms and libraries, as the Venetian is that of Venice or the Neapolitan is that of Naples—representing the common things of association, the things easily understood and felt, and charged as no other vehicle could be with the fund of local reference. There is always the difference, of course, that at Venice and at Naples, "in society," an alternative, either that of French or of the classic, the more or less academic Italian, is offered to the uninitiated stranger, whereas in Philadelphia he is candidly, consistently, sometimes almost contagiously entertained in the free vernacular. The latter may easily become, in fact, under its wealth of idiosyncrasy and if he have the favouring turn of mind, a tempting object of linguistic study; with the bridge built for him, moreover, that, unlike the Venetian, the Neapolitan and most other local languages, it contains, itself, colloquially, a notable element of the academic and the classic. It struck me even, truly, as, with a certain hardness in it, *constituting* the society that employed it—very much as the egg is made oval by its shell; and really, if I may say all, as taking its stand a bit consciously sometimes, if not a bit defiantly, on its own proved genius. I remember the visible dismay of a gentleman, a pilgrim from afar, in a drawing-room, at the comment of a lady, a lady of one of the new generations indeed, and mistress of the tone by which I had here and there occasion to observe that such ornaments of the new generation might be known. "Listen to the creature: he speaks English!"—it was the very opposite of the indulgence or encouragement with which, in a Venetian drawing-room (I catch my analogies as I can) the sound of French or of Italian might have been greeted. The poor "creature's" dismay was so visible, clearly, for the reason that such things have only to be said with a certain confidence to create a certain confusion—the momentary consciousness of some such misdeed, from the point of view of manners, as the speaking of Russian at Warsaw. I have said that Philadelphia didn't bristle, but the heroine of my anecdote caused the so genial city to resemble, for the minute, linguistically, an unreconciled Poland.

III

But why do I talk of the new generations, or at any rate of the abyss in them that may seem here and there beyond one's shallow sounding, when, all the while, at the back of my head, hovers the image in the guise of which antiquity in Philadelphia looks most seated and most interesting? Nowhere throughout the country, I think, unless it be perchance at Mount Vernon, does our historic past so enjoy the felicity of an "important" concrete illustration. It survives there in visible form as it nowhere else survives, and one can doubtless scarce think too largely of what its mere felicity of presence, in these conditions, has done, and continues, and will continue, to do for the place at large. It may seem witless enough, at this time of day, to arrive from Pennsylvania with "news" of the old State House, and my news, I can only recognize, began but with being news for myself—in which character it quite shamelessly pretended both to freshness and to brilliancy. Why *shouldn't* it have been charming, the high roof under which the Declaration of Independence had been signed?—that was of course a question that might from the first have been asked of me, and with no better answer in wait for it than that, after all, it might just have happened, in the particular conditions, not to be; or else that, in general, one is allowed a margin, on the spot, for the direct sense of consecrated air, for that communication of its spirit which, in proportion as the spirit has been great, withholds itself, shyly and nobly, from any mere forecast. This it is exactly that, by good fortune, keeps up the sanctity of shrines and the lessons of history, to say nothing of the freshness of individual sensibility and the general continuity of things. There is positively nothing of Independence Hall, of its fine old Georgian amplitude and decency, its large serenity and symmetry of pink and drab, and its actual emphasis of detachment from the vulgar brush of things, that is *not* charming; and there is nothing, the city through, that doesn't receive a mild sidelight, that of a reflected interest, from its neighbourhood.

This element of the reflected interest, and more particularly of the reflected distinction, is for the most part, on the American scene, the missed interest—despite the ingenuities of wealth and industry and "energy" that strain so touchingly often, and even to grimace and contortion, somehow to supply it. One finds one's self, when it *has* happened to intervene, weighing its action to the last grain of gold. One even puts to one's self fantastic cases, such as the question, for instance, of what might, what might *not* have happened if poor dear reckless New York had been so distinguished or so blest—with the bad conscience she is too intelligent not to have, her power to be now and then ashamed of her "form," lodged, after all, somewhere in her interminable boots. One has of course to suppress there the prompt conviction that the blessing—that of the possession of an historical monument of the first order—would long since have been replaced by the higher advantage of a row of sky-scrapers yielding rents; yet the imagination none the less dallies with the fond vision of some respect somehow instilled, some deference somehow suggested, some revelation of the possibilities of a public *tenue* somehow effected. Fascinating in fact to speculate a little as to what a New York held in respect by something or other, some power not of the purse, might have become. It is bad, ever, for lusty youth, especially with a command of means, to grow up without knowing at least one "nice family"—if the family be not priggish; and this is the danger that the young Philadelphia, with its eyes on the superior connection I am speaking of, was enabled to escape. The charming old pink and drab heritage of the great time was to be the superior connection, playing, for the education of the place, the part of the nice family. Socially, morally, even æsthetically, the place was to be thus more or less inevitably built round it; but for which good fortune who knows if even Philadelphia too might have not been vulgar? One meets throughout the land enough instances of the opposite luck—the situation of immense and "successful" communities that have lacked, originally, anything "first-rate," as they might themselves put it, to be built round; anything better, that is, than some profitable hole in the earth, some confluence of rivers or command of lakes or railroads: and one sees how, though this deficiency may not have made itself felt at first, it has inexorably loomed larger and larger, the drawback of it growing all the while with the growth of the place. Our sense of such predicaments, for the gatherings of men, comes back, I think, and with an intensity of interest, to our sense of the way the human imagination absolutely declines everywhere to go to sleep without some apology at least for a supper. The collective consciousness, in however empty an air, gasps for a relation, as intimate as possible, to something superior, something as central as possible, from which it may more or less have proceeded and round which its life may revolve—and its dim desire is always, I think, to do it justice, that this object or presence shall have had as much as possible an heroic or romantic association. But the difficulty is that in these later times, among such aggregations, the heroic and romantic elements, even under the earliest rude stress, have been all too tragically obscure, belonged to smothered, unwritten, almost unconscious private history: so that the central something, the social *point de repère*, has had to be extemporized rather pitifully after the fact, and made to consist of the biggest hotel or the biggest common school, the biggest factory, the biggest newspaper office, or, for climax of desperation, the house of the biggest billionaire. These are the values resorted to in default of higher, for with *some* coloured rag or other the general imagination, snatching its chance, must dress its doll.

As a real, a moral value, to the general mind, at all events, and not as a trumped-up one, I saw the lucky legacy of the past, at Philadelphia, operate; though I admit that these are, at best, for the mooning observer, matters of appreciation, mysteries of his own sensibility. Such an observer has early to perceive, and to conclude on it once for all, that there will be little for him in the American scene unless he be ready, anywhere, everywhere, to read "into" it as much as he reads out. It is at its best for him when most open to that friendly penetration, and not at its best, I judge, when practically most closed to it. And yet how can I pretend to be able to say, under this discrimination, what was better and what was worse in Independence Hall?—to say how far the charming facts struck me as going of themselves, or where the imagination (perhaps on this sole patch of ground, by exception, a meddler "not wanted anyhow") took them up to carry them further. I am reduced doubtless to the comparative sophism of making my better sense here consist but of my sense of the fine interior of the building. One sees them immediately as "good," delightfully good, on architectural and scenic lines, these large, high, wainscoted chambers, as good as any could thinkably have been at the time; embracing what was to be done in them with such a noble congruity (which in all the conditions they might readily have failed of, though they were no mere tent pitched for the purpose) that the historic imagination, reascending the centuries, almost catches them in the act of directly suggesting the celebrated *coup*. One fancies, under the high spring of the ceiling and before the great embrasured window-sashes of the principal room, some clever man of the period, after a long look round, taking the hint. "*What* an admirable place for a Declaration of something! What could one here—what *couldn't* one really declare?" And then after a moment: "I say, why not our Independence?— capital thing always to declare, and before any one gets in with anything tactless. You'll see that the fortune of the place will be made." It really takes some such frivolous fancy as that to represent with proper extravagance the reflection irresistibly rising there and that it yet would seem pedantic to express with solemnity: the sense, namely, of our beautiful escape in not having had to "declare" in any way meanly, of our good fortune in having found half the occasion made to our hand.

High occasions consist of many things, and it was extraordinary luck for our great date that not one of these, even as to surface and appearance, should have been wanting. There might easily have been traps laid for us by some of the inferior places, but I am convinced (and more completely than of anything else in the whole connection) that the genius of historic decency would have kept us enslaved rather than have seen us committed to one of those. In that light, for the intelligent pilgrim, the Philadelphia monument becomes, under his tread, under the touch of his hand and the echo of his voice, the very prize, the sacred thing itself, contended for and gained; so that its quality, in fine, is irresistible and its dignity not to be uttered. I was so conscious, for myself, I confess, of the intensity of this perception, that I dip deep into the whole remembrance without touching bottom; by which I mean that I grope, reminiscentially, in the full basin of the general experience of the spot without bringing up a detail. Distinct to me only the way its character, so clear yet so ample, everywhere hangs together and keeps itself up; distinct to me only the large sense, in halls and spreading staircase and long-drawn upper gallery, of one of those rare precincts of the past against which the present has kept beating in vain. The present comes in and stamps about and very stertorously breathes, but its sounds are as naught the next moment; it is as if one felt there that the grandparent, reserved, irresponsive now, and having spoken his word, in his finest manner, once for all, must have long ago had enough of the exuberance of the young grandson's modernity. But of course the great impression is that of the persistent actuality of the so auspicious room in which the Signers saw their tossing ship into port. The lapse of time here, extraordinarily, has sprung no leak in the effect; it remains so robust that everything lives again, the interval drops out and we mingle in the business: the old ghosts, to our inward sensibility, still make the benches creak as they free their full coat-skirts for sitting down; still make the temperature rise, the pens scratch, the papers flutter, the dust float in the large sun-shafts; we place them as they sit, watch them as they move, hear them as they speak, pity them as they ponder, know them, in fine, from the arch of their eyebrows to the shuffle of their shoes.

I am not sure indeed that, for mere archaic insolence, the little old Hall of the Guild of Carpenters, my vision of which jostles my memory of the State House, does not carry it even with a higher hand—in spite of a bedizenment of restoration, within, which leads us to rejoice that the retouchings of the greater monument expose themselves comparatively so little. The situation of this elegant structure—of dimensions and form that scarce differ, as I recall them, from those of delicate little Holden Chapel, of the so floridly-overlaid gable, most articulate single word, in College Yard, of the small builded sense of old Harvard—comes nearer to representing an odd town-nook than any other corner of American life that I remember; American life having been organized, *ab ovo*, with an hostility to the town-nook which has left no scrap of provision for eyes needing on occasion a refuge from the general glare. The general glare seemed to me, at the end of something like a passage, in the shade of something like a court, and in the presence of something like a relic, to have mercifully intermitted, on that fine Philadelphia morning; I won't answer for the exact correspondence of the conditions with my figure of them, since the shade I speak of may have been but the shade of "tall" buildings, the vulgarest of new accidents. Yet I let my impression stand, if only as a note of the relief certain always to lurk, at any turn of the American scene, in the appearance of any individual thing within, or behind, or at the end, or in the depth, of any other individual thing. It makes for the sense of complexity, relieves the eternal impression of things all in a row and of a single thickness, an impression which the usual unprecedented length of the American alignment (always its source of pride) does by itself little to mitigate. Nothing in the array is "behind" anything else—an odd result, I admit, of the fact that so many things affirm themselves as preponderantly before. Little Carpenters' Hall *was*, delightfully, somewhere behind; so much behind, as I perhaps thus fantastically see it, that I dare say I should not be able to find my way to it again if I were to try. Nothing, for that matter, would induce me to revisit in fact, I feel, the object I so fondly evoke. It might have been, for this beautiful posteriority, somewhere in the City of London.

IV

I can but continue to lose myself, for these connections, in my *whole* sense of the intermission, as I have called it, of the glare. The mellower light prevailed, somehow, *all* that fine Philadelphia morning, as well as on two or three other occasions—and I cannot, after all, pretend I don't now see why. It was because one's experience of the place had become immediately an intimate thing—intimate with that intimacy that I had tasted, from the first, in the local air; so that, inevitably, thus, there was no keeping of distinct accounts for public and private items. An ancient church or two, of aspect as Anglican still as you please, and taking, for another case, from the indifferent bustle round it, quite the look of Wren's mere steepled survivals in the backwaters of London churchyards; Franklin's grave itself, in its own backwater of muffled undulations, close to the indifferent bustle; Franklin's admirable portrait by Duplessis in the council-room of an ancient, opulent Trust, a conservative Company, vague and awful to my shy sense, that was housed after the fashion of some exclusive, madeira-drinking old gentleman with obsequious heirs: these and other matters, wholly thrilling at the time, float back to me as on the current of talk and as in the flood, so to speak, of hospitality. If Philadelphia had, in opposition to so many other matters, struck me as coherent, there would be surely no point of one's contact at which this might so have come home as in those mysterious chambers and before the most interesting of the many far-scattered portraits of Franklin— the portrait working as some sudden glimpse of the fine old incised seal, kept in its glass cabinet, that had originally stamped all over, for identification, the comparatively soft local wax. One thinks of Franklin's reputation, of his authority—and however much they may have been locally contested at the time—as marking the material about him much as his name might have marked his underclothing or his pocketbooks. Small surprise one had the impression of a Society, with such a figure as that to start conversation. He seemed to preside over it all while one lingered there, as if he had been seated, at the mahogany, relentingly enough, near his glass of madeira; seemed to be "in" it even more freely than by the so interesting fact of his still having, in Philadelphia, in New York, in Boston, through his daughter, so numerous a posterity. The sense of life, life the most positive, most human and most miscellaneous, expressed in his aged, crumpled, canny face, where the smile wittily profits, for fineness, by the comparative collapse of the mouth, represents a suggestion which succeeding generations may well have found it all they could do to work out. It is impossible, in the place, after seeing that portrait, not to feel him still with them, with the genial generations—even though to-day, in the larger, more mixed cup, the force of his example may have suffered some dilution.

It was a savour of which, at any rate, for one's own draught, one could but make the most; and I went so far, on this occasion, as fairly to taste it there in the very quality of my company—in that of the distinguished guidance and protection I was enjoying, which could only make me ask myself in what finer modern form one would have wished to see Franklin's humanity and sagacity, his variety and ingenuity, his wealth of ideas and his tireless application of them, embodied. There was verily nothing to do, after this, but to play over the general picture that light of his assumption of the general ease of things—of things at any rate thereabouts; so that I now see each reminiscence, whatever the time or the place, happily governed and coloured by it. Times and places, in such an experience, ranged themselves, after a space, like valued objects in one of the assorted rooms of a "collection." Keep them a little, tenderly handled, wrapped up, stowed away, and they then come forth, into the room swept and garnished, susceptible of almost any pleasing arrangement. The only thing is that you shall scarce know, at a given moment, amid your abundance, which of them to take up first; there being always in them, moreover, at best, the drawback of value from mere association, that keepsake element of objects in a reliquary. Is not this, however, the drawback for exhibition of almost any item of American experience that may not pretend to deal with the mere monstrosities?—the immensities of size and space, of trade and traffic, of organisation, political, educational, economic. From the moment one's record is not, in fine, a loud statistical shout, it falls into the order of those shy things that speak, at the most (when one is one's self incapable even of the merest statistical whisper), but of the personal adventure—in other words but of one's luck and of one's sensibility. There are incidents, there are passages, that flush, in this fashion, to the backward eye, under the torch. But what solemn statement is one to make of the "importance," for example, of such a matter as the Academy soirée (as they say in London) of the Philadelphia winter, the festive commemoration of some long span of life achieved by the Pennsylvania Academy of Fine Arts? We may have been thrilled, positively, by the occasion, by the interesting encounters and discoveries, artistic and personal, to which it ministered; we may have moved from one charmed recognition to another, noting Sargents and Whistlers by the dozen, and old forgotten French friends, foreign friends in general, older and younger; noting young native upstarts, creatures of yesterday and to-morrow, who invite, with all success, a stand and a stare; but no after-sense of such vibrations, however lively, presumes to take itself as communicable.

One would regret, on the other hand, failing to sound some echo of a message everywhere in the United States so audible; that of the clamorous signs of a hungry social growth, the very pulses, making all their noise, of the engine that works night and day for a theory of civilization. There are moments at which it may well seem that, putting the sense of the spectacle even at its lowest, there is no such amusement as this anywhere supplied; the air through which everything shows is so transparent, with steps and stages and processes as distinct in it as the appearance, from a street-corner, of a crowd rushing on an alarm to a fire. The gregarious crowd "tells," in the street, and the indications I speak of tell, like chalk-marks, on the demonstrative American blackboard—an impression perhaps never so much brought home to me as by a wondrous Sunday morning at the edge of a vast vacant Philadelphia street, a street not of Penn's creation and vacant of everything but an immeasurable bourgeois blankness. I had turned from that scene into a friendly house that was given over, from top to toe, to a dazzling collection of pictures, amid which I felt myself catch in the very act one of the great ingurgitations of the hungry machine, and recognize as well how perfect were all the conditions for making it a case. What could have testified less, on the face of it, than the candour of the street's insignificance?—a pair of huge parted lips protesting almost to pathos their innocence of anything to say: which was exactly, none the less, where appetite had broken out and was feeding itself to satiety. Large and liberal the hospitality, remarkably rich the store of acquisition, in the light of which the whole energy of the keen collector showed: the knowledge, the acuteness, the audacity, the incessant watch for opportunity. These abrupt and multiplied encounters, intensities, ever so various, of individual curiosity, sound the æsthetic note sometimes with unprecedented shrillness and then again with the most muffled discretion. Was the note muffled or shrill, meanwhile, as I listened to it—under a fascination I fully recognized—during an hour spent in the clustered palæstra of the University of Pennsylvania? Here the winter afternoon seemed to throw itself artfully back, across the centuries, the climates, the seasons, the very faiths and codes, into the air of old Greece and the age of gymnastic glory: artfully, I rather insist, because I scarce know what fine emphasis of modernism hung about it too. I put that question, however, only to deny myself the present luxury of answering it; so thickly do the visitor's University impressions, over the land, tend to gather, and so markedly they suggest their being reported of together. I note my palæstral hour, therefore, but because it fell through what it seemed to show me, straight into what I had conceived of the Philadelphia scheme, the happy family given up, though quite on "family" lines, to all the immediate beguilements and activities; the art in particular of cultivating, with such gaiety as might be, a brave civic blindness.

I became conscious of but one excrescence on this large smooth surface; it is true indeed that the excrescence was huge and affected me as demanding in some way to be dealt with. The Pennsylvania Penitentiary rears its ancient grimness, its grey towers and defensive moats (masses at least that uncertain memory so figures for me) in an outlying quarter which struck me as borrowing from them a vague likeness to some more or less blighted minor city of Italy or France, black Angers or dead Ferrara—yet seated on its basis of renown and wrapped in its legend of having, as the first flourishing example of the strictly cellular system, the complete sequestration of the individual prisoner, thought wonderful in its day, moved Charles Dickens to the passionate protest recorded in his *American Notes*. Of such substance was the story of these battlements; yet it was unmistakable that when one had crossed the drawbridge and passed under the portcullis the air seemed thick enough with the breath of the generations. A prison has, at the worst, the massive majesty, the sinister peace of a prison; but this huge house of sorrow affected me as, uncannily, of the City itself, the City of all the cynicisms and impunities against which my friends had, from far back, kept plating, as with the old silver of their sideboards, the armour of their social consciousness. It made the whole place, with some of its oddly antique aspects and its oddly modern freedoms, look doubly cut off from the world of light and ease. The suggestions here were vast, however; too many of them swarm, and my imagination must defend itself as it can. What I was most concerned to note was the complete turn of the wheel of fortune in respect to the measure of mere incarceration suffered, from which the worst of the rigour had visibly been drawn. Parts of the place suggested a sunny Club at a languid hour, with members vaguely lounging and chatting, with open doors and comparatively cheerful vistas, and plenty of rocking-chairs and magazines. The only thing was that, under this analogy, one found one's self speculating much on the implied requisites for membership. It was impossible not to wonder, from face to face, what these would have been, and not to ask what one would have taken them to be if the appearance of a Club had been a little more complete. I almost blush, I fear, for the crude comfort of my prompt conclusion. One would have taken them to consist, without exception, of full-blown basenesses; one couldn't, from member to member, from type to type, from one pair of eyes to another, take them for anything less. Where was the victim of circumstances, where the creature merely misled or betrayed? He fitted no type, he suffered in no face, he yearned in no history, and one felt, the more one took in his absence, that the numerous substitutes for him were good enough for each other.

The great interest was in this sight of the number and variety of ways of looking morally mean; and perhaps also in the question of how much the effect came from its being proved upon them, of how little it might have come if they had still been out in the world. Considered as criminals the moral meanness here was their explication. Considered as morally mean, therefore, would possible criminality, out in the world, have been in the same degree their sole sense? Was the fact of prison *all* the mere fact of opportunity, and the fact of freedom all the mere fact of the absence of it? One inclined to believe that—the simplification was at any rate so great for one's feeling: the cases presented became thus, consistently, cases of the vocation, and from the moment this was clear the place took on, in its way, almost the harmony of a convent. I talked for a long time with a charming reprieved murderer whom I half expected, at any moment, to see ring for coffee and cigars: he explained with all urbanity, and with perfect lucidity, the real sense of the appearance against him, but I none the less felt sure that his merit was largely in the refinement wrought in him by so many years of easy club life. He was as natural a subject for commutation as for conviction, and had had to have the latter in order to have the former—in the enjoyment, and indeed in the subtle criticism, of which, *as* simple commutation he was at his best. They were there, all those of his companions, I was able to note, unmistakably at their best. One could, as I say, sufficiently rest in it, and to do that kept, in a manner, the excrescence, as I have called it, on the general scene, within bounds. I was moreover luckily to see the general scene definitely cleared again, cleared of everything save its own social character and its practical philosophy—and at no moment with these features so brightly presented as during a few days' rage of winter round an old country-house. The house was virtually distant from town, and the conditions could but strike any visitor who stood whenever he might with his back to the fire, where the logs were piled high, as made to press on all the reserves and traditions of the general temperament; those of gallantry, hilarity, social disposability, crowned with the grace of the sporting instinct. What was it confusedly, almost romantically, like, what "old order" commemorated in fiction and anecdote? I had groped for this, as I have shown, before, but I found myself at it again. Wasn't it, for freedom of movement, for jingle of sleigh-bells, for breasting of the elements, for cross-country drives in the small hours, for *crânerie* of fine young men and high wintry colour of muffled nymphs, wasn't it, brogue and all, like some audible echo of close-packing, chancing Irish society of the classic time, seen and heard through a roaring blizzard? That at least, with his back to the fire, was where the restless analyst was landed.

X

Baltimore

I

I⸏T HAD doubtless not been merely absurd, as the wild winter proceeded, to find one's self so enamoured of the very name of the South that one was ready to take it in any small atmospheric instalment and to feel the echo of its voice in the yell of any engine that happened not to drag one either directly North or directly West. One tended at least, on these terms, in some degree, toward the land where the citron blooms, and that was something to go on with, a handful of small change accepted for the time as a pledge of great gold pieces to come. It is astonishing, along the Atlantic coast, how, from the moment the North ceases to insist, the South may begin to presume; ever so little, no doubt, at first, yet with protrusive feelers that tell how she only wants the right sensibility, the true waiting victim, to play upon. It is a question certainly of where, on the so frequently torpid stretch of shore I speak of, the North does cease to insist; or perhaps I should more correctly say a question of when it does. It appeared incapable of this fine tact almost anywhere, I confess, at the season, the first supposedly relenting weeks, of my facing in earnest to Florida; and the interest indeed of that slightly grim adventure was to be in the way it ministered to the coincidence, for me, of two quite opposed strains of reflection. On the one hand nothing could "say" more to the subject long expatriated, condemned by the terms of his exile to a chronic consciousness of grey northern seas, than to feel how, from New York, or even from Boston, he had but to sit still in his portentous car, had but to exercise a due concentrated patience, in order to become aware, without personal effort or suffered transfer, of that most charming of all watchable processes, the gradual soft, the distinctively demoralized, conversion of the soul of Nature. This conversion, if I may so put it without profanity, has always struck me, on any southward course, as a return, on the part of that soul, from a comparatively grim Theistic faith to the ineradicable principle of Paganism; a conscious casting-off of the dread theological abstraction—an abstraction still, even with all Puritan stiffening—in the interest of multiplied, lurking, familiar powers; divinities, graces, presences as unseen but as inherent as the scents clinging to the folds of Nature's robe. It would be on such occasions the fault of the divine familiars themselves if their haunts and shrines were empty, for earth and air and day and night, as we go, still affect us as moods of their sympathy, still vibrate to the breath of their passage; so that our progress, under the expanding sun, resembles a little less a journey through space than a retracing of the course of the ages.

These are fine fancies, however, and what is more to my point is that the theory (so agreeable to entertain at Jersey City) of a direct connection between the snow-banks and the orange-groves is a thing of sweetness only so long as practically unshaken. There is continuity, goodness knows, always in America—it is the last thing that is ever broken: the question for the particular case is but continuity of what? The basis of my individual hope had been that of the reign of the orange-grove; but what it proved, at the crisis I name, was positively that of the usurpation of the snow-bank. It was possible, indubitably, in such conditions, to go to Charleston on sledges—which made in fact, after all, for directness of connection. It made moreover, by the same token, for a certain sinister light on the general truth of our grand territorial unity. It was as if the winter, at the end of February, abroad for a walk, had marched as promptly and inevitably from the Arctic Circle to the Gulf as it might have proceeded, with pride in its huge clear course, from the top of Broadway to the Battery. This brought home again, as I myself went, I remember, one of those three or four main ideas, suggested by the recurrent conditions, which become as obsessions for the traveller in the States—if he have a mind, that is, so indecently exposed to ideas: the sense, constantly fed, and from a hundred sources, that, as Nature abhors a vacuum, so it is of the genius of the American land and the American people to abhor, whenever may be, a discrimination. They are reduced, together, under stress, to making discriminations, but they make them, I think, as lightly and scantily as possible. With the lively insistence of that impression, even though it quite undermined my fond view of a loose and overreaching citronic belt, I found my actually monotonous way beguiled. Practically, till I reached Charleston, this way, disclaiming every invidious intent, refused to be dissociated from anything else in the world: it was only another case of the painting with a big brush, a brush steeped in crude universal white, and of the colossal size this implement was capable of assuming. Gradations, transitions, differences of any sort, temporal, material, social, whether in man or in his environment, shrank somehow, under its sweep, to negligible items; and one had perhaps never yet seemed so to move through a vast simplified scheme. The illustration was once more, in fine, of the small inherent, the small accumulated resistance, in American air, to any force that does simplify. One found the signs of such resistance as little in the prospect enjoyed from the car-window as one distinguished them in the vain images of the interior; those human documents, deciphered from one's seat in the Pullman, which yet do always, in *their* way, for the traveller, constitute precious evidence. The spread of this single great wash of winter from latitude to latitude struck me in fact as having its analogy in the vast vogue of some infinitely-selling novel, one of those happy volumes of which the circulation roars, periodically, from Atlantic to Pacific and from great windy State to State, in the manner, as I have heard it vividly put, of a blazing prairie fire; with as little possibility of arrest from "criticism" in the one case as from the bleating of lost sheep in the other. Everything, so to speak, was monotonized, and the whole social order might have had its nose, for the time, buried, by one levelling doom, in the pages that, after the break of the spell, it would never know itself to mention again. Of course, one remembered meanwhile, there were spells and spells, and the free field—the particular freedom of which is the point of my remark—would on occasion be just as open to the far-exhaled breath of the South. That in fact is what I was to find it—though I thought all delightfully—later in the season, when the freedom of the field struck me as pure benefit. I was not, at the end of February,

really to meet it (as I had looked for it) before crossing the
Florida line; but toward the middle of June I was to meet it,
enchantingly, at Baltimore, and this, then, as I had not
stopped there in my previous course, was, even beyond the
wondrous February Florida, to reveal to me, grateful for any
such favour, the South in her freshness. The freshness was in
part, no doubt—and even perhaps to extravagance—mine; I
testify at all events first for Baltimore.

It would probably be again the freshness, of this confessedly subjective sort, it would probably be again the state of
alert response to any favour of the class just hinted at; but the
immediate effect of the Maryland capital was to place it, to
my troubled vision, and quite at the head of its group, in a
category of images and memories small at the best and the
charm of which casts a shadow, none the less, even as the rose
wears a thorn. I refer indeed in this slightly portentous figure
to the mere familiar truth that if representative values and the
traceable or the imaginable connections of things happen to
have, on occasion, for your eyes and your intelligence, an existence of any intensity, your case, as a traveller, an observer, a
reporter, is "bound" from the first, under the stirred impression, to loom for you in some distressful shape. These representative values and constructive connections, the whole of
the latent vividness of things, not only remain, under expression, subject to no definite chemical test, no mathematical
proof whatever, but almost turn their charming backs and
toss their wilful heads at one's poor little array of terms and
equivalents. There thus immediately rises for the lone visionary, betrayed and arrested in the very act of vision, that spectre of impotence which dogs the footsteps of perception and
whose presence is like some poison-drop in the silver cup.
Baltimore put on for me, from the first glance, the form of
the silver cup filled with the mildest, sweetest decoction; but I
had no sooner begun to taste of it than I began to taste also
of the infused bitter. It had, in its way, during that first early
hour or two of the summer evening, a perfect felicity: which
meant, for the touched intelligence, that it was full of
pleasantly-playing reference and reflection, that it exhaled on
the spot, as the word goes, an atmosphere; that it wore, to
contemplation, in fine, a character as marked with mild

accents as some faded old uniform is marked with tarnished buttons and braid—albeit these sources of interest were too closely of the texture to be snipped off, in the guise of patterns or relics, by any mere sharp shears of journalism.

I arrived late in the day, and the day had been lovely; I alighted at a large fresh peaceful hostelry, imposingly modern yet quietly affable, and, having recognized the deep, soft general note, even from my windows, as that of a kind of mollified vivacity, I sought the streets with as many tacit questions as I judged they would tolerate, or as the waning day would allow me to put. It took but that hour, as I strolled in the early eventide, to give me the sense of the predicament I have glanced at; that of finding myself committed to the view of Baltimore as quite insidiously "sympathetic," quite inordinately amiable—which amounted, in other words, to the momentous proposition that she was interesting—and still of wondering, by the same stroke, how I was to make any such statement plausible. Character is founded on elements and features, so many particular parts which conduce to an expression. So I walked about the dear little city looking for the particular parts—all with the singular effect of rather failing to find them and with my impression of felicity at the same time persistently growing. The felicity was certainly not that of a mere blank; there must accordingly have been items and objects, signs and tokens, there must have been causes of so charming a consequence; there must have been the little numbers (not necessarily big, if only a tall enough column) for the careful sum on my slate. What happened then, remarkably, was that while I mechanically so argued my impression was fixing itself by a wild logic of its own, and that I was presently to see how it would, when once settled to a certain intensity, snap its fingers at warrants and documents. If it was a question of a slate the slate was used, at school, I remembered, for more than one purpose; so that mine, by my walk's end, instead of a show of neat ciphering, exhibited simply a bold drawn image—which had the merit moreover of not being in the least a caricature. The moral of this was precious—that of the fine impunity with which, if one but had sensibility, the ciphering could be neglected and in fact almost contemned: always, that is (and only) *with* one's finer wits about one.

Without them one was at best, really, nowhere—even with "items" by the thousand; so that the place became, quite adorably, a lesson in the use of that resource. It would be "no good" to a journalist—for *he* is nowhere, ever, without his items; but it would be everything, always, to the mere restless analyst. He might by its aid stand against all comers; and this alike in pleasure and in pain, in the bruised or in the soothed condition. That was the real way to work things out, and to feel it so brought home would by itself sufficiently crown this particular small pilgrimage.

II

If my sensibility yielded so completely to Baltimore, however, I should add, this was no doubt partly because the air seemed from the first to breathe upon it a pledge of no bruises. I mounted, in the golden June light, the neatest, amplest, emptiest street-vista, the builded side of a steepish hill, and, having come in due course to a spacious summit, laid out with monumental elegance and completely void, for the time, of the human footstep, I saw that to suffer in any fibre I should have positively, somewhere, to hurl myself upon the spears. Not a point protruded then or afterwards; and the cunning of the restless analyst is essentially such that, with friction long enough in abeyance to leave him a start, he is already astride of his happier thesis, seated firm, having "elected" to be undismountable, and riding it as hard as it will go. The absence of friction, on my monumental hilltop and in the prospects it overhung, constituted, I was to find, an absolute circus-ring for this exercise; and it is much to be able to say, while performing in the circus (even if but mainly to the public of one's own conscience), that one has never had the sense of a safer hour. The safety of Baltimore, I should indeed mention, consisted perhaps a little overmuch, during that first flush, in its apparently vacant condition: it affected me as a sort of perversely cheerful little city of the dead; and from the dead, naturally, comes no friction. Was it cheerful, that is, or was it only resigned and discreet?—with the manner of the good breeding that doesn't publicly prate of family troubles. I found myself handling, in imagination, these large quantities only because, as I suppose, it was impossible not to remember on that spot of what native generation one had come. It took no greater intensity of the South than Baltimore could easily give to figure again, however fadedly, and all as a ghostly presence, the huge shadow of the War, and to reproduce that particular bloodstained patch of it which, in the very first days, the now so irresponsible and absent community about me had flung across the path of the North. This one echo of old Time made the connections, for the instant, all vibrate, and the scene before me, somehow, as it stood, had to account for the great revolution. It was as if *that*, for the restless analyst, had to be disposed of before anything else: whereby, precisely, didn't the amenity of his impression partly spring from the descent there, on the spot, in a quick white flash, of the most august of the Muses? It was History in person that hovered, just long enough for me to recognize her and to read, in her strange deep eyes, *her* intelligence at least of everything. It might have been there fairly as reassurance. "Yes, they have lived with *me*, and it has done them good, and we have buried together all their past—about which, wise creature as I am, I allow them, of course, all piety. But this—what you make out around us—is their real collective self, which I am delighted to commend to you. I've found Baltimore a charming patient." That was, in ten minutes, what it had come to; as if the brush of the sublime garment had by itself cleared the air. If there was a fine warm hush everywhere it was indeed partly that of this historic peace.

But for the rest it only meant that the world was at such a season out of town. Houses were everywhere closed, and the neat perspectives, all domiciliary and all, as I have hinted, tending mildly to a vague elegance, were the more neat and more elegant, though doubtless also the more mild and the more vague, for their being so inanimate. A certain vividness of high decency seemed in spite of it to possess them, and this suggestion of the real southern glow, yet with no southern looseness, was clearly something by itself—all special and local and all, or almost all, expressed in repeated vistas of little brick-faced and protrusively door-stepped houses, which, overhung by tall, regular umbrage, suggested rows of quiet old ladies seated, with their toes tucked-up on uniform footstools, under the shaded candlesticks of old-fashioned tea-parties. The little ladylike squares, though below any tide-mark of fashion, were particularly frequent; in which case it was as if the virtuous dames had drawn together round a large green table, albeit to no more riotous end than that each should sit before her individual game of patience. One sounds inevitably the note of the "virtue"—so little, in general, can any picture of American town-appearance hang together without it. It amounts, everywhere, to something intenser than the implied absence of "vice"; it amounts to a sort of registered absence of the conception or the imagination of it, and still more of the provision for it; though, all the while, as one goes and comes, one feels that no community can really be as purged of peccant humours as the typical American has for the most part found itself foredoomed to look. It has been caught in the mechanism of that consistency—to an effect of convenience, doubtless, much more than to any other; and has thus, in the whole vast connection, a relation to appearances that is all its own. The "European" scene, at a thousand points, looks all its sophistications straight out at us—or looks, in other words, at least as perverse as it practically is. The American, on the other hand, expressing physiognomically no sophistications at all—though plenty of quite common candours, crudities and vulgarities—makes one ask if the cash-register, the ice-cream freezer, the lightning-elevator, the "boys' paper," and other such overflows, do truly represent the sum of its passions. Incontestably, at all events, this immensely ingenuous aspect counts, for any country and any scheme of life, as a great force, just as the appearance of the stale and the congested residing in the comparatively battered mask of experience counts as a weakness: to conceive which the mind's eye has only to fix a little the colossal American face grimacing with anything of a subtler consciousness. That image, if actually presented, would become, as we feel, appalling. The inexorable fate of the countenance in question may be so to learn to grimace in time, but though few processes are slow, in the United States, and few exhibitions not contagious, any such transition, assuredly, will not be rapid, any more than any such tendency will easily predominate.

All of which would have carried me far from the simple sweetness of Baltimore, were it not that, for the restless analyst, there is no such thing as an unrelated fact, no such thing as a break in the chain of relations. Many a perceived American aspect, for that matter, would by itself have little to give; the student of manners, in other words, to make it presentable—by which I understand to make it *sufficiently* interesting—must first discover connections for it and then borrow from these, if possible, the elements of a wardrobe. And though it should sound a little monstrous, moreover, one had somehow not been prepared for so delicate an effect of propriety; since there are cases too, indubitably, in which propriety can show for almost as coarse as anything else. It couldn't have been, either, that one had expected any positive air of licence; but the fact was, I suppose, that, for a constitutional story-seeker, a certain still, small shock, a prompt need of readjustment of view, was involved in one's finding the element of the bourgeois crop up, so inveterately, in latitudes generally associated, so far as one knew them elsewhere, with some perceptible sacrifice to the sway of the senses. I had already, at this date, as I have noted, dipped deep into our own uttermost South, and had there had to reckon with that first slight disconcertment awaiting the observer whose southern categories happen to have been wholly European. His simplest expression for the anomaly he meets is that he sees the citronic belt all incongruously Protestantized: that big word (for so small a bewilderment perhaps) sticks to him and worries him—almost as absurdly, I grant, as if he had expected Charleston and Savannah to betray the moral accent of Naples or Seville. He had not, assuredly, done this; but he had as little allowed, in imagination, for the hyperborean note. A South without church-fronts and church-interiors had been superficially as strange, in its way, as a Methodism of the subtropic night, a Methodism of the orange and the palm. Such were the treacheries of association; though what indeed would observation be, for interest, if it were not, just by these armed surprises, constantly touched with adventure? The beauty of Baltimore was, all this time, that one could feel it as potentially harmonizing; the citronic belt would not embrace here more Methodism than might consort with it, nor the Methodism pretend to cultivate with any success the hibiscus and the pomegranate.

That I could entertain so many incoherent ideas in half-an-hour was in any case a proof that I felt, for the occasion, left in possession; quite as the visitor as yet unintroduced may feel during some long preliminary wait in a drawing-room. He looks at the furniture, pictures, books; he studies in these objects the character of the house and of his hosts, and if there be some domestic treasure visibly more important and conspicuous than the others, it engages his attention as either with a fatal or an engaging force. The top of the central eminence, with its air of an ample plan and of sweeping the rest of the circle, figured the documentary parlour and my enjoyed leave to touch and examine; so that when it was a question, in particular, of the monument to Washington, the high column, in the middle, with its surmounting figure and its spreading architectural base, this presence was, for all the world, like that of some vast and stately old-fashioned clock, a decorative "piece," an heirloom from generations now respectably remote, occupying an inordinate space in proportion to the other conveniences. The ornamental, the "important" clock is apt to be in especial, at such a crisis, a telltale object; its range of testimony, of possible treachery, is immense, and cases are not unknown, I gather, in which it has put the doubting visitor to flight. The greater the felicity, thereby, for the over-topping Baltimore timepiece, which hung about in mild reassurance, promptly aware that it wasn't a bit vulgar, but, on the contrary, of a pleasant jejune academic pomp that suggested to the fancy some melancholy, some spectral, man-at-arms mounting guard at the angles, in due military form, over suspected treasures of Style. One could imagine, somehow, under the summer stars, the mystic vigil of these mild heroes; and one could above all catch again the interesting hint of the terms on which, in the United States, the consecration of time may be found operating. It has a trick there all of its own, thanks to which the effect of duration is produced very much as, before the footlights, the prestidigitator produces the effect of extracting a live fowl from a hat. This is a law under which, the material permitting, the decades count as centuries and the centuries as æons. The misfortune is that too often the material, futile and treacherous, doesn't permit. Yet the law is in the happiest cases none the less strikingly vindicated. There, for instance—to pursue undiscouraged my figure of the guest in the empty parlour—were the best houses, the older, the ampler, the more blandly quadrilateral; which in spite of their still faces met one's arrest, at their commodious corners and other places of vantage, with an unmistakable *manner*. The quiet assurance of a position in the world—the world, the only one, with which they were concerned—testified again, in an interesting way, to the simple source of their impressiveness, showing how almost any modern interval could have been long enough to make them nobly antique if such interval might only have been vulgar enough. The age of "brown stone" was to have found no difficulty in *that*; the prolongation of its rage for a quarter of a century amply sufficed to dignify every antecedent thing it had spared (as the survivors of reigns of Terror grow by mere survival distinguished); while, steeped in dishonour up to the eyebrows, that is up to its false cornices of painted and sanded wood and iron, it was never to enjoy, for itself, the advantage it elsewhere conferred. Nothing has ever been vulgar enough to rehabilitate the odd ugliness, so distinct, yet after all so undemonstrable, of this luckless material; the way one shuddered, in particular, at the touch, on balustrade and elsewhere, of the sanded iron! It has been followed by other rages and other errors, but even the grace of the American time-measure can do nothing for it.

III

It was of course the fact that the "values" here were all such, and such alone, as might be reflected from the social conditions and the state of manners, even if reflected, for the hour, almost into empty space—it was this that gave weight to each perceived appearance and permitted none to show as trivial enough to project me, in reaction or in inanition, upon the comparative obviousness of the "burnt district." There is almost always a burnt district to eke out the interest of an

American city—it is the pride of the citizen and the resource of the visitor when all else fails; and I can scarce, I think, praise Baltimore so liberally as to note that this was the last of her beauties I was conscious of. She had lost by fire, a few months before, the greater part of her business quarter, which she was now rapidly and artfully calling back to existence; but the entertainment she offered me was guiltless, ever so gracefully and gallantly guiltless, as it struck me, of reference, even indirect, to the majesty either of ruin or of remedy. One was, on further acquaintance, thoroughly beguiled, but the burnt district had so little to do with it that the days came and went without my so much as discovering its whereabouts. Wonderful little Baltimore, in which, whether when perched on a noble eminence or passing from one seat of the humanities, one seat of hospitality, to another—a process mainly consisting indeed, as it seemed to me, of prompt drives through romantic parks and woodlands that were all suburban yet all Arcadian—I caught no glimpse of traffic, however mild, nor spied anything "tall" at the end of any vista. This was in itself really a benediction, since I had nowhere, from the first, been infatuated with tallness; I was infatuated only with the question of manners, in their largest sense—to the finer essence of which tallness had already defined itself to me as positively abhorrent. What occurred betimes, and ever so happily, was simply that the delicate blank of those first hours flushed into animation, and that with this indeed the embroidery of the fine canvas turned thick and rich. It came back again, no doubt, in the inveterate way, to the University presence, and to the eagerness with which, on the American scene, as I tire not, you see, of repeating, the visiting spirit, on such occasions, throws itself straight into sanctuary. It breaks in at any cost, this distracted appetite, and, recomposing the elements to their greater distinction, if need be, and with a high imaginative hand, makes of the combination obtained the only firm standpoint for the rest of the view. It has even in this connection an occasional sharp chill; air-borne rumours reach it of perversities and treacheries, conspiracies possibly hatching in the very bosom of the temple and against its very faith. One hears of the University idea threatened in more than one of the great institutions—reduced to some pettifogging conception of a short brisk term and a simplified culture; a lively thrifty training for "business-competition." This is a blow to the collective fond fancies set humming, at once, in almost any scholastic shade—under the effect of which one can but give one's own scant scholar's hood, while one winces, a further protesting pull over abashed brows. It would have been a question, very much, of what I call breaking-in (into the Johns Hopkins) at this moment, had I not here been indulged, in all liberality, with an impression the more charming, in a manner, for the fact of halls and courts brooding in vacation stillness. Perversely adorable always—and I scarce know why—the late afternoon light in deserted haunts of study; with the secret of supreme dignity lurking, above all, in high, dusky, wainscoted chambers where the sound of one's footfall lingers, to one's pleasure, like a caress, and where portraits of the appurtenant worthies, the heroes and patrons, grow vague in the twilight. It is a tribute to the forces of idealism lurking again and again, over the country, in the amenity of the general Collegiate appearance, that the last thing these conditions overtly suggest, or seem to accept as their imputed virtue, is this precipitation of the young intelligence into the mere vociferous market.

I scarcely know why, however, I should have appeared, even by waving it away, to make room at our banquet for the possible skeleton of the false, the barbarizing, note; since the natural pitch of Baltimore, the pictorial, so to speak, as well as the social, struck me, once a certain contact established, as that of disinterested sensibility, the passion of which her University is the highest and clearest example. There was on the splendid Sunday in particular a warm, soft fusion of aspects—a *con*fusion, in fact, while I now gather it in—which seems to defy, though all unconsciously, the sharper edge of discrimination and to offer itself, insistently, as a general wash of brave Southern shade, the play of a liquid brush of which the North knows nothing. The episodes melt together, yet they also, under a little pressure, come happily apart, and over the large sun-chequered picture the generous boughs hang heavy. Admirable I found them, the Maryland boughs, and so immediately disposed about the fortunate town, by parkside and lonely lane, by trackless hillside and tangled copse, that the depth of rural effect becomes at once bewildering. You wonder at the absent transitions, you look in vain for the shabby fringes—or at least, under my spell, I did; you have never seen, on the lap of nature, so large a burden so neatly accommodated. Baltimore sits there as some quite robust but almost unnaturally good child might sit on the green apron of its nurse, with no concomitant crease or crumple, no uncontrollable "mess," by the nursery term, to betray its temper. It was with something like that figure before me that I kept communing, as I say, with the bland presence. Even a morning hour or two at the great University Hospital—for one's experience of the higher tone, one's irrepressible pursuit of charm, in America, has, to its great enrichment, these odd sequences—even that beginning of the day did nothing to obtrude the ugly or to overemphasize the real; it simply contributed, under some perversion that I can neither explain nor defend, to the general grace of the picture. Why should the great Hospital, with its endless chambers of woe, its whole air as of *most* directly and advisedly facing, as the hospitals of the world go, the question of the immensities of pain—why should such an impression actually have turned, under the spell, to fine poetry, to a mere shining vision of the conditions, the high beauty of applied science? The conditions, positively, as I think of them after the interval, make the poetry—the large art, above all, by which, in a place bristling with its terrible tale, everything was made to seem fair, and fairest even while it most intimately concurred in the work. In short if the Hospital was fundamentally Universitarian—as of the domain of the great Medical Faculty—so it partook for me, in its own way, of the University glamour, and so the tempered morning, and the shaded splendour, and the passive rows, the grim human alignments that became, in their cool vistas, delicate "symphonies in white," and, more even than anything else, the pair of gallant young Doctors who ruled, for me, so gently, the whole still concert, abide with me, collectively, as agents of the higher tone.

No example could speak more of that enlargement of function, for constituting some picture of life, which many an American element or object, many an institution, has to be felt as practising—usually with high success. It comes back, one notes for the thousandth time, to that redistribution and reconsecration of values, of representative weight, which it is *the* interesting thing, over the land, to see take effect—to see in special take all the effect of which it is capable. There are a thousand "European" values that are absent, and, whether as a consequence or not of that, there are innumerable felt solutions of the social continuity. The instinct of missing—by which I mean not at all either the consciousness or the confession of lacking—keeps up, however, its own activity; for the theory at least of the native spirit is to consent wittingly to no privation. It has a genius, the native spirit, for desiring things of the existence, and even of the possibility of which it is actually unaware, and it views the totality of nature and the general life of man, I think, as more than anything else commissioned and privileged to wait on these awakenings. Thus new values arise as expansion proceeds; the marked character of which, for comparative sociology, is that they are not at all as other values. What they "count" for is the particular required American quantity; and we see again and again how large a quantity symbol and figure have to represent. The interesting thing is that, on the spot, the representation does practically cover the ground: it covers elements that in communities employing a different scale require for their expression (and perhaps sometimes to an effect of waste) a much greater number of terms. Hence the constant impression of elasticity, and that of those pressures of necessity under which value and virtue, character and quantity, greatness and glory even, to a considerable extent, are imputed and projected. There has to be a facility for the working of any social form— facility of comparison and selection in some communities, facility of rapid conversion in others. That is where the American material is elastic, where it affects one, as a whole, in the manner of some huge india-rubber cloth fashioned for "field" use and warranted to bear inordinate stretching.

One becomes aware thus wherever one turns, both of the tension and of the resistance; everything and every one, all objects and elements, all systems, arrangements, institutions, functions, persons, reputations, give the sense of their pulling hard at the india-rubber: almost always, wonderfully, without breaking it off, yet never quite with the effect of causing it to lie thick. The matter of interest, however, is just this fact that its thinness should so generally—in some cases, to all intents and purposes, so richly—suffice; suffice, that is, for producing unaided, impressions of a sort that make their way to us in "Europe" through superimposed densities, a thousand thicknesses of tradition. Which is what one means, again, by the differing "values"; the thinness doing perforce, on the one side, much of the work done by the thickness on the other: the work, in particular, of the appeal to the fond observer. He is by his very nature committed everywhere to his impression—which means essentially, I think, that he is foredoomed, in one place as in another, to "put in" a certain quantity of emotion and reflection. The turn his sensibility takes depends of course on what is before him; but when is it ever not in some manner exposed and alert? If it be anything really of a touchstone it is more disposed, I hold, to easy bargains than to hard ones; it only wants to be *somehow* interested, and is not without the knowledge that an emotion is after all, at the best or the worst, but an emotion. All of which is a voluminous commentary, I admit, on the modest text that I perhaps made the University Hospital stand for too many things. That establishes at all events my contention— that the living fact, in the United States, *will* stand, other facts not preventing, for almost anything you may ask of it. Other facts, at Baltimore, didn't prevent—there being none, outside the University circle, of any perceptibly public, any majestic or impressive or competitive order. So it was as if this particular experience had been (as the visitation of cities goes) that of *all* present art and organization, that of all antiquity, history, piety, sociability, that of the rich real and the rich romantic, in fine, at a stroke. Had there been more to see and to feel I should possibly have seen and felt more; yet what was absent, with this sense of feeling and seeing so much?

IV

There *were* other facts, in abundance, I hasten to add; only they were not, as I say, competitive, not of the public or majestic order—so that they the less imposed, for appreciation, any rearrangement of values. They were a matter still of the famous, the felicitous Sunday—into which as into an armful of the biggest and bravest June roses I seemed to find my perceptions cluster. Foremost among these meanwhile was that of the plentiful presence, freshly recognized, of absolute values too—which offer themselves, in the midst of the others, with a sharpness of their own, and which owe nothing, for interest, to any question of the general scale. The Country Club, for instance, as I have already had occasion to note, is everywhere a clear American felicity; a *complete* product of the social soil and air which alone have made it possible, and wearing whenever met that assured face of the full-blown flower and the proved proposition. These institutions speak so of American life as a success that they affected me at moments as crying aloud to be commemorated—since it is on American life only that they are founded, and since they render it, to my mind, the good office of making it keep all its graces and of having caused it to shed, by the same stroke, the elements that are contrary to these. Nothing is more suggestive than to recognize, each time, on the premises, the thing that "wouldn't do in Europe"—for a judgment of the reasons of its doing so well in the one hemisphere and so ill in the other promptly becomes illuminating. The illumination is one at which, had I space, I should have liked to light here a candle or two—partaking indeed by that character of a like baffled virtue in many another group of social phenomena. The Country Club testifies, in short, and gives its evidence, from the box, with the inimitable, invaluable accent of American authority. It becomes, for the restless analyst, one of the great garden-lamps in which the flame of Democracy burns whitest and steadiest and most floods the subject; taking its place thus on the positive side of a line which has its other side overscored with negatives. I may seem too much to brood upon it, but the interest of the American scene being, beyond any other, the show, on so immense a scale, of what Democracy, pushing and breaking the ice like an Arctic explorer, is making of things, any scrap that contributes to it wears a part of its dignity. To have been beforehand with the experiments, with several rather risky ones at least, and to have got on with these so beautifully while other rueful nations prowl, in the dusk, inquisitive but apprehensive, round the red windows of the laboratory, peeping, for the last news, between each other's shoulders—all this is, for the democratic force, to have stolen a march over no little of the ground, and to have gained time on such a scale as perhaps to make the belated of the earth, the critical group at the windows, still live to think of themselves as having too much wasted it.

There had been one—I mean a blest Country Club—in the neighbourhood of Boston (where indeed I believe there were a dozen, at least as exemplary, out of my range); there had been another, quite marvellous, on the Hudson—one of a numerous array, probably, within an hour's run of New York; there had been a supreme specimen, supreme for a documentary worth, even at Charleston (I reserve to myself to explain in due course, and ah, in such an exquisite sense, my "even"). This had made for me, if you will, a short list, but it had made a long admonition, to which the embowered institution near Baltimore was to add a wonderful emphasis. An admonition of what? it will meanwhile be asked: to which the answer may perhaps, for the moment, not be more precipitate than by one's saying that with any feeling for American life you soon enough see. You see its most complete attestation of its believing in itself unlimitedly, and also of its being right about itself at more points than it is wrong. You see it apply its general theory of its nature and strength—much of this doubtless quite an unconscious one—with a completeness and a consistency that will strike you also (or that ought to) as constituting an unconscious heroism. You will see it accept in detail, with a sublime serenity, certain large social consequences—the consequences of the straight application, in the most delicate conditions, of the prime democratic idea. As this idea is that of an universal eligibility, so you see it, under the application, beautifully resist the strain. So you see, in a word, everything staked on the conception of the young Family as a clear social unit—which, when all is said and done, remains, roundabout you, the ubiquitous fact. The conception of the Family is, goodness knows, "European" enough; but the difference resides in its working on one side of the world in the vertical and on the other in the horizontal sense. If its identity in "Europe," that is, resides more especially in its perpendicular, its backward and forward extension, its ascent and descent of the long ladder of time, so it develops in the United States mainly by its lateral spread, as one may say; expressing itself thus rather by number than by name, and yet taking itself for granted, when one comes to compare, with an intensity to which mere virtue of name elsewhere scarce helps it. American manners, as they stand, register therefore the apotheosis of the Family—a truth for which they have by no means received due credit; and it is in the light of Country Clubs that all this becomes vivid. These organizations accept the Family as the social unit—accept its extension, its *whole* extension, through social space, and accept it as many times over as the question comes up: which is what one means by their sublime and successful consistency. No, if I may still insist, nothing anywhere accepts anything as the American Country Club accepts these whole extensions.

That is why I speak of it as accepting the universal eligibility. With no palpable result does the democratic idea, in the States, more bristle than with the view that the younger are "as good" as the elder; family life is in fact, as from child to parent, from sister to brother, from wife to husband, from employed to employer, the eminent field of the democratic demonstration. This then is the unit that, with its latent multiplications, the Country Club takes over—and it is easy to see how such units must multiply. This is the material to which it addresses, with such effect, the secret of its power. I may of course be asked what I mean by an eligibility that is "universal"; but it seems needless to remark that even the most inclusive social scheme must in a large community always stop somewhere. Distinctly diverting, often, to Americans, the bewilderment of the "European" mind on the subject of "differences" and of the practicability of precautions for maintaining these; so beset is that mind, to the American view, with this theory, this habit or need of precautions, and so disposed apparently to fear, in its anxiety, that without the precautions the differences—dreadful thought—may cease. The American theory is, I think, but vague, and the inevitable consciousness of differences reduced to a matter of practice—a matter which, on the whole, very much takes care of itself. Glimpses and revelations come to it, across the sea, on the great wave of modern publicity—images of a

social order in which the precautions, as from above to below, are more striking than the differences and thereby out of
proportion to them: an appearance that reads a lesson, of a
sort, as to leaving precautions alone. It is true, at any rate,
that no application of the aristocratic, none of the democratic,
idea is ever practically complete; discriminations are produced
by the mere working of the machine, and they so engage alike
almost every one's interest, meet alike almost every one's convenience. Nature and industry keep producing differences as
fast as constitutions keep proclaiming equality, and there are
always, at the best, in any really liberal scheme or human
view, more conscious inaptitudes to convince of their privilege than conscious possibilities to remind of their limits. All
of which reflections, however, I agree, would probably have
remained a little dim even for the restless analyst, had not the
most shining of his examples bathed the subject, to his eyes,
in radiance. This could only be, as I have intimated, that of
the bright institution on the Hudson, as half-an-hour's vision
of it, one splendid Sunday of the May-time put it before
me—all in terms so eloquent that I would fain have translated them on the spot.

For there, to every appearance, was the high perfection of
the type—the ample, spreading, galleried house, hanging
over the great river, with its beautiful largeness of provision
for associated pleasures. The American note was *there*—in the
intensity and continuity of the association, and the interest of
the case was in its thus enjoying, for the effect, all the advantages that experience, chastening experience, and taste, "real"
taste, could heap upon it. Somewhere in one's mind, doubtless, lurked the apprehension that such a "proposition" might,
in that emphatic form, have betrayed a thousand flaws—
whereas all one *could* say face to face with it, treading its great
verandahs and conversation-rooms, its halls of refreshment,
repose and exercise, its kitchens and its courts and its baths
and its gardens, its wondrous inside and outside palæstra, was
that it positively revealed new forms of felicity. It was thus
a new and original thing—rare phenomenon—and actually
an "important" one; for what did it represent (all discriminations made and recognized) but the active Family, as a
final social fact, or in other words the sovereign People, as a

pervasive and penetrative mass, "doing" themselves on un-precedented lines? They had invoked, certainly, high and con-gruous countenance; but vain I thought the objection made when I exclaimed to a friend on these marvels. "It depends upon whom I call the People? Of course it depends: so I call them, exactly, the groups and figures we see, here before us, enjoying, and enjoying both so expertly and so discreetly, these conveniences and luxuries. That's their interest—that they *are* the people; for what interest, under the sun, would they have if they weren't? They are the people 'arrived,' and, what is more, disembarked: that's all the difference. It seems a difference because elsewhere (in 'Europe,' say again), though we see them begin, at the very most, to arrive, so-cially, we yet practically see them still on the ship—we have never yet seen them disembark thus *en masse*. This is the effect they have when, all impediments and objections on the dock removed, they do *that*." And later on, at the afternoon's end, on the platform of the large agreeable riverside station which spread there, close at hand, as the appanage of the club itself, I could but call attention to the manner in which every im-pression reinforced my moral. The Families, the parties, the groups and couples (the element of the Individual, as distin-guished from that of the Family, being remarkably absent) had gathered in the soft eventide for the return to New York, and it was impossible not to read each sign of the show in the vivid "popular" light. Only one did so—and this was the great point—with a positive uplifting of the spirit. Every-thing hung together and every one was charming. It was my explanatory word therefore to my companion. "That's what the People *are* when they've disembarked."

Having said so much—and with the sense, strange as it may appear, that there would still be much to say—I must add that I suddenly seem to see consternation in the charming face of the establishment, deep in the Baltimore countryside, my impression of which was to lay a train for these reflec-tions: so that with a conscience less clear I might take the image as a warning against the vice of reading too much meaning into simple intentions. Therefore let me admit that the conscious purpose of this house of hospitality didn't look beyond the immediate effect of luncheon or dinner on one of its deep southern verandahs, with great trees, close at hand, flinging their shade, with the old garden of the old country home that the Club had inherited forming one prospect, and with a deep woodland valley, stream-haunted if I am not mistaken, giving breadth of style to another. The Maryland boughs, for that matter, creating in the upper air great classic serenities of shade, give breadth of style; and the restless analyst, all grateful, and truly for the nonce at rest, could but ruefully note how little they had borrowed from any Northern, and least of all from any New England, model their almost academic grace. They might have borrowed it straight from far-away Claudes and Turners; yet one made no point of that either—their interest was so sufficiently their own. Distances of view have often in the North the large elegance, but nearnesses almost never; these are at their worst constitutionally coarse and at their best merely well-meaning. I was to find food all day for that observation; I was to remain under a charm of which breadth of style was the key. Earth and air, between them, had taken it in hand—so that one was always moving, somehow, under arches that were "triumphal" or sitting in bowers that made one think of temples. It was not that man, or that art, had done much, though indeed they had incurred no shame and had even been capable of a masterpiece, seen in the waning light, of which I shall presently speak. It was the diffused, mitigated glow, the happy medium itself that continued to be meanwhile half the picture. I wandered through it from one impression to another, and I keep, with intensity, that of the admirable outlying Park, treasure of the town, through which I had already three or four times driven, but the holiday life of which, on the warm Sunday night, humming, languidly, under the stars, as with spent voices of the homeward-bound, attested more than ever its valuable function.

That must have been, in the whole pleasant incoherence, on my way back from the sweet old Carroll house, climax of an afternoon drive, yet before another, an ultimate visit, which was the climax of everything. I have sufficiently noted already the charming law under which, in the States, any approach to really ripe architectural charm—for the real ripeness is indispensable—enjoys advantages, those of mystery and sanctity, that are achieved in "Europe" but on greatly harder terms. The observed practice of this art, at times singularly subtle, is in fact half the reward of one's attention, puzzled though the latter may none the less be to see how the trick is played. So much at any rate one remembers; yet where, after all, would the sweet old Carroll house, nestling under its wood in the late June afternoon, and with something vaguely haunted in its lonely refinement, not have made an insidious appeal? There are sweet old Carroll houses, I believe, on several other sites—the luckiest form perhaps in which a flourishing family may have been moved to write its annals. The intimation of "annals" hangs about the place, and again we try to capture, under the charming pillared portico, before the mild red brick and the pale pediment and facings, in the series of high chambers, quite instinct with style (small far-off cousins of such "apartments," say, as those of Kensington Palace, though they cover, bungalow-fashion, scarce more than one floor), some lingering, living accents of such a profession of history. We capture verily, I think, nothing; we merely project a little, from one room and from one mild aspect of the void to another, our old habit of suppositions. Bred of other historic contacts, it instinctively puts forth feelers; but the feelers drop, after a little, like hands that meet nothing; our suppositions themselves, as I have called them, and which but return to us like toy ships that won't sail, are all they find tangible. There is satisfaction of a sort, however, even in such arrested questions, when, as before this delicate faintly-resonant shell, each other element also helping, they have been vividly enough suggested. Later on, for the real crown of my day, no wonderments were checked and no satisfactions imperfect. Attained, for the high finish of the evening, by another plunge, behind vaguely-playing carriage-lamps, into the bosky, odorous, quite ridiculously-romantic suburban night, this was the case of an ancient home without lapses or breaks, where the past and the present were in friendliest fusion, so that the waiting future evidently slumbered with confidence; and where, above the easy open-air "Southern" hospitality, an impression now of shafts of mild candle-light across overlaced outer galleries and of throbs of nature's voice in the dark vaster circle, the Maryland boughs, at their best, presided in the unforgettable grand manner.

XI

Washington

I

I was twice in Washington, the first time for a winter visit, the second to meet the wonderful advance of summer, to which, in that climate of many charms, the first days of May open wide the gates. This latter impression was perforce much the more briefly taken; yet, though I had gathered also from other past occasions, far-away years now, something of the sense of the place at the earlier season, I find everything washed over, at the mention of the name, by the rare light, half green, half golden, of the lovely leafy moment. I see all the rest, till I make the effort to break the spell, through that voluminous veil; which operates, for memory, quite as the explosion of spring works, even to the near vision, in respect to the American scene at large—dressing it up as if for company, preparing it for social, for human intercourse, making it in fine publicly presentable, with an energy of renewal and an effect of redemption not often to be noted, I imagine, on other continents. Nowhere, truly, can summer have such work cut out for it as here—nowhere has it to take upon itself to repaint the picture so completely. In the "European" landscape, in general, some, at least, of the elements and objects remain upon the canvas; here, on the other hand, one seems to see intending Nature, the great artist of the season, decline to touch that surface unless it be first swept clean—decline, at any rate, to deal with it save by ignoring all its perceived pretensions. Vernal Nature, in England, in France, in Italy, has still a use, often a charmed or amused indulgence, for the material in hand, the furniture of the foreground, the near and middle distances, the heterogeneous human features of the face of the land. She looks at her subject much as the portrait-painter looks at the personal properties, this or that household object, the official uniform, the badges and ornaments, the favourite dress, of his sitter—with an "Oh, yes, I

627

can bring them in; they're just what I want, and I see how they will help me out." But I try in vain to recall a case in which, either during the New England May and June, or during those of the Middle States (since these groups of weeks have in the two regions a differing identity and value), the genius in question struck me as adopting with any frankness, as doing more than passively, helplessly accept, the supplied paraphernalia, the signs of existing life. The business is clearly to get rid of them as far as may be, to cover and smother them; dissimulating with the biggest, freest brush their impertinence and their ugliness.

I must ask myself, I meanwhile recognize, none the less, why I should have found Mount Vernon exquisite, the first of May, if the interest had all to be accounted for in the light of nature. The light of nature was there, splendid and serene; the Potomac opened out in its grandest manner; the bluff above the river, before the sweep of its horizon, raised its head for the historic crown. But it was not for a moment to be said that this was the whole story; the human interest and the human charm lay in wait and held one fast—so that, if one had been making light, elsewhere, of their suggestion and office, one had at least this case seriously to reckon with. I speak straightway, thus, of Mount Vernon, though it be but an outlying feature of Washington, and at the best a minor impression; the image of the particular occasion is seated so softly in my path. There was a glamour, in fine, for the excursion— that of an extraordinarily gracious hospitality; and the glamour would still have been great even if I had not, on my return to the shadow of the Capitol, found the whole place transfigured. The season was over, the President away, the two Houses up, the shutters closed, the visitor rare; and one lost one's way in the great green vistas of the avenues quite as one might have lost it in a "sylvan solitude"—that is in the empty alleys of a park. The emptiness was qualified at the most, here and there, by some encounter with a stray diplomatic agent, wreathed for the most part in sincerer smiles than we are wont to attribute to his class. "This"—it was the meaning of these inflections—"was the *real* Washington, a place of enchantment; so that if the enchantment were never less who could ever bring himself to go away?" The enchantment had been so much less in January—one could easily understand; yet the recognition seemed truly the voice of the hour, and one picked it up with a patriotic flutter not diminished by the fact that the speaker would probably be going away, and with delight, on the morrow.

The memory of some of the smiles and inflections comes back in that light; Washington being the one place in America, I think, where those qualities are the values and vehicles, the medium of exchange. No small part of the interest of the social scene there consists, inevitably, for any restless analyst, in wonder about the "real" sentiments of appointed foreign participants, the delegates of Powers and pledged alike to penetration and to discretion, before phenomena which, whatever they may be, differ more from the phenomena of other capitals and other societies than they resemble them. This interest is susceptible, on occasion, of becoming intense; all the more that curiosity must, for the most part, pursue its object (that of truly looking over the alien shoulder and of seeing, judging, building, fearing, reporting with the alien sense) by subtle and tortuous ways. This represents, first and last, even for a watcher abjectly irresponsible, a good deal of speculative tension; so that one's case is refreshing in presence of the clear candour of such a proposition as that the national capital *is* charming in proportion as you don't see it. For that is what it came to, in the bowery condition; the as yet unsurmounted bourgeois character of the whole was screened and disguised; the dressing-up, in other words, was complete, and the great park-aspect gained, and became nobly artificial, by the very complexity of the plan of the place—the perpetual perspectives, the converging, radiating avenues, the frequent circles and crossways, where all that was wanted for full illusion was that the bronze generals and admirals, on their named pedestals, should have been great garden-gods, mossy mythological marble. This would have been the perfect note; the long vistas yearned for it, and the golden chequers scattered through the gaps of the high arches waited for some bending nymph or some armless Hermes to pick them up. The power of the scene to evoke such visions sufficiently shows, I think, what had become, under the mercy of nature, of the hard facts, as one must everywhere call them; and yet though I could, diplomatically, patriotically pretend, at the right moment, that such a Washington *was* the "real" one, my assent had all the while a still finer meaning for myself.

I am hanging back, however, as with a sacred terror, from Mount Vernon, where indeed I may not much linger, or only enough to appear not to have shirked the responsibility incurred at the opening of these remarks. There, in ample possession, was masking, dissimulating summer, the envelope and disguise to which I have hinted that the American picture owes, on its human side, *all* its best presentability; and at the same time, unmistakably, there was the spell, as quite a distinct matter, of the hard little facts in themselves. How came it that if they could throw a spell they were yet so abject and so negligible? How came it that if they had no intrinsic sweetness, no visible dignity, they could yet play their part in so unforgettable an impression? The answer to this can only be, I think, that we happen here to "strike," as they say, one of the rarest of cases, a spot on which all sorts of sensibilities are touched and on which a lively emotion, and one yet other than the æsthetic, makes us its prey. The old high-placed house, unquestionably, is charming, and the felicity of the whole scene, on such a day as that of my impression, scarce to be uttered. The little hard facts, facts of form, of substance, of scale, facts of essential humility and exiguity, none the less, look us straight in the face, present themselves literally to be counted over—and reduce us thereby to the recognition of our supreme example of the rich interference of association. Association does, at Mount Vernon, simply what it likes with us—it is of so beautiful and noble a sort; and to this end it begins by making us unfit to say whether or no we would in its absence have noticed the house for any material grace at all. We scarce care more for its being proved picturesque, the house, than for its being proved plain; its architectural interest and architectural nullity become one and the same thing for us. If asked what we should think of it if it hadn't been, or if we hadn't known it for, Washington's, we retort that the inquiry is inane, since it is not the possessive case, but the straight, serene nominative, that we are dealing with. The whole thing *is* Washington—not his invention and his property, but his presence and his person; with discriminations (as distinguished from enthusiasms) as invidious and unthinkable as if they were addressed to his very ears.

The great soft fact, as opposed to the little hard ones, is the beauty of the site itself; that is definitely, if ever so delicately, sublime, but it fails to rank among the artificial items that I began by speaking of, those of so generally compromising an effect in the American picture. Everything else is *communicated* importance, and the magic so wrought for the American sensibility—by which I mean the degree of the importance and the sustained high pitch of the charm—place it, doubtless, the world over, among the few supreme triumphs of such communication. The beauty of the site, meanwhile, as we stand there, becomes but the final aspect of the man; under which everything conduces to a single great representative image, under which every feature of the scene, every object in the house, however trivial, borrows from it and profits by it. The image is the largest, clearest possible of the resting, as distinguished from the restless, consciousness of public service consummately rendered. The terms we commonly use for that condition—peace with honour, well-earned repose, enjoyment of homage, recognition of facts—render but dimly the luminous stillness in which, on its commanding eminence, we see our image bathed. It hangs together with the whole bright immensity of air and view. It becomes truly the great white, decent page on which the whole sense of the place is written. It does more things even besides; attends us while we move about and goes with us from room to room; mounts with us the narrow stairs, to stand with us in these small chambers and look out of the low windows; takes up for us, to turn them over with spiritual hands, the objects from which we respectfully forbear, and places an accent, in short, through the rambling old phrase, wherever an accent is required. Thus we arrive at the full meaning, as it were—thus we know, at least, why we are so moved.

It is for the same reason for which we are always inordinately moved, on American ground, I think, when the unconscious minor scale of the little old demonstrations to which we owe everything is made visible to us, when their disproportionate modesty is proved upon them. The reason worked at Mount Vernon, for the restless analyst, quite as it had worked a few months before, on the small and simple scene of Concord Fight: the slight, pale, bleeding Past, in a patched homespun suit, stands there taking the thanks of the bloated Present—having woundedly rescued from thieves and brought to his door the fat, locked pocket-book of which that personage appears the owner. The pocket-book contains, "unbeknown" to the honest youth, bank-notes of incredible figure, and what breaks our heart, if we be cursed with the historic imagination, is the grateful, wan smile with which the great guerdon of sixpence is received. I risk, floridly, the assertion that half the intensity of the impression of Mount Vernon, for many a visitor, will ever be in this vision there of Washington *only* (so far as consciously) so rewarded. Such fantastications, I indeed admit, are refinements of response to any impression, but the ground had been cleared for them, and it ministered to luxury of thought, for instance, that we were a small party at our ease there, with no other circulation—with the prowling ghosts of fellow-pilgrims, too harshly present on my previous occasion, all conveniently laid. This alone represented privilege and power, and they in turn, with their pomp and circumstance of a charming Government launch, under official attendance, at the Navy-Yard steps, amid those large, clean, protecting and protected properties of the State which always make one think much of the State, whatever its actual infirmities—these things, to say nothing of other rich enhancements, above all those that I may least specify, flung over the day I scarce know what iridescent reflection of the star-spangled banner itself, in the folds of which I had never come so near the sense of being positively wrapped. That consciousness, so unfamiliar, was, under the test, irresistible; it pressed the spring, absolutely, of intellectual exaltation—with the consequent loud resonance that my account of my impressions doubtless sufficiently translates.

II

Washington itself meanwhile—the Washington always, I premise, of the rank outsider—had struck me from the first as presenting two distinct faces; the more obvious of which was the public and official, the monumental, with features all more or less majestically playing the great administrative, or, as we nowadays put it, Imperial part. This clustered, yet at the same time oddly scattered, city, a general impression of high granite steps, of light grey corniced colonnades, rather harmoniously low, contending for effect with slaty mansard roofs and masses of iron excrescence, a general impression of somewhat vague, empty, sketchy, fundamentals, however expectant, however spacious, overweighted by a single Dome and overaccented by a single Shaft—this loose congregation of values seemed, strangely, a matter disconnected and remote, though remaining in its way portentous and bristling all incoherently at the back of the scene. The back of the scene, indeed, to one's quite primary sense, might have been but an immense painted, yet unfinished cloth, hung there to a confessedly provisional end and marked with the queerness, among many queernesses, of looking always the same; painted once for all in clear, bright, fresh tones, but never emerging from its flatness, after the fashion of other capitals, into the truly, the variously, modelled and rounded state. (It appeared provisional therefore because looking as if it might have been unhooked and removed as a whole; because any one object in it so treated would have made the rest also come off.) The foreground was a different thing, a thing that, ever so quaintly, seemed to represent the force really in possession; though consisting but of a small company of people engaged perpetually in conversation and (always, I repeat, for the rank outsider) singularly destitute of conspicuous marks or badges. This little society easily became, for the detached visitor, the city itself, *the* national capital and the greater part of the story; and that, ever, in spite of the comparatively scant intensity of its political permeation. The political echo was of course to be heard in it, and the public character, in his higher forms, to be encountered—though only in "single spies," not in battalions; but there was something that made it much more individual than any mere predominance of political or administrative colour would have made it; leaving it in that case to do no more than resemble the best society in London, or that in best possession of the field in Paris.

Two sharp signs my remoter remembrance had shown me the then Washington world, and the first met, as putting forth; one of these the fact of its being extraordinarily easy and pleasant, and the other that of one's appearing to make out in it not more than half-a-dozen members of the Lower House and not more than a dozen of the Upper. This kept down the political permeation, and was bewildering, if one was able to compare, in the light of the different London condition, the fact of the social ubiquity there of the acceptable M.P. and that of the social frequency even of his more equivocal hereditary colleague. A London nestling under the towers of Westminster, yet practically void of members of the House of Commons, and with the note of official life far from exclusively sounding, that might have been in those days the odd image of Washington, had not the picture been stamped with other variations still. These were a whole cluster, not instantly to be made out, but constituting the unity of the place as soon as perceived; representing that finer extract or essence which the self-respecting observer is never easy till he be able to shake up and down in bottled form. The charming company of the foreground then, which referred itself so little to the sketchy back-scene, the monstrous Dome and Shaft, figments of the upper air, the pale colonnades and mere myriad-windowed Buildings, was the second of the two faces, and the more one lived with it the more, up to a certain point, one lived away from the first. In time, and after perceiving *how* it was what it so agreeably was, came the recognition of common ground; the recognition that, in spite of strange passages of the national life, liable possibly to recur, during which the President himself was scarce thought to be in society, the particular precious character that one had apprehended could never have ripened without a general consensus. One had put one's finger on it when one had seen disengage itself from many anomalies, from not a few drolleries, the superior, the quite majestic fact of the City of Conversation pure and simple, and positively of the only specimen, of any such intensity, in the world.

That had remained for me, from the other time, the properest name of Washington, and nothing could so interest me, on a renewal of acquaintance, too long postponed and then too woefully brief, as to find my description wholly justified. If the emphasis added by "pure and simple" be invariably retained, the description will continue, I think, to embrace and exhaust the spectacle, while yet leaving it every inch of its value. Clearly quite immeasurable, on American ground, the value of such an assertion of a town-type directly opposed to the unvarying American, and quite unique, on any ground, so organized a social indifference to the vulgar vociferous Market. Washington may of course *know* more than she confesses—no community could perhaps really be as ignorant as Washington used at any rate to look, and to like to look, of this particular thing, of "goods" and shares and rises and falls and all such sordidities; but she knows assuredly still the very least she can get off with, and nothing even yet pleases her more than to forget what she does know. She unlearns, she turns her back, while London, Paris, Berlin, Rome, in their character of political centres, strike us as, on the contrary, feverishly learning, trying more and more to do the exact opposite. (I speak, naturally, as to Washington, of knowing actively and interestedly, in the spirit of gain—not merely of the enjoyed lights of political and administrative science, doubtless as abundant there as anywhere else.) It might fairly have been, I used to think, that the charming place—charming in the particular connection I speak of—had on its conscience to make one forget for an hour the colossal greed of New York. Nothing, in fact, added more to its charm than its appearing virtually to invite one to impute to it some such vicarious compunction.

If I be reminded, indeed, that the distinction I here glance at is negative, and be asked what then (if she knew nothing of the great American interest) Washington did socially know, my answer, I recognize, has at once to narrow itself, and becomes perhaps truly the least bit difficult to utter. It none the less remains distinct enough that, the City of Conversation being only in question, and a general subject of all the conversation having thereby to be predicated, our responsibility is met as soon as we are able to say what Washington mainly talks, and appears always to go mainly talking, about. Washington talks about herself, and about almost nothing else; falling superficially indeed, on that ground, but into line with the other capitals. London, Paris, Berlin, Rome, goodness knows, talk about themselves: that is each member of this sisterhood talks, sufficiently or inordinately, of the great number of divided and differing selves that form together her controlling identity. London, for instance, talks of everything in the world without thereby for a moment, as it were, ceasing to be egotistical. It has taken everything in the world to make London up, so that she is in consequence simply doomed never to get away from herself. Her conversation is largely, I think, the very effort to do that; but she inevitably figures in it but as some big buzzing insect which keeps bumping against a treacherous mirror. It is in positive quest of an identity of some sort, much rather—an identity other than merely functional and technical—that Washington goes forth, encumbered with no ideal of avoidance or escape: it is about herself *as* the City of Conversation precisely that she incessantly converses; adorning the topic, moreover, with endless ingenuity and humour. But that, absolutely, remains the case; which thus becomes one of the most thorough, even if probably one of the most natural and of the happiest, cases of collective self-consciousness that one knows. The spectacle, as it at first met my senses, was that of a numerous community in ardent pursuit of some workable conception of its social self, and trying meanwhile intelligently to talk itself, and even this very embarrassment, into a *subject* for conversation. Such a picture might not seem purely pleasing, on the side of variety of appeal, and I admit one may have had one's reserves about it; reserves sometimes reflected, for example, in dim inward speculation—one of the effects of the Washington air I have already glanced at—as to the amount of response it might evoke in the diplomatic body. It may have been on my part a morbid obsession, but the diplomatic body was liable to strike one there as more characteristically "abysmal" than elsewhere, more impenetrably bland and inscrutably blank; and it was obvious, certainly, that their concern to help the place intellectually to find itself was not to be expected to approach in intensity the concern even of a repatriated absentee. You were concerned only if you had, by your sensibility, a stake in the game; which was the last thing a foreign representative would wish to confess to, this being directly opposed to all his enjoined duties. It is no part of the office of such personages to assist the societies to which they are accredited to find themselves—it is much more their mission to leave all such vaguely and, so far as may be, grotesquely groping: so apt are societies, in finding themselves, to find other things too. This detachment from the whole mild convulsion of effort, the considerate pretence of not being too aware of it, combined with latent probabilities of alarm about it no less than of amusement, represented, to the unquiet fancy, much more the spirit of the old-time Legations.

What *was*, at all events, better fun, of the finer sort, than having one's self a stake in the outcome?—what helped the time (so much of it as there was!) more to pass than just to join in the so fresh experiment of constitutive, creative talk? The boon, it should always be mentioned, meanwhile went on not in the least in the tone of solemnity. That would have been fatal, because probably irritating, and it was where the good star of Washington intervened. The tone was, so to speak, of *conscious* self-consciousness, and the highest genius for conversation doubtless dwelt in the fact that the ironic spirit was ready always to give its very self away, fifty times over, for the love, or for any quickening, of the theme. The foundation for the whole happy predicament remained, more-over, of the firmest, and the essence of the case was to be as easily stated as the great social fact is, in America, whether through exceptions or aggravations, everywhere to be stated. Nobody was in "business"—that was the sum and substance of it; and for the one large human assemblage on the conti-nent of which this was true the difference made was huge. Nothing could strike one more than that it was the only way in which, over the land, a difference *could* be made, and than how, in our vast commercial democracy, almost any differ-ence—by which I mean almost any exception—promptly ac-quires prodigious relief. The value here was at once that the place could offer to view a society, the only one in the coun-try, in which Men existed, and that that rich little fact became the key to everything. Superficially taken, I recognize, the cir-cumstance fails to look portentous; but it looms large imme-diately, gains the widest bearing, in the light of any direct or extended acquaintance with American conditions. From the moment it is adequately borne in mind that the business-man, in the United States, may, with no matter what dim struggles, gropings, yearnings, never hope to be anything *but* a business-man, the size of the field he so abdicates is measured, as well as the fact of the other care to which his abdication hands it over. It lies there waiting, pleading from all its pores, to be occupied—the lonely waste, the boundless gaping void of "society"; which is but a rough name for all the *other* so numerous relations with the world he lives in that are imputable to the civilized being. Here it is then that the world he lives in accepts its doom and becomes, by his default, subject and plastic to his mate; his default having made, all around him, the unexampled opportunity of the woman—which she would have been an incredible fool not to pounce upon. It needs little contact with American life to perceive how she *has* pounced, and how, outside business, she has made it over in her image. She has been, up to now, on the vast residual tract, in peerless possession, and is occupied in developing and extending her wonderful conquest, which she appreciates to the last inch of its extent.

III

She has meanwhile probably her hours of amazement at the size of her windfall; she cannot quite live without wonder at the oddity of her so "sleeping" partner, the strange creature, by her side, with his values and his voids, but who is best known to her as having yielded what she would have clutched to the death. Yet these are mere mystic, inscrutable possibilities—dreams, for us, of her hushed, shrouded hours: the face she shows, on all the facts, is that of mere unwinking tribute to the matter of course. The effect of these high signs of assurance in her has been—and it is really her master-stroke—to represent the situation as perfectly normal. Her companion's attitude, totally destitute of high signs, does everything it can to further this feat; so that, as disposed together in the American picture, they testify, extraordinarily, to the *successful* rupture of a universal law, the sight is at first, for observation, most mystifying. Then the impunity of the whole thing gains upon us; the equilibrium strikes us, however strangely, as at least provisionally stable; we see that a society in many respects workable would seem to have been arrived at, and that we shall in any case have time to study it. The phenomenon may easily become, for a spectator, the sentence written largest in the American sky: when he is in search of the characteristic, what else so plays the part? The woman is two-thirds of the apparent life—which means that she is absolutely all of the social; and, as this is nowhere else the case, the occasion is unique for seeing what such a situation may make of her. The result elsewhere, in Europe generally, of conditions in which men have actively participated and to which, throughout, they personally contribute, she has only the old story to tell, and keeps telling it after her fashion. The woman produced by a women-made society alone has obviously quite a new story—to which it is not for a moment to be gainsaid that the world at large has, for the last thirty years in particular, found itself lending an attentive, at times even a charmed, ear. The extent and variety of this attention have been the specious measure of the personal success of the type in question, and are always referred to when its value happens to be challenged. "The American woman?—why, she has beguiled, she has conquered, the globe: look at her fortune everywhere and fail to accept her if you can."

She has been, accordingly, about the globe, beyond all doubt, a huge success of curiosity; she has at her best—and far beyond any consciousness and intention of her own, lively as these for the most part usually are—infinitely amused the nations. It has been found among them that, for more reasons than we can now go into, her manner of embodying and representing her sex has fairly made of her a new human convenience, not unlike fifty of the others, of a slightly different order, the ingenious mechanical appliances, stoves, refrigerators, sewing-machines, type-writers, cash-registers, that have done so much, in the household and the place of business, for the American name. By which I am of course far from meaning that the revelation has been of her utility as a domestic drudge; it has been much rather in the fact that the advantages attached to her being a woman at all have been so happily combined with the absence of the drawbacks, for persons intimately dealing with her, traditionally suggested by that condition. The corresponding advantages, in the light of almost any old order, have always seemed inevitably paid for by the drawbacks; but here, unmistakably, was a case in which—as at first appeared, certainly—they were to be enjoyed very nearly for nothing. What it came to, evidently, was that she had been grown in an air in which a hundred of the "European" complications and dangers didn't exist, and in which also she had had to take upon herself a certain training for freedom. It was not that she had had, in the vulgar sense, to "look out" for herself, inasmuch as it was of the very essence of her position not to be threatened or waylaid; but that she could develop her audacity on the basis of her security, just as she could develop her "powers" in a medium from which criticism was consistently absent. Thus she arrived, full-blown, on the general scene, the least criticized object, in proportion to her importance, that had ever adorned it. It would take long to say why her situation, under this retrospect, may affect the inner fibre of the critic himself as one of the most touching on record; he may merely note his perception that she was to have been after all but the sport of fate. For why need she originally, he wonders, have embraced so confidently, so gleefully, yet so unguardedly, the terms offered her to an end practically so perfidious? Why need she, unless in the interest of her eventual discipline, have turned away with so light a heart after watching the Man, the deep American man, retire into his tent and let down the flap? She had her "paper" from him, their agreement signed and sealed; but would she not, in some other air and under some other sky, have been visited by a saving instinct? Would she not have said "No, this is too unnatural; there must be a trap in it somewhere—it's addressed really, in the long run, to making a fool of me?" It is impossible, of course, to tell; and her case, as it stands for us, at any rate, is that she showed no doubts. It is not on the American scene and in the presence of mere American phenomena that she is even yet to be observed as showing them; but does not my digression find itself meanwhile justified by the almost clear certainty that the first symptoms of the revulsion—of the *con*vulsion, I am tempted to say—must break out in Washington?

For here—and it is what I have been so long in coming to —here alone in the American world, do we catch the other sex not observing the agreement. I have described this anomaly, at Washington, as that of Man's socially "existing"; since we have seen that his fidelity to his compact throughout the country in general has involved his not doing so. What has happened, obviously, has been that his reasons, at a stroke, have dropped, and that he finds himself, without them, a different creature. He has discovered that he *can* exist in other connections than that of the Market, and that all he has therefore to settle is the question of whether he may. The most delicate interest of Washington is the fact that it is quite practically *being* settled there—in the practical way which is yet also the dramatic. *Solvitur ambulando*; it is being settled—that is the charm—as it goes, settled without discussion. It would be awkward and gross to say that Man has dealt any conscious blow at the monopoly of his companion, or that her prestige, as mistress of the situation, has suffered in any manner a noted abatement. Yet none the less, as he has there, in a degree, socially found himself and, allured by the new sense, is evidently destined to seek much further still, the sensible effect, the change of impression on one's coming from other places, is of the most marked. Man is solidly, vividly present, and the presence of Woman has consequently, for the proposed intensity, to reckon with it. The omens on behalf of the former appearance are just now strikingly enhanced, as happens, by the accident of the rare quality, as it were, of the particular male presence supremely presiding there; and it would certainly be strange that this idea of the re-committal to masculine hands of some share at least in the interests of civilization, some part of the social property and social office, should not, from so high an example, have received a new impulse and a new consecration. Easily enough, if we had space here to consider it, might come up the whole picture of the new indications thus afforded, the question of the degree in which a sex capable, in the American air, of having so despoiled itself may really be capable of retracing its steps and repairing its mistake. It would appear inevitable to ask whether such a mistake on such a scale *can* prove effectively reparable—whether ground so lost can be effectively recovered. Has not the American woman, with such a start, gained such an irreducible advance, on the whole high plane of the amenities, that her companion will never catch up with her?

This last is an inquiry that I must, alas, brush aside, though feeling it, as I have already noted, *the* most oddly interesting that the American spectacle proposes to us; only saying, provisionally, that the aspect of manners through the nation at large offers no warrant whatever for any prompt "No" to it.

It is not, however, of the nation at large I here speak; the case is of the extremely small, though important and significant, fraction of the whole represented by the Washington group—which thus shows us the Expropriated Half in the very act of itself pondering that issue. Is the man "up to it," up to the major heritage, the man who *could*, originally, so inconceivably, and for a mere mess of pottage if there ever was one, let it go? "Are we up to it, really, at this time of day, and what on earth will awfully become of us if the question, once put to the test, shall have to be decided against us?" I think it not merely fanciful to say that some dim, distressful interrogative sound of that sort frequently reached, in the Washington air, the restless analyst—though not to any quickening of his own fear. With a perfect consciousness that it was still early to say, that the data are as yet insufficient and that the missing quantity must absolutely be found before it can be weighed and valued, he was none the less struck with the felicity of many symptoms and would fairly have been able to believe at moments that the character hitherto so effaced has but to show the confidence of taking itself for granted. That act of itself reveals, restores, reinstates and completes this character. Is it not, for that matter, essentially implied in our recognition of the place as the City of Conversation? The victim of effacement, the outcast at the door, has, all the while we have been talking of him, *talked himself* back; and if anything could add to this happy portent it would be another that had scarcely less bearing. Nowhere more than in Washington, positively, were the women to have struck me as naturally and harmoniously in the social picture—as happily, soothingly, proportionately, and no more than proportionately, participant and ministrant. Hence the irresistible conclusion that with the way really shown them they would only ask to take it; the way being their assent to the truth that the abdication of the Man proves ever (after the first flush of their triumph) as bad really for their function as

for his. Hence, in fine, the appearance that, with the proportions re-established, they will come to recognize their past
world as a fools' paradise, and their present, and still more
their future, as much more made to endure. They could not,
one reasoned, have been, in general, so perfectly agreeable
unless they had been pleased, and they could not have been
pleased without the prospect of gaining, by the readjusted
relation, more, on the whole, than they were to lose; without
the prospect even again perhaps of truly and insidiously gaining more than the other beneficiary. That *would* be, I think,
the feminine conception of a readministered justice. Washington, at such a rate, in any case, might become to them as
good as "Europe," and a Europe of their own would obviously be better than a Europe of other people's. There are,
after all, other women on the other continents.

IV

One might have been sure in advance that the character of a
democracy would nowhere more sharply mark itself than in
the democratic substitute for a court city, and Washington is
cast in the mould that expresses most the absence of salient
social landmarks and constituted features. Here it is that conversation, as the only invoked presence, betrays a little its in-
adequacy to the furnishing forth, all by itself, of an outward
view. It tells us it must be there, since in all the wide empty
vistas nothing else is, and the general elimination *can* but have
left it. A pleading, touching effect, indeed, lurks in this sense
of it as seated, at receipt of custom, by any decent door of any
decent domicile and watching the vacancy for reminder and
appeal. It is left to conversation alone to people the scene
with accents; putting aside two or three objects to be speci-
fied, there is *never* an accent in it, up and down, far and wide,
save such as fall rather on the ear of the mind: those projected
by the social spirit starved for the sense of an occasional emphasis. The White House is an accent—one of the lightest,
sharpest possible; and the Capitol, of course, immensely, another; though the latter falls on the exclusively political page,
as to which I have been waiting to say a word. It should
meanwhile be mentioned that we are promised these enhance-

ments, these illustrations, of the great general text, on the most magnificent scale; a splendid projected and announced Washington of the future, with approaches even now grandly outlined and massively marked; in face of which one should perhaps confess to the futility of any current estimate. If I speak thus of the Capitol, however, let me not merely brush past the White House to get to it—any more than feel free to pass into it without some preliminary stare at that wondrous Library of Congress which glitters in fresh and almost unmannerly emulation, almost frivolous irrelevance of form, in the neighbourhood of the greater building. About the ingenuities and splendours of this last costly structure, a riot of rare material and rich ornament, there would doubtless be much to say—did not one everywhere, on all such ground, meet the open eye of criticism simply to establish with it a private intelligence, simply to respond to it by a deprecating wink. The guardian of that altar, I think, is but too willing, on such a hint, to let one pass without the sacrifice.

It is a case again here, as on fifty other occasions, of the tribute instantly paid by the revisiting spirit; but paid, all without question, to the general *kind* of presence for which the noisy air, over the land, feels so sensibly an inward ache— the presence that corresponds there, no matter how loosely, to that of the housing and harbouring European Church in the ages of great disorder. The Universities and the greater Libraries (the smaller, for a hundred good democratic reasons, are another question), repeat, in their manner, to the imagination, East and West, the note of the old thick-walled convents and quiet cloisters: they are large and charitable, they are sturdy, often proud and often rich, and they have the incalculable value that they represent the only intermission to inordinate rapacious traffic that the scene offers to view. With this suggestion of sacred ground they play even upon the most restless of analysts as they will, making him face about, with ecstasy, any way they seem to point; so that he feels it his business much less to count over their shortcomings than to proclaim them places of enchantment. They are better at their worst than anything else at its best, and the comparatively sweet sounds that stir their theoretic stillness are for him as echoes of the lyre of Apollo. The Congressional

Library is magnificent, and would become thus a supreme sanctuary even were it ten times more so: there would seem to be nothing then but to pronounce it a delight and have done with it—or let the appalled imagination, in other words, slink into it and stay there. But here is pressed precisely, with particular force, the spring of the question that takes but a touch to sound: is the case of this remarkable creation, by exception, a case in which the violent waving of the pecuniary wand *has* incontinently produced interest? The answer can only be, I feel, a shy assent—though shy indeed only till the logic of the matter is apparent. This logic is that, though money alone can gather in on such a scale the treasures of knowledge, these treasures, in the form of books and documents, themselves organize and furnish their world. They appoint and settle the proportions, they thicken the air, they people the space, they create and consecrate all their relations, and no one shall say that, where they scatter life, which they themselves in fact *are*, history does not promptly attend. Emphatically yes, therefore, the great domed and tiered, galleried and statued central hall of the Congressional, the last word of current constructional science and artistic resource, already crowns itself with that grace.

The graceful thing in Washington beyond any other, none the less, is the so happily placed and featured White House, the late excellent extensions and embellishments of which have of course represented expenditure—but only of the refined sort imposed by some mature portionless gentlewoman on relatives who have accepted the principle of making her, at a time of life, more honourably comfortable. The whole ample precinct and margin formed by the virtual continuity of its grounds with those expanses in which the effect of the fine Washington Obelisk rather spends or wastes itself (not a little as if some loud monosyllable had been uttered, in a preoccupied company, without a due production of sympathy or sense)—the fortunate isolation of the White House, I say, intensifies its power to appeal to that musing and mooning visitor whose perceptions alone, in all the conditions, I hold worthy of account. Hereabouts, beyond doubt, history had from of old seemed to me insistently seated, and I remember a short spring-time of years ago when Lafayette Square itself, contiguous to the Executive Mansion, could create a rich sense of the past by the use of scarce other witchcraft than its command of that pleasant perspective and its possession of the most prodigious of all Presidential effigies, Andrew Jackson, as archaic as a Ninevite king, prancing and rocking through the ages. If that atmosphere, moreover, in the fragrance of the Washington April, was even a quarter of a century since as a liquor of bitter-sweet taste, overflowing its cup, what was the ineffable mixture now, with all the elements further distilled, all the life further sacrificed, to make it potent? One circled about the place as for meeting the ghosts, and one paused, under the same impulse, before the high palings of the White House drive, as if wondering at haunted ground. There the ghosts stood in their public array, spectral enough and clarified; yet scarce making it easier to "place" the strange, incongruous blood-drops, as one looked through the rails, on that revised and freshened page. But one fortunately has one's choice, in all these connections, as one turns away; the mixture, as I have called it, is really here so fine. General Jackson, in the centre of the Square, still rocks his hobby and the earth; but the fruit of the interval, to my actual eyes, hangs nowhere brighter than in the brilliant memorials lately erected to Lafayette and to Rochambeau. Artful, genial, expressive, the tribute of French talent, these happy images supply, on the spot, the note without which even the most fantasticating sense of our national past would feel itself rub forever against mere brown homespun. Everything else gives way, for me, I confess, as I again stand before them; everything, whether as historic fact, or present *agrément*, or future possibility, yields to this one high luxury of our old friendship with France.

The "artistic" Federal city already announced spreads itself then before us, in plans elaborated even to the finer details, a city of palaces and monuments and gardens, symmetries and circles and far radiations, with the big Potomac for water-power and water-effect and the recurrent Maryland spring, so prompt and so full-handed, for a perpetual benediction. This imagery has, above all, the value, for the considering mind, that it presents itself as under the wide-spread wings of the general Government, which fairly make it figure to the rapt vision as the object caught up in eagle claws and lifted into fields of air that even the high brows of the municipal boss fail to sweep. The wide-spread wings affect us, in the prospect, as great fans that, by their mere tremor, will blow the work, at all steps and stages, clean and clear, disinfect it quite ideally of any germ of the job, and prepare thereby for the American voter, on the spot and in the pride of possession, quite a new kind of civic consciousness. The scheme looms largest, surely, as a demonstration of the possibilities of that service to him, and nothing about it will be more interesting than to measure—though this may take time—the nature and degree of his alleviation. Will the new pride I speak of sufficiently inflame him? Will the taste of the new consciousness, finding him so fresh to it, prove the right medicine? One can only regret that we must still rather indefinitely wait to see—and regret it all the more that there is always, in America, yet another lively source of interest involved in the execution of such designs, and closely involved just in proportion as the high intention, the formal majesty, of the thing seems assured. It comes back to what we constantly feel, throughout the country, to what the American scene everywhere depends on for half its appeal or its effect; to the fact that the social conditions, the material, pressing and pervasive, make the particular experiment or demonstration, whatever it may pretend to, practically a new and incalculable thing. This general Americanism is often the one tag of character attaching to the case after every other appears to have abandoned it. The thing is happening, or will have to happen, in the American way— that American way which is more different from all other native ways, taking country with country, than any of these latter are different from each other; and the question is of how, each time, the American way will see it through.

The element of suspense—beguilement, ever, of the sincere observer—is provided for by the fact that, though this American way never fails to come up, he has to recognize as by no means equally true that it never fails to succeed. It is inveterately applied, but with consequences bewilderingly various; which means, however, for our present moral, but that the certainty of the *determined* American effect is an element to attend quite especially such a case as the employment of the arts of design, on an unprecedented scale, for public uses, the adoption on this scale of the whole æsthetic law. Encountered in America, phenomena of this order strike us mostly as occurring in the historic void, as having to present themselves in the hard light of that desert, and as needing to extort from it, so far as they can, something of the shading of their interest. Encountered in older countries, they show, on the contrary, as taking up the references, as consenting perforce to the relations, of which the air is already full, and as having thereby much rather to get themselves expressive by charm than to get themselves expressive by weight. The danger "in Europe" is of their having too many things to say, and too many others to distinguish these from; the danger in the States is of their not having things enough—with enough tone and resonance furthermore to give them. What therefore will the multitudinous and elaborate forms of the Washington to come have to "say," and what, above all, besides gold and silver, stone and marble and trees and flowers, will they be able to say it *with*? That is one of the questions in the mere phrasing of which the restless analyst finds a thrill. There is a thing called interest that has to be produced for him—positively as if he were a rabid usurer with a clutch of his imperilled bond. He has seen again and again how the most expensive effort often fails to lead up to interest, and he has seen how it may bloom in soil of no more worth than so many layers of dust and ashes. He has learnt in fact—he learns greatly in America—to mistrust any plea for it *directly* made by money, which operates too often as the great puffing motor-car framed for whirling him, in his dismay, quite away from it. And he has inevitably noted, at the same time, from how comparatively few other sources this rewarding dividend on his invested attention may be drawn. He thinks of these sources as few, that is, because he sees the same ones, which are the references by which interest is fed, used again and again, with a desperate economy; sees the same ones, even as the human heroes, celebrities, extemporized lions or scapegoats, required social and educational figure-heads and "values," having to serve in *all* the connections and adorn all the tales. That is one of the liveliest of his American impressions. He has at moments his sense that, in presence of such vast populations and instilled, emulous demands, there is not, outside the mere economic, enough native history, recorded or current, to go round.

V

It seemed to me on the spot, moreover, that such reflections were rather more than less pertinent in face of the fact that I was again to find the Capitol, whenever I approached, and above all whenever I entered it, a vast and many-voiced creation. The thing depends of course somewhat on the visitor, who will be the more responsive, I think, the further back into the "origins" of the whole American spectacle his personal vision shall carry him; but this hugest, as I suppose it, of all the homes of debate only asks to put forth, on opportunity, an incongruous, a various, an inexhaustible charm. I may as well say at once that I had found myself from the first adoring the Capitol, though I may not pretend here to dot all the i's of all my reasons—since some of these might appear below the dignity of the subject and others alien to its simplicity. The ark of the American covenant may strike one thus, at any rate, as a compendium of all the national ideals, a museum, crammed full, even to overflowing, of all the national terms and standards, weights and measures and emblems of greatness and glory, and indeed as a builded record of half the collective vibrations of a people; their conscious spirit, their public faith, their bewildered taste, their ceaseless curiosity, their arduous and interrupted education. Such were to my vision at least some of its aspects, but the place had a hundred sides, and if I had had time to look for others still I felt I should have found them. What it comes to—whereby the "pull," in America, is of the greatest—is that association really reigns there, and in the richest, and even again and again in the drollest, forms; it is thick and vivid and almost gross, it assaults the wondering mind. The labyrinthine pile becomes thus inordinately *amusing*—taking the term in its finer modern sense. The analogy may seem forced, but it affected me as playing in Washington life very much the part that St. Peter's, of old, had seemed to me to play in Roman: it offered afternoon entertainment, at the end of a longish walk, to any spirit in the humour for the uplifted and flattered

vision—and this without suggesting that the sublimities in
the two cases, even as measured by the profanest mind, tend
at all to be equal. The Washington dome is indeed capable, in
the Washington air, of admirable, of sublime, effects; and
there are cases in which, seen at a distance above its yellow
Potomac, it varies but by a shade from the sense—yes, absolutely the divine campagna-sense—of St. Peter's and the like-
coloured Tiber.

But the question is positively of the impressiveness of the
great terraced Capitol hill, with its stages and slopes, staircases and fountains, its general presentation of its charge. And
if the whole mass and prospect "amuse," as I say, from the
moment they are embraced, the visitor curious of the *democratic assimilation* of the greater dignities and majesties will
least miss the general logic. That is the light in which the
whole thing is supremely interesting; the light of the fact,
illustrated at every turn, that the populations maintaining it
deal with it so directly and intimately, so sociably and humor-
ously. We promptly take in that, if ever we are to commune in
a concentrated way with the sovereign people, and see their
exercised power raise a side-wind of irony for forms and arrangements other than theirs, the occasion here will amply
serve. Indubitably, moreover, at a hundred points, the irony
operates, and all the more markedly under such possible interference; the interference of the monumental spittoons, that of
the immense amount of vulgar, of barbaric, decoration, that
of the terrible artistic tributes from, and scarce less to, the
different States—the unassorted marble mannikins in particular, each a portrayal by one of the commonwealths of her
highest worthy, which make the great Rotunda, the intended
Valhalla, resemble a stonecutter's collection of priced sorts
and sizes. Discretion exists, throughout, only as a flower of
the very first or of these very latest years; the large middle
time, corresponding, and even that unequally, with the English Victorian, of sinister memory, was unacquainted with
the name, and waits there now, in its fruits, but for a huge
sacrificial fire, some far-flaring act-of-faith of the future: a
tribute to the æsthetic law which one already feels stirring the
air, so that it may arrive, I think, with an unexampled stride.
Nothing will have been more interesting, surely, than so

public a wiping-over of the æsthetic slate, with all the involved collective compunctions and repudiations, the general exhibition of a colossal conscience, a conscience proportionate to the size and wealth of the country. To such grand gestures does the American scene lend itself!

The elements in question are meanwhile there, in any case, just as the sovereign people are there, "going over" their property; but we are aware none the less of impressions—that of the ponderous proud Senate, for instance, so sensibly massive; that of the Supreme Court, so simply, one almost says so chastely, yet, while it breathes supremacy, so elegantly, so all intellectually, in session—under which the view, taking one extravagance with another, recurs rather ruefully to glimpses elsewhere caught, glimpses of authority emblazoned, bewigged, bemantled, bemarshalled, in almost direct defeat of its intention of gravity. For the reinstated absentee, in these presences, the mere recovery of native privilege was at all events a balm—after too many challenged appeals and abused patiences, too many hushed circuitous creepings, among the downtrodden, in other and more bristling halls of state. The sense of a certain large, final benignity in the Capitol comes then, I think, from this impression that the national relation to it is that of a huge flourishing Family to the place of business, the estate-office, where, in a myriad open ledgers, which offer no obscurity to the hereditary head for figures, the account of their colossal revenue is kept. They meet there in safe sociability, as all equally initiated and interested—not as in a temple or a citadel, but by the warm domestic hearth of Columbia herself; a motherly, chatty, clear-spectacled Columbia, who reads all the newspapers, knows, to the last man, every one of her sons by name, and, to the last boy, even her grandsons, and is fenced off, at the worst, but by concentric circles of rocking-chairs. It is impossible, as I say, not to be fondly conscious of her welcome—unless again, and yet again, I read into the general air, confusedly, too much of the happy accident of the basis of my introduction. But if my sensibility responds with intensity to this, so much the better; for what were such felt personal aids and influences, after all, but cases and examples, embodied expressions of character, type, distinction, products of the *working* of the whole thing?—specimens, indeed, highly concentrated and refined, and made thereby, I admit, more charming and insidious.

It must also be admitted that to exchange the inner aspects of the vast monument for the outer is to be reminded with some sharpness of a Washington in which half the sides that have held our attention drop, as if rather abashed, out of sight. Not its pleasant brightness as of a winter watering-place, not its connections, however indirect, with the older, but those with the newer, the newest, civilization, seem matter of recognition for its various marble fronts; it rakes the prospect, it rakes the continent, to a much more sweeping purpose, and is visibly concerned but in immeasurable schemes of which it can consciously remain the centre. Here, in the vast spaces—mere empty light and air, though such pleasant air and such pretty light as yet—the great Federal future seems, under vague bright forms, to hover and to stalk, making the horizon recede to take it in, making the terraces too, below the long colonnades, the admirable standpoints, the sheltering porches, of political philosophy. The compara-tively new wings of the building filled me, whenever I walked here, with thanksgiving for their large and perfect elegance: so, in Paris, might the wide mated fronts that are of such a noble effect on either side of the Rue Royale shine in multi-plied majesty and recovered youth over an infinite Place de la Concorde. These parts of the Capitol, on their Acropolis height, are ideally constructed for "raking," and for this sug-gestion of their dominating the American scene in playhouse gallery fashion. You are somehow possessed of it *all* while you tread them—their marble embrace appears so the comple-ment of the vast democratic lap. Though I had them in gen-eral, for contemplation, quite to myself, I met one morning a trio of Indian braves, braves dispossessed of forest and prairie, but as free of the builded labyrinth as they had ever been of these; also arrayed in neat pot-hats, shoddy suits and light overcoats, with their pockets, I am sure, full of photographs and cigarettes: circumstances all that quickened their resem-blance, on the much bigger scale, to Japanese celebrities, or to specimens, on show, of what the Government can do with people with whom it is supposed able to do nothing. They seemed just then and there, for a mind fed betimes on the

Leatherstocking Tales, to project as in a flash an image in itself immense, but foreshortened and simplified—reducing to a single smooth stride the bloody footsteps of time. One rubbed one's eyes, but there, at its highest polish, shining in the beautiful day, was the brazen face of history, and there, all about one, immaculate, the printless pavements of the State.

XII
Richmond

I

IT WAS, toward the end of the winter, fairly romantic to feel one's self "going South"—in verification of the pleasant probability that, since one's mild adventure had appeared beforehand, and as a whole, to promise that complexion, there would now be aspects and occasions more particularly and deeply dyed with it. The inevitability of his being romantically affected—being so more often than not—had been taken for granted by the restless analyst from the first; his feeling that he might count upon it having indeed, in respect to his visit, the force of a strong appeal. The case had come to strike him as perfectly clear—the case for the singular history, the odd evolution of this confidence, which might appear superficially to take some explaining. It was "Europe" that had, in very ancient days, held out to the yearning young American some likelihood of impressions more numerous and various and of a higher intensity than those he might gather on the native scene; and it was doubtless in conformity with some such desire more finely and more frequently to vibrate that he had originally begun to consult the European oracle. This had led, in the event, to his settling to live for long years in the very precincts, as it were, of the temple; so that the voice of the divinity was finally to become, in his ears, of all sounds the most familiar. It was quite to lose its primal note of mystery, to cease little by little to be strange, impressive and august—in the degree, at any rate, in which it had once enjoyed that character. The consultation of the oracle, in a word, the invocation of the possible thrill, was gradually to feel its romantic essence enfeebled, shrunken and spent. The European complexity, working clearer to one's vision, had grown usual and calculable—presenting itself, to the discouragement of wasteful emotion and of "intensity" in general, as the very stuff, the common texture, of the real world. Romance and mystery—in other words the *amusement* of interest—would have therefore at last to provide for themselves elsewhere; and what curiously befell, in time, was that the native, the forsaken scene, now passing, as continual rumour had it, through a thousand stages and changes, and offering a perfect iridescence of fresh aspects, seemed more and more to appeal to the faculty of wonder. It was American civilization that had begun to spread itself thick and pile itself high, in short, in proportion as the other, the foreign exhibition had taken to writing itself plain; and to a world so amended and enriched, accordingly, the expatriated observer, with his relaxed curiosity reviving and his limp imagination once more on the stretch, couldn't fail again to address himself. Nothing could be of a simpler and straighter logic: Europe had been romantic years before, because she was different from America; wherefore America would now be romantic because she was different from Europe. It was for this small syllogism then to meet, practically, the test of one's repatriation; and as the palpitating pilgrim disembarked, in truth, he had felt it, like the rifle of a keen sportsman, carried across his shoulder and ready for instant use.

What employment it was thus to find, what game it was actually to bring down, this directed and aimed appetite for sharp impressions, is a question to which these pages may appear in a manner to testify—constituting to that extent the "proof" of my fond calculation. It was in respect to the South, meanwhile, at any rate, that the calculation had really been fondest—on such a stored, such a waiting provision of vivid images, mainly beautiful and sad, might one surely there depend. The sense of these things would represent for the restless analyst, more than that of any others, intensity of impression; so that his only prime discomfiture was in his having had helplessly to see his allowance of time cut short, reduced to the smallest compass in which the establishment of a relation to any group of aspects might be held conceivable. This last soreness, however—and the point is one to be made—was not slow, I noted, to find itself healingly breathed upon. More promptly in America than elsewhere does the relation to the group of aspects begin to work—whatever the group, and I think I may add whatever the relation, may be. Few elements of the picture are shy or lurking elements—tangled among others or hidden behind them, packed close by time and taking time to come out. They stand there in their row like the letters of an alphabet, and this is why, in spite of the vast surface exposed, any item, encountered or selected, contributes to the spelling of the word, becomes on the spot generally informing and characteristic. The word so recognized stands thus, immediately, for a multitude of others and constitutes, to expert observation, an all-sufficient specimen. "Here, evidently, more quickly than in Europe," the visitor says to himself, "one knows what there is and what there isn't: whence there is the less need, for one's impression, of a multiplication of cases." A single case speaks for many—since it is again and again, as he catches himself repeating, a question not of clustered meanings that fall like over-ripe fruit into his lap, but of the picking out of the few formed features, signs of character mature enough and firm enough to promise a savour or to suffer handling. These scant handfuls illustrate and typify, and, luckily, they are (as the evidence of manners and conditions, over the world, goes) quickly gathered; so that an impression founded on them is not an undue simplification. And I make out, I think, the reflection with which our anxious explorer tacitly concludes. "It's a bad country to be stupid in—none on the whole so bad. If one doesn't know *how* to look and to see, one should keep out of it altogether. But if one does, if one *can* see straight, one takes in the whole piece at a series of points that are after all comparatively few. One may neglect, by interspacing the points, a little of the accessory matter, but one neglects none of the essential. And if one has not at last learned to separate with due sharpness, pen in hand, the essential *from* the accessory, one has only, at best, to muffle one's head for shame and await deserved extinction."

II

It was in conformity with some such induction as the foregoing that I had to feel myself, at Richmond, in the midst of abnormal wintry rigours, take in at every pore a Southern impression; just as it was also there, before a picture charmless at the best, I seemed to apprehend, and not redeemed now by mistimed snow and ice, that I was to recognize how much I had staked on my theory of the latent poetry of the South. This theory, during a couple of rather dark, vain days, constituted my one solace or support, and I was most of all occupied with my sense of the importance of carrying it off again unimpaired. I remember asking myself at the end of an hour or two what I had then expected—expected of the interesting Richmond; and thereupon, whether or no I mustered, on this first challenge, an adequate answer, trying to supply the original basis of expectation. By that effort, as happened, my dim perambulation was lighted, and I hasten to add that I felt the second branch of my question easy enough to meet. How was the sight of Richmond not to be a potent idea; how was the place not, presumably, to be interesting, to a restless analyst who had become conscious of the charge involved in that title as long ago as at the outbreak of the Civil War, if not even still more promptly; and to whose young imagination the Confederate capital had grown lurid, fuliginous, vividly tragic—especially under the process through which its fate was to close round it and overwhelm it, invest it with one of the great reverberating historic names? They hang together on the dreadful page, the cities of the supreme holocaust, the final massacres, the blood, the flames, the tears; they are chalked with the sinister red mark at sight of which the sensitive nerve of association forever winces. If the mere shadow had that penetrative power, what affecting virtue might accordingly not reside in the substances, the place itself, the haunted scene, as one might figure it, of the old, the vast intensity of drama? One thing at least was certain—that, however the sense of actual aspects was to disengage itself, I could not possibly have drawn near with an intelligence more respectfully and liberally prepared for hospitality to it. So, conformably with all this, how could it further not strike me, in presence of the presented appearances, that the needful perceptions were in fact at play?

I recall the shock of that question after a single interrogative stroll, a mere vague mile of which had thrown me back wondering and a trifle mystified. One had had brutally to put it to one's self after a conscientious stare about: "This then the tragic ghost-haunted city, this the centre of the vast blood-drenched circle, one of the *most* blood-drenched, for miles and miles around, in the dire catalogue aforesaid?" One had counted on a sort of registered consciousness of the past, and the truth was that there appeared, for the moment, on the face of the scene, no discernible consciousness, registered or unregistered, of anything. Richmond, in a word, looked to me simply blank and void—whereby it was, precisely, however, that the great emotion was to come. One could never consent merely to *taking* it for that: intolerable the discredit so cast on one's perceptive resources. The great modern hotel, superfluously vast, was excellent; but it enjoyed as a feature, as a "value," an uncontested priority. It was a huge well-pitched tent, the latest thing in tents, proclaiming in the desert the name of a new industry. The desert, I have mentioned, was more or less muffled in snow—that furthered, I admit, the blankness; the wind was harsh, the sky sullen, the houses scarce emphasized at all as houses; the "Southern character," in fine, was nowhere. I should doubtless have been embarrassed to say in what specific items I had imagined it would naturally reside—save in so far as I had attached some mystic virtue to the very name of Virginia: this instinctive imputation constituting by itself, for that matter, a symptom of a certain significance. I watched and waited, giving the virtue a chance to come out; I wandered far and wide—as far, that is, as weather and season permitted; they quite forbade, to my regret, the long drives involved in a visitation of the old battlefields. The shallow vistas, the loose perspectives, were as sadly simple as the faces of the blind. Was it practically but a question then, deplorable thought, of a poor Northern city?—with the bare difference that a Northern city of such extent would, however stricken, have succeeded, by some Northern art in pretending to resources. Where, otherwise, were the "old Southern mansions" on the wide verandahs and in the rank, sweet gardens of which Northern resources had once been held so cheap?

Well, I scarce remember at what point of my peregrination, at what quite vague, senseless street-corner it was that I felt my inquiry—up to that moment rather embarrassing—turn to clearness and the whole picture place itself in a light in which contemplation might for the time find a warrant and a clue. I at any rate almost like to live over the few minutes in question—for the sake of their relief and their felicity. So retracing them, I see that the spring had been pressed for them by the positive force of one's first dismay; a sort of intellectual bankruptcy, this latter, that one felt one really couldn't afford. There were no *references*—that had been the trouble; but the reaction came with the sense that the large, sad poorness was in itself a reference, and one by which a hundred grand historic connections were on the spot, and quite thrillingly, re-established. What was I tasting of, at that time of day, and with intensity, but the far consequences of things, made absolutely majestic by their weight and duration? I was tasting, mystically, of the very essence of the old Southern idea—the hugest fallacy, as it hovered there to one's backward, one's ranging vision, for which hundreds of thousands of men had ever laid down their lives. I was tasting of the very bitterness of the immense, grotesque, defeated project—the project, extravagant, fantastic, and to-day pathetic in its folly, of a vast Slave State (as the old term ran) artfully, savingly isolated in the world that was to contain it and trade with it. This was what everything round me meant—that that absurdity had once flourished there; and nothing, immediately, could have been more interesting than the lesson that such may remain, for long years, the tell-tale face of things where such absurdities *have* flourished. Thus, by a turn of my hand, or of my head, interest was evoked; so that from this moment I had never to let go of it. It was to serve again, it was to serve elsewhere, and in much the same manner; all aspects straightway were altered by it, and the pious pilgrim came round again into his own. He had wanted, his scheme had fairly required, this particular part of the country to be beautiful; he had really needed it to be, he couldn't afford, in due deference to the intellectual economy imposed on him, its not being. When things were grandly sad, accordingly—sad on the great scale and with a certain nobleness of ruin—an element of beauty seemed always secured, even if one could scarce say why: which truth, clearly, would operate fortunately for the compromised South.

It came back again—it was always, after this fashion, coming back, as if to make me extravagantly repeat myself—to the quantity to be "read into" the American view, in general, before it gives out an interest. The observer, like a fond investor, must spend on it, boldly, ingeniously, to make it pay; and it may often thus remind one of the wonderful soil of California, which is nothing when left to itself and the fine weather, but becomes everything conceivable under the rainfall. What would many an American prospect be for him, the visitor bent on appreciation frequently wonders, without his preliminary discharge upon it of some brisk shower of general ideas? The arid sand has, in a remarkable degree, the fine property of absorbing these latter and then giving them back to the air in proportionate signs of life. There be blooming gardens, on the other hand, I take it, where the foliage of Time is positively too dense for the general idea to penetrate or to perch—as if too many ideas had already been concerned and involved and there were nothing to do but to accept the complete demonstration. It was not to this order, at any rate, that my decipherable South was to belong; but Richmond at least began to repay my outlay, from point to point, as soon as the outlay had been made. The place was *weak*—"adorably" weak: that was the word into which the whole impression flowered, that was the idea, evidently, that all the rest of the way as well, would be most brought home. That was the form, in short, that the interest would take; the charm—immense, almost august—being in the long, unbroken connections of the case. Here, obviously, would be the prime source of the beauty; since if to be sad was to be the reverse of blatant, what was the sadness, taken all round, but the incurable after-taste of the original vanity and fatuity, with the memories and penalties of which the very air seemed still charged? I had recently been studying, a little, the record, reading, with other things, the volume of his admirable History in which Mr. James Ford Rhodes recounts the long preliminaries of the War and shows us, all lucidly and humanely, the Southern mind of the mid-century in the very convulsions of its perversity—the conception that, almost comic in itself, was yet so tragically to fail to work, that of a world rearranged, a State solidly and comfortably seated and tucked-in, in the interest of slave-produced Cotton.

The solidity and the comfort were to involve not only the wide extension, but the complete intellectual, moral and economic reconsecration of slavery, an enlarged and glorified, quite beatified, application of its principle. The light of experience, round about, and every finger-post of history, of political and spiritual science with which the scene of civilization seemed to bristle, had, when questioned, but one warning to give, and appeared to give it with an effect of huge derision: whereby was laid on the Southern genius the necessity of getting rid of these discords and substituting for the ironic face of the world an entirely new harmony, or in other words a different scheme of criticism. Since nothing in the Slave-scheme could be said to conform—conform, that is, to the reality of things—it was the plan of Christendom and the wisdom of the ages that would have to be altered. History, the history of everything, would be rewritten *ad usum Delphini*—the Dauphin being in this case the budding Southern mind. This meant a general and a permanent quarantine; meant the eternal bowdlerization of books and journals; meant in fine all literature and all art on an expurgatory index. It meant, still further, an active and ardent propaganda; the reorganization of the school, the college, the university, in the interest of the new criticism. The testimony to that thesis offered by the documents of the time, by State legislation, local eloquence, political speeches, the "tone of the press," strikes us to-day as beyond measure queer and quaint and benighted—innocent above all; stamped with the inalienable Southern sign, the inimitable *rococo* note. We talk of the provincial, but the provinciality projected by the Confederate dream, and in which it proposed to steep the whole helpless social mass, looks to our present eyes as artlessly perverse, as untouched by any intellectual tradition of beauty or wit, as some exhibited array of the odd utensils or divinities of lone and primitive islanders. It came over one that they *were* there, in the air they had breathed, precisely, lone—even the very best of the old Southerners; and, looking at them over the threshold of approach that poor Richmond seemed to form, the real key to one's sense of their native scene was in that very idea of their solitude and their isolation. Thus they affected one as such passive, such pathetic victims of fate, as so played upon and betrayed, so beaten and bruised, by the old burden of their condition, that I found myself conscious, on their behalf, of a sort of ingenuity of tenderness.

Their condition was to have waked up from far back to this thumping legacy of the intimate presence of the negro, and one saw them not much less imprisoned in it and overdarkened by it to-day than they had been in the time of their so fallacious presumption. The haunting consciousness thus produced is the prison of the Southern spirit; and how was one to say, as a pilgrim from afar, that with an equal exposure to the embarrassing fact one would have been more at one's ease? I had found my own threatened, I remember—my ease of contemplation of the subject, which was all there could be question of—during some ten minutes spent, a few days before, in consideration of an African type or two encountered in Washington. I was waiting, in a cab, at the railway-station, for the delivery of my luggage after my arrival, while a group of tatterdemalion darkies lounged and sunned themselves within range. To take in with any attention two or three of these figures had surely been to feel one's self introduced at a bound to the formidable question, which rose suddenly like some beast that had sprung from the jungle. These were its far outposts; they represented the Southern black as we knew him not, and had not within the memory of man known him, at the North; and to see him there, ragged and rudimentary, yet all portentous and "in possession of his rights as a man," was to be not a little discomposed, was to be in fact very much admonished. One understood at a glance how he must loom, how he must count, in a community in which, in spite of the ground it might cover, there were comparatively so few other things. The admonition accordingly remained, and no further appeal was required, I felt, to disabuse a tactful mind of the urgency of preaching, southward, a sweet reasonableness about him. Nothing was less contestable, of course, than that such a sweet reasonableness might play, in the whole situation, a beautiful part; but nothing, also, was on reflection more obvious than that the counsel of perfection, in such a case, would never prove oil upon the waters. The lips of the non-resident were, at all events, not the lips to utter this wisdom; the non-resident might well feel themselves indeed, after a little, appointed to silence, and, with any delicacy, see their duty quite elsewhere.

It came to one, soon enough, by all the voices of the air, that the negro had always been, and could absolutely not fail to be, intensely "on the nerves" of the South, and that as, in the other time, the observer from without had always, as a tribute to this truth, to tread the scene on tiptoe, so even yet, in presence of the immitigable fact, a like discretion is imposed on him. He might depart from the discretion of old, if he were so moved, intrusively, fanatically, even heroically, and he would depart from it to-day, one quite recognized, with the same effect of importunity, but not with the same effect of gallantry. The moral of all of which fairly became, to my sense, a soft inward dirge over the eternal "false position" of the afflicted South—condemned as she was to institutions, condemned to a state of temper, of exasperation and depression, a horrid heritage she had never consciously invited, that bound up her life with a hundred mistakes and make-believes, suppressions and prevarications, things that really all named themselves in the noted provincialism. None of them would have lived in the air of the greater world—which was the world that the North, with whatever abatements, had comparatively been, and had conquered by being; so that if the actual visitor was conscious now, as I say, of the appeal to his tenderness, it was by this sight of a society still shut up in a world smaller than what one might suppose its true desire, to say nothing of its true desert. I can doubtless not sufficiently tell why, but there was something in my whole sense of the South that projected at moments a vivid and painful image— that of a figure somehow blighted or stricken, discomfortably, impossibly seated in an invalid-chair, and yet fixing one with strange eyes that were half a defiance and half a deprecation of one's noticing, and much more of one's referring to, any abnormal sign. The deprecation, in the Southern eyes, is much greater to-day, I think, than the old lurid challenge; but my haunting similitude was an image of the keeping-up of appearances, and above all of the maintenance of a tone, the historic "high" tone, in an excruciating posture. There was food for sympathy—and the restless analyst must repeat that when he had but tasted of it he could but make of it his full meal. Which brings him back, by a long way round, to the grim street-corner at Richmond where he last left himself.

III

He could look down from it, I remember, over roofs and chimneys, through some sordid gap, at an abased prospect that quite failed to beckon—that of the James River embanked in snow and attended by waterside industries that, in the brown haze of the weather, were dingy and vague. There had been an indistinct sign for him—"somewhere there" had stood the Libby prison; an indication that flung over the long years ever so dreary a bridge. He lingered to take it in—from so far away it came, the strange apparition in the dress of another day; and with the interest of noting at the same time how little it mattered for any sort of intensity (whether of regret or of relief) that the structure itself, so sinister to the mind's eye, should have materially vanished. It was still there enough to parade its poor ghosts, but the value of the ghosts, precisely, was that they consented, all alike, on either side, to the grand epic dimness. I recognize, moreover, with the lapse of time, the positive felicity of my not having to connect them with the ruin of a particular squalid tobacco-house. The concrete, none the less, did, in the name of history, await me, and I indeed recollect pursuing it with pertinacity, for conscience' sake, all the way down a wide, steep street, a place of traffic, of shops and offices and altogether shabby Virginia vehicles, these last in charge of black teamsters who now emphasized for me with every degree of violence that already-apprehended note of the negro really at home. It fades, it melts away, with a promptitude of its own almost, any random reflection of the American picture; and though the restless analyst has arts of *his* own for fixing and saving it—as he at least on occasion fondly flatters himself—he is too often reduced to wondering what it can have consisted of in a given case save exactly that projected light of his conscience. Richmond—*there* at least was a definite fact—is a city of more or less nobly-precipitous hills, and he recalls, of his visit to the avenue aforesaid, no intellectual consequence whatever but the after-sense of having remounted it again on the opposite side.

It was in succession to this, doubtless, that he found himself consulting the obscure oracle of the old State House or Capitol, seat of the Confederate legislature, strange intellectual centre of the general enterprise. I scarce know in what manner I had expected it to regale either my outward or my inward sense; one had vaguely heard that it was "fine" and at the height, or in the key, of the old Virginian dignity. The approach to it had been adorned, from far back, moreover, as one remembered, with Crawford's celebrated monument to Washington attended by famous Virginians—which work indeed, I promptly perceived, answered to its reputation, with a high elegance that was quite of the mid-century, and yet that, indescribably archaic, made the mid-century seem remote and quaint and queer, as disconnected from us as the prolific age of Cyprus or of Crete. It is positive that of the "old" American sculpture, about the Union, a rich study might be made. What shall I say of this spot at large, and of the objects it presented to view, if not that here, where all the elements of life had been most in fiery fusion, everything was somehow almost abjectly frigid and thin? The small shapeless Square, ancient acropolitan seat, ill placed on its eminence, showed, I recollect, but a single figure in motion—that of a gentleman to whom I presently put a question and who explained to me that the Capitol, masked all round in dense scaffolding, though without a labourer visible, had been "very bad," a mere breakable shell, and was now, from top to bottom, in course of reconstruction. The shell, one could see, was empty and work suspended; and I had never, truly, it seemed to me, seen a human institution so coldly and logically brought low as this memorial mass, anything rewritten so mercilessly small as this poor passage of a great historic text. The effect was as of a page of some dishonoured author—printed "on grey paper with blunt type," and when I had learned from my informant that a fairly ample white house, a pleasant, honest structure in the taste of sixty or eighty years since, had been Jefferson Davis's official residence during part of the War, every source of interest had been invoked and had in its measure responded. The impression obeys, I repeat, a rigorous law —it irremediably fades, it melts away; but was there not, further, as a feature of the scene, one of those decent and dumb American churches which are so strangely possessed of the secret of minimizing, to the casual eye, the general pretension of churches?

The extent to which the American air affects one as a nonconductor of such pretensions is, in the presence of these heterogeneous objects, a constant lively lesson. Looking for the most part no more established or seated than a stopped omnibus, they are reduced to the inveterate bourgeois level (that of private, accommodated pretensions merely) and fatally despoiled of the fine old ecclesiastical arrogance. This, the richest attribute they elsewhere enjoy, keeps clear of them only to betray them, so that they remind one everywhere of organisms trying to breathe in the void, or of those creatures of the deep sea who change colour and shrink, as one has heard, when astray in fresh water. The fresh water makes them indeed pullulate, but to the loss of "importance," and nothing could more have fallen in with that generalization, for the restless analyst, than the very moral of the matter, as he judged, lately put before him at the national capital. Washington already bristles, for the considering eye, with national affirmations—big builded forms of confidence and energy; but when you have embraced them all, with the implication of all the others still to come, you will find yourself wondering what it is you so oddly miss. Numberless things are represented, and one interest after the other counts itself in; the great Congressional Library crowns the hill beside the Capitol, the Departments and Institutes cover their acres and square their shoulders, the obelisk to the memory of Washington climbs still higher; but something is absent more even than these masses are present—till it at last occurs to you that the existence of a religious faith on the part of the people is not even remotely suggested. Not a Federal dome, not a spire nor a cornice pretends to any such symbolism, and though your attention is thus concerned with a mere negative, the negative presently becomes its sharp obsession. You reach out perhaps in vain for something to which you may familiarly compare your unsatisfied sense. You liken it perhaps not so much to a meal made savourless by the failure of some usual, some central dish, as to a picture, nominally finished, say, where the canvas shows, in the very middle, with all originality, a fine blank space.

For it is most, doubtless, the æsthetic appetite in you— long richly fed elsewhere—that goes unassuaged; it is your sense of the comprehensive picture *as* a comprehensive picture that winces, for recognition of loss, like a touched nerve. What is the picture, collectively seen, you ask, but the portrait, more or less elaborated, of a multitudinous People, of a social and political order?—so that the effect is, for all the world, as if, with the body and the limbs, the hands and feet and coat and trousers, all the accessories of the figure showily painted, the neat white oval of the face itself were innocent of the brush. You marvel at the personage, you admire even the painting—which you are largely reduced, however, to admiring in the hands and the boots, in the texture of accompanying table-cloth, inkstand, newspaper (introduced with a careless grace) and other paraphernalia. You wonder how he would look if the face *had* been done; though you have compensation, meanwhile, I must certainly add, in your consciousness of assisting, as you apprehensively stand there, at something new under the sun. The size of the gap, the intensity of the omission, in the Washington prospect, where so much else is representative, dots with the last sharpness the distinct *i*, as it were, of one of the promptest generalizations of the repatriated absentee. The field of American life is as bare of the Church as a billiard-table of a centre-piece; a truth that the myriad little structures "attended" on Sundays and on the "off" evenings of their "sociables" proclaim as with the audible sound of the roaring of a million mice. Or that analogy reinsists—of the difference between the deep sea of the older sphere of spiritual passion and the shallow tide in which the inhabiting particles float perforce near the surface. And however one indicates one's impression of the clearance, the clearance itself, in its completeness, with the innumerable odd connected circumstances that bring it home, represents, in the history of manners and morals, a deviation in the mere measurement of which hereafter may well reside a certain critical thrill. I say hereafter because it is a question of one of those many measurements that would as yet, in the United States, be premature. Of all the solemn conclusions one feels as "barred," the list is quite headed, in the States, I think, by this particular abeyance of judgment. When an ancient treasure of precious vessels, overscored with glowing gems and wrought, artistically, into wondrous shapes, has, by a prodigious process, been converted, through a vast community, into the small change, the simple circulating medium of dollars and "nickels," we can only say that the consequent permeation will be of values of a new order. Of *what* order we must wait to see.

All of which remarks would constitute a long excursion, I admit, from the sacred edifice by the Richmond street, were it not for that saving law, the enrichment of each hour on the American scene, that wings almost any observed object with a power to suggest, a possible social *portée*, soaring superior to its plain face. And I seem to recover the sense of a pretext for incurable mooning, then and there, in my introduction, but little delayed, to the next in the scant group of local lions, the usual place of worship, as I understood, of the Confederate leader, from his proper pew in which Jefferson Davis was called, on that fine Sunday morning of the spring-time of 1865, by the news of Lee's surrender. The news had been big, but the place of worship was small, and, linger in it as one would, fraternize as one would with the mild old Confederate soldier, survivor of the epic age, who made, by his account, so lean a living of his office of sexton, one could but moodily resent, again, its trivialization of history—a process one scarce knows how to name—its inaccessibility to legend. Perhaps, after all, it represented, in its comfortable "denominational" commonness, the right scene of concentration for the promoters of so barren a polity, that idea of the perpetual Southern quarantine; but no leaders of a great movement, a movement acclaimed by a whole nation and paid for with every sacrifice, ever took such pains, alas, to make themselves not interesting. It was positively as if legend would have nothing to say to them; as if, on the spot there, I had seen it turn its back on them and walk out of the place. This is the horse, ever, that one may take to the water, but that drinks

not against his will. That was at least what it came back to—
for the musing moralist: if the question is of legend we dig
for it in the deposit of history, but the deposit must be thick
to have given it a cover and let it accumulate. It was on the
battle-fields and in all the blood-drenched radius that it would
be thick; here, decidedly, in the streets of melancholy Richmond, it was thin. Just so, since it was the planners and plot-
ters who had bidden unsuccessfully for our interest, it was for
the sacrificed multitude, the unsophisticated, irresponsible
agents, the obscure and the eminent alike, that distinction
might be pleaded. *They* were buried, if one would, in the "deposit"—where the restless analyst might scratch, all tenderly,
to find them.

He had fortunately at this moment his impression as to
where, under such an impulse, he had best look; and he
turned his steps, as with an appetite for some savour in his
repast still too much withheld to that Museum of the relics of
the Confederacy installed some years since in the eventual
White House of Richmond, the "executive mansion" of the
latter half of the War. Here, positively, the spirit descended—
and yet all the more directly, it seemed to me, strange to say,
by reason of the very nudity and crudity, the historic, the
pathetic poverty of the exhibition. It fills the whole large
house, each of the leagued States enjoying an allotted space;
and one assuredly feels, in passing from room to room, that,
up and down the South, no equal area can so offer itself as
sacred ground. Tragically, indescribably sanctified, these documentary chambers that contained, so far as I remember, not
a single object of beauty, scarce one in fact that was not altogether ugly (so void they were of intrinsic charm), and that
spoke only of the absence of means and of taste, of communication and resource. In these rude accents they phrased their
interest—which the unappeased visitor, from the moment of
his crossing the general threshold, had recognized in fact as
intense. He was at his old trick: he had made out, on the
spot, in other words, that here was a pale page into which he
might read what he liked. He had not exchanged ten words of
civility with a little old lady, a person soft voiced, gracious,
mellifluous, perfect for her function, who, seated by her fire in
a sort of official ante-room, received him as at the gate of

some grandly bankrupt plantation—he had not surrendered to this exquisite contact before he felt himself up to his neck in a delightful, soothing, tepid medium, the social tone of the South that *had* been. It was but the matter of a step over—he was afloat on other waters, and had remounted the stream of Time. I said just now that nothing in the Museum had beauty; but the little old lady had it, with her thoroughly "sectional" good manners, and that punctuality and felicity, that inimitability, one must again say, of the South in her, in the patriotic unction of her reference to the sorry objects about, which transported me as no enchanted carpet could have done. No little old lady of the North could, for the high tone and the right manner, have touched her, and poor benumbed Richmond might now be as dreary as it liked: with that small observation made my pilgrimage couldn't be a failure.

The sorry objects about were old Confederate documents, already sallow with time, framed letters, orders, autographs, extracts, tatters of a paper-currency in the last stages of vitiation; together with faded portraits of faded worthies, primitive products of the camera, the crayon, the brush; of all of which she did the honours with a gentle florid reverence that opened wide, for the musing visitor, as he lingered and strolled, the portals, as it were, of a singularly interesting "case." It was the case of the beautiful, the attaching oddity of the general Southern state of mind, or stage of feeling, in relation to that heritage of woe and of glory of which the mementos surrounded me. These mementos were the sorry objects, and as I pursued them from one ugly room to another—the whole place wearing the air thus, cumulatively, of some dim, dusty collection of specimens, prehistoric, paleolithic, scientific, and making one grope for some verbal rendering of the grey effect—the queer elements at play wrote themselves as large as I could have desired. On every side, I imagine, from Virginia to Texas, the visitor must become aware of them—the visitor, that is, who, by exception, becomes aware of anything: was I not, for instance, presently to recognize them, at their finest, for an almost comic ambiguity, in the passionate flare of the little frontal inscription behind which the Daughters of the Confederacy of the Charleston

section nurse the old wrongs and the old wounds? These af-
flictions are still, thus, admirably ventilated, and what is wonderful, in the air, to-day, is the comfort and cheer of this
theory of an undying rancour. Every facility is enjoyed for the
publication of it, but as the generation that immediately suffered and paid has almost wholly passed away, the flame-
coloured *idea* has flowered out of the fact, and the interest,
the "psychologic" interest, is to see it so disengage itself, as
legend, as valuable, enriching, inspiring, romantic legend, and
settle down to play its permanent part. Practically, and most
conveniently, one feels, the South is reconciled, but theoretically, ideally, and above all for the new generation and the
amiable ladies, the ladies amiable like the charming curatrix of
the Richmond Museum, it burns with a smothered flame. As
we meanwhile look about us there, over a scene as sad,
throughout, as some raw spring eventide, we feel how something of the sort must, in all the blankness, respond morally
and socially to a want.

The collapse of the old order, the humiliation of defeat, the
bereavement and bankruptcy involved, represented, with its
obscure miseries and tragedies, the social revolution the most
unrecorded and undepicted, in proportion to its magnitude,
that ever was; so that this reversion of the starved spirit to the
things of the heroic age, the four epic years, is a definite
soothing salve—a sentiment which has, moreover, in the
South, to cultivate, itself, intellectually, from season to season,
the field over which it ranges, and to sow with its own hands
such crops as it may harvest. The sorry objects, at Richmond,
brought it home—so low the æsthetic level: it was impossible, from room to room, to imagine a community, of equal
size, more disinherited of art or of letters. These about one
were the only echoes—daubs of portraiture, scrawls of memoranda, old vulgar newspapers, old rude uniforms, old unutterable "mid-Victorian" odds and ends of furniture, all ghosts
as of things noted at a country fair. The illiteracy seemed to
hover like a queer smell; the social revolution had begotten
neither song nor story—only, for literature, two or three bi-
ographies of soldiers, written in other countries, and only, for
music, the weird chants of the emancipated blacks. Only for
art, I was an hour later to add, the monument to General Lee

by M. Mercié of Paris; but to that, in its suburban corner, and to the strange eloquence of its isolation, I shall presently come. The moral of the show seemed to me meanwhile the touching inevitability, in such conditions, of what I have called the nursing attitude. "What on earth—nurse of a rich heroic past, nurse of a fierce avenging future, nurse of any connection that would make for *any* brood of visions about one's knee—wouldn't one have to become," I found myself inwardly exclaiming, "if one had this great melancholy void to garnish and to people!" It was not, under this reflection, the actual innocent flare of the altar of memory that was matter for surprise, but that such altars should strike one, rather, as few and faint. They would have been none too many for countenance and cheer had they blazed on every hilltop.

The Richmond halls, at any rate, appeared, through the chill of the season, scantly trodden, and I met in them no fellow-visitor but a young man of stalwart and ingenuous aspect who struck me so forcibly, after a little, as exhaling a natural piety that, as we happened at last to be rapt in contemplation of the same sad glass case, I took advantage of the occasion to ask him if he were a Southerner. His affirmative was almost eager, and he proved—for all the world like the hero of a famous novel—a gallant and nameless, as well as a very handsome, young Virginian. A farmer by occupation, he had come up on business from the interior to the capital, and, having a part of his morning on his hands, was spending it in this visitation—made, as I gathered, by no means for the first time, but which he still found absorbing. As a son of the new South he presented a lively interest of type—linguistically not least (since where doesn't the restless analyst grope for light?)—and this interest, the ground of my here recalling him, was promptly to arrive at a climax. He pointed out to me, amid an array of antique regimentals, certain objects identical with relics preserved in his own family and that had belonged to his father, who, enrolled at the earliest age, had fought to the end of the War. The old implements before us bore the number of the Virginia regiment in which this veteran had first seen service, and a question or two showed me how well my friend was acquainted with his parent's exploits. Enjoying, apparently—for he was intelligent and humorous and highly conversable—the opportunity to talk of such things (they being, as it were, so advantageously present there with a vague Northerner), he related, felicitously, some paternal adventure of which I have forgotten the particulars, but which comprised a desperate evasion of capture, or worse, by the lucky smashing of the skull of a Union soldier. I complimented him on his exact knowledge of these old, unhappy, far-off things, and it was his candid response that was charmingly suggestive. "Oh, I should be ready to do them all over again myself!" And then, smiling serenely, but as if it behoved even the least blatant of Northerners to understand: "That's the kind of Southerner *I* am!" I allowed that he was a capital kind of Southerner, and we afterwards walked together to the Public Library, where, on our finally parting, I could but thank him again for being so much the kind of Southerner I had wanted. He was a fine contemporary young American, incapable, so to speak, of hurting a Northern fly—*as* Northern; but whose consciousness would have been poor and unfurnished without this cool platonic passion. With what other pattern, personal views apart, *could* he have adorned its bare walls? So I wondered till it came to me that, though he wouldn't have hurt a Northern fly, there were things (ah, we had touched on some of these!) that, all fair, engaging, smiling, as he stood there, he would have done to a Southern negro.

IV

The Public Libraries in the United States are, like the Universities, a challenge to fond fancy; by which I mean that, if, taken together, they bathe the scene with a strange hard light of their own, the individual institution may often affect the strained pilgrim as a blessedly restful perch. It constitutes, in its degree, wherever met, a more explicit plea for the amenities, or at least a fuller exhibition of them, than the place is otherwise likely to contain; and I remember comparing them, inwardly, after periods of stress and dearth, after long, vacant stretches, to the mast-heads on which spent birds sometimes alight in the expanses of ocean. Their function for the student of manners is by no means exhausted with that attribute—

they project, through the use made of them, twenty interesting sidelights; but it was by that especial restorative, that almost romantic character I have just glanced at, that I found myself most solicited. It is to the inordinate value, in the picture, of the non-commercial, non-industrial, non-financial note that they owe their rich relief; being, with the Universities, as one never wearied of noting, charged with the *whole* expression of that part of the national energy that is not calculable in terms of mere arithmetic. They appeared to express it, at times, I admit, the strange national energy, in terms of mere subjection to the spell of the last "seller"—the new novel, epidemically swift, the ubiquity of which so mirrors the great continental conditions of unity, equality and prosperity; but this view itself was compatible with one's sense of their practical bid for the effect of distinction. There are a hundred applications of the idea of civilization which, in a given place, outside its Library, would be all wrong, if conceivably attempted, and yet that immediately become right, incur in fact the highest sanction, on passing that threshold. They often more or less fail of course, they sometimes completely fail, to assert themselves even within the precinct; but one at least feels that the precinct attends on them, waits and confessedly yearns for them, consents indeed to *be* a precinct only on the understanding that they shall not be forever delayed. I wondered, everywhere, under stress of this perception, at the general associations of the word that best describes them and that remains so quaintly and admirably *their* word even when their supreme right in it is most vulgarly and loudly disputed. They are the *rich* presences, even in the "rich" places, among the sky-scrapers, the newspaper-offices, the highly-rented pews and the billionaires, and they assert, with a blest imperturbable serenity, not only that everything would be poor without them, but that even with them much is as yet deplorably poor. They in fact so inexorably establish this truth that when they are in question they leave little to choose, I think, round about them, between the seats of wealth and the seats of comparative penury: they are intrinsically so much more interesting than either.

Was it then because Richmond at large, the "old" Richmond, seemed to lie there in its icy shroud with the very dim smile of modesty, the invalid gentleness, of a patient who has been freely bled—was it through profit of this impression that the town Library struck me as flushing with colour and resource, with confidence and temperament? The beauty of the matter is that these *penetralia*, to carry it off as they do, call to their aid, of necessity, no great store of possessions—play their trick, if they must, with the mildest rarities. It sufficed, really, at Richmond, that the solid structure—ample and detached indeed, and keeping, where it stood, the best company the place could afford—should make the affirmation furthest removed from the vain vaunt of the other time, the pretence of a social order founded on delusions and exclusions. Everything else was somehow, however indirectly, the bequest of that sad age and partook more or less of its nature; this thing alone either had nothing to do with it or had to do with it by an appealing, a quite affecting lapse of logic—his half-hour's appreciation of which had for the restless analyst a positive melancholy sweetness. The place had of course to be in its way a temple to the Confederate cause, but the charm, in the spacious, "handsome," convenient upper room, among books of value and pictures of innocence, and glass cases of memorabilia more refined than those of the collection I had previously visited, among gentle readers, transported and oblivious, and the still gentler specimens, if I rightly recollect, of the pale sisterhood of the appointed and attendant fair who predominantly, throughout the States, minister to intellectual appetite and perform the intellectual service, directing and controlling them and, as would appear, triumphantly minimizing their scope, feminizing their too possible male grossnesses—the charm, I say, was now in the beautiful openness to the world-relation, in the felt balm, really, of the disprovincializing breath. Once such a summer air as that had begun softly to stir, even the drearier little documents might flutter in it as confederately as they liked. The terrible framed canvases, portraits of soldiers and statesmen, strange images, on the whole, of the sectional great, might seem to shake, faintly, on the wall, as in vague protest at a possible doom. Disinherited of art one could indeed, in presence of such objects, but feel that the old South had been; and might not this thin tremor, on the part of several of those who had had so little care for it, represent some sense of what the more liberal day—so announced there on the spot—might mean for their meagre memories?

This was a question, however, that it naturally concerned me not to put to the old mutilated Confederate soldier who, trafficking in photographs in a corner of the room, rejoiced to proclaim the originals of the portraits. Nothing could have been a happier link than the old Confederate soldier—a link as from past to present and future, I mean, even when individually addicted to "voicing" some of the more questionable claims of the past. What will they be, at all events, the Southern shrines of memory, on the day the last old Confederate soldier shall have been gathered to his fate? Never, thanks to a low horizon, had the human figure endowed with almost anything at all in the nature of a presence or a silhouette such a chance to stand out; never had the pictorial accident, on a vast grey canvas, such a chance to tell. But a different matter from these, at Richmond, in fact the greatest matter of all, is the statue of General Lee, which stands, high aloft and extraordinarily by itself, at the far end of the main residential street—a street with no imputable "character" but that of leading to it. Faithful, experimentally, to a desperate practice, I yet had to renounce here—in the main residential street— the subtle effort to "read" a sense into the senseless appearances about me. This ranked, I scarce know why, as a disappointment: I had presumed with a fond extravagance, I have hinted, that they would give out here and there some unmistakable backward reference, show, from the old overclambered but dispeopled double galleries that I might liken to desecrated cloisters, some wan, faded face of shrunken gentility. Frankly, however, with the best will in the world—really too good a will, which found itself again and again quite grimly snubbed—frankly I could do nothing: everything was there but the material. The disposition had been a tribute to old Virginia, but old Virginia quite unceremoniously washed her hands of me. I have spoken of scratching, scratching for romance, and all tenderly, in the deposit of history; but, plainly, no deposit would show, and I tried to remember, for fairness, that Richmond had been after all but a modern and upstart capital. Indistinct there, below the hill, was the James River, and away in the mists of time "romantic" Jamestown, the creation of a Stuart king. That would have to do, though it also, in its way, was nothing; for meanwhile in truth, just here—here above all and in presence of the monument completing the vista—were other things to remember, provoked reflections that took on their own intensity.

The equestrian statue of the Southern hero, made to order in far-away uninterested Paris, is the work of a master and has an artistic interest—a refinement of style, in fact, under the impression of which we seem to see it, in its situation, as some precious pearl of ocean washed up on a rude bare strand. The very high florid pedestal is of the last French elegance, and the great soldier, sitting his horse with a kind of melancholy nobleness, raises his handsome head as he looks off into desolate space. He does well, we feel, to sit as high as he may, and to appear, in his lone survival, to see as far, and to overlook as many things; for the irony of fate, crowning the picture, is surely stamped in all sharpness on the scene about him. The place is the mere vague centre of two or three crossways, without form and void, with a circle half sketched by three or four groups of small, new, mean houses. It is somehow empty in spite of being ugly, and yet expressive in spite of being empty. "Desolate," one has called the air; and the effect is, strangely, of some smug "up-to-date" specimen or pattern of desolation. So long as one stands there the high figure, which ends for all the world by suggesting to the admirer a quite conscious, subjective, even a quite sublime, effort to ignore, to sit, as it were, superior and indifferent, enjoys the fact of company and thereby, in a manner, of sympathy—so that the vast association of the futile for the moment drops away from it. But to turn one's back, one feels, is to leave it again alone, communing, at its altitude, which represents thus some prodigious exemplary perched position, some everlasting high stool of penitence, with the very heaven of futility. So at least I felt brought round again to meeting my first surprise, to solving the riddle of the historic poverty of Richmond. It is the poverty that *is*, exactly, historic: once take it for that and it puts on vividness. The condition attested is the condition—or, as may be, one of the later, fainter, weaker stages—of having worshipped false gods. As I looked back, before leaving it, at Lee's stranded, bereft image, which time and fortune have so cheated of half the significance, and so, I think, of half the dignity, of great memorials, I recognized something more than the melancholy of a lost cause. The whole infelicity speaks of a cause that could never have been gained.

XIII
Charleston

I

To arrive at Charleston early in the chill morning was to appear to have come quite adventurously far, and yet to be not quite clear about the grounds of the appearance. Did it rest on impressions gathered by the way, on the number of things one had been, since leaving Richmond, aware of?—or was it rather explained by the long succession of hours, the nights and days, consumed as mere tasteless time and without the attending relish of excited interest? What, definitely, could I say I had seen, that my journey should already presume to give itself airs, to seat itself there as a chapter of experience? To consider of this question was really, I think, after a little, to renew one's appreciation of the mystery and the marvel of experience. That accretion may amount to an enormous sum, often, when the figures on the slate are too few and too paltry to mention. It may count for enrichment without one's knowing why; and so again, on occasion, with a long column of items, it may count for nothing at all. I reached Charleston ever so much (as it seemed to me) the wiser—the wiser, that is, for the impression of scarce distinguishable things. One made them out, with no great brilliancy, as just Southern; but one would have missed the point, I hasten to add, in failing to see what an application and what a value they derived from that name. One was already beginning—that was the truth—one's convenient induction as to the nature of the South; and, once that account was opened, how could everything, great or small, positive or negative, not become straightway a contribution to it? The large negatives, in America, have, as well as other matters, their meaning and their truth: so what if my charged consciousness of the long way from Richmond were that of a negative modified by small discomforts?

The discomforts indeed were as nothing, for importance—compared, candidly, with the importance of the rest of the impression. The process, certainly, however one qualified it,

679

had been interrupted by one of the most positive passages of one's life—which may not figure here, alas, unfortunately, as of the essence of my journey. Vast brackets, applied, as it were, to the very face of nature, enclosed and rounded this felicity; which was no more of the texture of the general Southern stuff than a patch of old brocade would be of the woof of the native homespun. I had, by a deviation, spent a week in a castle of enchantment; but if this modern miracle, of which the mountains of North Carolina happened to be the scene, would have been almost anywhere miraculous, I could at least take it as testifying, all relevantly, all directly, for the presence, as distinguished from the absence, of feature. One felt how, in this light, the extent and the splendour of such a place was but a detail; these things were accidents, without which the great effect, the element that, in the beautiful empty air, made all the difference, would still have prevailed. What was this element but just the affirmation of resources?—made with great emphasis indeed, but in a clear and exemplary way; so that if large wealth represented some of them, an idea, a fine cluster of ideas, a will, a purpose, a patience, an intelligence, a store of knowledge, immediately workable things, represented the others. What it thus came to, on behalf of this vast parenthetic Carolinian demonstration, was that somebody had *cared* enough—and that happily there had been somebody *to* care; which struck me at once as marking the difference for the rest of the text. My view of the melancholy of it had been conveniently expressed, from hour to hour, by the fond reflection, through the dreary land, that nobody cared—cared really for *it* or for anything. That fairly *made* it dreary, as the crazy timber viaducts, where the train crawled, and sometimes nervously stopped, spanned the deep gorges and the admirable nameless and more or less torrential streams; as the sense of landscape in mere quantity became, once more, the vehicle of effect; and as we pulled up at the small stations where the social scene might be sufficiently penetrated, no doubt, from the car window.

The social scene, shabby and sordid, and lost in the scale of space as the quotable line is lost in a dull epic or the needed name in an ageing memory, would have been as interesting, probably, as a "short story" in one of the slangy dialects promoted by the illustrated monthly magazines; but it affected me above all, and almost each time, I seem to remember, as speaking of the number of things not cared for. There were some presumably, though not at all discernibly, that *were*— enough to beget the loose human cohesion, the scant consistency of parts and pieces, to which the array by the railway platform testified; but questions came up, plentifully, in respect to the whole picture, and if the mass of interests that were absent was so remarkably large, this would be certainly because such interests were ruled out. The grimness with which, as by a hard inexorable fate, so many things were ruled out, fixed itself most perhaps as the impression of the spectator enjoying from his supreme seat of ease his extraordinary, his awful modern privilege of this detached yet concentrated stare at the misery of subject populations. (Subject, I mean, to this superiority of his bought convenience—subject even as never, of old, to the sway of satraps or proconsuls.) If the subject populations on the road to Charleston, seemingly weak indeed in numbers and in energy, had to be viewed, at all events, so vividly, as not "caring," one made out quite with eagerness that it was because they naturally couldn't. The negroes were more numerous than the whites, but still there *were* whites—of aspect so forlorn and depressed for the most part as to deprecate, though not cynically, only quite tragically, any imputation of value. It was a monstrous thing, doubtless, to sit there in a cushioned and kitchened Pullman and deny to so many groups of one's fellow-creatures any claim to a "personality"; but this was in truth what one was perpetually doing. The negroes, though superficially and doubtless not at all intendingly sinister, were the lustier race; but how could they care (to insist on my point) for such equivocal embodiments of the right complexion? Yet these were, practically, within the picture the only affirmations of life except themselves; and they obviously, they notoriously, didn't care for themselves. The moral of all of which was that really, through the more and more southward hours, the wondering stops and the blank renewals, it was only the restless analyst himself who cared—and enough, after all, he finally felt, to make up for other deficiencies.

He cared even when, in the watches of the night, he was

roused, under the bewilderment that was rarely to leave him, in America, at any stage of any transaction to which the cars and their sparse stern functionaries formed a party, for unpremeditated transfer to a dark and friendless void where, with what grace he could, he awaited the February dawn. The general American theory is that railway-travel within the confines of the Republic is a matter of majestic simplicity and facility—qualified at the worst by inordinate luxury; I should need therefore an excursion here forbidden me to present another and perhaps a too highly subjective view of it. There are lights in which the majesty, if the question be of that, may strike the freshly repatriated, or in other words the unwarned and inexpert, as quite grimly formidable; lights, however, that must be left to shine for us in some other connection. Let it none the less glimmer out of them for the moment that this implication of the penalty of imperfect expertness is really a clue to the essence of the matter; a core packed, in relation to the whole subject of expertness, with fruitful suggestion. No single admonition, in the States, I think, is more constant and vivid than the general mass of intimation of what may happen to you, in transit, unless you have had special and confirmed practice. You may have been without it in "Europe," for moving about, and yet not perish; but to be inexpert in the American battle would be, it struck me, much more quickly to go down. Your luggage, in America, is "looked after," but you are not, save so far as you receive on occasion a sharp order or a sharper shove: by sufferance of which discipline, moreover, you by no means always purchase a prompt delivery of your effects. This indeed is but a translation of the general truth that it is the country in the world in which you must do most things for yourself. It may be "better" for you to have thus to do for yourself the secondary as well as the primary things— but that is not here the question. It begins to strike you, at all events, as soon as you begin to circulate, that your fellow-travellers are for the most part, as to the complex act itself, professional; whereas you may perform it all in "Europe" successfully enough as an amateur. Whether to your glory or your shame you must of course yourself decide; but impunity, nay more, success, may at least attend your empiricism.

If it was not success, however, for the strayed amateur to

have found himself stranded in the small hours of morning by the vast vague wayside, he still nevertheless remembers how quickly even this interlude took on an interest. The gloom was scarce penetrable, but a light glimmered here and there, and formless sheds and shanties, dim, discomfortable things, straggled about and lost themselves. Indistinguishable engines hooted, before and behind, where red fires also flared and vanished; indistinguishable too, from each other, while one sought a place of temporary deposit for the impedimenta that attested one's absurd want of rehearsal, were the cold steel of the rails, the vague composition of the platform, and the kinder, the safer breast of earth. The place was apparently a junction, and it was but a question of waiting—of selecting as the wisest course, among the hoots and the flares, to stand huddled just where one was. That almost completely unservanted state which is so the mark, in general, of the American station, was here the sole distinctness. I had succeeded in artlessly becoming a perfectly isolated traveller, with nobody to warn or comfort me, with nobody even to command. But it was precisely in this situation that I felt again, as by the click of a spring, that my adventure had, in spite of everything, or perhaps indeed just because of everything, a charm all its own—and a charm, moreover, which I was to have from that moment, for any connection, no difficulty whatever in recognizing. It must have broken out more particularly, then and there, in the breath of the night, which was verily now the bland air of the South—mild, benignant, a benediction in itself as it hung about me, and with that blest quality in it of its appearing a medium through which almost any good might come. It was the air of the open gates—not, like that of the North, of the closed; and one inhaled it, in short, on the spot, as the very boon of one's quest.

A couple of hours later, in the right train, which had at last arrived, I had so settled to submission to this spell that it had wrought for me, I think, all its magic—ministered absolutely to the maximum of suggestion, which became thus, for my introduction to Charleston, the presiding influence. What had happened may doubtless show for no great matter in a bare verbal statement; yet it was to make all the difference, I felt, for impressions (happy and harsh alike) still to come. It couldn't have happened without one's beginning to wander; but the lively interest was that the further one wandered the more the suggestion spoke. The sense of the size of the Margin, that was the name of it—the Margin by which the total of American life, huge as it already appears, is still so surrounded as to represent, for the mind's eye on a general view, but a scant central flotilla huddled as for very fear of the fathomless depth of water, the too formidable future, on the so much vaster lake of the materially possible. Once that torch is at all vividly lighted it flares, for any pair of open eyes, over every scene, and with a presence that helps to explain their owner's inevitable failure to conclude. He feels it in all his uncertainties, and he never just escapes concluding without the sense that this so fallacious neatness would more or less absurdly have neglected or sacrificed it. Not by any means that the Margin always affects him as standing for the vision of a possible greater good than what he sees in the given case—any more than as standing for a possible greater evil; these differences are submerged in the immense fluidity; they lurk confused, disengaged, in the mere looming mass of the *more*, the more and more to come. And as yet nothing makes definite the probable preponderance of particular forms of the more. The one all positive appearance is of the perpetual increase of everything, the growth of the immeasurable muchness that shall constitute the deep sea into which the seeker for conclusions must cast his nets. The fact that, with so many things present, so few of them are not on the way to become quite other, and possibly altogether different, things, conduces to the peculiar interest and, one often feels tempted to add, to the peculiar irritation of the country.

II

Charleston early in the morning, on my driving from the station, was, it had to be admitted, no very finished picture, but at least, already, it was different—ever so different in aspect and "feeling," and above all for intimation and suggestion, from any passage of the American scene as yet deciphered; and such became on the spot one's appetite for local colour that one was fairly grateful to a friend who, by having promised to arrive from the interior of the State the night before, gave one a pretext for seeking him up and down. My quest, for the moment, proved vain; but the intimations and suggestions, while I proceeded from door to door in the sweet blank freshness of the day, of the climate, of the streets, began to swarm at such a rate that I had the sense of gathering my harvest with almost too eager a thrift. It was like standing steeped at the bookstall itself in the volume picked up and opened—though I may add that when I had presently retreated upon the hotel, to which I should in the first instance have addressed myself, it was quite, for a turning of pages, as if I had gone on with the "set." Thus, before breakfast, I entered upon my brief residence with the right vibrations already determined and unable really to say which of a couple of contacts just enjoyed would have most ministered to them. I had roused, guilelessly, through an easy misunderstanding, two more or less sleeping households; but if I had still missed my clue to my friend I had yet put myself into possession of much of whatever else I had wanted. What had I most wanted, I could easily ask myself, but some small inkling (a mere specimen-scrap would do) of the sense, as I have to keep forever calling my wanton synthesis, of "the South before the War"?—an air-bubble only to be blown, in any case, through some odd fragment of a pipe. My pair of early Charleston impressions were thus a pair of thin prismatic bubbles—which could have floated before me moreover but for a few seconds, collapsing even while I stood there.

Prismatically, none the less, they had shown me the "old" South; in one case by the mere magic of the manner in which a small, scared, starved person of colour, of very light colour, an elderly mulattress in an improvised wrapper, just barely held open for me a door through which I felt I might have looked straight and far back into the past. The past, that of the vanished order, was hanging on there behind her—as much of it as the scant place would accommodate; and she knew this, and that I had so quickly guessed it; which led her, in fine, before I could see more, and that I might not sound the secret of shy misfortune, of faded pretension, to shut the door in my face. So, it seemed to me, had I been confronted, in Italy, under quite such a morning air and light, quite the same touch of a tepid, odorous medium, with the ancient sallow crones who guard the locked portals and the fallen pride of provincial *palazzini*. That was all, in the one instance; there had been no more of it than of the little flare of a struck match—which lasted long enough, however, to light the sedative cigarette, smoked and thrown away, that renews itself forever between the picture-seeker's lips. The small historic whiff I had momentarily inhaled required the correction, I should add, of the sweeter breath of my commentary. Fresh altogether was the air behind the garden wall that next gave way to my pursuit; there being a thrill, for that matter, in the fact that here at last again, if nowhere else over the land, rose the real walls that alone make real gardens and that admit to the same by real doors. Close such a door behind you, and you are at once *within*—a local relation, a possibility of retreat, in favour of which the custom of the North has so completely ceased to discriminate. One sacrificed the North, with its mere hard conceit of virtuously meeting exhibition—much as if a house were just a metallic machine, number so-and-so in a catalogue—one sacrificed it on the spot to this finer feeling for the enclosure.

That had really sufficed, no doubt, for my second initiation; since I remember withdrawing, after my fruitless question, as on the completion of a mystic process. Initiation into *what* I perhaps couldn't have said; only, at the most, into the knowledge that what such Southern walls generally shut in proves exactly what one would have wished. I was to see this loose quantity afterwards in greater profusion; but for the moment the effect was as right as that of privacy for the habit of the siesta. The details escape me, or rather I tenderly withhold them. For the siesta there—what would it have been most like but some deep doze, or call it frankly some final sleep, of the idea of "success"? And how could one better have described the privacy, with the mild street shut off and with the deep gallery, where resignation might sit in the shade or swing without motion in a hammock, shut in, than as some dim dream that things were still as they had been— still pleasant behind garden walls—before the great folly? I was to find myself liking, in the South and in the most mon-

strous fashion, it appeared, those aspects in which the consequences of the great folly were, for extent and gravity, still
traccable; I was cold-bloodedly to prefer them, that is, to the
aspects, occasionally to be met, from which the traces had
been removed. And this, I need hardly say, from a point of
view having so little in common with the vindictive as to be
quite directly opposed to it. For what in the world was one
candidly to do? It is the manner of the purged and renovated,
the disconnected element, anywhere, after great trials, to express itself in forms comparatively vulgar; whereas those parts
of the organism that, having been through the fire, still have
kept the scorches and scars, resemble for tone, for colour and
value, the products of the potter's oven; when the potter, I
mean, or when, in other words, history, has been the right
great artist. They at least are not cheerful rawnesses—they
have been baked beautiful and hard.

I even tried, I fear, when once installed there, to look at my
hotel in that light; availing myself, to this end, of its appearance of "dating," with its fine old neo-classic front and of
a certain romantic grandeur of scale, the scale positively of
"Latin" construction, in my vast saloon-like apartment, which
opened to a high colonnade. The great canopied and curtained bed was really in the grand manner, and the ghost of a
rococo tradition, the tradition of the transatlantic South,
memory of other lands, glimmered generally in the decoration. When once I had—though almost exclusively under the
charm of these particular faded graces, I admit—again privately protested that the place might have been a "palace,"
my peace was made with Charleston: I was ripe for the last
platitude of appreciation. Let me say indeed that this consciousness had from the first to struggle with another—the
immediate sense of the degree in which the American scene is
lighted, on occasion, to the critical eye, by the testimony of
the hotel. As had been the case for me already at Richmond,
so here again the note of that truth was sounded; the visitor
interested in manners was too clearly not to escape it, and I
scarce know under what slightly sinister warning he braced
himself to the fact. He had not, as yet, for repatriation, been
thrown much upon the hotel; but this was the high sense of
looking further and seeing more, this present promise of that

adventure. One is thrown upon it, in America, as straight upon the general painted scene over which the footlights of publicity play with their large crudity, and against the freely-brushed texture and grain of which you thus rub your nose more directly, and with less of ceremony, than elsewhere. There are endless things in "Europe," to your vision, behind and beyond the hotel, a multitudinous complicated life; in the States, on the other hand, you see the hotel as itself that life, as constituting for vast numbers of people the richest form of existence. You have to go no distance for this to come over you—twenty appearances so vividly speak of it. It is not so much, no doubt, that "every one" lives at hotels, according to the witless belief of "Europe," but that you so quickly seem to measure the very limited extent to which those who people them, the populations they appeal to in general, may be conceived as "living" out of them. I remember how often, in moving about, the observation that most remained with me appeared to be this note of the hotel, and of the hotel-like chain of Pullman cars, as the supreme social expression. For the Pullmans too, in their way, were eloquent; they affected me ever, by the end of twenty-four hours, as carrying, if not Cæsar and his fortune, at least almost *all* the facts of American life. There were some of course that didn't fit into them, but so many others did, and these fitted somehow so perfectly and with such a congruity.

What it comes back to is that in such conditions the elements of the situation show with all possible, though quite unnoted, intensity; they tell you all about it (about the situation) in a few remarkably plain and distinct words; they make you feel in short how its significance is written upon it. It is as if the figures before you and all round you, less different from each other, less different too, I think, from the objects about them, whatever these in any case may be, than any equal mass of appearances under the sun—it is as if every one and everything said to you straight: "Yes, this is how we are; this is what it is to enjoy our advantages; this moreover is all there is of us; we give it all out. Make what you can of it!" The restless analyst would have had indeed an unusual fit of languor if he had not begun from the first to make of it what he could, divided even though he was between his sense of this largely-

written significance and his wonderment, none the less, as to
its value and bearing: which constituted, after all, a shade of
perplexity as to its meaning. "Yes, I see how you are, God
knows"—he was ready with his reply; "for nothing in the
world is easier to see, even in all the particulars. But what
does it *mean* to be as you are?—since I suppose it means
something; something more than your mere one universal
type, with its small deflections but never a departure; something more than your way of sitting in silence together at
table, than your extraordinary, your enormous passivity, than
your apparent absence of criticism or judgment of anything
that is put before you or that happens to you (beyond occasionally remarking that it's 'fine!') than, in a word, the fact of
what you eat and the fact of how you eat it. You are not final,
complacently as you appear so much of the time to assume
it—your mere inevitable shaking about in the Margin must
more or less take care of that; since you can't be so inordinately passive (everywhere, one infers, but in your particular
wary niche of your 'business-block') without being in *some*
degree plastic. Distinct as you are, you are not even definite,
and it would be terrible not to be able to suppose that you are
as yet but an instalment, a current number, like that of the
morning paper, a specimen of a type in course of serializa-
tion—like the hero of the magazine novel, by the highly-
successful author, the climax of which is still far off. Thus, as
you are perpetually provisional, the hotels and the Pullmans—the Pullmans that are like rushing hotels and the
hotels that are like stationary Pullmans—represent the stages
and forms of your evolution, and are not a bit, in themselves,
more final than you are. The particulars still to be added
either to you or to them form an insoluble question; and meanwhile, clearly, your actual stage will not be short." So much as
that, I recall, had hummed about my ears at Richmond,
where the strong vertical light of a fine domed and glazed
cortile, the spacious and agreeable dining-hall of the inn, had
rested on the human scene as with an effect of mechanical
pressure. If the scene constituted evidence, the evidence might
have been in course of being pressed out, in this shining
form, by the application of a weight and the turn of a screw.
There it was, accordingly; there was the social, the readable

page, with its more or less complete report of the conditions. The report was to be fuller as to some of these at Charleston; but I had at least grasped its general value. And I shall come back to the Charleston report.

It would have been a sorry business here, however, if this had been mainly the source of my impressions—which was so far from the case that I had but to go forth, after breakfast, to find insidious charm, the appeal of the outer, the larger aspect, await me at every turn. The day announced itself as warm and radiant, and, keeping its promise to the end, squared itself there as the golden frame of an interesting picture—interesting above all from the moment one desired with any intensity to find it so. The vision persists, with its charming, touching features; yet when I look back and ask myself what can have made my impression, all round, so positive, I am at a loss for elements to refer it to. Elements there were, certainly; in especial the fact that during these first bland hours, charged with the splendour of spring, I caught the wide-eyed smile of the South, that expression of a temperamental felicity in which shades of character, questions of real feature, other marks and meanings, tend always to lose themselves. But a deficiency was clear, which was neither more nor less than the deficiency of life; without life, all gracefully, the picture managed to compose itself. Even while one felt it do so one missed the precious presence; so that there at least was food for wonderment, for admiration of the art at play. To what, all the while, as one went, could one compare the mystification?—to what if not to the image of some handsome pale person, a beauty (to call her so) of other days, who, besides confessing to the inanimate state from closed eyes and motionless lips, from the arrest of respiration and gesture, was to leave one, by the day's end, with the sense of a figure prepared for romantic interment, stretched in a fair winding-sheet, covered with admirable flowers, surrounded with shining tapers. *That*, one reasoned, would be something to have seen; and yet one's interest was not so limited. Ruins, to be interesting, have to be massive; and poor bitter-sweet Charleston suffered, for the observer, by the merciless law of the thinness, making too much for transparency, for the effect of paucity, still inherent in American groupings; a law under which the attempt to subject them to portraiture, to see them as "composing," resembles the attempt to play whist with an imperfect pack of cards. If one had already, at the North, divined the general complexion as probably thin, in this sense, everywhere—thin, that is, for all note-taking but the statistical, under which it might of course show as portentously thick—it wouldn't turn dense or rich of a sudden, even in an air that could so drench it with benignity. Therefore if the scene, as one might say, was but the historic Desert without the historic Mausoleum, how was one's impression to give out, as it clearly would, the after-taste of experience?

To let this small problem worry me no longer than it might, I sought an answer, and quickly found one, in the fortunate fact of my not having failed, after all, of the admirably suggestive society of my distinguished and competent friend. He *had* arrived over-night, according to my hope, and had only happened to lodge himself momentarily out of my ken; so that as soon as I had his company to profit by I felt the "analytic" burden of my own blessedly lifted. I took over his analysis, infinitely better adjusted to the case and which clearly would suffice for everything—if only it should itself escape disintegration. Let me say at once that it quite averted—whether consciously or unconsciously, whether as too formidably bristling or as too perfectly pacific—that menace; which success was to provide for us both, I think, a rounded felicity. My companion, a Northerner of Southern descent (as well as still more immediately, on another side, of English), knew his South in general and his Carolina of that ilk in particular, with an intimacy that was like a grab-bag into which, for illustration, he might always dip his hand (a movement that, had the grab-bag been "European," I should describe rather as a plunge of his arm: so that it comes back again to the shallowness of the American grab-bag, as yet, for illustrations other than the statistical). He held up for me his bright critical candle, which even in the intrinsic Charleston vividness made its gay flicker, and it was under this aid that, to my extreme convenience, I was able to "feel" the place. My fortune had indeed an odd sequel—which I mention for its appreciatory value; the mishaps and accidents of appreciation being ever, in their way, I think, as contributive to judgment as the felicities. I was to challenge, too recklessly, the chances of a second day; having by the end of the first, and by the taking of example, quite learned to treat the scene as a grab-bag for my own hand. I went over it again, in an evil hour—whereupon I met afresh the admonition, already repeatedly received, that where, in the States, the interest, where the pleasure of contemplation is concerned, discretion is the better part of valour and insistence too often a betrayal. It is not so much that the hostile fact crops up as that the friendly fact breaks down. If you have luckily *seen*, you have seen; carry off your prize, in this case, instantly and at any risk. Try it again and you don't, you won't, see; for there is in all contemplation, there is even in any clear appreciation, an element of the cruel. These things demand that your exposed object shall, first of all, exist; and to exist for exposure is to be at the best impaled on the naturalist's pin. It takes superpositions, at any rate, to defy sufficiently this sort of attention; it takes either the stoutnesses of history or the rarest rarities of nature to resist fatal penetration. That was to come home to me presently in Florida—through the touched sense of the truth that Florida, ever so amiably, is weak. You may live there serenely, no doubt—as in a void furnished at the most with velvet air; you may in fact live there with an idea, if you are content that your idea shall consist of grapefruit and oranges. Oranges, grapefruit and velvet air constitute, in a manner, I admit, a feast; but press upon the board with any greater weight and it quite gives way—its three or four props treacherously forsake it. That is what I mean by the impression, in the great empty peninsula, of weakness; which I was to feel still clearer about on being able to compare it afterwards with the impression of California. California was to have—if I may decently be premature about it—her own treachery; but she was to wind one up much higher before she let one down. I was to find her, especially at the first flush, unlike sweet frustrated Florida, ever so amiably strong: which came from the art with which she makes the stoutnesses, as I have called them, of natural beauty stand you in temporary stead of the leannesses of everything else (everything that might be of an order equally interesting). This she is on a short acquaintance quite insolently able to do, thanks to her belonging so completely to the "handsome" side of the continent, of which she is the finest expression. The aspect of natural objects, up and down the Pacific coast, is as "aristocratic" as the comprehensive American condition permits anything to be: it indeed appears to the ingenious mind to represent an instinct on the part of Nature, a sort of shuddering, bristling need, to brace herself in advance against the assault of a society so much less marked with distinction than herself. If I was to conceive therefore under these later lights, that her spirit had put forth nowhere on the sub-tropical Atlantic shore anything to approach this conscious pride, so, doubtless, the Carolinian effect, even at its sweetest, was to strike me as related to it very much as a tinkle is related to a boom.

III

To stray but for an instant into such an out-of-the-way corner of one's notes, however, is to give the lie to the tenderness that asserted itself so promptly as the very medium of one's perception. There was literally no single object that, from morn to nightfall, it was not more possible to consider with tenderness, a rich consistency of tenderness, than to consider without it: *such* was the subtle trick that Charleston could still play. There echoed for me as I looked out from the Battery the recent speech of a friend which had had at the time a depressing weight; the Battery of the long, curved sea-front, of the waterside public garden furnished with sad old historic guns, with live-oaks draped in trailing moss, with palmettos that, as if still mindful of their State symbolism, seem to try everywhere, though with a melancholy sceptical droop, to repeat the old escutcheon; with its large, thrilling view in particular—thrilling to a Northerner who stands there for the first time. "Filled as I am, in general, while there," my friend had said, "with the sadness and sorrow of the South, I never, at Charleston, look out to the old betrayed Forts without feeling my heart harden again to steel." One remembered that, on the spot, and one waited a little—to see what was happening to one's heart. I found this to take time indeed; everything differed, somehow, from one's old conceived image—or if I had anciently grasped the remoteness of Fort

Sumter, near the mouth of the Bay, and of its companion, at the point of the shore forming the other side of the passage, this lucidity had so left me, in the course of the years, that the far-away dimness of the consecrated objects was almost a shock. It was a blow even to one's faded vision of Charleston viciously firing on the Flag; the Flag would have been, from the Battery, such a mere speck in space that the vice of the act lost somehow, with the distance, to say nothing of the forty years, a part of its grossness. The smitten face, however flushed and scarred, was out of sight, though the intention of smiting and the force of the insult were of course still the same. This reflection one made, but the old fancied perspective and proportions were altered; and then the whole picture, at that hour, exhaled an innocence. It was as blank as the face of a child under mention of his naughtiness and his punishment of week before last. The Forts, faintly blue on the twinkling sea, looked like vague marine flowers; innocence, pleasantness ruled the prospect: it was as if the compromised slate, sponged clean of all the wicked words and hung up on the wall for better use, dangled there so vacantly as almost to look foolish. Ah, there again was the word: the air still just tasted of the antique folly; so that in presence of a lesson so sharp and so prolonged, of the general *sterilized* state, of the brightly-lighted, delicate dreariness recording the folly, harshness was conjured away. There was that in the impression which affected me after a little as one of those refinements of irony that wait on deep expiations: one could scarce conceive at this time of day that such a place had ever been dangerously moved. It was the *bled* condition, and mostly the depleted cerebral condition, that was thus attested—as I had recognized it at Richmond; and I asked myself, on the Battery, what more one's sternest justice could have desired. If my heart wasn't to harden to steel, in short, access to it by the right influence had found perhaps too many other forms of sensibility in ambush.

To justify hardness, moreover, one would have had to meet something hard; and if my peregrination, after this, had been a search for such an element, I should have to describe it as made all in vain. Up and down and in and out, with my companion, I strolled from hour to hour; but more and more under the impression of the consistency of softness. One could have expressed the softness in a word, and the picture so offered would be infinitely touching. It was a city of gardens and absolutely of no men—or of so few that, save for the general sweetness, the War might still have been raging and all the manhood at the front. The gardens were matter for the women; though even of the women there were few, and that small company—rare, discreet, flitting figures that brushed the garden walls with noiseless skirts in the little melancholy streets of interspaced, overtangled abodes—were clad in a rigour of mourning that was like the garb of a conspiracy. The effect was superficially prim, but so far as it savoured of malice prepense, of the Southern, the sentimental *parti-pris*, it was delightful. What was it all most like, the incoherent jumble of suggestions?—the suggestion of a social shrinkage and an economic blight unrepaired, irreparable; the suggestion of by-ways of some odd far East infected with triumphant women's rights, some perspective of builded, plastered lanes over the enclosures of which the flowering almond drops its petals into sharp deep bands of shade or of sun. It is not the muffled ladies who walk about predominantly in the East; but that is a detail. The likeness was perhaps greater to some little old-world quarter of quiet convents where only priests and nuns steal forth—the priests mistakable at a distance, say, for the nuns. It was indeed thoroughly mystifying, the whole picture—since I was to get, in the freshness of that morning, from the very background of the scene, my quite triumphant little impression of the "old South." I remember feeling with intensity at two or three points in particular that I should never get a better one, that even this was precarious—might melt at any moment, by a wrong touch or a false note, in my grasp—and that I must therefore make the most of it. The rest of my time, I may profess, was spent in so doing. I made the most of it in several successive spots: under the south wall of St. Michael's Church, the sweetest corner of Charleston, and of which there is more to say; out in the old Cemetery on the edge of the lagoon, where the distillation of the past was perhaps clearest and the bribe to tenderness most effective; and even not a little on ground thereunto almost adjacent, that of a kindly Country-Club installed in a fine old semi-sinister mansion, and holding an afternoon revel at which I was privileged briefly to assist. The wrong touch and the false note were doubtless just sensible in this last connection, where the question, probed a little, would apparently have been of some new South that has not yet quite found the effective way romantically, or at least insidiously, to appeal. The South that is cultivating country-clubs is a South presumably, in many connections, quite in the right; whereas the one we were invidiously "after" was the one that had been so utterly in the wrong. Even there, none the less, in presence of more than a single marked sign of the rude Northern contagion, I disengaged, socially speaking, a faint residuum which I mention for proof of the intensity of my quest and of my appreciation.

There were two other places, I may add, where one could but work the impression for all it was, in the modern phrase, "worth," and where I had, I may venture to say, the sense of making as much of it as was likely ever to be made again. Meanings without end were to be read, under tuition, into one of these, which was neither more nor less than a slightly shy, yet after all quite serene place of refection, a luncheon-room or tea-house, denominated for quaint reasons an "Exchange"—*the* very Exchange in fact lately commemorated in a penetrating study, already much known to fame, of the little that is left of the local society. My tuition, at the hands of my ingenious comrade, was the very best it was possible to have. Nothing, usually, is more wonderful than the quantity of significant character that, with such an example set, the imagination may recognize in the scantest group of features, objects, persons. I fantastically feasted here, at my luncheon-table, not only, as the genius of the place demanded, on hot chocolate, sandwiches and "Lady Baltimore" cake (this last a most delectable compound), but on the exact *nuance* of oddity, of bravery, of reduced gentility, of irreducible superiority, to which the opening of such an establishment, without derogation, by the proud daughters of war-wasted families, could exquisitely testify. They hovered, the proud impoverished daughters, singly or in couples, behind the counter—a counter, again, delectably charged; they waited, inscrutably, irreproachably, yet with all that peculiarly chaste *bonhomie* of the Southern tone, on the customers' wants, even coming to ascertain these at the little thrifty tables; and if the drama and its adjusted theatre really contained all the elements of history, tragedy, comedy, irony, that a pair of expert romancers, closely associated for the hour, were eager to evoke, the scene would have been, I can only say, supreme of its kind. That desire of the artist to linger where the breath of a "subject," faintly stirring the air, reaches his vigilant sense, would here stay my steps—as this very influence was in fact, to his great good fortune, to stay those of my companion. The charm I speak of, the charm to cherish, however, was most exhaled for me in other conditions—conditions that scarce permit of any direct reference to their full suggestiveness. If I alluded above to the vivid Charleston background, where its "mystification" most scenically persists, the image is all rounded and complete, for memory, in this connection at which—as the case is of an admirably mature and preserved interior—I can only glance as I pass. The puzzlement elsewhere is in the sense that though the elements of earth and air, the colour, the tone, the light, the sweetness in fine, linger on, the "old South" could have had no such unmitigated mildness, could never have seen itself as subject to such strange feminization. The feminization is there just to promote for us some eloquent antithesis; just to make us say that whereas the ancient order was masculine, fierce and moustachioed, the present is at the most a sort of sick lioness who has so visibly parted with her teeth and claws that we may patronizingly walk all round her.

This image really gives us the best word for the general effect of Charleston—that of the practically vacant cage which used in the other time to emit sounds, even to those of the portentous shaking of bars, audible as far away as in the listening North. It is the vacancy that is a thing by itself, a thing that makes us endlessly wonder. How, in an at all complex, a "great political," society, can *everything* so have gone?—assuming indeed that, under this ægis, very much ever had come. How can everything so have gone that the only "Southern" book of any distinction published for many a year is *The Souls of Black Folk*, by that most accomplished of members of the negro race, Mr. W. E. B. Du Bois? Had the *only* focus of life then been Slavery?—from the point onward that Slavery had reached a quarter of a century before the War, so that with the extinction of that interest none other of any sort was left. To say "yes" seems the only way to account for the degree of the vacancy, and yet even as I form that word I meet as a reproach the face of the beautiful old house I just mentioned, whose ample spaces had so unmistakably echoed to the higher amenities that one seemed to feel the accumulated traces and tokens gradually come out of their corners like blest objects taken one by one from a reliquary worn with much handling. The note of such haunted chambers as these—haunted structurally, above all, quite as by the ghost of the grand style—was not, certainly, a thinness of reverberation; so that I had to take refuge here in the fact that everything appeared thoroughly to *antedate*, to refer itself to the larger, the less vitiated past that had closed a quarter of a century or so before the War, before the fatal time when the South, monomaniacal at the parting of the ways, "elected" for extension and conquest. The admirable old house of the stately hall and staircase, of the charming coved and vaulted drawing-room, of the precious mahogany doors, the tall unsophisticated portraits, the delicate dignity of welcome, owed nothing of its noble identity, nothing at all appreciable, to the monomania. However that might be, moreover, I kept finding the mere melancholy charm reassert itself where it could—the charm, I mean, of the flower-crowned waste that was, by my measure, what the monomania had most prepared itself to bequeathe. In the old Cemetery by the lagoon, to which I have already alluded, this influence distils an irresistible poetry—as one has courage to say even in remembering how disproportionately, almost anywhere on the American scene, the general place of interment is apt to be invited to testify for the presence of charm. The golden afternoon, the low, silvery, seaward horizon, as of wide, sleepy, game-haunted inlets and reed-smothered banks, possible site of some Venice that had never mustered, the luxury, in the mild air, of shrub and plant and blossom that the pale North can but distantly envy; something that I scarce know how to express but as the proud humility of the whole idle, easy loveliness, made even the restless analyst, for the hour, among the pious inscriptions that scarce ever belie the magniloquent clime or the inimitable tradition, feel himself really capable of the highest Carolinian pitch.

To what height did he rise, on the other hand, on being introduced another day, at no great distance from this point, and where the silvery seaward outlook still prevails, to the lapsed and readministered residence, also already named, that was to give him his one glimpse of any local modernism? This was the nearest approach for him to any reanimation of the flower-crowned waste, and he has still in memory, for symbol of the modernism, a vision of the great living, blazing fire of logs round which, as the afternoon had turned wet and chill, this contribution to his view of a possible new society, a possible youthful tone, a possible Southern future in short, had disposed itself. There were men here, in the picture—a few, and young ones: that odd other sense as of a becraped, feminized world was accordingly for the moment in abeyance. For the moment, I say advisedly—for the moment only; since what aspect of the social scene anywhere in the States strikes any second glance as exempt from that condition? It is overwhelmingly feminized or it *is* not—that is the formula with which its claim to existence pierces the ear. Lest, however, the recognition again of this truth should lead me too far, I content myself with noting a matter perhaps more relevant just here—one's inevitable consciousness, in presence of the "new" manifestations, that the South is in the predicament of having to be tragic, as it were, in order to beguile. It was very hard, I said to myself, and very cruel and very perverse, and above all very strange; but what "use" had the restless analyst here for a lively and oblivious type? Was there not something in the lively and oblivious that, given the materials employed for it and the effect produced by it, threw one back with renewed relish on the unforgetting and the devoted, on the resentful and even, if need might be, the vindictive? These things would represent certainly a bad *état d'âme*—and was one thus cold-bloodedly, critically, to wish such a condition perpetuated? The answer to that seemed to be, monstrously enough, "Well, yes—for these people; since it appears the only way by which they can be interesting. See when they try other ways! Their sadness and sorrow, as my friend called it, has at least for it that it has been expensively produced. Everything else, on the other hand, anything that may pretend to be better—oh, so cheaply!"

One had already, in moving about, winced often enough at sight of where one was, intellectually, to "land," under these last consistencies of observation and reflection; so I may put it here that I *didn't*, after all, land, but recoiled rather and forbore, making my skiff fast to no conclusion whatever, only pushing out again and letting it, for a supreme impression and to prepare in the aftertime the best remembrance, drift where it would. So, accordingly, the aftertime having a little arrived, it touches now once more of its own motion, carries me back and puts me ashore on the one spot where the impression had been perfectly felicitous. I have already named the place—under the mild, the bright south wall of St. Michael's Church, where the whole precinct offered the full-blown Southern spring, that morning, the finest of all canvases to embroider. The canvas here, yes, was of the best; not only did Charleston show me none other so good, but I was doubtless to have met, South or North, none of an equal happy grain and form. The high, complicated, inflated spire of the church has the sincerity, approved of time, that is so rare, over the land, in the work of man's hands, laden though these be with the millions he offers as a vain bribe to it; and in the sweet old churchyard ancient authority seemed to me, on the occasion of my visit, to sit, among the sun-warmed tombs and the inter-related slabs and the extravagant flowers, as on the sole cushion the general American bareness in such connections had left it. There was more still of association and impression; I found, under this charm, I confess, character in every feature. Even in the much-maintained interior revolutions and renovations have respected its sturdy, rather sombre essence: the place feels itself, in the fine old dusky archaic way, the constituted temple of a faith—achieves, in a word, the air of reality that one had seen in every other such case, from town to town and from village to village, missed with an unconsciousness that had to do duty for success.

XIV
Florida

I

IT IS the penalty of the state of receiving too many impressions of too many things that when the question arises of giving some account of these a small sharp anguish attends the act of selection and the necessity of omission. They have so hung together, have so almost equally contributed, for the fond critic, to the total image, the chapter of experience, whatever such may have been, that to detach and reject is like mutilation or falsification; the history of any given impression residing often largely in others that have led to it or accompanied it. This I find the case, again and again, with my American memories; there was something of a hundred of those I may not note in each of those I may, and I feel myself, amid the swarm, pluck but a fruit or two from any branch. When I think of Florida, for instance, I think of twenty matters involved in the start and the approach; I think of the moist, the slightly harsh, Sunday morning under the portico of the Charleston Hotel; I think of the inauspicious drizzle about the yellow omnibus, archaic and "provincial," that awaited the departing guests—remembering how these antique vehicles, repudiated, rickety "stages" of the age ignorant of trolleys, affected me here and there as the quaintest, most immemorial of American things, the persistent use of which surely represented the very superstition of the past. I think of the gentleman, in the watchful knot, who, while our luggage emerged, was moved to say to me, for some reason, "I guess we manage our travelling here better than in *your* country!"— whereby he so easily triumphed, blank as I had to remain as to the country he imputed to me. I think of the inimitable detachment with which, at the very moment he spoke, the negro porter engaged at the door of the conveyance put straight down into the mud of the road the dressing-bag I was obliged, a few minutes later, in our close-pressed company, to nurse on my knees; and I go so far, even, as almost

701

to lose myself in the sense of other occasions evoked by that reminiscence; this marked anomaly, the apparently deep-seated inaptitude of the negro race at large for any alertness of personal service, having been throughout a lively surprise.

One had counted, with some eagerness, in moving south-ward, on the virtual opposite—on finding this deficiency, en-countered right and left at the North, beautifully corrected; one had remembered the old Southern tradition, the house alive with the scramble of young darkies for the honour of fetching and carrying; and one was to recognize, no doubt, at the worst, its melancholy ghost. Its very ghost, however, by my impression, had ceased to walk; or, if this be not the case, the old planters, the cotton gentry, were the people in the world the worst ministered to. I could have shed tears for them at moments, reflecting that it was for *this* they had fought and fallen. The negro waiter at the hotel is in general, by an oddity of his disposition, so zealous to break for you two or three eggs into a tumbler, or to drop for you three or four lumps of sugar into a coffee-cup, that he scarce waits, in either case, for your leave; but these struck me everywhere as the limit of his accomplishment. He lends himself sufficiently to the rough, gregarious bustle of crowded feeding-places, but seemed to fall below the occasion on any appeal to his individual promptitude. Which reflections, doubtless, exactly illustrate my profession of a moment ago as to the insidious continuity, the close inter-relation, of observed phenomena. I might with a little audacity insist still further on that—which was in fact what I had originally quite promised myself to do. I certainly should have been half heart-broken at the hour itself, for example, had I *then* had to estimate as pure waste my state of sensibility to the style and stamp of my compan-ions; aspects and sounds burned into my memory, as I find, but none the less overstraining, I am obliged to feel, the frame of these remarks. So vivid on the spot was the sense of these particular human and "sectional" appearances, and of certain others of the same cluster, that they remained for me afterwards beautifully *placed*—placed in this connection of the pilgrimage to Palm Beach, and not the less relevant for being incidental. I was to find the obvious "bagman," the lusty "drummer" of the Southern trains and inns (if there be not, as yet unrevealed to me, some later fond diminutive of designation for the ubiquitous commercial traveller)—I was to find, I say, this personage promptly insist on a category of his own, a category which, at the moments I here recall, loomed so large as to threaten to block out of view almost every other object.

Was I the victim of grave mischance? was my infelicity exceptional?—or was the type with which the scene so abounded, were the specimens I was thus to treasure, all of the common class and the usual frequency? I was to treasure them as specimens of something I had surely never yet so *undisputedly* encountered. They went, all by themselves, as it were, so far—were, as to facial character, vocal tone, primal rawness of speech, general accent and attitude, extraordinarily base and vulgar; and it was interesting to make out why this fact took on, for my edification, so unwonted an intensity. The fact of the influence, on the whole man, of a sordid and ravenous habit, was naturally no new thing; one had met him enough about the world, the brawny peddler more or less gorged with the fruits of misrepresentation and blatant and brazen in the key of his "special line of goods" and the measure of his need. But if the figure was immemorial, why did it now usurp a value out of proportion to other values? What, for instance, were its remorseless reasons for treating the restless analyst, at the breakfast-hour perhaps above all, to so lurid a vision of its triumph? He had positively come to associate the breakfast-hour, from hotel to dining-car and from dining-car to hotel, with the perfect security of this exhibition, the sight of the type in completely unchallenged possession. I scarce know why my sensibility, at the juncture in question, so utterly gave way to it; why I appealed in vain from one of these so solemnly-feeding presences to another. They refused to the wondering mind any form of relief; they insisted, as I say, with the strange crudity of their air of commercial truculence, on being exactly as "low" as they liked. And the affirmation was made, in the setting of the great greasy inelegant room, as quietly as possible, and without the least intention of offence: there were ladies and children all about—though indeed there may have been sometimes *but* the lone breakfasting child to reckon with; the little pale, carnivorous, coffee-drinking ogre or ogress who prowls down in advance of its elders, engages a table—dread vision!—and has the "run" of the bill of fare.

The great blank decency, at all events, was no more broken than, on the general American scene, it ever is; yet the apprehension of marks and signs, the trick of speculation, declined none the less to drop. Whom were they constructed, such specimens, to talk with, to talk over, or to talk under, and what form of address or of intercourse, what uttered, what intelligible terms of introduction, of persuasion, of menace, what developed, what specific human process of any sort, was it possible to impute to them? What reciprocities did they imply, what presumptions did they, could they, create? what happened, inconceivably, when such Greeks met such Greeks, such faces looked into such faces, and such sounds, in especial, were exchanged with such sounds? What women did they live with, what women, living with them, could yet leave them as they were? What wives, daughters, sisters, did they in fine make credible; and what, in especial, was the speech, what the manners, what the general dietary, what most the monstrous morning meal, of ladies receiving at such hands the law or the licence of life? Questions, these latter, some of which, all the while, were not imperceptibly answered—save that the vainest, no doubt, was that baffled inquiry as to the thinkable ground, amid such relations, of preliminary confidence. What *was* preliminary confidence, where it had to reckon so with the minimum of any finished appearance? How, when people were like that, did any one trust any one enough to begin, or understand any one enough to go on, or keep the peace with any one enough to survive? Wasn't it, however, at last, none the less, the sign of a fallacy somewhere in my impression that the peace *was* kept, precisely, while I so luxuriously wondered?—the consciousness of which presently led me round to something that was at the least a temporary, a working answer. My friends the drummers bore me company thus, in the smoking-car, through the deepening, sweetening South (where the rain soon gave way to a refinement of mildness) all the way to Savannah; at the end of which time, under the enchantment of the spreading scene, I had more or less issued from my maze.

It was not, probably, that, inflated though they might be, after early refreshment, with the inward conflict of a greater number of strange sacrifices to appetite than I had ever before seen perpetrated at once, they were really more gruesome examples of a class at best disquieting than might elsewhere have been discovered; it was only that, by so sad a law of their situation, they were at once more exposed and less susceptible of bearing exposure. They so became, to my imagination, and by a mere turn of the hand of that precious faculty, something like victims and martyrs, creatures touchingly, tragically doomed. For they hadn't *asked*, when one reflected, to be almost the only figures in the social landscape—hadn't wanted the fierce light to beat *all* on themselves. They hadn't actively usurped the appearance of carrying on life without aid of any sort from other *kinds* of persons, other types, presences, classes. If these others were absent it wasn't *their* fault; and though they devoured, at a matutinal sitting, thirty little saucers of insane, of delirious food, this was yet a law which, over much of the land, appeared to recognize no difference of application for age, sex, condition or constitution, and it had not in short been their pretension to take over the whole social case. It would have been so different, this case, and the general effect, for the human scene, would have been so different, with a due proportion of other presences, other figures and characters, members of other professions, representatives of other interests, exemplars of other possibilities in man than the mere possibility of getting the better of his fellow-man over a "trade." Wondrous always to note is this sterility of aspect and this blight of vulgarity, humanly speaking, where a single type has had the game, as one may say, all in its hands. Character is developed to visible fineness only by friction and discipline on a large scale, only by its having to reckon with a complexity of forces—a process which results, at the worst, in a certain amount of social training.

No kind of person—that was the admonition—is a very good kind, and still less a very pleasing kind, when its education has not been made to some extent by contact with other kinds, by a sense of the existence of other kinds, and, to that degree, by a certain relation with them. This education may easily, at a hundred points, transcend the teaching of the big brick school-house, for all the latter's claim to universality. The last dose ever administered by the great wooden spoon so actively plied *there* is the precious bitter-sweet of a sense of proportion; yet to miss that taste, ever, at the table of civilization is to feel ourselves seated surely too much below the salt. We miss it when the social effect of it fails—when, all so dismally or so monstrously, every one strikes us as "after" but one thing, and as thus not only unaware of the absent importances and values, but condemned and restricted, as a direct consequence of it, to the mere raw stage of their own particular connection. I so worked out, in a word, that what was the matter with my friends was not at all that they were viciously full-blown, as one might say, were the ultimate sort of monstrosity they had at first appeared; but that they were, on the contrary, just unformed, undeveloped, unrelated above all—unrelated to any merciful modifying terms of the great social proposition. They were not in their place—not relegated, shaded, embowered, protected; and, dreadful though this might be to a stray observer of the fact, it was much more dreadful for themselves. They had the helpless weakness and, I think even, somewhere in dim depths, deeper down still than the awful breakfast-habit, the vaguely troubled sense of it. They would fall into their place at a touch, were the social proposition, as I have called it, completed; they would then help, quite subordinately assist, the long sentence to read—relieved of their ridiculous charge of supplying all its clauses. I positively at last thought of them as appealing from this embarrassment; in which sublime patience I was floated, as I say, to Savannah.

II

After that it was plain sailing; in the sense, I mean, of the respite—temporary at least—of speculation; of feeling impressions file in and seat themselves as quietly as decorous worshippers (say mild old ladies with neat prayer-books) taking possession of some long-drawn family pew. It was absurd what I made of Savannah—which consisted for me but of a quarter of an hour's pause of the train under the wide arch of the station, where, in the now quite confirmed blandness of the Sunday noon, a bright, brief morning party appeared of a sudden to have organized itself. Where was the charm?—if it wasn't already, supremely, in the air, the latitude, the season, as well as in the imagination of the pilgrim capable not only of squeezing a sense from the important city on these easy terms and with that desperate economy, but of reading heaven knows what instalment of romance into a mere railroad matter. It is a mere railroad matter, in the States, that a station should appear at a given moment to yield to the invasion of a dozen or so of bare-headed and vociferous young women in the company of young men to match, and that they should all treat the place, in the public eye, that of the crowded contemplative cars, quite as familiar, domestic, intimate ground, set apart, it might be, for the discussion and regulation of their little interests and affairs, and for that so oddly, so innocently immodest ventilation of their puerile privacies at which the moralizing visitor so frequently gasps. I recall my fleeting instants of Savannah as the taste of a cup charged to the brim; I recall the swarming, the hatless, pretty girls, with their big-bowed cues, their romping swains, their inveterate suggestion of their having more to say about American manners than any other single class; I recall the thrill produced by the hawkers of scented Southern things, sprigs and specimens of flower and fruit that mightn't as yet be of the last exoticism, but that were native and fresh and over-priced, and so all that the traveller could ask.

But most of all, I think, I recall the quite lively resolve not to give way, under the assault of the beribboned and "shirt-waisted" fair, to the provocation of *their* suggestiveness—even as I had fallen, reflectively speaking, straight into the trap set for me by the Charleston bagmen; a resolve taken, I blush to say, as a base economic precaution only, and not because the spectacle before me failed to make reflections swarm. They fairly hummed, my suppressed reflections, in the manner of bees about a flower-bed, and burying their noses as deep in the *corolla* of the subject. Had I allowed myself time before the train resumed its direction, I should have thus found myself regarding the youths and the maidens—but especially, for many reasons, the maidens—quite in the light of my so earnestly-considered drummers, quite as creatures extraordinarily disconcerting, at first, as to the whole matter of their public behaviour, but covered a little by the mantle of charity as soon as it became clear that what, like the poor drummers, they suffer from, is the tragedy of their social, their cruel exposure, that treachery of fate which has kept them so out of their place. It was a case, I more than ever saw, like the case of the bagmen; the case of the bagmen lighted it here, in the most interesting way, by propinquity and coincidence. If the bagmen had seemed monstrous, in their occupancy of the scene, by their disproportioned possession of it, so was not the hint sufficient that this also explains much of the effect of the American girl as encountered in the great glare of her publicity, her uncorrected, unrelated state? There had been moments, as I moved about the country, when she had seemed to me, for affirmation of presence, for immunity from competition, fairly to share the field but with the bagman, and fairly to speak as my inward ear had at last heard him speak.

"Ah, once *place* me and you'll see—I shall be different, I shall be better; for since I am, with my preposterous 'position,' falsely beguiled, pitilessly forsaken, thrust forth in my ignorance and folly, what do I know, helpless chit as I can but be, about manners or tone, about proportion or perspective, about modesty or mystery, about a condition of things that involves, for the interest and the grace of life, other forms of existence than this poor little mine—pathetically broken reed as it is, just to find itself waving all alone in the wind? How can I do *all* the grace, *all* the interest, as I'm expected to?— yes, literally all the interest that isn't the mere interest on the money. I'm expected to supply it all—while I wander and stray in the desert. Was there ever such a conspiracy, on the part of a whole social order, toward the exposure of incompetence? Were ever crude youth and crude presumption left so unadmonished as to their danger of giving themselves away? Who, at any turn, for an hour, ever pityingly overshadows or dispossesses me? By what combination of other presences ever am I disburdened, ever relegated and reduced, ever restored, in a word, to my right relation to the whole? All I want— that is all I need, for there is perhaps a difference—is, to put it simply, that my parents and my brothers and my male cousins

should consent to exist otherwise than occultly, undiscoverably, or, as I suppose you'd call it, irresponsibly. That's a
trouble, yes—but *we* take it, so why shouldn't they? The
rest—don't you make it out for me?—would come of itself.
Haven't I, however, as it is, been too long abandoned and too
much betrayed? Isn't it too late, and am I not, don't you
think, practically lost?" Faintly and from far away, as through
dense interpositions, this questioning wail of the maiden's ultimate distressed consciousness seemed to reach me; but I had
steeled my sense, as I have said, against taking it in, and I did
no more, at the moment, than all pensively suffer it again to
show me the American social order in the guise of a great
blank unnatural mother, a compound of all the recreant individuals misfitted with the name, whose ear the mystic plaint
seemed never to penetrate, and whose large unseeing complacency suggested some massive monument covered still with
the thick cloth that precedes a public unveiling. We wonder at
the hidden marble or bronze; we suppose, under the cloth,
some attitude or expression appropriate to the image; but as
the removal of the cloth is perpetually postponed the character never emerges. The American mother, enshrouded in her
brown holland, has, by this analogy, never emerged; only the
daughter is meanwhile seated, for the inspection of the world,
at the base of the pedestal, hypothetically supporting some
weight, some mass or other, and we may each impute to her,
for this posture, the aspect we judge best to beseem her.

My point here, at any rate, is that I had quite forgotten her
by the time I was seated, after dinner that evening, on a
bench in the small public garden that formed a prospect for
my hotel at Jacksonville. The air was divinely soft—it was
such a Southern night as I had dreamed of; and the only oddity was that we had come to it by so simple a process. We had
travelled indeed all day, but the process seemed simple when
there was nothing of it, nothing to speak of, to remember,
nothing that succeeded in getting over the footlights, as the
phrase goes, of the great moving proscenium of the Pullman.
I seemed to think of it, the wayside imagery, as something
that had been there, no doubt, as the action or the dialogue
are presumably there in some untoward drama that spends
itself at the back of the stage, that goes off, in a passion,

at side doors, and perhaps even bursts back, incoherently, through windows; but that doesn't reach the stall in which you sit, never quickens to acuteness your sense of what is going on. So, as if the chair in the Pullman had been my stall, my sense had been all day but of intervening heads and tuning fiddles, of queer refreshments, such as only the theatre and the Pullman know, offered, with vociferation, straight through the performance. I was a little uncertain, afterwards, as to when I had become distinctively aware of Florida; but the scenery of the State, up to the point of my first pause for the night, had not got over the footlights. I was promptly, however, to make good this loss; I felt myself doing so quite with intensity under the hot-looking stars at Jacksonville. I had come out to smoke for the evening's end, and it mattered not a scrap that the public garden was new and scant and crude, and that Jacksonville is not a name to conjure with; I still could sit there quite in the spirit, for the hour, of Byron's immortal question as to the verity of his Italian whereabouts: *was* this the Mincio, *were* those the distant turrets of Verona, and should I sup—well, if the train to Palm Beach, arriving there on the morrow in time, should happen to permit me? At Jacksonville I had, as I say, already supped, but I projected myself, for the time, after Byron's manner, into the exquisite sense of the dream come true.

I was not to sup at all, as it proved, at Palm Beach—by the operation of one of those odd, anomalous rigours that crop up even by the more flowery paths of American travel; but I was meanwhile able, I found, to be quite Byronically foolish about the St. John's River and the various structures, looming now through the darkness, that more or less adorned its banks. The river served for my Mincio—which it moreover so greatly surpassed in extent and beauty; while the remoter buildings figured sufficiently any old city of the South. For that was the charm—that so preposterously, with the essential notes of the impression so happily struck, the velvet air, the extravagant plants, the palms, the oranges, the cacti, the architectural fountain, the florid local monument, the cheap and easy exoticism, the sense as of people feeding, off in the background, very much *al fresco*, that is on queer things and with flaring lights—one might almost have been in a corner of Naples or of Genoa. Everything is relative—this illuminating commonplace, the clue to any just perception of effects anywhere, came up for the thousandth time; by the aid of which I easily made out that absolute and impeccable poetry of site and circumstance is far to seek, but that I was now immeasurably nearer to some poetic, or say even to some romantic, effect in things than I had hitherto been. And I had tried to think Washington relaxed, and Richmond itself romantic, and Charleston secretly ardent! There always comes, to any traveller who doesn't depart and arrive with the mere security and punctuality of a registered letter, some moment for his beginning to feel within him—it happens under some particular touch—the finer vibration of a sense of the real thing. He thus knows it when it comes, and it has the great value that it never need fail. There is no situation, wherever he may turn, in which the note of that especial reality, the note of character, for bliss or bale, may not insist on emerging. The note of Florida emerged for me then on the vulgar little dusky—and dusty—Jacksonville *piazzetta*, where other vague persons sat about, amid those spikey sub-tropical things that show how the South can be stiff as nothing else is stiff; while my rich sense of it incited me to resent the fact that my visit had been denounced, in advance, as of an ungenerous brevity. I had few days, deplorably few, no doubt, to spend; but it was afterwards positive to me that, with my image, as regards the essence of the matter, richly completed, I had virtually foretasted it all on my dusky Jacksonville bench and in my tepid Jacksonville stroll. Such reserves, in a complex of few interweavings, must impose themselves, I think, even upon foolish fondness, and Florida was quite remorselessly to appear to me a complex of few interweavings.

III

The next day, for instance, was all occupied with but one of these; the railway run from Jacksonville to Palm Beach begins early and ends late, yet I waited, the livelong time, for any other "factor" than that of the dense cypress swamp to show so much as the tip of an ear. I had quite counted on being thrilled by this very intensity and monotony of the charac-

teristic note; and I doubtless *was* thrilled—I invoked, I cultivated the thrill, as we went, by every itinerant art that experience had long since taught me; yet with a presentiment,
all the while, of the large field, in the whole impression, that
this simplicity would cover. Possible diversions doubtless occurred, had the attuned spirit been moved to avail itself; Or-
mond, for instance, off to our right, put in, toward the dim
centre of the stretch, a claim as large as a hard white racing-
beach, an expanse of firm sand thirty miles long, could make
it. This, I recognized, might well be an appeal of the grand
and simple order—the huge band of shining silver beside the
huge band of sapphire sea; and I inquired a little as to what
filled in the picture. "Oh, the motor-cars, the bicycles and the
trotting-waggons, tearing up and down." And then, as one
seemed perhaps to yearn for another touch: "Ah, the hotels of
course—plenty of *them*, plenty of people; very popular resort." It sounded charming, with its hint again of two or
three great facts of composition—so definite that their paucity constituted somehow a mild majesty; but it ministered
none the less to a reflection I had already, on occasion, found
myself perhaps a little perversely making. One was liable, in
the States, on many a scene, to react, as it were, from the
people, and to throw one's self passionately on the bosom of
contiguous Nature, whatever surface it might happen to offer; one was apt to be moved, in possibly almost invidious
preference, or in deeper and sweeter confidence, to try what
might be made of *that*. Yet, all unreasonably, when any source
of interest did express itself in these mere rigorous terms, in
these only—terms all of elimination, just of sea and sky and
river-breast and forest and beach (the "beaches" in especial
were to acquire a trick of getting on one's nerves!) that produced in turn a wanton wonder about the "human side," and
a due recurrence to the fact that the human side had been
from the first one's affair.

So, therefore, one seemed destined a bit incoherently to
proceed; asking one's self again and again what the play
would have been without the scenery, sometimes "even such"
scenery, and then once more not quite seeing why such scenery (in especial) should propose to put one off with so little of
a play. The thing, absolutely, everywhere, was to provide

one's own play; anything, everything made scenery for that, and the recurrence of such questions made scenery most of all. I remember no moment, over the land, when the mere Pullman itself didn't overarch my observations as a positive temple of the drama, and when the comedy and the tragedy of manners didn't, under its dome, hold me raptly attent. With which there were other resources—a rising tide that, before we got to Palm Beach, floated me back into remembered depths of youth. Why shouldn't I hold it not trivial that, as the day waned, and the evening gathered, and the heat increased, and my companions removed, one after the other, the articles of clothing that had consorted with our early start, I felt myself again beneath the spell of Mayne Reid, captain of the treasure-ship of romance and idol of my childhood? I might again have held in my very hand *The War Trail*, a work that had seemed matchless to my fourteenth year, for was not the train itself rumbling straight into *that* fantastic Florida, with its rank vegetation and its warm, heroic, amorous air?—the Florida of the Seminoles and the Everglades, of the high old Spanish Dons and the passionate Creole beauties gracing the primal "society"; of Isolina de Vargas, whose voluptuous form was lashed Mazeppa-like, at the climax of her fortunes, to the fiery mustang of the wilderness, and so let loose adown the endless vista of our young suspense. We had thus food for the mind, I recall, if we were reduced to that; and I remember that, as my buffet-car (there was none other) was hours late, the fond vision of the meal, crown of the endless day, awaiting me ultimately at the famous hotel, yielded all the inspiration necessary for not appealing again, great though the stress and strain, to the indescribable charity of the "buffet." The produce of the buffet, the procedure of the buffet, were alike (wherever resorted to) a sordid mockery of desire; so I but suffered desire to accumulate till the final charming arrest, the platform of the famous hotel, amid generous lights and greetings, and excellent arrangements, and balmy Southern airs, and the breath of the near sea, and the vague crests of great palms, announced the fulfilment of every hope.

The question of whether one's hope was really fulfilled, or of whether one had, among all those items of ease, to go

supperless to bed, would doubtless appear beneath the dignity of even such history as this, were it not for a single fact—
which, then and there looming large to me, blocked out, on
the spot, all others. It is difficult to render the intensity with
which one felt the great sphere of the hotel close round one,
covering one in as with high, shining crystal walls, stretching
beneath one's feet an immeasurable polished level, revealing
itself in short as, for the time, for the place, the very order of
nature and the very form, the only one, of the habitable
world. The effect was like nothing else of the sort one had
ever known, and of surpassing interest, truly, as any supreme
illustration of manners, any complete and organic projection
of a "social" case is apt to be. The whole picture presented
itself as fresh and luminous—as was natural to phenomena
shown in the splendid Florida light and off there at the end of
a huge peninsula especially appointed to them, and kept clear,
in their interest, as it struck me, of any shadow of anything
but themselves. One had been aware enough, certainly, for
long years, of that range of American aspects, that diffusion
of the American example, to which one had given, from far
back, for convenience, the name of hotel-civilization; why, accordingly, was this renewed impression so hugely to impose
itself; why was it, to the eye of the restless analyst, to stand
for so much more than ever yet? Why was it, above all, so to
succeed in making, with insistence, its appeal?—an appeal if
not to the finer essence of interest, yet to several of the fond
critic's livelier sensibilities. Wasn't, for that matter, his asking
of such questions as these the very state of being interested?—and all the more that the general reply to them was
not easy to throw off.

The vision framed, the reflections suggested, corresponded
closely with those to which, in New York, some weeks before,
on its harsh winter afternoon, the Waldorf-Astoria had prescribed such a revel; but it was wondrous that if I had there
supposed the apogee of the impression (or, better still, of the
*ex*pression) reached, I was here to see the whole effect written
lucidly larger. The difference was doubtless that of the
crowded air and encumbered ground in the great Northern
city—in the fact that the demonstration is made in Florida as
in a vast clean void expressly prepared for it. It has nothing

either in nature or in man to reckon with—it carries everything before it; meaning, when I say "it," in this momentarily
indefinite way, the perfect, the exquisite adjustability of the
"national" life to the sublime hotel-spirit. The whole appearance operates as by an economy so thorough that no element
of either party to the arrangement is discoverably sacrificed;
neither is mutilated, docked in any degree of its identity, its
amplitude of type; nothing is left unexpressed in either
through its relation with the other. The relation would in fact
seem to stimulate each to a view of the highest expression as
yet open to it. The advantage—in the sense of the "upper
hand"—may indeed be, at a few points, most with the hotel-
spirit, as the more concentrated of the two; there being so
much that is comparatively undeveloped and passive in the
social organism to which it looks for response, and the former
agency, by its very nature full-blown and expert, "trying it
on" the latter much more than the latter is ever perceptibly
moved to try it on the former. The hotel-spirit is an omni-
scient genius, while the character of the tributary nation is
still but struggling into relatively dim self-knowledge. An illustration of this met me, precisely, at the very hour of my
alighting: one had entered, toward ten o'clock in the evening,
the hotel-world; it had become the all in all and made and
imposed its law.

This took the form, for me, at that hungry climax, at the
end of the long ordeal of the buffet-car, of a refusal of all food
that night; a rigour so inexorable that, had it not been for the
charity of admirable friends, able to provide me from a private store, I should have had to go, amid all the suggestions
of everything, fasting and faint to bed. There one seemed to
get the hotel-spirit *taking* the advantage—taking it unfairly;
for whereas it struck me in general as educative, distinctly, in
respect to the society it deals with, keeping for the most part
well in advance of it, and leading it on to a larger view of the
social interest and opportunity than might otherwise accrue,
here, surely, it was false to its mission, it fell behind its pretension, its general pretension not only of meeting all American ideals, but of creating (the Waldorf-Astoria being in this
sense, for example, a perfect riot of creation) new and superior ones. Its basis, in those high developments, is not that it

merely gratifies them as soon as they peep out, but that it lies in wait for them, anticipates and plucks them forth even before they dawn, setting them up almost prematurely and turning their face in the right direction. Thus the great national ignorance of many things is artfully and benevolently practised upon; thus it is converted into extraordinary appetites, such as can be but expensively sated. The belated traveller's appetite for the long-deferred "bite" could scarce be described as *too* extraordinary; but the great collective, plastic public, so vague yet about many things, didn't *know* that it couldn't, didn't know that, in communities more knowing, the great glittering, costly caravansery, where the scale of charges is an implication of a high refinement of service, grave lapses are not condoned.

One appears ridiculously to be regretting that unsupplied mouthful, but the restless analyst had in truth quickly enough left it behind, feeling in his hand, already, as a clue, the long concatenation of interlinked appearances. Things short in themselves might yet have such large dimensions of meaning. The revelation, practically dazzling to the uninformed many, was constantly proving, right and left, if one gave it time, a trick played on the informed few; and there was no quarter of the field, either the material or the "social," in which that didn't sooner or later come out. The fact that the individual, with his preferences, differences, habits, accidents, might still fare imperfectly even where the crowd could be noted as rejoicing before the Lord more ingenuously than on any other human scene, added but another touch to one's impression, already so strong, of the success with which, throughout the land, even in conditions which might appear likely, on certain sides, to beget reserves about it, the all-gregarious and generalized life suffices to every need. I by no means say that it is not touching, the so largely witless confidence with which the universal impulse hurls its victims into the abyss of the hotel-spirit, trusting it so blandly and inviting it to throw up, round and about them and far and wide, the habitable, the practicable, the agreeable sphere toward which other arts of construction fail. There were lights in which this was to strike me as one of the most affecting of all social exhibitions; lights, positively, in which I seemed to see again (as, once more, at the universal Waldorf-Astoria) the whole housed populace move as in mild and consenting suspicion of its captured and governed state, its having to consent to inordinate fusion as the price of what it seemed pleased to regard as inordinate luxury. Beguiled and caged, positively thankful, in its vast vacancy, for the sense and the definite horizon of a cage, were there yet not moments, were there yet not cases and connections, in which it still dimly made out that its condition was the result of a compromise into the detail of which there might some day be an alarm in entering? The detail of the compromise exacted of the individual, throughout American life, affects the observer as a great cumulative sum, growing and growing while he awaits time and opportunity to go into it; and I asked myself again and again if I couldn't imagine the shadow of that quantity by no means oppressively felt, yet already vaguely perceived, and reflected a bit portentously in certain aspects of the native consciousness.

The jealous cultivation of the common mean, the common mean only, the reduction of everything to an average of decent suitability, the gospel of precaution against the dangerous tendency latent in many things to become too good for their context, so that persons partaking of them may become too good for their company—the idealized form of all this glimmered for me, as an admonition or a betrayal, through the charming Florida radiance, constituting really the greatest interest of the lesson one had travelled so far to learn. It might superficially seem absurd, it might savour almost of blasphemy, to put upon the "romantic" peninsula the affront of that particular prosaic meaning; but I profess that none of its so sensibly thin sources of romance—thin because everywhere asking more of the imagination than they could be detected in giving it—appealed to me with any such force or testified in any such quantity. Definitely, one had made one's pilgrimage but to find the hotel-spirit in sole *articulate* possession, and, call this truth for the mind an anti-climax if one would, none of the various climaxes, the minor effects—those of Nature, for instance, since thereabouts, far and wide, was no hinted history—struck me as for a moment dispossessing it of supremacy. So little availed, comparatively, those of the jungle, the air, the sea, the sky, the sunset, the orange, the pineapple, the palm; so little such a one, amid all the garden climaxes, as that of the divine bougainvillæa which, here and there, at Palm Beach, smothers whole "homes" in its purple splendour. For the light of the hotel-spirit really beat upon everything; it was the only torch held up for the view or the sense of anything else. The case, therefore, was perfect, for what did this mean but that its conscience, so to speak, its view of its responsibility, would be of the highest, and that, given the whole golden frame of the picture, the appearances could be nowhere else so grandly in its favour? That prevision was to be in fact afterwards confirmed to me.

IV

On a strip of sand between the sea and the jungle in one quarter, between the sea and the Lake in another, the clustered hotels, the superior Pair in especial, stand and exhale their genius. One of them, the larger, the more portentously brave, of the Pair, is a marvel indeed, proclaiming itself of course, with all the eloquence of an interminable towered and pinnacled and gabled and bannered sky-line, the biggest thing of its sort in the world. Such is the responsive geniality begotten by its apparently perfect adequacy to this pretension, or to any other it might care to put forth, that one took it easily as leaving far behind mere figures of speech and forms of advertisement; to stand off and see it rear its incoherent crest above its gardens was to remember—and quite with relief—nothing but the processional outline of Windsor Castle that could appear to march with it. I say with relief because the value of the whole affirmation, which was but the scale otherwise expressed, seemed thereby assured: no world *but* an hotel-world could flourish in such a shadow. Every step, for a mile or two round, conduced but to show how it did flourish; every aspect of everything for which our reclaimed patch, our liberal square between sea and jungle, yielded space, was a demonstration of that. The gardens and groves, the vistas and avenues between the alignments of palms, the fostered insolence of flame-coloured flower and golden fruit, were perhaps the rarest attestation of all; so recent a conquest did this seem to me of ground formerly abandoned, in the States, to the general indifference. There came back to me from other years a vision of the rude and sordid margins, the untended approaches surrounding, at "resorts," the crowded caravansery of the earlier time—and marking even now, I inferred, those of the type that still survive; and I caught verily at play that best virtue of the potent presence. The hotel was leading again, not following—imposing the standard, not submitting to it; teaching the affluent class how to "garden," how, in fact, to tidy up its "yard"—since affluence alone was supposable there; not receiving at other hands the lesson. It was doing more than this—discriminating in favour of the beautiful, and above all in favour of the "refined," with an energy that again, in the most interesting way, seemed to cause the general question of the future of beauty in America to heave in its unrest.

Fifty times, already, I had felt myself catching this vibration, received some vivid impression of the growing quantity of force available for that conquest—of all the latent powers of freedom of space, of wealth, of faith and knowledge and curiosity, verily perhaps even of sustained passion, potentially at its service. These possibilities glimmer before one at times, in presence of some artistic effect expensively yet intelligently, yet even charmingly produced, with the result of your earnestly saying: "Why not more and more then, why not an immense exploration, an immense exhibition, of such possibilities? What is wanting for it, after all, in the way of——?" Just there it is indeed that you pull yourself up—ah, in the way of what? You are conscious that what you recognize in especial is not so much the positive as the negative strength of the case. What you see is the space and the freedom—which at every turn, in America, make one yearn to take other things for granted. The ground is so clear of preoccupation, the air so clear of prejudgment and doubt, that you wonder why the chance shouldn't be as great for the æsthetic revel as for the political and economic, why some great undaunted adventure of the arts, meeting in its path none of the aged lions of prescription, of proscription, of merely jealous tradition, should not take place in conditions unexampled. From the moment it is but a question of some one's, of every one's caring, where was the conceivable quantity of care, where were the means and chances of application, ever so great? And the precedent, the analogy, of the universal organizing passion, the native aptitude for putting affairs "through," indubitably haunts you: you are so aware of the acuteness and the courage that you fall but a little short of figuring them as æsthetically contributive. But you do fall short; you remember in time that great creations of taste and faith never express themselves *primarily* in terms of mere convenience and zeal, and that all the waiting money and all the general fury have, at the most, the sole value of being destined to be good for beauty *when it shall appear*. They have it in them so little, by themselves, to make it appear, that your unfinished question arrives easily enough, in that light, at its end.

"What is wanting in the way of taste?" is the right form of the inquiry—that small circumstance alone being *positively* contributive. The others, the boundless field, the endless gold, the habit of great enterprises, are, you feel, at most, simple negations of difficulty. They affect you none the less, however, as a rank of stalwart soldiers and servants who, as they stand at attention, plead from wistful eyes to be enrolled and used; so that before any embodied symptom of the precious principle they are there in the background of your thought. These lingering instants spent in the presence of such symptoms, these brief moments of æsthetic arrest—liable to occur in the most diverse connections—have an interest that quite picks them, I think, from the heap of one's American hours. And the interest is always fine, throwing one back as, by a further turn, it usually does, on the question of the trick possibly played, for your appreciation, by mere negation of difficulty. To what extent may the absence of difficulty, to what extent may not facility of purchase and sweet simplicity of pride, surprise you into taking them momentarily for a demonstration of taste? You remain on your guard, very properly; but the interest, as I have called it, doesn't flag, none the less, since there is one mistake into which you never need fall, and one charming, one touching appearance that you may take as representing, wherever you meet it, a reality. When once you have interpreted the admonitory sign I have just named as the inordinate *desire for taste*, a desire breaking into a greater number of quaint and candid forms, probably, than have ever been known upon earth, the air is in a manner clearer, and you know sufficiently where you are. Isn't it cleared, moreover, beyond doubt, to the positive increase of the interest, and doesn't the question then become, almost thrillingly, that of the degree to which this pathos of desire may be condemned to remain a mere heartbreak to the historic muse? *Is* that to be, possibly, the American future—so far as, over such a mystery of mysteries, glibness may be permitted? The fascination grows while you wonder—as, from the moment you have begun to go into the matter at all, wonder you certainly must. If with difficulties so conjured away by power, the clear vision, the creative freshness, the real thing in a word, *shall* have to continue to be represented, indefinitely, but by a gilded yearning, the inference is then irresistible that these blessings are indeed of their essence a sovereign rarity. If with so many of the conditions they yet hang back, on what particular occult furtherance must they not incorruptibly depend? What are the other elements that make for them, and in what manner and at what points does the wrong combination of such elements, on the American scene, work for frustration? Entrancing speculation!—which has brought me back by a long circuit to the shining marble villa on the edge of Lake Worth.

I was about to allude to this wondrous creation as the supreme instance of missionary effort on the part of the hotel-spirit—by which I mean of the effort to illustrate and embody a group of its ideals, to give a splendid concrete example of its ability to flower, at will, into concentration, into conspicuous privacy, into a care for all the refinements. The palace rears itself, behind its own high gates and gilded, transparent barriers, at a few minutes' walk from the great caravan-series; it sits there, in its admirable garden, amid its statues and fountains, the hugeness of its more or less antique vases and sarcophagi—costliest reproductions all—as if to put to shame those remembered villas of the Lake of Como, of the Borromean Islands, the type, the climate, the horticultural elegance, the contained curiosities, luxuries, treasures, of which it invokes only to surpass them at every point. New with that consistency of newness which one sees only in the States, it seems to say, somehow, that to some such heaven, some such public exaltation of the Blest, those who have conformed with due earnestness to the hotel-spirit, and for a sufficiently long probation, may hope eventually to penetrate or perhaps actually retire.

It has sprung from the genius of the divine Pair, the Dioscuri themselves—as Castor and Pollux were the sons of Zeus; and has this, above all, of exemplary, that whereas one had in other climes and countries often seen the proprietor of estates construct an hotel, or hotels, on a piece of his property, and even, when rigid need was, in proximity to his "home," one had not elsewhere seen the home adjoined to the hotel, and placed, with such magnificence, under its protection and, as one might say, its star. In the former case—it was easy to reflect—there had been ever, at best, an effect of incoherence; while the beauty of logic, of the strictly consequent, was all on the side of the latter. So much as that one may say; but I should find it hard to express without some air of extravagance my sense of the beauty of the lesson read to the general Palm Beach consciousness from behind the gilded gates and between the large interstices of the enclosure. It had the immense merit that it was suited, admirably, to the "boarders"; it preached them the gospel of civilization all in their own terms and without the waste of an accent; it was in short the apotheosis, the ideal form of the final home that may pretend to crown a career of sufficiently expensive boarding. Anything less gorgeous wouldn't have been proportioned to so much expense, nor anything more sequestered in the key of such a mode of life. But I detach myself, with reluctance, from the view of this interesting creation—interesting in its sense of bathing the whole question of manners in a light. Anything that does that is a boon to the restless analyst; and I remember rejoicing that he should have been introduced promptly to the marble palace, which struck him as rewarding attention the more attention was privileged and the further it might penetrate. Such an experience was, all properly, preliminary to a view of the rest of the scene; since otherwise, frankly, in relation to what at all represented ideal were the boarders, in their vast multitude, to be viewed?

For the boarders, verily, were the great indicated show, as I had gathered in advance, at Palm Beach; it had been promised one, on all sides, that there, as nowhere else, in America, one would find Vanity Fair in full blast—and Vanity Fair not scattered, not discriminated and parcelled out, as among the comparative privacies and ancientries of Newport, but compressed under one vast cover, enclosed in a single huge *vitrine*, which there would be nothing to prevent one's flattening one's nose against for days of delight. It was into Vanity Fair, accordingly, that one embraced every opportunity to press; it was the boarders, frankly, who engaged one's attention in default of any great array of other elements. The other elements, it must be confessed, strike the visitor as few; he has soon come to the end of them, even though they consist of the greater part of the rest of the sense of Florida. And he seems to himself to pursue them, mainly, at the tail, and in the constant track of the boarders; these latter are so numerous, and the clearing in the jungle so comparatively minute, that there is scant occasion for the wandering apart which always forms, under the law of the herd, the intenser joy. The velvet air, the colour of the sea, the "royal" palms, clustered here and there, and, in their nobleness of beauty, their single sublime distinction, putting every other mark and sign to the blush, these are the principal figures of the sum—these, with the custom of the short dip into the jungle, at two or three points of which, approached by charming, winding wood-ways, the small but genial fruit-farm offers hospitality—offers it in all the succulence of the admirable pale-skinned orange and the huge sun-warmed grape-fruit, plucked from the low bough, where it fairly bumps your cheek for solicitation, and partaken of, on the spot, as the immortal ladies of Cranford partook of dessert—with a few steps aside, the back turned and a betrayed ingurgitation. It is by means of a light perambulator, of "adult size," but constructed of wicker-work, and pendent from a bicycle propelled by a robust negro, that the jungle is thus visited; the bicycle follows the serpentine track, the secluded ranch is swiftly reached, the peaceful retirement of the cultivators multitudinously admired, the perambulator promptly re-entered, the darkey restored to the saddle and his charge again to the hotel.

V

It is all most agreeable and diverting, it is almost, the boarders apart, romantic; but it is soon over, and there is not much more of it. The uncanny conception, the rank eccentricity of a walk encounters neither favour nor facility—but on the subject of the inveteracy with which the conditions, over the land, conspire against that sweet subterfuge there would be more to say than I may here deal with. One of these gentle ranches was approached by water, as Palm Beach has a front on its vast, fresh lake as well as seaward; a steam-launch puts you down at the garden foot, and the place is less infested by the boarders, less confessedly undefended, less artlessly ignorant in fine (thanks perhaps to the mere interposing water) of any possible right to occultation; the general absence of conception of that right, nowhere asserted, nowhere embodied, everywhere in fact quite sacrificially abrogated, qualifying at last your very sense of the American character—qualifying it very much as a pervading unsaltedness qualifies the taste of a dinner. This brief excursion remains with me, at any rate, as a delicate and exquisite impression; the neck of land that stretched from the languid lake to the anxious sea, the approach to real detachment, the gracious Northern hostess, just veiled, for the right felicity, in a thin nostalgic sadness, the precious recall in particular of having succeeded in straying a little, through groves of the pensive palm, down to the sandy, the vaguely-troubled shore. There was a certain concentration in the hour, a certain intensity in the note, a certain intimacy in the whole communion; I found myself loving, quite fraternally, the palms, which had struck me at first, for all their human-headed gravity, as merely dry and taciturn, but which became finally as sympathetic as so many rows of puzzled philosophers, dishevelled, shock-pated, with the riddle of the universe. This scantness and sweetness and sadness, this strange peninsular spell, *this*, I said, was sub-tropical Florida—and doubtless as permitted a glimpse as I should ever have of any such effect. The softness was divine—like something mixed, in a huge silver crucible, as an elixir, and then liquidly scattered. But the refinement of the experience would be the summer noon or the summer night—it would be then the breast of Nature would open; save only that, so lost in it and with such lubrication of surrender, how should one ever come back?

As it was, one came back soon enough, back to one's proper business: which appeared to be, urgently, strictly, severely, the pursuit of the boarders up and down the long corridors and round about the wide verandahs of their crowded career. I had been admirably provided for at the less egregious of the two hotels; which was vast and cool and fair, friendly, breezy, shiny, swabbed and burnished like a royal yacht, really immaculate and delightful; full of interesting lights and yet standing but on the edge of the whirlpool, the centre of which formed the heart of the adjacent colossus. One could plunge, by a short walk through a luxuriance of garden, into the deeper depths; one could lose one's self, if so minded, in the labyrinth of the other show. There, if Vanity Fair was not encamped, it was not for want of booths; the long corridors were streets of shops, dealing, naturally, in commodities almost beyond price—not the cheap gimcracks of the usual watering-place barrack, but solid (when not elaborately ethereal), formidable, incalculable values, of which it was of an admonitory economic interest to observe the triumphant appeal. They hadn't terrors, apparently, for the clustered boarders, these idols and monsters of the market—neither the wild fantastications of the milliner, the uncovered fires, disclosed secrets of the gem-merchant, the errant tapestries and *bahuts* of the antiquarian, nor, what I found most impressive and what has everywhere its picture-making force, those ordered dispositions and stretched lengths of old "point" in the midst of which a quiet lady in black, occupied with some small stitch of her own, is apt to raise at you, with expensive deliberation, a grave, white Flemish face. The interest of the general spectacle was supposed to be, I had gathered, that people from all parts of the country contributed to it; and the value of the testimony as to manners was that it brought to a focus so many elements of difference. The elements of difference, whatever they might latently have been, struck me as throughout forcibly simplified by the conditions of the place; this prompt reducibility of a thousand figures to a common denominator having been in fact, to my sense, the very moral of the picture. Individuality and variety is attributed to "types," in America, on easy terms, and the reputation for it enjoyed on terms not more difficult; so that what I was most conscious of, from aspect to aspect, from group to group, from sex to sex, from one presented boarder to another, was the continuity of the fusion, the dimness of the distinctions.

The distinction that was least absent, however, would have been, I judge, that of the comparative ability to spend and purchase; the ability to spend with freedom being, as one made out, a positive consistent with all sorts of negatives. That helped to make the whole thing documentary—that you had to be financially more or less at your ease to enjoy the privileges of the Royal Poinciana at all; enjoy them through their extended range of saloons and galleries, fields of high publicity all; pursue them from dining-halls to music-rooms, to ball-rooms, to card-rooms, to writing-rooms, to a succession of places of convenience and refreshment, not the least characteristic of which, no doubt, was the terrace appointed to mid-morning and mid-afternoon drinks—drinks, at the latter hour, that appeared, oddly, never to comprise tea, the only one appreciated in "Europe" at that time of day. (The quest of tea indeed, especially at the hour when it is most a blessing, struck me as attended, throughout the country, with difficulties, even with dangers; over ground where one's steps are beset, everywhere, with an infinite number of strange, sweet iced liquidities—many of these, I hasten to add, charmingly congruous, in their non-alcoholic ingenuity, with the heats of summer: a circumstance that doesn't prevent their flourishing equally in the rigour of cold.) The implication of "ease" was thus a light to assist inquiry; it is always a gained fact about people—as to "where" they are, if not as to who or what—that they are either in confirmed or in casual possession of money, and thereby, presumably, of all that money may, in this negotiable world, represent. Add to this that the company came, in its provided state, by common report, from "all over," that it converged upon Palm Beach from every prosperous corner of the land, and the case was clear for a compendious view of American society in the largest sense of the term. "Society," as we loosely use the word, is made up of the fortunate few, and, if that number be everywhere small at the best, it was yet the fortunate who, after their fashion, filled the frame. Every obligation lay upon me to "study" them as so gathered in, and I did my utmost, I remember, to render them that respect; yet when I now, after an interval, consult my notes, I find the page a blank, and when I knock at the door of memory I find it perversely closed. If it consents a little to open, rather, a countenance looks out—that of the inscrutable warden of the precinct—and seems to show me the ambiguous smile that accompanies on occasion the plea to be excused.

From which I infer that the form and pressure of the boarders, for all I had expected of the promised picture, failed somehow to affect me as a discussable quantity. It is of the nature of many American impressions, accepted at the time as a whole of the particular story, simply to cease to be, as soon as your back is turned—to fade, to pass away, to leave not a wreck behind. This happens not least when the image, whatever it may have been, has exacted the tribute of wonder or pleasure: it has displayed every virtue but the virtue of being able to remain with you. Its pressure and power have failed of some weight, some element of density or intensity, some property or quality in short that makes for the authority of a figure, for the complexity of a scene. The "European" vision, in general, of whatever consisting, and even when making less of an explicit appeal, has behind it a driving force—derived from sources into which I won't pretend here to enter—that make it, comparatively, "bite," as the plate of the etcher is bitten by aquafortis. That doubtless is the matter, in the States, with the vast peaceful and prosperous human show—in conditions, especially, in which its peace and prosperity most shine out: it registers itself on the plate with an incision too vague and, above all, too uniform. The paucity of one's notes is in itself, no doubt, a report of the consulted oracle; it describes and reconstitutes for me the array of the boarders, this circumstance that I only grope for their features and seek in vain to discriminate between sorts and conditions. There were the two sexes, I think, and the range of age, but, once the one comprehensive type was embraced, no other signs of differentiation. How should there have been when the men were consistently, in all cases, thoroughly obvious

products of the "business-block," the business-block unmitigated by any other influence definite enough to name, and the
women were, under the same strictness, the indulged ladies of
such lords? The business-block has perhaps, from the north-
east to the south-west, its fine diversities, but any variety so
introduced eluded even the most brooding of analysts.

And it was not of course that the marks of uniformity,
among so many persons, were not on *their* side perfectly appreciable; it was only that when one had noted them as marks
of "success," no doubt, primarily, and then as those of great
gregarious decency and sociability and good-humour, one
had exhausted the list. It was the scant diversity of type that
left me short, as a story-seeker or picture-maker; contributive
as this very fact might be to admiration of the costly processes, as they thus appear, that ensure, and that alone ensure,
in other societies, the opposite of that scantness. With this, as
the foredoomed observer may never escape from the dreadful
faculty that rides him, the very simplifications had in the highest degree their illustrative value; they gave all opportunity to
anything or any one that might be salient. They gave it to the
positive bourgeois propriety, serenely, imperturbably, massively seated, and against which any experimental deviation
from the bourgeois would have dashed itself in vain. This
neutrality of respectability might have been figured by a great
grey wash of some charged moist brush causing colour and
outline, on the pictured paper, effectually to run together.
What resisted it best was the look of "business success" in
some of the men; when that success had been very great (and
there were indicated cases of its prodigious greatness) the
look was in its turn very great; when it had been small, on the
other hand, there was doubtless no look at all—since there
were no other conceivable sources of appearance. The people
had not, and the women least of all, one felt, in general, been
transferred from other backgrounds; the scene around them
and behind them constituted as replete a medium as they
could ever have been conscious of; the women in particular
failed in an extraordinary degree to engage the imagination,
to offer it, so to speak, references or openings: it faltered—
doubtless respectfully enough—where they for the most part
so substantially and prosaically sat, failing of any warrant to

go an inch further. As for the younger persons, of whom there were many, as for the young girls in especial, they were as perfectly in their element as goldfish in a crystal jar: a form of exhibition suggesting but one question or mystery. Was it they who had invented it, or had it inscrutably invented *them*?

VI

The case of St. Augustine afterwards struck me as presenting, on another side, its analogy with the case at Palm Beach: if the "social interest" had in the latter place appeared but of a weak constitution, so the historic, at the former, was to work a spell of a simpler sort than one had been brought up, as it were, to look to. Hadn't one been brought up, from far back, on the article of that faith in St. Augustine, by periodical papers in the magazines, fond elucidations of its romantic character, accompanied by drawings that gave one quite proudly, quite patriotically, to think—that filled the cup of curiosity and yearning? The old town—for the essence of the faith had been that there *was* an "old town"—receded into an all but untraceable past; it had been of all American towns the earliest planted, and it bristled still with every evidence of its Spanish antiquity. The illustrations in the magazines, wondrous vignettes of old street vistas, old architectural treasures, gateways and ramparts, odds and ends, nooks and corners, crowned with the sweetness of slow decay, conveyed the sense of these delights and renewed at frequent intervals their appeal. But oh, as I was to observe, the school of "black and white" trained up by the magazines has much, in the American air, to answer for: it points so vividly the homely moral that when you haven't what you like you must perforce like, and above all misrepresent, what you have. Its translation of these perfunctory passions into pictorial terms saddles it with a weight of responsibility that would be greater, one can only say, if there ever were a critic, some guardian of real values, to bring it to book. The guardians of real values struck me as, up and down, far to seek. The whole matter indeed would seem to come back, interestingly enough, to the general truth of the æsthetic need, in the country, for much greater values, of certain sorts, than the country and its manners, its aspects and arrangements, its past and present, and perhaps even future, really supply; whereby, as the æsthetic need is also intermixed with a patriotic yearning, a supply has somehow to be extemporized, by any pardonable form of pictorial "hankey-pankey"—has to be, as the expression goes, cleverly "faked." But it takes an inordinate amount of faking to meet the supposed intensity of appetite of a body of readers at once more numerous and less critical than any other in the world; so that, frankly, the desperate expedient is written large in much of the "artistic activity" of the country.

The results are of the oddest; they hang all traceably together; wonderful in short the general spectacle and lesson of the scale and variety of the faking. They renew again the frequent admonition that the pabulum provided for a great thriving democracy may derive most of its interest from the nature of its testimony to the thriving democratic demand. No long time is required, in the States, to make vivid for the visitor the truth that the nation is almost feverishly engaged in producing, with the greatest possible activity and expedition, an "intellectual" pabulum after its own heart, and that not only the arts and ingenuities of the draftsman (called upon to furnish the picturesque background and people it with the "aristocratic" figure where neither of these revelations ever meets his eye) pay their extravagant tribute, but that those of the journalist, the novelist, the dramatist, the genealogist, the historian, are pressed as well, for dear life, into the service. The illustrators of the magazines improvise, largely—that is when not labouring in the cause of the rural dialects—improvise the field of action, full of features at any price, and the characters who figure upon it, young gods and goddesses mostly, of superhuman stature and towering pride; the novelists improvise, with the aid of the historians, a romantic local past of costume and compliment and sword-play and gallantry and passion; the dramatists build up, of a thousand pieces, the airy fiction that the life of the people in the world among whom the elements of clash and contrast are simplest and most superficial abounds in the subjects and situations and effects of the theatre; while the genealogists touch up the picture with their pleasant hint of the number, over the land, of families of royal blood. All this constitutes a

vast home-grown provision for entertainment, rapidly superseding any that may be borrowed or imported, and that indeed already begins, not invisibly, to press for exportation. As
to quantity, it looms immense, and resounds in proportion,
yet with the property, all its own, of ceasing to be, of fading
like the mist of dawn—that is of giving no account of itself
whatever—as soon as one turns on it any intending eye of
appreciation or of inquiry. It is the public these appearances
collectively refer us to that becomes thus again the more attaching subject; the public so placidly uncritical that the whitest thread of the deceptive stitch never makes it blink, and
sentimental at once with such inveteracy and such simplicity
that, finding everything everywhere perfectly splendid, it
fairly goes upon its knees to be humbuggingly humbugged. It
proves ever, by the ironic measure, quite incalculably young.

That perhaps was all that had been the matter with it in
presence of the immemorial legend of St. Augustine as a mine
of romance; St. Augustine proving primarily, and of course
quite legitimately, but an hotel, of the first magnitude—an
hotel indeed so remarkable and so pleasant that I wondered
what call there need ever have been upon it to prove anything
else. The Ponce de Leon, for that matter, comes as near producing, all by itself, the illusion of romance as a highly modern, a most cleverly-constructed and smoothly-administered
great modern caravansery can come; it is largely "in the
Moorish style" (as the cities of Spain preserve the record of
that manner); it breaks out, on every pretext, into circular
arches and embroidered screens, into courts and cloisters, arcades and fountains, fantastic projections and lordly towers,
and is, in all sorts of ways and in the highest sense of the
word, the most "amusing" of hotels. It did for me, at St.
Augustine, I was well aware, everything that an hotel could
do—after which I could but appeal for further service to the
old Spanish Fort, the empty, sunny, grassy shell by the low,
pale shore; the mild, time-silvered quadrilateral that, under
the care of a single exhibitory veteran and with the still milder
remnant of a town-gate near it, preserves alone, to any effect
of appreciable emphasis, the memory of the Spanish occupation. One wandered there for meditation—it is not congruous with the genius of Florida, I gathered, to permit you to

wander very far; and it was there perhaps that, as nothing prompted, on the whole, to intenser musings, I suffered myself to be set moralizing, in the manner of which I have just given an example, over the too "thin" projection of legend, the too dry response of association. The Spanish occupation, shortest of ineffectual chapters, seemed the ghost of a ghost, and the burnt-out fire but such a pinch of ashes as one might properly fold between the leaves of one's *Baedeker*. Yet if I made this remark I made it without bitterness; since there was no doubt, under the influence of this last look, that Florida still had, in her ingenuous, not at all insidious way, the secret of pleasing, and that even round about me the vagueness was still an appeal. The vagueness was warm, the vagueness was bright, the vagueness was sweet, being scented and flowered and fruited; above all, the vagueness was somehow consciously and confessedly weak. I made out in it something of the look of the charming shy face that desires to communicate and that yet has just too little expression. What it would fain say was that it really knew itself unequal to any extravagance of demand upon it, but that (if it might so plead to one's tenderness) it would always do its gentle best. I found the plea, for myself, I may declare, exquisite and irresistible: the Florida of that particular tone was a Florida adorable.

VII

This last impression had indeed everything to gain from the sad rigour of steps retraced, an inevitable return to the North (in the interest of a directly subsequent, and thereby gracelessly roundabout, move Westward); and I confess to having felt on that occasion, before the dire backwardness of the Northern spring, as if I had, while travelling in the other sense, but blasphemed against the want of forwardness of the Southern. Every breath that one might still have drawn in the South—might if twenty other matters had been different— haunted me as the thought of a lost treasure, and I settled, at the eternal car window, to the mere sightless contemplation, the forlorn view, of an ugly—ah, such an ugly, wintering, waiting world. My eye had perhaps been jaundiced by the breach of a happy spell—inasmuch as on thus leaving the sad fragments there where they had fallen I tasted again the quite saccharine sweetness of my last experience of Palm Beach, and knew how I should wish to note for remembrance the passage, supremely charged with that quality, in which it had culminated. I asked myself what other expression I should find for the incident, the afternoon before I left the place, of one of those mild progresses to the head of Lake Worth which distil, for the good children of the Pair, the purest poetry of their cup. The poetic effect had braved the compromising aid of the highly-developed electric launch in which the pilgrim embarks, and braved as well the immitigable fact that his shrine, at the end of a couple of hours, is, in the vast and exquisite void, but an institution of yesterday, a wondrous floating tea-house or restaurant, inflated again with the hotel-spirit and exhaling modernity at every pore.

These associations are—so far as association goes—the only ones; but the whole impression, for simply sitting there in the softest lap the whole South had to offer, seemed to me to dispense with any aid but that of its own absolute felicity. It was, for the late return at least, the return in the divine dusk, with the flushed West at one's right, a concert of but two or three notes—the alignment, against the golden sky, of the individual black palms, a frieze of chiselled ebony, and the texture, for faintly-brushed cheek and brow, of an air of such silkiness of velvet, the very throne-robe of the star-crowned night, as one can scarce commemorate but in the language of the loom. The shore of the sunset and the palms, what was that, meanwhile, like, and yet with what did it, at the moment one asked the question, refuse to have anything to do? It was like a myriad pictures of the Nile; with much of the modern life of which it suggested more than one analogy. These indeed all dropped, I found, before I had done—it would have been a Nile so simplified out of the various fine senses attachable. One had to put the case, I mean, to *make* a fine sense, that here surely then was the greater antiquity of the two, the antiquity of the infinite *previous*, of the time, before Pharaohs and Pyramids, when everything was still to come. It was a Nile, in short, without the least little implication of a Sphinx or, still more if possible, of a Cleopatra. I had the foretaste of what I was presently to feel in California—when the general aspect of that wondrous realm kept suggesting to me a sort of prepared but unconscious and inexperienced Italy, the primitive *plate*, in perfect condition, but with the impression of History all yet to be made.

Of how grimly, meanwhile, under the annual rigour, the world, for the most part, waits to be less ugly again, less despoiled of interest, less abandoned to monotony, less forsaken of the presence that forms its only resource, of the one friend to whom it owes all it ever gets, of the pitying season that shall save it from its huge insignificance—of so much as this, no doubt, I sufficiently renewed my vision, and with plenty of the reviving ache of a question already familiar. To what extent was hugeness, to what extent *could* it be, a ground for complacency of view, in any country not visited for the very love of wildness, for positive joy in barbarism? Where was the charm of boundless immensity as overlooked from a car-window?—with the general pretension to charm, the general conquest of nature and space, affirmed, immediately round about you, by the general pretension of the Pullman, the great monotonous rumble of which seems forever to say to you: "See what I'm making of all this—see what I'm making, what I'm making!" I was to become later on still more intimately aware of the spirit of one's possible reply to that, but even then my consciousness served, and the eloquence of my exasperation seems, in its rude accents, to come back to me.

"I see what you are *not* making, oh, what you are ever so vividly not; and how can I help it if I am subject to that lucidity?—which appears never so welcome to you, for its measure of truth, as it ought to be! How can I not be so subject, from the moment I don't just irreflectively gape? If I were one of the painted savages you have dispossessed, or even some tough reactionary trying to emulate him, what you are making would doubtless impress me more than what you are leaving unmade; for in that case it wouldn't be to *you* I should be looking in any degree for beauty or for charm. Beauty and charm would be for me in the solitude you have ravaged, and I should owe you my grudge for every disfigurement and every violence, for every wound with which you have caused the face of the land to bleed. No, since I accept your ravage, what strikes me is the long list of the arrears of

your undone; and so constantly, right and left, that your pretended message of civilization is but a colossal recipe for the
creation of arrears, and of such as can but remain forever out
of hand. You touch the great lonely land—as one feels it still
to be—only to plant upon it some ugliness about which,
never dreaming of the grace of apology or contrition, you
then proceed to brag with a cynicism all your own. You convert the large and noble sanities that I see around me, you
convert them one after the other to crudities, to invalidities,
hideous and unashamed; and you so leave them to add to the
number of myriad aspects you simply spoil, of the myriad
unanswerable questions that you scatter about as some monstrous unnatural mother might leave a family of unfathered
infants on doorsteps or in waiting-rooms. This is the meaning
surely of the inveterate rule that you shall multiply the perpe-
trations you call 'places'—by the sign of some name as senseless, mostly, as themselves—to the sole end of multiplying to
the eye, as one approaches, every possible source of displeasure. When nobody cares or notices or suffers, by all one
makes out, when no displeasure, by what one can see, is ever
felt or ever registered, why shouldn't you, you may indeed
ask, be as much in your right as you need? But in that fact
itself, that fact of the vast general unconsciousness and indifference, looms, for any restless analyst who may come along,
the accumulation, on your hands, of the unretrieved and the
irretrievable!"

I remember how it was to come to me elsewhere, in such
hours as those, that south of Pennsylvania, for instance, or
beyond the radius of Washington, I had caught no glimpse of
anything that was to be called, for more than a few miles and
by a stretch of courtesy, the honour, the decency or dignity of
a road—that most exemplary of all civil creations, and greater
even as a note of morality, one often thinks, than as a note of
facility; and yet had nowhere heard these particular arrears
spoken of as matters ever conceivably to be made up. I was
doubtless aware that if I had been a beautiful red man with a
tomahawk I should of course have rejoiced in the occasional
sandy track, or in the occasional mud-channel, just in proportion as they fell so short of the type. Only in that case I
shouldn't have been seated by the great square of plate-glass

through which the missionary Pullman appeared to invite me to admire the achievements it proclaimed. It was in this respect the great symbolic agent; it seemed to stand for all the irresponsibility behind it; and I am not sure that I didn't continue, so long as I was in it, to "slang" it for relief of the o'erfraught heart. "You deal your wounds—that is the 'trouble,' as you say—in numbers so out of proportion to any hint of responsibility for them that you seem ever moved to take; which is the devil's dance, precisely, that your vast expanse of level floor leads you to caper through with more kinds of outward clumsiness—even if also with more kinds of inward impatience and avidity, more leaps and bounds of the spirit at any cost to grace—than have ever before been collectively displayed. The expanse of the floor, the material opportunity itself, has elsewhere failed; so that what is the positive effect of their inordinate presence but to make the lone observer, here and there, but measure with dismay the trap laid by the scale, if he be not tempted even to say by the superstition, of continuity? Is the germ of anything finely human, of anything agreeably or successfully social, supposably planted in conditions of such endless stretching and such boundless spreading as shall appear finally to minister but to the triumph of the superficial and the apotheosis of the raw? Oh for a split or a chasm, one groans beside your plate-glass, oh for an unbridgeable abyss or an insuperable mountain!"—and I could so indulge myself though still ignorant of how one was to groan later on, in particular, after taking yet further home the portentous truth that this same criminal continuity, scorning its grandest chance to break down, makes but a mouthful of the mighty Mississippi. That was to be in fact my very next "big" impression.

AMERICA:
EARLY TRAVEL WRITINGS

Contents

Lake George

I FIND so great a pleasure in travelling, and maintain so friendly and expectant an attitude toward possible "sensations," that they haven't the heart to leave me altogether unvisited, though I confess that they are frequently such as may seem to lack flavor to fastidious people or to those sated with many wanderings. I found it a sensation, for instance, to come from Saratoga (for the first time) in a "drawing-room car." I found it a luxury of an almost romantic intensity to sit in one of those revolving *fauteuils* and gaze through that generous, oblong plate of glass at the midsummer wilderness which bordered my route, while through a nether screen of delicate wire the summer breeze rushed in, winnowed of the grossness of cinders, and an artfully frescoed ceiling invited my gaze to rest at moments from the excessive *abandon* of nature. I observed that my companions on top of the coach which I subsequently mounted, were unanimous in voting Glenn's Falls a remarkably pretty town: I therefore observed it with the view at once of enjoying its prettiness and of appraising my neighbor's judgment. Pretty it is for a town of elements so meagre. Like Saratoga, the village is blissfully bedimmed and overshadowed with a noble abundance of wayside verdure—by serried lines of elms and maples, and their goodly domestic umbrage in gardens and yards. It has not, however, that rounded and harmonious charm which would perhaps have made it appear a little less incongruous to me than it did to behold a public work of art at our egress from the village. Like so many other little American towns, it has its own little æsthetic fact—shining with newness—in the shape of a soldier's monument: an obelisk, if I recollect, of a pleasant cream-colored stone, surmounted on its apex by a species of napkin, which an eagle is in the act of rending in his claws, and decorated toward the bases with four niches, enclosing four of the usual warriors contemplating the graves of their comrades. It is not very wisely conceived, perhaps, nor very cunningly executed; but there it stands, neighbored by a grosser ugliness, which, in its fair monumental breadth and permanence, it may connect with some lurking germs of future beauty. The drive to Lake George is full of a grand rough prettiness—leading you straight into the midst of the thickening hills and along the bases of half-grown mountains. When you emerge upon the lake, you find yourself fairly launched into the romance of mountain scenery.

I find here, at this little village of Caldwell, an immense hotel of a good deal of external architectural pretension— French-roofed, with a sort of high-piled and gabled complexity which, as country hotels go, makes it look vaguely picturesque. It stands directly on the lake, and boasts a really magnificent piazza—a terrace of contemplation—worthy of the beautiful view it commands. This, I believe, is not the choice quarter of the lake. Yet such as it is, it is thoroughly lovely. Great simple masses of wooded hills rise with a plain green nearness, to right and left; further, as the lake recedes, they increase in size and in magic of colors, and in the uttermost background they figure nobly in outline and hue, with the magnitude and mystery of a mountain chain. A friend at Saratoga informed me that Lake George is considered strongly to resemble the Lake of Como. A year ago, almost at the present moment, I spent a week on the shores of that divinest of lakes, and I think that, even unreminded by my friends, I should occasionally be prompted to an attempt at comparison and contrast. It is in a certain way unwise and even unkind to play this sort of game with the things of America and of Italy, but it seems to me that comparisons are odious only when they are sterile, and intruders only when they are forced. Lake George is quite enough like the Lake of Como to impel you, if the image of the latter is fresh in your mind, to pursue the likeness to its inevitable phase of unlikeness. The mountains which melt into those blue Italian waters are clad with olives and vines, with groves of mulberry and chestnut and ilex, with a verdure productive of a wholly different range of effects from that of the sombre forests of the North. And yet, such is the infinite mercy of the sun, its inscrutable cunning and power, that, to-day, as the morning light spent itself through the long hours over the sullen darkness of these American hills, it tempered and tinted and soft-

ened them, and wrought upon them such a sweet confusion
of exquisite tones, such a dimness of distant blue, such a brilliant tissue of noonday vapors, such a fine-drawn purity of
outline, that they seemed to borrow their beauty from a
Southern air and to shine with that mild, iridescent, opaline
glow which you enjoy from the little headland above Bellagio.
It is the complete absence of detail which betrays the identity
of American scenery. On those Italian slopes the fancy travels
with the eye from one bright sign of human presence to another, from a gleaming mountain hamlet to the lonely twinkle
of a mountain shrine. In our own landscape, if the background in its greatest beauty is in a sense common, undetermined, and general, the foreground is even more so, inasmuch as in the foreground there is usually an attempt at
detail. Here, on the left shore of the lake, is a saw-mill with a
high black chimney, a dozen little white wooden houses, and
a little promontory of planks on posts, in the nature of a
steamboat-pier. This brave little attempt at civilization looks
as transient and accidental as the furniture of a dream. Above
it mounts the long-drawn roundness of the wooded hills.
Their woods of course supply the saw-mill, and the saw-mill
supplies the excellent plank-road. I followed this road yesterday through the village to a point where, having entered the
relapsing woods, it throws out two tributary arms. The plank-
road pursues its way to other little settlements, expectant of
the coach. One of the other roads keeps along the lake—"a
little piece away," as a young girl of the country told me. The
third observes a middling course, along the lower slope of the
hills, above the lake road. I wandered along the last, to excellent purpose as regards the pursuit of the picturesque:
through the coolness of thinly divided woods, past little bald
grey farm-houses, lonely and sunny in their midsummer plenitude, past an occasional cottage of gentility—a built and
dedicated point of view. I shall long remember a certain little
farm-house before which I stayed my steps to stare and enjoy.
If the pure picturesque means simply the presentation of a
picture, self-informed and complete, I have seen nothing in
Italy or England which better deserves the praise. Here, for
once, the picture swarmed with detail—less, however, with
the scattered accessories of the usual warm-toned farmstead of

tradition than with the rich invasive presence of spontaneous nature and the tangled overgrowth of rank vegetation. No Tuscan *podere* could have been more densely and gracefully luxuriant. The little unpainted dwelling stood on a grassy slope—leaden-grey in the shade, silver-grey in the sun. Against the darkness of the open doorway, from where I stood, I saw a white butterfly soar and sink—I almost heard in the noonday stillness the soundless whirr of his wings. The milk-pans glittered in the sun; beside the house-wall a magnificent clump of pink hollyhocks lifted its blooming stalks, touching almost the roof, and adding the hint of another color to the abounding green and yellow and blue. The deeper grass, toward the fence and roadside, was a great expansive blaze of golden-rod. It seemed to glitter upward toward the milder yellow of the crowded apples in the crowded trees of the orchard. This orchard—its trees all high and noble in spite of their bended breadth—lost itself in a tangled confusion of verdurous background, so that it was hard to say whether it was an orchard run wild with excessive productiveness, or a piece of the mountain wilderness come down to be tame and prolific. At any rate, I have seldom seen a more potent emanation of reflected composite light and color, of leafed and bladed and fruited green.

I made my way down a sloping lane to the road which adheres to the lake and thence by a path across a wooded field to the verge of the water. Here I wandered along the narrow strip of beach to a little sandy cove, and lay down with my head in the shade of a thicket of bushes. The pebbles lay unstirred at my feet; the water was sheeted with the noonday light; the opposite mountains were clothed with wonderful tones of atmospheric blue. I tried to study them, to distinguish them, to remember them; but I felt only that they were wonderful, and that they don't belong to the province of words. The mountains at all hours have a way of trying to put off the observer with a certain *faux air* of simplicity: a single great curve for an outline, a dozen alternate planes of deeper or fainter blue for its contents. The persistent observer very soon learns, however, what to make of this brave simplicity—or rather, he very soon learns how hard it is to make anything positive of it, to resolve it into its thousand magical

parts. It is an old story that the mountains are for ever changing, that they live and move in a series of shifting and melting
and amazing "effects;" but I never so deeply felt its meaning
as while I lay on that couch of unrolled pebbles and gazed at
them across that shining level which assures the freedom of
the interval of air. The clouds were stationed in a windless
volume just above the line of their summits. Above the empty
lake was an empty field of sky. The result, of course, on the
slopes of the hills was a series of exquisite operations in
light—doubly fine and delicate from the stillness of the air.
The general tone was immensely soft and luminous—so that,
as I say, I might very well have been on the Lake of Como or
on Lago Maggiore. A green island lay blooming in the middle of the lake—which was not the Isola Bella, but apparently
a plain small thicket of firs. The oars of a little boat twinkled
in the sun and wrinkled the waveless deep. I chased the great
slow shadows on the mountains into little shadows, and the
little shadows into shadows which still were great. I followed
the even blue into violet and pink and amber. I disintegrated
with a steady gaze the long pure sky-lines into linked miles of
innumerable lonely spires. And then at last I rose to my feet
feeling that I had learned chiefly to misreport these mountain
wonders.

In the late afternoon, I went upon the lake lazily, with a
red-necked, brown-eyed young rustic as an oarsman. It was,
of course, delicious. The closing day had drained the water of
its early glare and dyed it with cool blue shadows. The hotel,
from the lake, looked decidedly vulgar. The mountains, in the
gross richness of their deepening blue, made at last an approach to a large massive simplicity. It is not till the sun departs, I think, that you see them in their essential masses. The
aerial charm is gone, but they gain in formal grandeur. In the
evening, at the hotel, there was the usual array of placid,
sauntering tourists—the usual spectacle of high-heeled young
ladies in those charming puffed and panniered overdresses of
white muslin which are now so picturesquely worn. I confess,
however, that to myself the most interesting feature of the
evening was the band of musicians on the piazza. The New
York papers had just come in, and I had been reading of the
great deeds of Prussia and the confusion of France. I was

filled with a sense of Prussian greatness. Strolling toward the place where the band was stationed, I beheld behind every trumpet a sturdy German face and heard in every note an uplifted German voice. My sense of German greatness was hugely magnified. Here, while their strong fellow-citizens were winning battles and making history in Alsace and Lorraine, they were making music in a distant land for a crowd of unmelodious strangers. What a splendid range of prowess and powers! What an omen for the Prussian future! The air seemed a brazen pæan of triumph and joy. Their simple Teutonic presence seemed a portent.

From Lake George to Burlington

BURLINGTON, VT., August 12, 1870.

I HAVE spent to-day amid lakes and mountains. I left the further end of Lake George in a little steamer in the early morning. The three hours' sail which you thus obtain is full of delightful beauty. The whole lake is framed in the noblest, purest mountain-masses. On the sides of the mountains, as we started, the clouds lay heavy and low, shutting us in, almost, to our little world of water; and during our transit they occasionally broke into rapid momentary rain; but on the whole I think they gave us quite as many effects as they concealed. At moments, when they thinned and lifted, the pale watery light yellowed the heavy darkness of the ranged forests into a languid counterfeit of autumn. The circling mountains faded and deepened in this passage like arriving and departing ghosts. The great hills group themselves about the upper portions of Lake George with a multitudinous majesty and variety which I shall not attempt to describe. They recede in dimly vaporous bays, where you barely feel their grim walls darkening through the cold gray sheets of cloud; they protrude in great headlands and break the mist with their cliffed and crested foreheads. The especial beauty of Lake George is believed to consist in its innumerable little islands. Many of these are extremely small—a growing-place for a dozen trees; several are large enough to contain a couple of houses. On one of them we saw some brave pleasure-seekers encamped, who came down to the water's edge in the rain and cheered us with a beautiful, cheerful bravado. The scenery about the lake, as a whole, is such a vast simple undisturbed wilderness, that you are almost startled to behold these various little makeshifts of civilization; you half wonder at our capital little steamer and at the young ladies from the hotel on the deck, with copies of "Lothair" in their hands. Landing at the head of the lake, we mounted on stages and drove some four miles to Ticonderoga and the edge of Lake Champlain—passing on our way through a little village which seemed to me, save for its setting of hills, more drearily, dirtily, glaringly void of any poor, pitiful little incident of village prettiness than a village with as fine a name—it was called Ticonderoga—had a right to be. The last mile of the four brings you into a bit of country prettier to my eye, almost, than any other in all this beautiful region. Through a poor wooden gateway, erected as if with a sort of sense of its guarded treasure, you enter a great tract of grassy slopes and scattered trees, which seem to tell you that nature herself has determined for once to aim at pure privacy, and to bestow upon a great rough expanse of American woodland the distinction of aspect of a nobleman's park. The short grass rolls downward in easy slopes, shaded by dense yet desultory groups of walnut and oak. You glance down the short vistas, as if to discover a browsing deer, or, perhaps, in the purer essence of romance and of baronial landscape, the sauntering daughter of an earl. But the pleasant avenue brings you only to the simple ruins of the grass-grown fort and to a sudden view of Champlain at your feet.

Of the fort I shall not speak: I dined, perforce, in the half-hour during which I might fastingly have explored it. I saw it only from the top of the coach as we passed. It seemed to me in quite the perfection of decay—of stony decrepitude and verdurous overgrowth—and to exhale with sufficient force a meagre historic melancholy. I prefer to speak of the lake, though of this, indeed, there is but little to say, and I have little space to say it. My sail hitherward of four hours showed me the most and the best of it. There is something, to my sense, in the physiognomy of Lake Champlain delightfully free, noble, and open. It is narrow for a lake and broad for a river, yet it strikes you more as a river. The water is less blue and pure than that of Lake George—a concession of quality to quantity. But its great beauty is the really great style of the landscape: this grand unflowing river, as it seems, with the generous, prolonged simplicity of its shores—green and level, without being low, on the east (till you come abreast of the Green Mountains), on the west bordered by an immense panorama of magnificent hills, receding more dimly from line to line till they meet the steady azure of the great wall of the Adirondacks. At Burlington your seeming river broadens as if to the meeting of the sea, and the forward horizon becomes a long water-line. Hereabouts the Green Mountains rise up in the east to gaze across the broad interval at their marshalled peers in New York. The vast reach of the lake and this double mountain view go far to make Burlington a supremely beautiful town. I know of it only so much as I learned in an hour's stroll, after my arrival. The lower portion by the lake-side is savagely raw and shabby, but as it ascends the long hill, which it partly covers, it gradually becomes the most truly charming, I fancy, of New England country towns. I followed a long street which leaves the hotel, crosses a rough, shallow ravine, which seems to divide it from the ugly poorness of the commercial quarter, and ascends a stately, shaded, residential avenue to no less a pinnacle of dignity than the University of Vermont. The university is a plain red building, with a cupola of beaten tin, shining like the dome of a Greek church, modestly embowered in scholastic shade—shade as modest as the number of its last batch of graduates, which I wouldn't for the world repeat. It faces a small enclosed and planted common; the whole spot is full of civic greenness and stillness and sweetness. It pleased me deeply, considering what it was; it reminded me the least bit in the world of a sort of primitive development of an English cathedral close. On the summit of the hill, where it leaves the town, you embrace the whole circling presence of the distant mountains; you see Mount Mansfield looking over lake and land at Mount Marcy. Equally with the view, though—I had been having views all day—I enjoyed, as I passed again along the avenue, the pleasant, solid American homes, with their blooming breadth of garden, sacred with peace and summer and twilight. I say "solid" with intent; the most of them seemed to have been tested and ripened by time. One of them there was—but of it I shall say nothing. I reserve it for its proper immortality in the first chapter of the great American novel. It perhaps added a touch to my light impression of the old and the graceful that, as I wandered back to my hotel in the dusk, I heard repeatedly, as the home-faring laborers passed me in couples, the sound of a tongue of other than Yankee inflections. It was Canadian French.

Saratoga

THE SENTIMENTAL TOURIST makes images in advance; they grow up in his mind by a logic of their own. He finds himself thinking of an unknown, unseen place, as having such and such a shape and figure rather than such another. It assumes in his mind a certain complexion, a certain colour which frequently turns out to be singularly at variance with reality. For some reason or other, I had supposed Saratoga to be buried in a sort of elegant wilderness. I imagined a region of shady forest drives, with a bright, broad-terraced hotel gleaming here and there against a background of mysterious groves and glades. I had made a cruelly small allowance for the stern vulgarities of life—for the shops and sidewalks and loafers, the complex machinery of a city of pleasure. The fault was so wholly my own that it is quite without bitterness that I proceed to affirm that the Saratoga of experience is sadly different from this. I confess, however, that it has always seemed to me that one's visions, on the whole, gain more than they lose by being transmuted into fact. There is an essential indignity in indefiniteness; you cannot allow for accidents and details until you have seen them. They give more to the imagination than they receive from it. I frankly admit, therefore, that the Saratoga of reality is a much more satisfactory place than the all-too-primitive Elysium I had constructed. It is indeed, as I say, immensely different. There is a vast number of brick—nay, of asphalt—sidewalks, a great many shops, and a magnificent array of loafers. But what indeed are you to do at Saratoga—the morning draught having been achieved—unless you loaf? "Que faire en un gîte à moins que l'on ne songe?" Loafers being assumed, of course shops and sidewalks follow. The main avenue of Saratoga does not scruple to call itself Broadway. The untravelled reader may form a very accurate idea of it by recalling as distinctly as possible, not indeed the splendours of that famous thoroughfare, but the secondary charms of the Sixth Avenue. The place has what the French would call the "accent" of the Sixth Avenue. Its two main features are the two monster

hotels which stand facing each other along a goodly portion
of its course. One, I believe, is considered much better than
the other,—less of a monster and more of a refuge,—but in
appearance there is little choice between them. Both are immense brick structures, directly on the crowded, noisy street,
with vast covered piazzas running along the façade, supported
by great iron posts. The piazza of the Union Hotel, I have
been repeatedly informed, is the largest "in the world." There
are a number of objects in Saratoga, by the way, which in
their respective kinds are the finest in the world. One of these
is Mr. John Morrissey's casino. I bowed my head submissively
to this statement, but privately I thought of the blue Mediterranean, and the little white promontory of Monaco, and the
silver-gray verdure of olives, and the view across the outer sea
toward the bosky cliffs of Italy. The Congress waters, too, it
is well known, are excellent in the superlative degree; this I
am perfectly willing to maintain.

The piazzas of these great hotels may very well be the biggest of all piazzas. They have not architectural beauty; but
they doubtless serve their purpose—that of affording sitting-
space in the open air to an immense number of persons. They
are, of course, quite the best places to observe the Saratoga
world. In the evening, when the "boarders" have all come
forth and seated themselves in groups, or have begun to stroll
in (not always, I regret to say, to the sad detriment of the
dramatic interest, bisexual) couples, the big heterogeneous
scene affords a great deal of entertainment. Seeing it for the
first time, the observer is likely to assure himself that he has
neglected an important item in the sum of American manners.
The rough brick wall of the house, illumined by a line of
flaring gas-lights, forms a natural background to the crude,
impermanent, discordant tone of the assembly. In the larger
of the two hotels, a series of long windows open into an immense parlour—the largest, I suppose, in the world, and the
most scantily furnished in proportion to its size. A few dozen
rocking-chairs, an equal number of small tables, tripods to the
eternal ice-pitcher, serve chiefly to emphasise the vacuous
grandeur of the spot. On the piazza, in the outer multitude,
ladies largely prevail, both by numbers and (you are not slow
to perceive) by distinction of appearance. The good old times

of Saratoga, I believe, as of the world in general, are rapidly passing away. The time was when it was the chosen resort of none but "nice people." At the present day, I hear it constantly affirmed, "the company is dreadfully mixed." What society may have been at Saratoga when its elements were thus simple and severe, I can only vaguely and mournfully conjecture. I confine myself to the dense, democratic, vulgar Saratoga of the current year. You are struck, to begin with, at the hotels, by the numerical superiority of the women; then, I think, by their personal superiority. It is incontestably the case that in appearance, in manner, in grace and completeness of aspect, American women surpass their husbands and brothers; the relation being reversed among some of the nations of Europe. Attached to the main entrance of the Union Hotel, and adjoining the ascent from the street to the piazza, is a "stoop" of mighty area, which, at most hours of the day and evening, is a favoured lounging-place of men. I should add, after the remark I have just made, that even in the appearance of the usual American male there seems to me to be a certain plastic intention. It is true that the lean, sallow, angular Yankee of tradition is dignified mainly by a look of decision, a hint of unimpassioned volition, the air of "smartness." This in some degree redeems him, but it fails to make him handsome. But in the average American of the present time, the typical leanness and sallowness are less than in his fathers, and the individual acuteness is at once equally marked and more frequently united with merit of form. Casting your eye over a group of your fellow-citizens in the portico of the Union Hotel, you will be inclined to admit that, taking the good with the bad, they are worthy sons of the great Republic. I have found, at any rate, a great deal of entertainment in watching them. They suggest to my fancy the swarming vastness—the multifarious possibilities and activities—of our young civilisation. They come from the uttermost ends of the Union—from San Francisco, from New Orleans, from Alaska. As they sit with their white hats tilted forward, and their chairs tilted back, and their feet tilted up, and their cigars and toothpicks forming various angles with these various lines, I seem to see in their faces a tacit reference to the affairs of a continent. They are obviously persons of experience—of a somewhat narrow and monotonous experience certainly; an experience of which the diamonds and laces which their wives are exhibiting hard by are, perhaps, the most substantial and beautiful result; but, at any rate, they have *lived*, in every fibre of the will. For the time, they are lounging with the negro waiters, and the boot-blacks, and the news-vendors; but it was not in lounging that they gained their hard wrinkles and the level impartial regard which they direct from beneath their hat-rims. They are not the mellow fruit of a society which has walked hand-in-hand with tradition and culture; they are hard nuts, which have grown and ripened as they could. When they talk among themselves, I seem to hear the cracking of the shells.

If the men are remarkable, the ladies are wonderful. Saratoga is famous, I believe, as the place of all places in America where women adorn themselves most, or as the place, at least, where the greatest amount of dressing may be seen by the greatest number of people. Your first impression is therefore of the—what shall I call it?—of the abundance of petticoats. Every woman you meet, young or old, is attired with a certain amount of richness, and with whatever good taste may be compatible with such a mode of life. You behold an interesting, indeed a quite momentous spectacle; the democratisation of elegance. If I am to believe what I hear—in fact, I may say what I overhear—many of these sumptuous persons have enjoyed neither the advantages of a careful education nor the privileges of an introduction to society. She walks more or less of a queen, however, each uninitiated nobody. She often has, in dress, an admirable instinct of elegance and even of what the French call "chic." This instinct occasionally amounts to a sort of passion; the result then is wonderful. You look at the coarse brick walls, the rusty iron posts of the piazza, at the shuffling negro waiters, the great tawdry steamboat-cabin of a drawing-room—you see the tilted ill-dressed loungers on the steps—and you finally regret that a figure so exquisite should have so vulgar a setting. Your resentment, however, is speedily tempered by reflection. You feel the impertinence of your old reminiscences of English and French novels, and of the dreary social order in which privacy was the presiding genius and women arrayed themselves for the appreciation of the few. The crowd, the tavern-loungers, the surrounding ugliness and tumult and license, constitute the social medium of the young lady you are so inconsistent as to admire; she is dressed for publicity. The thought fills you with a kind of awe. The social order of tradition is far away indeed, and as for the transatlantic novels, you begin to doubt whether she is so amiably curious as to read even the silliest of them. To be dressed up to the eyes is obviously to give pledges to idleness. I have been forcibly struck with the apparent absence of any warmth and richness of detail in the lives of these wonderful ladies of the piazzas. We are freely accused of being an eminently wasteful people; and I know of few things which so largely warrant the accusation as the fact that these conspicuous *élégantes* adorn themselves, socially speaking, to so little purpose. To dress for every one is, practically, to dress for no one. There are few prettier sights than a charmingly-dressed woman, gracefully established in some shady spot, with a piece of needle-work or embroidery, or a book. Nothing very serious is accomplished, probably, but an æsthetic principle is recognised. The embroidery and the book are a tribute to culture, and I suppose they really figure somewhere out of the opening scenes of French comedies. But here at Saratoga, at any hour of morning or evening, you may see a hundred rustling beauties whose rustle is their sole occupation. One lady in particular there is, with whom it appears to be an inexorable fate that she shall be nothing more than dressed. Her apparel is tremendously modern, and my remarks would be much illumined if I had the learning necessary for describing it. I can only say that every evening for a fortnight she has revealed herself as a fresh creation. But she especially, as I say, has struck me as a person dressed beyond her life and her opportunities. I resent on her behalf—or on behalf at least of her finery—the extreme severity of her circumstances. What is she, after all, but a "regular boarder"? She ought to sit on the terrace of a stately castle, with a great baronial park shutting out the undressed world, and bandy quiet small-talk with an ambassador or a duke. My imagination is shocked when I behold her seated in gorgeous relief against the dusty clapboards of the hotel, with her beautiful hands folded in her silken lap, her head drooping slightly beneath the weight of her *chignon*, her lips parted in a vague contemplative gaze at Mr. Helmbold's well-known advertisement on the opposite fence, her husband beside her reading the New York *Herald*.

I have indeed observed cases of a sort of splendid social isolation here, which are not without a certain amount of pathos—people who know no one, who have money and finery and possessions, only no friends. Such at least is my inference, from the lonely grandeur with which I see them invested. Women, of course, are the most helpless victims of this cruel situation, although it must be said that they befriend each other with a generosity for which we hardly give them credit. I have seen women, for instance, at various "hops," approach their lonely sisters and invite them to waltz, and I have seen the fair invited surrender themselves eagerly to this humiliating embrace. Gentlemen at Saratoga are at a much higher premium than at European watering-places. It is an old story that in this country we have no "leisure-class"—the class from which the Saratogas of Europe recruit a large number of their male frequenters. A few months ago, I paid a visit to an English "bath," commemorated in various works of fiction, where, among many visible points of difference from American resorts, the most striking was the multitude of young men who had the whole day on their hands. While their sweethearts and sisters are waltzing together, our own young men are rolling up greenbacks in counting-houses and stores. I was recently reminded in another way, one evening, of the unlikeness of Saratoga to Cheltenham. Behind the biggest of the big hotels is a large planted yard, which it is the fashion at Saratoga to talk of as a "park," and which is perhaps believed to be the biggest in the world. At one end of it stands a great ballroom, approached by a range of wooden steps. It was late in the evening; the room, in spite of the intense heat, was blazing with light and the orchestra thundering a mighty waltz. A group of loungers, including myself, were hanging about to watch the ingress of the festally-minded. In the basement of the edifice, sunk beneath the ground, a noisy auctioneer, in his shirt and trousers, black in the face with heat and vociferation, was selling "pools" of the races to a dense group of frowsy betting-men. At the foot of the steps was stationed a man in a linen coat and straw hat, without waistcoat or necktie, to take the tickets of the ball-goers. As the latter failed to arrive in sufficient numbers, a musician came forth to the top of the steps and blew a loud summons on a horn. After this they began to straggle along. On this occasion, certainly, the company promised to be decidedly "mixed." The women, as usual, were much bedizened, though without any constant adhesion to the technicalities of full-dress. The men adhered to it neither in the letter nor the spirit. The possessor of a pair of satin-shod feet, twinkling beneath an uplifted volume of gauze and lace and flowers, tripped up the steps with her gloved hand on the sleeve of a railway "duster." Now and then two ladies arrived alone; generally a group of them approached under convoy of a single man. Children were freely scattered among their elders, and frequently a small boy would deliver his ticket and enter the glittering portal, beautifully unembarrassed. Of the children of Saratoga there would be wondrous things to relate. I believe that, in spite of their valuable aid, the festival of which I speak was rated rather a "fizzle." I see it advertised that they are soon to have, for their own peculiar benefit, a "Masquerade and Promenade Concert, beginning at 9 P.M." I observe that they usually open the "hops," and that it is only after their elders have borrowed confidence from the sight of their unfaltering paces that the latter dare to dance. You meet them far into the evening, roaming over the piazzas and corridors of the hotels—the little girls especially—lean, pale, formidable. Occasionally childhood confesses itself, even when maternity resists, and you see at eleven o'clock at night some poor little bedizened precocity collapsed in slumber in a lonely wayside chair. The part played by children in society here is only an additional instance of the wholesale equalisation of the various social atoms which is the distinctive feature of collective Saratoga. A man in a "duster" at a ball is as good as a man in regulation-garments; a young woman dancing with another young woman is as good as a young woman dancing with a young man; a child of ten is as good as a woman of thirty; a double negative in conversation is rather better than a single.

   An important feature in many a watering-place is the facility for leaving it a little behind you and tasting of the unmitigated country. You may wander to some shady hillside and sentimentalise upon the vanity of a high civilisation. But at Saratoga civilisation holds you fast. The most important feature of the place, perhaps, is the impossibility of carrying out any such pastoral dream. The surrounding country is a charming wilderness, but the roads are so abominably bad that walking and driving are alike unprofitable. Of course, however, if you are bent upon a walk, you will take a walk. There is a striking contrast between the concentrated prodigality of life in the immediate neighbourhood of the hotels and the pastoral solitudes into which a walk of half an hour may lead you. You have left the American citizen and his wife, the orchestras, the pools, the precocious infants, the cocktails, the importations from Worth, but a mile or two behind, but already the forest is primeval and the landscape is without figures. Nothing could be less manipulated than the country about Saratoga. The heavy roads are little more than sandy wheel-tracks; by the tangled wayside the blackberries wither unpicked. The horizon undulates with an air of having it all its own way. There are no white villages gleaming in the distance, no spires of churches, no salient details. It is all green, lonely, and vacant. If you wish to enjoy a detail, you must stop beneath a cluster of pines and listen to the murmur of the softly-troubled air, or follow upward the scaly straightness of their trunks to where the afternoon light gives it a colour. Here and there on a slope by the roadside stands a rough unpainted farmhouse, looking as if its dreary blackness were the result of its standing dark and lonely amid so many months—and such a wide expanse—of winter snow. It has turned black by contrast. The principal feature of the grassy unfurnished yard is the great wood-pile, telling grimly of the long reversion of the summer. For the time, however, it looks down contentedly enough over a goodly appanage of grainfields and orchards, and I can fancy that it may be amusing to be a boy there. But to be a man, it must be quite what the lean, brown, serious farmers physiognomically hint it to be. You have, however, at the present season, for your additional beguilement, on the eastern horizon, the vision of the long bold chain of the Green Mountains, clad in that single coat of simple, candid blue which is the favourite garment of our

American hills. As a visitor, too, you have for an afternoon's excursion your choice between a couple of lakes. Saratoga Lake, the larger and more distant of the two, is the goal of the regular afternoon drive. Above the shore is a well-appointed tavern—"Moon's" it is called by the voice of fame—where you may sit upon a broad piazza and partake of fried potatoes and "drinks;" the latter, if you happen to have come from poor dislicensed Boston, a peculiarly gratifying privilege. You enjoy the felicity sighed for by that wanton Italian lady of the anecdote, when, one summer evening, to the sound of music, she wished that to eat an ice were a sin. The other lake is small, and its shores are unadorned by any edifice but a boat-house, where you may hire a skiff and pull yourself out into the minnow-tickled, wood-circled oval. Here, floating in its darkened half, while you watch on the opposite shore the tree-stems, white and sharp in the declining sunlight, and their foliage whitening and whispering in the breeze, and you feel that this little solitude is part of a greater and more portentous solitude, you may recall certain passages of Ruskin, in which he dwells upon the needfulness of some human association, however remote, to make natural scenery fully impressive. You may recall that magnificent page in which he relates having tried with such fatal effect, in a battle-haunted valley of the Jura, to fancy himself in a name-less solitude of our own continent. You feel around you, with irresistible force, the eloquent silence of undedicated nature— the absence of serious associations, the nearness, indeed, of the vulgar and trivial associations of the least complete of all the cities of pleasure—you feel this, and you wonder what it is you so deeply and calmly enjoy. You make up your mind, possibly, that it is a great advantage to be able at once to enjoy Mr. Ruskin and to enjoy Mr. Ruskin's alarms. And hereupon you return to your hotel and read the New York papers on the plan of the French campaign and the Nathan murder.

1870

Newport

THE SEASON at Newport has an obstinate life. September has fairly begun, but as yet there is small visible diminution in the steady stream—the splendid, stupid stream—of carriages which rolls in the afternoon along the Avenue. There is, I think, a far more intimate fondness between Newport and its frequenters than that which in most American watering-places consecrates the somewhat mechanical relation between the visitors and the visited. This relation here is for the most part slightly sentimental. I am very far from professing a cynical contempt for the gaieties and vanities of Newport life: they are, as a spectacle, extremely amusing; they are full of a certain warmth of social colour which charms alike the eye and the fancy; they are worth observing, if only to conclude against them; they possess at least the dignity of all extreme and emphatic expressions of a social tendency; but they are not so untouched with Philistinism that I do not seem to overhear at times the still, small voice of this tender sense of the sweet, superior beauty of the natural things that surround them, pleading gently in their favour to the fastidious critic. I feel almost warranted in saying that here the background of life has sunk less in relative value and suffered less from the encroachments of pleasure-seeking man than the scenic dispositions of any other watering-place. For this, perhaps, we may thank rather the modest, incorruptible integrity of the Newport landscape than any very intelligent forbearance on the part of the summer colony. The beauty of this landscape is so subtle, so essential, so humble, so much a thing of character and expression, so little a thing of feature and pretension, that it cunningly eludes the grasp of the destroyer or the reformer, and triumphs in impalpable purity even when it seems to make concessions. I have sometimes wondered, in rational moods, why it is that Newport is so much appreciated by the votaries of idleness and pleasure. Its resources are few in number. It is extremely circumscribed. It has few drives, few walks, little variety of scenery. Its charms and its interest are confined to a narrow circle. It has of

759

course the unlimited ocean, but seafaring idlers are not true Newporters, for any other sea would suit them as well. Last evening, it seemed to me, as I drove along the Avenue, that I guessed the answer to the riddle. The atmospheric tone, the careful selection of ingredients, your pleasant sense of a certain climatic ripeness—these are the real charm of Newport, and the secret of her supremacy. You are affected by the admirable art of the landscape, by seeing so much that is lovely and impressive achieved with such a frugality of means—with so little parade of the vast, the various, or the rare, with so narrow a range of colour and form. I could not help thinking, as I turned from the harmonies and purities which lay deepening on the breast of nature, with the various shades of twilight, to the heterogeneous procession in the Avenue, that, quite in their own line of effect, the usual performers in this exhibition might learn a few good lessons from the daily prospect of the great western expanse of rock and ocean in its relations with the declining sun. But this is asking too much. Many persons of course come to Newport simply because others come, and in this way the present brilliant colony has grown up. Let me not be suspected, when I speak of Newport, of the untasteful heresy of meaning primarily rocks and waves rather than ladies and gentlemen.

The ladies and gentlemen are in great force—the ladies, of course, especially. It is true everywhere, I suppose, that women are the animating element of "society;" but you feel this to be especially true as you pass along Bellevue Avenue. I doubt whether anywhere else so many women have a "good time" with so small a sacrifice of the luxury of self-respect. I heard a lady yesterday tell another, with a quiet ecstasy of tone, that she had been having a "most perfect time." This is the very poetry of pleasure. It is a part of our complacent tradition that in those foreign lands where women are supposed to be socially supreme, they maintain their empire by various clandestine and reprehensible arts. With us—we say it at Newport without bravado—they are both conspicuous and unsophisticated. You feel this most gratefully as you receive a confident bow from a pretty girl in her basket-phaeton. She is very young and very pretty, but she has a certain habitual assurance which is only a grace the more. She combines, you reflect with respectful tenderness, all that is possible in the way of modesty with all that is delightful in the way of facility. Shyness is certainly very pretty—when it is not very ugly; but shyness may often darken the bloom of genuine modesty, and a certain frankness and confidence may often incline it toward the light. Let us assume, then, that all the young ladies whom you may meet here are of the highest modern type. In the course of time they ripen into the delightful matrons who divide your admiration. It is easy to see that Newport must be a most agreeable sojourn for the male sex. The gentlemen, indeed, look wonderfully prosperous and well-conditioned. They gallop on shining horses or recline in a sort of coaxing Herculean submission beside the lovely mistress of a curricle. Young men—and young old men—I have occasion to observe, are far more numerous than at Saratoga, and of vastly superior quality. There is, indeed, in all things a striking difference in tone and aspect between these two great centres of pleasure. After Saratoga, Newport seems really substantial and civilised. Æsthetically speaking, you may remain at Newport with a fairly good conscience; at Saratoga you linger under passionate protest. At Newport life is public, if you will; at Saratoga it is absolutely common. The difference, in a word, is the difference between a group of undiscriminating hotels and a series of organised homes. Saratoga perhaps deserves our greater homage, as being characteristically democratic and American; let us, then, make Saratoga the heaven of our aspiration, but let us yet a while content ourselves with Newport as the lowly earth of our residence.

The villas and "cottages," the beautiful idle women, the beautiful idle men, the brilliant pleasure-fraught days and evenings, impart, perhaps, to Newport life a faintly European expression, in so far as they suggest the somewhat alien presence of leisure—"fine old Leisure," as George Eliot calls it. Nothing, it seems to me, however, can take place in America without straightway seeming very American; and, after a week at Newport, you begin to fancy that to live for amusement simply, beyond the noise of commerce or of care, is a distinctively national trait. Nowhere else in this country—nowhere, of course, within the range of our better civilisation—does business seem so remote, so vague, and unreal. It is the

only place in America in which enjoyment is organised. If
there be any poetry in the ignorance of trade and turmoil and
the hard processes of fortune, Newport may claim her share
of it. She knows—or at least appears to know—for the most
part nothing but results. Individuals here, of course, have private cares and burdens to preserve the balance and the dignity
of life; but collective society conspires to forget everything
that worries. It is a singular fact that a society that does nothing is decidedly more pictorial, more interesting to the eye of
contemplation, than a society which is hard at work. Newport, in this way, is infinitely more fertile in combinations
than Saratoga. There you feel that idleness is occasional, empirical. Most of the people you see are asking themselves, you
imagine, whether the game is worth the candle and work is
not better than such difficult play. But here, obviously, the
habit of pleasure is formed, and (within the limits of a severe
morality) many of the secrets of pleasure are known. Do what
we will, on certain lines Europe is in advance of us yet. Newport lags altogether behind Trouville and Brighton in her exhibition of the unmentionable. All this is markedly absent
from the picture, which is therefore signally destitute of the
enhancing tints produced by the mysteries and fascinations of
vice. But idleness *per se* is vicious, and of course you may
imagine what you please. For my own part, I prefer to imagine nothing but the graceful and the pure; and with the help
of such imaginings you may construct a very pretty sentimental undercurrent to the superficial movement of society. This I
lately found very difficult to do at Saratoga. Sentiment there
is pitifully shy and elusive. Here, the multiplied relations of
men and women, under the permanent pressure of luxury and
idleness, give it a very fair chance. Sentiment, indeed, of masterly force and interest, springs up in every soil, with a sovereign disregard of occasion. People love and hate and aspire
with the greatest intensity when they have to make their time
and opportunity. I should hardly come to Newport for the
materials of a tragedy. Even in their own kind, the social elements are as yet too light and thin. But I can fancy finding
here the motive of a drama which should depend more on
smiles than tears. I can almost imagine, indeed, a transient
observer of the Newport spectacle dreaming momentarily of a

great American novel, in which the heroine might be infinitely realistic and yet neither a schoolmistress nor an outcast. I say intentionally the "transient" observer, because it is probable that here the suspicion only is friendly to dramatic point; the knowledge is hostile. The observer would discover, on a nearer view, I rather fear, that his possible heroines have too perfect a time.

This will remind the reader of what he must already have heard affirmed, that to speak of a place with abundance you must know it, but not too well. I suffer from knowing the natural elements of Newport too well to attempt to describe them. I have known them so long that I hardly know what I think of them. I have little more than a simple consciousness of enjoying them very much. Even this consciousness at times lies dumb and inert. I wonder at such times whether, to appeal fairly to the general human sense, the horizon has not too much of that mocking straightness which is such a misrepresentation of the real character of the sea—as if, forsooth, it were level. Life seems too short, space too narrow, to warrant you in giving in an unqualified adhesion to a *paysage* which is two-thirds ocean. For the most part, however, I am willing to take the landscape as it stands, and to think that, without the water to make it precious, the land would be much less lovable. It is, in fact, a land exquisitely modified by marine influences. Indeed, in spite of all the evil it has done me, I could almost speak well of the ocean when I remember the charming tricks it plays with the Newport promontories.

The place consists, as the reader will know, of an ancient and honourable town, a goodly harbour, and a long, broad neck of land, stretching southward into the sea and forming the chief habitation of the summer colony. Along the greater part of its eastward length, this projecting coast is bordered with cliffs of no great height, and dotted with seaward-gazing villas. At the head of the promontory the villas enjoy a magnificent reach of prospect. The pure Atlantic—the old world westward tides—expire directly at their feet. Behind the line of villas runs the Avenue, with more villas yet—of which there is nothing at all to say but that those built recently are a hundred times prettier than those built fifteen years ago, and give one some hope of a revival of the architectural art. Some years ago, when I first knew Newport, the town proper was considered remarkably quaint. If an antique shabbiness that amounts almost to squalor is a pertinent element, as I believe it is, of this celebrated quality, the little main street at least— Thames Street by name—still deserves the praise. Here, in their crooked and dwarfish wooden mansions, are the shops that minister to the daily needs of the expanded city; and here of a summer morning, jolting over the cobble stones of the narrow roadway, you may see a hundred superfine ladies seeking with languid eagerness what they may buy—to "buy something," I believe, being a diurnal necessity of the conscientious American woman. This busy region gradually melts away into the grass-grown stillness of the Point, in the eyes of many persons the pleasantest quarter of Newport. It has superficially the advantage of being as yet uninvaded by fashion. When I first knew it, however, its peculiar charm was even more undisturbed than at present. The Point may be called the old residential, as distinguished from the commercial, town. It is meagre, shallow and scanty—a mere pinch of antiquity—but, so far as it goes, it retains an exquisite tone. It leaves the shops and the little wharves, and wanders close to the harbour, where the breeze-borne rattle of shifted sails and spars alone intrudes upon its stillness, till its mouldy-timbered quiet subsides into the low, tame rocks and beaches which edge the bay. Several matter-of-course modern houses have recently been erected on the water-side, absorbing the sober, primitive tenements which used to maintain the picturesque character of the place. They improve it, of course, as a residence, but they injure it as an unexpected corner. Enough of early architecture still remains, however, to suggest a multitude of thoughts as to the severe simplicity of the generation which produced it. The plain gray nudity of these little warped and shingled boxes seems to make it a hopeless task on their part to present any positive appearance at all. But here, as elsewhere, the magical Newport atmosphere wins half the battle. It aims at no mystery—it simply makes them scintillate in their bareness. Their homely notches and splinters twinkle till the mere friendliness of the thing makes a surface. Their steep gray roofs, barnacled with lichens, remind you of old barges, overturned on the beach to dry.

One of the more recent monuments of fashion is the long drive which follows the shore. The Avenue, where the Neck abruptly terminates, has been made to extend itself to the west, and to wander for a couple of miles over a lovely region of beach and lowly down and sandy meadow and salt brown sheep-grass. This region was formerly the most beautiful part of Newport—the least frequented and the most untamed by fashion. I by no means regret the creation of the new road, however. A walker may very soon isolate himself, and the occupants of carriages are exposed to a benefit quite superior to their power of injury. The peculiar charm of this great westward expanse is very difficult to define. It is in an especial degree the charm of Newport in general—the combined lowness of tone, as painters call it, in all the elements of *terra firma*, and the extraordinary elevation of tone in the air. For miles and miles you see at your feet, in mingled shades of yellow and gray, a desolate waste of moss-clad rock and sand-starved grass. At your left is nothing but the shine and surge of the ocean, and over your head that wonderful sky of Newport, which has such an unexpected resemblance to the sky of Venice. In spite of the bare simplicity of this prospect, its beauty is far more a beauty of detail than that of the average American landscape. Descend into a hollow of the rocks, into one of the little warm climates, five feet square, which you may find there, beside the grateful ocean glare, and you will be struck quite as much by their fineness as by their roughness. From time to time, as you wander, you will meet a lonely, stunted tree, which is sure to be a charming piece of the individual grotesque. The region of which I speak is perhaps best seen in the late afternoon, from the high seat of a carriage on the Avenue. You seem to stand just outside the threshold of the west. At its opposite extremity sinks the sun, with such a splendour, perhaps, as I lately saw—a splendour of the deepest blue, more luminous and fiery than the usual redness of evening, and all streaked and barred with blown and drifted gold. The whole large interval, with its rocks and marshes and ponds, seems bedimmed with a kind of purple glaze. The near Atlantic fades and turns cold with that desolate look of the ocean when the day ceases to care for it. In the foreground, a short distance from the road, an old

orchard uplifts its tangled stems and branches against the violet mists of the west. It seems strangely grotesque and enchanted. No ancient olive-grove of Italy or Provence was ever
more hoarily romantic. This is what people commonly behold
on the last homeward bend of the drive. For such of them as
are happy enough to occupy one of the villas on the cliffs, the
beauty of the day has even yet not expired. The present summer has been emphatically the summer of moonlights. Not
the nights, however, but the long days, in these agreeable
homes, are what especially appeal to my fancy. Here you find
a solution of the insoluble problem—to combine an abundance of society with an abundance of solitude. In their
charming broad-windowed drawing-rooms, on their great
seaward piazzas, within sight of the serious Atlantic horizon,
which is so familiar to the eye and so mysterious to the heart,
caressed by the gentle breeze which makes all but simple, social, delightful *now* and *here* seem unreal and untasteful—the
sweet fruit of the lotus grows more than ever succulent and
magical. How sensible they ought to be, the denizens of these
pleasant places, of their peculiar felicity and distinction! How
it should purify their temper and refine their tastes! How
delicate, how wise, how discriminating they should become!
What excellent manners—what enlightened opinions—their
situation should produce! How it should purge them of vulgarity! Happy *villeggianti* of Newport!

1870

Quebec

I.

A TRAVELLER who combines a taste for old towns with a love of letters ought not, I suppose, to pass through "the most picturesque city in America" without making an attempt to commemorate his impressions. His first impression will certainly have been that not America, but Europe, should have the credit of Quebec. I came, some days since, by a dreary night-journey, to Point Levi, opposite the town, and as we rattled toward our goal in the faint raw dawn, and, already attentive to "effects," I began to consult the misty window-panes and descried through the moving glass little but crude, monotonous woods, suggestive of nothing that I had ever heard of in song or story, I felt that the land would have much to do to give itself a romantic air. And, in fact, the feat is achieved with almost magical suddenness. The old world rises in the midst of the new in the manner of a change of scene on the stage. The St. Lawrence shines at your left, large as a harbour-mouth, gray with smoke and masts, and edged on its hither verge by a bustling water-side *faubourg* which looks French or English, or anything not local that you please; and beyond it, over against you, on its rocky promontory, sits the ancient town, belted with its hoary wall and crowned with its granite citadel. Now that I have been here a while I find myself wondering how the city would strike one if the imagination had not been bribed beforehand. The place, after all, is of the soil on which it stands; yet it appeals to you so cunningly with its little stock of transatlantic wares that you overlook its flaws and lapses, and swallow it whole. Fancy lent a willing hand the morning I arrived, and zealously retouched the picture. The very sky seemed to have been brushed in like the sky in an English water-colour, the light to filter down through an atmosphere more dense and more conscious. You cross a ferry, disembark at the foot of the rock on unmistakably foreign soil, and then begin to climb into the city proper—the city *intra muros*. These walls, to the American vision, are of course the sovereign fact of Quebec; you take off your hat to them as you clatter through the gate. They are neither very high nor, after all, very hoary. Our clear American air is hostile to those mellow deposits and incrustations which enrich the venerable surfaces of Europe. Still, they are walls; till but a short time ago they quite encircled the town; they are garnished with little slits for musketry and big embrasures for cannon; they offer here and there to the strolling bourgeoisie a stretch of grassy rampart; and they make the whole place definite and personal.

Before you reach the gates, however, you will have been reminded at a dozen points that you have come abroad. What is the essential difference of tone between street-life in an old civilisation and in a new? It seems something subtler and deeper than mere external accidents—than foreign architecture, than foreign pinks, greens, and yellows plastering the house-fronts, than the names of the saints on the corners, than all the pleasant crookedness, narrowness and duskiness, the quaint economised spaces, the multifarious detail, the brown French faces, the ruddy English ones. It seems to be the general fact of detail itself—the hint in the air of a slow, accidental accretion, in obedience to needs more timidly considered and more sparingly gratified than the pressing necessities of American progress. But apart from the metaphysics of the question, Quebec has a great many pleasant little ripe spots and amenities. You note the small, box-like houses in rugged stone or in stucco, each painted with uncompromising *naïveté* in some bright hue of the owner's fond choice; you note with joy, with envy, with momentary self-effacement, as a New Yorker, as a Bostonian, the innumerable calashes and cabs which contend for your selection; and you observe when you arrive at the hotel, that this is a blank and gloomy inn, of true provincial aspect, with slender promise of the "American plan." Perhaps, even the clerk at the office will have the courtesy of the ages of leisure. I confess that, in my case, he was terribly modern, so that I was compelled to resort for a lodging to a private house near by, where I enjoy a transitory glimpse of the *vie intime* of Quebec. I fancied, when I came in, that it would be a compensation for worse quarters to possess the little Canadian vignette I enjoy from my windows.

Certain shabby Yankee sheds, indeed, encumber the foreground, but they are so near that I can overlook them. Beyond is a piece of garden, attached to nothing less than a
convent of the cloistered nuns of St. Ursula. The convent
chapel rises inside it, crowned with what seemed to me, in
view of the circumstances, a real little *clocher de France*. The
"circumstances," I confess, are simply a couple of stout
French poplars. I call them French because they are alive and
happy; whereas, if they had been American they would have
died of a want of appreciation, like their brothers in the
"States." I do not say that the little convent-belfry, roofed and
coated as it is with quaint scales of tin, would, by itself, produce any very deep illusion; or that the whispering poplars,
per se, would transport me to the Gallic mother land; but
poplars and belfry together constitute an "effect"—strike a
musical note in the scale of association. I look fondly even at
the little casements which command this prospect, for they
too are an old-world heritage. They open sidewise, in two
wings, and are screwed together by that bothersome little
iron handle over which we have fumbled so often in European inns.

If the windows tell of French dominion, of course larger
matters testify with greater eloquence. In a place so small as
Quebec, the bloom of novelty of course rubs off; but when
first I walked abroad I fancied myself again in a French sea-
side town where I once spent a year, in common with a large
number of economically disposed English. The French element offers the groundwork, and the English colony wears,
for the most part, that half-genteel and migratory air which
stamps the exiled and provincial British. They look as if they
were still *en voyage*—still in search of low prices—the men in
woollen shirts and Scotch bonnets; the ladies with a certain
look of being equipped for dangers and difficulties. Your very
first steps will be likely to lead you to the market-place, which
is a genuine bit of Europeanism. One side of it is occupied by
a huge edifice of yellow plaster, with stone facings painted in
blue, and a manner of *porte-cochère*, leading into a veritable
court—originally, I believe, a college of the early Jesuits, now
a place of military stores. On the other stands the French cathedral, with an ample stone façade, a bulky stone tower, and

a high-piled, tin-scaled belfry; not architectural, of course, nor imposing, but with a certain gray maturity, and, as regards the belfry, a quite adequate quaintness. Round about are shops and houses, touching which, I think, it is no mere fancy that they might, as they stand, look down into some dull and rather dirty *place* in France. The stalls and booths in the centre—tended by genuine peasants of tradition, brown-faced old Frenchwomen, with hard wrinkles and short petticoats, and white caps beneath their broad-brimmed hats, and more than one price, as I think you'll find—these, and the stationed calèches and cabriolets complete a passably fashionable French picture. It is a proof of how nearly the old market-women resemble their originals across the sea that you rather resentfully miss one or two of the proper features of the type—the sabots for the feet and the donkey for the load. Of course you go into the cathedral, and how forcibly that swing of the door, as you doff your hat in the cooler air, recalls the old tourist strayings and pryings beneath other skies! You find a big garish church, with a cold high light, a promiscuity of stucco and gilding, and a mild odour of the seventeenth century. It is, perhaps, a shade or so more sensibly Catholic than it would be with ourselves; but, in fine, it has pews and a boarded floor, and the few paintings are rather pale in their badness, and you are forced to admit that the old-world tone which sustains itself so comfortably elsewhere falters most where most is asked of it.

Among the other lions of Quebec—notably in the Citadel—you find Protestant England supreme. A robust trooper of her Majesty, with a pair of very tight trousers and a very small cap, takes charge of you at the entrance of the fortifications, and conducts you through all kinds of incomprehensible defences. I cannot speak of the place as an engineer, but only as a tourist, and the tourist is chiefly concerned with the view. This is altogether superb, and if Quebec is not the most picturesque city in America, this is no fault of its incomparable site. Perched on its mountain of rock, washed by a river as free and ample as an ocean-gulf, sweeping from its embattled crest, the villages, the forests, the blue undulations of the imperial province of which it is warden—as it has managed from our scanty annals to squeeze out a past, you pray in the name of all that's majestic that it may have a future. I may add that, to the mind of the reflective visitor, these idle ramparts and silent courts present other visions than that of the mighty course of the river and its anchorage for navies. They evoke a shadowy image of that great English power, the arches of whose empire were once built strong on foreign soil; and as you stand where they are highest and look abroad upon a land of alien speech, you seem to hear the echoed names of other strongholds and provinces—Gibraltar, Malta, India. Whether these arches are crumbling now, I do not pretend to say; but the last regular troops (in number lately much diminished) are just about to be withdrawn from Quebec, and in the private circles to which I have been admitted I hear sad forebodings of what society will lose by the departure of the "military." This single word is eloquent; it reveals a social order distinctly affiliated, in spite of remoteness, to the society reproduced for the pacific American in novels in which the hero is a captain of the army or navy, and of which the scene is therefore necessarily laid in countries provided with these branches of the public service. Another opportunity for some such reflections, worthy of a historian or an essayist, as those I have hinted at, is afforded you on the Plains of Abraham, to which you probably adjourn directly from the Citadel—another, but I am bound to say, in my opinion, a less inspiring one. A battlefield remains a battlefield, whatever may be done to it; but the scene of Wolfe's victory has been profaned by the erection of a vulgar prison, and this memento of human infirmities does much to efface the meagre column which, with its neat inscription, "Here died Wolfe, victorious," stands there as a symbol of exceptional virtue.

II.

To express the historical interest of the place completely, I should dwell on the light provincial—French provincial—aspect of some of the little residential streets. Some of the houses have the staleness of complexion which Balzac loved to describe. They are chiefly built of stone or brick, with a stoutness and separateness of structure which stands in some degree in stead of architecture. I know not that, externally, they have any greater charm than that they belong to that category of dwellings which in our own cities were long since pulled down to make room for brown-stone fronts. I know not, indeed, that I can express better the picturesque merit of Quebec than by saying that it has no fronts of this luxurious and horrible substance. The greater number of houses are built of rough-hewn squares of some more vulgar mineral, painted with frank chocolate or buff, and adorned with blinds of a cruder green than we admire. As you pass the low windows of these abodes, you perceive the walls to be of extraordinary thickness; the embrasure is of great depth; Quebec was built for winter. Door-plates are frequent, and you observe that the tenants are of the Gallic persuasion. Here and there, before a door, stands a comely private equipage—a fact agreeably suggestive of a low scale of prices; for evidently in Quebec one need not be a millionaire to keep a carriage, and one may make a figure on moderate means. The great number of private carriages visible in the streets is another item, by the way, among the Europeanisms of the place; and not, as I may say, as regards the simple fact that they exist, but as regards the fact that they are considered needful for women, for young persons, for gentility. What does it do with itself, this gentility, keeping a gig or not, you wonder, as you stroll past its little multicoloured mansions. You strive almost vainly to picture the life of this French society, locked up in its small dead capital, isolated on a heedless continent, and gradually consuming its principal, as one may say—its vital stock of memories, traditions, superstitions. Its evenings must be as dull as the evenings described by Balzac in his *Vie de Province*; but has it the same ways and means of dulness? Does it play loto and "boston" in the long winter nights, and arrange marriages between its sons and daughters, whose education it has confided to abbés and abbesses? I have met in the streets here little old Frenchmen who look as if they had stepped out of Balzac—bristling with the habits of a class, wrinkled with old-world expressions. Something assures one that Quebec must be a city of gossip; for evidently it is not a city of culture. A glance at the few booksellers' windows gives evidence of this. A few Catholic statuettes and prints, two or three

Catholic publications, a festoon or so of rosaries, a volume of Lamartine, a supply of ink and matches, form the principal stock.

In the lower class of the French population there is a much livelier vitality. They are a genuine peasantry; you very soon observe it, as you drive along the pleasant country-roads. Just what it is that makes a peasantry, it is, perhaps, not easy to determine; but whatever it is, these good people have it—in their simple, unsharpened faces, in their narrow patois, in their ignorance and naïveté, and their evident good terms with the tin-spired parish church, standing there as bright and clean with ungrudged paint and varnish as a Nürnberg toy. One of them spoke to me with righteous contempt of the French of France—"They are worth nothing; they are bad Catholics." These are good Catholics, and I doubt whether anywhere Catholicism wears a brighter face and maintains more docility at the cost of less misery. It is, perhaps, not Longfellow's *Evangeline* for chapter and verse, but it is a tolerable prose transcript. There is no visible squalor, there are no rags and no curses, but there is a most agreeable tinge of gentleness, thrift, and piety. I am assured that the country-people are in the last degree mild and peaceable; surely, such neatness and thrift, without the irritability of the French genius—it is true the genius too is absent—is a very pleasant type of character. Without being ready to proclaim, with an enthusiastic friend, that the roadside scenery is more French than France, I may say that, in its way, it is quite as picturesque as anything within the city. There is an air of completeness and maturity in the landscape which suggests an old country. The roads, to begin with, are decidedly better than our own, and the cottages and farmhouses would need only a bit of thatch and a few red tiles here and there to enable them to figure creditably by the waysides of Normandy or Brittany. The road to Montmorency, on which tourists most congregate, is also, I think, the prettiest. The rows of poplars, the heavy stone cottages, seamed and cracked with time, in many cases, and daubed in coarse, bright hues, the little bourgeois villas, rising middle-aged at the end of short vistas, the sun-burnt women in the fields, the old men in woollen stockings and red nightcaps, the long-kirtled curé nodding to doffed hats, the more or less bovine stare which greets you from cottage-doors, are all so many touches of a local colour reflected from over the sea. What especially strikes one, however, is the peculiar tone of the light and the atmospheric effects—the chilly whites and grays, the steely reflections, the melancholy brightness of a frigid zone. Winter here gives a stamp to the year, and seems to leave even through spring and summer a kind of scintillating trail of his presence. To me, I confess it is terrible, and I fancy I see constantly in the brilliant sky the hoary genius of the climate brooding grimly over his dominion.

The falls of Montmorency, which you reach by the pleasant avenue I speak of, are great, I believe, among the falls of the earth. They are certainly very fine, even in the attenuated shape to which they are reduced at the present season. I doubt whether you obtain anywhere in simpler and more powerful form the very essence of a cataract—the wild, fierce, suicidal plunge of a living, sounding flood. A little platform, lodged in the cliff, enables you to contemplate it with almost shameful convenience; here you may stand at your leisure and spin analogies, more or less striking, on the very edge of the white abyss. The leap of the water begins directly at your feet, and your eye trifles dizzily with the long, perpendicular shaft of foam, and tries, in the eternal crash, to effect some vague notation of its successive stages of sound and fury; but the vaporous sheet, for ever dropping, lapses from beneath the eye, and leaves the vision distracted in mid-space; and the vision, in search of a resting-place, sinks in a flurry to the infamous saw-mill which defaces the very base of the torrent. The falls of Montmorency are obviously one of the greatest of the beauties of nature; but I hope it is not beside the mark to say that of all the beauties of nature, "falls" are to me the least satisfying. A mountain, a precipice, a river, a forest, a plain, I can enjoy at my ease; they are natural, normal, self-assured; they make no appeal; they imply no human admiration, no petty human cranings and shrinkings, head-swimmings and similes. A cataract, of course, is essentially violent. You are certain, moreover, to have to approach it through a turnstile, and to enjoy it from some terribly cockneyfied little booth. The spectacle at Montmorency appears to be the private property of a negro innkeeper, who "runs" it evidently with great pecuniary profit. A day or two since I went so far as to be glad to leave it behind, and drive some five miles farther along the road, to a village rejoicing in the pretty name of Château-Richer. The village is so pretty that you count on finding there the elderly manor which might have baptized it. But, of course, in such pictorial efforts as this Quebec breaks down; one must not ask too much of it. You enjoy from here, however, a revelation of the noble position of the city. The river, finding room in mid-stream for the long island of Orleans, opens out below you with a peculiar freedom and serenity, and leads the eye far down to where an azure mountain gazes up the channel and responds to the dark headland of Quebec. I noted, here and there, as I went, an extremely sketchable effect. Between the road and the river stand a succession of ancient peasant-dwellings, with their back-windows looking toward the stream. Glancing, as I passed, into the apertures that face the road, I saw, as through a picture-frame, their dark, rich-toned interiors, played into by the late river light and making an admirable series of mellow *tableaux de genre*. The little curtained alcoves, the big household beds, and presses, and dressers, the black-mouthed chimney-pieces, the crucifixes, the old women at their spinning-wheels, the little heads at the supper-table, around the big French loaf, outlined with a rim of light, were all as warmly, as richly composed, as French, as Dutch, as worthy of the brush, as anything in the countries to which artists resort for subjects.

I suppose no patriotic American can look at all these things, however idly, without reflecting on the ultimate possibility of their becoming absorbed into his own huge state. Whenever, sooner or later, the change is wrought, the sentimental tourist will keenly feel that a long stride has been taken, roughshod, from the past to the present. The largest appetite in modern civilisation will have swallowed the largest morsel. What the change may bring of comfort or of grief to the Canadians themselves, will be for them to say; but, in the breast of this sentimental tourist of ours, it will produce little but regret. The foreign elements of eastern Canada, at least, are extremely interesting; and it is of good profit to us Americans to have near us, and of easy access, an ample something which is not our expansive selves. Here we find a hundred mementoes of an older civilisation than our town, of different manners, of social forces once mighty, and still glowing with a sort of autumnal warmth. The old-world needs which created the dark-walled cities of France and Italy seem to reverberate faintly in the steep and narrow and Catholic streets of Quebec. The little houses speak to the fancy by rather inexpensive arts; the ramparts are endued with a sort of silvery innocence; but the historic sense, conscious of a general solidarity in the picturesque, ekes out the romance and deepens the colouring.

1871

Niagara

M Y JOURNEY hitherward by a morning's sail from To-
ronto across Lake Ontario, seemed to me, as regards a
certain dull vacuity in this episode of travel, a kind of calculated preparation for the uproar of Niagara—a pause or hush
on the threshold of a great impression; and this, too, in spite
of the reverent attention I was mindful to bestow on the first
seen, in my experience, of the great lakes. It has the merit,
from the shore, of producing a slight ambiguity of vision. It is
the sea, and yet just not the sea. The huge expanse, the land-
less line of the horizon, suggest the ocean; while an indefinable shortness of pulse, a kind of fresh-water gentleness of
tone, seem to contradict the idea. What meets the eye is on
the scale of the ocean, but you feel somehow that the lake is a
thing of smaller spirit. Lake-navigation, therefore, seems to
me not especially entertaining. The scene tends to offer, as
one may say, a sort of marine-effect missed. It has the blankness and vacancy of the sea, without that vast essential swell
which, amid the belting brine, so often saves the situation to
the eye. I was occupied, as we crossed, in wondering whether
this dull reduction of the main contained that which could
properly be termed "scenery." At the mouth of the Niagara
River, however, after a sail of three hours, scenery really begins, and very soon crowds upon you in force. The steamer
puts into the narrow channel of the stream, and heads upward
between high embankments. From this point, I think, you
really enter into relations with Niagara. Little by little the elements become a picture, rich with the shadow of coming
events. You have a foretaste of the great spectacle of colour
which you enjoy at the Falls. The even cliffs of red-brown
earth are crusted and spotted with autumnal orange and crimson, and, laden with this gorgeous decay, they plunge sheer
into the deep-dyed green of the river. As you proceed, the
river begins to tell its tale—at first in broken syllables of foam
and flurry, and then, as it were, in rushing, flashing sentences
and passionate ejaculations. Onwards from Lewiston, where
you are transferred from the boat to the train, you see it from

the edge of the American cliff, far beneath you, now superbly unnavigable. You have a lively sense of something happening ahead; the river, as a man near me said, has evidently been in a row. The cliffs here are immense; they form a *vomitorium* worthy of the living floods whose exit they protect. This is the first act of the drama of Niagara; for it is, I believe, one of the commonplaces of description that you instinctively convert it into a series of "situations." At the station pertaining to the railway suspension-bridge, you see in mid-air, beyond an interval of murky confusion produced at once by the farther bridge, the smoke of the trains, and the thickened atmosphere of the peopled bank, a huge far-flashing sheet which glares through the distance as a monstrous absorbent and irradiant of light. And here, in the interest of the picturesque, let me note that this obstructive bridge tends in a way to enhance the first glimpse of the cataract. Its long black span, falling dead along the shining brow of the Falls, seems shivered and smitten by their fierce effulgence, and trembles across the field of vision like some enormous mote in a light too brilliant. A moment later, as the train proceeds, you plunge into the village, and the cataract, save as a vague ground-tone to this trivial interlude, is, like so many other goals of æsthetic pilgrimage, temporarily postponed to the hotel.

With this postponement comes, I think, an immediate decline of expectation; for there is every appearance that the spectacle you have come so far to see is to be choked in the horribly vulgar shops and booths and catchpenny artifices which have pushed and elbowed to within the very spray of the Falls, and ply their importunities in shrill competition with its thunder. You see a multitude of hotels and taverns and stores, glaring with white paint, bedizened with placards and advertisements, and decorated by groups of those gentlemen who flourish most rankly on the soil of New York and in the vicinage of hotels; who carry their hands in their pockets, wear their hats always and every way, and, although of a stationary habit, yet spurn the earth with their heels. A sideglimpse of the Falls, however, calls out your philosophy; you reflect that this may be regarded as one of those sordid foregrounds which Turner liked to use, and which may be effective as a foil; you hurry to where the roar grows louder, and,

I was going to say, you escape from the village. In fact, however, you don't escape from it; it is constantly at your elbow, just to the right or the left of the line of contemplation. It would be paying Niagara a poor compliment to say that, practically, she does not hurl away this chaffering by-play from her edge; but as you value the integrity of your impression, you are bound to affirm that it suffers appreciable abatement from such sources. You wonder, as you stroll about, whether it is altogether an unrighteous dream that with the slow progress of taste and the possible or impossible growth of some larger comprehension of beauty and fitness, the public conscience may not tend to confer upon such sovereign phases of nature something of the inviolability and privacy which we are slow to bestow, indeed, upon fame, but which we do not grudge at least to art. We place a great picture, a great statue, in a museum: we erect a great monument in the centre of our largest square, and if we can suppose ourselves nowadays to build a cathedral, we should certainly isolate it as much as possible and expose it to no ignoble contact. We cannot enclose Niagara with walls and a roof, nor girdle it with a palisade; but the sentimental tourist may muse upon the contingency of its being guarded by the negative homage of empty spaces and absent barracks and decent forbearance. The actual abuse of the scene belongs evidently to that immense class of iniquities which are destined to grow very much worse in order to grow a very little better. The good humour engendered by the main spectacle bids you suffer it to run its course.

Though hereabouts so much is great, distances are small, and a ramble of two or three hours enables you to gaze hither and thither from a dozen standpoints. The one you are likely to choose first is that on the Canada cliff, a little way above the suspension-bridge. The great fall faces you, enshrined in its own surging incense. The common feeling just here, I believe, is one of disappointment at its want of height; the whole thing appears to many people somewhat smaller than its fame. My own sense, I confess, was absolutely gratified from the first; and, indeed, I was not struck with anything being tall or short, but with everything being perfect. You are, moreover, at some distance, and you feel that with the lessening interval you will not be cheated of your chance to be dizzied with mere dimensions. Already you see the world-famous green, baffling painters, baffling poets shining on the lip of the precipice; the more so, of course, for the clouds of silver and snow into which it speedily resolves itself. The whole picture before you is admirably simple. The Horseshoe glares and boils and smokes from the centre to the right, drumming itself into powder and thunder; in the centre the dark pedestal of Goat Island divides the double flood; to the left booms in vaporous dimness the minor battery of the American Fall; while on a level with the eye, above the still crest of either cataract, appear the white faces of the hither-most rapids. The circle of weltering froth at the base of the Horseshoe, emerging from the dead white vapours—absolute white, as moonless midnight is absolute black—which muffle impenetrably the crash of the river upon the lower bed, melts slowly into the darker shades of green. It seems in itself a drama of thrilling interest, this blanched survival and recovery of the stream. It stretches away like a tired swimmer, strug-gling from the snowy scum and the silver drift, and passing slowly from an eddying foam-sheet, touched with green lights, to a cold, verd-antique, streaked and marbled with trails and wild arabesques of foam. This is the beginning of that air of recent distress which marks the river as you meet it at the lake. It shifts along, tremendously conscious, relieved, disengaged, knowing the worst is over, with its dignity in-jured but its volume undiminished, the most stately, the least turbid of torrents. Its movement, its sweep and stride, are as admirable as its colour, but as little as its colour to be made a matter of words. These things are but part of a spectacle in which nothing is imperfect. As you draw nearer and nearer, on the Canada cliff, to the right arm of the Horseshoe, the mass begins in all conscience to be large enough. You are able at last to stand on the very verge of the shelf from which the leap is taken, bathing your boot-toes, if you like, in the side-ooze of the glassy curve. I may say, in parenthesis, that the importunities one suffers here, amid the central din of the cataract, from hackmen and photographers and vendors of gimcracks, are simply hideous and infamous. The road is lined with little drinking-shops and ware-houses, and from these retreats their occupants dart forth upon the hapless traveller with their competitive attractions. You purchase release at last by the fury of your indifference, and stand there gazing your fill at the most beautiful object in the world.

The perfect taste of it is the great characteristic. It is not in the least monstrous; it is thoroughly artistic and, as the phrase is, thought out. In the matter of line it beats Michael Angelo. One may seem at first to say the least, but the careful observer will admit that one says the most, in saying that it *pleases*— pleases even a spectator who was not ashamed to write the other day that he didn't care for cataracts. There are, however, so many more things to say about it—its multitudinous features crowd so upon the vision as one looks—that it seems absurd to begin to analyse. The main feature, perhaps, is the incomparable loveliness of the immense line of the shelf and its lateral abutments. It neither falters, nor breaks nor stiffens, but maintains from wing to wing the lightness of its semi-circle. This perfect curve melts into the sheet that seems at once to drop from it and sustain it. The famous green loses nothing, as you may imagine, on a nearer view. A green more vividly cool and pure it is impossible to conceive. It is to the vulgar greens of earth what the blue of a summer sky is to artificial dyes, and is, in fact, as sacred, as remote, as impalpable as that. You can fancy it the parent-green, the head-spring of colour to all the verdant water-caves and all the clear, sub-fluvial haunts and bowers of naiads and mermen in all the streams of the earth. The lower half of the watery wall is shrouded in the steam of the boiling gulf—a veil never rent nor lifted. At its heart this eternal cloud seems fixed and still with excess of motion—still and intensely white; but, as it rolls and climbs against its lucent cliff, it tosses little whiffs and fumes and pants of snowy smoke, which betray the convulsions we never behold. In the middle of the curve, the depth of the recess, the converging walls are ground into a dust of foam, which rises in a tall column, and fills the upper air with its hovering drift. Its summit far overtops the crest of the cataract, and, as you look down along the rapids above, you see it hanging over the averted gulf like some far-flowing signal of danger. Of these things some vulgar verbal hint may be attempted; but what words can render the rarest charm of all—the clear-cut brow of the Fall, the very act and figure of the leap, the rounded passage of the horizontal to the perpendicular? To say it is simple is to make a phrase about it. Nothing was ever more successfully executed. It is carved as sharp as an emerald, as one must say and say again. It arrives, it pauses, it plunges; it comes and goes for ever; it melts and shifts and changes, all with the sound as of millions of bass-voices; and yet its outline never varies, never moves with a different pulse. It is as gentle as the pouring of wine from a flagon—of melody from the lip of a singer. From the little grove beside the American Fall you catch this extraordinary profile better than you are able to do at the Horseshoe. If the line of beauty had vanished from the earth elsewhere, it would survive on the brow of Niagara. It is impossible to insist too strongly on the grace of the thing, as seen from the Canada cliff. The genius who invented it was certainly the first author of the idea that order, proportion and symmetry are the conditions of perfect beauty. He applied his faith among the watching and listening forests, long before the Greeks proclaimed theirs in the measurements of the Parthenon. Even the roll of the white batteries at the base seems fixed and poised and ordered, and in the vague middle zone of difference between the flood as it falls and the mist as it rises you imagine a mystical meaning—the passage of body to soul, of matter to spirit, of human to divine.

Goat Island, of which every one has heard, is the menagerie of lions, and the spot where your single stone—or, in plain prose, your half-dollar—kills most birds. This broad insular strip, which performs the excellent office of withholding the American shore from immediate contact with the flood, has been left very much to itself, and here you may ramble, for the most part, in undiverted contemplation. The island is owned, I believe, by a family of co-heirs, who have the good taste to keep it quiet. More than once, however, as I have been told, they have been offered a "big price" for the privilege of building an hotel upon this sacred soil. They have been wise, but, after all, they are human, and the offer may be made once too often. Before this fatal day dawns, why should not the State buy up the precious acres, as California has done the Yo-Semite? It is the opinion of a sentimental tourist that no price would be too great to pay. Otherwise, the only hope for their integrity is in the possibility of a shrewd provision on the part of the gentlemen who know how to keep hotels that the music of the dinner-band would be injured by the roar of the cataract. You approach from Goat Island the left abutment of the Horseshoe. The little tower which, with the classic rainbow, figures in all "views" of the scene, is planted at a dozen feet from the shore, directly on the shoulder of the Fall. This little tower, I think, deserves a compliment. One might have said beforehand that it would never do, but, as it stands, it makes rather a good point. It serves as a unit of appreciation of the scale of things, and from its spray-blackened summit it admits you to an almost downward peep into the green gulf. More here, even, than on the Canada shore, you perceive the unlimited *wateriness* of the whole spectacle. Its liquid masses take on at moments the likeness of walls and pillars and columns, and, to present any vivid picture of them, we are compelled to talk freely of emerald and crystal, of silver and marble. But really, all the simplicity of the Falls, and half their grandeur, reside in their unmitigated fluidity, which excludes all rocky staging and earthy commixture. It is water piled on water, pinned on water, hinging and hanging on water, breaking, crashing, whitening in shocks altogether watery. And yet for all this no solid was ever so solid as that sculptured shoulder of the Horseshoe. From this little tower, or, better still, from various points farther along the island-shore, even to look is to be immersed. Before you stretches the huge expanse of the upper river, with its belittled cliffs, now mere black lines of forest, dull as with the sadness of gazing at perpetual trouble, eternal danger. Anything more horribly desolate than this boundless livid welter of the rapids it is impossible to conceive, and you very soon begin to pay it the tribute of your own suddenly-assumed suspense, in the impulse to people it with human forms. On this theme you can work out endless analogies. Yes, they are alive, every fear-blanched billow and eddy of them—alive and frenzied with the sense of their doom. They see below them that nameless pause of the arrested current, and the high-tossed drift of sound and spray which rises up lamenting, like the ghosts of their brothers who have been dashed to pieces. They shriek, they sob, they clasp their white hands and toss their long hair; they cling and clutch and wrestle, and, above all, they appear to *bite*. Especially tragical is the air they have of being forced backward, with averted faces, to their fate. Every pulse of the flood is like the grim stride of a giant, wading huge-kneed to his purpose, with the white teeth of a victim fastened in his neck. The outermost of three small islands, interconnected by short bridges, at the extremity of this shore, places one in singularly intimate relation with this portentous flurry. To say that hereabouts the water leaps and plunges and rears and dives, that its uproar makes even one's own ideas about it inaudible, and its current sweeps those ideas to perdition, is to give a very pale account of the universal agitation.

The great spectacle may be called complete only when you have gone down the river some four miles, on the American side, to the so-called rapids of the Whirlpool. Here the unhappy stream tremendously renews its anguish. Two approaches have been contrived on the cliff—one to the rapids proper, the other, farther below, to the scene of the sudden bend. The first consists of a little wooden cage, of the "elevator" pattern, which slides up and down a gigantic perpendicular shaft of horrible flimsiness. But a couple of the usual little brides, staggering beneath the weight of gorgeous cashmeres, entered the conveyance with their respective consorts at the same time with myself; and, as it thus carried Hymen and his fortunes, we survived the adventure. You obtain from below—that is, on the shore of the river—a specimen of the noblest cliff-scenery. The green embankment at the base of the sheer red wall is by itself a very fair example of what they call in the Rocky Mountains a foot-hill; and from this continuous pedestal erects itself a bristling palisade of earth. As it stands, Gustave Doré might have drawn it. He would have sketched with especial ardour certain parasitical shrubs and boskages—lone and dizzy witnesses of autumn; certain outward-peering wens and warts and other perpendicular excrescences of rock; and, above all, near the summit, the fantastic figures of sundry audacious minor cliffs, grafted upon the greater by a mere lateral attachment and based in the empty air, with great slim trees rooted on their verges, like the tower of the Palazzo Vecchio at Florence. The actual whirlpool is a third of a mile farther down the river, and is best seen from the cliff above. From this point of view, it seems to me by all odds the finest of the secondary episodes of the drama of Niagara, and one on which a scribbling tourist, ineffectively playing at showman, may be content to ring down his curtain. The channel at this point turns away to the right, at a clean right-angle, and the river, arriving from the rapids just above with stupendous velocity, meets the hollow elbow of the Canada shore. The movement with which it betrays its surprise and bewilderment—the sudden issueless maze of waters—is, I think, after the Horseshoe Fall, the very finest thing in its progress. It breaks into no small rage; the offending cliffs receive no drop of spray; for the flood moves in a body and wastes no vulgar side-spurts; but you see it shaken to its innermost bowels and panting hugely, as if smothered in its excessive volume. Pressed back upon its centre, the current creates a sort of pivot, from which it eddies, groping for exit in vast slow circles, delicately and irregularly outlined in foam. The Canada shore, shaggy and gaudy with late September foliage, closes about it like the rising shelves of an amphitheatre, and deepens by contrast the strong blue-green of the stream. This slow-revolving surface—it seems in places perfectly still—resembles nothing so much as some ancient palace-pavement, cracked and scratched by the butts of legionary spears and the gold-stiffened hem of the garments of kings.

1871

Americans Abroad

SOME WEEKS ago (No. 668) there appeared in these columns a short account of the American colony in Paris, which called forth at the time a rejoinder, and upon which it has been our fortune to hear privately a good many comments. Some of these comments have been sympathetic; others have been highly dissentient. In every case, however, there was a discussion of the question raised—a discussion which, in the circle in which it took place, could not fail to be extremely interesting. However the question raised may in any case be settled—the question of Americans appearing "to advantage" or otherwise in Europe—there is no doubt that nothing could be well more characteristic of our nationality than the sight of a group of persons more or less earnestly discussing it. We are the only people with whom such a question can be in the least what the French call an actuality. It is hard to imagine two or three Englishmen, two or three Frenchmen, two or three Germans comparing notes and strongly differing as to the impression made upon the civilized world by the collective body of their countrymen. In the first place, the Englishman or the Frenchman sees no reason to suppose that such an impression is in any way peculiar, or that one member of European society distinguishes himself noticeably from another. In the second place, if he were to be made aware that foreigners were criticising him, he would be extremely indifferent to their verdict. He would comfortably assume that the standard of manners—the shaping influences—in his own country are the highest, and that if he is a gentleman according to these canons he may go his way in peace. The season is drawing to a close during which, chiefly, Americans disseminate themselves in foreign lands, and for the last three or four months the national character has had free play in European hotels and railway stations. The impression, whatever it is, produced upon the European community must have been sensibly deepened. In spite of the commercial tribulations at home, the number of American travellers abroad has been very large, and numerous also have been the

Americans (more numerous every year) who have betaken themselves to Europe for an indefinite residence. Those observers of whom we just now spoke, who are always ready to be a party to national self-analysis, have probably, in many cases, collected some new ideas. They have encountered, for instance, a few more specimens of the unattached young American lady—the young lady travelling for culture, or relaxation, or economy—and, according to their different points of view, she has seemed to them a touching or a startling phenomenon. The writer of these lines feels that he has added to the number of his own observations; that the data upon which his general conclusions rest have been multiplied; and that, thanks to his having passed some weeks in a great city in which the American tourist is frequently met and easily recognized, he might, in such a discussion as was just now alluded to, be beguiled into giving an even indiscreet extension to remarks originally prompted simply by a friendly interest in that class of Parisians known as Americans.

Americans in Europe are *outsiders*; that is the great point, and the point thrown into relief by all zealous efforts to controvert it. As a people we are out of European society; the fact seems to us incontestable, be it regrettable or not. We are not only out of the European circle politically and geographically; we are out of it socially, and for excellent reasons. We are the only great people of the civilized world that is a pure democracy, and we are the only great people that is exclusively commercial. Add the remoteness represented by these facts to our great and painful geographical remoteness, and it will be easy to see why to be known in Europe as an American is to enjoy an imperfect reciprocity. It may be the Europeans who are the losers by this absence of reciprocity; we do not prejudge that point, and we do not know, indeed, who is to settle it. A great many Americans—by no means all—maintain that the Europeans *are* the losers, and declare that if they don't know us and don't care about us, so much the worse for them. This is in many ways a very proper and very natural attitude; but nothing can be more characteristic of our civilization than the fact that an American may be almost defied to maintain it consistently. Let him be even more patriotic than is necessary, he is constantly lapsing from it, and,

when he is in company with Europeans who do nothing to
ruffle his usually great good-nature, he constantly takes a tone
which indicates that he values their good opinion and that he
is rather flattered than otherwise by possessing it. This, however, is a matter to be discussed apart. We wish to mention
the last fact which leads Europeans to look upon Americans
as aliens—the fact that large and increasing numbers of them
elect, as the phrase is, to spend large parts of their lives in
foreign lands. When a European sees an American absentee
settle down in the country of which he himself is a native it is
not surprising that, in the face of this practical tribute, he
should be found doubting whether the country the American
has left is as agreeable, as comfortable, as civilized, as desirable a one to belong to as his own. The American may carefully explain that he is living abroad for such and such special
and limited reasons—for culture, for music, for art, for the
languages, for economy, for the education of his children; the
fact remains that in pursuit of some *agrément* or other he has
forsaken his native-land, and the European retains, ineffaceably, the impression that if America were really a pleasant
place he would never do so. He would come to travel—yes,
frequently and extensively; but he (or rather *she*, for as a general thing, in this case, that is the proper pronoun) would
never take up an abode in a strange city and remain there year
after year, looking about, rather hungrily, for social diversion
and "trying to get into society." Such a spectacle makes the
European take the American, as an American, by so much the
less *au sérieux*. An Englishman, a Frenchman, a German finds
his intellectual, his æsthetic ideal in living in his own country.
A great many Englishmen live out of England for economy; a
great many Germans emigrate to make a living. But the ideal
in each of these cases is to be rich enough to live at home; the
dream of felicity is to have a large income and spend it within
one's native borders. If we perhaps except the Russians, who
do not altogether come into our category, the Americans are
the only highly-civilized people among whom the ideal takes
another turn. It will probably never be the case that the country will lack a sufficient number of rich residents to "run" it;
but we shall probably for a long time continue to see numbers
of Americans absenting themselves from the United States in

proportion as fortune puts into their hands the means of what is called enjoying life. A great many of them prefer to enjoy life in Paris, where our correspondent who described the "colony" gave a sketch of their situation. They are naturally a puzzle to many of the people they live among, who are at a loss to imagine the compensation that Americans find in a society with which they do not amalgamate for the forfeiture of those social advantages which, as is supposed, gentlemen and ladies enjoy in their own country. The compensation that comes from shops and theatres and restaurants seems insufficient to the average European mind, preoccupied as that mind is with the belief that nothing can be so agreeable as the *life* of one's native land—the animated circle of which one is a member as a matter of course. The average European mind can never understand that for many enriched Americans life at home has never been strikingly agreeable, and that public amusements in a European capital may not unfairly be held to outweigh the social advantages relinquished even in certain capitals of States.

Curiously combined with that argumentative national self-consciousness of which we began by speaking is a profound, imperturbable, unsuspectingness on the part of many Americans of the impression they produce in foreign lands. With this state of mind it is impossible to find fault; it has always been, we suspect, the mark of great nationalities. It has become a commonplace to say that the English are conspicuous for it, and it is highly probable that the ancient Romans—the *cives Romani*—were equally so. But it may sometimes provoke a smile, when the impression produced is a good deal at variance with European circumstances. There is the conscious and the unconscious American; for we, of course, do not mean that the two characters are combined in the same individual. The conscious American is apologetic, explanatory—a pessimist might sometimes say snobbish. But perhaps, after having traversed a certain phase by a sort of Hegelian unfolding, this type is on its way to become unconscious again. Extremes meet, and that is a symptom of great experience as well as of great innocence. The great innocence of the usual American tourist is perhaps his most general quality. He takes all sorts of forms, some of them agreeable and some the reverse, and it is probably not unfair to say that by sophisticated Europeans it is harshly interpreted. They waste no time in hair-splitting; they set it down once for all as very vulgar. It may be added that there are a great many cases in which this conclusion hardly seems forced. A very large proportion of the Americans who annually scatter themselves over Europe are by no means flattering to the national vanity. Their merits, whatever they are, are not of a sort that strike the eye—still less the ear. They are ill-made, ill-mannered, ill-dressed. A very good way to get a collective impression of them is to go and sit for half an hour in the waiting-room of any European banker upon whom Americans hold letters of credit. During certain hours of the morning our compatriots swarm, getting their drafts cashed and asking for their letters—those letters which they apparently suspect the banker's clerks of a consti- tutional indisposition to surrender. The writer of these lines lately enjoyed on several occasions this opportunity of obser- vation, and—from the point of view of amenity—the specta- cle was not gratifying. *Are* we the worst-looking people in the world? the sophisticated spectator, on such an occasion, en- quires; and lest he should be beguiled into giving an answer too monstrous he abstains from giving any at all. One Amer- ican (of the "conscious" class) has a way of explaining these things—the common facial types, the vulgar manners, the "mean" voices, the want of acquaintance with the rudiments of the science of dress—to another. He says that in America "every one travels," and that the people at the bankers are much better than the corresponding class in Europe, who lan- guish in downtrodden bondage and never have even a chance to show themselves to the world. The explanation is highly sufficient, for it is very certain that for many Americans a journey to Europe is the reward of a period of sordid toil. An American may take great satisfaction in this circumstance; he may be proud of belonging to a country in which the advan- tages of foreign travel are open to all, irrespective of "social standing"; instead of being, as in Europe (according, at least, to his theory), only within the reach of the luxurious and the privileged. But the European only perceives that a great many American travellers are remarkably "rough," and quite fails to congratulate either his own country or theirs upon possessing them. The people in question neither know nor care what he thinks about them, and, having examined the antiquities of the Old World, they go westward across the Atlantic with a perfectly good conscience. The European critic, however, sometimes opens himself with striking candor to an American of the introspective class. It is a hundred to one that his tone is patronizing; but there are degrees of patronage. If it is grossly patronizing the American is offended, and invites him to keep his approbation for himself; but if it is subtly patronizing the American listens to it with a complacency decidedly at variance with the theory of his more exalted hours—the theory of the sufficiency of the great Republic in every way to itself.

It may be that we shall some day become sufficient to ourselves and lose the sense of being the most youthful, most experimental, and, somehow, most irregular of the nations. But until that time comes some of us may occasionally be caught listening without protest to compliments paid us at the expense of some others. It is only just to say, however, that the American in Europe often enters into what we have called the conscious phase by a great deal of irritation. He finds Europeans very ignorant of a country, very indifferent to a country which, in spite of irregularities, he may be pardoned for thinking a magnificent one. A few Englishmen and Germans know a good deal about the United States—a good deal more than most Americans do; but it is hardly too much to say that as a general thing, as regards this subject, the European mind is a perfect blank. A great many Americans are very ignorant of Europe, but in default of knowledge it may be said that they have a certain amount of imagination. In respect to the United States the European imagination is motionless; and it may well seem to an American that there is something ridiculous in a scheme of the universe which leaves out a country as large as an aggregation of European kingdoms. There are many anomalies and crookednesses in the lot of the conscious American, and not the least of them is the fact that the country on whose behalf he is expected to be humble and patient—to wait for further results and withhold inopportune boasts—is an affair which, at times and in certain lights, seems to make this sweet reasonableness an affectation. It is comparatively easy to confess yourself a provincial if you really come from a province; but if you have been brought up among "big things" of every kind the admission requires an effort. On the whole, the American in Europe may be spoken of as a provincial who is terribly bent upon taking, in the fulness of ages, his revenge.

1878

Chronology

1843   Born April 15 at 21 Washington Place, New York City, the second child (after William, born January 11, 1842, N.Y.C.) of Henry James of Albany and Mary Robertson Walsh of New York. Father lives on inheritance of $10,000 a year, his share of litigated $3,000,000 fortune of his Albany father, William James, an Irish immigrant who came to the U.S. immediately after the Revolution.

1843–45 Accompanied by mother's sister, Catharine Walsh, and servants, the James parents take infant children to England and later to France. Reside at Windsor, where father has nervous collapse ("vastation") and experiences spiritual illumination. He becomes a Swedenborgian (May 1844), devoting his time to lecturing and religious-philosophical writings. James later claimed his earliest memory was a glimpse, during his second year, of the Place Vendôme in Paris with its Napoleonic column.

1845–47 Family returns to New York. Garth Wilkinson James (Wilky) born July 21, 1845. Family moves to Albany at 50 N. Pearl St., a few doors from grandmother Catharine Barber James. Robertson James (Bob or Rob) born August 29, 1846.

1847–55 Family moves to a large house at 58 W. 14th St., New York. Alice James born August 7, 1848. Relatives and father's friends and acquaintances—Horace Greeley, George Ripley, Charles Anderson Dana, William Cullen Bryant, Bronson Alcott, and Ralph Waldo Emerson ("I knew he was great, greater than any of our friends")—are frequent visitors. Thackeray calls during his lecture tour on the English humorists. Summers at New Brighton on Staten Island and Fort Hamilton on Long Island's south shore. On steamboat to Fort Hamilton August 1850, hears Washington Irving tell his father of Margaret Fuller's drowning in shipwreck off Fire Island. Frequently visits Barnum's American Museum on free days. Taken to art shows and theaters; writes and draws stage scenes. Described by father as "a devourer of libraries." Taught in assorted private schools and by tutors in lower Broadway and Greenwich Village. But father claims in 1848 that American schooling fails to provide "sensuous education" for his children and plans to take them to Europe.

1855–58   Family (with Aunt Kate) sails for Liverpool, June 27. James is intermittently sick with malarial fever as they travel to Paris, Lyon, and Geneva. After Swiss summer, leaves for London where Robert Thomson (later Robert Louis Stevenson's tutor) is engaged. Early summer 1856, family moves to Paris. Another tutor engaged and children attend experimental Fourierist school. Acquires fluency in French. Family goes to Boulogne-sur-mer in summer, where James contracts typhoid. Spends late October in Paris, but American crash of 1857 returns family to Boulogne where they can live more cheaply. Attends public school (fellow classmate is Coquelin, the future French actor).

1858–59   Family returns to America and settles in Newport, Rhode Island. Goes boating, fishing, and riding. Attends the Reverend W. C. Leverett's Berkeley Institute, and forms friendship with classmate Thomas Sergeant Perry. Takes long walks and sketches with the painter John La Farge.

1859–60   Father, still dissatisfied with American education, returns family to Geneva in October. James attends a pre-engineering school, Institution Rochette, because parents, with "a flattering misconception of my aptitudes," feel he might benefit from less reading and more mathematics. After a few months withdraws from all classes except French, German, and Latin, and joins William as a special student at the Academy (later the University of Geneva) where he attends lectures on literary subjects. Studies German in Bonn during summer 1860.

1860–62   Family returns to Newport in September where William studies with William Morris Hunt, and James sits in on his classes. La Farge introduces him to works of Balzac, Merimée, Musset, and Browning. Wilky and Bob attend Frank Sanborn's experimental school in Concord with children of Hawthorne and Emerson and John Brown's daughter. Early in 1861, orphaned Temple cousins come to live in Newport. Develops close friendship with cousin

Mary (Minnie) Temple. Goes on a week's walking tour in July in New Hampshire with Perry. William abandons art in autumn 1861 and enters Lawrence Scientific School at Harvard. James suffers back injury in a stable fire while serving as a volunteer fireman. Reads Hawthorne ("an American could be an artist, one of the finest").

1862–63   Enters Harvard Law School (Dane Hall). Wilky enlists in the Massachusetts 44th Regiment, and later in Colonel Robert Gould Shaw's 54th, one of the first black regiments. Summer 1863, Bob joins the Massachusetts 55th, another black regiment, under Colonel Hollowell. James withdraws from law studies to try writing. Sends unsigned stories to magazines. Wilky is badly wounded and brought home to Newport in August.

1864   Family moves from Newport to 13 Ashburton Place, Boston. First tale, "A Tragedy of Error" (unsigned), published in *Continental Monthly* (Feb. 1864). Stays in Northampton, Massachusetts, early August–November. Begins writing book reviews for *North American Review* and forms friendship with its editor, Charles Eliot Norton, and his family, including his sister Grace (with whom he maintains a long-lasting correspondence). Wilky returns to his regiment.

1865   First signed tale, "The Story of a Year," published in *Atlantic Monthly* (March 1865). Begins to write reviews for the newly founded *Nation* and publishes anonymously in it during next fifteen years. William sails on a scientific expedition with Louis Agassiz to the Amazon. During summer James vacations in the White Mountains with Minnie Temple and her family; joined by Oliver Wendell Holmes Jr. and John Chipman Gray, both recently demobilized. Father subsidizes plantation for Wilky and Bob in Florida with black hired workers. (The idealistic but impractical venture fails in 1870.)

1866–68   Continues to publish reviews and tales in Boston and New York journals. William returns from Brazil and resumes medical education. James has recurrence of back ailment and spends summer in Swampscott, Massachusetts. Begins friendship with William Dean Howells. Family moves to 20 Quincy St., Cambridge. William, suffering from nervous ailments, goes to Germany in spring 1867. "Poor Richard," James's longest story to date, published in *Atlantic Monthly* (June–Aug. 1867). William begins intermittent criticism of Henry's story-telling and style (which will continue throughout their careers). Momentary meeting with Charles Dickens at Norton's house. Vacations in Jefferson, New Hampshire, summer 1868. William returns from Europe.

1869–70   Sails in February for European tour. Visits English towns and cathedrals. Through Nortons meets Leslie Stephen, William Morris, Dante Gabriel Rossetti, Edward Burne-Jones, John Ruskin, Charles Darwin, and George Eliot (the "one marvel" of his stay in London). Goes to Paris in May, then travels in Switzerland in summer and hikes into Italy in autumn, where he stays in Milan, Venice (Sept.), Florence, and Rome (Oct. 30–Dec. 28). Returns to England to drink the waters at Malvern health spa in Worcestershire because of digestive troubles. Stays in Paris en route and has first experience of Comédie Française. Learns that his beloved cousin, Minnie Temple, has died of tuberculosis.

1870–72   Returns to Cambridge in May. Travels to Rhode Island, Vermont, and New York to write travel sketches for *The Nation*. Spends a few days with Emerson in Concord. Meets Bret Harte at Howells' home April 1871. *Watch and Ward*, his first novel, published in *Atlantic Monthly* (Aug.–Dec. 1871). Serves as occasional art reviewer for the *Atlantic* January–March 1872.

1872–74   Accompanies Aunt Kate and sister Alice on tour of England, France, Switzerland, Italy, Austria, and Germany from May through October. Writes travel sketches for *The Nation*. Spends autumn in Paris, becoming friends with James Russell Lowell. Escorts Emerson through the Louvre. (Later, on Emerson's return from Egypt, will show him the Vatican.) Goes to Florence in December and from there to Rome, where he becomes friends with actress Fanny Kemble, her daughter Sarah Butler Wister, and William Wetmore Story and his family. In Italy sees old family friend Francis Boott and his daughter Elizabeth (Lizzie), expatriates who have lived for many years in Florentine villa on Bellosguardo. Takes up horseback riding on the Campagna. Encounters Matthew Arnold in April 1873 at Story's. Moves from Rome hotel to rooms of his own. Continues writing and now earns enough to support himself. Leaves Rome in June, spends summer in Bad Homburg. In October goes to Florence, where William joins him. They also visit Rome, William returning to America in March. In Baden-Baden June–August and returns to America September 4, with *Roderick Hudson* all but finished.

1875　　*Roderick Hudson* serialized in *Atlantic Monthly* from January (published by Osgood at the end of the year). First book, *A Passionate Pilgrim and Other Tales*, published January 31. Tries living and writing in New York, in rooms at 111 E. 25th Street. Earns $200 a month from novel installments and continued reviewing, but finds New York too expensive. *Transatlantic Sketches*, published in April, sells almost 1,000 copies in three months. In Cambridge in July decides to return to Europe; arranges with John Hay, assistant to the publisher, to write Paris letters for the *New York Tribune*.

1875–76　Arriving in Paris in November, he takes rooms at 29 Rue de Luxembourg (since renamed Cambon). Becomes friend of Ivan Turgenev and is introduced by him to Gustave Flaubert's Sunday parties. Meets Edmond de Goncourt, Émile Zola, G. Charpentier (the publisher), Catulle Mendès, Alphonse Daudet, Guy de Maupassant, Ernest Renan, Gustave Doré. Makes friends with Charles Sanders Peirce, who is in Paris. Reviews (unfavorably) the early Impressionists at the Durand-Ruel gallery. By midsummer has received $400 for *Tribune* pieces, but editor asks for more Parisian gossip and James resigns. Travels in France during July, visiting Normandy and the Midi, and in September crosses to San Sebastian, Spain, to see a bullfight ("I thought the bull, in any case, a finer fellow than any of his tormentors"). Moves to London in December, taking rooms at 3 Bolton Street, Piccadilly, where he will live for the next decade.

1877　　*The American* published. Meets Robert Browning and George du Maurier. Leaves London in midsummer for visit to Paris and then goes to Italy. In Rome rides again in Campagna and hears of an episode that inspires "Daisy

Miller." Back in England, spends Christmas at Stratford
with Fanny Kemble.

1878   Publishes first book in England, *French Poets and Novelists*
(Macmillan). Appearance of "Daisy Miller" in *Cornhill
Magazine*, edited by Leslie Stephen, is international success, but by publishing it abroad loses American copyright
and story is pirated in U.S. *Cornhill* also prints "An International Episode." *The Europeans* is serialized in *Atlantic*.
Now a celebrity, he dines out often, visits country houses,
gains weight, takes long walks, fences, and does weight-
lifting to reduce. Elected to Reform Club. Meets Tennyson, George Meredith, and James McNeill Whistler. William marries Alice Howe Gibbens.

1879   Immersed in London society (". . . dined out during the
past winter 107 times!"). Meets Edmund Gosse and
Robert Louis Stevenson, who will later become his close
friends. Sees much of Henry Adams and his wife, Marian
(Clover), in London and later in Paris. Takes rooms in
Paris, September–December. *Confidence* is serialized in
Scribner's and published by Chatto & Windus. *Hawthorne*
appears in Macmillan's "English Men of Letters" series.

1880–81   Stays in Florence March–May to work on *The Portrait of
a Lady*. Meets Constance Fenimore Woolson, American
novelist and grandniece of James Fenimore Cooper. Returns to Bolton Street in June, where William visits him.
Washington Square serialized in *Cornhill Magazine* and
published in U.S. by Harper & Brothers (Dec. 1880). *The
Portrait of a Lady* serialized in *Macmillan's Magazine* (Oct.
1880–Nov. 1881) and *Atlantic Monthly*; published by Macmillan and Houghton, Mifflin (Nov. 1881). Publication
both in United States and in England yields him the then-
large income of $500 a month, though book sales are dis-
appointing. Leaves London in February for Paris, the
south of France, the Italian Riviera, and Venice, and returns home in July. Sister Alice comes to London with
her friend Katharine Loring. James goes to Scotland in
September.

1881–83   In November revisits America after absence of six years.
Lionized in New York. Returns to Quincy Street for
Christmas and sees ailing brother Wilky for the first time

in ten years. In January visits Washington and the Henry
Adamses and meets President Chester A. Arthur. Summoned to Cambridge by mother's death January 29 ("the
sweetest, gentlest, most beneficent human being I have
ever known"). All four brothers are together for the first
time in fifteen years at her funeral. Alice and father move
from Cambridge to Boston. Prepares a stage version of
"Daisy Miller" and returns to England in May. William,
now a Harvard professor, comes to Europe in September.
Proposed by Leslie Stephen, James becomes member,
without the usual red tape, of the Atheneum Club. Travels
in France in October to write *A Little Tour in France*
(published 1884) and has last visit with Turgenev, who is
dying. Returns to England in December and learns of
father's illness. Sails for America but Henry James Sr. dies
December 18, 1882, before his arrival. Made executor of
father's will. Visits brothers Wilky and Bob in Milwaukee
in January. Quarrels with William over division of property—James wants to restore Wilky's share. Macmillan
publishes a collected pocket edition of James's novels and
tales in fourteen volumes. *Siege of London* and *Portraits of
Places* published. Returns to Bolton Street in September.
Wilky dies in November. Constance Fenimore Woolson
comes to London for the winter.

1884–86   Goes to Paris in February and visits Daudet, Zola, and
Goncourt. Again impressed with their intense concern
with "art, form, manner" but calls them "mandarins."
Misses Turgenev, who had died a few months before.
Meets John Singer Sargent and persuades him to settle in
London. Returns to Bolton Street. Sargent introduces
him to young Paul Bourget. During country visits encounters many British political and social figures, including W. E. Gladstone, John Bright, and Charles Dilke.
Alice, suffering from nervous ailment, arrives in England
for visit in November but is too ill to travel and settles
near her brother. *Tales of Three Cities* ("The Impressions
of a Cousin," "Lady Barbarina," "A New England Winter") and "The Art of Fiction" published 1884. Alice goes
to Bournemouth in late January. James joins her in May
and becomes an intimate of Robert Louis Stevenson, who
resides nearby. Spends August at Dover and is visited by
Paul Bourget. Stays in Paris for the next two months.
Moves into a flat at 34 De Vere Gardens in Kensington

early in March 1886. Alice takes rooms in London. *The Bostonians* serialized in *Century* (Feb. 1885–Feb. 1886; published 1886), *The Princess Casamassima* serialized in *Atlantic Monthly* (Sept. 1885–Oct. 1886; published 1886).

1886–87   Leaves for Italy in December for extended stay, mainly in Florence and Venice. Sees much of Constance Fenimore Woolson and stays in her villa. Writes "The Aspern Papers" and other tales. Returns to De Vere Gardens in July and begins work on *The Tragic Muse*. Pays several country visits. Dines out less often ("I know it all—all that one sees by 'going out'—today, as if I had made it. But if I had, I would have made it better!").

1888   *The Reverberator*, *The Aspern Papers*, *Louisa Pallant*, *The Modern Warning*, and *Partial Portraits* published. Elizabeth Boott Duveneck dies. Robert Louis Stevenson leaves for the South Seas. Engages fencing teacher to combat "symptoms of a portentous corpulence." Goes abroad in October to Geneva (where he visits Woolson), Genoa, Monte Carlo, and Paris.

1889–90   Catharine Walsh (Aunt Kate) dies March 1889. William comes to England to visit Alice in August. James goes to Dover in September and then to Paris for five weeks. Writes account of Robert Browning's funeral in Westminster Abbey. Dramatizes *The American* for the Compton Comedy Company. Meets and becomes close friends with American journalist William Morton Fullerton and young American publisher Wolcott Balestier. Goes to Italy for the summer, staying in Venice and Florence, and takes a brief walking tour in Tuscany with W. W. Baldwin, an American physician practicing in Florence. Miss Woolson moves to Cheltenham, England, to be near James. *Atlantic Monthly* rejects his story "The Pupil," but it appears in England. Writes series of drawing-room comedies for theater. Meets Rudyard Kipling. *The Tragic Muse* serialized in *Atlantic Monthly* (Jan. 1889–May 1890; published 1890). *A London Life* (including "The Patagonia," "The Liar," "Mrs. Temperly") published 1889.

1891   *The American* produced at Southport is a success during road tour. After residence in Leamington, Alice returns to London, cared for by Katharine Loring. Doctors discover she has breast cancer. James circulates comedies (*Mrs. Vibert*, later called *Tenants*, and *Mrs. Jasper*, later named *Disengaged*) among theater managers who are cool to his work. Unimpressed at first by Ibsen, writes an appreciative review after seeing a performance of *Hedda Gabler* with Elizabeth Robins, a young Kentucky actress; persuades her to take the part of Mme. de Cintré in the London production of *The American*. Recuperates from flu in Ireland. James Russell Lowell dies. *The American* opens in London, September 26, and runs for seventy nights. Wolcott Balestier dies, and James attends his funeral in Dresden in December.

1892   Alice James dies March 6. James travels to Siena to be near the Paul Bourgets, and Venice, June–July, to visit the Daniel Curtises, then to Lausanne to meet William and his family, who have come abroad for sabbatical. Attends funeral of Tennyson at Westminster Abbey. Augustin Daly agrees to produce *Mrs. Jasper*. *The American* continues to be performed on the road by the Compton Company. *The Lesson of the Master* (with a collection of stories including "The Marriages," "The Pupil," "Brooksmith," "The Solution," and "Sir Edmund Orme") published.

1893   Fanny Kemble dies in January. Continues to write unproduced plays. In March goes to Paris for two months. Sends Edward Compton first act and scenario for *Guy Domville*. Meets William and family in Lucerne and stays a month, returning to London in June. Spends July completing *Guy Domville* in Ramsgate. George Alexander, actor-manager, agrees to produce the play. Daly stages first reading of *Mrs. Jasper*, and James withdraws it, calling the rehearsal a mockery. *The Real Thing and Other Tales* (including "The Wheel of Time," "Lord Beaupré," "The Visit") published.

1894   Constance Fenimore Woolson dies in Venice, January. Shocked and upset, James prepares to attend funeral in Rome but changes his mind on learning she is a suicide. Goes to Venice in April to help her family settle her affairs. Receives one of four copies, privately printed by Miss Loring, of Alice's diary. Finds it impressive but is concerned that so much gossip he told Alice in private has been included (later burns his copy). Robert Louis Stevenson dies in the South Pacific. *Guy Domville* goes into rehearsal. *Theatricals: Two Comedies* and *Theatricals: Second Series* published.

1895   *Guy Domville* opens January 5 at St. James's Theatre. At play's end James is greeted by a fifteen-minute roar of boos, catcalls, and applause. Horrified and depressed, abandons the theater. Play earns him $1,300 after five-week run. Feels he can salvage something useful from playwriting for his fiction ("a key that, working in the same *general* way fits the complicated chambers of *both* the dramatic and the narrative lock"). Writes scenario for *The Spoils of Poynton*. Visits Lord Wolseley and Lord Houghton in Ireland. In the summer goes to Torquay in Devonshire and stays until November while electricity is being installed in De Vere Gardens flat. Friendship with W. E. Norris, who resides at Torquay. Writes a one-act play ("Mrs. Gracedew") at request of Ellen Terry. *Terminations* (containing "The Death of the Lion," "The Coxon Fund," "The Middle Years," "The Altar of the Dead") published.

1896–97   Finishes *The Spoils of Poynton* (serialized in *Atlantic Monthly* April–Oct. 1896 as *The Old Things*; published 1897). *Embarrassments* ("The Figure in the Carpet," "Glasses," "The Next Time," "The Way It Came") published. Takes a house on Point Hill, Playden, opposite the old town of Rye, Sussex, August–September. Ford Madox Hueffer (later Ford Madox Ford) visits him. Converts play *The Other House* into novel and works on *What Maisie Knew* (published Sept. 1897). George du Maurier dies early in October. Because of increasing pain in wrist, hires stenographer William MacAlpine in February and then purchases a typewriter; soon begins direct dictation to MacAlpine at the machine. Invites Joseph Conrad to lunch at De Vere Gardens and begins their friendship. Goes to Bournemouth in July. Serves on jury in London before going to Dunwich, Suffolk, to spend time with Temple-Emmet cousins. In late September 1897 signs a twenty-one-year lease for Lamb House in Rye for £70 a year ($350). Takes on extra work to pay for setting up his house—the life of William Wetmore Story ($1,250 advance) and will furnish an "American Letter" for new magazine *Literature* (precursor of *Times Literary Supplement*) for $200 a month. Howells visits.

1898	"The Turn of the Screw" (serialized in *Collier's* Jan.–April; published with "Covering End" under the title *The Two Magics*) proves his most popular work since "Daisy Miller." Sleeps in Lamb House for first time June 28. Soon after is visited by William's son, Henry James Jr. (Harry), followed by a stream of visitors: future Justice Oliver Wendell Holmes, Mrs. J. T. Fields, Sarah Orne Jewett, the Paul Bourgets, the Edward Warrens, the Daniel Curtises, the Edmund Gosses, and Howard Sturgis. His witty friend Jonathan Sturges, a young, crippled New Yorker, stays for two months during autumn. *In the Cage* published. Meets neighbors Stephen Crane and H. G. Wells.
1899	Finishes *The Awkward Age* and plans trip to the Continent. Fire in Lamb House delays departure. To Paris in March and then visits the Paul Bourgets at Hyères. Stays with the Curtises in their Venice palazzo, where he meets and becomes friends with Jessie Allen. In Rome meets young American-Norwegian sculptor Hendrik C. Andersen; buys one of his busts. Returns to England in July and Andersen comes for three days in August. William, his wife, Alice, and daughter, Peggy, arrive at Lamb House in October. First meeting of brothers in six years. William now has confirmed heart condition. James B. Pinker becomes literary agent and for first time James's professional relations are systematically organized; he reviews copyrights, finds new publishers, and obtains better prices for work ("the germ of a new career"). Purchases Lamb House for $10,000 with an easy mortgage.
1900	Unhappy at whiteness of beard which he has worn since the Civil War, he shaves it off. Alternates between Rye and London. Works on *The Sacred Fount*. Works on and then sets aside *The Sense of the Past* (never finished). Begins *The Ambassadors*. *The Soft Side*, a collection of twelve tales, published. Niece Peggy comes to Lamb House for Christmas.
1901	Obtains permanent room at the Reform Club for London visits and spends eight weeks in town. Sees funeral of Queen Victoria. Decides to employ a typist, Mary Weld, to replace the more expensive overqualified shorthand stenographer, MacAlpine. Completes *The Ambassadors* and begins *The Wings of the Dove*. *The Sacred Fount* published.

Has meeting with George Gissing. William James, much improved, returns home after two years in Europe. Young Cambridge admirer Percy Lubbock visits. Discharges his alcoholic servants of sixteen years (the Smiths). Mrs. Paddington is new housekeeper.

1902   In London for the winter but gout and stomach disorder force him home earlier. Finishes *The Wings of the Dove* (published in August). William James Jr. (Billy) visits in October and becomes a favorite nephew. Writes "The Beast in the Jungle" and "The Birthplace."

1903   *The Ambassadors, The Better Sort* (a collection of twelve tales), and *William Wetmore Story and His Friends* published. After another spell in town, returns to Lamb House in May and begins work on *The Golden Bowl*. Meets and establishes close friendship with Dudley Jocelyn Persse, a nephew of Lady Gregory. First meeting with Edith Wharton in December.

1904–05 Completes *The Golden Bowl* (published Nov. 1904). Rents Lamb House for six months, and sails in August for America after twenty-year absence. Sees new Manhattan skyline from New Jersey on arrival and stays with Colonel George Harvey, president of Harper's, in Jersey shore house with Mark Twain as fellow guest. Goes to William's country house at Chocorua in the White Mountains, New Hampshire. Re-explores Cambridge, Boston, Salem, Newport, and Concord, where he visits brother Bob. In October stays with Edith Wharton in the Berkshires and motors with her through Massachusetts and New York. Later visits New York, Philadelphia (where he delivers lecture "The Lesson of Balzac"), and then Washington, D.C., as a guest in Henry Adams' house. Meets (and is critical of) President Theodore Roosevelt. Returns to Philadelphia to lecture at Bryn Mawr. Travels to Richmond, Charleston, Jacksonville, Palm Beach, and St. Augustine. Then lectures in St. Louis, Chicago, South Bend, Indianapolis, Los Angeles (with a short vacation at Coronado Beach near San Diego), San Francisco, Portland, and Seattle. Returns to explore New York City ("the terrible town"), May–June. Lectures on "The Question of Our Speech" at Bryn Mawr commencement. Elected to newly founded American Academy of Arts and Letters

(William declines). Returns to England in July; lectures had more than covered expenses of his trip. Begins revision of novels for the New York Edition.

1906–08   Writes "The Jolly Corner" and *The American Scene* (published 1907). Writes eighteen prefaces for the New York Edition (twenty-four volumes published 1907–09). Visits Paris and Edith Wharton in spring 1907 and motors with her in Midi. Travels to Italy for the last time, visiting Hendrik Andersen in Rome, and goes on to Florence and Venice. Engages Theodora Bosanquet as his typist in autumn. Again visits Wharton in Paris, spring 1908. William comes to England to give a series of lectures at Oxford and receives an honorary Doctor of Science degree. James goes to Edinburgh in March to see a tryout by the Forbes-Robertsons of his play *The High Bid*, a rewrite in three acts of the one-act play originally written for Ellen Terry (revised earlier as the story "Covering End"). Play gets only five special matinees in London. Shocked by slim royalties from sales of the New York Edition.

1909   Growing acquaintance with young writers and artists of Bloomsbury, including Virginia and Vanessa Stephen and others. Meets and befriends young Hugh Walpole in February. Goes to Cambridge in June as guest of admiring dons and undergraduates and meets John Maynard Keynes. Feels unwell and sees doctors about what he believes may be heart trouble. They reassure him. Late in year burns forty years of his letters and papers at Rye. Suffers severe attacks of gout. *Italian Hours* published.

1910   Very ill in January ("food-loathing") and spends much time in bed. Nephew Harry comes to be with him in February. In March is examined by Sir William Osler, who finds nothing physically wrong. James begins to realize that he has had "a sort of nervous breakdown." William, in spite of now severe heart trouble, and his wife, Alice, come to England to give him support. Brothers and Alice go to Bad Nauheim for cure, then travel to Zurich, Lucerne, and Geneva, where they learn Robertson (Bob) James has died in America of heart attack. James's health begins to improve but William is failing. Sails with William and Alice for America in August. William dies at Chocorua soon after arrival, and James remains with the family for the winter. *The Finer Grain* and *The Outcry* published.

1911   Honorary degree from Harvard in spring. Visits with Howells and Grace Norton. Sails for England July 30. On return to Lamb House, decides he will be too lonely there and starts search for a London flat. Theodora Bosanquet obtains two work rooms adjoining her flat in Chelsea and he begins autobiography, *A Small Boy and Others*. Continues to reside at the Reform Club.

1912   Delivers "The Novel in *The Ring and the Book*," on the 100th anniversary of Browning's birth, to the Royal Society of Literature. Honorary Doctor of Letters from Oxford University June 26. Spends summer at Lamb House. Sees much of Edith Wharton ("the Firebird"), who spends summer in England. (She secretly arranges to have Scribner's put $8,000 into James's account.) Takes 21 Carlyle Mansions, in Cheyne Walk, Chelsea, as London quarters. Writes a long admiring letter for William Dean Howells' seventy-fifth birthday. Meets André Gide. Contracts bad case of shingles and is ill four months, much of the time not able to leave bed.

1913   Moves into Cheyne Walk flat. Two hundred and seventy friends and admirers subscribe for seventieth birthday portrait by Sargent and present also a silver-gilt Charles II porringer and dish ("golden bowl"). Sargent turns over his payment to young sculptor Derwent Wood, who does a bust of James. Autobiography *A Small Boy and Others* published. Goes with niece Peggy to Lamb House for the summer.

1914   *Notes of a Son and Brother* published. Works on "The Ivory Tower." Returns to Lamb House in July. Niece Peggy joins him. Horrified by the war ("this crash of our civilisation," "a nightmare from which there is no waking"). In London in September participates in Belgian Relief, visits wounded in St. Bartholomew's and other hospitals; feels less "finished and useless and doddering" and recalls Walt Whitman and his Civil War hospital visits. Accepts chairmanship of American Volunteer Motor Ambulance Corps in France. *Notes on Novelists* (essays on Balzac, Flaubert, Zola) published.

1915–16   Continues work with the wounded and war relief. Has occasional lunches with Prime Minister Asquith and family, and meets Winston Churchill and other war leaders. Discovers that he is considered an alien and has to report to police before going to coastal Rye. Decides to become a British national and asks Asquith to be one of his sponsors. Receives Certificate of Naturalization on July 26. H. G. Wells satirizes him in *Boon* ("leviathan retrieving pebbles") and James, in the correspondence that follows, writes: "Art *makes* life, makes interest, makes importance." Burns more papers and photographs at Lamb House in autumn. Has a stroke December 2 in his flat, followed by another two days later. Develops pneumonia and during delirium gives his last confused dictation (dealing with the Napoleonic legend) to Theodora Bosanquet, who types it on the familiar typewriter. Mrs. William James arrives December 13 to care for him. On New Year's Day, George V confers the Order of Merit. Dies February 28. Funeral services held at the Chelsea Old Church. The body is cremated and the ashes are buried in Cambridge Cemetery family plot.

Note on the Texts

Throughout his life Henry James wrote about the places he visited. This volume prints, in the last versions revised by him, all of his travel writings about Great Britain and America. Most of these writings appeared first in periodical form; many of them were later revised for book publication, and some appeared in more than one book version.

English Hours, published in October 1905 by William Heinemann in London and by Houghton, Mifflin and Company in Boston, contains sixteen previously published essays, fourteen of which had also appeared in earlier books. James carefully and often extensively revised these essays from their earlier published versions to create a more consistent whole. The first two essays, "London" (originally in *Century Magazine*, Dec. 1888) and "Browning in Westminster Abbey" (originally in *The Speaker*, Jan. 1890), had appeared in *Essays in London and Elsewhere* (New York, 1893). The next four essays, "Chester," "Lichfield and Warwick," "North Devon," and "Wells and Salisbury," had appeared in *Transatlantic Sketches* (Boston, 1875; they were slightly revised in the Tauchnitz edition, *Foreign Parts*, published in Leipzig in 1883). All four essays had first been published in *The Nation*, July 4, July 25, August 8, and August 22, 1872, with the additional unifying title, "A European Summer, I–IV." The next eight essays had appeared in *Portraits of Places* (Boston, 1883) after first being published in periodicals: "An English Easter," *Lippincott's Magazine*, July 1877; "London at Midsummer," *Lippincott's Magazine*, November 1877; "Two Excursions," *The Galaxy*, September 1877 (part of a longer essay titled "Three Excursions"); "In Warwickshire," *The Galaxy*, November 1877; "Abbeys and Castles," *Lippincott's Magazine*, October 1877; "English Vignettes," *Lippincott's Magazine*, April 1879; "An English New Year," *The Nation*, January 12, 1879 (as "The New Year in England"); and "An English Watering Place" (as "An English Winter Watering Place"), *The Nation*, April 3, 1879. Only "Winchelsea, Rye and 'Dennis Duval,'" *Scribner's*, January 1901, and "Old Suffolk," *Harper's Weekly*, September

25, 1897, had not been previously published in book form. Henry James was living in England when *English Hours* was published and by that time preferred British spelling and a light use of commas. Because collation shows that the English edition more closely follows this practice, the texts and illustrations printed in this volume are from the Heinemann edition.

The texts of the early articles printed here under the title "Great Britain: Uncollected Travel Writings" were never collected in book form by James and are taken from their original periodical appearances: "London Sights," *The Nation*, December 16, 1875; "The Oxford-Cambridge Boat-Race," *The Nation*, April 12, 1877 (where it appeared under the heading "Notes"); "The Suburbs of London," *The Galaxy*, December 1877; "London in the Dead Season," *The Nation*, September 26, 1878; "In Scotland," Parts I and II, *The Nation*, October 10 and 24, 1878. The late pieces were written by James in support of the war effort in Britain during World War I. "The Question of the Mind," originally written as a preface to a proposed larger collection of essays by others, appeared with one other essay in a pamphlet, *England at War*, July 1915; "Refugees in England" appeared in the *Boston Sunday Herald Supplement* as "Novelist Writes of Refugees in England" and in *The New York Times Magazine* as "Henry James Writes of Refugees in England" (both published Oct. 17, 1915), and it was posthumously printed as "Refugees in Chelsea," with a long paragraph dropped and other lines inserted, in *The Times Literary Supplement*, March 23, 1916. This volume prints the text from *The New York Times Magazine* because of James's more direct contact with that periodical during this time. "Within the Rim" was written February–March 1915 and submitted for inclusion in a larger project that was never carried out (see note 329.1 in this volume). The essay appeared posthumously in *The Fortnightly Review* (Aug. 1917). The last piece in this section, "The Long Wards," was written at the request of Edith Wharton for inclusion in *The Book of the Homeless*, edited by her and published by Charles Scribner's Sons on January 22, 1916, in an effort to raise money for refugees.

The American Scene was conceived by James from the beginning as a book rather than a gathering of articles written over a number of years. He had returned to America in the fall of 1904 after an absence of twenty years and traveled not only to familiar places of his past but to places he had never been before. Ten of the fourteen chapters were first published in periodicals: "New England: An Autumn Impression," *North American Review*, April and June 1905; "New York Revisited," *Harper's Magazine*, February, March, and May 1906; "New York and the Hudson: A Spring Impression," *North American Review*, December 1905; "New York: Social Notes," *North American Review*, January and February 1906 (the January section was also published in *The Fortnightly Review*, Feb. 1906); "The Sense of Newport," *Harper's Magazine*, August 1906; "Boston," *North American Review* and *The Fortnightly Review*, March 1906; "Philadelphia," *North American Review* and *The Fortnightly Review*, April 1906; "Baltimore," *North American Review*, August 1906; "Washington," *North American Review*, May and June 1906; and "Richmond" (as "Richmond, Virginia"), *The Fortnightly Review*, November 1906. James carefully revised the serial versions in preparing the book for his publishers, Chapman and Hall, Ltd., of London and Harper & Brothers in New York. The English edition was published January 30, 1907, and the American edition appeared one week later, set from the English sheets, but omitting James's carefully prepared running titles (summarizing page contents) and the seventh section of the chapter on Florida. This volume prints the text of the English edition.

"America: Early Travel Writings" includes seven essays originally written for *The Nation*, four of which were revised by James for inclusion in *Portraits of Places*, published in London by Macmillan and Company in 1883. The American edition, published in Boston by James R. Osgood in 1884, used the Macmillan plates. The texts printed here of "Lake George" and "From Lake George to Burlington" are from *The Nation*, August 25 and September 1, 1870. The texts of "Saratoga" (*The Nation*, Aug. 11, 1870), "Newport" (*The Nation*, Sept. 15, 1870), "Quebec" (*The Nation*, Sept. 28–Oct. 5, 1871), and "Niagara" (*The Nation*, Oct. 12 and 19, 1871) are printed here from the English edition of *Portraits of Places*. The text of "Americans Abroad" is from *The Nation*, October 3, 1878.

This volume presents the texts of the printings chosen for inclusion here, but it does not attempt to reproduce features of their typographic design, such as the display capitalization of chapter openings. An illustration that was miscaptioned "Senate House, Oxford" and placed in the chapter "English Vignettes" in *English Hours* is here corrected to "The Sheldonian Theatre" and moved to "Two Excursions" at page 159. A line dropped in the original *Galaxy* text of "The Suburbs of London," December 1877, is indicated at 287.11 in this volume by [   ]. Otherwise the texts are reproduced without change except for the correction of typographical errors. Spelling, punctuation, and capitalization often are expressive features and they are not altered, even when inconsistent or irregular. The following is a list of typographical errors corrected, cited by page and line number: 6.6, (1879); 35.14, one eye's; 132.6, in (compliment; 143.19, futher; 161.14, at it in; 182.1, Everthing; 188.18, seem; 236.20, imformed; 246.31, shipyard; 319.9, than; 321.40, house; 325.34−35, apprehand; 325.39, as once; 326.27, sustainly; 345.2, acceptance submission; 406.22, speads; 504.31, were,; 520.37−38, sublety; 554.14, threatre; 586.25, of symbolic; 605.15, oncemore; 660.35, Rhoades; 677.25, "up-to-date; 727.2, "study' ; 745.25, brawn-eyed. Errors corrected second printing: 7.6, Poolock; 29.33, like (*LOA*); 570.19, interest like,.

Notes

In the notes below, the reference numbers denote page and line of the present volume (the line count includes chapter headings or titles and captions). Footnotes in the text are the author's own. No note is made for material included in standard desk-reference books such as *Webster's Ninth New Collegiate* and *Webster's Biographical* dictionaries. For further background than is provided in the notes, see *Henry James Letters*, ed. Leon Edel (Cambridge: The Belknap Press of Harvard University Press, Vol. I—1843–1875 [1974]; Vol. II—1875–1883 [1975]; Vol. III—1883–1895 [1980]; Vol. IV—1895–1916 [1984]).

ENGLISH HOURS

13.6—8   earlier . . . beginning.]   James had first visited London as a boy in 1855, and arrived there for a second time in 1869.

16.5   "The Ingoldsby Legends."]   Verse narratives (1837; collected 1840), subtitled *or mith and marvels, by Thomas Ingoldsby esquire*, humorous and grotesque treatments of medieval legends by R. H. Barham (1788–1845), a minor canon of St. Paul's.

16.10   Temple Bar]   Gateway that adjoined the Temple Inns of Court between Fleet Street and the Strand, built by Christopher Wren in 1670 and removed in 1878, that marked the western boundary of the City of London.

16.11   "Henry Esmond"]   *The History of Henry Esmond Esquire* (3 vols., 1852), a novel by William Makepiece Thackeray.

16.12—13   masterpiece . . . Wren]   St. Paul's Cathedral was designed by Wren and built 1675–1710, replacing the earlier medieval cathedral that had been destroyed by the Great Fire of 1666.

16.35   Exeter Hall]   A large hall in the Strand, opened in 1831, for concerts and religious and philanthropic meetings; the name was used allusively for Evangelicalism.

18.22   "careful of the type,"]   Cf. Tennyson's *In Memoriam*, Canto LV, stanza 2: "Are God and Nature then at strife, / That Nature lends such evil dreams, / So careful of the type she seems, / So careless of the single life . . ." and Canto LVI, stanza 1: " 'So careful of the type?' but no, / From scarped cliff and quarried stone / She cries, ' A thousand types are gone; / I care for nothing, all shall go.' "

19.34   Mayfair]   A general reference to fashionable London; specifically, a district north of Piccadilly between Bond Street and Park Lane, the most fashionable in London.

21.24–25   the home . . . Hawthorne]   In *Our Old Home: A Series of English Sketches* (1863), "A London Suburb," Hawthorne calls London "the dream-city of my youth" and writes ". . . I acquired a home-feeling there, as nowhere else in the world,—though afterwards I came to have a somewhat similar sentiment in regard to Rome; and as long as either of those two great cities shall exist, the cities of the Past and of the Present, a man's native soil may crumble beneath his feet without leaving him altogether homeless upon earth."

25.8   Serpentine]   An artificial lake in Hyde Park that extends into Kensington Gardens.

26.12   Du Maurier]   George Du Maurier (1834–96), English illustrator of *Punch*, *Loisure Hour*, *Cornhill Magazine*, and of his own novels and those of others, including James's *Washington Square*.

28.9–11   the arch . . . Iron Duke]   The Green Park Arch, erected opposite Hyde Park Corner in 1846, was surmounted by an equestrian statue of the Duke of Wellington by Wyatt. The statue was removed in 1883 when the gate was moved to the west end of Constitution Hill.

28.38   *The monument]   A bronze equestrian statue of the Duke of Wellington with figures of a Highlander, Welsh fusilier, grenadier, and Inniskilling dragoon at the corners of its pedestal.

30.10   Arnold's fine poem]   "Heine's Grave" (1867).

34.12   *par quatre chemins.*]   By four roads, i.e., beating around the bush.

34.21   *que voulez-vous?*]   What can you expect?

42.32–33   Swiss Cottage]   A tavern built in the style of a chalet in 1840; it gave its name to the surrounding area and to a railroad station, opened in 1868.

42.38–43.1   Joanna Baillie . . . muse,]   The Scottish dramatist and poet's home in Hampstead was a meeting place for literary figures including Walter Scott, who became a close friend of Baillie (1762–1851) after reading her *Plays on the Passions* (1798), which he admired.

43.11   Lady Castlewood]   Heroine of *Henry Esmond* (see note 16.11).

48.17   the bishop . . . St. Praxed's.]   A reference to the fictional Bishop Gandfold in Browning's poem "The Bishop Orders His Tomb at Saint Praxed's Church."

48.18   Macaulay's . . . reconciliation"] From Thomas Babington Macaulay's "On Warren Hastings" (October 1841) in *Essays Contributed to the Edinburgh Review, Critical and Historical* (1843).

48.34   the Poets' Corner] Among those interred in the Aisle of the Poets' Corner, besides Browning, are Chaucer, Matthew Prior, Edmund Spencer, Abraham Cowley, John Dryden; among others commemorated there are Milton and Thomas Gray.

57.31   *Stat . . . umbra.*] "He stands, the shadow of a mighty name" (Lucan, *Pharsalia*, I, 35).

64.24   *mens . . . recti*] "A mind conscious of its own rectitude" (Virgil, *Aeneid*, Bk. I, line 608).

64.38–65.6   Canon Kingsley's . . . "Hypatia"] Charles Kingsley (1819–75), clergyman, poet, and novelist. *Westward Ho!* (1855) is a patriotic tale of Jesuit intrigue and naval enterprise during the reign of Elizabeth I and *Hypatia* (1853), a story of 5th-century Alexandria, concerning the conflict of Christian faith and Greek philosophy.

66.9–10   Jeremy Taylor] English divine (1613–67) known for the splendor and simplicity of his prose style.

68.22   "Rasselas"] Johnson's *The History of Rasselas, King of Abyssinia* (1759), a didactic romance, the theme of which is the unobtainability of temporal happiness, begins with Rasselas, the king's son, escaping "the soft vicissitudes of pleasure and repose" of Abyssinia for Egypt.

68.35–36   certain primitive martyrs] The cathedral is dedicated to Saint May and Saint Chad, who established the see at Lichfield.

70.34–35   long-drawn . . . poet] Thomas Gray, "Elegy in a Country Churchyard" (1751), stanza 10.

73.17   Haddon Hall] Considered the most complete and authentic example of a medieval manorial home in England.

74.20–21   Dorothy . . . Manners] The elopement in the 16th century of Dorothy Vernon, heiress of Haddon Hall, with Lord John Manners would be revived in the operetta *Haddon Hall* (1892) by Arthur Sullivan and in the historical romance *Dorothy Vernon of Haddon Hall* (1902) by Charles Major.

76.25–27   Countess Olivia . . . Benedick] Olivia and Malvolio are characters in *Twelfth Night*, and Beatrix and Benedick, in *Much Ado About Nothing*.

76.28   Chatsworth] Seat of the Dukes of Devonshire, a Renaissance-style palace begun in 1588 and completed by Sir Joseph Paxton, designer of the Crystal Palace, in 1854.

76.36   Blenheim.] Blenheim Park, seat of the Duke of Marlborough, is an estate near Woodstock in Oxfordshire, with a castle designed by Sir John Vanburgh.

78.26−27   residence . . . fire] Warwick Castle, which stands on a rock in the Avon, was begun in the 14th century on the site of a fortress built in 915 by Aethelflaed. The interior is primarily by Fulke Greville, who converted it to a mansion after it was granted him by James I in 1604. The fire of December 3, 1871, destroyed some of the most ancient parts of the castle.

80.2   Salons Carrés and Tribunes] The choicest exhibition rooms of, respectively, the Louvre and the Uffizi Gallery.

86.32−33   defeat of the Atalanta] The New York Atalanta rowing club was defeated by the London rowing club in a four-oared race on the Thames, June 10, 1872.

90.2   *morgue*] Haughtiness.

91.16−17   drawing . . . Doré's] Doré (1832−83), French illustrator and painter, was known for his grotesque and visionary scenes. Among the more than 90 works he illustrated was Tennyson's *Idylls of the King* in 1868−69.

93.11   Sir Roger de Coverly] Coverly, baronet and bachelor "of ancient descent," a member of the Spectator Club, was a mildly eccentric fictional character who represented the country gentry and was pictured around town, at home, in church, and so on, by Joseph Addison and Richard Steele in a number of *Spectator* issues, 1711−12; his death is reported in number 517. (The imaginary Spectator Club members purportedly conducted the daily periodical.)

100.33−34   Abbey . . . Henry VIII.] After failing to obtain a papal divorce from Catherine of Aragon, Henry VIII secured passage through Parliament in 1534 of the Act of Supremacy, making him supreme head of the Church of England. In 1536 he began to dissolve the English monasteries on the grounds that they owed allegiance to foreign religious orders. Richard Whyting, the abbot of Glastonbury, accepted the Act of Supremacy but refused to surrender the abbey. In 1539 Whyting and two of his monks were executed for treason and the abbey was confiscated by the crown.

103.16   Apollo . . . Medici.] The "Apollo Belvedere" is a Roman copy in marble, dating from the early empire, of the Greek bronze original, representing Apollo as a beautiful young man; it is in the Belevedere court at the Vatican. The marble "Medicean Venus," in the Uffizi Gallery at Florence, represents the goddess as a beautiful young woman. It dates from around the time of Augustus and is believed to have derived from Praxiteles' "Aphrodite of Cnidus" which was destroyed.

106.4−6   *The Critic* . . . wonderful.] *The Critic; or a Tragedy Rehearsed*, burlesquing the problems of producing "Mr. Puff's new play," II, 2.

106.8   the Reverend Arthur Tooth]   A priest serving at Hatcham, Tooth
was jailed January 22 to February 17, 1877, for refusing to comply with the
Public Worship Regulation Act, passed in 1874 to restrict the practice of High
Church ritual in Church of England services. On May 14, 1877, Tooth forcibly
entered his church and celebrated communion. The legal proceedings
brought against him were dismissed on appeal on jurisdictional grounds in
November 1877.

106.9   Mr. Henry Irving]   Irving (1838–1905), who was celebrated for his
first roles on the London stage in the early 1870s, was later attacked by many
critics for his unconventional treatments of *Hamlet*, *Othello*, and *Macbeth*.
Although opinion turned in his favor, throughout his career he would continue to be both acclaimed and critically attacked. In 1895 he became the first
English actor to be knighted.

111.26   *agréments*]   Pleasures.

111.31   *blanchisseuse*]   Laundress.

118.33–38   The question . . . delicacy]   In *Portraits of Places* (1883) this
reads: "The capacity of an Englishwoman for being handsome strikes me as
absolutely unlimited, and even if (I repeat) it is in the luxurious class that it is
most freely exercised, yet among the daughters of the people one sees a great
many fine points. Among the men fine points are strikingly numerous—especially among the younger ones. Here the same distinction is to be made—
the gentlemen are certainly handsomer than the vulgarians. But taking one
young Englishman with another, they are physically very well turned out.
Their features are finished, composed, as it were, more harmoniously than
those of many of their nearer and remoter neighbours, and their figures are
apt to be both powerful and compact. They present to view very much fewer
accidental noses and inexpressive mouths, fewer sloping shoulders and ill-
planted heads of hair, than their American kinsmen. Speaking always from
the sidewalk, it may be said that as the spring increases in London and the
symptoms of the season multiply, the beautiful young men who adorn the
West End pavements, and who advance before you in couples, arm-in-arm,
fair-haired, gray-eyed, athletic, slow-strolling, ambrosial, are among the most
brilliant features of the brilliant period."

120.24   Tichborne claimant]   Roger Charles Tichborne, born into a
prominent English Roman Catholic family in 1829, sailed from Rio de Janeiro
in April 1854 aboard the *Bella*, which was lost at sea with no known survivors.
His mother, Lady Henriette Tichborne, refused to believe that her son was
dead and sought news of him through newspaper advertisements. In 1865 she
was told that a man resembling Roger Charles Tichborne was working as a
butcher in Wagga Wagga, Australia, under the name Thomas Castro. Lady
Tichborne paid for his passage to England and in 1867 acknowledged him as
her son, although the rest of the family rejected his claim. The claimant eventually brought suit against the trustees of the estate, seeking the Tichborne

baronetcy and title to property in Hampshire worth £24,000 a year (the current baronet, Roger Charles' nephew, was a minor). In a civil trial that began on May 11, 1871, about 100 witnesses testified that the claimant was Roger Charles Tichborne, while the family introduced evidence that he was actually Arthur Orton, born 1834, the son of a London butcher. The suit was dismissed on March 6, 1872, after the jury indicated that it believed the claimant was an impostor. The claimant was then indicted, as Arthur Orton, for perjury, and went on trial on April 23, 1873. He was convicted on February 28, 1874, and sentenced to 14 years imprisonment at hard labor. Despite the jury's finding that he was Arthur Orton, the claimant retained considerable popular support, and it was alleged that his conviction was the result of a Jesuit plot. He was released in 1884 and died in poverty in 1898.

120.32   obelisk . . . Concorde]   The obelisk of Luxor, built under Ramses II of Egypt (reigned 1304–1237 B.C.), was erected at the Place de la Concorde in 1836. It replaced a statue of Liberty (erected 1792).

121.27   towers of Julius.]   According to legend, the Tower of London was founded by Julius Caesar. Actual construction began under William the Conqueror in 1077 with the building of the central keep, later known as the White Tower.

122.5–10   castle, . . . Dickens;]   The ruins of Cooling Castle, the home of Sir John Oldcastle, supposedly the prototype of Falstaff, and Cooling Marshes, which figures in *Great Expectations* (1860–61), are about four miles from Gadshill (or Gad's Hill), which is mentioned in Chaucer's *Canterbury Tales*, is the scene of a mock robbery of Falstaff in Shakespeare's *I Henry IV*, II. ii, and also the site of the house where Dickens lived in his later years and where he died in 1870.

124.1   proctors]   In the 16th and 17th centuries, one who collected alms for lepers and others not allowed to collect for themselves; someone with a license to collect alms; an agent to collect tithes and other church dues.

130.13–14   Edward . . . *mye*,"]   Edward (1330–76; also known as Edward of Woodstock and Edward IV), Prince of Wales, and Prince of Aquitaine 1362–72, son of Edward III of the house of Plantagenet or Anjou: "Of death I never had a thought."

130.33   Moreville and Fitzurse]   Becket's assassins Reginald Fitz Urse and Hugh de Morville, two knights in the court of Henry II.

132.7   "Fleur-de-Lis"]   The emblem of kings of France, also used by English kings who laid claim to France.

135.4–5   *plaisanterie*]   Joke.

143.2   Hospital]   Greenwich Hospital was established in 1694 as a home for aged and disabled sailors. In 1865 a resolution of the Admiralty allowed pensioners the choice of remaining in the hospital or receiving an "outdoor pension." By 1869 the last pensioners had left and in 1873 the building became the Royal Naval College.

144.24   last of the Bonapartes]   Napoléon Eugene Louis (1856–79), the Prince Imperial, Napoléon III's only son with the Empress Eugénie, fled to England with his mother after the first French defeats in the Franco-Prussian War of 1870 and became the Bonaparte pretender on the death of his father, January 9, 1873. He graduated from the Royal Military College at Woolwich, which trained artillery and engineering officers, in 1875. (The Prince Imperial was killed in Natal, South Africa, on June 1, 1879, while observing the British war against the Zulus.)

146.33–34   Spectator . . . Egypt]   Influential weekly periodical founded by Robert S. Rintoul in 1828 as an organ of "educated radicalism," and edited by Richard Holt Hutton from 1865 to 1897. In 1875 Ismail, the Ottoman viceroy of Egypt, sold his interest in the Suez Canal to the British government in order to pay the costs of his extensive construction of public works in Egypt and his military campaigns in the Sudan. Despite the sale and his continuing harsh taxation of the peasantry, Ismail soon faced bankruptcy and was forced in 1876 to accept increased foreign control over his finances and judicial system. An Arab revolt against Ottoman rule in 1882 (five years after the initial publication of James's essay) led to the British occupation of Egypt.

148.7   Derby day]   Since 1839 the Derby has been run at Epsom Downs on Wednesday in the week in which May 31 falls (in 1877, May 30).

148.15–16   empires . . . East?]   In 1875–76 Christians in Bosnia-Herzegovina, Bulgaria, Serbia, and Montenegro fought against Turkish rule in a series of rebellions and wars. On April 9, 1877, Turkey rejected the latest attempt by six European powers (Britain, France, Italy, Germany, Austria-Hungary, and Russia) to arrange a peace settlement for the Balkans. Russia then declared war on Turkey on April 24, renewing the intense debate in British politics over the "Eastern Question." The Conservative prime minister, Benjamin Disraeli, earl of Beaconsfield, sought to preserve British power in the Middle East and India by maintaining the Ottoman Empire as a bulwark against Russian expansion in the Balkans and in southwest Asia. His pro-Turkish policy was opposed by the Liberal William Gladstone, who in 1876 had aroused public opinion against Turkish atrocities in Bulgaria. The war ended in a Russian victory on January 31, 1878, although the final peace terms agreed to at the Congress of Berlin, June–July 1878, reflected the interest of Britain and Austria-Hungary in maintaining a balance of power in the Balkans between Russia and Turkey.

151.2   ébats]   Pleasures, revels.

154.16–17   dégringolade]   Collapse, downfall.

160.1–2   Bowery Theatre]   See pages 515–19 and note 515.21 in this volume.

164.15   Kenilworth]   The ruins of an English castle built in 1120, the scene of entertainments given to Queen Elizabeth in 1575, described in Scott's novel *Kenilworth* (1821).

166.32   Mrs. Quickly]   Hostess of the Boar's Head Tavern in Shakespeare's *2 Henry IV*; she also appears in *Henry V*.

167.29–38   George Eliot's . . . Deronda.]   Characters in her novel *Daniel Deronda* (1876).

171.1   *justesse*.]   Precision.

172.15   "The Small . . . Allington."]   Novel (1864) by Anthony Trollope of which Lily Dale and Adolphus Crosbie are characters.

174.12   Hawthorne's account]   "About Warwick" in *Our Old Home* (1863).

176.34   church . . . buried,]   Church of the Holy Trinity.

178.19–38   "Adam Bede" . . . Chettam,]   Hetty Sorrel is the tragic heroine of *Adam Bede* (1859), which is set in the village of Hayslope, and the others named are characters in *Middlemarch, A Study of Provincial Life* (1871–72).

179.18   Cross . . . nursery-rhyme.]   "Ride a Cockhorse to Banbury Cross." The original cross was destroyed by Puritans in 1602 and a new one was installed in 1859.

185.30   merely "good."]   The following passage appeared here in *Portraits and Places*: "Is it that English country life seems to possess such irresistible charms? I have not always thought so; I have sometimes suspected that it is dull; I have remembered that there is a whole literature devoted to exposing it (that of the English novel 'of manners'); and that its recorded occupations and conversations occasionally strike one as lacking a certain indispensable salt. But, for all that, when, in the region to which I allude, my companion spoke of this and that place being likely sooner or later to come to the hammer, it seemed as if nothing could be more delightful than to see the hammer hanging upon one's own liberality. And this in spite of the fact that the owners of the places in question would part with them because they could no longer afford to keep them up. I found it interesting to learn, in so far as was possible, what sort of income was implied by the possession of country-seats such as are not in America a concomitant of even the largest fortunes; and if in these revelations I sometimes heard of a very long rent-roll, on the other hand I was frequently surprised at the shortness of purse attributed to people living in the depths of an oak-studded park. Then, certainly, English country-life seemed to me the most advantageous thing in the world; on conditions such as these one would gladly be dull; surrounded by luxury of so moderate a cost one would joyfully stagnate."

192.2   *gentilhommière*] Country seat.

195.14   Fanny . . . Cecilia.] Fanny Price and Emma Woodhouse appear, respectively, in *Mansfield Park* (1814) and *Emma* (1816) by Jane Austen, and Evelina and Cecilia in *Evelina* (1778) and *Cecilia* (1782) by Fanny Burney.

196.17–18   *temporis acti*] Events of the times.

198.1   attitude of Nebuchadnezzar)] In Daniel 5:23, Nebuchadnezzar in his madness eats grass.

201.20   *rentières*] Women living on independent means.

206.8   Flying Dutchman] The legendary captain of a spectral ship (also called *The Flying Dutchman*) who is condemned to sail the seas forever.

212.7–8   *débrouiller*] Disentangle, unravel.

223.14   "Oliver Twist."] Novel (1838) by Charles Dickens.

224.19   Lady Bountiful] A character in George Farquhar's comedy *The Beaux' Stratagem* (1707) who expends half her income in charitable uses.

225.23–24   London *super mare*] London by the sea.

228.31   Que voulez-vous?] What more can you ask?

231.3   Mrs. Langtry] British actress Emily Charlotte Le Bon Langtry, stage name Lillie Langtry, (1853–1929), a famous beauty known as "the Jersey Lily," was an intimate friend of Queen Victoria's eldest son, Albert Edward (1841–1910), Prince of Wales (crowned Edward VII in 1901).

233.14   Thackeray's . . . "Denis Duval"] The unfinished novel (posthumously published in *Corhnhill Magazine*, 1864) was the last work of Thackeray, who died suddenly December 24, 1863.

234.20–23   "Lovel . . . "Esmond"] The story "Lovel the Widower" (1860) and *The Adventures of Philip* (1861–62), Thackeray's last complete novel. Thackeray was the first editor of *The Cornhill Magazine* (1860–1975), a monthly literary periodical that specialized in serialized novels (among other contributors were Henry James, George Eliot, Trollope, Tennyson, Robert Browning, Swinburne, Hardy, and Ruskin). The English artist Frederick Walker (1840–75) gained success for his illustrations of Thackeray's work in the magazine. For *Henry Esmond*, see note 16.11.

236.10   Edict at Nantes] The edict, signed by Henry IV of France in April 1598, granted freedom of conscience, full civil rights, and limited freedom of worship to French Huguenots (Protestants). It was revoked by Louis XIV in October 1685.

236.36−37   Longfellow's . . . Wellington.] "The Warden of the Cinque Ports" (written 1852).

238.1−2   Edward . . . design] The first town of Winchelsea was washed away by several English Channel storms between 1232 and 1297. A new town was then founded by Edward I (reigned 1272−1307).

238.23   "The Roundabout Papers"] A series of discursive essays that Thackeray wrote for *Cornhill* (1860−63).

241.15−16   Mrs. Richmond Ritchie] Anne Thackeray Ritchie (1837−1919), Thackeray's eldest child, author of novels and essays.

244.36   fragment of Beauvais] Gothic cathedral of St. Pierre, begun 1225 and never completed, in the city of Beauvais in northern France.

245.28   Holloway's History] H. R. Holloway, *Walks Around Rye* (1849).

248.33−34   preachment . . . Wesley.] John Wesley (1703−91), the founder of Methodism, preached some 40,000 sermons, often in the open air.

248.34   Black Prince] See note 130.13−14.

248.35   Spaniards] Castilian allies of Philip VI of France. In 1337 Edward III laid claim to the French throne, beginning a series of Anglo-French conflicts that lasted until 1453 and became known as the Hundred Years War.

250.8   *en plein ancien régime*] At the height of the old (pre-Revolutionary) regime.

250.29−30   very celebrated lady] Ellen Terry (1847−1928).

254.17   Phiz.] The pseudonym of Hablot Knight Browne (1815−82), illustrator of novels, including several of Dickens' works.

256.36   Swinburne, in verses] "By the North Sea" in *Studies in Song* (1880).

259.2   Reform Bill] The 1832 Reform Act disenfranchised 56 small boroughs that had been represented in the House of Commons for centuries.

260.35   Birket Foster] Myles Birket Foster (1825−99), English painter and illustrator.

261.9   Marquis of Carabas] The name by which the cat represents its master in the traditional folk tale recounted by Charles Perrault (1628−1703), "Puss in Boots."

261.17   Hodge . . . *frais*] Hodge and Gaffer are typical names for the English rustic. *Font les frais* means "bear the expense."

GREAT BRITAIN: UNCOLLECTED TRAVEL WRITINGS

272.3–4   "Tapis Vert"]   "Green Carpet."

275.11–12   Trinity and Jesus.] Two of the colleges at Cambridge University.

276.17   terrace at Saint Germain] Terrace designed by Le Nôtre, a mile and a half long, with a panoramic view of the Seine Valley and Paris, at St. Germain-en-Laye.

278.36   *faîner*]   Loaf, idle.

280.9   Homer sometimes nods,] Cf. Horace, *Ars Poetica*, 359: "If Homer, usually good, nods for a moment, I think it shame; and yet it may well be that over a work of great length one should grow drowsy now and then."

290.36–37   *ultima ratio*]   "Last resort" or "final argument," from *ultima ratio regum*, "the final argument of kings" (i.e., force; an inscription on French cannon in the time of Louis XIV).

293.15   interlunar . . . Shelley says,]   ". . . the silent Moon / In her interlunar swoon . . . " from "With a Guitar, to Jane" (1822), lines 23–24.

300.2   Meurice and Francatelli]   Continental restaurateurs.

301.3   ému]   Moved, stirred.

301.14   Arthur's Seat]   Hill overlooking the southeast section of the city, where King Arthur is said to have watched his army defeat the Picts.

302.3–4   *perfervidum ingenium*]   Sharpest wit. *Perfervidium ingenium Scotorum*, a proverb of unknown origin, has been translated "The very ardent disposition of the Scotch."

302.6   Principal Shairp]   John Campbell Shairp (1819–85), professor of humanities from 1861 and principal from 1868; he was the author of, among other works, *Kilmahoe and Other Poems* (1864), *Studies on Poetry and Philosophy* (1868), *Lectures on Culture and Religion* (1870), *Life of James Forbes* (1873), and *Poetic Interpretation of Nature* (1877).

302.17–18   Matthew Arnold . . . Glasgow.]   In "Equality," collected in *Mixed Essays* (1879).

303.27   Thiers . . . least]   Adolphe Thiers (1797–1877), French statesman and historian, the first president of the Third Republic: "The Republic is the system of government that divides us least."

304.24   Sassenach]   The name given by Gaelic inhabitants of Great Britain to their "Saxon" or English neighbors.

305.14   Mayfair]   See note 19.34.

306.21   "Sawbath,"]   A pronunciation of Sabbath.

307.8–9   union . . . France]   Scottish nobles resisting Edward I of England made an alliance with Philip IV of France in 1295. The alliance was renewed at various times until the accession of Stuarts to the English throne in 1603.

311.35   *portée*]   Bearing.

313.22   *comité de lecture*]   Reading committee, which determines the plays to be performed.

315.9   *constatation*]   Verification; declaration; findings of an inquiry.

319.3–4   Belgians . . . unprovoked]   After declaring war on France, August 3, 1914, Germany invaded neutral Belgium in an attempt to outflank the French armies; this violation of Belgian neutrality brought Great Britain into the war on August 4.

329.1   *Within the Rim*]   In an introductory note to "Within the Rim" in *The Fortnightly Review*, August 1, 1917, Elizabeth Asquith explained that James had written the essay in February or March 1915 for a proposed album to benefit a fund for "artists in distress owing to the war." One of the last things he wrote, and one of the few about the war, the subject was, she explained, his decision: " 'It must be about the war,' he said, 'I can think of nothing else.' " James left the manuscript with Asquith, and when the idea of an album was abandoned, refused to take it back, saying " 'It is yours, my dear child, to do with as you will.' . . . Now that he is dead," Asquith concluded, "I am publishing it for the purpose for which he originally intended it. It is his legacy to the literature of the war and to the English nation, for it shows him not only as a great artist, but as a great soldier fighting our battles." Elizabeth Asquith was a daughter of Raymond Asquith, prime minister of Great Britain (1908–16) and a friend of James.

329.4–10   Civil War . . . South Carolina]   Lincoln issued a proclamation calling forth 75,000 militia on April 15, 1861, three days after the Confederate attack on Fort Sumter in Charleston, South Carolina. The flood of volunteers (more than 200,000 by July 4, 1861) in response to it and a subsequent proclamation of May 3 became known as "the uprising of the North."

336.30–32   Germanic . . . five years]   Under the terms of the May 10, 1871, treaty that ended the 1870–71 Franco-Prussian War, France ceded to Germany almost all of its eastern provinces of Alsace and Lorraine, promised to pay a war indemnity of five billion francs, and agreed to have German troops remain in northern France until the indemnity was paid in full. Despite expectations that payment of the indemnity would take five years, it was paid in full by September 1873, and by early 1875 France had also begun to rebuild its army and create stable republican political institutions. The French revival created alarm among some German political and military leaders, who believed that French desires to regain Alsace-Lorraine and to become the dominant power in Europe made another Franco-German war inevitable. In the spring of 1875 speculation was widespread in the German press that an attack would be launched against France to prevent its further recovery and to impose a second indemnity. Both Russia and Britain discouraged such an attack, and the war scare dissipated during the summer.

341.17—18   President Lincoln's . . . short period] See note 329.4—10; the service term for the militia called forth by Lincoln's proclamation of April 15, 1861, was three months. James was in Newport, Rhode Island, when the war broke out, and a camp of soldiers was nearby.

THE AMERICAN SCENE

362.31   in *villeggiatura*]   In country residence.

367.33—34   Mademoiselle de Scudéri] Madeleine de Scudéry (1607–1701), author of very long romances including *Clélie, historie romaine* (10 vols., 1654—60), *Ibrahim ou l'illustre Bassa* (1641), and *Artamène ou le Grand Cyrus* (10 vols., 1649—53), which depict persons of the author's own time disguised as characters in the novels.

370.9   Pomona.]   Roman goddess of fruit and fruit trees (*pomum* is Latin for apple).

370.33—34   W. C. Bryant . . . water-fowl.]   "To a Waterfowl" (1818).

372.8   "Oh . . . woman-land!"]   Cf., for example, "By the Fireside," Stanza 6.

377.25   *maîtresse de maison*]   Woman of the house.

382.24   *quelconque*]   Mediocre, like any other.

393.27   house on a hilltop]   Now Hill-Stead Museum.

395.13   Cenci-drama]   A story of incest and murder that occurred in the rich and noble Roman family of the Cenci in 1599. It was dramatized by Shelley in *The Cenci* (1819, 1821).

403.22   Rappacini-garden]   In the allegorical tale "Rappaccini's Daughter" (1844) by Hawthorne, the rank and poisonous garden in which the hero falls in love with the learned Dr. Rappaccini's daughter Beatrice.

405.30—31   Higginson . . . gifts)]   Henry Lee Higginson (1834–1919), a fellow of Harvard College, also gave the university the land for Soldiers' Field, founded (1890) and financially supported the Boston Symphony Orchestra, and made significant donations to a number of colleges, including Radcliffe, and to secondary schools.

409.23   *portée*]   Significance, import.

412.38   J. R. L.]   James Russell Lowell (1819–91), American poet.

413.21   Elmwood]   The home of James Russell Lowell (1819–91) on Elmwood Avenue off Brattle Street.

413.23–24   Longfellow's . . . residence,]   Craigie House on Brattle Street was Longfellow's home 1837–82.

415.4   W. D. H.]   William Dean Howells (1837–1920).

420.27–28   bell-tower of Giotto]   The Campanile, known as "Giotto's tower," next to the Duomo Cathedral, was designed by Giotto (c. 1266–1337) toward the end of his life.

420.34–35   creator . . . Trinity Church,]   English-born architect Richard M. Upjohn (1802–78) built the 60-foot high Gothic church (1839–46) with a 285-foot spire on the site of the original building (consecrated 1689), the first Anglican church in New York City. (It had also been rebuilt in 1788–90 after a fire.)

421.36   Castle Garden,]   On the Battery at the south end of Manhattan. Originally a fort called Castle Clinton (built 1808), the building was named Castle Garden when it was made into an opera house and amusement hall in 1823. From 1855 to 1892, before Ellis Island was opened, it served as an immigrant processing station, and from 1896 to 1914 housed the New York Aquarium; after World War II it became Castle Clinton National Monument.

424.27–28   Le Ventre . . . L'Argent,]   In Les Rougon-Macquart, Zola's cycle of 20 naturalistic novels. Le Ventre de Paris (1873) is about the meat and provisions market Les Halles in Paris; Au Bonheur des Dames (1883), about a department store that ruins its small competitors; Pot-Bouille (1887), about bourgeois life in a Paris apartment block; and L'Argent, about avarice, speculation, the power of money, and the stock exchange.

430.26   Arch of Triumph]   Washington Memorial Arch. The permanent structure was erected 1890–92 after a temporary wooden arch, erected 1889 to celebrate the centennial of George Washington's inauguration, was removed. Both were designed by Stanford White.

431.31   University building]   The Gothic New York University building on the east side of the square, erected 1832–35 and demolished 1894–95.

432.38   two . . . churches]   Episcopal Church of the Ascension at 10th Street, which no longer exists there, and the First Presbyterian Church at 12th Street.

434.23–26   Park . . . saving it,]   Park Street (Congregational) Church was built 1809–10 from the design of Peter Banner, or Bonner, who came to Boston from England around 1794; its spire, once the highest object in Boston's skyline, has been compared to the Wren tower of Saint Bride's Church on Fleet Street, London. In 1894, when some church deacons wished to sell the church to real-estate speculators, it narrowly escaped destruction.

438.22   Waldorf-Astoria] The hotel of red brick and sandstone in German Renaissance style, then on Fifth Avenue between 33d and 34th streets, was actually two hotels operated as a unit: William Waldorf Astor's Waldorf, completed 1893, and John Jacob Astor's Astoria, completed 1897.

440.10   *Un bon mouvement*] A vigorous effort.

443.11   Trianon] Built for Louis XV in 1751 and 1766, and given to Marie Antoinette by Louis XVI as her private domain, the Petit Trianon, in Trianon, a hamlet near Versailles, is a pavilion and small country house with elaborate gardens. There, free of the demands of royal etiquette, the queen kept cows, gave parties, and acted in musical comedies.

443.28   *vente de charité*] Charity bazaar.

451.4   *fin mot*] Exact expression, last word.

461.12   *chez lui*] At home.

469.35   *enquête*] Inquiry, investigation.

474.4–6   Columbia . . . moved up] Founded as King's College in 1754, with classes held at Trinity Church, and incorporated as Columbia College in 1784, the school moved to Madison Avenue and 49th Street in 1857. The name Columbia University in the City of New York was adopted in 1896 (officially, 1912), and the school moved to its present location in Morningside Heights in 1897.

479.4   *raffiné*] Refined, cultivated person.

483.26   "Hudson River School"] A group of realistic American landscape painters, circa 1825–75, including Thomas Cole, usually considered the founder of the school, Asher Durand, Frederick Church, John Kensett, Sanford Gifford, and others. Their subjects were rustic and rural American scenery, particularly the Hudson River and the Catskill Mountains.

485.2–3   Wolfert's . . . purchase,] Irving (1783–1859) bought the cottage and 110 acres about two miles outside of Tarrytown in 1835 and first called it Wolfert's Roost after its original owner, Wolfert Acker.

501.38   *cabotine*] Strolling player.

502.8   Plaza] At Fifth Avenue and 59th Street, site of the original Plaza hotel (open 1900–05; the present hotel opened in 1907).

506.4   *endimanchés*] In their Sunday best.

509.4–5   old Reservoir,] The Reservoir of the Croton Aqueduct (known as the Croton Reservoir) on Fifth Avenue between 40th and 42d streets was completed in 1842 and demolished 1899–1901.

509.5   *ultima Thule*]   Farthest limit.

510.13–14   Robinson . . . sand.]   In *The Life and strange and surprising Adventures of Robinson Crusoe* (1719) by Daniel Defoe.

511.34–35   Metropolitan Museum]   Incorporated 1871, the museum moved to Fifth Avenue and 81st Street in 1879; before 1900 it had been enlarged three times.

511.36   *flânerie*]   Idle strolling.

512.36   *étape*]   Stage, stopover.

513.29   Cesnola Collection]   Italian-born soldier, archaeologist, and writer Luigi Palma di Cesnola (1832–1904) was secretary of the Metropolitan Museum of Art, 1877–79, and director, 1879–1904. The authenticity of his collection of Cypriote antiquities and Phoenician and archaeic Greek art, collected while he was U.S. consul at Cyprus (1865–76), and which he sold to the museum for a modest sum (less than he was told it would have brought in auction), was frequently attacked, as was his personal honor and his administration of the museum. The collection's authenticity was sustained by a jury in a libel suit in 1883–84 and by the findings of an investigative committee of sculptors and stone-cutters, but the public remained skeptical and attacks in the press continued; later researchers also vindicated it.

513.31   Marquand's rare munificence)]   Philanthropist Henry Gurdon Marquand (1819–1902), called "one of the ablest and most generous supporters" of the Metropolitan Museum in his time, from 1869 helped to organize and raise an endowment for the museum and served as its treasurer, 1882–89, and president, 1889–1902; his personal gifts included endowments, several collections, and individual works of art.

514.29–30   funeral-pile of Sardanapalus,]   According to the *Persica* of Greek historian Ctesias (fl. 400 B.C.), Sardanapalus was an Assyrian king known for his luxury. After being besieged at Nineveh by the Medes for two years, he set fire to his palace, burning with it himself, his court, and all his treasures.

515.21   *the* Bowery Theatre]   The New York Theatre, Bowery, known as the Bowery Theatre, opened in 1826 and was one of the most famous theaters in the city; it was rebuilt after fires in 1828, 1836, 1838, and 1845. When the theater district began moving from the area around 1839, the Bowery acquired a new audience that became famous for shouting insults or encouragement at the actors; when encouraged, actors were expected to step out of their roles and engage in dialogue with the audience. The theater closed in 1878 and was reopened the next year as the Thalia, which produced plays in German; it was destroyed by fire in 1929.

516.32–34   "Jack Sheppard . . . orange-peel,]   The melodramas *Jack Sheppard* and *Claude Duval* (first produced there 1839 and 1848 respectively). The

Bowery was the last major theater to retain "the pit" until the 1860s, where fruit, nuts, and candy were sold by "street urchins," and the remains sometimes thrown at the stage.

517.16   *vieux jeu*]   Old-fashioned, out of date.

518.26   *trucs*]   (Theatrical) machinery.

521.2   *enquête*]   See note 469.35.

526.22   Delmonico tradition]   A reference to Delmonico's Restaurant in New York City, which was opened at Williams Street around 1834 by Swiss emigré Lorenzo Delmonico (1813–81) and his uncles John and Peter Delmonico. It popularized salads, vegetable dishes, fine European, and later American, cuisines, and was immediately popular, gradually acquiring an international reputation (from 1855 it was located at various other places in the city).

528.29   *raffiné*]   See note 479.4.

535.1   State House]   Built 1738–43; Newport was, along with Providence, a capital of Rhode Island until 1900.

535.19   Vernon house]   The headquarters of Rochambeau after his landing in Newport in July 1780.

539.16   *Revue des Deux Mondes*]   French periodical and literary review, founded 1829. Its contributors included George Sand, Balzac, Hugo, Sainte-Beuve, and Alfred de Vigny.

544.23–24   Hooker and Devens]   Massachusetts natives and Union Army officers Joseph Hooker (1814–79) and Charles Devens (1820–91).

544.40   "Park Street" Church]   See note 434.23–26.

546.40   present Public Library]   The white building in Roman Renaissance style was designed by McKim, Mead, and White and built 1888–95.

547.30   *honnête*]   May be translated, for example, honest, respectable, modest, genteel, proper, befitting, decorous, honorable, obliging, suitable, handsome, fair, comely.

551.25–26   St. Clement Danes . . . St. Mary-le-Strand]   Churches on the Strand in London.

551.34–36   Park . . . London examples]   See note 434.23–26.

554.13–14   Museum Theatre.]   The Boston Museum (and Gallery of Fine Arts) opened June 14, 1841, and closed in 1893. Among the outstanding actors who appeared with or were part of its stock company were Mrs. J. R. Vincent (Mary Ann Farley, 1818–87), called the most beloved of Boston actresses (she played 44 roles there, 1852–87), and William Warren, Jr. (1812–88), considered the foremost comedian of his time (he appeared in about 600 plays there, 1847–82).

555.11   beautifully . . . Jacob's Ladder.]   In Jacob's dream (Genesis 21:12) angels climb the ladder between earth and heaven.

560.16   *penetralia*]   Innermost or private parts; sanctuary.

560.21   South Kensington]   A center for museums and colleges in London's West End that grew out of the 1851 International Exhibition in nearby Hyde Park. By the beginning of the 20th century institutions in the area included the Victoria and Albert Museum (known as the South Kensington Museum until 1899), the Royal College of Music, the University of London, and the Natural History Museum of the British Museum.

560.38–39   Massachusetts . . . lions]   The two lions, carved in Siena marble by Louis St. Gaudens, honor the 2d and 20th Massachusetts Infantry. Thirteen of the sixteen officers of the 2d Massachusetts killed in action were Harvard graduates; among the officers of the 20th Massachusetts was Oliver Wendell Holmes, Jr.

561.40–562.1   Laurentian, . . . Ambrosian Library]   Michelangelo's Laurentian Library (built 1523–71) in Florence and the Ambrosian Library (founded around 1609) in Milan, one of the earliest public libraries.

563.24–25   bigger . . . overtop it.]   The Museum of Fine Arts was moved to a new building on Commonwealth Avenue in 1909.

564.24–25   Gardner Collection]   Art collector and socialite Isabella Stewart Gardner (1840–1924) would leave her home and gallery (now called the Isabella Stewart Gardner Museum) on the Fenway to the City of Boston.

568.3–5   Lamb . . . woman."]   Charles Lamb's (1775–1884) farce *Mr. H* flopped at the Theatre Royal, Drury Lane, a leading London theater, in 1806; none of his other dramas was ever produced. In 1819 William Hazlitt (1778–1830), who was living apart from his wife, fell obsessively in love with Sarah Walker, the daughter of his landlord. Hazlitt planned to marry her, but after his divorce in 1822 learned that she had taken another lover. His agonized account of the affair is *Liber Amoris; or, The New Pygmalion* (1823). In 1824 he married Isabella Bridgewater, a widow he met on a stagecoach; they separated in 1827.

568.29   "American Weimar"]   Weimar, a small ancient city in Thüringen, on the Ilm River, in beautiful country of wooded hills and where Herder, Goethe, and Schiller lived, was a center of German intellectual and literary life.

568.36   *tutti quanti*]   All such (persons).

571.4–8   manse . . . Hawthorne's]   The house where Ralph Waldo Emerson (1803–82) lived, 1834–35, was built in 1765 by his grandfather and was the birthplace of his father, the Rev. William Emerson (1769–1811); Nathaniel Hawthorne (1804–64) named it the Old Manse and wrote *Mosses from an Old Manse* (1846; tales and sketches) when he lived there, 1842–46.

571.15–17   house . . . Miriam]   Hawthorne spent about two years in Italy after serving as consul in Liverpool, 1853–57, then settled in Concord in a house called The Wayside in 1860. Donatella and Miriam are characters in *The Marble Faun* (1860).

571.38–39   Wahrheit and Dichtung]   Truth and Poetry; Goethe's *Dichtung und Wahrheit* (1811–22) concerns his development as an artist.

573.22   Hester . . . needle]   The letter A, signifying adultress, that Hester Prynne is condemned to wear on her dress is "in red cloth, surrounded with an elaborate embroidery and fantastic flourishes of gold . . . "

588.34   *tutoiement*]   Second-person-singular (intimate) address.

591.1–4   Russian . . . Poland.]   In 1815 Warsaw and much of central Poland became part of the Russian empire under the terms of the Congress of Vienna. After the suppression of the 1863 insurrection against Russian rule, the use of the Russian language was made mandatory in higher education and civil administration in Poland as part of a widely resisted campaign of Russification.

592.23   *tenue*]   Proper bearing.

595.31   Hall . . . Carpenters]   Where the First Continental Congress assembled, September 5, 1774.

597.32   his daughter,]   Sarah (Sally) Franklin (1743–1808) married Richard Bache (1737–1811) in 1767; they had at least six children.

600.25   Pennsylvania Penitentiary]   Eastern Penitentiary on Cherry Hill was established in 1829 in an attempt to reform inmates by "discriminatory treatment" (they were allowed contact only with prison officials and occasional visitors). Cells were 12 ft. by 7 1/2 ft., and 16 ft. high, with individual exercise yards that were enclosed to prevent contact among prisoners. It was the first penitentiary to use the system of solitary confinement and became a model for other prisons in the United States and Europe.

600.30   Angers . . . Ferrara]   In other essays, James had complained about contemporary changes and building in the ancient cities of Angers (called "Black Angers" and "the Black City" for its slate quarries), western France, and Ferrara in northern Italy near the Po.

602.34   *crânerie*]   Swaggering display.

609.6–9   War, . . . North.]   Four Massachusetts militiamen were killed by pro-secessionist rioters while marching with their regiment through Baltimore on April 19, 1861. They were the first Union soldiers to be killed in the

Civil War, and their deaths, which occurred on the anniversary of the battles of Lexington and Concord, were widely publicized in the North. Secessionist sympathizers also destroyed several railroad bridges near Baltimore on April 19, severing rail communications between Philadelphia and Washington, D.C., until April 25.

614.4−5   fire, . . . before,]   On February 7, 1904.

646.29   *agrément*]   Felicity, pleasure.

653.1   Leatherstocking Tales]   A series of novels by James Fenimore Cooper: *The Pioneers* (1823), *The Last of the Mohicans* (1826), *The Prairie* (1827), *The Pathfinder* (1840), and *The Deerslayer* (1841).

660.34−36   History . . . War]   *History of the United States from the Compromise of 1850* (7 vols., 1893−1906), covering American history 1850 to 1877.

661.18−19   *ad usum Delphini*]   For the Dauphin's use.

668.17   *portée*]   Bearing.

668.22−24   pew . . . Lee's surrender.]   On April 2, 1865, Jefferson Davis, while attending morning service at St. Paul's Protestant Episcopal church in Richmond, received a message from General Robert E. Lee that he could no longer hold the Petersburg siege lines against the Union Army and that Richmond would have to be evacuated. (Davis, who had been baptized and received into the church three years earlier, was described as a devout worshipper.) When Lee surrendered his army at Appomattox Court House on April 9, Davis was in Danville, Virginia.

677.2   Jamestown . . . king.]   Jamestown was established May 13, 1607, in the time of the first Stuart king of England, James I (reigned 1603−25).

693.38−694.1   Fort Sumter . . . companion]   Fort Moultrie, on Sullivan's Island, was built to defend Charleston Harbor along with Fort Sumter. On December 26, 1860, six days after South Carolina declared its secession, Major Robert Anderson evacuated the fort and moved its garrison to the more defensible Fort Sumter. See also note 329.4−10.

699.34   *état d'âme*]   State of soul.

710.19−20   was . . . sup]   Cf. Samuel Rogers, *Italy* (1822−28), "In Italy."

713.22   Mazeppa-like]   In Byron's poem *Mazeppa* (1819), Mazeppa is punished for an intrigue by being bound naked to the back of a wild horse from the Ukraine, which, lashed until mad and set loose, gallops through forest and river until it reaches the Ukrainian steppe, where it falls down dead; Mazeppa, himself nearly dead, is rescued.

721.36   Borromean Islands] Four small islands noted for their scenery in Lake Maggiore, northwest Italy.

723.30   ladies of Cranford] In *Cranford* (1851–53) by English novelist Mrs. Gaskell (Elizabeth Cleghorn Stevenson Gaskell, 1810–65).

725.26   *bahuts*] Cupboards.

732.8   *Baedeker*] German publisher Karl Baedeker (1801–59) in 1829 published the first of the famous series of travel guidebooks in French, English, and German; the series was continued by his son Fritz Baedeker.

732.24   VII] This section is omitted in the first American edition.

AMERICA: EARLY TRAVEL WRITINGS

741.11   *fauteuils*] Armchairs.

744.3   *podere*] Farm.

744.35   *faux air*] False appearance.

745.40   deeds of Prussia] In response to a diplomatic provocation arranged by Prussian minister-president Otto von Bismarck, France declared war on Prussia on July 15, 1870. By August 10, the date of James's letter, the Prussians had won battles at Wissembourg, Spicheren, and Froeschwiller (August 4–6) and were advancing into France.

747.33   "Lothair"] One of Benjamin Disraeli's last novels, published in 1870 and reviewed by James in *Atlantic Monthly*, August 1870.

750.29–30   "Que . . . songe?"] "What's there to do in a place like this unless you dream?"

758.34–35   Nathan murder.] Benjamin Nathan, a wealthy stockbroker, was brutally murdered in his mansion at 12 West 23d Street on the night of July 28, 1870, evidently during a burglary. A large reward was offered, but no one was ever charged with the crime.

761.33   "fine old Leisure,"] In *Adam Bede* (1859), ch. 52.

766.25   *villeggianti*] Vacationers.

768.38   *vie intime*] Intimate life.

769.6   *clocher de France*] French steeple or belfry.

770.6   *place*] Square.

772.30   *Vie de Province*] The *Scènes de la Vie de Province* is a subsection of works in the *Études de Moeurs* group in *La Comédie Humaine* (collected edition, 17 vols., 1842–48).

773.12   Nürnberg toy.]   The manufacture of toys was one of the chief industries of Nuremberg, or Nürnberg, Germany.

778.4   *vomitorium*]   An opening or vent for discharge or emission.

786.2–3   these columns]   In *The Nation*.

788.18   *agrément*]   See note 646.29.

789.28   *cives Romani*]   Roman citizens. According to Cicero, *Civis Romanus sum* (I am a Roman citizen) was an "appeal that helped or even saved many a man among the barbarians in the remotest lands" (*In Verrem*, II, v, 147).

Index

CATALOGING INFORMATION

James, Henry, 1843–1916.
   Collected travel writings: Great Britain and America.
   Edited by Richard Howard.

   (The Library of America ; 64)
   Contents: English hours—The American scene—Other travels.
   1. Great Britain—Description and travel. 2. United States—Description
and travel. 3. James, Henry, 1843–1916—Journeys. I. Title. English hours.
II. Title. The American scene. III. Series.
DA625.J37   1993   917.304—dc20   93–9192

ISBN 0–940450–76–3 (alk. paper)

*This book is set in 10 point Linotron Galliard,
a face designed for photocomposition by Matthew Carter
and based on the sixteenth-century face Granjon. The paper
is acid-free Ecusta Nyalite and meets the requirements for permanence of the American National Standards Institute. The binding
material is Brillianta, a 100% woven rayon cloth made by
Van Heek-Scholco Textielfabrieken, Holland. The composition is by Haddon Craftsmen, Inc., and The
Clarinda Company. Printing and binding
by R. R. Donnelley & Sons Company.
Designed by Bruce Campbell.*

THE LIBRARY OF AMERICA SERIES